AMERICAN ARCHITECTURE NOW II

AMERICAN ARCHITECTURE NOW II

BARBARALEE DIAMONSTEIN

FOREWORD BY PAUL GOLDBERGER

RIZZOLI NEW YORK

Cover: Madison Plaza, Chicago, Ill. by Skidmore, Owings
& Merrill. Photograph by Gregory Murphey ©1983

First published in the United States of America in 1985 by
RIZZOLI INTERNATIONAL PUBLICATIONS, INC.
597 Fifth Avenue, New York, NY 10017

Designed by Gilda Hannah
Set in type by Roberts/Churcher
Printed and bound in the USA

Library of Congress Cataloging in Publication Data
Diamonstein, Barbaralee.
    American architecture now II.

    Consists of interviews with various famous architects.
    1. Architecture, Modern—20th century—United States.
2. Architecture—United States. 3. Architecture—United
States—Interviews. I. Diamonstein, Barbaralee.
American architecture now. II. Title. III. Title:
American architecture now 2. IV. Title: American
architecture now two.
NA712.D472   1985   720'.973   85–42870
ISBN 0–8478–0612–X (pbk.)

for Carl Spielvogel
a master-builder
in his own right

These conversations, a number of which were originally videotaped as part of the Van Day Truex Memorial Lecture Series at the New School/Parsons School of Design, were held during a two-year period, from 1982 through late 1984. They were an extension of a series of other interviews that I had conducted with painters, sculptors, architects, photographers, craftspersons, and interior and fashion designers, which focused on those who have made significant contributions to contemporary American culture.

For their help in transforming this project into a reality, my thanks to my able assistants—Linda Reid, Jill Shaffer, and Jean Zimmerman—and to the Mary Biddle Duke Foundation and Helene Curtis, Inc., whose generous support was invaluable. My thanks, too, to Pierre and Fred, who provided a tranquil haven, as well as personal enhancement.

Barbaralee Diamonstein
11 June 1985

CONTENTS

FOREWORD

It is generally a wise idea to judge architects by their work, not by their words; few architects, even the most gifted, are the most reliable analysts and critics of their own efforts. And in some cases, ranging from the brilliant if flawed autobiography of Frank Lloyd Wright to innumerable works of self-promotion by lesser architects, architects' own words have been downright misleading.

But what this book reveals is that architects understand a lot more about their time, their culture, and even about their own designs than they usually let on. There is not one among the twenty-nine architects whose words fill the following pages who does not shed at least some welcome light on his or her own work, who does not give us at least some new perspective, and who does not reveal a reasonable amount of self-knowledge. Indeed, these conversations with Barbaralee Diamonstein are so incisive that they give us what I must admit is a flattering picture of the architectural profession: we see here a profession deeply aware of the social and historical context in which it works, determined to practice in neither a cultural nor an aesthetic vacuum. Though their work differs enormously in type, style, and philosophy (not to mention quality), as a group these architects seem united by the knowledge that it is a struggle to produce architecture that has both artistic and economic validity—and they seem determined to try to do it. They pursue their quest with zeal, but without the myopia of the missionary.

These interviews do not tell us in so many words what the current state of architecture is, or where the profession should be going. The absence of any attempt to do this is refreshing, and it saves these conversations from the pomposity that afflicts so many books of this type. But if the tone is casual and the movement brisk, these conversations do not want for substance. Barbaralee Diamonstein is both well informed and articulate, and she knows how to make easy conversations yield weight. These interviews, collectively, may manage to tell us far more about what architecture means at this instant in our history than many books that tackle such an issue head on.

This is a time of passionate interest in architecture, but only a tentative sense of what it should be. There is no orthodoxy prevalent at this moment, and these interviews surely reflect this: none of the architects speak in absolute terms; they convey no sense that their practice is a moral calling, as it was in the early days of modernism. But there is clearly a common ground that is expressed here, a similarity of concerns that provides a fair summary of the values currently governing architecture: virtually all of these architects speak of the importance of history to them, as a general inspiration if not as a specific physical source; of the necessity for buildings to communicate on a sensual as well as a cerebral level; and of the need to design buildings not as isolated objects but as elements in a larger urban whole.

That the architects interviewed here have met with varying degrees of success at achieving these goals goes without saying; some, in fact, we are better off knowing through their words rather than their buildings. But a comparative judgment of these architects is not the point of the interviews, nor is the point to compare what an individual architect says with what he or she does. What these written conversations can do is broaden and deepen our knowledge of each architect's sensibility and give us some verbal context within which to place his or her work. They enlighten us as to why Romaldo Giurgola wants to design a building one way and Bruce Graham wants to do it another way, or how William Conklin's upbringing gave him one set of perceptions while William Pedersen's gave him another.

Pedersen, incidentally, is one of the more pleasing conversationalists here; he comes off as amiable and self-assured without the arrogance one might expect from an architect who is the dominant design force in Kohn Pedersen Fox, a firm that is rapidly becoming one of the nation's preeminent. He speaks of hockey sticks, of English furniture, of skyscrapers, and of whole cities.

Helmut Jahn of the Chicago firm of Murphy/Jahn is, if anything, an even more fashionable shaper of skyscraper form right now. But he is more directed than Pedersen, less willing to ponder, blunter in admitting his interest in the towers themselves. About skyscraper design he concedes, revealing perhaps more than he intends: "We are forced to come up with something new, something marketable, and something different from other buildings."

Brief quotations out of context do not do justice to any of these interviews, for the impressive thing is that all of them really do read as conversations, as a natural flow of dialogue that does not easily admit to dissecting. Not the least of the pleasures here is the discovery that many architects are superb raconteurs—Ulrich Franzen, for example, who recounts the history of his own career with relaxed ease; or Emilio Ambasz, who describes his metaphorical architecture with striking clarity; or Hugh Jacobsen, whose prancing wit sometimes masks a strong critical intelligence; or Kevin Roche, who comes off displaying an ironic sense of the world that is nowhere present in his architecture.

Some interviews tell us as much about other figures as about their subjects. John Hedjuk offers considerable insight into such architects as Michael Graves and Richard Meier, whereas Meier himself speaks of Le Corbusier, at once acknowledging Corbusier's great influence on him and challenging those critics who see him as solely a neo-Corbusian. James Ingo Freed is splendid on the subject of Mies van der Rohe, as is Stanley Tigerman. Mies is a fairly constant presence in these pages; the extent to which he still hovers over the consciousness of architects is remarkable. The impression he made was so intense that several architects describe in detail visits made to him two, even three decades ago.

The realities of professional practice are well explained by Norman Pfeiffer, who neatly analyzes both the structure of his own firm, Hardy Holzman Pfeiffer Associates, and the nature of its eclectic, sometimes brash work; and Henry Cobb, I. M. Pei's longtime partner, who explains with grace and clarity the difficult balance between aesthetic and commercial concerns he has sought for most of his career. John Burgee's best moments are his frank discussion of his relationship with his partner, Philip Johnson, who he clearly delights in working with yet feels somewhat overshadowed by. Johnson, for his part, lavishes praise on Burgee, refers to himself as "the most hated architect in America," and calls Robert Venturi the most important architect in the world. (Venturi, as always, is straightforward and unpretentious.) Others are a bit less revealing, at least about the nature of their own practices. Bruce Graham of Skidmore, Owings & Merrill, for example, glosses over the complex internal politics of that vast firm, while Gyo Obata, the design partner of the huge Hellmuth, Obata & Kassabaum,

is actually most articulate—and most moving—when he goes back in time to describe the tragic detention of his Japanese-American family during World War II.

Benjamin Thompson, the architect who many years ago founded the retail enterprise Design Research, speaks convincingly of his effort at creating popular urban space in such designs as the Fanueil Hall Marketplace, though the high point of this conversation is his discussion of the difficult struggle to make modern furniture and high-design objects available to a broad spectrum of the public. James Wines, cofounder of the unconventional sculpture/architectural practice called SITE, speaks clearly of his firm's work, which he defends as not as purely conceptual as critics often have it. Richard Saul Wurman comes off as an eager cheerleader and promoter of architectural appreciation, Romaldo Giurgola as graciously didactic.

The architects whose words fill these pages constitute an eclectic group, sharing a set of general values but hardly in agreement as to the specific built form that should emerge from these values. If there is anything that unites these architects, it is something highly personal: it is impossible to read this book without being struck by the fact that all of them appear to be quite happy doing what they do. Although it may seem hardly a surprise that twenty-nine people who have reached high positions in a prestigious profession would feel confident about their careers, the insistence with which each of these architects proclaims his or her absence of regrets is striking. Architecture is not an easy pursuit, yet there is not one of the architects interviewed who is sad not to have written poetry, or sailed a boat around the world, or become an itinerant carpenter. Could a group of prominent lawyers or business executives feel a similar confidence? I have no reason to doubt these architects when they tell Barbaralee Diamonstein how satisfied they are with the course their lives have taken, for they say it with certainty but without smugness or restlessness. At every moment a sense of pleasure at architecture emanates from these pages.

Paul Goldberger
July 1985

INTRODUCTION

More than half a century has passed since Philip Johnson and Henry-Russell Hitchcock, Jr. organized "Modern Architecture: International Exhibition" for New York City's Museum of Modern Art (MoMA). The 1932 exhibition celebrated such stars of modernism as Le Corbusier, Oud, Gropius, Mies, Hood, Howe, and Lescaze in their ascendancy and unveiled to the American public the new spatial schemes that a young, optimistic generation of architects was fostering for the post–World War I international community. In an article on the MoMA exhibition, *Art News* wrote: "There is . . . a distinct architectural challenge in the air, a new and resonant note sounding in this drafting-room and that—be it in Paris, Berlin, Stockholm, Moscow or New York—is calling to the more radically-minded to rise up and assume the aesthetic responsibilities of our immediate time. Through the agency of the Museum of Modern Art . . . this new architectural stirring, known as the International Style, is being given a preliminary showing."

The International Style, it was prophesied, would obliterate regional distinctions to create a universally accepted architectural vocabulary and aesthetic. This new architecture was praised by many observers because it, unlike most modern architecture, did not camouflage the building principles of contemporary construction. The MoMA exhibition and *The International Style: Architecture Since 1922,* a provocative book by Johnson and Hitchcock that accompanied the exhibition, heralded the rise of an architecture characterized by simple, unadorned rectangular forms constructed of glass, steel, and other "modern" materials—an architecture that would turn its back on the past to speak clearly and specifically of the present. "This contemporary style, which exists throughout the world, is unified and inclusive, not fragmentary and contradictory like so much of the production of the first generation of modern architects," Johnson and Hitchcock proclaimed in their introduction to *The International Style.*

For the second generation of twentieth-century architects, the creation of a new architectural idiom was to lead not only to the re-creation of the built environment but also to the establishment of a new and better world. The rejection by these architects of recent design efforts was a condemnation of both bourgeois architectural expression and of the social order that had produced and sustained it; in introducing a new aesthetic,

the architect of the 1920s would assume the role of torch-bearer of a new, socialist order. As Johnson notes in his interview: "[The International Style] was almost a moral movement. We thought we had saved the world. . . . In the twenties, when the best International Style work was done in Europe, the rules were very strict and the hopes for the future were endless. It was the old socialist dream, that everybody could be happy."

The socialist dream failed. Although modernism spread throughout the United States in the succeeding decades, it never dominated American architecture to the extent its early proponents had anticipated. The architects who created America's world-famous skylines during the thirties, forties, and fifties did indeed adapt the blueprints of the European socialist philosophy for modern living, but in the United States these designs were manifested as a sleek aesthetic for the capitalist corporation's working environment. By the mid-sixties, modernism was in its decline. In his introduction to the 1966 edition of *The International Style,* Hitchcock wrote that he, through his writings, and Johnson, through his architectural designs, had "offered the conclusion that the International Style is over."

The glass-and-steel monoliths of the modernist period are now perceived as the buildings of an ideological aesthetic past. Although contemporary architects continue to use the high-technology building materials that defined the structures of modernism, they do not adhere to the International Style's austere and rigid rules of composition. Even neo-modernists like Richard Meier and Michael Graves have forgotten, if not abandoned, the moral/leftist political posture of the modernists. In the 1980s we no longer have, says Johnson, an earlier generation's illusions of the possibility of universal happiness, or its faith in the ability of architecture to "make a difference."

Perhaps it was the disillusionment and the "revolutions" of the 1960s that first led architects to join in the reevaluation of America and to help create the country's new sense of self. Stanley Tigerman, who began his career during that decade, cites the changing cultural, social, and political climate of those years as an important factor in the recent history of his profession: "Before the late sixties, American architecture was very sure of itself. Mies and Le Corbusier had won, and their descendants were everywhere. But at the end of the sixties, the cultural revolution, inner-city problems, black revolutionaries, advocacy planning, and numerous social concerns caused a rejection of prior products. . . . I would contend that the situation today is a product of the struggle between all of those trends."

Since the sixties, we've experienced a period of transition, during which modernism has been debated and reappraised. American architects have moved with increasing confidence toward an age of calculated diversity; eclecticism and individualism have invalidated the dominance of any single design ideology.

A conscious effort to reject the absoluteness of any new orthodoxy is suggested by the opposition of many of today's leading architects to the use of "postmodernism" as a broad, all-encompassing label for their work and that of their contemporaries. Some of these designers, whose buildings have contributed significantly to the delineation of a contemporary architectural idiom, find such a label glib and restrictive. "There's been such a lot of dialogue about postmodernism that when you use the word it conjures up only a certain style or a certain group of architects," complains Gyo Obata. "I think that's too limiting. I have always hated to be categorized. . . . I want to be free." The ease with which critical lines are drawn and talent embraced or discarded, praised or maligned, has created a wariness that Obata intimates and other architects underscore. "With the general discontent expressed now about postmodernism and the deluge of facile spin-offs, it goes without saying that in the next few years there will be a combination of backlash and future-oriented changes in architecture that will make the whole label and movement passé," James Wines comments. "All the ins will be outs. This is tragic; I would rather circumvent such trauma."

Many architects reject the classification of postmodernism on theoretical grounds: in defining itself as the negation of modernism and rejecting the tenets of that vocabulary, postmodernism has, they claim, repeated the very weakness—an ideological rigidity that denies the importance of architectural precedents—it sought to indict by its example. As Helmut Jahn explains, "A lot of people call me a postmodernist and, like many architects, I refuse that label. Postmodernism . . . fails in the end because of its own orthodoxy. Just as modernism refused to acknowledge anything that had to do with history, postmodernism refuses to acknowledge anything that has to do with modernism." Robert Venturi elaborates on this theme. "*Plus ça change, plus c'est la même chose.* The postmodernists may use pink, green, and other pastels instead of white, but they are still dogmatic and ideological. They see only one way—their kind of neoclassicism, which comes out of their limited perspective more than the multifarious circumstances of their time. They are still modern architects big on unity, with a yen for the universal; they're bent on an International Style, this time in pastels." The dogmatism of modernists and postmodernists—an orthodoxy of homogeneity—dissatisfies Venturi. "We're living in a time of intense communication that promotes unity in one sense, but there is a concurrent trend of people trying to acknowledge and understand their own heritage, their own unique qualities. This is a time when heterogeneity reigns over homogeneity, eclecticism over neoclassicism, when many kinds of symbolism and formal systems can be employed in architecture. But the postmodernists don't get it."

At the other end of the spectrum are architects who deny that a style clearly distinguishable from modernism has yet evolved. "I don't like the terms 'modernist' and 'postmodernist,'" James Ingo Freed remarks. " It seems to me that what is

called postmodernism is actually very modern; it's a kind of latter-day modernism. The best buildings of our time tend to be evolutionary. There are some very good buildings labeled postmodernist that are simply developments and enrichments of a modernist tradition." Perhaps, as Venturi suggests, "architects should leave the naming of what they do to future historians."

Certainly architecture is currently in a state of flux: futuristic, historicist, and "developmental modernist" strains have all been evident in recent designs. In the interviews that follow, many architects address this delicate transitional state, articulating and illuminating the architectural currents that have replaced the purist modernist aesthetic for those who are among the country's foremost practitioners today. These architects have begun a reconstructive process, stripping architecture of many of its complex layers in an attempt to reveal its most basic forms, sometimes even to begin anew.

This process has required a recognition and analysis of the past. As John Burgee notes, today's architects are "more and more conscious" of architectural trends and precedents and readily acknowledge that awareness. "The root of architecture," says Freed, "lies in certain simple remembered things," historical precedents being among the most important elements he names.

Yet today's architects have distinguished themselves from their immediate predecessors not by their awareness of historical precedents but by the respect they give the same works the modernists rejected, sometimes disparagingly, as inappropriate in a twentieth-century context. Emilio Ambasz describes this recent phenomenon: "Many architects—my beloved colleagues—are engaged in an operation of recovering the memory of architecture. As you know, the modern movement started with the assumption that the evolution of a new man was possible. This new man would not remember the history of architecture. During the forty or fifty years that the modern movement lasted, in the hope of arriving at that magnificent promised land, we neglected all the lessons of history. At present many architects are interested in a recovery of those lessons."

Recent efforts to recover the past have resulted in a reappraisal not only of the architecture and theoretical currents of other periods but of the architects of an earlier day as well. Some of the architects included in this series of conversations could be described as the progeny of the American masters— Frank Lloyd Wright and the great immigrant architects Walter Gropius, Ludwig Mies van der Rohe, Louis Kahn, and Eliel and Eero Saarinen. These pioneers, who shaped and expressed a modernist sensibility from its infancy through its maturity, are recognized by today's architects as the giants of twentieth-century architecture. Ambasz expresses the esteem in which they are held in his tribute to Mies and Wright: "They strike a chord that says 'architecture.' Even if the styles are completely different, the emotional pursuit is the same."

It may be true, as Johnson says, that "we're not in what the English call a 'heroic' period. There's no Le Corbusier, Mies, or Frank Lloyd Wright. Nobody would dispute that. We granted these people a genius status as you would Michelangelo and Veronese. Today I don't think any of us measure up to that standard." Johnson and the other architects interviewed here may not see themselves as "up to that standard," but their work is informed to a large degree by their close association as students and observers with the brilliant architects of the modernist era.

The younger generation has recognized that the vitality of the modernists' professional spirit—the intensity of their approach to architecture—is as important a part of their legacy as their body of work. This is appropriate in an age that has rejected many of the tenets of modernism but has embraced its practitioners' sense of commitment to architecture. Throughout the interviews we hear allusions to contemporary architects' modernist forebears.

"Gropius was more effective in describing the role and responsibilities of the architect than he was in prescribing an architectural style," William Conklin says of the former chairman of Harvard's Department of Architecture. "His brilliance was in pointing out to students the range of opportunities and responsibilities before them." For Benjamin Thompson, who worked with Gropius for twenty years at The Architects Collaborative, "the most fascinating thing about Gropius was his total intensity, the sense of purpose and seriousness he exhibited. But he was also a very natural fellow. He wasn't what the legend says—a character who went around making great 'form-follows-function' pronouncements. He was a person you could talk to about almost anything, and we did."

Bruce Graham observed in Mies van der Rohe the same professional consciousness—and conscientiousness—for which Gropius was noted. "Mies was . . . very conscious of his responsibility as a great artist. It's that sort of consciousness that I was most impressed with. It was the art that was important to him, not the individual." The theme of architecture as art is reiterated in Kevin Roche's recollection of Mies: "He was truly a very great architect and had such an intensity about architecture. . . . For Mies it was a very serious art. It was interesting to begin my life in architecture with the sense that this was *the* most serious of all the arts, the one to which we must devote the most effort and time."

Perhaps more than any of his contemporaries, Mies came to epitomize modernism, particularly the International Style. Chicago, where he served as director of architecture at the Illinois Institute of Technology and worked in private practice, became the showcase for the best efforts by Americans of the modernist school. As Tigerman notes, in Chicago, "there are forty-five buildings by [Mies] completed while he was alive. There are over fifty by Frank Lloyd Wright. There are over seventy-five by the first Chicago School—John Wellborn Root, Louis Sullivan. And then there are buildings by the descendants. One is confronted by this enormous tradition everywhere in Chicago." When Burgee began to practice architecture during the late 1950s, "Chicago was the first city of American architecture. . . . Much of the great architecture of modern times has been built in Chicago; it was the home of Mies van der Rohe. . . . That architectural heritage was always apparent to me."

The great achievements of Mies and his modernist contemporaries both inspired and challenged the subsequent generation of architects, who aspired to reach comparable—but distinct—heights. "When I came back from Yale," says Tigerman, "Chicago was a product of what can only be called the German invasion: Mies van der Rohe and his elite troops from the Black Forest. I really wanted to make a home for myself, my own home, in the city where I was born. It was important to me to do that. So I saw that group as the enemy, in a sense. On the other hand, of course, much of my work has been couched in their language."

Freed studied with Mies at the Illinois Institute of Technology and later worked with him on the Seagram Building in New York City. Freed's appreciation of and respect for Mies are tempered by his recent recognition of the limitations of modernism in general and of Mies's architectural philosophy in particular. Freed acknowledges Mies's impact on his beliefs but says: "I have found myself consciously leaving it behind. [Mies] was incredibly persuasive, not only because he composed a formal solution, but because that solution contained a fully realized language of architecture, including all the bits and pieces, even the decorative. . . . The tangibility of space . . . the poetry of the tectonic, the making of a building . . . I don't want to lose those strong concepts and perceptions. But I do want to lose the limiting and diminishing ways of thinking, which disallowed history as a source for design inspiration and proposed structural expressionism as the only legitimate methodology."

Eero Saarinen, son of noted architect and Cranbrook Academy of Art founder Eliel Saarinen, accepted no limits in creating his architectural designs; many critics have hailed his originality as genius. Roche, who was principal design associate to the younger Saarinen from the mid-fifties until Saarinen's death in 1961, has acknowledged him as a significant influence on his early career. Saarinen's authority and guidance were commanding forces for Roche as a young staff member: "Eero provided tremendous leadership, and we had a sense of total involvement. It was almost a religious experience, being so possessed by this activity." Saarinen attacked each assignment as a unique challenge, constantly bidding himself and those who worked with him to explore new solutions. "He always began," Roche recalls, "at the foundations of the problem by considering the forces behind it, the elements bringing it about, and how to use these forces to generate a building."

Louis Kahn, like Eero Saarinen, was praised for the creativity of his designs. "What is most meaningful to me," says Richard Saul Wurman, "is the process [Kahn] went through, how he thought and expressed himself." Romaldo Giurgola, who worked with Kahn at the University of Pennsylvania, echoes Wurman's appreciation of Kahn's contribution to the profession. Kahn "was concerned with making architecture as a response to new situations," he explains. "He was always searching for the nature of things, why things were the way they were—what it meant, for instance, for an association to meet in a monastery or a convention hall; what happened in order for them to start doing so; what kind of space they developed; what fundamental shapes and forms created that space; how the particular kind of space they determined became evocative of the particular action that took place in that space." It is Kahn's concept of architectural space to which contemporary architecture is especially indebted, Giurgola believes. " 'Room' was the word that Kahn used all the time. He thought in terms of rooms, architecture as an assembly or an association of rooms. Insisting upon the value of the room as a primordial element of architecture was a tremendous breakthrough. From Kahn came a host of architects who think in the same way, take that idea as a point of departure." Giurgola optimistically speculates that we will increasingly hear talk of Louis Kahn and that there will be a rediscovery of his value.

Like their mentors, many of the architects interviewed are also educators, deeply involved in passing on their knowledge and expertise to a younger generation. These architects speak of their own teachers as having been very important influences, and they are excited, in turn, by the role they play in shaping the future of architecture through their current teaching duties.

Freed left his successful architecture practice in 1970 to teach full-time at his alma mater, the Illinois Institute of Technology. What prompted his decision? "I felt an indebtedness to the profession," Freed explains. "It's been my life, and I wanted to repay some of that." The classroom gave Freed the opportunity to reassess, experiment, and explore—to "see things with a fresh perspective and to question what you believe," an experience he considers the most valuable aspect of teaching.

Jaquelin Robertson and Peter Eisenman, distinguished academics as well as partners in a recently formed architectural firm, share the belief that practicing architects must teach in order to find and express a proper balance between theory and practice. Eisenman characterizes the relationship between the practice and the teaching of architecture as a mutually beneficial symbiosis: "You cannot teach only from a theoretical perspective, and you cannot practice only from a commercial perspective. The two inform each other," he declares. "One of the problems in a practice is that there's too little theory, and in the schools there's too little practice. Our commitment," he continues, "is to finding that middle ground."

Robertson, in agreement with his partner, boldly states that "nearly every architect worth spitting on has taught, and the only architects doing interesting work are those who've been associated with schools at one time or another." His commitment to teaching emerged early in his career. "I realized when I graduated from college that the one thing I learned in school was that I didn't know anything. I certainly didn't know what architecture is. . . . I thought one way to do this . . . was to teach. The students began questioning why this was good or that bad. I had opinions—but no convincing, easy answers. Slowly I began to evolve an idea about architecture."

In training the architects of the future, the architecture school not only teaches design but promotes self-knowledge; the classroom can be an invaluable forum for critical self-examination. "I believe in bringing diverse views into our school, but I want to do it in a way that doesn't allow them to simply slide by each other without getting into a dialogue, without challenging, without communicating," explains Henry Cobb, chairman of the Department of Architecture at Harvard's Graduate School of Design and a founding principal of I. M. Pei & Partners. "I want to create a *discourse*. This I would say is my single most important goal."

Michael Pittas, former director of the National Endowment for the Arts Design Arts Program and dean of the Otis Art Institute of the Parsons School of Design in Los Angeles, has called architecture a service industry. The reader of these conversations will see that for most architects now, shaping a "serviceable" architecture—making architecture that is beautiful, enjoyable, and usable—is a high-priority goal. The architects differ from one another in their approaches to this objective; yet, in responding to current social imperatives and environmental realities, they have in common a perspective devoid of the often self-righteous ideals and principles that inspired and bound their modernist teachers.

The public's perspective has also changed. As *New York Times* architecture critic Paul Goldberger has written, "We ask of our architecture today something much more particular, something much less moralistic. We expect it to shelter us and, quite frankly, we expect it also to please and even entertain us. At its best—when its aspirations to art are the most serious—we hope that it will uplift us. But we still do not look to it for a cleansing of the soul. Neither do we look to it for a sense of absolutes."

The absence of an attitude of moral and intellectual superiority in creating our built environment markedly distinguishes the contemporary architect from the modernist. If today's architect recognizes his building as an element of a larger, encompassing architectural fabric, he also recognizes himself as part of a larger, encompassing social fabric. This recognition is suggested by Tigerman's comment: "Architecture, paint-ing, and sculpture tend to advance an attitude that says there is one correct, overriding answer, often couched in the language of the era in which the works are created. I no longer believe in that single answer. The struggle of combining all the things that produce a work of architecture, especially the accommodation of a client, has become much more important to me."

Contemporary architecture must acknowledge a multiplicity of social, political, economic, and cultural realities as well as aesthetic, functional, and spatial factors; consequently, its parameters are best defined not by an omniscient individual but through the collaborative efforts of many individuals who present a multitude of perspectives and needs. In Graham's words, "Architecture is a participatory art, not the art of an individual. It's the art of a society, and it's epochal." Giurgola concurs. "Society is the real motor of any new architectural idea," he avers. "You can see that the houses architects build for themselves are usually pretty awful. An architect without a client is really a nonentity. Architecture is the confluence of a tremendous number of factors and includes the contributions of a great number of people."

The professional-client relationship is, then, highly valued as an integral part of a cooperative process. Indeed, Joan Goody firmly believes that "it is *not* ideal not to have a client"; the point of view of the inhabitants or users of a structure is needed to counter the whims of the architect and to give a design focus. "It really takes two groups of people to build: the clients and the architects," says Kevin Roche. "Both need to be enlightened in order to produce good architecture." Venturi posits that "most good buildings derive from an understanding collaboration between architect and client."

Many of the architects interviewed describe the ideal client: Norman Pfeiffer, for example, says that the ideal client is "one who can see. It is amazing how difficult it is for people to read drawings and understand models, and it is rare to find a client who is capable of either projecting the reality of the finished product into those drawings or of anticipating what it is that the architects have in mind." Often the architect's ideal is a composite of the best qualities of those clients with whom he's worked most successfully and happily to produce a mutually satisfying design. For Venturi and his partner and spouse, Denise Scott Brown, the ideal client may be "the president of a college or the head of an urban renewal agency. The client could be in the private or the public sector. He could be a poet, which one of our best clients was, or a would-be professor running his family's factory, like another. But they all have an entrepreneurial sense, a view that they're going to do it themselves, and the architect is very special to them. They also like to match ideas, to match wits. They ask telling questions."

In many of the interviews the establishment of a dialogue between the architect and his client is cited as an essential component of their collaboration. "You *do* listen to the client," Hugh Jacobsen states emphatically. "It is his building. He is going to live in it. You listen to his program and try to isolate the problem, identify the needs." The ideal clients, Jacobsen concludes, "participate and they make me listen."

The most successful collaboration between an architect and his client is also often a difficult one for the architect, because ultimately it is he who must challenge his creative and analytic skills to address the problems and articulate the ideas presented to him by the nonprofessional. Thus, although the ideal client may, as Giurgola describes, sit down with the architect to "think with you about the resolution of problems or about the manifestation of aspirations," it is up to the designer to realize the envisioned course. For Stanley Tigerman, the ideal client compels him to fulfill his potential as a problem solver; he is a hard-driving catalyst—"the toughest son-of-a-bitch out there, the one that really works you out, not the one that lets you get away with murder." He continues, "That kind of client forces me to think it out again and again until I get to a deeper level of understanding of the problem and of the project."

How much does a client contribute to the design of a building? The answer to that question varies with each project, of course, depending on the architect, the client, and a variety of project-specific and general factors. Yet many of the architects interviewed are able to discuss in broad terms how, and to what extent, they are influenced by their clients.

Ulrich Franzen says that "human beings have to express themselves when making a house, and you as the architect attempt to represent someone else's ideas to the extent that you create a stage where the ideas can flower. But the shape of the stage, its illumination, and how the client can use it is up to the architect to create."

Getting a client to accept a design proposal is often, Franzen contends, a matter of packaging—the architect must "legitimize a radical idea" by presenting it in terms the layman can understand and accept. But, Franzen insists, he does not like to sell a project that has been developed independent of any client contribution, independent of a client's particular needs and desires. "I don't think that is really architecture," Franzen says. "Architecture is the coming together of an idea and reality. The exciting thing is where that intersection occurs. . . . That is crucial."

Establishing that intersection hinges on compromise. The successful collaboration is a relationship in which a balance of wills is struck; flexibility, research, and resourcefulness serve the architect well in this endeavor. "We believe in communication, interaction, and understanding," Gyo Obata says. "We respond to the feelings and psychology of each client. . . . We also do a tremendous amount of research. . . . I think some American architects have a conception of a model in their head and impose that on the owner without a lot of interaction or communication. . . . I'm not saying that we're anonymous. I'm saying that in the end you get everything you want as an architect if you really listen and understand, because then the client will go along with you."

The architect and his client strive for a meeting of the minds; on another plane, the architect strives to achieve a similarly harmonious and mutually satisfying relationship with the society and the culture within which he is working. "The participants in building are more than just those who pay the bills," as Graham observes. "They're also the members of the society within which you are building." In recognition of their ultimate responsibility to the general public, it has become a common practice at firms such as Hardy Holzman Pfeiffer Associates and Venturi, Rauch and Scott Brown to discuss impending projects at public gatherings.

As glimpsed in these interviews, the architect of the 1980s speaks of, for, and often with his society. Of himself and his partner Eisenman, Robertson says, "We emphasize the idea of the architect as someone who understands the world. . . . The architect must first be of his time, then an architect; architecture must always be in the service of life, not the other way around."

The architects in this series offer ample evidence that the best among them are seriously committed to improving the quality of life for the general public. Over and over again we hear of the "responsibility" of the architect. "After all, in everything we do we are part of our society and our culture," says Roche. "We have a tremendous responsibility in what we pass along to our children and our grandchildren, the future of our society. If what we leave to posterity isn't done well or isn't done right, we are leaving the future with a problem." Says Giurgola, "Much of architecture stems from the individual's attempt to fit in, to make a place part of himself, to be at home. That's the real issue. . . . You have to take things slowly in order to develop the kind of environment that makes life enjoyable. The fundamental task of architecture has always been to create an aspiration to a better life." Giurgola emphasizes that "you have to feel responsible. Otherwise you are not an architect."

Most of the architects interviewed feel that the task of today's architect is a constructive, positive one rooted in optimism, an appreciation of the existing environment, and a belief in man's ability—and obligation—to create a better quality of life. "Social upheaval and negativism brought certain things into focus," explains Thompson. "I concluded that an architect's greatest service would be the expression of possibility, of potential. It was easy to mouth all the negatives, the 'God's own junkyard' kind of criticism. But I am naturally positive, and I wanted to make real three-dimensional examples, which people could see and feel, showing how the world really could be put together if we worked at it."

During the fifties and early sixties, America's effort to use architecture to create a better life for its people was pursued with renewed vigor as a nationwide program of urban renewal reached its apex. Through urban renewal, the modernist disregard of historical precedents was expressed in tangible form: the past was erased as buildings and neighborhoods were destroyed and communities displaced in a wholesale movement to build the Great Society from the ground up.

Despite the allocation of considerable government funds and the concerted efforts of architects, city planners, legislators, government agencies, and private groups, urban renewal was largely a failure—an aesthetically bankrupt, expensive, and inadequate solution to cities' worsening housing problems. "During the civil rights and social movements of the sixties, [Herbert] Gans and other social scientists criticized the architecture of urban renewal in America," Scott Brown comments. "They pointed out that the new towers in the centers of our cities, although reminiscent of social housing in Europe, did not house the poor, and that the beautiful utopian vision of the planners had become a nightmare in which the poor were removed to make way for urban renewal. The architects' vision of the good city seemed to conspire in this situation."

In city after city, housing projects rapidly became breeding grounds for crime and alienation, accelerating the decay of downtown districts. They hastened the flight to the suburbs of those who could afford to get out and aggravated the despair of those who could not. Minoru Yamasaki's award-winning Pruitt-Igoe projects (St. Louis), an overcrowded, poorly maintained housing complex ill suited to many of the needs of its southern migrant tenants, exemplified the blight of urban renewal. With no sense of neighborhood, no mix of shops and restaurants, no intermingling of economic groups as is found in areas that have grown more naturally, Pruitt-Igoe became a low-income ghetto, plagued by crime and ultimately uninhabitable. In 1972, seventeen years after it had opened to critical acclaim, the project was razed by explosives.

One of the criticisms frequently leveled by urban renewal's detractors was that the destruction it wrought to alleviate social ills created cultural deprivations: in many instances, buildings of historical and architectural significance were demolished to make way for new, insignificant construction. It was this aspect of urban renewal that inspired the rise of a broadly based preservation movement.

During the last twenty years, preservation—reconstruction, renovation, rehabilitation, and adaptive reuse—has, in Conklin's words, "enlarged and broadened my definition of the word 'contemporary.'" Today the meaning of forms and materials created in the past persists when applied appropriately to contemporary living. Because of current economic limitations, because of our new sensitivity to history, because of a widespread cultural nostalgia for times we perceive to have been easier, if not precisely better, and—last, but not least—because the buildings of our past represent a tangible link with the shared life of our culture, the enthusiasm for landmarks preservation and adaptive reuse today is unprecedented.

We have, in Pittas's words, come "a long way from seeing architecturally and historically significant buildings as needing fossilization." Preservation has been embraced by both the professional and the layman as a viable, and often preferable, alternative to destruction, construction, or "fossilization." Joan Goody, since 1976 a member of Boston's Landmarks Commission and partner in the leading Boston firm Goody, Clancy and Associates, Inc., which has done much work in the area of adaptive reuse and other preservation architecture, speaks for many when she says, "Believing as I do that part of the quality of any place is its visible history, I don't want to eradicate the past while building for the present and preparing for the future. We should plan in such a way that we enhance those parts of an environment that have a distinctive quality, make an effort to reuse them, and build the new in a scale and with materials and forms that are sensitive to the past. That doesn't mean no building at all, but it means perhaps building less than some developers . . . would like. I think it requires self-restraint—or governmental regulation."

For Conklin, preservation is of special import to our architectural centers—the cities. "We have to put higher value on the existing structures of our communities," he advises. "Everybody in cities—architects as well as residents—increasingly realizes and appreciates that the buildings of our environment are of great value. They are like friends. Just as we respect the structure of our social relationships in the world, so should we value our urban context. When we wipe out buildings, we wipe out not just the physical objects but many more subtle urban networks."

The skyscraper remains the foremost American architectural form and symbol, the structure through which the architect most prominently shapes the environments in which we live and work. Across the continent, these tall towers have had an evocative power over the American imagination since the first steel skeleton was used by William Le Baron Jenney in the design of Chicago's ten-story Home Insurance Building in 1884. Louis Sullivan, the nineteenth-century pioneer in the architecture of the skyscraper, asserted that each giant structure "must be every inch a proud and soaring thing, rising in sheer exultation that from bottom to top it is a unit without a single dissenting line." Henry James, upon his return from Europe in 1904, marveled at New York City's skyline, describing "the multitudinous skyscrapers standing up to the view, from the water, like extravagant pins in a cushion already overplanted." Today the skyscraper still elicits eloquent and passionate responses. In Conklin's words, "High buildings should inspire. They are noble, and they should *be* noble as well as look noble."

Helmut Jahn attributes a new vitality in architecture to the skyscraper "because it offers never-ending possibilities for exploration in terms of its urban symbolism, its form, and its image. It's not a question of whether or not the skyscraper is here to stay. The skyscraper is the urban phenomenon of the twentieth century. With land values and zoning the way they are, the skyscraper is definitely going to stay, and the technological possibilities exist to extend its limits even further."

Although the extension of one limit—height—can still be impressive today, rarely does that characteristic become the hallmark of an architecturally distinguished building. John Burgee, who, with Philip Johnson, has designed a number of the most notable skyscrapers of the last decade, explains: "When you enter a city, you look at the skyline and say, 'Hey, there's the Empire State Building, there's the Chrysler Building.' You may say the Seagram Building is the best building in New York, but you can't identify it from across the river. . . . It gets its quality from its fine detail."

Consideration of "details"—exterior ornamentation and interior design—is an increasingly significant component of contemporary architecture. As William Conklin puts it, "What used to be called 'irrelevant detail,' to use Gropius's term, is actually the elaboration of the language of architecture. The forms convey ideas; they have history, they have precedents. They're not just shapes but are really ideas in shapes. They also have value simply as delight and entertainment to the eye." Though America's fascination with modernism continues, there has been a resurgence of interest in classical architecture, a renewed enthusiasm for the eclectic impulse that motivated earlier generations of architects, and a concomitant renaissance of the decorative characteristics that enriched the designs of pre-modernist structures. The picturesque Georgian mansions of Delano & Aldrich, the sumptuous Renaissance buildings of McKim, Mead & White, and the lush Gothic structures of James Gamble Rogers are all in vogue now; recent works by Burgee and Johnson, Robert Stern, and Alan Greenberg are praised for their classical elements.

The buildings looked to by many contemporary architects for inspiration carry a set of values and express a nobility beyond their function; together they convey an order and dignity of which we are in need. A major aim of today's architects is to address and redress the structural discontinuity of alienation—the diminution of architectural order—created by the modernist builders of the twentieth-century American city. One expression of this effort is an emerging commitment to what could be called organic urban architecture—the concept of the city as a single entity composed of distinct but complementary parts. This theme recurs throughout the interviews.

"Modern architecture, largely inspired by Cubism, dealt with its facades abstractly," William Pedersen observes. "Because they were abstractly conceived, these facades were never able to establish connections to each other." Pedersen has rejected this total structural independence in the design of an individual building or in the more complex, long-term strategy of redesigning a city. One of the tenets of his philosophy, he states, "is that a building must be able to gather its meaning specifically from its context." The energies of Pedersen and his colleagues "are aimed at creating a temporal and physical continuity within cities. . . . Our work is . . . focused on a rather specific philosophical objective: to create buildings that generate contextual linkage within the urban fabric."

In this postmodernist, eclectic era, the measure of a structure's success is determined, in part, by how well it stands as part of its environment. "A building should relate to its existing context and be respectful of that context. It should not make the adjacent buildings look ridiculous; it should not cast other buildings in its shadow," Conklin insists. "But," he hastens to add, "it should also make a positive contribution, not only by its function, but by being something special on the street." The contemporary building should define, as well as be defined by, its environment.

Much of contemporary architecture is defined by designers' attempts to balance contending and often opposite forces: urban design integrity and stylistic independence; historic reference and progressive innovation; aesthetic considerations and functional requirements; growing populations and dwindling space; escalating construction costs and economic limitations; private aspirations and public interests. It is the creativity with which these various elements are being reconciled that gives this period its textural richness and diversity.

The current architectural scene is marked most vividly by a dialogue between the future and the past, the new and the old. "We cannot not use history," Cobb says of contemporary architects. But of course," he concedes, "within that broad truism there lurks an infinity of possible choices and interpretations." Today's dialogue between innovation and tradition exists between buildings but also, increasingly, within the confines of single structures. Thus, the stone facade of Johnson and Burgee's AT&T Building in New York City may summon visions of the seventeenth century and its massive colonnade may conjure up ancient Egypt, but its interior is inspired by modern master Mies van der Rohe. Indeed, an historicist vision has become a highly visible and increasing component of contemporary architecture; echoes of the past are apparent in such recent major projects as Venturi, Rauch and Scott Brown's Stratford, Connecticut, bank. Despite—or perhaps because of—the acclaim accorded these structures, building design in the 1980s faces criticism that it is unimaginative and derivative.

Recent technological advances have increased the choices available to today's architects. In the 1980s, architects have more design options than ever before. "We have the tools to build bigger, to span farther, to dig deeper, and to use a greater variety of materials than ever before. So if we make mistakes . . . it's going to be more visible," Joan Goody points out. "A greater degree of anarchy is possible." Norman Pfeiffer also sounds a note of caution in his discussion of the future of architecture. "Invention just for the sake of invention is disastrous," says Pfeiffer, whose firm has broadened the palette of color and material in contemporary architecture. "If there is a simple way to solve a problem, there is no point in making it complicated by doing it differently. Being overly inventive can cause more problems than it solves. One always has to be very cautious about moving in new directions."

To most architects it is clear that in coming decades the American architect's major forum will continue to be the city. To work effectively there architects will have to widen their perspective and broaden their area of expertise: the master architect of the twenty-first century will be inspired by a macro view of urban architecture.

This development is anticipated and proposed by several of the architects interviewed. Peter Eisenman, for example, describes this emerging current as a necessary change: "The architect has traditionally not been in planning and policy-making. Architects are usually thought of as facilitators. For some strange reason they arrogate that role to themselves, as much as society gives it to them. Architects have got to start being interested in policy-making without losing their creative role in the making of physical reality."

With the acknowledgement of the importance of urban planning as a concern of the architect comes a recognition of the problems inherent in addressing a matter of its scope and complexity. James Ingo Freed, for example, anticipates that the heterogeneity of American society will profoundly affect the future of urban design: "Great cities are usually the products not of individual architects but of great cultures; great cultures have goals or ends that are shared in some way by most of the people. Unfortunately, I'm not persuaded that we have a common view today." James Wines shares Freed's view and believes that our social and ideological pluralism creates an ambience difficult for, if not deleterious to, the process of environmental design. "Truly successful collaborations respond to the larger needs of a community and reflect a universal agreement in what constitutes a communicative imagery. In this epoch I think it is very hard to bond people together with any single philosophy or mission. Nothing seems universal anymore. Everything is fragmented, disparate, and pluralistic," Wines comments. "Great collaborations have always come out of situations where there was a church or state with a universal mandate." In contrast, our society, Wines says, "is too fragmented now to inspire that kind of cooperation between artists and architects."

Certainly the heterogeneity of our society presents an inescapable challenge for architects as they consider both form and function; perhaps, more than any other factor, it will shape a new aesthetic. Robert Venturi, in his influential and controversial books *Complexity and Contradiction in Architecture* and *Learning from Las Vegas,* has developed an argument for a new architectural aesthetic, one in which complexity and contradiction serve as timely expressions of our heterogeneity. Venturi discusses this during his interview. "The aesthetic ideal of orthodox modernism was a combination of unity and clarity. This was a perfectly valid ideal. Renaissance architecture was based on the same ideal—the Pazzi Chapel is remarkable for the unity and clarity of its forms and symbols. But there is another, equally valid ideal apparent in Byzantine architecture. In terms of unity or clarity, a Byzantine chapel is a disaster in its combinations of materials, media, symbols, and forms. But it is appealing because of its richness and ambiguity. This 'messy vitality' is an ideal we think is valid for today. This is what people want—an architecture that has many levels of meaning and that achieves its effect through richness rather than unity, ambiguity rather than clarity."

One frequent result of our heterogeneity is a struggle for representation and power among subcultures and interest groups. The resolution of these conflicts is a significant factor in urban planning, as Jaquelin Robertson discovered when he designed a project for New York City. "Politics in a pluralistic society like this is very tough on planning," Robertson says in frustration. "You can't predict anything. Some of the most public policies are impossible to carry out in a city like New York because people are really afraid of planning decisions. Representatives change votes at the last minute because they don't have time to understand the issues, they only listen to the wind."

Alexander Cooper, who has had extensive experience in the public sector, maintains that the problem of realizing effective designs in the urban environment is due in part to a lack of knowledge about elements that are not generally in the realm of architectural training but are nevertheless pertinent to the manipulation of large-scale design: "traffic, zoning, law, development, finance, politics, and management in the public sector. Each of these has to be understood by architects before they can control any environment beyond a building's property lines," he insists.

As Cooper's comments suggest, architects must address a broad range of contemporary issues in designing the structure of a city. Hugh Jacobsen's concerns are a further illustration of this. "Problems of security and the rising crime rate have

. . . had a tremendous influence on how buildings are designed," Jacobsen reflects. "Something I'm working seriously on now is based on the fact that when I was born my life expectancy would have been about fifty years. Now that I'm in my fifties, my life expectancy is seventy-eight. By the time I'm seventy-eight, I hope it will be a hundred. This means that all our buildings must be designed to take care of very old and, I hope, very independent people. We have to come to terms with this, or our buildings are going to be destroyed by the introduction of ramps, chair-lifts, and the like," he warns. "It's valid as a design problem to make these things part of the architecture."

Michael Pittas also addresses the challenges posed by the changing demographics of American society and, like Jacobsen, perceives them as something with which architects should be concerned. Indeed, Pittas claims that "architects are the only professional group that can give formal manifestation to the new demographics of the country and reflect such factors as changing lifestyles, household formulations, age distribution. These are critically important issues that are not being discussed at all in the vocabulary of architecture. What does it mean when the predominant household type in the country is *not* Mom, Dad, two kids, and a dog?"

Newly emerging social and demographic patterns—whether they have to do with the changing composition of the contemporary family or the ethnic, sexual, generational, and economic makeup of the populace—must be reflected in an environment that can adapt to change. In response to changing urban mandates, Cooper says, architects must ask themselves "whether life in cities is improving, whether priorities are sensible, whether architects are contributing to the dialogue." How—and how successfully—contemporary architects will meet this challenge remains to be seen; we are currently, as John Hejduk says, "in a period of architectural search and re-search." In what direction is this search headed? When the architects who speak in *American Architecture Now: II* consider the future of building in the United States, they inevitably voice a commitment to the diversity we are already witnessing. Philip Johnson's prophecy captures the essence of this vision: "We are entering an unbelievably glorious age of mélange, eclecticism, random choices, and leadership. It's impossible to pin down, but it should be the greatest period architecture has ever seen."

Architecture may yet make a difference.

Barbaralee Diamonstein
June 1985

EMILIO AMBASZ

The work of architect, designer, and curator Emilio Ambasz is celebrated for its poetic as well as practical qualities. Called an inspired pragmatist, Ambasz draws on natural and technological, ancient and futuristic sources for his buildings.

BLDD: You came from your native Argentina in the mid-1960s to Princeton University, where you received a bachelor's degree and a master's degree in architecture in something like two years. How did you manage that?

EA: Cheating and lying. How else? I came in as a freshman and took courses in sociology, Romance languages, and architecture. Among the people teaching there at the time were Michael Graves and Peter Eisenman. They proposed that I be moved over to the graduate school. The dean of the college called all the other departments. Everybody said I was an A-plus student. What they very generously didn't mention was that I was writing all my papers and exams in Spanish because I could barely put three English sentences together.

BLDD: It must have been quite an adjustment to make when you first came from Argentina. How much of a challenge was it to overcome the language barrier, not to mention the cultural barrier? Is it true that you could barely speak English?

EA: Well, no. I taught myself English mainly by watching American films on Argentine television. I spoke like Gary Cooper in his films of the 1940s. I used to say things like "How do you like them apples?" which I picked up from an Edward Albee play. What I could never adjust to was the Princeton food. That was the greatest cultural shock.

BLDD: What was it like for you when you first came to the United States?

EA: I felt they had made a mistake by accepting me, but after three days I realized that *I* had made a mistake. I thought I was coming to the Institute for Advanced Study, which is what I had always imagined Princeton to be. I never knew how the American university system worked and thought it was similar to the Argentine system, where you go to university for six years and get a professional degree. I didn't understand the distinction between college and graduate school. I was ad-

vised by the American cultural affairs attaché in Buenos Aires that I should apply directly to American colleges, so I got application forms from many schools. But Princeton said that they didn't want me to apply for undergraduate studies—I did not know exactly what they meant—and that they would be happy to receive my application once I got a degree from the University of Buenos Aires. I got it into my head that I was going to get admitted there, so I sent Princeton responses to every question I could imagine they would have asked in the application form they had never sent. When I met the admissions officer years later, he told me he had never known anybody with so much nerve. That might be the reason they admitted me.

BLDD: Did you know you wanted to study architecture when you first came?

EA: Oh yes. I've known that since I was eleven.

BLDD: What inspired such an ambition at that age?

EA: I used to wake up an architect. I used to go to bed as an architect. I never thought about anything else.

BLDD: Was there a tradition of architecture in your family?

EA: No, not at all.

BLDD: Was there a particular individual, institution, circumstance, or building that gave you such an idea?

EA: No. It was single-mindedness. I got one idea into my head and never left room for any other.

BLDD: But what gave you the idea in the first place?

EA: Oh, building blocks, naturally—isn't that always the way?

BLDD: You decided that you were going to become an architect when you were eleven years old. You also once said that you received your most important design tools when you were a child of ten. What were they?

EA: My goodness . . . I've been trying to forget my childhood. I was probably referring to a little set of construction toys; they were boring, as I remember. They had perfectly cutout windows made of cardboard and columns made of wood. The natural thing was to build yourself a house, but my obsession was to use the elements to make something against the nature of what the toy dictated. I built towers or airplanes—where the windows had to double as wings—or many other things. The perversion of the material is the only way you can actually create a new work.

BLDD: Like many architects, you did not begin your career by designing buildings. You began by organizing exhibitions. From 1970 to 1976, you were the Museum of Modern Art's curator of design. How did that experience influence your architectural life? What did you do while you were there?

EA: There is a traditional role established for a curator of design—basically, bringing to a certain level of consciousness the meanings and values embodied in the objects man makes. I thought it also my duty to celebrate objects—to communicate the sense of joy I had in them—and to actually collect as well as exhibit them. But there was also a special aspect to the Museum of Modern Art, which is that it organized exhibitions around certain types of problems. I felt that the museum had to use its prestige as an institution to support the undertakings of a number of architects and designers who were interested in certain kinds of inquiry but didn't have an institutional forum. One of the shows I produced along these lines was called "Italy: The New Domestic Landscape." We wanted to critically examine the extraordinary cultural phenomenon of Italian design in the sixties and early seventies. On one hand, we planned to present a number of objects produced in that decade that were of remarkable quality. On the other hand, I thought that Italian designers would also be interested in exploring questions that could not be answered within the scale of objects, but had to be dealt with on the larger scale of whole environments. When we invited designers to participate, we requested that they design environments proposing alternative modes of existence and new types of domestic rituals. We perform various rituals and ceremonies in our culture of which we are usually not aware. I was mainly interested in the rituals of the twenty-four hours of the day. The modern movement had been promising utopia for forty years, but in the meantime it had neglected the twenty-four hours of the day. I prepared a program asking the designers to look into the twenty-four-hour day in terms of the poetics of the house. It was a difficult task because their design, or anti-design, proposals had to be represented in twelve-foot cube spaces.

BLDD: How many objects and environments did you show?

EA: We commissioned twelve environments or events, in some cases, and brought in about 180 objects.

BLDD: Which were the most successful?

EA: There was one that proposed a number of mobile pieces of furniture in the same unit. They looked like steamer trunks on casters and all the twelve or fourteen pieces could be moved around and organized in several ways. They fit into a way of life that European designers imagine every American inhabits—a loft space in SoHo. Another design I thought interesting was a mobile home. When the capsule arrived someplace, the walls would come down and it would open up like an accordion. You could live there for a certain amount of time, then close it up and move to another place. Again, a European idea of the mobile American society.

BLDD: Your idea of American mobility was such that it engendered another idea—a better form of mobility. Can you tell us about the taxi show?

EA: Taxis represent a very important form of semipublic transportation. We discovered that in the United States forty percent of semipublic transportation is done by taxis. It's one means of transportation that is privately financed, not requiring a public investment. The result is that existing taxis utilized in urban circumstances are not suitable for city use. I prepared a program for a better urban vehicle, requiring that in the design the seated taxi driver could open the door for passengers, who could enter without having to lose their foreheads and could travel with their suitcases inside. Also necessary would be air-conditioning systems and a barrier or division between driver and passenger. This program was presented to a number of manufacturers. I insisted on having real, working prototypes that the Urban Mass Transit Administration in Washington would test.

BLDD: Were any of them successful?

EA: Many were successful. Two were especially good. One of them was by Volvo, the Swedish company, and the other was by Alfa Romeo. The Alfa Romeo taxi utilized the chassis and engine of an existing vehicle with a redesigned habitat, demonstrating that in a very small chassis it was possible to have comfort with no need to make a substantial investment to achieve it.

BLDD: Were any manufactured?

EA: They were not manufactured on a large scale. We did manufacture prototypes to show that the American or European car industries could manufacture the taxis, in some cases with minor investment. In the case of the Volkswagen taxi, it was a hybrid electric-diesel engine that produced almost no pollution, and the only extra expense was $800 for the electric engine. The Alfa Romeo or the Volvo could have been manufactured and sold to the public or to taxi drivers for $10,000 to $12,000. In order to produce a prototype we would have required a guarantee that it would be sold to twenty thousand buyers, or that some sort of subsidy would be made available to buyers of such taxis in the form of loans or tax abatements.

BLDD: From your early days as an architect you have written fables as a means of describing projects. What's the purpose of this method?

EA: It's a kind of irony, a device of stating courageously what may not be read within the lines.

BLDD: What is an example of an Ambasz fable?

EA: This one is called "Fabula Rosa." There once was a village in the grip of fear, a fear of the divine as well as the human: the villagers were afraid of the gods and they were afraid of men. One villager went to the center of the village and started building a construct made of mud, stones, and branches. It had a more or less cylindrical form and a semispherical roof. When the villager finished, he emerged from his construction and announced that this was where the gods dwelled and that the temple he had built had the shape of the universe. He then pulled a branch off the temple and drew a circle around the village with it. With the help of the other villagers he built defense walls made of mud and stone. Once he completed his travails, he came again into the village and built a hut and covered it with earth, except for the entrance. On top he put six vertical slabs of stone. That he called his home. The people called it the palace. When the man died, his son put his body inside the hut, took the stones off the top, and covered the entrance. That is the way some people say architecture started.

BLDD: And what would you say?

EA: That such was the way.

BLDD: Is it fair to say that most, if not all, of your buildings are metaphors?

EA: Yes, I think they are metaphors. They act as standards for approximation. They stand for the celestial dwelling we aspire to, we desire. Perhaps I'm more interested in evoking the architectural domain by using nontraditional means than by using the more canonical elements of architecture. By now we have an established, classical language of architecture; it's possible to create an architecture by using windows, columns, cornices, and other details within that language. I'm more interested in the more basic primeval hope, expectation, need, and desire for an abode. I don't know the word in English, but in Italian it's called *dimora,* in French *demeure*—the place where you dwell while waiting for the end to come. It is a deliberate construct, a place where you embellish your allotted time before you render your account at the end. I'm not frightened of the end. I believe that any system that does not contemplate the way it's going to end is a self-deluding system, and this brings about vanity.

BLDD: How much of the work of architecture is fable and how much of it is practice?

EA: In reality some images or drawings have a greater impact than many buildings that are built. For example, Mies van der Rohe's designs for the Friedrichstrasse skyscraper had a tremendous impact on the work of the modern movement. It was never built. The Barcelona Pavilion was built, but it lasted only three months. Yet it had an immense influence. I don't think something actually has to be built to create an impact. However, if it's built, it casts a shadow; it operates on a sensory level and adds another enormously important dimension.

BLDD: What buildings do you think reflect the best in modern architecture?

EA: I think Mies's Farnsworth House is the expression of the perfect abode. It has a perfect roof and a perfect floor, completely separate from the ground. It is a universal type of space that allows everything to happen. It suffers by neglecting its context in terms of sun or wind, as well as other things. But it is a conceit of the mind. Culture usually is a conceit of the mind, and I think the house is a high expression of culture. Other places that have moved me in some way would include Luis Barragan's fountains. These are places where you get the feeling of a presence having been there a minute before you arrived. They have a very staged, dramatic quality that interests me very much.

BLDD: What architects or periods of architecture have been most influential or inspiring for you?

EA: The pre-Adamic period is the only one I'm interested in. Sometimes I have a feeling that I would like to build for the last inhabitants of our culture and for the first ones of the culture to come. I don't think I am terribly interested—consciously—in periods of architecture. Subconsciously, I am. I have, after all, acquired a métier by looking at architecture, and therefore I am part of the tradition I have inherited, even if I scream that I am not.

BLDD: To the work of which architects do you most respond?

EA: Frank Lloyd Wright, from the bottom of my heart. Will I be loyal to him forever and ever? Only until the next architect walks by.

BLDD: That's interesting, considering that you are in many ways a protégé of the Museum of Modern Art. As I recall, one of your predecessors at the museum once referred to Mr. Wright as "the best architect—of the nineteenth century." How do *you* respond to that appraisal?

EA: I can simultaneously admire Mies van der Rohe and Frank Lloyd Wright because they strike a chord that says "architecture." Even if the styles are completely different, the emotional pursuit is the same. That one comes from the nineteenth century and the other from the twentieth I find a meaningless distinction.

BLDD: Among your cryptic phrases is the declaration that you're interested not in recovery but in discovery. What do you mean by that statement?

EA: Many architects—my beloved colleagues—are engaged in an operation of recovering the memory of architecture. As you know, the modern movement started with the assumption that the evolution of a new man was possible. This new man would not remember the history of architecture. During the forty or fifty years that the modern movement lasted, in the hope of arriving at that magnificent promised land, we neglected all the lessons of history. At present many architects are interested in a recovery of those lessons. I think it is the recovery of architecture's memories that is important. As I said before, we have neglected the twenty-four hours of the day and, therefore, the emotional and sensory materials of which the twenty-four hours are made. People engaged in recovery are interested in recapturing the sensory quality that architecture once had in the form of ornaments or decorations. But the way they go about that, I think, is rather simplistic and too academic. They recover fragments from history and apply them, as it were, with glue. Regrettably, the glue holding the product together will dry up in a few years and the thing will fall with a sound few people will hear. What I'm interested in is the invention of ornaments connected with a new type of structure. And by structure I do not mean the built structure, but a theoretical structure of the building. There is a need for ornament. I have absolutely no doubt about that.

BLDD: You've said that in the course of reinvention, the search the architect must undertake is not so much for sources as for secrets. Can you explain this?

EA: By sources I mean historical sources—not so much historical elements such as windows or doors, but that which defines a door as a passage, that which defines a window as a device to look from one place to another. Although these elements can be created by utilizing frames or proper ornaments, or anything traditional architectural culture has to offer, the important thing is not to actually make a window but to create the possibility of looking through. I'm interested in the secret of looking through matter, the secret of going through matter, not in the door or the window. Architecture has to do with the way we exist, the way we transact with materials, not with a devised code of door, frame, or window.

BLDD: In some ways your work is more theoretical than that of most architects. You talk of myths and fantasies, of private worlds and inner desires. But there is another aspect of it that is very direct and very solid. How would you best describe the work you do?

EA: What I do is not reductive as much as it is evocative and essential. I try to create a certain type of statement that will evoke the feeling of the roof, the entrance, or the approach to the house, sometimes by utilizing nontraditional elements. If I have to indicate an entrance, I would prefer to use two bales of hay. If I have to make a roof, I would prefer to use grapevines.

BLDD: In addition to traditional and technological building materials, you are interested in natural materials as an important component in architecture—not only bales of hay, but earth, air, water, and light. You just made reference to using a grapevine. Would you tell us about your low-cost housing solution for a community of grape growers in California?

EA: A group of nine families, with state help, bought land that was not very good for grape growing. They went to the University of Southern California to discuss how they could best cultivate their grapes. Someone there remembered that I had once mentioned how marvelous it is to exist under the vines of southern France and southern Italy, which grow about twelve feet above the ground on trellises. The grapes hang among the leaves, which cover up the grapes and cast a very nice shadow. I proposed to these nine families that they plant their grapes in the same way. Columns would support a grid of

Private Residence, Córdoba, Spain, model

wires. Once the grapes grew, the families could move their trailer homes under the roofs created by the leaves. I defined their private plots with hedges that, when fully grown, would create gardens. This was one way to achieve an architecture by utilizing natural materials. We also created a chapel by excavating until we reached the water table. Since the water level changes often, we put the cross there. A certain amount of instability would assure the perpetuity of the church.

BLDD: The idea of excavation and subterranean life has influenced a number of your projects. Can you tell us about this fascination and what prompted your interest in underground solutions?

EA: The only underground house I've built is the one in Córdoba, and it's not really underground. It has a roof covered with three feet of earth, but it looks onto a patio open to the sky, as in a traditional southern Spanish house. The fact that the house is below ground is in no way perceivable, either experientially or culturally, by the inhabitants, because they are in a normal southern Spanish patio house. But I assure you that in most cases I build above ground. It's cheaper and many times it's drier.

BLDD: What is your idea of a berm? How do you use it?

EA: Imagine that I build a normal house with four sides. One side is oriented toward the sun and will not get covered, but against the other three sides, especially the one to the north, and the roof I start piling up at least four inches of earth. This has a number of advantages: you don't have problems with insulation; you don't have to spend money on outside finishes; you can keep approximately the same temperature in the house throughout the year, sixty-eight to seventy degrees; you can combine the house and the garden. The windows are on the open side that faces south. So it's a traditional house, except that the back is inaccessible. In many cases, even in normal houses, it makes sense not to have windows on the north side, where wind can come in.

BLDD: No matter what the locale, how do you see the relationship between landscape and building?

EA: I feel that I am an intruder in the landscape in all cases, so a reconciliation has to be established, not a separation of landscape and house. I prefer a place that welcomes me rather than one that forces me to interact constantly with the outer elements as well as with society. So I like to turn the land and the house into one element with minimum cultural intervention. It's not possible in all types of projects. You can do it with houses but not with large buildings like office buildings.

BLDD: Actually you *are* trying to do it with an office building.

Can you tell us about your proposal for the new home for the Museum of American Folk Art?

EA: The Museum of American Folk Art has two assets. One is its collection and the other is its real estate on an extraordinarily desirable site, next to the Museum of Modern Art. The only way for the museum to finance itself is to sell its air rights. We are proposing an office building, about twenty-six stories high, which would house the museum. Since the museum would be much smaller than the building, I have designed the office building in such a way that its volume would be subordinated to the museum's. As the museum is small and relatively unknown, it requires a strong theatrical gesture. There is a need for a transitional procession as one passes from the street into the building. It shouldn't be like passing through a single membrane; it should be a series of steps. So the design calls for a great portico.

BLDD: Is this how you managed to subordinate the office function to that of the museum?

EA: No. The portico is the grand portal that goes around the entrance to both the office building and the museum. I have reversed the traditional organization of the New York wedding-cake or zigzag-type building by dividing the mass into three blocks. The blocks are projected over one another in such a way that they create a canopy over the entrance. The buildings shelter the entrance to the museum like a big cornice.

BLDD: It is right up the street from one of the most distinguished museums of modern art in the world, the Museum of Modern Art, and in the shadow of the American Craft Museum, which will also have a new home soon. How do you plan to compete with those more established and—at least publicly—more auspicious neighbors?

EA: I think it's a marvelous collection of friends to have nearby. They do not cast shadows. They lend us their light. The problem of contest that seems to concern some architects . . .

BLDD: Does it concern you?

EA: When the contest is worthwhile, yes. In certain cases where there's a vacuum, it is up to the architect to make the first statement that will then generate a context. This street is a treasure.

BLDD: But other architects *have* already generated that context—Cesar Pelli, for example, in the tower for the Museum of Modern Art, and Kevin Roche, in the addition to the CBS Building that will house the new American Craft Museum. How do you conceive of your tower as an addition to the history of the Manhattan skyscraper and as an addition to the context that includes those two buildings, those two friends, as you put it?

EA: The Manhattan skyscraper is based on a nineteenth-century notion that you build a tall building like a column, with a base, a shaft, and a capital. What I have done is provide a building with a base, a shaft, and a capital. And Manhattan itself has the tradition of the wedding-cake building, which, as I explained before, I tried to reverse, so the cake is upside-down, creating an awning over the entrance. The problems and the vagaries of American, especially New York, real estate are such that I prefer to provide a frame enclosing and defining my building. The building is like two pillars—one on the right, one on the left—that go all the way up. They contain the elevators and all the vertical movement systems, and the floors span between the two. The pillars create a frame, ensuring that whatever is placed to the right or to the left of the building will not affect it that much. The building's contribution to the context is that it is an entity unto itself; it has an architectural identity that doesn't result from borrowing reflections from the sky or from appealing too much to memory.

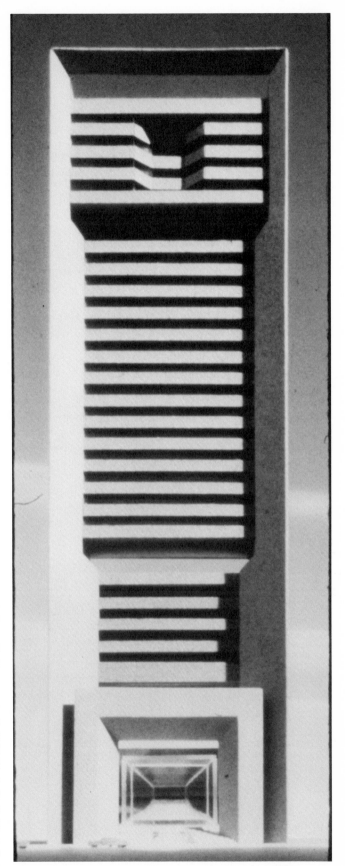

Museum of American Folk Art, New York, N.Y., model

This building could have a great effect on such a short street; as with three or four words well spoken, the meanings that may arise, as well as the contradictions, are what matters.

BLDD: Could you explain a recent commission of yours—a

botanical garden in San Antonio? First of all, how can San Antonio sustain a botanical garden?

EA: Actually, San Antonio has a rather good climate. It's not that terribly hot. Come winter it gets to be thirty-two degrees and pretty windy. And the people there do have a longing for plants. But in this case, more than a botanical garden, we are talking about an enchanted place where plants could provide the serenity and pleasure always associated with gardens. San Antonio has some advantages for a botanical garden. You can grow plants without the need for a tremendous amount of glass coverage. So rather than having a container all of glass, a glass roof might be enough. As there are no great collections of plants from the southern United States, the hope is that San Antonio could organize such a collection.

BLDD: You've also created a large garden and greenhouse in Houston called Celestial Garden, which you have described as a metaphor for fossil fuel. Could you elaborate on that?

EA: Greenhouses are really hothouses. Houston certainly doesn't need a greenhouse to grow any plants; it is a hothouse by itself—it has that type of climate. But because of the climate, the city would benefit from a garden where people could go and find a hospitable environment. In a greenhouse in Houston the problems are compounded because the sun will warm it up and tremendous loads of air-conditioning will be necessary. What I proposed, in order to reduce the need for air-conditioning and heating, was to cool the outside of the greenhouse. I built a second glass house outside the first one. Between the two there is a space of about fifty feet, and the volume is filled with cold water mist. This fulfills a number of functions: one, it diffuses the sun; two, it cools the greenhouse; three, it could act as a three-dimensional screen for the projection of light shows. The mist also diffracts the light in such a way that rainbows are constantly created. Between the two glass skins there are a number of pieces of optical machinery that represent the sun and the planets—in essence a planetarium. So you have the sun above, the trees underneath, and at the bottom is a fire pit, courtesy of the gas company. With the sun, the plants, and the fire, what you have in essence is the history of fossil fuels.

BLDD: It also sounds like it fulfills your need for the theatrical gesture.

EA: That's the way architecture started.

BLDD: How do you apply drama to other kinds of projects—for instance, one as specifically and as carefully defined as the Schlumberger Engineering Research Laboratory in Austin, Texas?

EA: Sometimes in a very silent place just the sketch of a smile can reverberate throughout.

BLDD: That is more persuasive as a thought, I suspect, than as a building. How did you actually do it?

EA: The research laboratory wanted to attract a number of bright and energetic engineers, and the hope was that Schlumberger would provide them with a place conducive to conversation, discussion, maybe a certain degree of exasperation. It was assumed that a collegiate type of atmosphere was appropriate. In order to create this, I dammed a very small flow of water that existed on the site to make a rather large pond. I separated all the functions of the laboratory into a kind of "garden-text," a park scattered with objects for particular uses and a system of linking paths.

BLDD: What's the most satisfying assignment you've ever had?

EA: I think the house in Córdoba, the one that is covered with earth. It's the quintessential house, perhaps because the idea came out right. That's why I found it satisfying. Although even if a work is satisfying, one has peace for only a few minutes before the eyes of the indifferent Almighty close again, demanding yet another image.

Botanical Garden, San Antonio, Tex., model

Celestial Garden, Houston, Tex., model

BLDD: You served as the president of the Architectural League of New York. What special value and function does an architecture-oriented organization like that have?

EA: There are many ideas generated by designing buildings. A society expresses itself with its buildings; often you can recognize the values of a society by looking at what it builds. The goal of the Architectural League is to bring to a level of awareness some of the meanings embodied in proposed buildings, to expand cultural values by analyzing them, and often just to criticize what is being done. You need places like the Architectural League as chambers for criticism. They provide a platform for people who have ideas and hypotheses. Architecture is different from painting or writing. Many times architects present their ideas by means of drawings or models, and I feel that you need a place where such things can be discussed as if they already had a full-fledged existence.

BLDD: You are a persuasive fellow and a very influential teacher. Many of your students have described your effect on them. Tell us how they have influenced you.

EA: They reveal to me that I have a very paternalistic side, in that I try to protect them from all that happens to them, myself included. They have taught me that I'd rather deal with inanimate objects. Objects will not betray me. They will not die. They will be there and they will be indifferent to me, which is a very healthy situation.

BLDD: You don't mean one word of that! Yet another expression of your need for drama! You've done a great deal to encourage public dialogue about architecture. Do you think it is more active and significant today than it has been in years past?

EA: There's great attention focused on architecture and on the quality of daily existence in the home. It is really significant in terms of the number of books published on the subject and

the attention many large publications are giving it. There's also an improvement in the general level of education of the public. It reflects a recognition that we do dwell in cities and that the possibility of action within cities is pretty restricted. The interior is perhaps the last degree of freedom people have, a place where you can enact your dreams. The fact that people have taken refuge in the interior and abandoned the hope of acting upon the larger, urban scale frightens me.

BLDD: In other words, you think that the attention to interior design is not the new freedom, but the last freedom?

EA: You said it very nicely, yes. Perhaps the last freedom will be the sweater. I leave that for the fashion designer.

BLDD: Would you comment on the recent controversy over architects appropriating other architects' designs? In your view, what constitutes plagiarism rather than inspiration or derivation?

EA: The notion of a monopoly on ideas is an artificial concept. The moment something is invented is the moment of maximum joy for the inventor. If an idea is later appropriated by somebody else, and this second person achieves the recognition by society that the first one didn't, I hope it will all be balanced in the next world. At present, I am only interested in the invention of the first word. When I designed the Vertebra chair with Piretti, I think it was the first of its kind. Since then there have been many other chairs with moving backs and tilting seats. In no case do I think that I am owed anything by the others, just by the people who first used my idea.

BLDD: The designing of chairs is among your many interests; your seating has won many prizes. One of your designs was for the Lumb-r chair, and now you've designed the Dorsal chair. Would you describe your special concerns in developing these chairs?

EA: Dorsal chairs are for people who have to sit for long periods of time. When most people sit for more than eight minutes, they fidget. I wanted a chair that would move with me. I wanted the back to tilt when I leaned back, and I wanted the whole chair to lean forward if I leaned over a desk to write. I wanted a chair whose front edge wouldn't bite into the thighs and inhibit blood circulation. I designed a chair that accomplishes these things without the need for levers or arms. I thought the chair would force any user into a certain form of exercise. For people who have to work sitting—some of us spend almost a third of our lives sitting—I wanted the chair to be a working instrument that doesn't require a lot of attention.

BLDD: You've said that you do not make graphic designs, industrial products, or architecture. You've described yourself as an object maker, whether it be a building or a product. What do you mean when you call yourself that?

EA: The word for that is "invention."

BLDD: One of your more recent inventions was the design of a poster for Formica to announce a new type of laminate that shows no black lines where one piece joins another. What did you do to show this concept?

EA: The basic feature of this product is that when two planes of this material meet, there are no black joining lines. The poster had to demonstrate this. Since the poster is also a piece of

Lumb-r Chair

paper, I folded it and showed that there was no visible seam of any sort. It was just a fold. The poster was therefore designed like an accordion. It arrives small and compact but when extended becomes a three-dimensional item. The most important concept behind this material is the possibility of creating three-dimensional elements, rather than two-dimensional elements joined at a treacherous edge.

BLDD: At the moment you are engaged as the chief design consultant for the Cummins Engine Company in Columbus, Indiana. How does your approach differ in designing a technological object like an engine and designing a building? Are there similar concerns?

EA: Certain basic concerns are the same, but the main similarity is my interest in fundamental principles. If you understand the basic principle of a house and you remain loyal to the pursuit of quintessence, then like a perfect act, you will generate a number of perfect coincidences.

BLDD: One problem architects have been preoccupied with for much of history is . . .

EA: Clients . . .

BLDD: Actually I was going to say the difference between the inside and the outside of a building. How do you see this relationship?

EA: With the outside you interact with society at large. With the inside you interact with yourself. The same thing is true in many types of products. When I design diesel engines, the inside of the skin has to do with explosion chambers, combustion, and all that. The outside has to do with regulation, a number of attachments and elements that have to regulate the performance of this explosion chamber. The situation at present is that architects have compressed the outside and the inside into one very thin, perhaps two-inch-thick, domain that they call the skin. I believe it's possible to read all types of meanings between the inside and the outside of those two inches.

BLDD: Do inside and outside have to speak the same language?

EA: No. There should be a certain degree of contradiction. Usually between the two there will only be microscopic differences, but they will be assigned immense meanings. Architects are willing to accept the domain of the skin as one way of reconciling themselves to the difficulties of commercial building. They have to accept the two inches that developers will allow them. I imagine that we're going to have interior architects and exterior architects, and there will be cards exchanged that say "So-and-So, Interior Architect" or "So-and-So, Exterior Architect."

BLDD: What will *your* card say?

EA: Mine will be just a handful of earth that will disintegrate in your hands as you receive it.

BLDD: Are there any frustrations you find associated with the work of an architect?

EA: Clients.

BLDD: What would you do without them?

EA: I would like to be my own client, although I've been very lucky—I have extraordinarily understanding and enlightened clients. So I'm really voicing complaints for the profession without myself having been too much of a victim.

BLDD: An architect who is his own client might be likened to the lawyer who had himself as a client: he was said to have a fool as a client and a fool as a lawyer. Don't you think you need that outside exchange?

EA: Many of the best examples of architecture I've seen came about because of the interaction between a great architect and a remarkable client. That's absolutely true. With the products I design, I'm able to postulate an idea of what type of chair I believe should exist and then go out and find the financial and

N-14 Engine for the Cummins Engine Company

technical means to bring it into being. But in the case of my architecture, the type of housing I believe should be created, I do need a certain amount of collaboration from the outside. Unfortunately, I don't think I've been endowed with much patience, and I certainly have no tact.

BLDD: According to an article about you in the Italian design magazine *Domus,* there are two personas in Emilio Ambasz. To whom, or what, were they referring?

EA: I think they meant that one was Emilio and the other one was Ambasz. Emilio the architect and Ambasz the product maker. Ambasz is anxious because he would like his products to be well received by man; Emilio is anguished because he would like his architecture to be well received by angels.

BLDD: By the way, which of those personas has been present here today?

EA: Oh, Emilio is seen rarely. I think most of the time there was a guarded Ambasz.

BLDD: We had glimpses of Emilio, too, I suspect. Did you expect your life to follow the path it has?

EA: I usually live in dire terror of doing something that will make the whole thing come unstuck.

BLDD: Do you think that's the way most people are?

EA: No. I think that in some way I have a messianic, completely maniacal attitude. I feel I have a destiny to fullfill.

BLDD: Was this engendered by your Argentine forebears?

EA: Well, that is a hard thing to prove. No, I think it's engendered by a sense that architecture is a very long road and that hopefully you get better with age, although as you get older you may change so much that you don't remember where you started.

BLDD: Is there a prevailing philosophy that ties all your work together?

EA: No. There are only images. It is only through images that the meaning or the truth will emerge. I do not want to express it in language.

BLDD: Is there such a thing as an architectural spirit of the time?

EA: Yes, I would hope so. But it cannot be expressed in words, only in images, and when the images appear, they will grip the heart. I think those images are rare.

BLDD: Do you see your own work as being in the forefront of that spirit? Or an alternative to it?

EA: I feel myself to be on the edge, to the side, or to the front of that spirit, but quite outside the common, ongoing discourse, even of the so-called avant-garde.

BLDD: Is that by choice or by circumstance?

EA: By destiny. That's the way it is.

BLDD: If you had it to do over again, what would you do differently?

EA: I would be born the son of a banker.

BLDD: Or a developer?

EA: Right. I would never hang out the shingle that says "Architect." I would claim to be a developer and smuggle in my architecture under that umbrella.

BLDD: If there were one project you would someday like to do, some secret dream, what would that be?

EA: My house.

BLDD: What would that house look like?

EA: No answer until the image arrives. That house is a mystery to me.

JOHN BURGEE

John Burgee, in collaboration with Philip Johnson, has designed buildings acclaimed for their elegance and sophistication. Their designs are distinguished by innovative, daring features; striking forms are often created through the juxtaposition of modern materials with elements from an earlier architectural vocabulary.

BLDD: After receiving your degree in architecture from the University of Notre Dame in 1956, you remained in Chicago, the city in which you were raised, to practice architecture. What was so compelling about Chicago that made you decide to practice there?

JB: Chicago was the first city of American architecture. It had the tradition of the Chicago School. Much of the great architecture of modern times has been built in Chicago; it was the home of Mies van der Rohe. My father was a member of one of the oldest firms in Chicago, Holabird, Root & Burgee. That architectural heritage was always apparent to me. It seemed that the people of Chicago—perhaps because of the second-city syndrome—were proud of their buildings and had great feeling for architecture, more so than in any other city.

BLDD: Do you think that this is still the case?

JB: It has changed a great deal. Architecture has become much more commercial. I like to think that's because I left! But it had already started.

BLDD: Are there any other cities that you think now have that kind of pride?

JB: Houston has picked up this spirit, the ambition to create great buildings. Builders there, don't mind, it seems, spending a little more for better buildings. They have not always been successful, but the same spirit exists that I think existed in Chicago.

BLDD: Does that exist in New York also?

JB: Not to the same extent. Except for individual people or places, New York has never had an overall feeling for it. Chrysler built a building to glorify himself and his company. Rockefeller built his center, still unsurpassed. Vanderbilt built Grand Central Station. But as for the general run of office buildings, the standard was lower in New York.

BLDD: But there is, you maintain, a prevailing attitude of civic pride in Houston now that is manifested in its architecture.

JB: It is a civic pride. You know how people think in Houston—in a lot of Texas, for that matter. They feel a pride in their buildings. That's why our firm has built so much, so successfully, there.

BLDD: Do you think they're on their way to accomplishing their ambitions?

JB: Yes. They have built some fine buildings already and are in the process of building more.

BLDD: For example?

JB: Pennzoil was called the building of the decade. The Shell Building, although not my favorite, was recognized as one of the best buildings of its time. The original Tenneco is a very fine building, probably one of Skidmore, Owings & Merrill's best buildings. Unfortunately, they had to put a sign on the top. Other than that, it is excellent. When Tenneco built their second building, it wasn't of the same quality. Indeed, it was just the opposite, a plain speculative building. They weren't building headquarters for themselves, and it shows. The program for Pennzoil was to give them some identity, something to be proud of. With Transco, it was the same thing. They kept asking us, "Are you still sure that this is your best building?" That sentiment is more prevalent now in Houston than any place else.

BLDD: When you began to practice architecture in Chicago you did not join the firm that your father was once with.

JB: No. My brother was there; he was involved in the design department. I wanted to be a designer, too, so I thought it would be better to go elsewhere.

BLDD: Eventually you became a partner in another distinguished firm, C. F. Murphy Associates.

JB: Yes, I started with C. F. Murphy, now called Murphy/Jahn. When I came back from the army, I found that Murphy had all the best work but nobody to do it. It seemed to be a great opportunity. I moved right in, and the first job I worked on was a $100 million airport. It was a good project to cut your teeth on!

BLDD: You were with Murphy for almost ten years. What

were some of the other major projects during that time?
JB: The Civic Center Building, that's the rusty steel building; the First National Bank, the one with the sloping walls; and a number of projects for the University of Illinois. My first project was O'Hare Airport and it was certainly the one that taught me most. The nice part about it was that it was a combination of small and large buildings with big management and construction problems. Yet because of the variety of buildings, the project had a scale a young person could relate to. To start working as a young architect on a $100 million project in a very responsible position is not something that happens very often. It was a bit overwhelming, but O'Hare gave me almost a whole career in a single project.
BLDD: How would you characterize the design approach of C. F. Murphy Associates when you were part of the firm?
JB: None of the Murphy family were designers; they were business people. This appealed to me, as I could contribute in the design phase of the work. I did not design the airport, but I was able to contribute. The design approach of the firm fluctuated as strong designers joined or left the staff.
BLDD: Can you tell us who some of them were?
JB: Jaq Brownson, who had been dean at Illinois Institute of Technology, was a student of Mies's and a strong advocate of his work. I worked on the Civic Center with him. Then Gene Summers came to do the new McCormick Place. He had been a partner of Mies's. Before that there was Stan Gladych, who had come from SOM straight from the Air Force Academy and worked with me on O'Hare.
BLDD: Did Mies himself have a relationship with Murphy? If so, on what project?
JB: The Murphy office did the Federal Office Building in Chicago from Mies's design. The office had a strong production reputation and many young people from IIT were trying to build a design image, so it was a strong and natural relationship with Mies. We did several projects with him.
BLDD: Did you know Mies?
JB: I met him several times. He was substantially older than me. I was never as friendly with him as Philip was.
BLDD: Is there anything that you remember clearly?
JB: He was so adored. He had such a presence that when he came into the room we all felt something special was happening. But he was very uncommunicative.
BLDD: What made his presence so enriching?
JB: He had a strong physical presence. But he was so revered by Chicago architects of my generation I don't know how to describe it.
BLDD: What do you see as the major difference between working as an architect in Chicago and in New York, either in the past or today?
JB: Philip Johnson put it best when I came to New York. He said to me, "Being an architect in Chicago means building in Chicago. Being an architect in New York means building in the world." That has proven to be the case. Some Chicago friends do practice outside the city, but not to a great extent. Since I've been in New York I've practiced everywhere. In fact, I've done fewer buildings in New York than I've done in other places. At the moment we have one Chicago building on the drawing board, an office on LaSalle Street for a developer named John Buck. He worked for the realtor on the Sears Tower and wants to build up his image as the best developer in Chicago. He has some property on Adams and LaSalle, which is one of the finest locations in the city. It's very exciting. The design of the building is reminiscent of the work of the pre-Mies Chicago School of the twenties. It's kind of Gothic in feeling.
BLDD: Can you describe the project?

JB: It's only in the preliminary stages. But it will be stone and will try to capture the quality and proud feeling of that earlier period.
BLDD: How did you first come to meet Philip Johnson?
JB: I had been asked to come to an interview for the Philadelphia airport project. Carter Manny, one of my partners at Murphy's office, had been a classmate of Philip's at Harvard. I was Carter's assistant on O'Hare Airport. Philip had asked Carter to join him because he'd never done an airport and his office wasn't able to handle such a large project. He asked us to come and be interviewed. Carter recommended me. Philip and I hit it off very well. We seemed to have similar professional aims. That was in 1965.
BLDD: Did you ever expect events to unfold the way they did?
JB: Not at all. We nearly got that airport commission. Philip called me one time and said, "My God, we might get that job commission. Then we could never get together!" We had been talking about joining. At the time I was a little disenchanted with the large practice of Murphy's.
BLDD: For what reasons?
JB: When I joined that firm there were about seventy or eighty people, and when I left we had over three hundred. While I was responsible for a good portion of the work, I was not able to be as personally involved as I wanted. The firm was just too big, although I had helped to set it up to be large, on the scale of a Skidmore, Owings & Merrill. I found I was only getting involved in the beginning and at the end of projects. The buildings were being designed by others, with very little input from me. I was going to building openings and thinking, My God, how did that happen? I felt I was becoming a manager or caretaker of this huge beast and was not really practicing architecture, which I consider a "hands-on" profession.
BLDD: What made the two of you decide to work together? What was the nature of your first association, and what did you expect from it?
JB: I didn't know what to expect. This was 1967. Philip and I talked for over a year. No decision had been made on the Philadelphia airport. Finally, the airport fell through. He called me the next day. I flew to New York and we decided to work together. It was a big step because my wife and I were both firmly entrenched Chicagoans.
BLDD: What gave you the courage to act?
JB: I think it was the opportunity to work with someone like Philip and to get back into the profession on a real working level, in a smaller firm. There were only twelve people here when I came in 1967.
BLDD: And now?
JB: Sixty, which I think is ten more than the number I have always set as my ideal. I am trying to cut back now.
BLDD: You are twenty-seven years younger than Philip Johnson, who has always had the energy and vigor of a man at least half his age. What do you think is his secret?
JB: He has enormously good health, and architecture is his single interest. Philip's life is his architecture—no family, no distractions of any kind. His concentration is immense, as is his dedication to this single pursuit. He has an enormous devotion. His friends are architects. When he goes to dinner he talks architecture. His weekends are spent with people involved in architecture.
BLDD: How do you contrast that to your life?
JB: I have a family and other outside interests. I sail a boat, for instance. But I do think that any successful architect has to have dedication, a purpose, and devotion to his profession. This is not the kind of business you can practice as though you

were running a publishing house or a manufacturing company. It isn't something you turn on or off. It's part of your life. I would compare it more to medicine.

BLDD: When you joined with Philip Johnson in 1967, what was your first project as a team? Did you have an assignment before you became a firm?

JB: No. I came with the understanding with Philip that we didn't know how it would work out because he had never had a partner before.

BLDD: Did he have a real structure to his practice?

JB: He was an individual who had assistants. My understanding when I joined him was that I wasn't coming as an assistant, although I didn't insist on being made a partner immediately. I didn't think this was important. The understanding was that if it worked, I would be his partner.

BLDD: How long did it take?

JB: We said we would give it a year, but in six months we went ahead. What I found was that I was a better architect because of my relationship with Philip. He was very stimulating, as I think I am to him. Together we probably have a better output or a better product, better buildings, than either of us would have had alone. And our practice is unusual in that we both work on every single project.

BLDD: How does it work? Who does what?

JB: We talk in shorthand, in an almost telepathic way. I compared it once to a couple of bakers. One baker might come in and say, "Let's make a cake," and before the next word is spoken the other baker has taken out the chocolate, although the first baker had not said, "Let's make a chocolate cake." This is how Philip and I have worked in the past. We talk about the kind of project it should be before we draw. Pennzoil is a good example. The client wanted a distinctive building, a building with an identity. We knew it couldn't be the highest building in the city, because there would be a higher one within a week. Houston is like that. So while it was a big building, we had to decide what would make it distinguished. We talked about it for a long time.

BLDD: What did you conclude?

JB: Well, when you enter a city, you look at the skyline and say, "Hey, there's the Empire State Building, there's the Chrysler Building." You may say the Seagram Building is the best building in New York, but you can't identify it from across the river, in fact, not even from two blocks away. It gets its quality from its fine detail. So we started out by putting a top on Pennzoil. Many of our succeeding buildings have needed the same kind of identification.

BLDD: Do you still have your "mansardmania"?

JB: Yes, we are doing several buildings with mansards now.

BLDD: Who prevails when there are differences of opinion?

JB: If I question a design that Philip has been working on, he will rework it or we both will. If I say something that he does not like, he will tell me freely, so that we reach a consensus. Perhaps an idea I didn't like in the first place might have been all right, but we will work on it until we're both sure.

BLDD: Have you ever had any sharp ruptures of opinion?

JB: Yes. It was during the first weeks I was here. I was trying to get to know this man and how to work with him. I told him that I intended to be a total part of the office, including the design. He agreed to this. One day we were working, sketching on paper, and I said, "How about this idea?" And he said, "That is stupid! That's the dumbest thing I've ever heard!" You know, he dismisses things that he doesn't like in a very abrupt manner. I thought, Uh-oh, how will this ever work? I was put down a bit, but I thought, I'm not going to stop, because if I do, that's the end. Then I offered another sugges-

tion. And Philip said, "That's brilliant, damn it! Why didn't I think of it?" So that's how our relationship has been. We've been very direct and open with each other, and it's been like that: "That's dumb, it's stupid, it doesn't work," or "It's brilliant, it's good, let's go."

BLDD: What is it like to work with the so-called bad boy of architecture?

JB: I love it this way. The variety is what is so stimulating. If I had to turn out the same thing over and over, it would be no fun. Philip has this marvelous quality, particularly at his age, which is that he is able to accept such variety and start off on a new direction. It has been very broadening for me and taught me not to be satisfied with pat solutions. It is easy when you have developed a successful design to then just repeat it and repeat it with small variations. Part of the criticism of our work has been that there are no clear identifying marks. How can I tell it's a Johnson/Burgee building? I know a Mies van der Rohe building when I see one, and I know a Hugh Stubbins even, or I know I. M. Pei has a certain way, or Harry Cobb has a certain style. It is so stimulating to me to attack each problem as brand-new.

BLDD: There has been a change made in the organization of your firm; John Burgee Architects with Philip Johnson was created just a few years ago. Is it more a change of title or of function—is Philip Johnson now a design consultant?

JB: It's more a change in title, but it reflects the function as it has developed, really.

BLDD: In what way?

JB: Philip is, as you pointed out, twenty-seven years my senior. I intend to practice at least another twenty-seven years, and I don't know that Philip will. He is a celebrity. He was a celebrity before I joined him. He is well known, better known than I am, and many of the buildings that we have done together are regarded as Philip's buildings. So this new name gives a continuity to the firm, which is really a firm that I built around Philip. I run the firm and the office, take care of assignment of staff and all office operations. The new name reflects the firm's organization, a group of architects and me, with Philip Johnson, who is a partner, fully involved, but not in the support operations.

BLDD: What is it like to practice with someone who you describe as a celebrity? I can imagine the positive side of being associated with such a well-known and unusual figure as Philip Johnson, but I can imagine the negative side as well. Can you tell us some of the advantages and some of the limitations?

JB: Well, the "up" side is obvious, and it's fun. The people Philip knows, I get to know; I'm included in interesting situations that I might not have been in without Philip. But I often don't get credited when I should. For example, the AT&T Building is usually referred to as Philip Johnson's building.

BLDD: That must not feel so good.

JB: That hurts, because I've done half of it, let's say—if you can divide things in half. People have asked me, "Who did the hole in the top of AT&T?" I don't remember. Philip and I worked on it together.

BLDD: Who did the design for the entrance?

JB: I don't know. I had an idea once to lift it off the street. How is that done? Is that a possibility? Before I knew it, there it was. It was done. I can't say who did the top, who did the bottom, or who did the middle.

BLDD: Have you found increasing recognition of your contribution since your firm name has changed? Or do you see that as a function of evolution, ultimately?

JB: Yes, it is increasing because of the change. The firm name has often been dropped in the past because everybody recog-

Pennzoil Place, Houston, Tex.

nizes the name Philip Johnson and it gets used more than the firm name. With this new name the firm is recognized.

BLDD: Your firm is interesting because both partners design and you design together. Tell us a little about your unusual collaboration.

JB: We started to talk about Pennzoil. Let's use that example because it was one where we really took a jump. Philip was devoted to being as close as possible to Mies van der Rohe. That was how you measured how good you were. The project was a little outside the development pattern of Houston. In searching for a special identity for the building, Philip suggested expanding the business area by connecting the cultural community, which was on one side of our site, with the financial community, on the other side of the site. Perhaps the diagonal circulation system could become a feature of the design. This set the site plan and started the design parti. The diagonal cut through the site created not a single building but two buildings. This also helped the developer's package in that each building was going to be named after its major tenant. Since oil companies are the major renters in Houston, another oil company wasn't going to rent major space in a Pennzoil tower. The second building offered another identity. It was rented to the Zapata Oil Company and is called the Zapata Tower. We then started developing the top. We did the top on an airplane, actually, coming back from Houston. We had been working on how to relate the tops of the two buildings—pointed tops or pyramids or triangles.

BLDD: I've come to believe that more designs of significant buildings are done on envelopes or napkins, in airplanes or airports.

JB: Sometimes the airplane martinis help, by the way.

BLDD: Which architects, periods, or theories have been most influential in your development as an architect?

JB: Since I was from Chicago, Mies came first. I also studied Philip Johnson before I knew him. But the man I admired most in my early days and to whom I arrogantly applied for a job was Eero Saarinen. I wrote him saying that I was now finished with my training and ready to go to work, and if he could guarantee that I would personally work with him, I'd be glad to come to his office.

BLDD: How did he reply?

JB: His reply was that he had no openings for the position I described. I also admired Kevin Roche's work. In fact, when I was becoming disillusioned with Murphy's firm in Chicago, I called him and asked if there was a possibility of working for him. He told me that I was already spoiled and overqualified; he wanted only someone he could train. Since then we have become quite friendly, and he remembers this, too.

BLDD: How important is an awareness of architectural traditions, or precedents, when designing a building?

JB: Years ago we would have had to say not at all. That would have been popular. But now we're more and more conscious of architectural traditions. People criticize us because of the inconsistency of our work. I don't really see this. It is true that our buildings don't look alike, but they're always consistent in their processional quality—a word we like to use to denote the way in which a building is seen from your very first glance as you approach it, arrive at it, enter it.

BLDD: Observers have described your buildings as classical, traditional, historicist, and, recently, eclectic. What do you think of these descriptions? How, other than processional, would you describe your work?

JB: They're all fair descriptions, but we also build buildings that none of these words would describe. I think this is one of the great developments of our firm at this moment—that we

are able to expand and be pluralistic in choosing materials or styles appropriate for a particular project. It makes it not easier but harder, by the way.

BLDD: You have talked about the pride of the craftsmen on the AT&T project, which must be very encouraging, because it obviously reflects your intent. What do you think of the AT&T Building now that it is completed?

JB: It seems better and better all the time. I was surprised at the strong public reaction. I thought it would cause some comment, but I didn't realize the depth of feeling. The controversy, while lessening as the building neared completion, is still evident. The reactions are really polar, not the way people judge other buildings—it's O.K., or it's not O.K. AT&T you either like or hate.

BLDD: Don't you think it's about to become one of our contemporary beloved buildings?

JB: By many people, but there are still some that are upset by it. When it was first published we even received hate mail! People said that we were ruining the profession and, worse, that we were making some kind of perverse joke.

BLDD: You heard this from architects?

JB: Yes, oh yes. Moshe Safdie for one. He said this was a joke, arrogant, damaging to the profession, arbitrary, and not within the rules.

BLDD: Has he been in communication since?

JB: Philip wrote to him in response, suggesting that perhaps his arches in Jerusalem, handsome or not, are just as arbitrary. The letter was published in *Skyline*.

BLDD: What would you do differently if the project were commissioned today?

JB: I don't think I'd do anything differently. It's very, very successful in achieving what it set out to do. Perhaps I would add more detail to the stone. We might have been too timid in not carrying the moldings a little further. Of course, some of them were removed for cost reasons. However, it was a quantum leap for us to move into designing that kind of building. We were headed towards it, but then we were almost pushed into it by John deButts, then chairman of AT&T, who said, "I simply want the finest building in the world for the finest company in the world." Almost all the AT&T people said, "Don't give us a glass box." So I would ask what they thought of the Seagram Building. Their answer was often, "Oh, that's not a glass box." DeButts's answer was different. He said, "The Seagram Building was the finest building of its time, and it took a step in architecture at the time it was built. I want to take the next step."

BLDD: Even though he's no longer at AT&T, how does John deButts feel about what he has helped bring about?

JB: I haven't talked to him, but people tell me he's pleased. Philip and I really responded to his charge. It was a responsibility that we took very seriously.

BLDD: You mentioned building costs, economics. While the public has been engaged in this debate over the AT&T Building's design, few are as knowledgeable as you about the business end of such a mammoth enterprise, the details of which you yourself helped to work out. Give us an idea how a building like AT&T gets built and what the process is like from start to finish.

JB: First we interviewed the clients to find out what they were looking for. From there we decided that a stone building was proper. We decided historic reference was the right direction—looking back to the earlier great days of New York skyscrapers—and proceeded to develop a design along those lines. However, it meant resurrecting a type of building that just hadn't been done in recent times. People said that stone

AT&T Corporate Headquarters, New York, N.Y.

carving was a lost art, but we discovered that it wasn't. The will to do it exists, but it costs money. People have criticized the AT&T Building as being expensive; some have said it is the most expensive in the world.

BLDD: Is it?

JB: No, it really isn't. Everything in the building, regardless of how it may appear, has been studied from a cost standpoint. Yes, the stone is more expensive than the stone on the IBM building next door, though on a project like this it's a couple of million dollars out of a total cost of over $100 million.

BLDD: How much over $100 million?

JB: Around $150 million, including all the interiors and special finishes.

BLDD: Are you responsible for the interiors as well?

JB: Yes.

BLDD: I understand that there are incredible innovations in the interior—like using desk lamps.

JB: That's right. This was something else that grew from the program. Because they're constantly changing their company organization and moving offices, AT&T wanted a ceiling that didn't need to be taken down every time they changed. They wanted to have extra air-conditioning outlets so they could

580 California Street, San Francisco, Calif., model

the Baroque period. Even Mr. Chippendale was inspired by architectural elements for his furniture. So perhaps there is a connection, but we didn't start with the furniture.

BLDD: You said that you should have been bolder with the AT&T Building in terms of moldings. Can we expect to see you moving in that direction in upcoming projects?

JB: We will see more decoration, because stone is a sculptural material. We deliberately used carved stone at AT&T. Why not exploit the very nature of the material? Its intrinsic quality is such that it can be carved. It's not mass-produced, and it doesn't come out uniform like pieces of glass. Why use a piece of stone as you would a metal panel or a piece of glass?

BLDD: Can you think of a cost-effective way of accomplishing that?

JB: Industry will devise the systems we need once we decide we want them. Industry will automate the process. For our job in San Francisco, 580 California Street, now under construction, we wanted round stone columns. It's obviously a difficult task. It used to require cutting by hand and it hadn't been done recently. We tried to eliminate the hand work. A company in Italy came up with a great big saw and a machine and made a model of the form to be cut. The machine can be set up to cut unattended. That's how we get our round columns.

BLDD: What are some of your upcoming projects?

JB: We are doing two projects in Boston, one using more carved stone. But we couldn't afford to carve all of it. We are getting an effect by carving some of it, where it is most visible, letting you know that it's there without overdoing it.

BLDD: But would you carve it all if cost were not the factor?

JB: Cost is only part of the problem. As we found out at AT&T, we've been spoiled by the International Style. In the last thirty years office tenants were given endless rows of five-foot modules. Corporate clients have been accustomed to

Forty-second Street Development Project, New York, N.Y., model

move a wall without taking down the ceiling to change all the duct work. One of the problems with a universal system is lighting, and this building was being designed at the time the energy crunch was being felt the most. We talked with our lighting consultant and I said that it would be nice if we took everything off the ceiling. The trouble with normal task lighting is it's so industrial. A great deal of light has to be reflected off the ceiling and it is not very pleasant. How could it be made more pleasant? At home I have a little desk lamp, which gives plenty of light and a nice atmosphere. We developed the system based on that.

BLDD: How does all the publicity surrounding a project like the AT&T affect the work itself?

JB: It didn't really affect the work very much, other than the first publication about the top. One of the writers said it was silly or . . .

BLDD: Said it was reminiscent of a Chippendale highboy.

JB: That was a funny term. Philip and I died laughing because it had never entered our minds. A broken pediment like that is an architectural device used since Roman times, often during having ten-, fifteen-, or twenty-foot offices. They have become status symbols. In the old days, when they built stone buildings, they built them from the outside in. The facade didn't always relate to the function within. I don't know how the president got along without a corner office with a window, for instance, but there were buildings without windows in the corner. We had to try to devise a modern interior with a more historical facade. We did it at AT&T by varying the width of the stone on panels between the windows.

BLDD: How much of a building is designed by economics, developers, builders, bankers, and planning commissions, and how much is left to the architects?

JB: These are all restraints. There are always restraints—money, developers, economics, rentability—but I would say that the architect, in the end, has the responsibility of organizing those restraints and using them to make the architecture. At the same time as we were doing Pennzoil, which was more costly than other speculative buildings, we were doing a purely speculative building that was one of the cheapest in Houston. So we had to build a very inexpensive one concurrently with a very expensive one.

BLDD: Given the opportunity, and without limitations of funds, assistance, or time, what would be your ideal project?

JB: I'd like to build a Rockefeller Center. Something like that would be great. I think we may have that opportunity. We're working on a Forty-second Street project with George Klein. George happens to be the type of builder who demands quality. If everything goes well, maybe we'll have a great urban statement like Rockefeller Center. It's four million square feet in four buildings on Forty-second Street between Broadway and Seventh Avenue, right on Times Square.

BLDD: Who is your ideal client?

JB: We used to say it was somebody that gives you your program, pays your bill, and then goes to Europe until the building is finished!

BLDD: And now?

JB: Someone like George Klein or Gerald Hines. Both are sophisticated developers who know quality in architecture is a good investment. Most architects say they don't like to work for developers because they impose their will so strongly. Hines and Klein have a desire to build quality, but they also know the building industry well enough that they don't let you go off on your own to design a building that will never get built. That's most wasteful of your time, which is so precious to an architect. What I most want to avoid is drawing a project and then not having it built because of some impractical reason.

BLDD: You don't want to publish *Unbuilt Burgee?*

JB: No.

BLDD: Which of the Johnson/Burgee projects do you see as the most enduring, or those that will survive most gracefully and usefully the passage of the years?

JB: I'd like to say all of them.

BLDD: Which are your own favorites?

JB: I like AT&T, not because of the building itself but because of what it did for me personally and what it did for the profession. It gave credibility to the attempt of some architects to break out of a standard mold. Even before the building was finished, it had made its contribution. I also like Transco. It has a certain presence. It provided a special opportunity. It is a sixty-five-story building built on a plain, standing by itself with nothing nearly as tall around it. Most tall buildings are built in urban settings and become part of the group, but here it stands all alone.

BLDD: Are there any buildings you would like to forget?

JB: No. I've made mistakes, but I am not going to tell you about those! I'm conscious of them, however. That's the nice part about business at this level. When I was at Murphy, so much of the work was delegated that you weren't able to oversee it all directly. You were not aware of all the mistakes generated. Now if I go and see something at one of our buildings that I don't like, I take the blame.

BLDD: Is there anything you've done that you would do otherwise if you had the opportunity to do it again?

JB: No, I can't think of anything.

BLDD: Would you have come to New York earlier?

JB: I think I came at the right time, frankly. If I had come earlier I might not have been in a position to build an office like this. My time in Chicago and the opportunity at twenty-eight years old of taking over responsibility for O'Hare Airport were very important. If I hadn't had that experience behind me, I couldn't have organized this office. I've tried to maintain an extremely high level of quality along with the ability to do projects of any size, to accept projects for their interest, not because we've got to run a large office. This is where my fifty people come in—we need fifty to do a $150 million project. But we can also accept a one or two million dollar project if it's architecturally interesting.

BLDD: Did you ever expect your life to unfold the way it has?

JB: No, not at all. I never thought I would leave Chicago.

BLDD: What next?

JB: I intend to stay here doing what I'm doing for as long as I can. It is still enormously fun, every minute of it.

HENRY COBB

Architect/urbanist/educator Henry Cobb, one of the founding partners of I. M. Pei & Partners, has contributed to the distinguished work of that firm since its formation thirty years ago.

BLDD: I've described you as an architect/urbanist/educator. How would *you* describe yourself?

HC: There's nothing wrong with your description. I would only emphasize that architect comes first and that the other two roles derive from being an architect.

BLDD: It was thirty years ago—in 1955—that you started working at one of the most celebrated architectural firms of our age.

HC: Before that, actually. It was in 1955 that we began to use the name I. M. Pei & Partners. But in fact Pei and I have been working together for thirty-five years. I first became acquainted with him in 1946, when I was a student at the Harvard Graduate School of Design and he was a very young faculty member. He had just earned his master's degree at Harvard under Gropius. His thesis project, which Gropius particularly admired, had been a museum of art for Shanghai, which is interesting in view of Pei's later career. It was also interesting because although it was done in Gropius's master's class, one would have to say that it was much more influenced by Mies than by Gropius.

BLDD: How do you explain that?

HC: In this respect, Pei was like many students at Harvard at that time. Although we were drawn to the GSD because of Gropius and we subscribed, by and large, to his pedagogical program, Gropius the architect was never a major influence by comparison with the other so-called heroes of modern architecture—Wright, Le Corbusier, Aalto, and Mies van der Rohe. In Pei's case, and in mine as well, the influence of Mies was particularly strong. The early work of our firm in the 1950s came quite directly from the Miesian ethic. I use the word "ethic" rather than "aesthetic" because Mies's belief system had—or at least we interpreted it as having—a very significant moral dimension. This was both its strength and its limitation. Within this belief system, there was a right and a wrong way of making things, and that notion of right and wrong permeated the entire

enterprise of architecture, from its broadest conception at the scale of urban planning to its ultimate materialization in the smallest detail. In retrospect, it seems an irony of history that this rigorously moral attitude toward architecture should have been adopted by so many American architects as the lodestone for practice in an era now viewed as having been pragmatic to the point of expediency. Be that as it may, in our early work for William Zeckendorf, Miesian notions of order clearly constituted the essential design strategy for dealing with tough, real-world development problems. That design strategy certainly had its origins at Harvard, though not necessarily in the teachings of Walter Gropius. Although Gropius created a significant center of architectural thought at Harvard through his persona and his philosophy, the GSD was also concerned with ideas and influences that came largely from outside sources.

BLDD: What were some of those influences, other than Mies?

HC: Certainly Le Corbusier, through his books *Vers Une Architecture* and the early volumes of the *Oeuvre Complète*. In the late forties, just after World War II, there were relatively few current books and monographs devoted to the culture of architecture—nothing like the avalanche of publications that assaults us today. In those days we immersed ourselves over a period of years in a very few documents, which because of their small number were enormously influential. I can still name every one. For example, in the same format as Le Corbusier's *Oeuvre* there was Alfred Roth's *New Architecture*, a compendium of early modern buildings that served as models not only for our design but equally for our style of drawing and presentation. It was especially fortuitous for me that in 1941, when I was a sophomore at Exeter, two books came out: Henry-Russell Hitchcock's *In the Nature of Materials*, which was the first catalogue raisonné of Wright's work, and Sigfried Giedion's *Space, Time and Architecture*. When these books appeared in the Exeter library, they immediately seized my imagination, indeed provoked my decision to become an architect.

BLDD: Then it was while you were at Exeter that you made that decision?

HC: Yes.

BLDD: Can you identify any particular influence, either familial or experiential, that inclined you to that career?

HC: In 1935, at the age of nine, I was taken on a summer tour of Europe. I suppose I dreamed about architecture after that.

BLDD: Where did you go that so influenced you?

HC: Italy, Switzerland, France. But I think the most influential places were Venice and Paris—above all Venice.

BLDD: Does it still continue to affect you?

HC: Of course! The wonderful thing about great cities is that they have the power to engage the imagination at many levels and therefore never dry up in terms of their interest. Nonetheless, when I reflect on all my subsequent travels—and there have been many—nothing remains in my consciousness as vividly as my first sojourn in Venice.

BLDD: Does Mies still continue to affect and influence you, too?

HC: Yes, but in ways that are by now somewhat complex and indirect. Just as a sailor may chart his outward course from a familiar landmark, I have remained in a certain way connected even as I have distanced myself from Mies's ideas and work.

BLDD: Did you know Mies personally?

HC: I met him only once, at a dinner given by mutual friends in Chicago more than thirty years ago—I think it was in 1950. What I remember most vividly from that rather trivial occasion is not Mies but his apartment, to which the party repaired for after-dinner drinks.

BLDD: What was his apartment like?

HC: There were no Barcelona or Brno chairs elegantly disposed in space—just a large empty living room with several black upholstered sofas of the most conventional design pushed up against the walls. Each sofa was flanked by a pair of end tables, and on each table was a large shaded lamp. Behind each shade, hung so that you couldn't see it without moving the lamp, was an exquisite Klee watercolor. I can't recall anything Mies said that evening—in fact he didn't say much—but I will never forget his living room!

BLDD: How did that influence your later designs and the way you live?

HC: Not at all, so far as I can tell. But it brought home the realization that a man's life and his art are two different realms. Perhaps this is why I have never built a house for myself—or for anyone else, for that matter. But then there are other more important reasons as well, having to do with my early fascination with building on a large scale.

BLDD: How did that come about?

HC: The influence of Harvard was crucial. It was at Harvard that Joseph Hudnut sponsored the notion of design as a field embracing the three professions of architecture, landscape architecture, and city planning. The curriculum of the GSD encouraged the student to think of planning and architecture as interdependent and mutually nourishing disciplines—and this was at least as much Hudnut's doing as Gropius's. Although this idea was not particularly popular with most of my fellow students, it appealed to me greatly, with the result that I emerged from school with a youthful enthusiasm for large undertakings, a desire to practice architecture at the urban scale and, in so doing, to remake the world.

BLDD: Do you now think that was a naive ambition?

HC: Of course it was naive! What else could it be at age twenty-three? But it nonetheless shaped my career, as such naive ambitions are apt to do. It was in this enthusiasm that my interests and Pei's found a significant common ground, re-inforcing the friendship we had already formed at Harvard. I. M. had been motivated to go to work for William Zeckendorf in New York by much the same aspiration—he wanted to tackle significant urban building projects. That was in the fall of 1948, and when a year later Pei needed help in drawing up his first important "dream project" for Zeckendorf, he called on me to organize a team of his former students in Cambridge. Out of that effort came the "Helix," an unbuilt but widely published design for a circular apartment tower. Subsequently I. M. asked me to join him in New York, and on April 1, 1950, we commenced the association that has now persisted, in one form or another, for thirty-five years.

William Zeckendorf was a man of remarkable intelligence, energy, and vision. He was also a bold and resourceful entrepreneur. For both Pei and me Zeckendorf was an extraordinary mentor throughout our first decade in practice. He satisfied in spades our appetite for large undertakings. Thus came about the curious upside-down profile of my career: my first building, Place Ville Marie in Montreal, remains to this day my largest, while my most recent building, the Portland Museum of Art, is my smallest. Before I was thirty, and just six years out of school, I became the principal architect of a mixed-use development covering seven acres in the heart of Montreal, incorporating some four million square feet of floor space and including the tallest and largest building in Canada. Place Ville Marie consumed about seven years of my professional life; building it was a marvelous experience. Not surprisingly, it emerged as a somewhat immature and derivative work of architecture. But despite its shortcomings, the project did reanimate downtown Montreal, and I couldn't help feeling gratified when, twenty years after its completion, placards appeared bearing the motto "Vingt Ans: Fêtons la Grande Dame!"

Place Ville Marie, Montreal, Canada

John Hancock Tower, Boston, Mass.

BLDD: Did your firm's experience with Place Ville Marie lead to other large-scale development projects of that kind?

HC: Yes. Commerce Court in Toronto—that was Pei's design—comes immediately to mind. A more recent example, in the 1970s, is Collins Place, my project in Melbourne, Australia. Both were complexes of many buildings covering several acres of land and involving, like Place Ville Marie, the reordering of urban systems and the reshaping of urban space as well as the intensification of urban activity. We continue to keep our hand in this kind of work: Pei's Raffles Center in Singapore and my Campeau/Criswell Development in Dallas are both current projects of this type in our office. This shared interest in center-city development and the whole set of aspirations associated with it is undoubtedly the essential glue that has kept our partnership together for so many years—and it extends of course beyond Pei and myself to include Eason Leonard, Jim Freed, and virtually the entire senior staff of our office. It has enabled each of us to grow and to pursue our own personal interests within the context of a group practice in which we continue to provide each other with important mutual support.

BLDD: You didn't include the Hancock Tower among the projects you just mentioned. Isn't it one of your most significant works?

HC: Yes, but I place it in a different category because it is an institutional project built for owner occupancy rather than a real-estate investment project built for diverse tenancy. The spirit of the enterprise is therefore very different. But you are right, the Hancock Tower is an important building in my career. It is another that seems to have occupied about seven years of my life. Unlike Place Ville Marie, it is a highly distilled work in that it crystallizes the predicament of the big institution as a citizen in its community. The Hancock Tower is significant not because it solves a problem but because it *illustrates* a problem. I believe this is a legitimate role for architecture—to illustrate, with eloquence and precision, the uncomfortable paradoxes of our human condition. I think the Hancock Tower succeeds in doing this, which is why, despite its controversial beginnings and its traumatic construction problems, the building is now admired by some who at first opposed it. Especially because I am a native of Boston, I am proud to have built a skyscraper that strengthens rather than diminishes the distinctive personality of that city.

BLDD: The projects you've discussed so far have all been for private entrepreneurial or institutional clients. Haven't you also been active in your firm's extensive planning work for public authorities? I am thinking of such early urban renewal projects as Government Center in Boston, as well as more recent revitalization projects in Augusta, Georgia, and Denver, Colorado. What were your major concerns, and how were they resolved?

HC: Yes, in retrospect I have spent a good deal of my life on work that falls into the category of urban planning and design, often setting the framework for buildings to be designed by others. This kind of work came to us originally in the early sixties, as an outgrowth of our work for Zeckendorf. He was one of the first to understand and exploit the opportunities for development offered by Title One of the Federal Housing Act of 1949—the basic legislation that launched the era of urban renewal. As a result of our involvement with him we became familiar with the urban renewal process. Later, after our separation from Zeckendorf's firm, we were invited by local planning agencies in several cities—Cleveland and Boston are two that come immediately to mind—to assist in preparing the urban renewal plans that were a prerequisite to obtaining

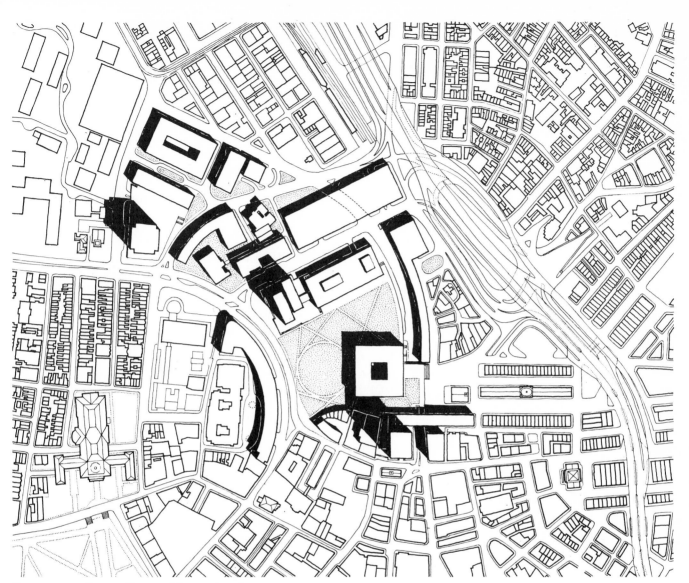

Government Center, Boston, Mass., site plan

federal assistance under the terms of the law. Pei and I worked together on the Government Center plan in Boston. Ed Logue, as director of the Boston Redevelopment Authority, was our client. Those were heady days, in the years 1961 to 1963, the apogee of the urban renewal era. Our responsibilities encompassed all aspects of planning—circulation, land use, open space, and controls mandating the location, height, and bulk of buildings. Logue, together with Mayor Collins, managed the process brilliantly. Government Center was one of the few urban renewal projects in the nation to be executed more or less as planned. It therefore stands as a model of both the virtues and the shortcomings of that process and of the goals that motivated it. It is a measure of how much societal values have changed in twenty years that such an undertaking would be practically unthinkable today.

In both Augusta and Denver, the problem was to find ways of revitalizing the life of the downtown without engaging in massive clearance and rebuilding. These more recent projects are naturally much more characteristic of current urban planning and development practice, which tends to be incremental and conservative rather than comprehensive and radical. In both cases, the projects were focused on the reinterpretation of existing streets, leaving the flanking buildings untouched,

with the objective of inducing more people to come downtown for purposes other than employment, specifically for shopping, dining, entertainment. Of the two, the Denver project is the more significant, in both design and planning terms. It involved converting the principal downtown shopping street into a three-quarter-mile-long transitway/mall for pedestrians and electric-powered mini-buses. Aside from these innovative planning features, the project was important for me because it offered the opportunity to propose a street design that is in striking contrast to the prevailing trend. In my view, most downtown malls—there are now a number in cities around the country—have suffered from the tendency of planners to stuff them full of too many disparate objects for the sake of variety and eventfulness. Thus, the street becomes cluttered with things that don't last and that in the end make it tackier than ever. Our approach to this problem was just the opposite. We said that the whole idea of this mall should be to focus people's attention on the shops, which provide the animation and variety. We felt that the street should bring to the urban scene what the shops cannot bring—a sense of community, of identity, of a larger public realm that is shared and enhances a sense of citizenship. Drawing on our observation of urban spaces that seem to exhibit these qualities, we proposed a design composed of three basic ingredients—paving, planting, lighting—applied consistently along the entire length of the street. Each of these elements is placed and designed in such a way as to complement rather than compete with the flanking shop fronts. For example, the trees and lights are arranged in double rows close to the center, so as not to obstruct or detract from the window displays lining both sides. The polychrome granite paving—light gray, dark gray, and red—is laid in a very simple and nonassertive pattern near the two street walls, but with an increasingly bold geometry as it approaches the center, somewhat like the skin of a diamondback rattlesnake or the pattern of a Navaho blanket.

BLDD: Your mention of Navaho blankets is interesting. Do you often use historical sources to form your vision or your design?

HC: Philip Johnson said, "We cannot not know history." I would go further: we cannot not use history. But of course within that broad truism there lurks an infinity of possible choices and interpretations. I think the record of our work shows that, along with almost everyone else in our profession, my partners and I are making different choices and different interpretations in our uses of history than we were, say, ten or fifteen years ago. The most obvious evidence of that is to be found in two recent projects—Pei's Fragrant Hill Hotel, near Beijing, and my Portland Museum of Art in Maine. Both are rather deliberate meditations on the vernacular traditions of building in their respective locales. Yet both are completely modern in that their programmatic, technical, and spatial characteristics are unequivocally of our time. An aspect of no little importance in these projects is that they are located in our respective homelands, so that the interpretive issues involved

have an especially personal meaning. I have vacationed in Maine all my life, and Portland was the home of my forebears during several generations in the eighteenth and nineteenth centuries. As it happens, on the exact site of the new museum, my great-great-great-grandfather built 182 years ago a splendid house to the design of Alexander Parris. How's that for historical sources!

BLDD: How did you use those connections in the design of the Portland Museum?

HC: In many ways, both direct and indirect. The most direct and easily perceived is in the choice of exterior building materials. The walls are of water-struck brick, laid up in American bond—that is, with headers every sixth course—and trimmed with granite lintels, sills, copings, and stringcourses. Both these materials are indigenous to Maine and commonly found in the vernacular architecture of Portland. My aim was to reinterpret, reanimate if you will, the tradition of masonry building that significantly shaped the character of that city. If you were to ask Pei what he had in mind in the design of the Fragrant Hill Hotel, I think he would make very much the same statement, though neither of us talked much to the other about these particular buildings. Most of the interior surfaces of the Portland Museum are gypsum wallboard—we are condemned, it would seem, to live in a sheetrock world!—but on the floors I was able to extend the regional theme by laying wide naturally finished pine planks in panels bordered by granite bands. This gives the exhibition galleries a certain material richness without in any way challenging the primacy of the works of art on the walls. The most important use of history in the Portland Museum is of a quite different kind. Because the new building stands in a very rich urban context, surrounded by landmark

Transitway/Mall, Denver, Colo.

**Above and right: Charles Shipman Payson Building,
Portland Museum of Art, Portland, Me.**

structures, I planned to make the awareness of history an integral part of the museum experience. A visitor strolling through the galleries cannot fail to encounter window openings placed so as to remind one that this museum is not an isolated temple of art but part of a living city. These windows offer views first into the museum garden with its Federal-period mansion as a focus, then into a public square surrounded by nineteenth-century commercial buildings, and finally—on the top floor—over the entire Portland peninsula to the harbor and ocean beyond. Because this is a specifically regional museum, dedicated to the many American artists who have lived and worked in Maine, I believe the making of these connections is, in this case, a special obligation of the architecture. It is also an opportunity of which I have been acutely conscious and to which I believe I have been able to respond. Here again, as in the case of the Hancock Tower but with a totally different set of specifics, I have found myself preoccupied with the way in which, through architecture, an institution presents itself in the city and how that presentation, in turn, portrays, perhaps even shapes, the character and value system of the society that sponsors it. In this sense, if in no other, I would argue that architecture is inescapably a representational art.

BLDD: Speaking of institutions, I am reminded of your current activity at Harvard, where you have been chairman of the department of architecture since 1980.

HC: Ah, Harvard. Sooner or later we would have to get back to Harvard. Now, there's an institution!

BLDD: How do you divide your time between your responsibilities at Harvard and your large-scale, demanding practice?

HC: With difficulty! My usual routine, when school is in session, is to spend the middle of the week in Cambridge and the beginning and end in New York. In principle, this kind of divided life is impossible but, like many things that are in principle impossible, it is done. The reasons are not complicated. As an architect with over thirty years of practice behind me, I believe that I benefit—and my practice in the years left to me will benefit—from the critical distance obtained by my engagement with the academic world. Of course it's not just the academic world; it's the whole world of architectural discourse with which one becomes involved as a result of being in the academic world. On the other side, I have always believed that professional schools need to be in close touch with the practicing profession. That can only happen if architects who have active practices are willing to devote some part of their careers to education. There is in this a kind of natural symbiosis—teaching humbles the practitioner and practice humbles the teacher. Of couse the aim is not humility—a most unattractive condition!—but learning and the capacity to apply it, which is my definition of wisdom.

BLDD: What are some of your specific goals as chairman of the department?

HC: On one level—perhaps the most superficial, though still important—my goal is to stir things up, to make connections that otherwise might not be made, to bring to the school people who don't fit and who challenge the status quo. This may seem trivial as a goal, perhaps even a bit irresponsible, but I think not, especially in the context of a graduate school like ours at Harvard, where the student body is composed of extraordinarily intelligent, quite mature, relatively experienced young people, not necessarily experienced in architecture but experienced in life. I think it is *not* our obligation as teachers to protect these young people from the conflicts, paradoxes, and uncertainties that beset architecture. On the contrary, it is our first duty to expose them to those uncertainties, so that they may be challenged to develop their own sense of responsibility, their own convictions, and ultimately their own mode of intervention as architects. As you can see, I am not of the view that our school should espouse any one theory or adopt one posture to the exclusion of others. I don't believe I would have favored that kind of pedagogical program at any time, but I

certainly don't today. On the other hand, I'm not trying to promote anarchy either. I believe in bringing diverse views into our school, but I want to do it in a way that doesn't allow them to simply slide by each other without getting into a dialogue, without challenging, without communicating. I want to create a *discourse*. This I would say is my single most important goal. It has to do—and here again I'm afraid I have to drag in my preoccupation with institutions—with my conception of the graduate professional school as an institution and its role in the culture of architecture. I am struck by a paradox inherent in the title "graduate professional school": graduate implies advanced study and research in a field of knowledge already partly mastered; professional refers to basic and clearly instrumental training for a specified practice. The two concepts do not live well together, yet it seems that it is the particular obligation of a school like Harvard to make them live together. In the simplest terms, we must aim to shape as well as serve our profession. In order to do this, we must offer superb instrumental training—competence is a quality that I will never demean—but at the same time we must promote a discourse of sufficient substance to nourish the intellect and, above all, to develop the capacity for self-criticism. In our profession, with its overwhelmingly pragmatic conditions of practice, we will always need more questioning, more ferment, and less self-satisfaction.

BLDD: Have you found this kind of ferment missing for the past thirty years?

HC: Never entirely missing, but at times nearly suffocated by the prevailing ethos. Anyway, there can never be enough of it. When it comes to intellectual ferment, I subscribe to Mae West's famous pronouncement: "Too much of a good thing is wonderful!"

BLDD: What has been the greatest satisfaction of your career?

HC: Those occasions—all too rare—when I have sensed that through my work I have been able to change the way people look at the world, to enrich their perceptions of the human condition.

BLDD: What's been the greatest frustration of your career?

HC: Those occasions—fortunately few—when I have felt that my work failed to transcend mere building.

BLDD: If you had it to do over, what would you do differently?

HC: I would have more of the former and less of the latter.

WILLIAM CONKLIN

Architect, archaeologist, and preservationist William J. Conklin is known for his far-reaching ideas and his fine designs. He's also known for his dedication to small-scale amenities as well as to large-scale urban planning.

BLDD: How does someone who grew up in Hubbell, Nebraska—a town with a population of eighty, fifteen miles from the county seat—end up as an international architect, archaeologist, and textile scholar?

WJC: It's all because that little town was a well-structured community. It was a kind of model town—a perfect plan of square blocks, a straight main street with a school at one end and a railroad station at the other. Along that main street were stores, a church, a blacksmith's shop, a giant elm tree, a bank. All the parts of the community seemed to fit together in a beautiful way. The architecture, the form of the town, and the community life were all very coherent. It was a wonderful world for me as a child, and it remains a model of how a community and its urban design can work together.

BLDD: How many of your ideas about planning are based on this early experience with the very clear urban structure of your hometown?

WJC: I don't think that the exact physical form of the town was translated in my adult life into city planning and urban design. But the idea of forming a community with a wonderful sense of place and a pedestrian scale, one in which architecture and total design work together to reinforce the sense of community, is very much a part of everything that my office and I do.

BLDD: Was there an architectural tradition in your own family?

WJC: As a matter of fact, there was a slight one: my father designed the facade of his new bank building, although he was a banker, not an architect. As a hobby he occasionally engaged in a little bit of architecture. He did a symmetrical bank facade with flattened-out Greek columns, slightly postmodernist, if you will! He probably used copy books, but nevertheless he did design that little bank front.

BLDD: Were you conscious of it at the time?

WJC: Yes, very much so.

BLDD: Does it still exist?

WJC: It still exists.

BLDD: From early on you had an interest in the built environment. I assume it developed not only from the experience with your father's bank but from other things in your childhood as well. How did this early interest manifest itself?

WJC: I suppose if you were to look back at my childhood, you would see the thousands of hours I spent in my great sandpile building mounds, rivers, villages, and little buildings.

BLDD: In a sandpile?

WJC: Yes. I spent hours alone in the sandpile. Growing up in a town with a population that small, you often must make do by yourself.

BLDD: What did you build in that imaginary village?

WJC: Oh, wonderful things with rivers and dams, with forests and farms, with little groups of houses. None of them looked like the town itself, nor did they look like anything I've done since. They were imaginary environments.

BLDD: Lincoln, the capital of Nebraska, is one hundred miles from Hubbell and is the site of a very distinguished building by Bertram Goodhue. Do you have any early recollections of that structure?

WJC: By all means. The State Capitol is perhaps Goodhue's greatest building. The first time I saw the structure I was a little child. *The Sower,* the statue that is now on top of the tower, was at that time still on the ground. I remember looking up at it and then being told that I was actually looking up at only the big toe. I was thrilled and excited beyond belief at the idea of the tremendous difference in scale. I remember that moment very keenly.

BLDD: Is there anything else about that building that impressed you?

WJC: It's very successful in conveying meaning. It projects a very strong image and says very clearly that it is indeed the capitol building of the state. Every person in the state knows that building. It isn't an anonymous building. It makes a very triumphant statement—"I am the center of this world of Nebraska"—that remains strong to this day. That is an admirable role for architecture to fulfill.

BLDD: You left Hubbell at a young age to go away to school. How did you end up in New Hampshire?

WJC: I went there to attend the Phillips Exeter Academy, which in terms of sophistication was at the opposite end of the spectrum from my rural Nebraska background. I attended prep school there for a few years because my father had also attended Exeter, in the early part of the century. He got there because of his father, who wanted to provide the best education for his son. My grandfather traveled up to Omaha to seek the advice of the president of the Omaha National Bank, who recommended Phillips Exeter Academy. Thus the tradition began.

BLDD: When and how did you decide to become an architect?

WJC: After I returned to the Midwest and attended Doane—a great little liberal arts college in Nebraska.

BLDD: What lured you back?

WJC: The Depression. It even affected bankers' sons. And I had not entirely cut off my roots in Nebraska, in spite of the attraction of the East. In college I found myself interested in a variety of fields. I studied theology. I was interested in art—I did a certain amount of painting and I took courses in art history—but I was also interested in physics and engineering. When I spoke to an adviser in the school about what I might do in life, he said, "If you want to bring together art, engineering, and science in one field, you should choose architecture." Sure enough, that turned out to be the answer. I decided that I would be an architect, although I finished undergraduate school with one major in chemistry and one in art, a strange combination. I chose to study architecture at the Graduate School of Design at Harvard under Walter Gropius. Harvard was then, and still is, a critically important architectural school.

BLDD: The 1950s were a particularly significant time in American architectural education and represented a coming of age in American architectural practice as well. What was the specific influence of Gropius?

WJC: Gropius was more effective in describing the role and responsibilities of the architect than he was in prescribing an architectural style. His brilliance was in pointing out to students the range of opportunities and responsibilities before them. In establishing the school, he brought in many other disciplines—city planning and art, for instance—and tried to accommodate all within the framework of a school of architecture. He used as a model the Bauhaus, which he had administered in the previous decade. To some extent this new school was a direct continuation of Bauhaus ideas, but Gropius's educational direction in the United States was oriented much more toward large-scale city planning and less toward art and artifact design.

BLDD: Did you know Gropius? Did you have any dealings with him?

WJC: Oh yes, quite a lot. He was a warm, generous, tolerant person, a great leader of debates and discussions. The school had rather formal juries and criticism in which each student would put up his work and the faculty would comment. Gropius always led the discussion in a way that was generous to the student but also invited the other professors to participate. He always kept the level of discussion high and was, therefore, very much the leader of the school. He had profound educational instincts. Not every architect has those.

BLDD: What was Gropius like? How did he live?

WJC: I knew him only as a teacher, although the school was small and teacher/student relationships were close. I was at his home a few times. His house was a modernist structure of the late thirties, built of redwood but painted pure white, with curved glass brick walls. There were white wooden space

frames in the garden. It was a well-manicured place, but not elaborate or luxurious. The interior details were not so very interesting. Perhaps when it came to fine design points, Gropius didn't have unique and special answers. Once a student asked him, "What should we be doing at the present time with interiors, with color, with finishes?" Gropius answered, "I think it's best to keep things tweedy for now." An answer that was a bit of a dodge but judicial.

BLDD: What were space frames doing in the backyard?

WJC: Defining the volumes that moved out from the house and encompassing the garden and the pool in various ways—a cubistic concept of spatial organization.

BLDD: What problems were students trying to solve then?

WJC: At that time the school was structured in such a way that one began with a set of problems that were community oriented; the very first problem was a community center. This emphasis no doubt reflected the vaguely socialist leanings of early modernism.

BLDD: Not a field house?

WJC: Not a field house or an art gallery, as it might be today, but a community center for a specific group of people in a given neighborhood in a given area. The student was challenged to solve a range of social problems of the community as well as the architectural and physical problems of the building. You proceeded through the school, tackling larger and larger projects, until you finally worked on a large-scale city planning project in the final year. It was all clearly structured in a hierarchical way.

BLDD: What kind of school did Gropius set up at Harvard?

WJC: He took over the existing architectural school, which had been in existence for a long time, and transformed it into something after his own educational image. I've described this briefly in terms of the way problems were structured. But one of the most controversial aspects was to eliminate all study of the history of architecture. To Gropius, who grew up in Europe and practiced architecture there, Europe's architectural tradition was simply overwhelming, too dominating. He felt that it was necessary to clear one's mind of all that and begin afresh. When he came to this country and started the school, he established the rule that no student would be allowed to study the history of architecture. The courses were still taught at Harvard, but in other departments.

BLDD: Was that a good idea? Do you think your education suffered as a result of denying the past?

WJC: One attempts to make up for deficiencies as one goes along. It's hard to evaluate the sum total. Of course students did sneak around the rule, and Gropius did permit courses in the history of urban design. There we could hear about how Greek towns were planned, how Roman cities were organized; we could learn something of the history of Italian town planning. Through urban design, of which architecture was considered a part, we did see something of the history of European design, although we weren't involved in detailed studies of the architecture itself.

BLDD: You've said that you did a lot of things at that school that America did later. What did you mean by that? What were you doing?

WJC: For the advanced students one of the problems concerned clearing away areas of buildings in old cities and establishing a new order of architecture. As students we did many studies in which we would—I shudder to recall—wipe out half of old Boston and examine what it might look like ideally, as if we were the architects for the whole city, starting once again. We participated in many studies of that sort. Somewhat later the laws of this country were changed and a powerful urban

Lake Anne Center, Reston, Va.

renewal act was passed by Congress. The idea of clearing away old buildings to permit new ones to rise became the law of the land. Urban renewal certainly began as an academic and utopian dream and then for a few decades, alas, it became the American way. Another influential idea we studied was the shopping center as a solution to suburban problems—and this was before shopping centers existed in suburbia. Gropius and his associated planners could see the need for such solutions—people in the growing suburban areas needed to shop locally and could no longer always come to town. They devised a shopping center program and we studied how to create them, what sort of form they might have. We now know the results of investigating such compelling solutions: shopping centers took over and spread across the country.

BLDD: As a student you were trained to design new towns. What were some of your first assignments after graduation?

WJC: You're referring, I guess, to my work on the new town of Reston, Virginia. That opportunity to plan and design a new town outside Washington, D.C., arose through Robert E. Simon Jr. (The R-E-S in the name of the town are his initials.) The design was a tremendous opportunity, very much in line with the kinds of problems we had studied in school. My partner, Jim Rossant, and I jumped into it with great enthusiasm and spent many years working on it. We did the master plan for the new town and then concentrated specifically on the design of the first portion to be constructed, the Lake Anne Center.

BLDD: How close did your vision of a new town, Reston in this instance, come to the prototype that Hubbell, Nebraska, represented for you?

WJC: That does tie things into a bit of a circle, doesn't it? Reston doesn't literally look like Hubbell, but conceptually the Lake Anne Center and that little town in Nebraska have a lot in common. Lake Anne is a pedestrian center and a wonderful world for kids. It's a mixture of playgrounds, schools, and shops. All of these elements are within walking distance of each other. The architecture encloses the spaces of the main town plaza, as well as the lake we created, in such a way that it gives a strong sense of security and a sense of place to those who live there.

BLDD: With the population explosion of twenty years ago, we thought we needed new towns. Is Reston a success?

WJC: I think Reston is a success. It stands head and shoulders above most American new towns started around that time. Reston is a success because it's loved by its inhabitants; the people are proud of its strong identity. The town has established many creative community services and activities, and it has a vigorous group of people who constantly think of new solutions to problems.

BLDD: Does America need any more new towns?

WJC: Probably not, in terms of statistics, at least. If you were to add up all the towns that exist in America, it would be hard to say that we need even a few more. In that sense there are surely enough towns. However, if a new town were constructed to teach us something new, something not found in an existing town, then on the level of experimentation maybe it would be justifiable.

BLDD: What could we learn from such a utopian community? What would make it a coherent, significant place to live?

WJC: One unsuccessful aspect of Reston was its inability to expand rapidly and yet remain coherent. We didn't figure out clearly how it should have expanded from our original village center. As architects we designed a complete model of a town center with all its various parts, facilities, and arrangements—complete to the town fountain. But it didn't grow successfully; the newer parts are not as good. Perhaps the problem all cities face is that of growth and change. Every city has a period during which wonderful buildings are built and wonderful places are created, but over time they change or are destroyed. A *new* new town should tackle that problem from the beginning.

BLDD: If new towns aren't the answer to America's urban problems, toward what should we be directing our energies?

WJC: We have to put higher value on the existing structures of our communities. Everybody in cities—architects as well as residents—increasingly realizes and appreciates that the buildings of our environment are of great value. They are like friends. Just as we respect the structure of our social relationships in the world, so should we value our urban context. When we wipe out buildings, we wipe out not just the physical objects but many more subtle urban networks. I think we are all learning to reread old buildings and to see them in a way that was lost during the heyday of modernism. What used to be called "irrelevant detail," to use Gropius's term, is actually the elaboration of the language of architecture. The forms convey ideas; they have history, they have precedents. They're not just shapes but are really ideas in shapes. They also have value simply as delight and entertainment to the eye.

BLDD: In light of your interest in community planning and urban design, do you ever wish that as a student you had concentrated on city and regional planning rather than architecture?

WJC: Oh no, not at all. I think architecture is a rich and complex art form. With a project like Reston—designing and building a whole group of buildings—one is really creating a living community, which is enormously satisfying. But simply planning can be unsatisfying and frustrating because one only controls the broadest outline. The details or the language are not there. A message cannot be conveyed simply by the shape of a paragraph; words are necessary for meaning.

BLDD: Raised in Nebraska, educated in New Hampshire and Massachusetts—how did you end up in New York?

WJC: I was offered a job in New York. It's that elementary. At Harvard I did a paper for a geography course on factors that influence the location of architectural practice. I came to the conclusion, by looking at all of the statistical projections for the United States, that there were two logical places to establish a practice: Seattle and Houston. However, the job that came along was in New York, so I quickly tossed out the academic paper and took the job. I haven't regretted it. The paper may have been statistically correct, but one follows the heart.

BLDD: Did you expect to stay in New York?

WJC: I don't know if I thought that through. I was offered a job in New York by an organization sponsored by Nelson Rockefeller for the construction of low-cost housing. It was a fancy office at the top of the RCA Building. What more could a student just graduating from school want than a job in such a location, designing new communities around the world? It was a wonderful opportunity.

BLDD: Among the work you've done in New York are 333 East Sixty-ninth Street, on the Upper East Side, and Butterfield House, in Greenwich Village—two buildings praised for their respect for architectural traditions. Why are they so often cited and what lessons can we learn from them today?

WJC: Both of those buildings were done when I was an associate partner in charge of design for the firm of Mayer, Whittlesey and Glass. Each building involved serious analysis of the existing context—the scale of the street and the architectural elements of the surrounding buildings. The design solution did not come from replicating but from dealing with the essence. In the case of 333 East Sixty-ninth Street we introduced into the base of the building a group of small townhouses that have direct access to the street and therefore re-create some of the social as well as visual characteristics of a townhouse-lined street. Those small-scale building elements bring the building into interaction with the existing structures of the street. Butterfield House has rather rich patterns of bay windows on its Twelfth Street facade. This was suggested by a then-existing building on Twelfth Street, a cast-iron structure with bay windows. Taking our cue from that kind of building, Jim Rossant and I worked out a solution to Butterfield House that involves a classic version of bay windows and limestone spandrels and a richly landscaped interior garden. Both buildings continue to live very well on their streets and to hold their place in the world of architecture.

BLDD: Has the quality of housing throughout the country declined in the last few years at the same time that interest in architecture has grown?

WJC: The quality of housing has probably declined. There has been a shift on the part of the profession away from housing because of its economic difficulties. With a factory it is the

Butterfield House, New York, N.Y.

Market Square, Washington, D.C., model

manufactured product that has to make money, not the building. But in housing the building itself has to be immediately paid for by the consumer. Housing involves a difficult financial equation.

BLDD: You've said that the first function of every urban building is to play a constructive role in the city. Would you elaborate?

WJC: First of all, a building should relate to its existing context and be respectful of that context: it should not make the adjacent buildings look ridiculous; it should not cast other buildings in its shadow. But it should also make a positive contribution, not only by its function, but by being something special on the street.

BLDD: It should go beyond being well-mannered and respectful of its context.

WJC: Well-mannered and respectful, always; but really significant design should come from the building's function in society. This is an aspect that is almost lost today. Schools and churches should be distinguishable from housing, corporate headquarters from bulk rental space, and hotels from palaces. High buildings should inspire. They are noble, and they should *be* noble as well as look noble.

BLDD: In several of your designs, such as the New School for Social Research in New York, you've included indoor gardens. The concern with outdoor space also extends to your own home, where you've designed a very ingenious portable wooden pavilion for your townhouse garden. Won't you tell us about this architectural experiment, this playhouse for adults?

WJC: It is precisely that. It is about five feet square and covered with latticework, and it has a spire on top. It can be

carried around and placed in different parts of the garden. It's big enough for four people to sit in. You can put it in the shade or in the sun. It changes the garden and the vistas of the occupants. It's a miniature, toy temple, I suppose.

BLDD: You've always been aware of the importance of symbolic structure. Recently you've been designing a memorial for the United States Navy. What are your concerns as you design this, and how has the assignment unfolded so far?

WJC: The initial design was for a memorial arch to be constructed in Market Square on Pennsylvania Avenue, approximately halfway between the White House and the Capitol. The arch proposal arose from research into the history of great military monuments. It was a monument designed to connect us with our memories. The historic form precisely fit the need. We also examined the context of the site itself—its space and its scale. Market Square is located where Eighth Street crosses Pennsylvania Avenue, a place of central importance in L'Enfant's plan. It is a setting for a great urban statement, and I felt our placement of the arch—across Eighth Street, standing to one side of Pennsylvania Avenue but allowing a vista through—was a very strong and appropriate statement. It was to be just a little over a hundred feet high, say eleven or twelve stories, not as big as the Arc de Triomphe in Paris.

BLDD: How would your design fit in with the historic design and scale of Pennsylvania Avenue, and how was your concept for this heroic monument received?

WJC: The arch was very much the same scale as the classic Archive building, which it faced across Pennsylvania Avenue. The avenue itself is enormous, both in width and in length. Its scale is indeed heroic. It is called America's main street, but

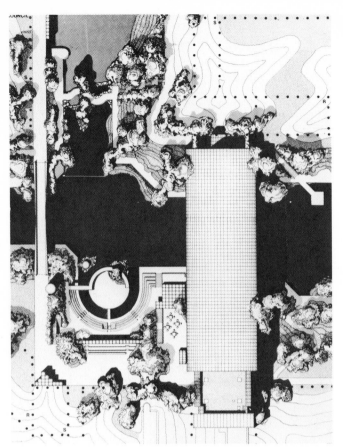

Myriad Gardens, Oklahoma City, Okla., plan

the country has no other main street that size. The design proposal was well received by the Pennsylvania Avenue Development Commission and the Navy Memorial Foundation and was approved by the Fine Arts Commission.

BLDD: But it was finally disapproved?

WJC: Yes. The process of obtaining approval in Washington is very complex; many agencies and representative groups must be satisfied. The arch design eventually met vigorous opposition from the National Capital Planning Commission, which represents the local community interests.

BLDD: To what did they object?

WJC: To be philosophical about it, I think their inability to approve it is understandable. The proposal was a very simple and powerful idea, perhaps too simple and strong for our pluralistic age. To build something in a city today, you must satisfy many interests. This is not a time when society is unified, not even a time when symbols that imply unity can be accepted. The decision not to build it was personally heartbreaking, but it may be a decision that is true to our time. At any rate, we are now working on an entirely different kind of answer. We are going to create a circular plaza with both a performance facility for the navy bands and a setting for memorial sculpture. The sculpture will be related to oceanic and naval themes and will be low in scale. It will be a busy, urban, multipurpose space. The scale requirements of the site, which is very large, will be satisfied by the semicircular form of the buildings that surround the plaza. As you look from the Archive building northward up Eighth Street, your gaze will extend to the circular forms surrounding the low sculpture.

BLDD: Did you learn anything from the controversy surrounding the Vietnam Veterans Memorial?

WJC: The Vietnam Memorial addresses a very different kind of problem. Although it is powerful, it is an anti-memorial, the opposite of a celebration. But the failure of the design has to do with the fact that it does not add anything to the urban design. Though it is a large structure, it doesn't form a part of the city fabric. It is hidden in a park setting, where its black message is conveyed. I like the fact that in Washington you move from the Lincoln Memorial to the Washington Monument along the spinal axes of the city laid down by L'Enfant. The monuments reinforce the form of the city in addition to being great individual memorials. The Vietnam Memorial speaks, but it avoids addressing the city itself.

BLDD: Are you working on projects in other American cities that do attempt to speak to their environments?

WJC: Yes, but in a different way. One of our most important efforts is in Oklahoma City, where we are building a new four-block centerpiece for the downtown area called Myriad Gardens. We have excavated the area and revealed the natural water level, creating a sunken lake, and have built civic facilities into the parklike surroundings. The city has very severe wind conditions, and the sunken plazas and waterways provide retreat and protection.

BLDD: How, then, does Myriad Gardens speak to Oklahoma City?

WJC: Primarily by giving the downtown an oasis, a new view of green and a breath of fresh air. There also will be a botanical bridge, a cylindrical glass building that spans across the lake. It will contain all of the plants, flowers, and green wonders that the downtown now lacks. Its style is very abstract and modern, for Oklahoma looks only forward.

BLDD: You have had an interest in theology since your student days. In fact, you've continued that interest as chairman of the Society for Art, Religion and Contemporary Culture. Who founded that organization, and what is its purpose?

WJC: It was founded by a group of people—Alfred Barr, Paul Tillich, Amos Wilder, and Marvin Halverson—who believed that the level of art in churches was dreadful and that most religious institutions didn't know anything about art and needed to have their vision and understanding of its importance greatly expanded. They also believed that art itself contained messages and meanings as important and as spiritually significant as the words of the Bible or other religious literature. The founders tried to find religious meaning in art and also to incorporate significant art into religious structures.

BLDD: Has the society helped achieve this goal?

WJC: It has certainly helped people think about the subject. But one cannot as yet point to great churches that have been created as a result of the society. It hasn't been explicitly directed toward the creation of architectural examples, but rather toward providing a place where people who wanted to think about the subject could do so.

BLDD: Do you see architecture itself as a kind of mission?

WJC: Oh, architecture's too much fun to describe it in such a serious way. Architecture is best seen as part of an urban structure that provides meaning to the people who live in the community. If that constitutes a mission, then perhaps the word is correct.

BLDD: You've said that museums are modern-day cathedrals. Is that meant as praise?

WJC: It's meant as an observation of fact. Certainly in our society the museum is the place to which one goes to worship the "wholly other." That which one doesn't understand one finds most effectively in confrontation with art today.

BLDD: Have you ever designed any religious institutions?

WJC: Only a couple of small churches and a religious school, which contains within it a small chapel. The Ramaz School, on Seventy-eighth Street between Madison and Park Avenues in Manhattan, contains a complete range of facilities for an Orthodox Jewish education, as well as an underground gym, classrooms, and other facilities.

BLDD: It has a sleek aluminum facade punctuated by unusual, odd-shaped windows. What's the meaning of its facade and its window patterns?

WJC: The facade has to be understood in light of several considerations. One is the context, the kind of street and the surrounding buildings. If we look at that street we discover many townhouses with small vertical windows in groupings of fours and fives. That kind of punctuation is also found on the facade of the school. There's one grouping of five windows on the Ramaz School facade that represents a bay window drawn in a two-dimensional fashion, forming a kind of shadow image of a bay and recalling one of the themes of the street. Secondly, the internal function of the building, with its variety of rooms and spaces, is directly expressed on the outside. A third consideration is represented by a group of windows that form a reference to the tablet form of the Torah.

BLDD: As the one-time vice chairman of the New York City Landmarks Preservation Commission, how do you think preservation has affected the architectural profession?

WJC: I think it's had a great effect on the profession. The close look at our existing architectural heritage has enlarged every architect's range of design ideas and vocabulary of forms. Architects all across the United States are working hard at restoring old buildings, giving them new uses and solving their technical problems so that they can be saved. This process of detailed study is a case of constant discovery and learning.

BLDD: What sort of impact has the preservation movement had on you as an architect?

WJC: Preservation has changed my views considerably. It has enlarged and broadened my definition of the word "contemporary." There was a time when I thought that being contemporary meant being on the cutting edge. That is not really my view now. I think that what constitutes contemporary is much broader: in some situations, designing in a manner consistent with the strong stylistic characteristics of an existing environment may be the most "up-to-date" solution.

BLDD: How valuable is an active landmark preservation program to the quality of city life?

WJC: It's enormously valuable. Here in New York, it has brought an extraordinary richness to the architectural, artistic, and cultural life of the city. I assume it is similar in other American cities, although I'm most familiar with it in New York.

BLDD: Now that the preservation movement has been around for more than twenty years, and a lot of buildings have been identified and designated, what do you see as its future?

WJC: We will develop more appropriate uses for our old buildings, uses that are more in concert with the meaning of the structures' forms. Consider an example here in New York. A Greek Revival church with beautiful white columns and a classic steeple gets designated as a landmark and is therefore saved. But in order to save it, the developer has to gut the inside and convert it into condos and efficiency apartments. So the building is saved, but what does that mean? The result is a radical separation of function and form; the internal function of the building no longer has anything to do with the external form. The Americans who built that church believed that they were reviving Greek democracy and that they were indeed the reincarnation of ancient Greek society. Once stuffed full of condos, that church, which embodied an early American dream, is beyond recognition. As the landmarks movement progresses, I hope we'll find some way to make a closer fit between function and form.

BLDD: You're also interested in and knowledgeable about South American architecture and artifacts, especially textiles. How did that interest develop?

WJC: The interest in South American archaeology probably stems from something as simple as seeing a poster of Machu Picchu. I then traveled to Peru and became fascinated by the cultural remnants. I have had a curiosity about ancient arts for a long time, but the particular interest in ancient Peruvian architecture and textiles is relatively recent.

BLDD: How did you translate a general interest in the meaning of physical form into such a profound involvement with textiles?

WJC: It may seem at first that textile art is very far from architecture and city planning, but it really isn't. All of these elements together are concerned with the meaning of physical form. Whether you're talking about a city plan, the architectural details of an ancient ruin, or a textile structure, it's really the same subject, only at different scales. As a creative architect you try to impart meaning into the form you're working with. As an archaeologist, you look at the ancient forms and try to ascertain what they were trying to convey, what kind of society it was, what their religion was, and so forth. You try to extract the meaning. Architectural design and archaeological analysis are just two sides of the same coin.

In ancient Peruvian cultures textiles were of great importance, not at all like their minor position in our culture today. Textile structure was the high technology of ancient Peru. Everybody knew how to weave, and almost everything they needed was created with structure similar to textiles: they made boats and bridges like textiles, they kept records and accounts with textiles, in addition to using textiles for clothing. It's great fun to analyze patterns of ancient fragments and to discover not only the iconography, symbols, and religions of the culture, but also how the different cultures manipulated the various textile elements and how the technology evolved. In Peru we have an amazing record spanning thousands of years.

BLDD: How do you study a fragment of a textile?

WJC: The study of a fragment can reveal a great deal about the whole object, particularly if you know its origin, its context, and with what it was associated. The microscope can add and reveal a whole new landscape. It's really no different from being in an airplane and looking down on a city.

BLDD: Have you ever worked at repairing or conserving textiles?

WJC: Such fragile textiles do have special conservation requirements, and though I haven't done much myself, I have taken courses in the field of textile conservation. I've designed textile storage facilities for my own studio and for the Textile Museum in Washington, D.C., where in addition to being their architect, I have participated in scholarly work at the museum. The design for the museum consisted of converting two existing house structures in northwest Washington, creating display spaces and storage facilities with controlled conditions. The textiles are fragile and require special light, humidity, and temperature controls, yet one wants to exhibit them in a way that makes them as beautiful and as brilliant as possible.

BLDD: Are you interested in the textiles of other cultures?

WJC: Not to the extent that I am in those from ancient Peru. I really can't explain why, except that there's only a certain amount of room in one's mind.

BLDD: Well, there is sufficient room to explore other cul-

Ramaz School, New York, N.Y.

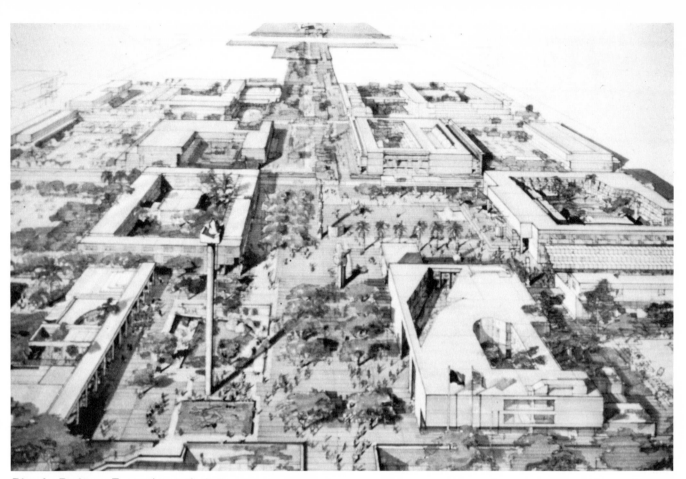

Plan for Dodoma, Tanzania, rendering

tures and to develop a new capital for Tanzania. Can you tell us how that came about and what scheme you developed there?

WJC: Jim Rossant was first called upon as a consultant to the United Nations and to the Government of Tanzania. From that relationship evolved the firm's work in the planning of a new capital, Dodoma, for that country.

BLDD: Why was there a need for a new capital in Tanzania?

WJC: The old capital, Dar-es-Salaam, had the ugly tradition of having been a slave-trading port. It is a hot, tropical place at the eastern edge of the country. The goals of this new socialist country were to create a new image for itself and to build a city closer to the center of the country in a milder climate. Our plans for that new capital are consonant with the goals of the country and government. It's a capital of low structures, a maximum of four stories high—no great towering glass monoliths, which American architects so often export.

BLDD: No high-rise buildings?

WJC: None at all.

BLDD: Why did you decide to do that?

WJC: For reasons of scale, energy conservation—the city will have no elevators—and finance. It's not a rich country. The site was selected because it has a beautiful climate and won't require

air-conditioning. We evolved a richly patterned but low-scale urban structure that will have a series of governmental buildings surrounded by housing, as well as commercial facilities.

BLDD: How did the history and culture of Tanzania play a part in the development of the plan?

WJC: The traditional indigenous housing consists of low, rectilinear structures called *tembes*. Our buildings, although in no way duplicates, have something in common with *tembes*. The plan of the town relates more to the future of the country than to its past, because the country really has no native urban past.

BLDD: Did you ever expect your life to unfold the way it has?

WJC: No. Life has new surprises at every turn. I don't think it's possible to anticipate all that.

BLDD: What's been the greatest satisfaction of your career?

WJC: I suppose Reston, because there we really built a whole group of buildings that have different faces and different functions but still engage in elaborate architectural conversations across the plaza. That's the greatest pleasure of all. One dreams of the opportunity to design not just one object but a group of objects that then converse. If you're lucky, they even form a chorus.

ALEXANDER COOPER

Alexander Cooper is a partner in Cooper, Eckstut Associates, a firm founded in 1979 on a venturesome premise: that a single firm could achieve excellence in three distinct but related fields—architecture, urban planning, and urban design.

BLDD: You have long been associated with improved urban planning and design. Where did this interest and commitment originate? Were you an urban flower from the beginning?

AC: I was born in Pittsburgh, which is a physical city. It wasn't until I was older that I realized it's also a very European city. Europeans who visit Pittsburgh love it—not the downtown, but the surrounding hills. Pittsburgh has hills very much like Salzburg's. There are little church steeples everywhere. When you grow up in Pittsburgh you are very aware of what cities are about. But that's not what drove me to architecture; that happened later.

BLDD: At what point in your life did you decide to pursue a career in architecture and planning? Was there anything in your childhood that influenced you to think in terms of architecture?

AC: No, actually not. I was not one of those prodigies who drew and drew and didn't think about anything else. In fact, I was an English major at Yale, and that's what I thought about and enjoyed most. My interest in architecture came very late. It happened when I was at Yale. Louis Kahn was there, and the Yale University Art Gallery was being finished. I thought it was an extraordinary building, and it inspired me to switch from being an English major to an architecture major. It happened simply, no magic. I was a junior at that point, and my older brother was in the architecture school at the time. He has a firm in Philadelphia now.

BLDD: Have you ever done anything in collaboration with your brother?

AC: We've tried, but we haven't actually built anything. My brother's firm is very different from ours, but we'll eventually do something together. We do a lot of large-scale publicly oriented work and his firm is more traditionally architectural.

BLDD: After graduating from Yale, you worked with two very celebrated architects: Philip Johnson and then Edward Lar-

rabee Barnes. How did you decide to work in those offices?

AC: I have to talk about Yale first, a difficult experience for me, except for the people I met there. Yale was a very trendy and stylish place under Paul Rudolph, and I came away with some very negative feelings about certain aspects of the profession. The transitory and the fashionable were spoon-fed to the students to an extreme degree. I felt I wasn't learning the right things. So when I came to New York, I was quite cynical. I went to work for a man named René de Blonet, a wonderful Swiss architect who did classical interiors. I spent a year drawing wood moldings, full size and in perspective, which brought me back to a level of reality I could appreciate. After a year with him I decided I'd better do something more serious and went to work for Philip Johnson, where I stayed for three years.

BLDD: How did you first come in contact with Philip, who at that point in his career wasn't the same Philip Johnson we know today?

AC: He was in fact my second choice. What I really wanted was to work for Mies, so I went to Chicago and got a job with him. The day before I was to move to Chicago I got cold feet about moving to the Midwest and sent a telegram saying I couldn't make it. They were not pleased, since they offered so few jobs in those days.

BLDD: Why weren't you willing to venture forth?

AC: It seemed like too big a jump from the values that I instinctively understood and was comfortable with. I love Chicago, but I knew that it would be too big a change for me. So the idea of Philip as a New York Mies seemed logical. The extraordinary thing about Philip's office at that time, and it may still be true today, was that it was incredibly well managed. All the lessons I learned from Philip were business lessons. You have to work for Philip to understand that. To this day, Philip can compete on fees that knock your socks off because he can produce a job more efficiently than any other design-oriented firm. I was in awe of the expertise and brilliance of Philip's office management. Behind the gadfly is a rock. He heads an organization that is highly tuned to producing things very quickly and very consistently on a budget. It was an eye-opener for me.

BLDD: What were your responsibilities?

AC: I was one of the drafting corps. I think for six months I wrapped drawings before they even gave me a desk. I worked on the addition to the Boston Public Library for a while. Then I got to work on Philip's underground painting gallery on his own property, the Glass House in New Canaan. I worked on that for a year after helping to catalogue his own collection, which was another education. I was the only one working on it, so I did all the working drawings and all the design work with him, and supervision on the site. That was a very complete experience for a young architect at the time. The reason I went on to Barnes's office was that Jaque Robertson, a close friend from Yale who was working with Barnes, called me and said, "You've got to come here and work. We've got all kinds of problems and projects." So I moved to Barnes's office, where there was an extraordinary crew working—Jaque, Gio Passanella, Charlie Gwathmey, and a number of other top designers.

BLDD: I've often heard that it was one of the best post-graduate schools around for young architects.

AC: It was. At the time, Ed was doing smaller things, mostly houses, camps, small galleries, some schools—but not big college campus projects. Ed has such a mastery over the small-scale object. It was wonderful to see him working on that. I probably learned more about design in Ed's office than in Philip's. I spent three years there and then went from Barnes's office into city government.

BLDD: You are now known as an architect and planner. I suspect that those who have followed your career over an extended period are more familiar with your significant contributions as a so-called planner. I suspect, too, that you're less than comfortable with that term. Is it one that you use to describe yourself?

AC: Not at all. But the fact that I was a commissioner on the New York City Planning Commission has reinforced the perception of me as a planner. In fact, even after a number of years in practice, we still have a significant problem being recognized as architects. That is a continuing battle. To this day even good friends of mine don't realize we follow buildings all the way through as architects because our image as planners and urban designers is so powerful.

BLDD: Do you think one role generally precludes the other in the minds of your potential public?

AC: Yes. The public likes very simple, neat definitions. It's either one or the other.

BLDD: And in the mind of the practitioner?

AC: Architecture and urban design are completely related. This mixture—the combination of a lot of different skills—is in fact the foundation of our practice. "Planning," however, is a word we haven't used alone to refer to ourselves for several years.

BLDD: What prompted you to abandon its use, and what have you substituted for it?

AC: Right now planning has lost touch with the physical world in this country. It used to be a profession run by engineers working on large-scale projects such as roads and airports. People who go into planning now, however, have little training in the physical aspects of things. They have become social planners, dealing with public policy, budget allocation, education, economic development, and so on. When we used the word "planning" for our firm, we would get calls to do things we just don't do—we don't have people to do land-use studies and interminable analyses. Unless something leads to a physi-cal product, we aren't interested. So we dropped the word, but people don't let go of it easily because it is a word people understand. It's a word with a history. There's even an American Institute of Planners. Urban design is less understood, generally, because it's more complicated. Nobody really knows what it is. There are no standards for it. There's no American Institute of Urban Design. It was really at Columbia that the definition of urban design came together clearly. We had to define it in order to teach it. When the graduate urban design program there was headed by Aldo Giurgola, urban design was taught basically as architectural study on a grander scale—more buildings, larger sites. When I took over as head of the program, I crafted a different definition of urban design, one based on what I had learned working for the city. We set up a program that had architectural training as a requirement. Then we taught new skills needed to manipulate large-scale design, such as traffic, zoning, law, development, finance, politics, and management in the public sector. Each of these has to be understood by architects before they can control any environment beyond a building's property lines. But urban design also includes the ability to manipulate three-dimensional objects architecturally and to make space. Urban design is what this firm does—we did it at Battery Park City, at Forty-second Street, and at Baltimore Harbor. All of the things that we do we call urban design. In terms of marketing the firm's services, we do urban design and architecture, and the second flows from the first.

BLDD: How is Cooper, Eckstut different from other firms that specialize in urban design?

AC: There's a general perception in private industry that people who come from the public sector are difficult to work with and don't know the realities of the private sector. This can be particularly true with architecture, but in our firm we look for only the best people from the public sector. Probably more than half the firm consists of people who have had experience in the public sector, and from there they bring values and judgments that we respect. So I think our staff mix makes us different from other firms.

BLDD: What is the proportion of public to private sector work that your firm does?

AC: When the firm started we had predominantly public sector work. That has shifted now to the point where two-thirds of our work is in the private sector, where we'd like to keep it. But we never want to stop the public work. We're very good at it and we enjoy it, and there are a lot of private sector projects that would be very unlikely for us. Doing a speculative office building in an office park, for instance, would be very hard for us to take on as a firm. We've never done a private house, and I don't imagine we ever will. We just don't have time for that kind of problem.

BLDD: Would it be fair to describe you as a philosophical, analytic fellow?

AC: "Analytic" is a good word.

BLDD: If that's the case, you would not start a firm without having a carefully conceived design philosophy and approach. Can you tell us about it?

AC: Philosophies usually come after you've been in practice a while. We had something less than a philosophy, but more than a notion, to start with. The firm was based on three things that if mixed properly would lead to a special kind of practice. First was the public sector experience. Both Stan Eckstut and I put in a lot of years working for agencies—and we shared the values and commitment fostered by those experiences. The second had to do with involvement in the academic world, which we continue. The third was trying to understand design from an owner's point of view. When we began we had a special relationship with Rockefeller Center as retainer clients. I had known John Burnett, the president of the Rockefeller Center Development Corporation, for many years, again from public service. Early on, when the Development Corporation was formed, he called me and said, "We're not going to have an internal design staff, but I want you to work with us on everything we do to make sure that we achieve a standard of quality acceptable to the board of directors. Because we're developers, we've got to be very careful to make sure we continually produce quality projects." Over a period of three or four years I sat with them as their representative on projects around the country and learned from an owner's perspective, as opposed to a professional's perspective, what was important to them and what they wanted to achieve. That mix of public sector experience, academic work, and understanding private ownership was what gave the firm its particular cast.

BLDD: Has your relationship with Rockefeller Center continued?

AC: I'm still a consultant to them on everything they do.

BLDD: What's the most significant project you've worked on with them?

AC: I've worked in a couple of roles with them. They've now hired us as architects on a number of projects that go beyond design consulting. The project that was the most fun was the Wells Fargo Building in Los Angeles, which I think is the best building in Los Angeles. I worked with the architect, A. C. Martin, a prominent Los Angeles firm that has done downtown buildings since 1920. I was out there every other week for two years and worked on all the pieces, including circulation, massing, and exterior skin. Also, they hired us to initially look at a piece of property, seventeen acres on Camelback Road in Phoenix. Based on our analysis, Rockefeller Center bought the land, although part of our recommendation had been to change the zoning. This project is a good example of what we do. We looked at the property and decided that under the city's existing height limit—forty-eight feet—and given the parking requirements, an economic investment could not be made there. But if the zoning were changed and the development clustered, a significant center could be built. Phoenix's height limit applied everywhere but on one street, Central Avenue. So we sat down with public officials and worked out a plan to do what they called "high-rise" and we called "mid-rise" development.

BLDD: Mid-rise? Would you call that a euphemism?

AC: Yes. After a year's battle—and it was a very big issue—Rockefeller Center ended up with permission to build nine stories high on a site that was not on Central Avenue.

BLDD: It may have been a good thing for your client, but was it good for Camelback Road?

AC: It was essential for the future of Phoenix. Before we came to town, the city had done a plan to the year 2000. They already realized that if they continued growing as they had been, expanding and filling up all the valleys surrounding the city, they would soon go as far as they could in terms of city limits, natural limits, and cost. A city can't spread that far and pay for it; there are extraordinary public costs in that form of development, where you have to expand forty miles in every direction because of limited-height zoning. If Phoenix were to grow beyond its current size—and maybe that isn't sensible, but that was the objective they had set—if it were to continue to prosper, it would have to grow back in. The fight became an issue of lifestyle. There were those who said, "We came here to get away from nine-story buildings. We want a two-story world." But nobody could pay for the two-story world any-

more. So it came down to a question of design quality. We demonstrated clearly that although we could have achieved the same density on the property within the height limit, the development would have been a nightmare. By going to nine stories, we created much more open space. We made a public park on three acres right on the Camelback frontage. Nobody had ever done that in Phoenix. It was actually quite a civic project, even with the heat it generated.

BLDD: What is the current state of it?

AC: After the zoning was settled, Rockefeller Center hired us as architects to do the first building, a 200,000-square-foot office building, which is now finished and occupied. The park is constructed. The city required that it be done in the first stage. The back half of it, which is in the second stage, will be dug up and replanted with parking under it. The entire front of Camelback, however, is quite beautiful right now, filled with cottonwood trees.

BLDD: What do you see as the project's impact?

AC: Now other people in Phoenix who want to build higher than the forty-eight-foot limit must obtain a permit that is issued only if they offer something the city considers comparable in quality to this project. It remains to be seen if others will want to pay the price.

BLDD: You raised an issue that relates to public benefit and private interest. It seems there's a whole subculture of former public servants who early on helped create certain kinds of legislation and have now become part of the private sector. In some instances, they are attempting to dismantle the very legislation, or very ideas, they helped to create. Would you comment on that?

AC: The zoning work that you're referring to—what a number of people worked on in the late sixties and early seventies—was called, I guess euphemistically, "incentive zoning." It was a system set up in New York to create benefits specific to areas smaller than the general zoning ordinance could deal with. For instance, there is a special district for Fifth Avenue, for the theater district, for Lincoln Square, the premise being that no generalized zoning rules should be applied uniformly to areas as different as these, that you simply need a more highly tuned piece of legislation to encompass the special character of each place. New York needed special districts because of its size. The zoning for all of San Francisco is like the zoning for one of New York's special districts; San Francisco is small enough for them to define street by street and view by view exactly what they want. In New York we got very involved in trying to decide what was special about each district. But the problem is that even in those districts the zoning has to be more general than a specific architectural design would be. Right now, for instance, in our design for a building within the Lincoln Square special district, we are asking for three exceptions to the basic rules. None increases the density, none makes the project less acceptable, but each represents a refinement in the design that the zoning language couldn't be specific about. And each was in a sense anticipated generally, and the reasons for the exceptions were already written into the existing text. I really don't think it's the case that the people previously involved with this legislation have been at the forefront of trying to abuse it.

BLDD: Your earliest involvement in the New York City government was during the John Lindsay administration, as a member of the Urban Design Group. Can you tell us the history of that group and what its goals were?

AC: It was started by five people—Jaquelin Robertson, Richard Weinstein, Jonathan Barnett, Gio Passanella, and Miles Weintraub—who had a vision of architects working in public service.

Anroc Center, Phoenix, Ariz.

When Lindsay ran his first campaign, those five people got in touch with him and said they were willing to do white papers about design for him. John was a person of extraordinary sympathy and sensitivity to the things we were interested in and was tough as nails about them. Without that as motivation, none of us would have gone to work in the public sector. In 1967 Jaque Robertson called me. The group by then was established in the City Planning Department, after having survived a constant bureaucratic fight to get themselves set up and recognized. Those five, with the tender loving care of Don Elliott, then chairman of the City Planning Commission, really fought to make it happen. The Urban Design Group was an idea—architects in public service—and a tool—the Zoning Resolution. Lindsay saw that the members shared very powerful urbanistic ideas, respected what they were headed for, and gave them a lot of leeway.

BLDD: Was the group controversial? In retrospect, what do you see as its contribution?

AC: Of course it was controversial. But the group managed to heighten design awareness in government and made it clear that government controls an enormous amount of the physical environment.

BLDD: What were some of the specific things the group accomplished?

AC: The first thing the members worked on was to conceptualize a theater district. Very early on their perception that the theater district was evaporating led them to come up with a mechanism for building new theaters in the district. That legislation now needs to be modified to incorporate preservation of existing theaters as well. The problem at that time, however, was how to get new theaters. The Lincoln Center district, another early one, was created to capitalize on the public investment in Lincoln Center and to organize development in that area over the following ten or fifteen years. That work is almost completed. There are virtually no sites left in the Lincoln Center district.

BLDD: What was your specific role within the group?

AC: They brought me in after they were established, and I ran a project, Coney Island. I spent most of my time on the site in 1967–68.

BLDD: Even though the group didn't have a leader, was Jaque the motivating force?

AC: That's probably true, and I think others recognize that as a matter of fact.

BLDD: Would an urban design group make sense in New York today? Would it make a difference? What would it do?

AC: Oh, I think it would. Every city government can use such a thing. In fact most city governments around the country carry out some design function, and the issue is really whether their systems are competent. They should have design professionals who know what they are looking at when they renew proposals in the public sector. The key is attracting and holding on to motivated people.

BLDD: How did you make the move from the Urban Design Group to the Housing and Development Administration?

AC: Based on my work on the Urban Design Group, Bob Hazeen, who was housing commissioner at the time, asked me to come to the HDA and run the design department there. It was a difficult decision because the Urban Design Group was so cohesive. Basically the decision, which was made as a group, was that it made sense to spread our kind of thinking to other agencies. In fact that then became one of the objectives of the group. Subsequently we made sure that urban designers got into the Transportation Department and any other agency we could find in the cause of urban design.

BLDD: What was the relationship of the HDA design department to the City Planning Department?

AC: Everything HDA did had to be submitted to City Planning for approval. HDA was in charge of the forty-eight urban renewal areas in the city, each of which had ten to twelve sites on it. That meant about five hundred sites in the city over which the HDA had design control. That was an awesome task for me—I was thirty-two and probably the youngest of a staff of forty people I inherited overnight—but a wonderful opportunity for learning about the city in all its parts.

BLDD: Now, nearly twenty years later, what would you do if you had a similar assignment today?

AC: I'd panic just as much, because at a certain fundamental level the task was impossible. I would probably know that beforehand, though, instead of afterwards. I don't think I'd do anything differently; I would try to relate the physical products to the particular morality in each area. It turned out that my biggest adversaries in trying to achieve good design were other governmental agencies. That was the real battle. I can give you an example of that. In most renewal areas, public housing was the exclusive source of new housing. Community groups were just coming into their own socially and politically, and I worked with them in all those areas. Their objectives, usually very different from what the federal rule books allowed, were made very clear to me. I spent a lot of time in Washington at the Federal Housing Administration and the Public Housing Administration trying to change their guidelines and rules to fit New York lifestyles. Spanish families, for instance, would tell us that they spend most of their time in the kitchen and would rather have a big kitchen than a big living room. But you couldn't get the federal government to mortgage a unit that had a big kitchen, that responded culturally to what these families wanted.

I stayed at HDA for three years. In 1971, Don Elliott asked me to come back from HDA to City Planning and head the Urban Design Group. By that time, Jaque had become the head of the mayor's midtown development group, and Richard Weinstein was the head of the lower Manhattan office. Lindsay gave me three things to do simultaneously. Heading the Urban Design Group was one. The other two were basically tasks for the mayor, as opposed to City Planning, which was where the Urban Design Group was. He made me the head of the Urban Design Council, which had a dozen members and had been functioning for a while but didn't have much direction at that point. Lindsay wanted to resurrect it to follow through the original recommendations made by William Paley's committee. So the second thing I agreed to do was to be the executive director of the Urban Design Council, working with Paley as chairman. Paley was unhappy about that and ended up resigning.

BLDD: Why did Paley decide to resign?

AC: He may have had a lot of reasons, but I remember that Paley, Lindsay, and I met at Gracie Mansion one afternoon, and Paley was quite clear that from a management perspective he felt it was wrong to have a paid city employee running a body constituted as an independent ombudsman. That's not an unreasonable point. Lindsay, however, felt that it could be done. John and I had worked together on a lot of things, and we knew that independence wasn't going to be an issue or a problem. So we proceeded and Paley resigned, and a man named Jack Blum became the chairman. The Urban Design Council was given a small staff. We worked up an agenda; housing quality became the council's major undertaking.

As the third responsibility, Lindsay made me head of the West Side Highway Office. That was an awesome responsibility: it took a lot of time and a separate staff to get the West Side Highway project organized, oriented, and started. Lindsay had a good perception about that project as a land-use and development enterprise rather than a transportation project. So I had three separate things to do, each with a separate staff. What were my personal objectives? Again, to survive. Good things were going on in all three.

BLDD: After all this experience you became a logical appointment to the City Planning Commission.

AC: Apparently.

BLDD: Was that something that you actively sought?

AC: Oh no. I had worked with the commission too often to seek being part of it. Having seen it from the staff side, the idea couldn't have been further from my mind.

BLDD: Who approached you, and why did you choose to accept? What did you do during that period?

AC: That seat had been vacant for about eight months, but I was busy thinking about other things and the commission was functioning perfectly well. Curiously, it was during the last weeks of Lindsay's administration that he called me out of the blue one night to ask if I would do it. I said, "I thought we were friends." We met a few days later and talked about what he thought the job needed and why somebody with design experience had to sit there.

BLDD: That sounds like a very thoughtful gesture on his part, and a very unpolitical appointment.

AC: Totally unpolitical—it was his last month in office.

BLDD: Did it reflect a deep commitment to design factors that influence the city?

AC: Yes. And I think we were all worried, as you would naturally be when you're loyal to one mayor, that the next mayor would not have the same level of commitment. We wanted to protect some of the things that had been started and were ongoing. I ended up accepting the job, of course. It was very difficult for me to say no to John, partly because his sensitivities and sympathies were so compatible with mine.

BLDD: How do you think history will view his administration in terms of its attitude toward urbanism?

AC: I'm very clear on that. His image will become more and more positive. One of the things he will come to be recognized for, in addition to his general urban sensitivity, is his superb management. I think he ran the government extremely well and brought an effective concept of management to government.

BLDD: What was your term of office in the City Planning Commission?

AC: The terms are normally eight years, but John Zuccotti resigned to become chairman, which created a five-year remaining term as opposed to a full eight. I was there from 1973 to 1978.

BLDD: Did you serve on the commission when John Zuccotti was the chairman?

AC: Yes, we worked very closely.

BLDD: And how would you characterize his role as chairman? What were his philosophy and goals?

AC: John was extraordinarily qualified for that job, through his housing experience, through a year or two as commissioner, and through his own personal commitments. He was probably more qualified for that job than any of the previous chairmen. John had some very clear ideas as to what could be done, his

**Battery Park City, New York, N.Y. Above: model of the
performance arena, right: model of the proposal**

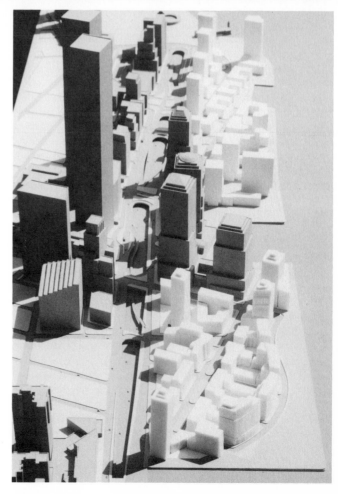

major contribution being to scale city planning down to the
block level. It was an extraordinary tour de force at a time
when community boards were starting to have real, as opposed
to imaginary, power. John was committed to getting to know
every one of the boards, the needs of every street. It was the
most formidable display of breadth of knowledge about the city
that I have seen from anybody in government. In the sixties we
had experienced all the bravado of large-scale planning. In the
seventies John was involved in tempering that down to something people could relate to. The plans—I think we called them
"mini-plans"—became very tactile, very intimate, and very
responsive to local needs.

BLDD: By the time you were through with your city involvement, you must have known more about zoning and development policy than almost anyone. A dozen years later, one of
your first assignments in the private sector was for a public
client. Tell us about Battery Park City and the master plan you
created for it.

AC: I wasn't happy when that assignment came because I'd
had too much experience with Battery Park City already. It
was one of the great lost opportunities of New York that had
been going on for ten or fifteen years already. So I wasn't sure
we wanted to do it at all. But we were reassured by our client
for Battery Park City, Richard Kahan, who at that time had a
dual role as the head of the New York State Urban Development Corporation and the Battery Park City Authority. He
assured us that we were selected in the hope of changing the
previous plan into something more sensible and desirable.
Over the years he has been an unbelievable client in terms of
his ability to prompt design people to achieve ever higher

Forty-second Street Development Project, New York, N.Y., model

standards. And what any architect looks for is great clients. The Authority was bankrupt, heading for default, and Kahan had decided as an alternative to try development, rather than defaulting on the bonds. We were given ninety days to redo a plan for ninety-two acres. We worked for three months virtually nonstop. At the end of that time a plan was taken to the mayor and the governor. It was approved by both of them within a month. For us the assignment had been clear. The old proposal was one of those overly complex, visionary sixties schemes. We approached it differently, as an extension of lower Manhattan, as more of New York City. We just couldn't believe that ninety-two acres on the waterfront could be all bad. The theme in redoing Battery Park City was to make it simpler, more familiar, more real; to make it as good as all the best neighborhoods in New York; and to make it a place that developers would relate to and want to come back to. Our master plan had a lot to do with the kind of firm we are. When we did the plan, we refused to show any buildings, which is highly unusual, not what master plans by architects are supposed to be. We drew only streets and open space because we knew that those were the elements we needed to create beautiful spaces, wonderful addresses, great real estate, and a marvelous, complex urban environment. Over the mile-and-a-half of landfill we structured a road and park system that we knew would be desirable regardless of the buildings. The buildings became secondary to the public spaces. That is still the format at Battery Park City. It is a magical place because of the relationship of the river to all the public pieces of Battery Park City. The public pieces lured the necessary private investment, which was the theory on which we crafted the emphasis on parks and streets.

BLDD: How do you see it evolving? Do you think it will be erosive to other neighborhoods?
AC: Not at all. I think one element of what was conceived in the sixties about Battery Park City was correct: the attempt to create residential space close to the workplace. Residential living in lower Manhattan is going to reinforce lower Manhattan; it won't erode other neighborhoods.
BLDD: What effects would you like to see from Battery Park City?
AC: One thing I would love is for the whole public walkway system of Battery Park City to be continued around lower Manhattan. A lot of people are thinking about that. It is still elevating for me to go down to the Battery Park Esplanade. If you go there in the summer, even before you see the esplanade you can smell the suntan oil. It's like going to the beach. People are there with towels, radios, umbrellas, and picnics spread out on the asphalt paths. It's a magical place.
BLDD: What do you see as your mission on Forty-second Street, another recent project?
AC: I think the word "mission" is a little elaborate. We were hired by the city and the state to do the physical parts of a plan for Forty-second Street. It was the most complicated thing I have ever worked on—it made Battery Park City look like a suburb. We dealt with lawyers, environmentalists, financial people, civic groups, the general public. We had a nine-month schedule to create a plan whereby the street could become a location for more desirable activities. The strategy was to take all the development rights of the midblock part of the project—between Seventh and Eighth Avenues, where there are ten historic theaters—and transfer those to the corner of Seventh Avenue, Broadway, and Forty-second, and the corner of Eighth

Forty-second Street Development Project, New York, N.Y., drawing

Avenue and Forty-second. That transfer, without changing the zoning, would allow development that would then come back and subsidize midblock. It was an extraordinary project in that a public body that didn't own the property and had no money to develop was advertising the land and getting developers to respond. I think it will happen, but it's going to take time. In the end, it will be a tremendous success. The centerpiece will always be the early-century theaters in midblock. That, along with the transit improvements, is what's important in the project. If we can end up with a redevelopment that doesn't cost us Times Square, the city will be way ahead.

BLDD: Would the city have been better off without another redevelopment, the one at the South Street Seaport?

AC: I think it could have been done very differently. Rouse is going to have trouble there because there are plenty of other retail areas in New York—Madison Avenue, Fourteenth Street, or any of the other locations where there are restaurants and retail and "real" buildings. The problem with the Seaport is that it's been made synthetic. You feel like you're in an exhibit, like you should have paid admission. You don't feel as if you can walk in and out easily. You miss the sense of choice, spontaneity, and flexibility. New Yorkers won't go back often, and tourists are going to be very disappointed. You can hear people saying, "This is just like Baltimore."

BLDD: How important is art in your life and career, not only from your early experience cataloguing Philip Johnson's collection, but as a member of the Art Commission and creator of some very beautiful drawings?

AC: Art is extraordinarily important to me personally. I believe that's true for most architects. We bring that sort of interest into a lot of our projects where we've worked with artists. For example, in the Phoenix project we worked with the Heard Museum to find sculptures for the park and paintings for the interiors. And several years ago I suggested to Richard Kahan, then the head of the Battery Park City Authority, that he put together an art program for Battery Park City. At first he said, "That's a great idea, I'll get back to you." Then he came back and said, "Alex, no good. We cannot have a bankrupt agency sponsoring art programs. It's not credible to the legislature. But," he said, "write down your thoughts about it." I wrote that if artists could work in direct collaboration with architects and landscape architects in Battery Park City, it would enrich the place in subtle and sensitive ways. Six months later, Richard came back and said, "We now have enough credibility that the issue of bankruptcy won't come up, and we can do art programs. Let's work on it." So Battery Park City now has top artists working on the open spaces throughout the entire development. The commitment has been made, with the active participation of a prestigious committee, to carry this out for the next fifteen years.

BLDD: Has there been any particular person who has affected the aesthetic you demonstrated in Battery Park City?

AC: Yes, John Nash and Daniel Burnham. Do you know how clever Burnham was? He offered to do master plans for cities at no cost—for Manila, Cleveland, Chicago—on the condition that if public buildings were to be erected to implement the plans, his firm would do the architecture. Battery Park City has been a confirming piece of work for us, because we've done everything from plans and designing the streets and parks to choosing the esplanade handrails. We believe that the handrail embodies the same concepts as the master plan. The work we would most like to do is the large-scale organization of civic spaces in a number of cities, followed by the design of parks, streets, and public buildings. We seem to need a significant public agenda to get motivated as a firm. That's when we do our best work.

BLDD: What do you see as the state—and the significance—of American architecture now?

AC: It's very troubled. There are some brilliant architects out there working, producing extraordinarily beautiful objects. But in the main, architecture now is very self-involved, without a social or cultural mandate. You have to ask whether life in cities is improving, whether priorities are sensible, whether architects are contributing to the dialogue. I'm afraid we've basically moved off stage.

BLDD: How do you see your career evolving?

AC: As a firm, we hope to grow into a national practice, even though we recognize the incredible difficulty in becoming equally effective in all parts of the country. This is especially true for us, since our design approach requires extracting the essence of each place, each time. Personally, my own priorities have significantly altered my attitude toward buildings. I used to be very object oriented. Now I concentrate on background architecture, with variations particular to the location. I think this is an approach that leads to a more rational urbanism and a more gentle architecture. I am still as moved by a beautifully composed street as by a beautifully articulated building. I hope to do a number of each.

ARTHUR DREXLER

For almost thirty years Arthur Drexler has been the director of the Department of Architecture and Design of the Museum of Modern Art. As director, he is responsible for the Mies van der Rohe Archive, a collection of more than twenty thousand architectural drawings; a selection of furniture, machine-made and handcrafted objects, and textiles; and thousands of posters and other forms of graphic design. The Department of Architecture, the first of its kind in the country, was founded in 1932 under the chairmanship of Philip Johnson. In 1951 Arthur Drexler joined the staff of the museum as curator of the Department of Architecture and Design.

BLDD: Three years after the Museum of Modern Art was founded, work to establish a department of architecture and design was under way. Would you explain who made the decision to create such a department and why it was deemed a useful and significant addition to the museum?

AD: When the museum was founded in 1929, it was based on Alfred Barr's program. From the very beginning, the museum was intended to deal with all of the arts of the twentieth century. In practice, it did not end up dealing in any comprehensive way with theater arts, but it has dealt with painting and sculpture, prints and drawings, photography, cinema, and the applied arts—architecture, industrial design, and graphic design (typography and posters). Not all of these activities started simultaneously because, to begin with, there wasn't a proper museum building. The museum was housed in rented space in either a townhouse or an office building until it got going and a staff was assembled. By 1936, when the museum building was in construction, all these departments existed formally. They were about to come into their own in the new museum building quarters—each department with offices and storage and exhibition space—when the war years interrupted the activities of the museum. By 1947 the department was reorganized somewhat by Philip Johnson. There were for a time two separate departments, one for architecture and one for what was called "industrial arts," a name that was always a little problematic. What was settled on finally was "industrial design," and the two subjects were combined into one department, still called the Department of Architecture and Design. We have to explain constantly that this also includes graphic design, which is separate from the print collection: graphic design includes only posters and typography, combinations of word and image. It was agreed that all of these elements fit properly under the rubric of architecture, since historically it was architects who dominated these fields, more or less. You can make a good case that it should be organized this way, and so it has remained.

BLDD: How did Philip Johnson's chairmanship affect the overall purpose, focus, and direction of the department in its early stages?

AD: Philip was involved with the museum before a department even existed, and he knew that Alfred Barr had in mind that there would be exhibitions pertaining to these subjects. At that time, as far as I know, Philip had a minor interest in design but a strong interest in architecture. He and Henry-Russell Hitchcock made at least one trip to Europe together, and subsequently Philip made several visits on his own, to look at buildings and to familiarize himself with new work. The museum's program and its comprehensive view of the arts were not entirely new; the museum was, after all, restating the Bauhaus, which taught all these arts simultaneously. But the museum's perspective on all the arts was supplied by Alfred Barr. There would not have been an international architecture show—the famous show for which Alfred gave its name to the International Style—without his active involvement. And the "Machine Art" show at the museum presented Alfred's perspective on what was significant about design in our time. Very few people take the trouble to go back and read the catalogue preface written by him. It is the basic statement, as he saw it, of what constituted a design standard for the twentieth century. It differs from, say, the more materialist Bauhaus point of view in that he cites Plato and Thomas Aquinas as intellectual precedents, supplying abstract modern design with a moral, theological, and philosophical basis.

BLDD: Are you saying that from that preface came the American architect's sense of mission?

AD: I'm simply saying that the definition of what the museum was interested in was provided by Alfred Barr. Philip was the gifted executant of that project. The first efforts to establish the nucleus of a design collection, which came out of the "Machine Art" show, were under Alfred's guidance. It's what he had in mind to accomplish when he began the museum and before he had any staff available.

BLDD: What was Philip Johnson's own point of view at that time?

AD: Philip Johnson's point of view at that time was Alfred Barr's point of view, although from every indication I can find in his correspondence and his achievement he did have remarkable taste and judgment. He could distinguish between the superb, the merely good, and the indifferent with the greatest of ease. My emphasis on Alfred Barr's primacy in establishing content and direction should be supported by the observation that he had the perfect executant for the job. Their comprehension of what they were looking at was so similar that their relationship, if it started off as one of teacher and pupil, quickly grew to be an exchange on pretty much equal footing. As the years went by and demands on his time became overwhelming, Barr had to rely increasingly on other people in their assigned areas of expertise. After being director of the museum, Alfred was briefly out of office but was then appointed director of museum collections. He could not pay equal attention to every department in the museum and decided to concentrate on painting, sculpture, and drawings.

BLDD: After the modern architecture show of 1932, the next significant exhibition was in 1934, the exhibition entitled "Machine Art." What was the significance of that exhibition, and how did it eventually provide the nucleus for the design collection?

AD: The "Machine Art" exhibition dealt with two classes of objects. One comprised utilitarian objects made by machines or with machine tools—kitchen faucets, stoves, cooking pots, that sort of thing. The layman had certainly not considered such objects works of art with aesthetic qualities worthy of being singled out for such attention. The second class of objects was the machine or tool itself—coil springs, propellers, tools of all kinds. Exhibiting objects like these in an art museum was even more of a shock. At that time it was extremely difficult, if not impossible, to find products such as telephones or typewriters to put forward as examples of twentieth-century artifacts that had been beautifully designed and made. Whatever was available was in one way or another unsatisfactory as design. The exhibition had to confine itself to the rigorously utilitarian because there was little else to show. The idea that utilitarian objects can be very beautiful was scarcely new; why people seemed shocked by it I cannot imagine. I don't know why anyone who had seen Shaker furniture or Yankee clipper ships would find it a novel notion that well-made, unadorned useful objects are beautiful.

BLDD: In the 1940s, the Department of Architecture and the Department of Design conducted competitions. What was the purpose of these and at what point did they end?

AD: The competitions were conducted in order to encourage the production, and then the acceptance, of well-designed useful objects. It was felt that providing exposure for these things would encourage the audience to buy and use them. Furniture was one of the most conspicuous problems. There were plenty of people available to design good modern furniture, but it was very difficult to persuade a manufacturer to make it and a department store to stock it. The buyers in the

department stores were not interested in allocating space for this kind of furniture, and the public was very uncertain of it. The museum undertook to remedy the situation through the "Organic Design" competition, which was organized by Eliot Noyes and done in collaboration with department stores and manufacturers. It was an enormous success. Out of it came furniture by Charles Eames, who had won a prize in partnership with Eero Saarinen.

BLDD: Was that when the five-dollar-type design selections were being shown?

AD: No, that program started earlier, in the late thirties, under John McAndrew. His shows were called "Useful Household Objects Under Five Dollars," although the price had to be raised as inflation took over. Their purpose was to call attention to the fact that there were perfectly fine modern objects that you could buy in the dime store. When such things were taken out of the dime store and shown handsomely, they suddenly looked very different.

BLDD: When were the collections named the Department of Architecture and Design, and what motivated the creation of this all-inclusive department?

AD: It was renamed around 1947, when Philip formally rejoined the staff. It was renamed because, for one thing, Eliot Noyes, who had been head of the Department of Design, had left during the war and didn't come back to the museum, but went into private practice. Combining architecture and design made more sense, and it imposed a more rigorous and more consistent standard of judgment. At the time Edgar Kaufmann was conducting something called the "Good Design" program. Consistent standards had been somewhat blurred in this program, which has always generated an enormous amount of confusion. To this day, people assume that the Museum of Modern Art gives awards for good design. We do nothing of the sort, and never have. The museum has never given awards to anybody for anything.

BLDD: You may not give awards, but you do seem to give seals of approval . . .

AD: Not if I can help it, we don't. In fact, that was one of the reasons why the "Good Design" program was brought to an end. The museum did not want to become an official promoter. If you wish to conclude that something is worthy of emulation because you saw it here, that's your business.

BLDD: In a sense every museum, by selecting objects for exhibition, certifies, validates, and ratifies them as worthy of very close and important consideration.

AD: Yes, but that's not the same as saying, "This is now the approved standard because it has been selected for your admiration by such-and-such an institution." That's an untenable position for an institution to hold; it's unfair to everyone, including design professionals. The fact that one chair is selected for the design collection doesn't mean that ten other chairs are not good, just that they may not have quite the same significance, historical or otherwise, to the museum.

BLDD: You are known as a thoughtful interpreter of architecture and as someone interested in raising the level of the intellectual debate about architecture. I would liken it to a mission to which you have devoted yourself. How did you first become involved in this calling?

AD: First of all, I studied painting at the High School of Music and Art in New York, and then went on to Cooper Union, where my studies were rudely interrupted by World War II. During the war, I was in the Army Corps of Engineers, in the intelligence section of a combat battalion, and we built bridges and highways from one end of Luzon to the other. When I came back after the war I returned to painting but eventually ran out of money and had to get a job. The easiest thing to do was architecture.

BLDD: How did an artist get work as an architect? Were you a draftsman?

AD: I got my first job on the basis of some renderings of buildings and was soon assigned the "arts" desk in that office. After a year or so I went to France, where I stayed for about eight months. When I came back I went to work for George Nelson, who had a very small office. There were only four or five people, including the secretary, and they were all delightful. George had a lot of writing assignments, because before he had opened his office he had been an editor of *Architectural Forum* magazine. I began to help him by doing the research. After a while I was spending as much time writing as drafting. When George got a contract to do a year's worth of articles on holiday houses for *Holiday Magazine,* they hired me to do the research and I traveled around the United States for months. It was tedious, but I saw a great deal of work. Even if I could have afforded it, I would never have thought to do that on my own. By the time it was all over, I had a very good picture of what was going on in the United States.

When I came back to New York I went to work as architectural editor of *Interiors* magazine, which at that time was a somewhat classier publication than it subsequently became. I was there for several years and found out that, yes, I could meet deadlines and get a magazine out once a month, but if I did it for more than two years I would end up killing myself out of boredom. It was worse than that: I came to hate journalism because it generates a demand for which there is no supply.

BLDD: How did you eventually move from *Interiors* to the Museum of Modern Art?

AD: I had already met Philip. When I started at the magazine I knew that his Glass House in New Canaan was nearing completion. I phoned Philip, went up on a Saturday to see his house, brought a camera with me and took 35mm color photographs. Since I had just begun on the magazine and the publisher was very eager to please me so that we would be off on a friendly footing, he agreed to allocate twelve pages to this house, with two color photos. This was the first time the house was published; it was about 1948 or '49. I subsequently published one other building by Philip in *Interiors,* the guest house for Mrs. John D. Rockefeller on East Fifty-second Street in Manhattan. After two years at *Interiors* I couldn't stand it any longer, so I began to look for another job. One day I bumped into Philip on Fifth Avenue. He had heard I had been looking for a job in Paris and said, "Would you like to come to the museum? I need a curator for the department." That conversation was in the fall of 1950. I finally started at the Museum of Modern Art in early 1951.

BLDD: What was your first assignment at the museum?

AD: There were two projects right away. One was the "Eight Automobiles" show, which Philip had in the works already. I wrote the catalogue for the show, but he had already made the selection of cars and had designed the installation. As my very first exhibition at the museum I did a tiny little show in a room about eighteen by twenty-four feet—if it was that big. It was a show of Le Corbusier material in the collection, including the model of the Villa Savoye and some furniture and a painting. This assemblage of objects had no organizing principle other than that it was an interestingly diverse selection of material owned by the museum.

BLDD: So you worked with Philip for approximately three years before he left the museum?

AD: Yes. When I came here, it was with the understanding that Philip was in the process of setting up his own architecture

The Philip Johnson Gallery, the Museum of Modern Art, New York, N.Y.

practice in New Canaan. He was in the museum four days a week, then three days a week, then two days a week. It was unclear as to whether he would leave completely. Nobody knew, including Philip, although I think pretty soon it became clear to him and to everybody else that he would have to leave because he was putting himself in an awkward position. It was a conflict of interests. As soon as he had enough work and enough reason to leave, he did. At that point I had to decide whether I wanted to stay here or go someplace else.

BLDD: Did you have a specific offer, or was it a general life choice you were making?

AD: It was a choice. The museum paid starvation wages in those days, much less than the academic world. It had a history of gentlemen directors and secretaries in mink and sable. I had no private resources whatsoever, which made life rather a hassle. But I was willing to put up with poverty because I was interested in and committed to the museum, and I decided to stay. During those years I had become very friendly with René d'Harnoncourt, then director of the museum, whom I liked enormously and who liked me. Largely because of René's assurances about his plans for the future of the museum, which I found extremely appealing and exactly what I had hoped for, I wanted to stay. I wanted to be involved in what he was doing. I was much closer to René d'Harnoncourt than I was to Alfred Barr. So I stayed and became director of the department in 1956.

BLDD: When Philip Johnson left in 1954, he said, "I left it to Arthur, whom I picked. And I can't imagine anyone who would have done better what I would have done than Arthur Drexler." Why do you think Philip envisioned you as the ideal replacement? And did he think he could ever be replaced? (Don't answer the last part!)

AD: I'm not sure he did. He may have seen it as a possibility, if only because I was interested. In those days no one was trained to head a department of architecture and design in any museum, let alone the Museum of Modern Art. There were no such curatorial positions and people weren't studying for them. No other institution had the slightest intention of maintaining such a program on a full-time basis. No other institution was collecting as we were. Obviously, museum studies have expanded enormously over the years—we're now drowning in Ph.D.'s who want to work at museums. But at that time it was a very different proposition. Interested people were likely to come out of publishing, or perhaps they were architectural historians. But to find somebody who also had practical experience was more difficult. I had, after all, earned a living as a designer of furniture and architectural detail. Philip liked my taste; we seemed to see eye-to-eye about the collection. But lots of things have changed over the years in the administration of the collection, principally in response to the changing resources of the museum. When Philip and Alfred first began to form the collection, there was no place for it to be shown. It was not shown as a collection until I insisted on it in 1958. I maintained that it was unethical to go on collecting material and never showing it. The "Good Design" program showed people a design selection annually in the museum, biannually in Chicago. It was the best that had been produced in one year, but the collection was the best that had been produced, period. That's a rather big difference. I insisted that it was improper for a museum to keep feeding the public these happenstance selections, when in fact in the storerooms we had masterpieces they never got to see.

BLDD: What were the immediate challenges you faced as the new director of the department nearly thirty years ago?
AD: The department was always understaffed: at that time we had one secretary; an associate curator of design, the late Greta Daniel; and an associate curator of graphic design, Mildred Constantine. The associate curators and I did everything. It was backbreaking. Things didn't improve until 1964, when the first museum expansion was completed and we reopened with larger facilities and additions to the staff. It wasn't until the mid-sixties that salaries and staffing in curatorial positions were brought into some sort of alignment with university positions, which is what's normally used as the basis of comparison.

Apart from these, there weren't any problems. It was a wonderful place to do what you wanted to do. Life was in some respects much easier in those days. The trustees were accustomed to paying the cost of exhibitions. There was no federal money. I spent relatively little time on fundraising. Now it sometimes seems like I spend ninety percent of my time worrying about funding.
BLDD: It may be one of the prices of success. . . . Not only have the realities of funding changed over the years, but also the realities of museum attendance. You were originally addressing yourself to such a small public; now you serve an ever-increasing audience. How do you feel about what you've helped unleash?
AD: Depressed. I preferred it when there were fewer people

Installation view of "The Architecture of the Ecole des Beaux-Arts," the Museum of Modern Art, New York, N.Y.

and much, much less attention from the press. It was much better. I think sometimes the whole world will be consumed by the seething mass of art lovers.

BLDD: But don't you think with that broader-based constituency will come an increased awareness?

AD: No. I don't know anybody who believes that anymore. Museums have become subject to too many of the influences of show biz—blockbuster productions, concern with box office, perpetual fundraising. The role of the media is far more important today than it was forty or fifty years ago.

BLDD: The media didn't pay much attention to what you were doing early on, nor was there much of an audience to receive whatever the media did say about it.

AD: You can't expect good things to last forever. Museums have become wrapped up with merchandising—not just for tourists, but for the local population as well. In fact, for the national population: all the museums put out mail-order catalogues now.

BLDD: Do you think of the Museum of Modern Art as an international institution, particularly in the Department of Architecture and Design?

AD: Yes, of course. The entire museum is an international institution. Very often, exhibitions that we've done here have had an international impact. A case in point would be the "Architecture of the École des Beaux-Arts" exhibition in 1975 and the accompanying publication. It opened up this subject for further study not just here, but in France, England, everywhere. The show surprised even the French, who had not paid much attention to their own history. Since that show the previously neglected production of the nineteenth century has become a subject for serious study.

BLDD: Now that you have succeeded in bringing back the Beaux-Arts, would you like to see more of that tradition return to architecture?

AD: No, not really.

BLDD: The training?

AD: Well, yes, that more than anything else. I was prompted to do the Beaux-Arts exhibition because the failure of the Bauhaus as a teaching system had become painfully apparent by the sixties. The Bauhaus had not renewed itself in its American manifestation. The École des Beaux-Arts succeeded in renewing itself for over two hundred years before it was swept away, so it had a rather better record of self-renewal than modernism did. People forget that modernism began as a teaching system. The new movement, the new attitudes, were intimately connected with teaching, with an academy. One reason Mies had such enormous success, particularly in the United States, was that his ideas could be taught. They didn't rely on subjective whims or ill-defined principles but on very clear, basic methods that were easily taught. You could argue that the consequences were no better than the consequences of any other attitude, and in fact might have been worse. Nevertheless it was possible to teach Mies's approach to architecture not only in Chicago but all around the world.

By the mid-sixties it was apparent there was a real problem in the education of architects. Architecture had not yet become a fashionable subject, although you could see that was likely to happen. By the early seventies in Europe the production of so-called architects was overwhelming. In Milan I think there were nine thousand students enrolled in architecture schools, in Venice seven thousand, in Rome eight thousand. Very few of them actually ended up practicing architecture, thank heavens. The best regulated economy in the world could not possibly absorb the vast numbers of students from the middle class who had decided to become architects. And that's

just Italy. Add to that Germany, France, England, the United States, and Japan, and suddenly you have this army of untalented people, all eager to become architects because it confers middle-class, professional status and, I suppose, the possibility of posing for a whiskey ad someday.

BLDD: To have one's work exhibited in the Museum of Modern Art is of singular importance to the career of any architect or designer. And you justifiably pride yourself on your imperviousness to pressures—political, personal, aesthetic, and economic—that often influence the selection process. How do you manage to do that?

AD: It's simple. Whenever it's necessary, you say no. "No" is any easy word to say, and nothing happens to you when you say it. If you're lucky, people will go away. If you're not lucky, they'll try to come in the side door, or the window, or in a trustee's pocket—but the trustees here have been pretty good about that sort of thing. But a little honesty goes a long way. You quickly get a reputation for not being for sale, and that ends it.

BLDD: What criteria do you use to make your selections?

AD: Originally the standards of the department were exaggeratedly high, which was primarily a consequence of space. If you get a turn at bat once every two or three years because all the curatorial departments are competing for the same very small exhibition space, you do become extremely selective. If you can have only one exhibition a year, you are not likely to devote it to work that seems marginal. You are more likely to concentrate on what seems important—good, rather than interesting, as Mies would have said.

BLDD: How do you decide whose work is exhibited in your department?

AD: In the thirties and forties the assumption was that a museum should show the best of modern architecture. Since there wasn't very much modern architecture around, you had to make do with what you had. As modern architecture gained acceptance and more of it was built, your choices became greater and you could become more selective. We were probably at our most selective in the fifties. The fifties was the decade in which modernism established itself in this country under the patronage of business and government. In that same period many architects hoped that their work would be the subject of an exhibition at the Museum of Modern Art. We had several survey shows, but we did not give anybody a one-man show, other than Frank Lloyd Wright, Mies van der Rohe, and Le Corbusier. Of the following generation, no one, as far as I can recall, got a one-man show. What we did do was group two or three architects and present a number of buildings by each. Sometimes they would be chosen because their work contrasted so much with each other's, sometimes because it was variations on a theme. The most recent example of that type of show was the "Three New Skyscrapers" exhibition in 1983. I thought that the three architects—Norman Foster, Philip Johnson, and Gordon Bunshaft—had each produced a skyscraper of remarkable interest, and each of them for very different reasons. Foster's bank building in Hong Kong is undoubtedly the most ambitious, elaborate, and far-reaching high-technology effort in tall building design ever attempted. It is an effort to make a technologically oriented modern architecture that is richer than the simplistic abstractions of the orthodox International Style. The Philip Johnson building was exactly the opposite. It was an eclectic, stage-set design of the most problematic nature in terms of the attitudes it represents. But they are attitudes that are currently very popular, partly because of Johnson's own efforts and partly because that sort of mood prevails at the moment.

Installation view of Gordon Bunshaft's work in "Three New Skyscrapers," the Museum of Modern Art, New York, N.Y.

BLDD: How would you characterize that mood?

AD: Some would characterize it as a failure of nerve, taking it easy. I would say it's just playtime again in the nurseries of the West. One can certainly go against the spirit of the time, but that won't make it go away. Norman Foster is utterly unmoved by Philip's kind of architecture, but he would probably agree that Philip's work captures the mood of the day and that his own architecture fits into the countermovement rather than the mainstream.

BLDD: Where would Gordon Bunshaft fit into that scheme?

AD: Gordon Bunshaft is also against the present mood. He produced a building for the National Commercial Bank in Jeddah, Saudi Arabia, that was monumental in scale and not contextual. That is, it didn't look like something else. Paul Goldberger dismissed the building as being simply a monument—by which he meant something bad. But the context of downtown Jeddah is a little hard to understand. Jeddah is an even more recent and synthetic environment than Miami Beach. Since the Saudis commissioned the bank with the express hope of getting a modern, monumental, twentieth-century Western building, Paul Goldberger's dismissal was perhaps a little cavalier. The Bunshaft building is, in fact, one of a handful of genuinely original ideas about the design of vertical buildings since Mies's glass skyscraper of the twenties. Bunshaft came up with a plan that dealt with vertical mass in seven-story increments, rather than in single floors repeated identically or in a massing imposed by factors outside the plan requirements. The result is a vertical form without precedent. The elevations are not subject to whim or to subjective judgments; they are the inevitable consequence of the plan, and they introduce a scale peculiar to that plan. There's no way to arrive at that scale other than through that plan. It is, indeed, monumental.

BLDD: You are familiar with the work of many, many archi-

tects, but from what I understand you are particularly familiar with the work of Gordon Bunshaft and began but did not finish a book about his work. Why is that?

AD: It is more because of happenstance than anything else. I've known Gordon for many years. We met at about the same time I came to the museum, and we have been good friends ever since. I admire many of his buildings very much. I think they're extraordinarily forceful statements about basic ideas. Lever House is the prototypical modern office building of the United States. It has had worldwide impact; there is no city in the Western world that does not have an imitation of Lever House. The Pepsi-Cola Building on Park Avenue is probably one of the most elegant, most refined small-scale buildings done in the twentieth century. In the development of flat, paper-thin, refined detail and the means to make it work, Gordon is second to none. He's interested not in elaborating detail and revealing what would normally be concealed—the method pursued by Norman Foster, for instance—but in abstraction and simplification. There is something both refined and brutal in Bunshaft's response to architectural problems. He is not an intellectual. He is not a public figure. He doesn't write articles. He doesn't lecture. He doesn't teach.

BLDD: What do you see as the current state of architectural criticism?

AD: There are two classes of critics. One is the media journalist, whether it be newspaper or magazine or TV, and the other is the academic, who is writing for other academics in journals of narrow circulation. The required style for the academics is inarticulateness passing as great verbal felicity and even greater philosophical depth. You discover that behind the style there is very little content. That's understandable, because there is a limit as to what can be said about architecture. The other kind of criticism is oversimplified, almost of necessity, because if you are expected to produce eight inches of copy three times a week, you tend to standardize its production in various ways. We have one or two journalists who write the same article five times. They also write the same article five times within the same article.

BLDD: Who are the most significant architectural critics today?

AD: That is a question I prefer not to answer.

BLDD: Don't you look to the corpus of anyone's work with esteem?

AD: There is no one I would cite as being a great critic today—no one on the level of Henry-Russell Hitchcock. Kenneth Frampton has made valiant efforts to write more comprehensively. There are others, no doubt. Occasionally an individual will write interestingly and persuasively in a very narrow area where they have some personal commitment. One example is Neil Levine, now at Harvard, who wrote one of the essays for the École des Beaux-Arts book. I thought he wrote brilliantly on the subject. He is steeped in nineteenth-century theory and writes beautifully. Among older critics Colin Rowe has influenced many of us, including myself.

BLDD: Are there any teachers or writers that you think have had a significant impact on the development of an audience to appreciate architecture?

AD: One person who certainly has had a tremendous influence is Vincent Scully. As an enthusiast he generates great excitement and makes people regard architecture as they never have before. And Ada Louise Huxtable makes the subject accessible, if not exhilarating in the way Vince does. I think her pieces in the *New York Times* were well written and persuasive, even when I didn't agree with her. Her work has helped to enlarge the audience.

BLDD: What do you think the role of this museum has been in enlarging that audience?

AD: I'm sure the museum has helped enlarge the audience, because museum attendance keeps growing and growing. But I think that's a mixed blessing. There are a great many people who come to museums because it's something to do, like going to the movies or shopping. This museum has maintained a consistency of attitudes in its curatorial departments. We have resisted most of the popularizing efforts that have taken over almost everywhere else, and, interestingly, the more we resist, the larger the audience. When Bill Rubin [director of the Department of Painting and Sculpture] did the show called "Late Cézanne," the board and the curators were worried that the esoteric nature of the show would discourage the general public. Contrary to expectations, the public broke the doors down trying to get in. The point is that being serious does not necessarily mean you will reduce the audience to professionals. The public will respect and trust what you're doing, and attendance will increase rather than diminish. It is also true, however, that attendance will increase if you show junk. Whichever way you turn, attendance increases.

BLDD: There was a time when the Museum of Modern Art's Department of Architecture and Design was the only one in the city, in fact the only one in the country. Obviously that is no longer the case. Has that diminished your influence?

AD: I'm sure it has diminished our influence in some ways and increased it in others. It's very bad to be the only show in town. I think it's bad for New York City to have only one serious newspaper, the *New York Times*. The *Times* was a better newspaper when it had the competition of the *Herald Tribune*. It was bad for New York City to have only one museum dealing with the arts of the twentieth century.

BLDD: What is the process you go through to create a balanced exhibition schedule?

AD: Each curatorial department submits its proposals for exhibitions to the museum's administration. The director of the museum is supposed to assure that it is a balanced program and that space and resources are allocated fairly, a task that no one has ever felt was accomplished with perfect harmony and justice. I certainly don't believe it's been accomplished now, even with the new building. You have to remember that initially this phase of rebuilding was supposed to have been completed by the end of the sixties. Instead, inflation and the Vietnam War and revolving-door directors prolonged the agony. Now, twenty years later, we have completed the expansion.

BLDD: How involved was the Department of Architecture and Design in the design of the new Museum of Modern Art complex? It seems logical that a museum would look to its own experts as participants in the process.

AD: I was very much involved in the early stages of planning for the allocation of space. I prepared some studies for my colleagues so that we could discuss how our space might be distributed. Eventually, a consensus was arrived at and adhered to with only minor changes.

BLDD: Did you help choose the architect?

AD: Yes, I did, as one member of a committee of trustees and staff. Cesar Pelli was a good and rather obvious choice. We all wanted someone whose building style, while it would inevitably depart to some extent from what was here, would still be in harmony with what had already been done. We did not want to undercut the general character of the building and the garden. Another requirement—and here this museum differs from all other museums I know of—was that the design of the galleries was to be controlled by the individual department heads. My gallery is entirely my design. Outside the doors of my gallery it's Cesar's design; within the doors it's mine.

BLDD: Was this process subject to review?

AD: It was reviewed by the museum.

BLDD: How will it work for subsequent curators of those departments?

AD: There may be some problems, especially in my department, because my installation is very elaborate and virtually impossible to dislodge. That's less the case with painting and sculpture, or drawings. But the style of our galleries is largely fixed. We do things a certain way because we have found by experience that that's the best way. We think our pictures look very good in our galleries and will look even better now that there's more space for them.

BLDD: Would you explain why your department's galleries needed to be expanded and how the expansion came about?

AD: Well, obviously the collection is now much more substantial in number as well as in kind. From 1964 until we closed for the construction of the new building, we had 250 objects on view, ranging in scale from a teaspoon to an automobile, in a space of approximately 1,700 square feet. Before the expansion no architectural material was exhibited on a permanent basis as a part of a collections gallery. There simply wasn't space for it. Out of the 2,700 square feet we had, we used 1,700 for the collection and the remainder for changing shows. These were supposed to have been drawn from the collection, but because of the general shortage of space throughout the museum, the remaining thousand feet were used for noncollection, topical shows, whatever they might have been. With the new arrangement we have gone to a total of 6,500 square feet. The whole 6,500 square feet will be used for the collection and for nothing but the collection. We must now fight again for exhibition space in galleries on the ground floor and in the new basement galleries. Our space for the collection is divided into

Entrance to the architecture and design galleries, the Museum of Modern Art, New York, N.Y.

two sections—roughly 4,000 square feet for the design collection and 2,500 square feet for the new architecture gallery, where models and drawings will be shown. The new gallery has been named in honor of Philip Johnson. The design gallery will continue to be called the Goodwin Gallery. The elevator/escalator landing accommodates some very large objects, like a car and a Bell 47-D-1 helicopter we recently acquired, and a lot of posters.

BLDD: Is that helicopter model better designed than others?

AD: It is to helicopters what the Jeep is to automobiles. It is a workhorse object, intelligently designed, without styling but with a definite sense of how it should look.

BLDD: How has the new design for the museum turned out? What are the most significant changes?

AD: The most important was the improvement of internal circulation. It used to be that getting around inside the building made a visit to the Museum of Modern Art rather unpleasant, unless you happened to be here when the place was not crowded, which was not very often. If you have an attendance of over a million people a year in a very small building, you cannot handle the crowds by elevator, which was what we were relying on. So we decided to install escalators. Now you can move easily to wherever you want to go without having to stand on line. And we still will have elevators for the handicapped and for those who don't like to use escalators. Staff and business traffic is now separated from the public. You no longer have to go to the top of the building to get to the members' restaurant. Now the restaurants are off to one side on the first and second floors. The Garden Hall, the main circulation spine of the building, is the single most important element that we have added. It's the extension that runs along the back and houses the escalators. But it's also a greenhouse structure and provides beautiful views. You look out over the garden, over the city, which you couldn't do before, and at each landing there are balconies where you can sit and look at works of art or at the view.

BLDD: Do you consider that the most successful part?

AD: It's the most interesting architecturally. The galleries are ordinary spaces; our intention was to maintain the continuity of the space. People won't know whether they're in the old or the new galleries. What the public will perceive as a new experience is the lobby, which is greatly enlarged and much improved, and the Garden Hall circulation system, which is spectacular.

BLDD: What do you think are the least successful aspects of the new program?

AD: Not enough space. That was known from the beginning.

BLDD: And what is the solution?

AD: We own another fifty feet on Fifty-third Street west of the museum. Sometime in the twenty-first century somebody can worry about expanding there. The other thing that can be done is to build underneath the garden, to put a colossal amount of space there and then put the garden back on top of it. You could put two floors of galleries below the garden level. It would be very expensive construction, but it certainly could be done.

BLDD: It's often been said that architecture is a seasoned man's profession. Would you agree with that assessment?

AD: I think it is true that architects take more time to mature than do writers and probably other kinds of artists. They could mature a lot faster if they could get commissions when they were younger.

BLDD: What's a young architect to do until a commission comes along?

AD: Marry rich.

BLDD: How do architects get their first commissions?

The Garden Hall, the Museum of Modern Art, New York, N.Y.

AD: A normal experience is to build something for a relative, usually one's parents. You get it published. You hope that it leads to more.

BLDD: What do you see as the most urgent problems facing architects today in this country?

AD: There are overwhelming problems not just for architects but also for the people who commission and pay for buildings. The structure of labor, the union system, is decisive. Large-scale building in a big city in the United States puts you at the mercy of the unions. The effects on building technology and every other aspect of finance and use are incalculable.

BLDD: Do you think architecture is a profession that's bereft of new ideas at this moment?

AD: Yes. You cannot artificially synthesize talent, no matter how much money you spend on education, exhibitions, books, lectures, symposia. And there are reasons to believe that original talent comes along only at certain intervals.

BLDD: Which exhibitions here have generated the most praise or the most controversy?

AD: In the fifties, when I came here, the museum was dearly loved. Everything we did seemed to get a favorable response. During that period, our show "Buildings for Business and Government" was very popular with the public and did the profession a lot of good. It established the fact that modern architecture had arrived and was no longer a controversial subject. From then on the issues were how good is it, and how do you make it better. Over the years we've had four automobile shows, and I would say they had absolutely no effect on

Installation view of "Transformations in Modern Architecture," the Museum of Modern Art, New York, N.Y.

automobile design whatsoever. No museum effort that I can imagine would have any bearing on it. We have tried every conceivable thing, including getting the Department of Transportation to spend a million dollars to develop a taxicab that would be of more rational design and to pay for the development of prototypes of real cars that could be tested, all of which were shown here in Emilio Ambasz's taxi show. It was a brilliant effort, but there are some kinds of problems that are not amenable to museum exhibitions or museum interventions, no matter how well organized, how elaborate, or how well intentioned they are. An exhibition that was popular in a later period, and no doubt influential, was "The Architecture of the École des Beaux-Arts" in 1975. This show made people feel that the rules and regulations of modern architecture no longer held true, that now everyone was on their own. That was not the intention of the exhibition. What I had hoped would happen was that the entire system of architectural education would be reexamined. That hasn't happened, and I can't say that the show even accelerated the process. It didn't reform the educational system; it simply let people off the hook, legitimizing their pursuit of something that they found a little easier.

BLDD: Have any exhibitions had results that surprised you, that you never had in mind?

AD: The only surprises I can recall were about the degree of interest or the intensity of a response—the "Transformations in Modern Architecture" show in 1979, for instance. This show was a radical departure not just for this museum but for any kind of survey show, because it attempted to cover a twenty-year period of architecture around the world in volume and with a rapid-fire, one-image-per-work presentation. There were 406 images in the show. The intent was to show how an architectural idea becomes devalued through a process of repetition and variation, until it loses its original quality and intent and becomes something very different. What was intended was to show what happens to an idea. It was clear that some ideas turned out to be not as fruitful as people had thought they were. All survey shows make professionals very nervous, and the longer they know about its preparation, the longer they have to work themselves into a frenzy. The emotional tension that this exhibition generated among architects was not to be believed. The letters, the telephone calls, the personal visits, the solicitations, the carryings-on were extraordinary. They reached their apogee when Peter Eisenman organized a group of his friends to refuse to participate in the exhibition. Peter conducted one of his round-the-clock terror campaigns. Of course, they all privately repudiated his prohibition.

BLDD: Did they end up participating?

AD: Yes, of course, and so did Peter, but when it was all over he and I didn't talk to each other for a year.

BLDD: What do you see as the future direction of the department?

AD: I would like very much to establish the degree of flexibility we had in the fifties, when we could schedule exhibitions on a more impromptu basis and do many smaller exhibitions. Under those circumstances you can deal with younger talent; you don't have to make a statement for the ages every time you mount a show.

BLDD: Isn't that part of your mandate, to deal with and encourage younger talent?

AD: Certainly we think it is. It's not part of the museum's charter, but all of us are here because we're sympathetic to new things in the arts.

BLDD: Are you as sympathetic to new things in the arts and architecture as you were before?

AD: I think ideas are being produced at about the same rate as they were thirty years ago. What is different is the level of talent and the amount of time and energy that talent expends on ideas. I suspect this is due to the media more than anything else. Architects today, unlike architects in the forties and fifties, work for the media, although they may think they're working for their clients. Probably the most important architecture journal in the United States today is *Architectural Digest.* It's much more important for an architect to be published in that magazine than in any of the other journals we subscribe to in this department. This tells us that merchandising rules the universe and that the architect trying to establish himself feels he has to think in terms of the novelty of his approach and the maximum public exposure. More time is spent twisting and turning architecture to serve those purposes than used to be the case. I sympathize with architects who feel this way. I don't earn my living practicing architecture, so I'm in a privileged position. Nevertheless, it's impossible not to see the consequences. A lot of the work shown to me in the hope of recognition by the Museum of Modern Art was formulated with an eye toward media coverage.

BLDD: Can you resist being manipulated by that process and becoming a part of it yourself?

AD: In one sense it is unavoidable. If this is what architecture is becoming and if I want to deal with architecture, I will have to face it. But there are people who are not doing that kind of work. Someone like Richard Meier sticks to his guns. You may or may not like Meier's work, but you have to salute a man who does what he does and is not deflected by media hype. But you could also argue that what I'm describing is part of the new social condition in which architecture can be practiced and that by not accepting the social conditions that produce this architecture, I'm making a judgment that rules out accepting the art of the time.

BLDD: How do you stem the tide?

AD: You don't. You just wait. Everything comes in waves. Sometimes the waves break over your head, so you dry yourself off.

BLDD: What have you not done yet that you would care to?

AD: If you had asked me that question about ten years ago, I would have said that, like most critics, I'm a frustrated architect and would like to go back and pick up where I left off as an architect. I still feel a twinge but, to my great surprise, not as much as I would have ten years ago.

BLDD: Is that because the profession has evolved in a way that you would not be very comfortable with?

AD: It's because I feel a need for more distance between myself and the hype, the turmoil.

BLDD: But what about the present? Is there something now that you'd still like to do?

AD: There is one thing I would very much like to do before I leave the museum. The last time we did a publication on the design collection was in 1959, a ninety-two page catalogue called *Twentieth-Century Design from the Collection of the Museum of Modern Art.* It's been out of print for about twenty years. I'd like to do a comprehensive book about the collection that would also include material not in our collection—things that I wish were in the collection; things that are uncollectable because of size, like battleships and jet planes; things that are uncollectable because the sole example is already in somebody else's collection. I want to incorporate all of this material into the story.

BLDD: That sounds like a mammoth undertaking.

AD: Yes, it would be. It's going to be a big, complicated book.

BLDD: Where did you get all your passion for this field?

AD: I suppose a psychiatrist would say that the curatorial personality is a sublimation of the acquisitive instinct. I've never been a collector privately, with the exception of a collection of Japanese ceramics that I started immediately after World War II. For years I never thought of myself as a collector, but about five or six years ago I realized I couldn't move through my apartment. The ceramics were all over the floors.

BLDD: If you had your life to live over again, what would you do differently?

AD: I would be born rich, and I would arrange my life so that I was a trustee and patron of the Museum of Modern Art rather than a staff member.

BLDD: And what would your impact be?

AD: Because of my wealth and generosity—and indescribable tact—I would contrive to put in place people who could do everything.

BLDD: Like Arthur Drexler.

AD: Like myself. And then I would make it possible for them to have unlimited money and time.

BLDD: Have you ever come across this fantasy trustee?

AD: Well, the Philip Goodwins and the Philip Johnsons have been rather astonishing. And many others have been helpful beyond the call of duty. On the other hand, this collection was formed with very little money. It's hard to believe. It happened that way in part because of the nature of the material, most of which was given to us by manufacturers or by designers. We have bought material very occasionally.

BLDD: Has this influenced the collection?

AD: Not in the least. Most of the work people offer us we turn down. That's the normal procedure. When we see something we want that hasn't been offered, we ask for it. Almost invariably the manufacturer or designer makes it available to us. If we can manage it, we only buy something if it's so cheap that it just isn't worth the time and trouble to negotiate a gift. Where a substantial amount of money has been required—and it gets to be more and more money as the years go by—is in filling the gaps in the historical part of the collection.

BLDD: What's your greatest gap now?

AD: I would say the most serious is that we have no example of work by E. W. Godwin. Very few of his pieces have survived, and most of them are in the Victoria and Albert Museum. Godwin was a very important figure in the evolution of a certain kind of design, but he was ignored by this institution when collection policies were being formed. Even then his works were scarce, but we would have had a better chance of getting it thirty years ago than we have now.

BLDD: Did you expect your life to turn out the way it has?

AD: No. I started life intending to be a painter but was disturbed by a simultaneous desire to be an architect. When I met Le Corbusier he understood my desire to do both. Since he was a painter-architect he saw no conflict at all. But I found I couldn't do both. Later, when I came to the museum, the work was so demanding that it filled every hour. I got completely absorbed in what I was doing. I have no regrets about it.

BLDD: Do you ever think of doing anything else now?

AD: Yes. If I can still stand on my feet when I retire, I will indeed do something else. I'd like to go back to what I was doing right after the war—painting.

BLDD: Do you paint now?

AD: No. I stopped when I came to the museum. I found it a psychological conflict of interest. Now I would like to pick up where I left off.

BLDD: What would the work look like?

AD: If I could describe it I wouldn't want to do it.

PETER EISENMAN
AND
JAQUELIN ROBERTSON

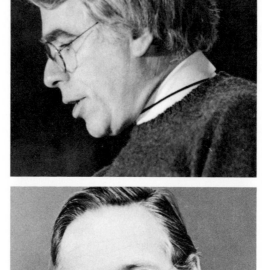

Fifteen years ago the collaboration of architects Peter Eisenman and Jaquelin Robertson would have been highly unlikely. In the 1960s, Jaque Robertson, an urban designer and planner, was often referred to as Mayor Lindsay's "Golden Boy," while Peter Eisenman was a favorite of architecture's avant-garde, one of their premier spokesmen and the designer—in theory—of buildings. Currently they are partners in Design Development Resources, working together to create structures that are visually distinctive as well as responsive to community needs.

BLDD: Now the two of you are partners. Considering your past experience, what has changed to make your recent collaboration desirable or even possible?

JR: We're older.

PE: And we've grown up.

JR: Also, we've identified important situations that we can probably handle better together than singly.

PE: When Jaque and I were working separately, we were working primarily in the public domain, working for planning commissions, developers, institutions. We were never ready to put our own names on something. When we were ready, we did not want to do it in the traditional manner of the individual architect, the mythic architectural figure, the Howard Roark figure. We wanted to be identified individually but also have this collaboration.

BLDD: Are you an odd couple, or do you balance each other well?

JR: We *are* an odd couple—perhaps therefore a good balance!

BLDD: What does that mean?

JR: Peter and I do share a fundamental interest in institutions and in the structure of society, as well as certain formal attitudes about the importance of architecture as a vehicle for describing in physical terms ideas about society and about how men and women might live together.

BLDD: How did the two of you meet?

JR: We have known each other since we met in Cambridge, England, in 1961. I was working for Sir Leslie Martin on my first job out of architecture school, and Peter was getting his Ph.D. in architecture at Cambridge. We were two Yanks abroad and we became close friends.

PE: One of the significant points of our interaction came out of the *Five Architects* book. The New York Five wasn't really a group, but the book was an interesting project anyway. Jaque wrote a response to it, as part of a section in *Architectural Forum* called "Five on Five." We had often met and talked when he was with the Urban Design Group and I was at the Institute for Architecture and Urban Studies. In fact, the institute's first commission was given to us by Jaque when he was at the Urban Design Group. It was a design opportunity study in the Kingsbridge Heights/Jerome Park area of the Bronx. Jaque and I have always had a mutual respect. In fact, Jaque is one of the few people I have always been able to talk to about architecture. Even though we never agreed, we agreed to disagree. He is still a very important catalyst, critic, corrector, and refiner for my ideas. I think we are a very interesting couple. We work symbiotically and are probably one of the few partnerships in which there are two equally strong designers, two equally strong thinkers—neither of us takes a back seat to the other. We also have two very strong egos, and that's sometimes difficult for both of us. It probably wouldn't have worked if we hadn't already had gray hair.

BLDD: In 1967 you both were involved in a symposium at the Museum of Modern Art at the time of an exhibition called "Forty Under Forty." Can you tell us about that exhibition and why it was a catalyst in your relationship?

PE: That exhibition took place in 1967, but it is important to go back to 1964, when Jaque and I were part of a group of young architects called the CASE group [Conference of Architects for the Study of the Environment]. Probably every leading architect of our generation in this country was at one time or another involved in that group. We were all young and wet behind the ears. We would meet in the country with no publicity and talk about architecture. It was one of the first such groups formed in this country.

BLDD: Who was involved?

PE: At various times the group included Bob Venturi, Richard Meier, Michael Graves, Tim Vreeland, Charles Moore, Mike McKinnell, Vincent Scully, and Colin Rowe. That group honed our capacity to criticize one another. We had nothing to lose. There was no camera on us. Nobody knew we were doing it. It wasn't only for the initiated; it wasn't an "in" group. We were doing it because we wanted to get together. When Arthur Drexler had the idea for a show at the Museum of Modern Art featuring young architects involved in urban problems, he did not know how many young architects actually were interested in these issues. At the time, Michael Graves and I were designing a city stretching between New York and Philadelphia. That's the kind of craziness that was going on in 1965. Jaque, along with Richard Weinstein, Jonathan Barnett, and Gio Passanella, was involved in urban issues in New York and was getting involved with John Lindsay's campaign. Arthur Drexler's idea was to do an exhibition to show that young architects *were* involved in the city. That is how it started.

BLDD: How far did you get with Michael Graves in the plan for that mythical city?

JR: Got money out of the Feds, I remember.

PE: How far did we get? Oh, we got into the "Forty Under Forty" show.

BLDD: Was that project really a vehicle for you?

PE: We did not think of it that way, no. We were very serious. We got a lot of money—we were raising money from everybody we could. It was a time when people were listening to crazy kids. Even the president of Princeton gave us money to have this group of young architects.

BLDD: Would that be possible today?

PE: I would say not.

JR: No.

BLDD: Is it a loss?

JR: It's just a different time.

PE: When Bob Geddes came to Princeton as dean in 1967, he walked into the basement of the architecture school, where Michael and I had a setup of eight or ten people working on huge models. It was wild! There was a real underground in that school. There was something going on at the teaching level, but it was also that the heat was there. We were lucky.

JR: It was exciting.

PE: Young architects today are caught in a trap. They can work on little garage additions, kitchens, renovations, but they do not get the chance to work on large-scale projects because nobody is funding them. Period. I think that is a loss.

JR: The museum show was a kind of origin in both Peter's and my separate careers. Peter and Michael did quite an elegant, highly theoretical scheme for the river, and Jonathan, Richard, Gio, and I did what we *thought* was a nuts-and-bolts, hard-hitting, practical solution to deck the Park Avenue railroad track with replacement housing. We were concerned with relocation and how much it would cost, trying to show that a "practical" solution could be achieved. At the end of that show, Peter and I were talking one day over a cup of coffee and Peter said, "Listen, why don't you join me? I'm going to start an institute." And I said, "Peter, why don't you join me? We're putting together a group that will work for the city on practical problems." We went out and set up these two new institutions that were really examining some of the same issues but from very different perspectives. We were very pragmatic and obsessed with trying to understand how the world worked.

PE: Both of us were also interested in the notion of creating institutions. The Urban Design Group was a unique institution and public agency, while the Institute for Architecture and Urban Studies was a unique quasi-academic institution of advanced studies in architecture. Neither existed before, and both have had some interesting spin-offs.

JR: Peter was trying to bring theory and ideas back into the practice of architecture. In looking at each other's work over the years, we've carried on a constant critique and dialogue.

BLDD: Peter, you referred earlier to a loosely knit group of like-minded architects—Michael Graves, Charles Gwathmey, John Hejduk, Richard Meier, and you—who were interested in a purely formal approach to architecture. How did the group evolve?

PE: Very quickly. It came out of the CASE group. After eight or nine meetings the group splintered. We got tired of talking, I guess.

JR: We wanted to fight!

PE: And then we got tired of fighting, and by that time each of us had done a house and we . . .

BLDD: Real or on paper?

PE: Real. Real. Real. Built houses. And we wanted to show our work. Arthur Drexler was host at a meeting of ours at the Museum of Modern Art. Jim Stirling was there along with Joseph Rykwert and Colin Rowe. All the gurus came. Ken Frampton made the introduction and Arthur Drexler the concluding remarks. It was a very heavy occasion for five young people. At that time we hardly knew Charles Gwathmey and John Hejduk, since they had not been in the CASE group. But because we needed more than Richard, Michael, and myself, we added the two of them. "The Five" as a title was fabricated by the media. The book was almost casual in its origins. I walked into Wittenborn's, a book store on Manhattan's Upper East Side, one morning, as was my wont, and said to George Wittenborn, "Hey, I've got a wonderful idea for a book." We wanted to make a book like we made architecture. The five of us worked on this book. We published only five hundred copies because we never thought it would be anything like a best-seller. Then it was hyped. Paul Goldberger picked it up, and suddenly we became the New York Five.

BLDD: Who first named the group?

PE: Paul Goldberger.

BLDD: Jaque, you were one of those who disagreed with the approach of the New York Five. You said then that the work raised several questions: Was the architecture of this group one of drawing or of living? And how would their type of building age, both physically and stylistically? Would your response be any different now?

JR: The critique stands.

BLDD: How do you respond to that now, Peter?

PE: Well, Jaque said to go ahead.

JR: The only one of the five that profoundly interested me was Peter, as I said in "Five on Five." His work was of an entirely different nature, investigating at a very deep level certain central issues that related structure—particularly the structure of language, semantics—to architectural issues. Both of us were interested in linguistic philosophy. What he was doing was a very, very different exercise than that of the rest of them.

BLDD: There's been a great deal of controversy about the work of one of the New York Five—Michael Graves—especially his recent Portland Municipal Building in Oregon. What do you think about the project?

JR: It's a very urban building. It seems to make a lot of sense. It's the right size for a building in that particular city. It fills up the block, the 200-foot grid, very well. I think it will be beautiful. I haven't seen it since it was finished, but the pictures are very promising.

PE: Jaque's always very generous. We're the wrong people to ask, though. I basically grew up with Michael. Michael is a very good and serious architect, but my own view of architecture is 180 degrees from where Michael is today. I think that his Portland Building is a form of pastiche with misplaced symbolism, although I admire his effort and I enjoy the discourse.

JR: You can't ask architects who are contemporaries to give an objective critique.

BLDD: Do you know of any professionals that are more harshly critical of their peers than architects?

JR: Opera singers.

PE: Painters, fashion designers, graphic designers.

JR: But, Peter, she's right. Architects are unbelievably bitchy, and they hate to see each other succeed.

BLDD: But, Jaque, you praised Peter Eisenman even way back then. You saw him as breaking new ground, trying to bring architectural theory up to date. Is that what most interested you in his work?

JR: Yes. And I still am interested in the idea of what architecture *is*. I realized when I graduated from college that the one thing I learned in school was that I didn't know anything. I certainly didn't know what architecture was as someone who must make it, simply because I hadn't made it. From then on I would spend my time learning what architecture is. I thought one way to do this, other than apprenticeship (I was working for Ed Barnes), was to teach. Paul Rudolph gave me that chance at Yale, and later Aldo Giurgola did at Columbia. The students began questioning why this was good or that bad. I had opinions—but no convincing, easy answers. Slowly I began to evolve an idea about architecture.

BLDD: Both of you have been involved in education, but at very different kinds of institutions. There is a counterpoint in your experiences up until now, including your experiences with educational institutions. Should a school of architecture advocate one particular approach?

JR: Depends on what the approach is!

PE: You're dodging.

JR: No. It's not a popular notion to advocate a single approach now. At a basic educational level I want to open the doors to a variety of interesting possibilities. But by and large, teachers and deans of schools do have strong prejudices based on preference and experience. I have them. I'm deeply committed to a certain kind of urbanism. I would not be willing to work in an educational institution that didn't have that commitment. On the other hand, I'm not interested in only mandating my own views. People need exposure to ideas; life teaches them to choose.

PE: I think there are two schools of thought in education. One is to define a curriculum as in an academy and teach from a set of principles; the other is to get a group of teachers together and give them free reign—to bring the best people together and let them teach what they will. For myself I do not ever want to teach anybody else's curriculum; no teacher worth his salt ever wants to teach what he is told to teach. There are certain things you have to teach, but these ideas change all the time. The particular architects and buildings that are considered important change in cycles that can be documented.

BLDD: And what was your commitment and focus at the Institute?

PE: The students at the Institute were basically from liberal arts institutions. We were not concerned with the training of professionals. We were interested in taking young people before they had a commitment to anything and exposing them to a way of thinking visually. There is verbal thinking and there is visual thinking, and if you want to be an architect, you've got to think visually. We also were trying to expose them to the community at large—to the professional architectural community and to the city, where architecture is. I would like to think that the Institute was very effective in this dual role in the seventies.

JR: That is one of those areas of interest we share. At the University of Virginia we emphasize the idea of the architect as someone who understands the world by providing students with a strong liberal arts base. The architect must first be of his time, then an architect; architecture must always be in the service of life, not the other way around.

BLDD: Jaque, you have been dean of the University of Virginia School of Architecture since 1981. What educational approach do you encourage in that role?

JR: As an architect you really have to understand how the world works, not just the technical craft of architecture, or you're not very useful as an architect. You certainly have to understand, for example, what cities are about.

PE: There's a danger in getting students too late, which I think is a real problem with graduate schools. Students who have studied English literature or philosophy have minds and egos that are very well developed. It is difficult to break down that kind of thinking, to get them to give up the ego structure that they have spent four years forming, to think in a totally different way. That is a real problem.

JR: It's a problem, but the other extreme is equally difficult. Technocrats who only know how to put things together and can't think a problem through can be hopeless as students.

BLDD: How are you influenced by your students or by newcomers to the field?

PE: Both of us think of ourselves as architects first, educators second. I teach because I find great stimulation in asking and learning how to ask questions. Teaching students is a good way to focus questions. Learning is about asking questions, and you cannot do that if you are cut off from the vitality that students represent.

BLDD: Jaque, how do you manage to combine a commercial practice in New York City with your academic commitment in Virginia?

JR: It just takes a lot of work and a lot of time, an eight- or nine-day week—nothing serious. I spend four to five days a week in Charlottesville and the weekends plus a Monday or Friday in New York. The same thing is done by other deans; there's a long tradition of practicing deans.

PE: My sense is that the best teachers are practicing architects. You cannot teach only from a theoretical perspective, and you cannot practice only from a commercial perspective. The two inform each other. One of the problems in a practice is that there's too little theory, and in the schools there's too little practice. Our commitment is to finding that middle ground.

JR: Architecture is much more than that dual relationship between teaching and practice. Nearly every architect worth spitting on has taught, and the only architects doing interesting work are those who've been associated with schools at one time or another. It's rare to find a top architect who has not been involved in teaching.

BLDD: Both of you have led complex and rich lives. Jaque, you spent a part of your childhood in China, eventually became a Rhodes Scholar, then lived in the Middle East. But you say—at least since you've been back there—that you are really a Virginian. How has being raised there influenced your ideas? Did the architect/critic/historian/statesman/farmer Thomas Jefferson particularly influence you? What can Jefferson's work teach today's architect?

JR: How to concentrate on essential issues. What's important in architecture is to find and clarify the significant relationship between people and then to try to build it. The University of Virginia is the clearest example in the United States of ideas about how men and women live together translated into physical form. It's an absolutely modern complex; it has nothing to do with nostalgia. The University of Virginia—Jefferson called it his "academic village"—is one of the three best urban environments in the United States. In fact, the best or most sensible urban plans in America are in this Jefferson village, in Williamsburg, Savannah, and some of the New England villages like Edgartown or East Hampton. So I look at Charlottesville as a generic type of American urbanism, though it is in a beautiful natural setting.

PE: Jefferson's design for the University of Virginia is one of the least understood pieces of architecture in the country. There's no question it has nothing to do with romantic nostalgia or pastoral serenity. I was knocked out by it when I went there. I was overwhelmed by it. People look at it too quickly and say, "Oh, that's . . ."

JR: "That's old buildings."

PE: "That's Georgian" or "that's Palladian" or "that's neoclassical." They don't actually *see* anything. It is like reading James Joyce very literally and saying, "Those words do not make any sense to me." An architect has to look very carefully. Everything you draw you have to draw again and again. It's a dedication that very few of us in this media-hype society have.

BLDD: Most people think of Virginia as the mother of presidents, and you, Jaque, have referred to it as the mother of architects. What prompts that attitude?

JR: It's the mother of presidents *and* of architects. It's the oldest colony and probably has the best inventory of buildings, gardens, and landscape conceived together in the United States. It has a long tradition of people interested in architecture. There's no real interest in painting in Virginia, but there's an enormous interest in architecture. Architecture is the state's mother art. Jefferson said that you should use architecture in a young republic as a way to teach people about the arts, because there are never enough paintings in a young country. Architecture was thus the mother art with which to teach people about their own culture and other cultures and about the arts in general. Because they were so closely related to architecture, furniture and the decorative arts—how you fitted out architecture—also became important.

BLDD: Does that interest persist in Virginia?

JR: I think it does. Virginia is very conservative and architecture is very conservative. So the two are now perhaps getting back in sync.

BLDD: Peter, let's talk about your influences and your background. Was there a particular tradition of architecture in your family?

PE: No. I did not know what an architect was until I went to college. My grandfather was a builder, but that did not have any meaning for me.

BLDD: *Someone* had to design the buildings he developed.

PE: Yes, but I didn't know about it. I lived in a middle-class cocoon.

BLDD: Apparently that cocoon expanded enough to produce both you and your cousin Richard Meier.

PE: He lived in a middle-class cocoon, too. I disliked college until I realized that people were building models and drawing, that they were studying architecture. I said, "Do you mean you can do this and go to college?" I thought that was fantastic. I always liked to draw, but in the forties suburban high school boys never took art classes. I finally found something I wanted passionately to do. At spring vacation, the last day, the last hour, I told my parents, "I'm going to be an architect." They looked at me as if I were crazy. My father said, "Is this another one of your tricks?" And it was!

JR: It's interesting how important drawing really is. I was a cartoonist, managing editor of the *Yale Record* humor magazine, and I thought some day I would be a cartoonist—I'd go to the *New Yorker* and spend the rest of my life making fun of people. Drawing is enormously important to architecture. It's also intimately tied to thinking; it's a way of putting down ideas. You start drawing quite naturally. Both Peter and I do it all the time.

BLDD: Jaque, as the director of the Office of Midtown Planning, which was created in 1969, you worked with the group to suggest a plan for a mall on Madison Avenue. Whatever happened to that idea?

JR: Ah yes, the Madison Maul! The idea was not *just* for a mall. We did a systematic analysis of New York streets and how they operated. We found you couldn't have all kinds of traffic on all kinds of streets. Midtown needed more open space, more sidewalk space, more trees. We proposed a network of "green streets" (technically pedestrian transit streets) in the most congested areas, one of which was Madison Avenue. To be understood it had to be seen as part of a larger plan. It wasn't. The plan was defeated on the Board of Estimate by one vote, that of Queens Borough President Donald Manes—one of the stupidest votes ever cast in the city. It was a very, very important test—never made because of a very weak politician.

BLDD: How would our city—its grid, its side streets, its green areas—look or function differently if the plan had been enacted?

JR: We were at the cutting edge then. Ironically, what we proposed has been enacted in many other cities in the world that now have special bus streets, pedestrian transit streets with wider sidewalks, nice trees, good paving—all the things people seem to like.

BLDD: Around the country, many of the areas "mauled over" have been abandoned. Good ideas, and well conceived, but not really working on a day-to-day level . . .

JR: Remember that there is a big difference between purely pedestrian malls and what we proposed. There *are* lots of stupid malls. But this doesn't change the fact that high-density city streets should be designed differently than the way they are now. We did not propose to close the street to traffic. We proposed carrying more bodies in the same corridor, in a more pleasant atmosphere. And there are examples all over the world of those kinds of streets working fantastically well, for instance in Munich, Denver, Minneapolis. Half of the world's cities are experimenting with various types of special new streets, with traffic control and increased pedestrian amenity systems.

BLDD: You say that one vote was a crucial test. What did you learn from that experience that could be applied to the many other crucibles you have been part of since then?

JR: How to take your lumps. That was enormously depressing for us, especially for John Lindsay, because we were counting on the enormous benefit it might bring to the city. We also learned that politics, in a pluralistic society like this, is very tough on planning. You can't predict anything. Some of the most public policies are impossible to carry out in a city like New York because people are really afraid of planning decisions. Representatives change votes at the last minute because they don't have time to understand the issues, they only listen to the wind. Manes had said, "I'm with you." The next day he was visited by the taxi lobby, spun around, and changed his mind. You can't control that. Only strong character can.

BLDD: Can you plan for it in any way?

JR: Yeah. You can try to hold people on line and you can expect the worst. That's what American politics is about. Systematic, major changes are increasingly difficult in our capitalistic, pluralist society. It's almost impossible now to point to an attractive urban environment being produced by our system. Anywhere from Phoenix to Houston—Phoenix is the poor version, Houston's the rich version—the urban environment is garbage. It's expensive garbage or it's cheap garbage, but it's still garbage.

BLDD: So what do we have in store for us?

JR: We've got to rethink the ways in which we plan cities, and we've got to make better decisions.

BLDD: And what would you two propose?

PE: The architect has traditionally not been in planning and policy-making. Architects are usually thought of as facilitators. They arrogate that role for themselves for some strange reason as much as society gives it to them. Architects have got to start being interested in policy-making without losing their creative role in the making of physical reality. Jaque provides a good example of that. He attempted to move into policy-making because he thought he could accomplish something, but he also lost touch with what he really could do and needed to do—that is, making architecture. That is very important, and that is the problem.

JR: As soon as architects step out of the role of being the designers of cities, a lot is lost. You learn about buildings by starting with buildings and progressing to cities; with the lessons you learn from cities you come back to buildings again. Until the priority of city first and building second is established, you've got only spare parts. We've got vast cities that are collections of spare parts; almost nothing urbanistically worthwhile has been done in them since World War II. We have a lot of architecture. We have prizes every day—they're coming out of our ears—but we have no worthwhile cities.

PE: I don't think it's an architectural problem; it is an economic one.

JR: It's a conceptual problem.

PE: It's also economics: zoning, tax write-offs . . .

BLDD: How much of a building or city is designed by zoning laws, builders, developers, bankers, and so on? How much of it is left to the architect, the designer, or the planner?

JR: I used to think—and that's why, as Peter said, I went in the direction I did—that architects have to know a lot about law, economics, real-estate development, management, design, transport, garbage, and all those things. And, in fact, you do. But knowing all this doesn't mean that you produce better cities, because we've already got people who know all those things. The key is having some reasonable notion of what is an acceptable order for so many people living in a given area. Most successful cities have been based on a consensus about what that reasonable order is. We don't have that right now.

BLDD: What is your overriding notion of what a city should be? What is the grand design?

PE: Since I started doing small-scale buildings and moved toward larger-scale ideas, I've come to believe that man has always symbolized his condition on earth by the towns and structures he has built. Starting with the Greek or Etruscan cities right through to the nineteenth century, every change in culture brought about a change in city form. The ideal cities of the Renaissance mirrored man's idea that he was in harmony with God and nature. The neoclassical cities of the eighteenth century were representative of the Enlightenment man. The nineteenth-century cities, like nineteenth-century man, were technological, standardized. The city of the early twentieth century was an attempt by man to come to terms with nature. Le Corbusier, for example, tried to bring nature and man back into some sort of harmony. Now our cosmology of Man, God, and Nature has fundamentally changed. The three are no longer in the same harmony. Yet there has been no image of the city that reflects that change in cosmology. Before we can patch up and repair we have to try to think through what the city means to us, and what the image of the city should be for post-nuclear man.

JR: I don't think the greatest problem today is the potential for nuclear destruction. I think we're already destroying ourselves. The way in which we build cities is by far the most serious disease in our country now. If you ask me my idea of a grand design for a city, I'll take Savannah, Georgia. You can't build city precincts in which people don't live, in which there are no major parks with big trees, in which there are no homogenous building types. You can't have cities in which those precincts get too big, that is, you can't have cities the size of Mexico City. It's appalling that people don't understand that the way we build cities now is an unbelievable disease ravaging this country as well as most of the rest of the world to whom we export our form of urbanism.

BLDD: How do you communicate this sense of urgency to larger numbers of people?

JR: Take them to Mexico City. Make all the leaders, mortgage bankers, and developers live in Mexico City, in the traffic. Just walk around with them and say, "This is what it's going to be. This is the form of disease you've chosen as your setting. The cultural goal of this society is based on that model."

PE: It takes a certain amount of courage. This is where Jaque and I might become critical of each other—which I think is useful, because one of the good things about partnership is that you search for differences. I think what it takes is the courage to invent the kind of symbolism that will have some importance today. I'm not certain that taking Savannah and replicating it will solve the problem. That imagery, for me, has no potency any more. Ideas about Savannah and scale do not motivate my students, who are not certain that they will live out their natural lives. They're looking for something they can believe in, aspire to, hope for—a future—in what can be called a "futureless present." The shadow of biological destruction that Robert Jay Lifton, Jonathan Schell, any number of people talk about creates a situation in which the generations born after 1945 do not have the same beliefs that the three of us share. Getting in touch with the new condition may lead us to some courage. I hope Jaque and I will reach that state. It will take us an enormous amount of courage to do it because there are so many practical considerations that say we should just get on with working, get on with building buildings. That is what we like to do. But there is another consideration: what we really need to do together.

BLDD: And what is that?

PE: To try to build an urban environment, try to build a street.

JR: To try to build anything in which ideas about how people could—and should—live together are given physical form.

BLDD: There are several programs for building new cities in Europe. It seems there are none here. Do you see new cities as a possibility and, if so, do you see them as a solution?

JR: Title Seven was the name of the new towns program in this country. Every one of those new towns, with one exception, went bankrupt very quickly because we didn't understand how new cities are financed. There's probably not a lot of hope for new site cities in the near future in the United States. That doesn't depress me because I'd rather see people work on what exists. Most cities have so much underdeveloped land—and by that I don't mean that the only option is to put up high buildings, but that there are vast areas of Nagasaki-like open space to be developed. That's where our new town building effort ought to be, in the heart of the existing cities. I'd like to stop all suburban development for ten years and start reworking the cities to show how they can become valuable again.

PE: When you go to Europe, where do you go? To the cities. When visitors come to America, they go to the countryside.

BLDD: I thought the number-one tourist attraction in the United States was New York City.

PE: Well, outside of New York City. No one ever goes to Detroit, Kansas City, Albuquerque, because they are non-urban places, lacking in those qualities that make for an urban experience. I love walking in cities, but there are very few cities in this country. When I go to Europe, there are many I could walk in. The new towns in Europe are disasters because this idea of planning, either for obsolescence or for the good life, is difficult to do at the macro scale. I'd rather see incremental growth in the existing urban fabric, because that's where the action is.

BLDD: Jaque, one of your best designs was the 1975 plan for developing a 1,200-acre site into a new capital center for Teheran. What was the genesis of that project?

JR: The Shah of Iran and the mayor of Teheran decided to create a new city center in a vast empty space in the middle of the city in order to alleviate some of the congestion from around the old bazaar. After much deliberation they selected the English firm of Llewellyn Davies International to do the job. Lou Kahn and Kenzo Tange also had a shot at the project. Richard Llewellyn Davies asked me to assemble a team to design it.

BLDD: What did you learn from that experience?

JR: That you should never count on anything. It is very difficult to design a city or a major part of it and have the plans implemented. That's why urban design is so tough. Few architects have the stomach for it because they don't see results, they don't get any feedback. You work on something for fifteen years, and more likely than not it will all go down the tube. Teheran was important because it taught me that you can't write rules for other people. To build successfully you have to design the entire thing yourself. It took me some time to believe this. Most of the special zoning districts we tried to create included some good and some really monstrous proposals. The best parts of cities are designed either by one person or a small group, or there is a consensus among the people who are designing that this is the way to do buildings. Teheran was important because not only did we make the plan, but we also designed the whole bloody thing.

PE: I think Jaque also learned that he was really an architect, that it was very important for him to build buildings. We can believe in urbanism, in culture, but in the end, as individuals we need to be satisfied by certain tangible things. Sensual aspects need to be resolved, no matter what the scale. Jaque loves small-scale things. I marvel at the time he spends on a detail, on getting the color right or getting the right material. If Jaque's public commitment could have been tempered earlier by his need to build buildings, there would be a lot more of his fine buildings around.

BLDD: Let's talk about your practice. How do people go about engaging the services of an architectural firm?

JR: That's what we'd like to know! Where are they? There are three or four different kinds of firms. One is always staggered at the kind of marketing effort made by big commercial firms, even small ones, in the United States. We really have quite a bad marketing scheme. We usually get jobs on the recommendation of other people, through the networks of people we know. Every now and then someone sees something about us and says, "This man is crazy enough to work with me. Let's try him."

BLDD: An architect once said, "You must face the fact that architects get work by holding hands with other architects." How accurate is that?

PE: That's partially true. Many of the recommendations come from friends who are architects. We recommend other architects for work. I wish it were a closer society, because it's a very good way to get work.

JR: *I* wish it were a more even exchange! I spent ten years of my life recommending lots of architects for jobs when I wasn't in the business, and not many of them are recommending me now! It's not always a two-way street.

PE: No, it's that they feel you don't need to be recommended.

BLDD: How should potential clients prepare themselves for the experience of dealing with an architect?

JR: One of the crucial aspects for a private client is to understand it's a long-term process. The client has to be involved. Even in a community building you need a responsive client who is able to live with the architect, respond to the architect's integrity, and listen when he talks straight. It's taken me fifty years to really learn how to talk straight. When I was an architect of thirty, I wasn't talking this way. It's only when you're a little more mature that you get the sense you'd better tell the truth, because if you don't, and then you try to cut corners, you always get into trouble. The client should be looking for integrity, maturity, and a certain sense of compatibility.

PE: It's no different from choosing a dentist, a doctor, or a lawyer. You really can't know how good these people are. A lot of it is chemistry.

JR: The client must trust you. You've got to be able to tell them things that they may not want to hear and not be afraid of losing the job. One of the worst things is when architects, trying to protect their job, hide information about cost overruns or being behind schedule.

BLDD: Sometimes practical considerations must take precedence. Peter, in the instance of House VI the skylight began to leak and the owners of that house brought in a contractor who built a pitched roof atop the structure's original flat roof. How did you feel about that?

PE: People don't realize that it is very difficult to put a skylight in a roof and not have leaks. Sometimes you just do not know why they leak. By the way, that particular client later came into the office and said that for my birthday he would put the original flat roof back.

BLDD: Are you going to do that?

PE: Oh yes! So you never can tell about clients.

BLDD: Why did you name houses by numbers rather than by the clients?

PE: I could make up a story and say it was because I was much more interested in the object than the subject.

BLDD: Wasn't that the story you made up at the time?

House VI, Darien, Conn.

Flinn Residence, East Hampton, N.Y.

PE: Yes, that was the story I made up at the time. I was really interested in experiments. House I was not even a house. It was a toy museum, but I called it a house. I was interested in the notion of depersonalizing architecture.

JR: Decontextualizing.

PE: I was trying to build architecture. That has always been the problem for me. I was not trying to build expensive second homes for rich people. That was not what I was trying to do.

JR: That's what *I* was interested in!

BLDD: You have had that opportunity, Jaque. I'm thinking of the Shingle Style house you built in East Hampton. What made you choose to do that kind of house at this point in time?

JR: I live in East Hampton and I like it very much. I was doing a variation on a Shingle Style saltbox house . . .

PE: And I think there is something else you have got to say . . .

BLDD: Does it work this way in the office? How often do you agree?

PE: Oh, but this *is* agreeing.

JR: We agree with each other a lot.

PE: I am going to give you his line. He forgets his lines! He gets nervous on stage. His line to me is: "The house is one of the most important ways to learn about architecture." Despite all the large-scale buildings that we are interested in doing and that we are doing, we always said we would never do houses again. But one always goes back to houses because there is always something more to be learned from designing a house, because the program is so flexible. There isn't much flexibility in doing a commercial office building, a hotel, a multi-story apartment house, a factory—the kinds of things we have been working on. There's not much room to move except maybe in the skin.

JR: My line is even simpler than that. There is a long tradition

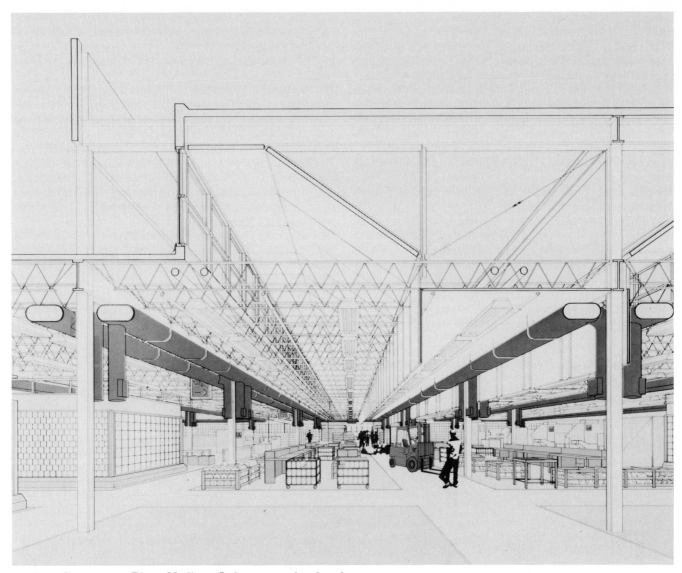

Madison Components Plant, Madison, Ind., perspective drawing

of architects building houses as a way of coming to grips with the most pressing architectural issues. One hopes it continues.

BLDD: Your solution for beautifying that hallmark of American cities, the so-called strip, is a very simple one. You suggested that we prohibit parking in front of stores and businesses. Why is it that America's builders, developers, and even architects have so rarely been interested in this kind of common-sense approach?

JR: I don't think they look at what's around them. Whatever rationalization or intellectualization you give it, the parking lot is not an attractive environment. You can't combine a street, a parking lot, and a building and have anything other than a no-man's land. The real test for all of these places is to consider whether you want to get out of your car and walk in them.

PE: Jaque talks about the parking lot as the institutionalization of bad taste.

BLDD: Let's talk about your current projects. First, you have designed a components factory for Cummins Engine in Madison, Indiana. You relied on information and suggestions from factory workers for guidance. Was that an effective form of collaboration?

PE: Yes, it was fantastic. Cummins is a company with a tradition of doing very interesting architecture.

BLDD: How did you involve them in the design of their own work space, and how did you get them to trust you?

PE: It took long hours of drinking beer and talking about things the workers are interested in.

JR: Basketball. Peter's very good on sports.

PE: I found real camaraderie with these people. They helped us decide where things went, what colors we used. Now they really believe in that plant.

BLDD: And did they always know best?

PE: Architects are always trying to find out what people want, but people can't always articulate it. Snags arose when I wasn't able to provide exactly what they wanted. This is the real key—not what I want or what they think they want, but what they might not be able to express.

BLDD: Since World War II, Berlin has been a symbol of a divided world. A competition was held there for the 1984 International Building Exhibition. Your firm was awarded a special place for your project, called the City of Artificial Excavation. By which aspects of Berlin's history were you most influenced or inspired?

JR: The title for the project is indicative of the search for a metaphor appropriate to such a historical location—one of the few instances in which a high-flying title is quite accurate.

BLDD: You've said that Berlin is a special place, that the city is now "the crossroads of every place and no place." How do you describe and combine two such very different themes?

PE: We were talking about a site right next to the Berlin Wall. That wall separates Berlin, which used to be the capital, from the rest of the country. It's an artificial capital; therefore it's no place. Yet in terms of history—the East-West confrontation, World War II, the intellectual revolutions of this century, the rise of nationalism in the nineteenth century—it is every place. So, its history is every place, yet as a place it is no place. We did not want to make a museum piece or put the bones of a dead city back together. To create something alive was really the challenge.

BLDD: Another project is a film institute for Sundance, Utah. What are your plans for that?

JR: Robert Redford is trying to build a new type of film institute. He has been talking with us about helping him do that. We haven't started working on it, although we've spent time there. Both of us are interested fundamentally in institution building, in the roles of people within institutions and in their relationship to society. Jefferson's university was a new institution. Bob Redford is trying something very brave—to offer a way to develop scripts and new material that is an alternative to the studio system, and to bring out younger talent and give them special exposure, technical professional briefing, and guidance.

BLDD: What kind of impact would the location of the studio have?

JR: Redford has conflicting sentiments about that. On the one hand, he's a great conservationist and doesn't want to see anything changed; on the other, he is trying to house this institute and must change the setting.

BLDD: How do you help the client reconcile that issue?

JR: I don't know yet, but it is the classic American dilemma. Sundance is very much a part of America. It's exaggerated America. It's enormously important as an out-of-kilter vision of Eden and how man builds in Eden. Redford is perfect in his role there. It's his quintessential role.

BLDD: A few years ago you submitted a proposal for the Beverly Hills Civic Center competition. What was your intent there?

PE: To win.

BLDD: What did you propose specifically in that project?

PE: This is one project where Jaque and I put our heads together and really came up with ideas that we were both

South Friedrichstadt, West Berlin, West Germany, rendering

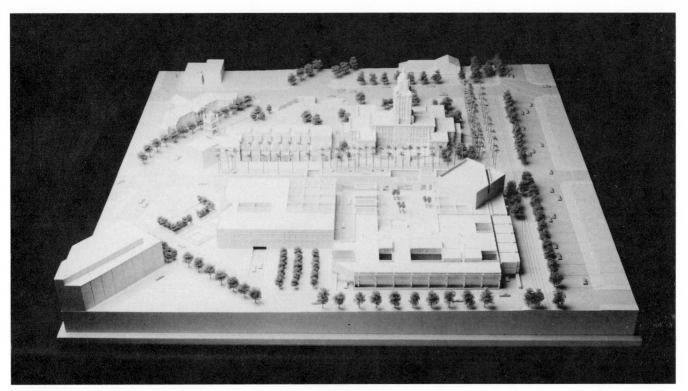

Competition entry for Beverly Hills Civic Center, Beverly Hills, Calif., model

interested in. One is the notion of the street as an American place—not a re-creation of European plazas or malls, but an acknowledgement that people in Beverly Hills see each other in their cars and want to be seen in their cars. We made the focus of the place an automobile plaza. We even put an arcade over the street itself. A second idea that was very important for both of us was that of totems. We felt that there were too many kitsch representations of our history and that we should go back to the primitive notion of the totemic or special place or special object that signifies a great deal about man and his relationship to God and nature. We wanted to find a way to bring the totemic object back into our civilization, to restore a connection with something other than day-to-day life.

JR: We also were interested in the dialogue between the language of architecture and the natural language of landscape. We attempted to exaggerate that confrontation between landscape and language by placing institutions in the most logical, formal, and psychologically appropriate relationship to one another. We thought about where a jail, a courthouse, or a library should be placed vis-à-vis a city hall.

PE: Jaque and I, if our partnership stands for anything distinguishable from the others, share a great belief in two components of the art form—landscape and language. He stands for landscape and I stand for language, if you want. We are looking at the dialogue between language, man's most sophisticated, refined, and abstract form of communication, and another form of communication, landscape, which is an attempt to represent man's relationship to nature and to God. We are trying to work with these things and bring them back into some sort of focus, but not as a form of kitsch nostalgia.

BLDD: Are you still thought of as mavericks, or are your ideas more widely accepted today?

JR: We're older, so I think we're probably less maverick-like than before.

BLDD: But no less experimental?

PE: I think we are thought of as Establishment, unfortunately.

JR: No. We haven't built enough. You cannot be Establishment until you build a lot and people get tired of it, and they start looking for something else.

PE: I do not think our ideas have ever been maverick. We've just grown up a lot. We are still concerned with ideas. We still debate among ourselves.

BLDD: If each of you had your lives to live over again, what, if anything, would you do differently?

JR: I would have had the Shah of Iran, my client, stay in power for twenty years so he could build my city.

PE: I was hoping you would say you wouldn't have gone to Iran!

BLDD: What would you say for yourself?

PE: I guess I would have tried to grow up sooner.

JR: Start building sooner?

PE: Yes, and taken responsibility for my actions.

BLDD: An architect, especially one who is a teacher, must be able to look to the future as well as at his own time. What do the coming years hold?

JR: My answer will probably be different from Peter's. The future is not very interesting to me in that you can't learn anything from it because you haven't been there. I'm interested in architects who attempt to solve today's problems in the most elegant and practical way possible. I have almost no interest in futurology. If I were to project trends, though, the one that is most terrifying to me is the proliferation of Mexico Cities, a destructive mode of building that this culture is addicted to and that is killing our world.

BLDD: Peter, what do you see for the future? What would you like to be doing ten years from now?

PE: My concern is to find an architecture *today*. I'm not interested in futurology either. If I could do two or three projects that I knew were architecture and that would cause one of my colleagues—Jaque would probably be the one whose opinion I would respect most—to say, "*That's* a piece of architecture," I would be very happy.

ULRICH FRANZEN

Ulrich Franzen has always pursued an architecture of multiple ideas. He sees architecture as a continuous process of trying, of rejecting and accepting, of learning always. Franzen's architecture is paralleled by the myriad activities he has engaged in throughout his career as an architect. He has written on architecture, taught and lectured at a number of institutions in the United States, and served on many urban planning boards and professional association committees.

BLDD: You were born in Germany after World War I. You spent your formative years in Germany at the very moment when the Bauhaus was beginning to exert its influence on contemporary architecture. Was that something you were aware of then? Did the architectural environment make any impression on you?

UF: I'm sure it must have. I don't see how any of these things can *not* make an impression. But my awareness of the Bauhaus didn't really dawn on me, in very graphic terms, until I came to the United States. When I was a child I lived in buildings that, I discovered later, were apparently by-products of the Bauhaus. I grew up in the International Style superblocks that we have all learned to dislike. We wound up living in an attached house with gardens, and a park nearby. That all seemed on the surface to be a perfectly reasonable way of living. I think when you grow up in Europe you automatically have a different attitude toward the traditions of building than Americans do. Because we traveled a lot when I was young, I knew Switzerland and Italy very well, and my parents were at home in many parts of Europe. Without it being pounded into our heads, my brother and I had a reasonable feeling for what the traditions in Europe were all about.

BLDD: What was your childhood in Düsseldorf like? And how did you eventually emigrate to the United States at the age of thirteen?

UF: My parents were intellectuals. My mother was a psychoanalyst and my father was a writer, a critic of contemporary literature. They were both active politically; my mother was very left-wing. It's strange, and I don't know what consequences this has had, but all I remember about when I was

little is turmoil, terrible turmoil. It was a very harrowing childhood. I remember street riots, my mother sending us to the grocery store to buy up everything we could to stock the house. I remember my parents laughing about how this paperhanger, Hitler, couldn't even speak properly. They were typical intellectuals who thought that anyone who couldn't spell or write properly would never be able to make it. Then, when Hitler took over and the world around us fell apart, my parents had to flee. They fled a short time after Hitler came to power. My brother and I were left behind in the care of friends. We were smuggled out of the country a year later, ostensibly on a vacation to Switzerland. The Germans at that time were already trying to hold onto their young men, their future cannon fodder. We left everything and snuck across the border. We spent half a year living in Switzerland with friends. My parents had come to the United States by then.

BLDD: How did you get from Switzerland to the United States?

UF: I am not totally sure. But we were fortunate. It had all been pretty much arranged. We finally were able to catch a train to Le Havre and then took a ship to New York, where my parents were fairly settled. It was only then that I really relaxed. When you're ten or eleven and the worst happens—the Nazis taking over—all you can do is think of survival. Once we were settled in Moorestown, New Jersey, I started to enjoy myself. I liked being a New Jersey high school kid. From high school I managed to get several scholarships to college. That's how I got to Williams College. This was due to an absolutely wonderful lady, the principal of Moorestown High School, who took me under her wing. I owe her a lot.

BLDD: Was it in college that you discovered you wanted to pursue architecture?

UF: I had wanted to be an architect for a long time. When I was a kid, six or seven, I used to sketch and make drawings. I drew what I saw around me—houses, gardens, this and that—but I was also interested simply in making pictures. I think I must have been influenced by the artists around me. My mother came from a very talented family with eight sisters, all suffragettes before World War I; all very strong, powerful ladies, some of whom became artists. But my mother, being a psychoanalyst, felt that the Bohemian life wasn't very promising. She may not have disapproved of it in relation to her sisters, but she didn't think it was the right direction for me. My mother discouraged me from becoming a fine artist. She lived in a world where things were so insecure. You've got to be very secure and have a secure setting to be able to say, "Okay, Son, go out there and tackle the world of painting." Mothers always want their sons to be able to do something more solid. I think she must have encouraged my interest in architecture. By the time I was in high school I wanted to be an architect.

BLDD: Can you trace your interest to anything tangible?

UF: I'm sure I was motivated on a psychological level by the fact that I was surrounded by typical European intellectuals. You know how boring they can be—endless intellectualizing that never seems concrete. I was smart enough to understand what they were talking about but also smart enough to know that there is a kind of futility to all this talk, particularly when you see the world falling apart and they're still talking about all the wonderful things that could have happened. Architecture appealed to me because it was concrete. To this day, while I am interested, for instance, in the kind of work Peter Eisenman does, I really have an aversion to it because I feel it's not relevant, it doesn't have the concreteness that I like about architecture.

BLDD: How did you start your formal architectural education?

UF: I was very fortunate again. While at Williams I was helped along by Dean Gregersen, the aesthetics-oriented dean of students. Before graduation he took me to Harvard—drove me all the way—and said, "My student is coming up, and we want you to accept and assist him." I needed all those scholarships to survive. So I began at Harvard. I was there for about six or seven months before I was drafted. Again I was lucky. Within a month I found myself in a super-secret intelligence training center, and I wound up doing really important work in operational intelligence all through the war. I directed some agents investigating certain areas of Nazi-occupied Europe, particularly France, and analyzed their reports. Before the invasion of Normandy I put together a booklet for the combat troops describing the many foreign legions the Germans had defending important areas of northern France. I had been the most fanatic Nazi-hater you could imagine. The war cured me of it a little bit. I was able to express my feelings by working at something day and night. To become fanatical is no good—you're not a human being any more.

BLDD: When you returned to Harvard after the war, was it still the era of Gropius there?

UF: It was the end of the era of Gropius. He left in 1948. The exciting thing about Harvard at the time was the unique student body. We grew and evolved together and learned a lot of things from each other, particularly because the Gropius era had come to an end. Breuer was there for a few years, but there were no real major figures left. The student body was very gung-ho.

BLDD: Who was there at the time?

UF: Everybody was there. Philip Johnson was still finishing up.

BLDD: Did you know him then?

UF: Everybody was in awe of him because, after all, he was one of the founders of the Museum of Modern Art and had given birth to that famous exhibition in 1932. He seemed like our father; he was close to twenty years older than most of us. I remember being one of the few students allowed to visit the first house he built, quite a lovely house in Cambridge, on Acorn Street. He had little soirees there—very desirable events. There I stood one evening nervously holding my drink, when suddenly a guest walked into the glass wall—one of the first glass walls—and fell to the floor. Johnson walked over to this person lying on the floor with his nose bleeding—the glass wall was intact—and said, "Damned fool," and walked away. That was a formative moment!

It was a very exciting time there. Paul Rudolph was in the master's class. Harry Cobb was a classmate; we were good friends and helped each other on our theses. Almost everybody in that generation touched base at Harvard. I. M. Pei was there as a teacher.

BLDD: Was it through Harry Cobb that you came to know I. M. Pei?

UF: I knew I. M. a bit at Harvard, but it was at Harry Cobb's suggestion that I came to work for I. M. Pei. But I got involved in a number of other things before I did that. While I was still in school I had gotten married. My former mother-in-law, who is still alive and in her nineties, was very aesthetically inclined and a great collector of American art. She represented an aesthetic idealism that appealed to me. She was eccentric; she made her family live in a farmhouse without central heating even though they were quite well off. My first wife's brother, Willard Cummings, was a portrait painter who, along with Sidney Simon, started the Skowhegan School of Painting and Sculpture on land owned by his family. They were basically traditional artists and were inviting traditional artists to Skowhegan. I couldn't understand this, since there were all these new artists on the scene. I've always been very interested in new painting. I used to go to the Eighth Street Club when I came to New York and listen to Kline, Rothko, Reinhardt, and all those people. I thought Rothko was God. He was a kind of marvelous aesthetic rabbi, a theologian, and I was a kid who had lost my roots. He was able to turn his theology into paintings with luminous color. I was entranced. I would get such a thrill out of going to see his work in the early fifties. Other people go into a temple or a church to have a religious experience; I had mine looking at those damned Rothkos. I was quite offended when he took his life later on. I just didn't think that was a way for a saint to leave this world. So, you see, I was very involved in the arts by the time I got out of Harvard. But believe it or not, the first thing I did when I got out was to actually build a house, a small little house—the minimum house. To suddenly get out of school and have a commission—I was the envy, as you can imagine, of my peers. The house was probably the smallest designed house ever built. It was published, while I was still a half-ready architect, in *McCall's* magazine. The postwar building boom had started, and they were publishing prototypical houses that veterans getting G. I. loans could afford. My house was one of those efforts. I came across drawings of it recently and thought that it was the kind of house people would be building again soon, the way things are going.

BLDD: When Harry Cobb suggested that you come and work with I. M. Pei, for what sort of project were you hired?

UF: I went to I. M. Pei as a designer and worked on several projects. The major project I worked on, together with Harry, was Mile High Center in Denver—we were sort of underpaid project designers. Pei's decision to work with William Zeckendorf was at that time very idealistic. He felt that in order to fulfill his responsibilities toward society he should work with the most pragmatic and important developers and make them build architecture. To go off and build a small architectural jewel was considered not very responsible in those days.

Similar ideas were very much on Harry's mind. Harry was really taken by social issues. He and other Harvard architecture students became followers of an American planner who, I think, finally turned out to be a spy. He seduced young, innocent Harvard students into taking tours to see the new social progress on the other side of the Iron Curtain in the late forties. I am mentioning this because by then, with the war behind me and the Nazis defeated, I wasn't interested in social issues. I wanted to help design a new world. Mies van der Rohe was my personal architectural savior at Harvard—although he, of course, was not there—and I always felt that Mies was not interested in social architecture. From Mies I learned that to speak clearly in architecture you have to have a vocabulary; you don't misspell words, and you put things together properly. His very tight vocabulary was aimed at solving a few problems extremely well. The intensity and the aesthetics of Mies's effort I also felt in the work of Mark Rothko and Franz Kline. Mies represented all those things I was excited about then. I used to spend a lot of time going to Chicago and looking at as many Mies buildings as I could, and I got to know people in his office.

BLDD: Did you get to know Mies?

UF: I met him several times. He was a very down-to-earth god. It was wonderful to walk into his apartment because it just looked comfortable. He had a wonderful collection of paintings—Klees, for instance—but they were scattered about. Some were leaning against a wall on the floor, others were propped up on the piano. He was a cigar smoker. He was a brandy drinker. The place smelled of cigar smoke and brandy. He was a wonderfully warm human being, a man of the earth, elemental.

BLDD: That's a different description than one would imagine by looking at his very austere architecture.

UF: Isn't it amazing? It's totally different. And that was very appealing to me. Gropius, by comparison, was a very charming, elegant duke type. There was something of the Prussian count about him. He was not an artist really. But Mies was.

BLDD: What was life like during the five years you spent in I. M. Pei's office?

UF: That was a very important period for me. Harry and I led the Miesian group in that office in terms of architectural expression. On Mile High Center we attempted to work within a Miesian vocabulary. We should have stayed within that vocabulary, but we were foolish enough to want to add something to it, and the building ended up being just a grid. It's very flat and has no plastic qualities at all. We thought what would make this building unique would be to express the mechanical systems, to put up a grid of the ducts on the outside of the building, over the structural grid. The structural grid was gray aluminum, the mechanical-systems grid was a beige porcelain enamel. That was the idea behind the building, and we thought we were breaking new ground with this crazy thing! In part it shows the difficulty of working within a Miesian vocabulary. You have to stick to all the parameters that Mies established and try to refine them. You can't add to the vocabulary. It's like taking the architectural vocabulary of a Greek temple and then adding a gridded system to it. The minute you add to it, you ruin it. That's what we did, I think: we wound up ruining it. When I saw this building a while ago, I did not like it at all.

BLDD: What has so changed in your aesthetic that the building no longer has meaning for you?

UF: Unlike some other people, I have never wanted to operate within a formula or work according to a manifesto. I feel that I'm still learning. And I certainly was learning a lot then. I like the idea of change. An architecture that does not change and in some way encapsulate the world as it evolves is not as energetic or as lively as it could be. It's the opposite point of view from that of Richard Meier. I had the option to go in that direction. I'm not saying that I necessarily would have been as skillful as he is. I'm just saying that it's a choice one has to make.

BLDD: Why did you not exercise that option?

UF: I really am not a dogmatist who must stick to what I have decided to do. Once that decision has been made, it's very difficult to make a major change. You can see the problems Richard has. He's taken the vocabulary that he very skillfully derived from the twenties and has made it so elaborate and so complicated that it has lost its tension. He's trying to achieve a new richness, to go into a more textural and sensual kind of composition, with his purist vocabulary. He's interested in the same things other people are interested in, but he's trapped by that one early decision. Because of that, his buildings are becoming fussy and contorted. I find them uncomfortable to look at. There's one thing that I have consistently held onto, and that is the notion of a constructionist vocabulary. This I learned from Mies: to build well and naturally, and if possible to detail elegantly. Wright's idea of the "nature of materials" comes into it as well. The detailing or the construction used in the setting of basic architectural elements such as windows and doors into a facade are major sources of architectural expression.

BLDD: You've told us what influence Mies had on your career. What did you learn while working for I. M. Pei?

UF: One of the things I learned from I. M. was his wonderful gift for approaching an architectural problem. He can sit down and listen to a group of people talking about a building project and can then summarize in one or two minutes the basic conceptual idea that would solve the client's problem. Although that ability brings the danger of oversimplifying, I did learn the ability to communicate architectural concepts to nonarchitects in a very, very simple and unencumbered fashion. I think that's how I. M. wins a lot of his major commissions. He walks into a board of directors meeting, listens to what they have to say, and then says, "This is what you need."

BLDD: You've talked about how your views have changed over the years. Were there specific people that influenced this evolution?

UF: In the early sixties I taught at Yale for a number of years when Paul Rudolph was there. I became very well acquainted with Vincent Scully, who was a major influence on me. His ideas deflected me substantially. This was my postgraduate education. Scully rejected the idea of the all-encompassing architectural style and talked about the cultural denominators, like inclusiveness, that must be considered in architecture. He is in many ways the father of Venturi, and he brought about a change in my work, as he did in the work of many others. When Louis Kahn suddenly appeared as a major figure on the scene he made a tremendous difference in my development away from Mies and toward something else. Louis Kahn was someone who built well. He had respect for what the building itself was about. Louis Kahn didn't care about beautiful buildings; he wanted buildings to have character. It was important to him that when you come upon a building you say "Oh, this building does this and that," rather than "Oh, what a wonderful composition." I also became interested in the beginnings of modern architecture in the Age of Enlightenment. During that period there was a theory of an *architecture parlante,* a reaction against classicism, which was felt to be without character. While I was at Yale Paul Rudolph had a lot to do with introducing the whole idea of context, which came out of the issue of purpose and character. Despite Rudolph's reputation as the pursuer of a personal style, he was really the person responsible for inventing certain prototypical ideas. He was very concerned with contextual issues. He was very taken with Camillo Sitte, the Austrian architect who at the turn of the century talked about city design. Suddenly the notion of context took hold, and its implications were endlessly argued about during student critiques by students and teachers alike. Out of that ferment at Yale in the sixties came a generation of important new architects, such as Stern, Gwathmey, and Tigerman, to name a few. I feel that I have been part of the intellectual and aesthetic changes in attitude that have occurred over the years.

BLDD: What led you to establish your own firm only seven years after starting your career?

UF: I wanted to do it so badly.

BLDD: Yes, but everybody wants to. Where did you get the optimism and the courage to take on such a venture?

UF: I was foolhardy, I suppose.

BLDD: Did you have any specific assignments or commissions?

UF: When I was still with Pei, I started designing a house for myself—the kind of thing one designs and then doesn't build. That became a process by which I began to work through a series of statements that I was then able to produce. I actually did build a house while I was still at Pei's office, and it drew a lot of attention. In fact that's how I met George Weissman. The house couldn't be seen from the road, but there was a little brook that ran past this site in a hollow. One day George Weissman, his wife, Mildred, and his children came walking along that brook, looking for a site for themselves—the New England Thruway was about to be built over their old house. When he saw my house he said, "My God, what is this?" We chatted and immediately hit it off. Before I knew it, I was talking to George and Mildred in their house in Greyrock Park. In those days George was a young man on his way up and, like all of us, didn't have much wherewithal. Whether he could become my client depended on how much the state would reimburse him for the road taking his house. Fortunately it worked out. I was in the process of building two or three other houses in Rye, which I think gave George a little confidence that I was able to do more than just build my own house. But I must say that it was an act of courage on his part. Aside from the fact that I obviously was not the most experienced architect in the world, the houses that I built in those days were these pavilion-type houses, certainly unusual for their time. We spent $80,000 on the house, which then was a phenomenal amount. Then, as it happens when you build a house for someone, I became a member of the family. First I have to help find the furniture and chairs. Then the oil burner doesn't work and George calls up and says, "What kind of a burner did you design for me?" And I say, "Listen, I didn't design the burner, but I'll come over." And so it goes. We became good friends. We also had children of the same ages who grew up together.

BLDD: Your early client ended up becoming the chairman and CEO of Philip Morris, Inc. and a major corporate sponsor of the arts. During the course of his career he remained your client and you had the opportunity to design large buildings for the company.

UF: It's important to realize that we didn't start by designing the large buildings; initially we did little renovations here and there. George brought us in because he was interested in introducing into the company new and fresh ideas about marketing and the physical environment. We started working with them in the early sixties. We were sent down to Richmond to take a look at the many old structures they owned in the

downtown area—some dilapidated and some quite grand—to see what could be done with them to create a more coherent image. We came up with the idea to paint the smokestacks and buildings in a distinctive color scheme to tell the passersby that this collection of buildings with a fresh look belonged to one company. We also got involved in designing huge highway signs, which allowed people to see Philip Morris as they drove from downtown Richmond. George included us in all of these things. George and I became so involved that at one time he said, "Why don't you see what you can do on the Parliament package?" So I designed a cigarette pack that I still think is very pretty—all silver on the outside, with "Parliament" embossed on it, and a dark, rich ultramarine blue on the inside. All of our work for Philip Morris led to a couple of test commissions for their office headquarters in New York, and eventually to the first major renovation of the entire corporate headquarters. That was a traumatic experience for some of the older executives, who had really set themselves up like a bank. They imagined themselves in a typical Wall Street-type environment, the style of the old tobacco traditionalists. But through me George brought in a very different aspect, which led to the operations center in Richmond, the research center, then the new building in New York.

BLDD: The Philip Morris building is a major international headquarters for a leading Fortune 500 company. It has a very significant location in New York City, Forty-second Street and Park Avenue. Could you describe the building?

UF: In the making of a building, all sorts of issues have to be considered. First of all, there was Philip Morris. The top people were very concerned about the character of the building. Basically they wanted a quiet, conservative building. They didn't want a wild building, as George called it. But the building also in a sense represented the culmination of both George Weissman's and Joe Cullman's careers. Joe, who built the

Philip Morris Corporate Headquarters, New York, N.Y.

800 Fifth Avenue, New York, N.Y.

business, is an adventuresome traditionalist; George brings in the new ideas, the new world. Joe was very involved in critiquing all the initial processes for this building, which he felt to a certain extent would be a monument to him as well. Another consideration was the Landmarks Preservation Commission, which, because Philip Morris had purchased air rights, had to approve the plan as being appropriate to Grand Central Station, the landmark building across the street. That in itself created quite an issue. Then there was this fantastic condition at the street level, where Forty-second Street and Park Avenue come together. The urban situation there offers a great confluence of images. Park Avenue immediately conjures up one set of associations, Forty-second Street another set. All of those things had to be expressed. The building is reticent and conservative in terms of the choice of stone (although the granite is a little darker than I wish it had been), but in terms of the compositional devices it is very avant-garde. It became very controversial. The use of two different facade treatments was a way of clearly indicating that there are two very different urban situations going on—Forty-second Street and Grand Central across the street, and Park Avenue, with all its big corporate headquarters standing like a bunch of girls at a junior prom waiting to be introduced. Creating two facades was also a way of making the building less conservative

in its attitude, a little touch that would suggest progressive and radical notions, something not entirely proper. I had by then already experimented with using screens and different facades in a number of buildings, such as 800 Fifth Avenue. One successful thing about 800 Fifth Avenue is the screen that stands out from the building.

BLDD: Your comments on 800 Fifth Avenue call to mind what you've said about the eighteenth-century French architect Ledoux. You cited him as one of the earliest architects whose work reflected a modern sensibility, a multiplicity of ideas in architecture. How was his influence reflected in your design for 800 Fifth Avenue?

UF: Ledoux made studies for a triumphal arch made up of a base of Tuscan farmhouses, topped with a Greek pediment and crowned by a Roman arch. A bizarre arrangement. He experimented with bringing into one composition different ideas that were current in his time—the era of the French Revolution. The farmhouses represented the style of the common people, the Greek pediment the Greek democratic ideal, and the Roman arch the antiquities of Italy. His was an age of fundamental social and cultural changes, with many valid but different ideas operating side by side. This parallels our time. We live in a city of violent contrasts and heterogeneous cultures. If you want to design a building here that engages its surroundings, that reaches out beyond the lot line, you have to make a composition that clearly embraces the diversity. That's what we attempted at 800 Fifth Avenue. It is on a very formal street where the doormen make you feel you have no business walking on the sidewalk. But if you go over one block, to Madison Avenue, there is a totally different life—restaurants, shops, much more variety. In one block you have a cross section of the city. I felt that a building going into that space had to somehow encapsulate the complexity of the setting in order to create a relationship with its context. The facade on Fifth Avenue is ironic in part: it recalls other development buildings along Fifth Avenue, which all have similar formal limestone detailing, a sort of "savings-bank classicism." But it also establishes continuity: it is built to the height of the adjoining Knickerbocker Club. The Madison Avenue facade is not formal but indicates a relaxed and comfortable apartment life. These were the ideas I was experimenting with, the ideas that brought 800 Fifth Avenue into being.

BLDD: You've written that "a building that fulfills only a functional need is merely a building. Architecture is something more." What *is* architecture? What distinguishes today's architecture from the architecture that you first became involved with almost forty years ago? You started with the Bauhaus, which had a program, a philosophy, something that could be taught because it was codified.

UF: The word "codified" can be used as a key. Modern architecture was for nearly forty years a code of how to build. It represented a singular, somewhat elitist but nonetheless enlightened point of view. I think I may have adopted that view when I started out, although I learned from Mies van der Rohe and not Gropius, and that's a world of difference. Today, living in a world where it is totally clear that on social, political, and human levels there is no such thing as a single codified way of

operating, architecture has simply become the manifestation in physical form of these uncertainties and this complexity of experience. Different buildings have different appearances and are representative of a variety of value systems. Architecture, being a part of its time, does suggest in some measure those qualities that have come upon us in the last twenty years from other fields.

BLDD: You've described architecture as an artistic and intellectual endeavor whose subtleties often escape its practitioners, not to mention the general public. Can architecture really only be appreciated by the professionally trained?

UF: That's a big issue. It is a failing of modernist architecture that the problems considered were of interest only to an academic priesthood, that only the high priests themselves had an inkling about what the architecture was saying. I don't think it was really saying a lot. In this light it is interesting to look at, say, Gothic architecture, which was an architecture determined by priests. The abbots would meet at convocations to discuss changes in the fluting on columns, which is a very intellectual approach. But at the same time the buildings were sensuous and anecdotal. Ordinary people were clearly affected by walking into those grand spaces with beautiful light coming through the stained-glass windows. And in the windows and sculpture were pictorial references to many of their religious beliefs. While all architecture is done by highly skilled artists and on some levels will be of interest only to those artists, on other levels it must also speak to the lay person, the user. If it doesn't, it is not complete.

BLDD: You've called the Multi-Categorical Research Center, which you designed for Cornell University in 1973, the first major illustration in your work of an architecture of multiple ideas. Can you explain your concept and how this project reflects it?

Multi-Categorical Research Laboratory, Cornell University, Ithaca, N.Y.

UF: In the case of that building there were two very different kinds of requirements. On the one hand, we had to design a series of specialized spaces—sealed laboratories for advanced virus research. Because of problems of contamination, the laboratories could not have windows or openings to the outside. Their environments are totally sustained by machines—it's like being in a submarine. On the other hand, there was the requirement for "normal" spaces—offices for professors, graduate student areas, seminar rooms, places to eat, and so on—that also provided daylight and views. It is a building type for which there is no historical precedent. In a traditional approach, one would have tried to find a stylistic formula that would have packaged those two requirements into a single architectural language. I decided to bring together two compositional systems, each expressive of its requirements in collage fashion. The final design was a narrow building with two facades, one a symbolic rendition of a giant machine, the other a nice academic office building overlooking the lake. It is pretty wild when you move from one side of the building to the other.

BLDD: You've also designed a corporate headquarters for the Société Lyonnaise des Eaux in Paris. How did working in a major European city influence your design?

UF: Our efforts in Paris involved a *Catch-22*. We were retained by our friends at the Lyonnaise because they wanted forward-looking American-style buildings, but we wanted this building to be based on a more Parisian kind of concept. When we made our first presentation to the president of this company, we invoked the Place Vendôme. We wanted the building to make a square and to contain artwork or symbolic things. At the time of the second presentation, the president of the company said that if I mentioned the Place Vendôme once more, we might just as well go back home. The problem that arose was that we as Americans had to try to sell the Parisians on their roots when the Parisians didn't want to hear of it. They thought the nineteenth-century "imperial architecture of Paris," as they called it, did not represent them. It was one horrendous effort, and the building was not built, incidentally, because the bank was nationalized at the last moment.

BLDD: How can healthy development and a spirit of progressiveness in contemporary architecture coexist with a covenant we all have with the past? What do you think of the current interest in preservation?

UF: Probably the most important advance that's been made in architecture in two hundred years is the question of contextual integrity, to which a building must address itself. That doesn't necessarily mean that you always have to ape the context, but you have to either establish a relationship or reject it for contextual reasons. This concern for context comes partly from living in the chaotic cities that modern life has created. A contextual attitude tries to recombine the existing city into something more harmonious and compositionally more beautiful. Preservation becomes a major element in cities such as New York, where there are so many extraordinary buildings of the nineteenth and early twentieth centuries that are disappearing. The question of how to build in settings like that is a complicated one. At present preservation has become, for a lot of people, a fanatic, vigilante-type interest. Some people spend their time walking up and down the streets making records of somebody having painted a window frame a wrong color, or somebody trying to change a door front. While in many ways that's very caring, it scares me a little. I come from a background where people used to be asked to spy on their neighbors, and I don't like it!

BLDD: You've written that all of us in America are the children of refugees; someone in our past has—perhaps even we ourselves have—made an attempt at a new beginning. Has your own history as an immigrant predisposed you to movement towards the new?

UF: I think America is about hope. People may be removed several generations from the immigrants that came to enjoy our society, but whether they are boat people from Vietnam or refugees from Costa Rica, iimigrants come here because they are full of extraordinary hope about what it might mean to be here. In terms of preservation, if you build new, you have to give the new a chance to be expressive and representative.

BLDD: Is the present economic situation both here and abroad conducive to the exploration of new ideas in architecture?

UF: The way an architect works is locked into the economy. When there is little building, architects turn to making drawings of their unbuilt dreams or, as in Italy, they design things like lamps and furniture. When the opportunity comes to build, most serious architects try to draw on the ideas developed when building was a dream.

BLDD: You've said that Charles Moore was in the forefront of the movement to make architecture eloquent again. To what degree has Moore succeeded in revitalizing that lost spirit of eloquence, and has anyone else made a significant contribution toward that end?

UF: Artists in the forefront of a movement are not necessarily the ones who realize the intentions of that movement. Charles Moore, with his Piazza d'Italia in New Orleans, for instance, has made a series of proposals on anecdotal architecture that are very, very unusual. But it seems that the person who has both codified a meaningful approach to combining the new and the old and come up with some interesting design proposals is Bob Stern. He has not built large buildings, but in his houses in the Hamptons he looks at the vernacular architecture and the context of the region and then takes that regional style and embellishes it with something of his own. It is a straightforward and intelligent approach that can produce admirable designs. Charles Moore's achievement is more complicated, more literary. He's a wonderful observer and has written well about the traditional qualities of architecture. He has also, of course, debunked modernism, but his buildings so far remain amusing, paper-thin stage sets of an architectural raconteur.

BLDD: You've said that in designing a house, if you give a woman the kitchen she wants, she'll give you a free hand with the rest. How much control—aesthetic, artistic, architectural—are you willing to relinquish to the client?

UF: That sounds like a terrible thing to say, but I think in part architecture is the art of either seduction or subversion! I don't know if it's possible to seduce somebody without their knowing that they're being seduced, but certainly the idea of subversion is that you don't realize what's happening. Human beings have to express themselves when making a house, and you as the architect attempt to represent someone else's ideas to the extent that you create a stage where the ideas can flower. But the shape of the stage, its illumination, and how the client can use it is up to the architect to create. The architect plays an important role. It has to be a very loving process.

BLDD: How do you persuade a client to accept your design notions when most of the clients you deal with, especially in corporate matters, are singular, strong-minded people themselves?

UF: If you tried to do in Switzerland or even in Paris what I try to do here, it would be hopeless. The corporate types in Europe are very rigid; you can't get through to them. Here, when you begin to talk about a slightly different arrangement, a new way of doing things, a fresh approach, even the most distinguished corporate type will get a gleam in his eye. What you have to do is find a way of making that gleam in his eye respectable to him. Here you are able to introduce new ideas, although you may have to legitimize a radical idea in the eyes of the board. This is a task that some architects cannot manage. They may have a wonderful idea, but they cannot package it in such a way that the corporate representative, who may be a secret ally, can take it back to his board.

BLDD: You've done a large number of corporate headquarters, including buildings for the Miller Brewing Company in Milwaukee, Grosset & Dunlap in New York, and Philip Morris, Inc., in New York. What difference is there between working on commissions and working from your own inspiration?

UF: I don't like working in the abstract with no program or site. I don't think that is really architecture. Architecture is the coming together of an idea and reality. The exciting thing is where that intersection occurs, between idea and reality. That is crucial. I appreciate what my friend John Hejduk does—his sometimes incomprehensible but still very intricate schemes and beautiful drawings are certainly an art—but it's not architecture.

BLDD: Nowadays so many artists' work resembles that of architects, and the work of many architects seems to resemble that of artists. Would you comment on this new direction and on the potential for collaboration between artist and architect?

UF: It is fascinating that architects are suddenly becoming interested in a lot of issues that ordinarily would only be the concern of a fine artist, whether it's making drawings or the way you organize a wall. Fine art is also now headed in a direction where collaboration could again become more natural, more easy, than it had been, say, in the days of rigorous reductionist modernism, when there was an almost total divorce of the two. Maybe we are working toward another kind of relationship, one that comes out of the fact that attitudes today are more pluralistic. The strangers of the recent past—architect and artist—perhaps will come together.

BLDD: In what ways does the residence you built for yourself represent your ideas about architecture?

UF: A lot of architects say that they don't want to "live in the store," that building for yourself is chickening out. But you've got to live in your store. If you design your own space, it reflects your values at that particular moment; it is a reading of what you think is important and not important in a composition.

BLDD: The new academic facilities at Hunter College are one of your recent innovative achievements. Among the challenges you faced there was designing some way to connect the two units, which stand on opposite corners of a major New York City thoroughfare, Lexington Avenue, and taking into account the insurmountable presence of a subway beneath the street. How did you finally arrive at a solution for this project?

UF: The new Hunter buildings are to serve a student population of fifteen thousand, plus five thousand teachers and administrators, brought together from scattered locations in the city. We calculated that, at most, about ten thousand people would be pouring out of the new buildings and attempting to cross Lexington Avenue at Sixty-eighth Street, creating human gridlock. We simply had to find a way out of this dilemma. Bridges were the only answer, as the subway system blocked any thought of tunnels. The design options were, therefore, concerned with the shape of the bridges and their role in the community. The bridges are designed as thin and elegant spaces, yet they add a new element to the area around Hunter:

They create a new urban space, a kind of forecourt for this major institution. This roofless urban room between the old building and the two new ones is a place—Hunter's place—providing an identity where there was none. All this was quite controversial when we initially proposed it. But people who at first complained are now beginning to like the whole arrangement, including our renovation of the subway station. The new Hunter complex is, in my mind, an illustration of a progressive solution inserted into an existing setting, bringing about a more harmonious setting for old and new.

BLDD: Do you see a new celebrity status given to architects by the general public? How has that affected the profession?

UF: There has been a lot of media attention to architecture, but most of the attention has been on two or three architects, like Michael Graves and Helmut Jahn. The disadvantage of all the media attention is that next year people will want something new, and it's not possible for a serious architect to take a new position every year. It's not like Yves Saint Laurent, who does something new every season—he's expected to come up with new ideas that will keep him in the limelight. Architects can't do that. The excessive media attention may end up working against a lot of reputations that were not justly derived.

BLDD: To the work of what architects do you most respond?

UF: In terms of young new architects, I think Bob Stern is a very responsible person. I don't do what he does, but I've learned from Bob's way of looking at architecture and the world. The person I admire most as an artist is Frank Gehry. He has created a completely modern dimension by exploiting areas within modernism that have not been fully explored. That's something I'm very interested in. His work is a crazy, wonderful jumble of all kinds of things put together, an explosion of the process of building—raw studs, cyclone fencing, bits of corrugated metal, exposed plumbing. His work has a lot of qualities that are generally attributed to postmodernism, but his tastes are not really postmodern. They're modern postmodern, or whatever you want to call it.

BLDD: Now that we are postmodern, what happens when we're post-postmodern, or are we already there?

UF: I think we're going to get modern postmodern.

BLDD: What is "modern postmodern" as you see it? Is postmodern already passé?

UF: Yes. There's been a lot of heat, but there have also been some significant insights. We've all learned a hell of a lot, even those of us who were not necessarily in the postmodern vanguard. I read an article Julian Schnabel recently wrote in *Artforum*. I was very moved by it. He really was talking to Franz Kline and Mark Rothko, saying that he is their offspring and that he is trying to carry on the things they did. That's the way architects should work. The postmodern theorists like Robert Venturi or Charles Moore have rewakened dimensions of architectural composition that were put to sleep by the International Style. I think that there was more to modernism than the International Style, and that these unexplored areas can now be fully viewed.

Frank Lloyd Wright, for instance—how does one classify him? You can't call him a postmodernist, even though, from his ornament to his consideration of context, he fulfills all the requirements of postmodernism. But Wright is Mr. Modern Architecture! When his work was first published in Europe at the turn of the century, it had the most tremendous impact. It ignited European modernism, which many years later and in a different form came to the U.S. The radical postmodernist may scream and yell about the sterility, the starkness, the lack of place of reductionist modernism, but he looks the other way

Detail of bridge addition to Hunter College, New York, N.Y.

Private Residence, East Hampton, N.Y.

when the question of Wright is brought up. No one dares pick on him because he doesn't fit the bill. Wright is the modern postmodern architect!

There are other areas of modernism, aside from the stark kind, that have not been fully explored. There's the work of Louis Kahn. (Philip Johnson speaks of him as a second-rate architect, but Johnson belongs to Kahn's generation, and he is worried that the only one who will be remembered in that generation is Kahn.) Kahn really is the bridge from modernism to postmodernism over which many of us traveled. He appealed to me because he was another theologian in visual form, much like Mark Rothko. Kahn was very important in my development. Aalto, too, is a modern postmodernist. His work, while it started in a minimalist mode, was concerned with other dimensions of modernism—the sensual, the tactile, and the site-specific.

BLDD: How will the role of architects in the next century differ from that of today's architects?

UF: There's a danger that architects will become such generalists that they'll do everything—the total environment—which I don't think architects should do. Architects should do architecture. We can get together with graphic designers and mural artists and sculptors and so on and split up what has to be done. It will be a richer, more in-depth effort. That would be my hope for the next century.

BLDD: For what would you like best to be remembered?

UF: I would like to have it said that at least some of my buildings were of my time and for my time.

BLDD: What would you care to do that you haven't done yet?

UF: I can't tell you how anxious I am to get to work on another project that poses a number of challenges, preferably in the city, because I feel I've learned so much since I built the last one that I really want to put all this experience to work.

BLDD: If you had your life to live over again, what would you do differently?

UF: I would spend more time on design and drawings. I probably would have wound up doing pretty much the same, except I would have done it a lot better.

BLDD: Did you expect your life to unfold the way it has?

UF: No, but I guess I did always expect good things to happen. Like everyone I can occasionally be depressed, but I basically believe that if you feel good about the world and about yourself, you can somehow project this feeling into what's going to happen around you.

JAMES INGO FREED

From his first work in New York as assistant to Mies van der Rohe on the Seagram Building, to his most recent project as a principal at I. M. Pei & Partners on the New York City Convention Center, James Ingo Freed has been known for his dedication to integrating structures of formal elegance into the urban environment.

BLDD: When did you first come to New York?

JIF: In 1955. I was in Alaska, where I had been stationed with the army, when I received a letter from Mies van der Rohe asking me to come to New York to work on the Seagram Building. It was a wonderful opportunity. I didn't know very much about New York, so I came.

BLDD: How did he know where to find you?

JIF: I had kept in touch with a friend who had graduated with me from the Illinois Institute of Technology, where Mies taught. It's like all small mafias and undergrounds—everyone knows everyone else.

BLDD: Is that how architects get jobs?

JIF: Oh yes. There are support groups, and support groups within support groups. People help each other.

BLDD: Do you think this approach is more prevalent among architects than among other professionals?

JIF: I think so. Architects are competitive, but they can also be supportive, particularly of those who stand on the same side when aesthetic or ideological lines have been drawn. They become extremely protective of members in their own camp.

BLDD: Ada Louise Huxtable said that architects nowadays are engaged in a "hand-to-hand, building-to-building polemic." She was referring to the modernist-versus-postmodernist debate. Where do you stand? Of which camp are you a part?

JIF: I don't like the terms "modernist" and "postmodernist." It seems to me that what is called postmodernism is actually very modern; it's a kind of latter-day modernism. Many architects love to label and draw overfine distinctions, to sharpen their differences. The best buildings of our time tend to be evolutionary. There are some very good buildings labeled postmodernist that are simply developments and enrichments

of a modernist tradition. I am particularly sensitive to and interested in the notion of polemics because I come from that kind of background. I was trained as an undeviating modernist. The school very often substituted polemics for reality. In the architectural debate, polemics can overwhelm the built object. The shoddiness of some buildings is overlooked because of the polemic surrounding them.

BLDD: We know what you *don't* like now, but what *do* you like?

JIF: I'm a latter-day modernist.

BLDD: How would you define that?

JIF: The purist position that the early modernists took, which was deeply embedded in social theory, is probably no longer credible or even possible. That abstracted purism led to the worst kind of contextual excesses; polemics overwhelmed the eye, and intellectual position overwhelmed experiential fact. If we look to the long-ago past and to the future, as well as to the immediate past and those things in it that remain valuable, we will have a richer palette of materials and forms and a broader range of metaphoric, symbolic, and logical structures. It is even possible to be inventive.

BLDD: You made reference to the Illinois Institute of Technology. What caused you to go to school there?

JIF: I had always been interested in art and architecture. I had first gone to the Art Institute of Chicago, but I became overwhelmed by the building images coming out of IIT. There was a quasi-religious fervor about it, a spirit that appealed to me. This was 1948, shortly after World War II, and the great, idiosyncratic American architects who had operated in the twenties and thirties were no longer visibly active. The great Art Deco buildings had already been done. There was a great outburst of building activity in the United States, but very bad work was coming out of the offices. It was the possibility of working with a reinvigorated architecture that attracted me to IIT.

BLDD: How influential were other images for you, particularly those from your native country, Germany?

JIF: That influence was pretty strong. I came from Germany in 1941, during World War II, and went to Chicago, a city where the art of building was evident. Just as nearly every educated Parisian in the late nineteenth century could talk about the novel as a form, so could most intelligent Chicagoans talk about architecture in the forties and fifties. They talked about Frank Lloyd Wright as a person and the Chicago School as a force. We all went to look at Wright's buildings and thought they were marvelous. We all took tours to Taliesin East and thought *it* was marvelous. But one was not attracted to Wright in those days because his teaching had somehow become academic. To become a fellow at Taliesin was really to become an acolyte. Curiously, the same thing happened later at IIT. That may be the way of all strong ideas and strong men—their followers tend to become academic. In any case, there was something at that time at IIT that was still being worked out. It was not a totally fixed situation, there were no absolute or given forms. A modernist architecture was still in the process of becoming, and that was exciting. After it became codified it ceased to be exciting. It was good to come to New York from a place like Chicago, because there had been a rigor in Chicago that made it possible to absorb and integrate the very fruitful and chaotic nature of New York. I did, however, work in Chicago for a little while before that.

BLDD: What was interesting or inspiring to you in Chicago?

JIF: Chicago was, and is, a city of building. Building is *the* art form of Chicago. It's very hard to say the same of New York.

BLDD: Or of almost any other American city.

JIF: In Chicago it *was* an art form, and Chicago as a city was all of a piece. In a way, it had some very Florentine qualities. It was very stern, very stark, and stylistically unified. It was deliberate and purposeful and had a strong unity of expression. The streets were firm and ordered, the corners marked. It was a wonderful city to walk in. It had a grid that was determined by the streetcar patterns. All of this began to disappear, however, at the hands of those who celebrated it the most. The designers of the Chicago School, with their abstracted, structurally expressive buildings, decided that these idealized or platonic buildings could not survive in the modifying chaos of the grid but had to stand by themselves. So they applied a theory of city planning that focused on individual buildings in three-dimensional isolation. They eroded the city fabric. They used didactic techniques similar to Rauschenberg's technique of erasure on a drawing. The city was operated on by erasing streets and putting parks in the fragmented voids. The existing city fabric was destroyed. The IIT campus destroyed the traditional part of the South Side of Chicago, where it was located, by creating an amorphous park with no life in it, breaking the area's continuity with the rest of the city.

BLDD: Did your experience at IIT shape your approach to architecture?

JIF: It is a truism that we are all the inheritors of our youth, that our education shapes us first. Initially I felt I had the tools with which to press ahead, but then I felt dissatisfied with those tools because the results were not what I expected.

BLDD: How did you act on that feeling?

JIF: It took a very long time. My education was unbendingly vigorous in its historic revisionism. We were taught, for example, that the Renaissance was *abhorrent.* That marvelous time was considered one of the decadent periods of architecture. Renaissance architects perceived certain problems and then solved them. The problem of turning corners on buildings, for instance, was solved by rotating the surface around a right angle. The problem was not identified before that. In my schooling, we were taught never to turn corners—there was a fascination with section and frontality. The notion of turning the corner symmetrically was considered decadent—

structures, it was pronounced, do not turn corners. My first unease with my education occurred when I decided to turn a corner and realized that what I had been taught was not useful, that I had to begin to reteach myself. It took ten to twenty years to shake myself loose from a belief system that had disposed me to perceive the architectural world in a very narrow way. I'm still shaking myself loose. I don't mean, however, to make that system sound entirely negative. There were some very good things in that other way of seeing the world. At that time we were made to feel the tangibility of space; we could swim in it like a fish swims in water. Space was a metaphysical solid. You didn't have to confine yourself to the surface of a wall to imbue a building with symbolism; space itself had iconic and symbolic value. Those modernists also understood the poetry of the tectonic, the making of a building, a building constructed and fabricated by man. I don't want to lose those strong concepts and perceptions. But I do want to lose the limiting and diminishing ways of thinking, which disallowed history as a source for design inspiration and proposed structural expressionism as the only legitimate methodology.

BLDD: What circumstances prompted you to move to New York?

JIF: I wanted to come to New York and I wanted to work on the Seagram Building.

BLDD: How much contact had you previously had with Mies?

JIF: He was my teacher at IIT; I had the good fortune to have him as a part-time critic. He was not very active in the school in those days, and I found that there was a significant difference between having him as a teacher and having one of his students. So the opportunity to work on the Seagram Building directly with him and to learn from him was very important.

BLDD: You have credited Mies as a major influence. Would you describe what kind of man he was?

JIF: He was the major influence on me at one time, but I have found myself resenting that terribly in the last decade or so. I have found myself consciously leaving it behind. He was incredibly persuasive, not only because he composed a formal solution, but because that solution contained a fully realized language of architecture, including all the bits and pieces, even the decorative. I speak of Mies in order to exorcise his ghost. He looked like a sturdy stonemason. I remember charretting at night while Mies sat with a shaker full of martinis, passing them around but keeping the larger part for himself. He was a man of the senses who spoke to the spirit. In the end he made a terrible mistake, the kind people make who become too narrowly focused. He perceived and sometimes spoke of the modern movement as being a war. He wanted to win that war. At that time the issue in architecture was the debate between the plasticism of Le Corbusier and the structuralism of Mies. He did not perceive that in the United States these architectural issues would be worked out in a different way. The modern movement, with its strong programmatic substructure, was not easily transferable to the New World, where the politically ideational and the overshadowing of social issues by theory were less important. Mies unwittingly made it possible in the long run to build in a shoddier way. When Mies's followers took over with their determinist aesthetic, developers realized that they didn't have to use stone or expensive details. They saw the new aesthetic as giving them free reign to put up simple, unadorned cheap glass boxes. Mies's theories led to buildings that were too abstracted. Buildings should have personality and should appeal to all the senses. That's not something you can arbitrarily put on the surface of a building. It has to be contained in the body of architecture. Architecture is, after all, an art.

National Bank of Commerce, Lincoln, Neb.

BLDD: What about architecture as a business?

JIF: If architecture is only a business, then why worry so much about it? Why struggle so hard? Somebody once said that the architecture of buildings is an unnecessary gift, and it is that unnecessary gift that makes it architecture. If architecture is an art, then what kind of an art is it? Is it a platonic art? If architecture is platonic, pure art, then it's like an easel painting, which can be picked up and moved around; it can be taken anyplace, and it will always be agreeable. Yet it has no flavor or personality. The root of architecture lies in certain simple remembered things—historical precedents, types of buildings, textures of spaces and surfaces. There are pre-prototypes, morphologies that exist in memory and are more or less schematic. These schematized notions of a building memory can coalesce and form a special place, which then modifies them in turn. If that process of coalescing is done sensitively, if the place created fits into that continuum of structure that we call a place, a landscape, or a city, then it's true architecture, true art.

BLDD: Let's come back for a moment to Mies. You referred to him as a great architect. What made him great?

JIF: What made him great was that he took a number of preexisting programmatic situations and turned them into an art form. You have to remember what the Bauhaus was like in the late twenties and early thirties. There was an attempt by the social historians who were running parts of the Bauhaus to make architecture a tool of social revolution. They did some things that may be interesting in books but would have been

pretty horrible if they had been built. It was a kind of army-barracks architecture. Many of the Bauhaus people believed fervently that to design consciously was to corrupt the design process. But Mies took what was in those days a simplified, schematized notion and turned it into an extremely elegant spatial and formal construct. Mies's Barcelona Pavilion was a great piece of work. He developed a brilliant notion of the horizontal extension of space. Frank Lloyd Wright dealt with the specifically horizontal in his spaces, but Mies dealt with the universality of the horizontal, which extended in all directions, unlimited. For him space was a complex of planes of walls counterpointed by columns. Rather than a rational relationship between the columns and the planes of the wall, there was an intuitive, poetic one. And he created his architecture out of industrial parts, which integrated industry into the poetic medium. He went on to create an architecture of considerable dignity that dealt with rapid industrialization at a time of extensive building. But his architectural thinking laid claims to an absolute, universal permanence that its productions could not support. His thinking sometimes reminds me of other claims to a thousand-year reich.

BLDD: What would he have thought of this enduring debate about the modernism that he engendered and fostered?

JIF: I don't think he would have any doubt that we are now backsliding into privilege and decadence—into nonarchitecture. It would be a view that I do not share.

BLDD: Is there anything in architecture that you would talk about with such certitude?

JIF: I would say that a schematized or totally abstracted architecture leads to a scaleless and uninteresting world. I would talk with certitude about the values of the traditional city, which I think is here to stay in some form. The city is composed of rooms and spaces, which should be of sufficient variety to generate a variety of experience. I believe that architecture is strongly experiential; in that I may differ from some of the latter-day modernists who think of it as primarily symbolic. I find it difficult to think of buildings primarily as objects. I think of them as space enclosures. Now, late in life, I'm developing a conviction about the necessity of bringing people into a building and having them engage with it. Architecture cannot stand at an austere distance from life. It has to have a real engagement with it. This means breaking down scale, concentrating on surface and detail, and grappling with the conflicts that arise when dealing with a number of ideas rather than one.

BLDD: What do great cities have that sets them apart? What makes you think they will endure?

JIF: Great cities are usually the products not of individual architects but of great cultures; great cultures have goals or ends that are shared in some way by most of the people. Unfortunately, I'm not persuaded that we have a common view today. This problem is glossed over by the idea that pluralism is a good thing. It may be good not to have a common view; it does open up possibilities. But what this will lead to is the loss of the classic notion of the unified great city. The great cities like Paris and Florence have a similarity of mass, form, and height; they have a common language of streets, gardens, and details. I don't think that is going to happen again. Our cities are going to be much more patched together.

BLDD: The city as a collage?

JIF: It's really like those paintings of the city by Léger. The city will have precincts of different character, each with some of the qualities associated with great cities. One reason cities can't be what they were is the rise of the tall building. The tall building creates a scale, a mass, a volume, a punctuation in the city that obliterates the sense of the roofline and the sky as a reference plane, making the city a place of precincts.

BLDD: Out of the window of your office on Madison Avenue, directly in your line of vision, there is a low-rise building—one of the few remaining in the area. You are surrounded almost everywhere by midtown overdevelopment. What do you think the effects of this building boom will be on the city in general? Will it be, in the end, an enhancement or a detraction?

JIF: I love seeing the sky from my window. I think there has to be a limit to the size and density of buildings. We have to be very careful not to abet the unalloyed overintensification of the city. A city can be very dense and still be humane. When you build densely, you have to give something in return. But there's a point when you ought to stop.

BLDD: And what is that point?

JIF: I think we've reached it in New York.

BLDD: What *are* the limits of growth?

JIF: When you can no longer stroll on the streets and stop to chat, when life begins to be a hectic movement from place to place, when frenzy replaces interest and stimulation.

BLDD: How do you return some balance and joy to urban existence?

JIF: You can ameliorate the situation by protecting what is left, by being more selective about densities. Greater density can exist in some places, but then you ought to give the ground level back to civic use. People should be able to expect gardens and resting places, and I'm not talking about patchwork atrium gardens. They're O.K., if that's all you can get, but they're silly as an overall concept. I'd like the streets to be places to occupy rather than hurry through. If the buildings were more interesting—functionally, spatially, and aesthetically—it would help a little, but not a lot. I don't know how to define the limit to growth, except pragmatically for a particular condition, time, and place. I'm working on a project for San Francisco—the Mission Bay—where we are deliberately creating lagoons, canals, gardens, and parks as impediments to unlimited growth. We're channeling growth. We've kept a lot of land from development to provide a skeleton of amenities that cannot be built upon. Think how horrible New York would be without Central Park.

BLDD: Your firm usually is associated with monumental buildings. Is there now a shift in emphasis?

JIF: We won't do a building that we think is wrong. We have been approached a number of times to do buildings that are wrong, and we've turned them down. I'm not at all bashful about saying when density should and should not exist.

BLDD: The National Bank of Commerce you created in Lincoln, Nebraska, is thought of as a lesson in how to design on a human scale, an idea that you continue to find compelling. Tell us some of your concerns in developing that project.

JIF: That project was situated at the crossroads of a small vital city. Most midwestern cities seem bombed out by the automobile and surrounded by parking lots. Lincoln, Nebraska, is not; it has many of the virtues we associate with smaller American cities. It has remained vital because it is the capital city and has a state university. The site is at the crossroad of O Street, the commercial street, and Thirteenth Street, the business street, really the center of town. The problem was how to mark this center and to provide passages on a site that is a sliver. The site is seventy-five feet wide by two hundred feet long, fifty feet wide at its most important point. Consequently, the building had to be broken into a series of parts: a public section in the center, an entry to the office building, a space for the bank. We acknowledged the lower-scale commercial street, the higher-scale cross street, and the back of the building, which was against a garage. This project forced me to think about the possibilities of a building that is different on each of its six faces. It forced me to speculate on how to unify the faces and how to make the building site-specific. When I started there was some discussion about a loose fit, but I was more interested in making a specific response to a specific site. The surrounding buildings were fairly nondescript, without much architectural quality. It became necessary to design a building that faced one way yet had its door at a right angle to that direction. One way of doing this was to modulate the height in section, working with space to transmit information about where you are and how you are to move. I loved working on that project. I still like it very much.

BLDD: Some of the projects you're now working on reflect your evolving idea of beauty. You're involved in several projects in California—in San Francisco and Los Angeles.

JIF: I have three projects in California. One is the Ferry Building project, a remarkable challenge because it is a great public monument. But the back of it is awful—it has been destroyed over the years. It's not feasible to reconstruct the back, which was one level higher because it consisted of dolphins, or buoys, that moored the ferryboats. Now there are no more ferries and there are no more dolphins. It seems unnecessary to reconstruct it.

BLDD: For what purpose will the building be used now?

JIF: It will be used as a commercial and public building. We've opened up the galleria and made a wonderful arcade through

Ferry Building, San Francisco, Calif., drawing

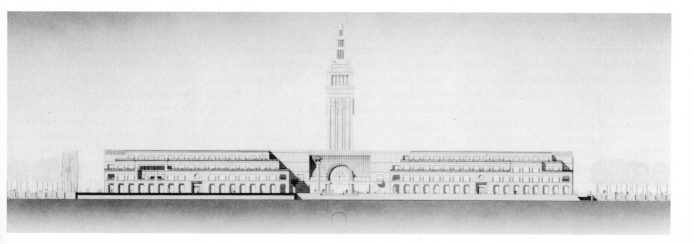

Mission Bay, San Francisco, Calif., model

the building. The front facade will be restored to its pristine condition.

BLDD: Are you becoming a preservationist?

JIF: I've always been a preservationist! Curiously, good modernists have always been good preservationists. We found a serendipitous thing in the Ferry Building. There's a pier to the left of it and an old building to the right. The front portions of these buildings are beautiful. The backs are factory-like additions. By restructuring the backs of these buildings we have developed an urban lagoon edged with useful buildings that will form a new environment for the city at the end of Market Street. The fronts of the buildings—not just the walls, but a significant depth of the buildings—are preserved and sometimes reconstructed. From the city side everything is as it was, and from the water side, everything is as it might have been; not a historicizing solution—that was never intended— but a complementary might-have-been.

BLDD: What are the two other projects in California?

JIF: The second one is the Mission Bay project. It is the development of a new sector of San Francisco, a 200-acre area on Mission Creek near China Basin, south of the Ferry Building. The area will have the flavor of San Francisco and the small, fragmented scale—the water, the townhouses, the

trees—that makes San Francisco what it is. We want an environment that is unique and that has an immediate, recognizable impact on the city. It is now a wasteland of tracks, near the bay. San Francisco has a bay that is accessible only in a few places. So we're bringing the bay into the land, creating waterways on this site to give it character and personality. There's housing on the lagoons and canals, and we're shielding the edges with parks. We're going to provide an urban environment in which water is the significant characteristic.

The third project is for a developer who has acreage near the Los Angeles airport. The airport is a fast-growing area, but it lacks identifiable character or atmosphere. It's pretty vacant; the roads and freeways are certainly nothing to look at. I decided at the very beginning that Continental City would have to be an inward-oriented city. The problem with this development is the uncertain program: at the time of design we don't have tenants for its office buildings and hotels. How do you build a city that is dense and low—because of FAA height limitations—and give it a coherent and memorable image when the program is uncertain? Our solution was to create large building elements that can combine in a variety of ways. The "building parts" are eight stories high and 180 feet long. They have recognizable, if fragmentary, forms, and they combine in a variety of predetermined ways so that buildings may be 120,000, 240,000, or 480,000 square feet in size. Despite the variables, the urban image is controlled. We attempted to capture certain qualities of a city like Paris, which has specific cornice lines and roof profiles. What goes on inside the buildings is less important than the urban edge those buildings give to the street. We are now involved in the first phase of Continental City. It's really an attempt to see whether a place that is full of internal small gardens, that is relatively dense, urban, and accessible to pedestrians, can survive the process of development. We think it can, and we think it will give coherence to what is now an incoherent urban structure.

BLDD: You are principal for design of the New York City Convention Center, a project that may bring about coherent development in a previously undeveloped urban area. I have heard that the convention center is "wide enough to hold two 747s, wingtip to wingtip, tall enough to accommodate the Statue of Liberty, with more than fifteen football fields of exhibition space." One basic question: why the size and the density there?

JIF: It has two exhibit halls—one approximately half a million square feet, another approximately a quarter of a million square feet—support spaces, and a hundred-odd meeting rooms. It is effectively not one building but five buildings, with a series of entrances off Eleventh Avenue. The exhibit halls are designed as if they were a series of buildings along that street. The building is very low, except at the formal or symbolic center, where it rises very high. Most convention centers are not used by the non-convention-going citizenry, as they're usually on the outskirts of cities, surrounded by parking lots. They don't generate development. In this case we placed public registration, entry, food, and theme display adjoining public, unprogrammed space on Eleventh Avenue, making the avenue a populated, theatrical part of the building and thereby bringing some life to that street. This building is located in an old railroad yard in a totally underdeveloped area. There's little to preserve there—no jobs, no factories, no housing—just outdated railyards. If density is too great in midtown, the place where density *can* occur is on the west side of Manhattan, south of Forty-second Street. But you need a catalyst for

Continental City, Los Angeles, Calif., isometric drawing

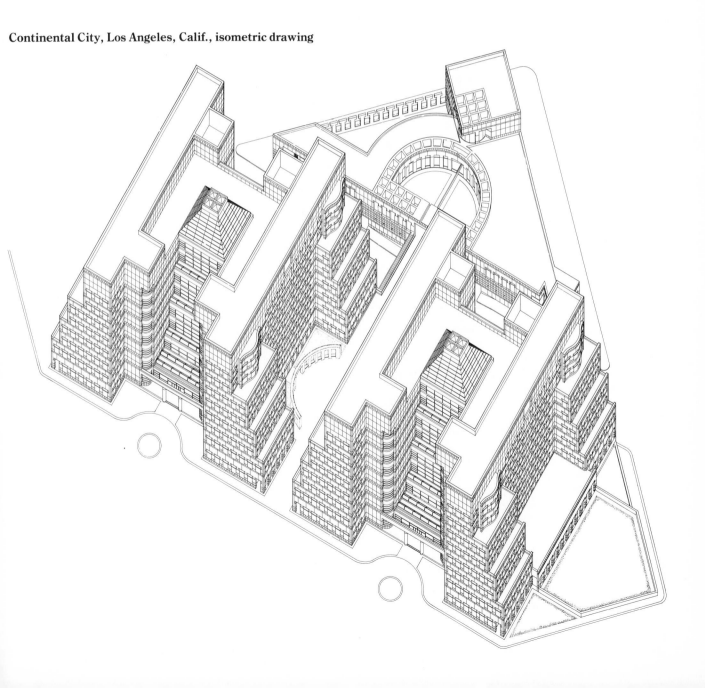

development. It's not enough just to say, "I'm going to build something." You have to prove that it's a viable area first. The Convention Center will generate enough traffic to create active, self-policing streets, which will then generate development activity. So movement can take place from the overdeveloped center of Manhattan to the edge, with its wonderful views of the Hudson. I think it's an appropriate place to have the Convention Center. It will not only develop a potential for new growth but will move growth away from other areas as well.

BLDD: What kind of growth do you think it will engender in that area?

JIF: It will engender a modest, slow growth. Some hotels will move there, then some related office buildings, and eventually restaurants, housing. Offices and businesses that cannot afford midtown rents, such as architecture and engineering firms, are already moving to that area. I think it is New York's next frontier. But the area needed something else to spur development: it needed a symbolic presence. And that is the purpose of the Great hall. Not only will we have a building and activity there, but we will have a symbolic space that is open to all the people of New York.

BLDD: You've called that symbolic presence a "great honorific space." The great hall of the Convention Center towers 160 feet above the pedestrian entrance level to create a ceremonial space. What do you see as the real function of this space? What do you predict or hope that the response will be of those who enter it?

JIF: It's important for New York City to have an unprogrammed space like the Grand Palais. It can hold ships, display airplanes; there could be laser shows, great sculptural events, large public gatherings. I hope the space will become part of the arsenal of New York cultural spaces. When people know a place is there, they'll use it.

BLDD: Why don't you give us some statistics? Describe the size, the scope, the cost of this enormous project, the largest one in New York.

JIF: It's between 1.7 and 1.8 million square feet. The upper floor, exclusive of the galleria and the great hall, is forty-five feet high, with ninety-foot spans. It stretches from Thirty-fourth to Thirty-eighth Street and from Eleventh to Twelfth Avenue. Someone calculated that you could walk twenty-five miles through booths on the upper level. The importance of the size is that it will allow New York to compete for the biggest trade shows, which generate a lot of income.

BLDD: How much will the project cost?

JIF: The building itself costs $239 million. The land costs, project costs, and associated costs make up the total of $375 million. It is important to remember that a building this vast, and essentially blank, needs some special nuance, but there isn't much money and a lot of it goes for technical support. The floors, for example, have to support 400 pounds per square foot. Air-conditioning and electrical loads are extremely high—compressed air must be provided everywhere, the plumbing requirements are large. Consequently, the technical aspects of the building tend to burn up most of the money.

BLDD: Have the recent budgetary cuts and fiscal crises faced by both the city and state of New York been burning up some of your budget, too?

JIF: Not really. But we did buy this building in bits and pieces during a time of unprecedented high inflation in construction costs in New York City. Because of this we've had to cut the building back a bit a number of times—not in its function but in its size, in its architecture.

BLDD: How did you do that?

JIF: What you lose are the nuances. The galleria was intended to be skylit, which it no longer is. It now becomes an interior theatrical place like Times Square, but I would have preferred it skylit. Some of the nuances of finish may have disappeared. What does remain is the conception we had from the beginning—a strong musculature defined in units of space that can symbolically articulate entrances, levels, and public spaces. I would not be willing to cut anything that compromised the essence of the architecture.

BLDD: Your design could have been a massive, hulking structure, but what you've attempted is a latter-day Crystal Palace that is transparent by night and reflects the skyline by day. What was most challenging about working with this space and structure?

JIF: I've always been very impressed with the Crystal Palace, which was wonderful because it was both airy and solid; it had a sense of being light but also had great form. The first drawing I made of the Convention Center—with a great barrel vault and a smaller barrel vault across it—was derived from the Crystal Palace. We then put it in a drawer and never looked at it again, but that was one of the triggering impulses.

The single most challenging aspect about working with this space was the scale. I discovered that at a certain point size becomes more important than scale. Then it's no longer possible to talk of a human scale. You talk of the relative size of things. The other problem was to make comprehensible spaces within the building. To do that, we developed many discrete spaces of a size not normally associated with that kind of spatial formation. The overwhelming problem was how to make this huge monolith, which had very little money for nuances of architecture, behave in the city. One of the devices we used was breaking it down into ninety-foot bays and successively articulating those bays. The last challenge, not architectural but practical, was to fit all of the technical requirements into this envelope.

BLDD: You've described the Convention Center as both a soap bubble and an elephant dancing on its toes. I wonder if you'll elaborate on these somewhat unusual, if not obscure, metaphors.

JIF: It's a soap bubble because it has a very thin, overall film of uniform structure. For example, the walls and the ceilings of the great hall are composed of the same material and structural framework and are covered by a thin membrane of glass, a soap bubble. From the inside that's what it looks like, and also from the outside at night. During the day, when it is reflective, it looks like a very large thing coming down on points—the inflection points around the entrances. That's the elephant dancing. The entrances are very important. A big building ought to tell you where to enter, and the interior spaces should reveal themselves clearly. You should not need a map to find your way. So we carved out large openings at the main hall level and at the lower mezzanine level.

BLDD: Could you explain how your office works? How do you divide or share the work on each project?

JIF: We are a group practice, which means that we practice together but more or less independently within the group. We have 260 people and six partners, three of whom are principally design partners, three principally management partners.

BLDD: Who comprises each group?

JIF: I. M. Pei, Harry Cobb, and I are principally design partners, although we do other things.

BLDD: Who are the other three partners, and what are their duties?

JIF: The other three partners are Eason Leonard, Leonard Jacobson, and Werner Wandelmaier. They're primarily management partners, although they're all architects and do other things as well. For example, I often team up with Werner

New York Exposition and Convention Center, New York, N.Y. Above: rendering of Great Hall interior, below: rendering of Great Hall at night

Warwick Post Oak Hotel, Houston, Tex.

Wandelmaier, who is the partner for management on the Convention Center. He manages the process, which is one of the most difficult I have ever encountered because it's such a very big job and it's in the public sector. He uses his judgment when we come to design or construction issues. We are all architects and we all participate in the making of architecture.

BLDD: Who decides who the partner in charge of design is for any given project?

JIF: Often an inquiry is addressed to a particular partner, who will then usually follow it up. It's not very formal.

BLDD: How did you "win" the Convention Center?

JIF: I didn't really win the Convention Center. I was a natural

for it because of my Miesian background. We knew from the beginning that the Convention Center was primarily a building that would have to depend on its own skeletal formation because there would be no money available for an applied emblematic architecture. It was the kind of large-scale project with lots of bones that I am presumably best at.

BLDD: So then are you the person who designed the Convention Center?

JIF: I was principally responsible for the design. I discussed it with I. M. in the very beginning of the project, and he had strong programmatic notions that he articulated.

BLDD: What were those notions?

JIF: That we ought to give ten percent of our project to the public and ought to make an accessible public space central to the design. This was strongly generative in the design process of the building. It's important to think of this building as one that has a public face. As soon as you think of it as a place that's always open to the public, your formal notions undergo a certain shift. A public space must be visible. It must have a certain address. We drove around the site, and as our taxi went up over the Thirty-fifth Street viaduct, at the highest point between Thirty-fourth and Thirty-eighth, we looked at each other and said, "This is the front door." So it's difficult to separate each other's contributions.

BLDD: How did you come together almost thirty years ago?

JIF: Harry Cobb joined up with I.M. at Harvard. They've been together longer than I have been with them. I was friendly with Leonard Brooks, who was in the fledgling Pei office working for Bill Zeckendorf, and in 1956 I was recruited. I met I. M. and Harry and liked them immensely. I was impressed with the work they were doing, which was not the doctrinaire modernist work common at the time. I was delighted to join the office, and it was a very good thing.

BLDD: Are you still delighted?

JIF: Yes, I am.

BLDD: Is it still a good thing?

JIF: Yes.

BLDD: What allows you to sustain that pleasure in this association? It's a long time . . .

JIF: It is a long time, and there are a variety of reasons. One, it is nice to work with people you like. Two, the fact that it is a group practice means that we have resources greater than any one of us could muster by himself. We are able to support an office with architects who have special information, special knowledge, and special talents, and make architecture in and with that group. We also can have a larger office to tackle bigger projects than any of us could tackle by ourselves. Consequently, we're able to deal with projects like the Convention Center—which can be an unforgiving project, mostly because it's so huge and in the public sector—and with projects like Mission Bay. We have talented planners and urban designers in the office. Because of this ability to handle both large and small work, we have a variety of projects in the public and private sectors, which enlivens our practice. I think we all share a certain value system and a desire to act in a larger realm. We often differ stylistically and intuitively. If you look at our buildings, you'll see they are not all alike. Since we are all growing and changing, it's hard to characterize our differences any more precisely. But we do share certain values that are definable. We share the idea that context is important; that it is not necessary for buildings to shout; that buildings should be good neighbors, which does not mean they have to be wallflowers. We share the notion of the city as a positive concept. We feel that the making of spaces and fragments of space creates the continuity of the city.

BLDD: Assuming this community of interest has prevailed, what do you see as the major differences?

JIF: The major differences may be ones of stylistic development. For example, all three of us naturally deal with geometries, but Harry's geometries are different from I. M. 's geometries, which in turn are different from my own. Harry is much more of a minimalist. I. M. uses his geometries in such a way that large forms tend to interact asymmetrically. I am beginning to work with images that are fragmented, that only act as a whole when seen with other building parts. Form is obviously only a part of architecture, but it's an important part—we know all buildings by their formal edges and limits. We share notions about directness of the use of materials and directness of expression in buildings. The value of our buildings comes from what they are, not from an arbitrary placement of a symbolic coat-of-arms over them. It's in the nuance of the development that we differ. Our new buildings bear some of these distinctions.

BLDD: Would you cite some of the buildings?

JIF: I. M. 's Fragrant Hill Hotel in Peking, Harry's work in Portland and some of his new towers. The work I'm doing in California is very different from what I've done before. A somewhat flawed building, but one that is very important for me, is the Warwick Hotel in Houston. Somehow it went out of control, but there were wonderful things in it that I loved.

BLDD: Why is it flawed, and in what way is it out of control?

JIF: Well, it's not all of a piece, and it therefore has problems of coherence and cohesiveness.

BLDD: What did you learn from it?

JIF: I learned how to look again at building surfaces. As for spaces, I learned to be looser about their aggregation within buildings. It became clear that programmatically complex buildings can support a variety of attitudes—in the way stone is handled, for instance, or the way buildings can be fragmented and formal spaces manipulated inside buildings. This building was an adventure into the unknown.

BLDD: Having as one of your partners a man who has such a public face has obvious benefits, and perhaps, some less obvious limitations. How do you feel about being in close association with such a well-known and admired public figure?

JIF: Sometimes it's wonderful and sometimes difficult. I owe a great deal to I. M. I'm not sure that I would have developed my views as I did if it hadn't been for my association with him. I think we all get along very well together. We are able to bounce ideas off each other. Many architects become isolated and find they have no dialogue with anybody. All of that is very important to me. I suppose you find a best way of working and, if it finally becomes unsatisfactory, you stop doing that. This is obviously not unsatisfactory for me at this point.

BLDD: You have mentioned a number of times the importance of architects taking risks. What are the biggest risks you've taken in your career?

JIF: The biggest risk I ever took was giving up a comfortable methodology. The greatest risk all architects take is embarking on a new way of looking at the making of architecture. That's an enormous risk, since we all know the language we inherit is worked out. The big risk is to abandon that and start again.

BLDD: When did you do that in a manifest way?

JIF: After I finished 88 Pine, which was my last overtly modernist building. That was in 1970.

BLDD: Soon thereafter, you left practice and returned to teaching. Almost twenty years after you were graduated from the Illinois Institute of Technology, you returned there as dean. That was from 1975 to 1978.

JIF: That's correct. I had been teaching all along, but never full time.

BLDD: What prompted you to do that?

JIF: A number of things. I felt an indebtedness to the profession. It's been my life, and I wanted to repay some of that. I went to IIT because I thought there was something I could contribute. I knew that the school had not moved, that it still had problems of being standardized and didactic, problems that were twenty and thirty years old. It had not built on its heritage in any significant way. I thought I could move the school and help it evolve.

BLDD: Were you able to do so?

JIF: I was able to bring in some good people and influence others, but in the end I was not able to give the school new life. The school was heavily tenured and the tenured people were all students of second- and third-generation students of the master. It had become an academy.

BLDD: At that time you criticized other schools of architecture for "trying to teach poetry." What did you mean by that statement?

JIF: You cannot teach poetry, but you can expose people to poetry. In schools of architecture you have to teach a number of things. You have to teach the art and making of architecture. If you don't know how to make architecture, the art becomes mere appliqué. There may be nothing wrong with appliqué, but it is not enough. Unless you learn how to think about buildings in a buildable way, you limit your possibilities as an architect. If I said that you cannot teach poetry, I probably meant it cannot be taught superficially or separated from its medium.

BLDD: What's the most important thing you've learned from your students?

JIF: Free inquiry, the ability to see things with a fresh perspective and to question what you believe. I'm always amazed that while students stumble a great deal and do some perfectly awful things, one student suddenly does something wonderful, something you hadn't thought out, hadn't thought was possible. It gets you thinking all over again.

BLDD: Did you ever expect your life to unfold the way it has?

JIF: Never. Years ago when I was in school I thought I would never want to come to New York City, never want to do big projects, never want to work with many people. Everything I thought I would never want to do I relish doing today.

BLDD: If you had to do it all over again, what would you do differently?

JIF: I'd probably do the same thing over again. I would have started experimenting a bit earlier. I regret that it took me so long to free my thinking processes.

BLDD: Is there any single dream project that you would like to do if you had the funds and the assistance?

JIF: Yes, the kind of projects that most architects would love to do: those relatively unprogrammed, highly symbolic buildings.

BLDD: They sound like religious structures to me.

JIF: Maybe museums, religious or small public structures, structures that allow for a great deal of manipulation of space, form, and meaning.

BLDD: And what next for you?

JIF: More of the same, and perhaps my dream . . .

ROMALDO GIURGOLA

Romaldo Giurgola is a distinguished architect and teacher. He is currently the Ware Professor of Architecture in Columbia University's Department of Architecture and was previously the chairman of that department. A widely admired designer of commercial and residential buildings, schools, libraries, and government centers, he was the recipient of the Gold Medal of the American Institute of Architects in 1982.

BLDD: You were born in Rome, a city noted for its architectural splendor. How much of an influence was that early environment on you?

RG: I don't think anyone could not be influenced by Rome. Even for one not born there, Rome leaves a very strong impression. Living in Rome caused me to consider architecture as a link with the past and to understand certain fundamental values with which I'm convinced architecture has to be approached. Rome communicates the spirit that an environment can, through manufactured elements, be just as human and as natural as one could possibly want it to be.

BLDD: You have many links to the past, including one very close to home. Your father was a Beaux-Arts architect. How did his work or ideas influence your own architectural philosophy?

RG: He had the good fortune of doing very few buildings and concentrating on only a few clients. He lived in a small town before coming to Rome. He built four or five buildings along one street for a friend. To him it seemed he had covered the whole world of experience in architecture. Those precise and fundamental experiences had a great educational value for me.

BLDD: By what architectural periods or styles have you been most influenced?

RG: That's difficult to say; I cannot profess an influence from any particular style. All styles have influenced my thinking in architecture, although I may have an inclination, a preference for some types of architecture. I feel most interested in, enthusiastic about, and emotionally connected to the architecture of the Renaissance.

BLDD: For what reasons?

RG: Because during the Renaissance a great number of ele-

ments coalesced in architecture: the pleasure of living, the notion of the importance of the workplace, the relationship between the building and the city, the attitude toward the landscape and the natural environment, and a sense of connection with the past (Renaissance architecture had strong roots in Roman and Greek architecture). All those factors were there in the precise architectural language that evolved. I feel sympathetic to that attitude.

BLDD: What factors do you think made possible the greatest architecture of the Renaissance?

RG: The fact that the architects were concerned with changing situations. They dealt with the new problems of life and they tried to respond directly to them. They used a language that they developed in part by looking at what had existed before. Their architecture had true resonance—the ability to link with another time to create continuity with the past, rather than a breach. They were able to appreciate their changing world. I don't think that the Duomo in Florence, considered the first building of the Renaissance, would have been possible without the breakthrough of viewing the church as an important place in the community, a place that had to be big enough for great meetings.

BLDD: So was the design engendered by the church, the people, or the architect?

RG: By the people—by the change in the dynamics of life, the change in the nature of assembly. The freedom brought about by this change produced new characteristics of space to which the architect responded. Brunelleschi, often thought of as the first Renaissance architect, worked very hard with the various committees that were building this cathedral, this public place. He worked for many years with the masons and everybody involved. He was not the dictator of forms, as one would imagine from later interpretations, particularly those of the Beaux-Arts professors. He was working directly in the field with the other workers and responding to the needs of society at that particular moment.

BLDD: In your view, does the contribution of the people still play a significant role in the design of the built environment?

RG: My opinion may not be a popular one, but I definitely think so. Society is the real motor of any new architectural idea. You can see that the houses architects build for themselves are usually pretty awful. An architect without a client is really a nonentity. Architecture is the confluence of a tremendous number of factors and includes the contributions of a great number of people.

BLDD: That's a very humanistic view. I suspect that some clients, in relation to their architects, feel like nonentities, to use your word.

RG: That may be possible. But I really think that architecture doesn't have an audience. Because it belongs to everyone, it has only participants. It's a peculiar art in this sense, with very peculiar connotations.

BLDD: Do you think that people sometimes feel they are outside of the participatory process, that they are simply recipients of, rather than collaborators in, the very buildings in which they live, work, and play?

RG: This is unfortunately so. In attacking this problem, I've always tried to bring as many people as possible into the making of architecture. I do that in the office by bringing in different talents—not just architects or technicians, but also people from different fields.

BLDD: For example?

RG: Archaeology and technology in particular, but also people from other areas of endeavor such as literature.

BLDD: What can someone who's involved or trained in literature contribute to the work of an architect?

RG: Having people from different disciplines produces a critical evaluation of the various ideas that occur within a project. We find that especially helpful in the beginning. The kind of criticism that emerges is spontaneous, not articulated by intellectual preconceptions.

BLDD: To pursue your idea of architects being responsive to the needs of the people, can you tell us what kinds of spaces people need or demand currently?

RG: More than need, I'm thinking more precisely of the aspirations of people, because needs alone never produce anything great. If you answer to a need, you satisfy the momentary situation. I think architecture should really be involved with aspirations. This you have to search for. People have aspirations of various sorts; sometimes they become group aspirations. These have to be identified in order to arrive at the development of form, the understanding of space, and so on. Functional problems are resolved by answering to pure needs, which any architect in this country is very experienced at doing. The hard part is responding to vague and latent aspirations that are either in the body of society or in individuals.

BLDD: What prompted you to come to the United States more than thirty years ago?

RG: It was a mixture of chance and circumstances. I was asked to come to teach at the University of Pennsylvania with G. Holmes Perkins and Louis Kahn.

BLDD: Did you first come to New York as a student?

RG: Yes. I was in New York as a Fulbright Fellow at Columbia from 1949 to 1951. Then I went back to Italy, and I returned here a few years later. I knew that Louis Kahn was teaching at Penn, and I was quite interested in that proximity to him.

BLDD: What was your first trip to this country like? What kind of impression did it make?

RG: The first thing that shocked me when I arrived on the boat was the huge advertisement over Riverside Drive—it was for a refrigerator. It obliterated all the architecture of the place.

This was unthinkable, coming from Europe, to see something that took up three or four blocks of frontage. It introduced the country in a picturesque but also formidable way. The dynamics were such that you had to respond to situations as they emerged, always being ready to give an answer.

BLDD: Did you see that as a challenge?

RG: I certainly did. I also thought, when I became more acquainted with the place, that here things get used and disposed of very quickly. But there is also an urge, a desire, an aspiration toward the assessment of fundamental aspects of life throughout this country's history. There have been periods, such as the time of the country's founding, in which there was great conviction in the building of America. There was an assessment then of the value of land, an assessment of the relationship of man and nature; literature was rich in this kind of reference and was developing a more intellectual and abstract character. These aspects have to be assessed for architecture to develop from fundamental issues and not from superficial ones.

BLDD: When you returned to America you went to Philadelphia and taught side by side with several architects, including Louis Kahn. What did you learn from his work? Was his most important contribution as a teacher, a theorist, or an architect?

RG: My answer to the previous question, in which I used the word "fundamental," comes very much from his teaching, his attitude toward architecture and toward life in general. He excelled in all three of the aspects you mentioned. He was a tremendous teacher and a tremendous architect. I think he has still to be discovered as an architect. Critics have associated his work too closely with Beaux-Arts architecture, only because he was not biased against it. But he went beyond the Beaux-Arts in his thinking and in his work as an artist.

BLDD: What leads you to that conclusion?

RG: He was concerned with making architecture as a response to new situations. He was always searching for the nature of things, why things were the way they were—what it meant, for instance, for an association to meet in a monastery or a convention hall; what happened in order for them to start doing so; what kind of space they developed; what fundamental shapes and forms created that space; how the particular kind of space they determined became evocative of the particular action that took place in that space. "Room" was the word that Kahn used all the time. He thought in terms of rooms, architecture as an assembly or an association of rooms. That was a tremendous revolution in architecture. Before that everybody was talking about floating space, about "copenetrated" spaces like the ranch house, the split level, and so on. One of the characteristics of the American house at that time was that there was no place to sit because all the spaces were combined. Insisting upon the value of the room as a primordial element of architecture was a tremendous breakthrough. From Kahn came a host of architects who think in the same way, who take that idea as a point of departure. I'm doing so myself, I hope.

BLDD: Do you see your architecture as using Kahn's work as a point of departure? Do you see your work as an extension or a continuation of the ideas expressed in his buildings?

RG: That would be too ambitious for me to say. I can say only that I hope I learned a lot from his work and I hope he would consider my work a worthy continuation.

BLDD: What do you think he would have thought about some of the recent developments in architecture?

RG: I think he would be very disconcerted by some of them. During his lifetime he was adamantly against "the circumstantial"—that was what he used to call the reliance upon circumstance, which, in turn, has fostered the pluralism we are witnessing now in architecture.

BLDD: Could you describe in more detail this circumstantial art that he always denounced? What did he mean?

RG: All that was accidental or incidental in architecture. According to Kahn, a room first of all had to evoke a special condition, whether it was for quietness, isolation, and contemplation or for a great, lively gathering. These characteristics were fundamental. The shape of a room, the color of the fabric, the molding—these were of descriptive value but were not the elements to start with.

BLDD: Do you share that perception?

RG: I think so.

BLDD: What is Kahn's role today? Is he as influential as he was at the time of his death more than ten years ago?

RG: Yes. In fact, I think we will increasingly hear talk of him and there will be a rediscovery of his value.

BLDD: When do you expect that to happen, and what will be the catalyst?

RG: Pretty soon. We will have to make many new assessments. The situation has often been like a merry-go-round in the last few years, but now we have to make a somber assessment of what we can afford. There will be an increasing need for spaces designed to respond to the aspirations of the public at large. Because many public areas have been deteriorating, there will be a need to move toward making sounder places for school or work. One of the future directions of architecture will be the development of the workplace. We assume that present office spaces are O.K. But if you think about this layering of floors with people isolated in the middle of the building, away from windows and with constant "conditioning" of the air, it really is not a good environment. The factory has the same problem. There will be a movement to develop better places in which to spend the workday. The design has to be approached not from a circumstantial or fashionable standpoint but from a very fundamental one, based on questions of what working people do and how they relate to each other.

BLDD: What functional innovations can you envision in the workplace?

RG: Many. For instance, the creation of a certain amount of intimacy and isolation. For many years architects have worked with the open plan idea in an interior space. We now can sense the importance of individual space, of individual rooms with windows. In the factories, the notion of smaller teams of workers will create smaller spaces, different kinds of workshops, and so forth. Working people desire more contact with the natural environment. Those aspirations will create new forms in architecture. Contact with nature will be one of the most important considerations in the future of architecture.

BLDD: When you were starting out in your working life, while waiting for the right building to come along, like other young architects you were busy in another field. Tell us about your early working experiences.

RG: I worked in a publishing company. I had to have my New York experience, I suppose, and a job was available. It was very freeing. I lost all my prejudices. In Europe I would never have done a thing like that, because there I was practically born an architect. You have to do just that one thing, nothing else.

BLDD: I was under the impression that there were so many architects currently being trained in Italy that it was perfectly acceptable to become a graphic or interior designer—not like this country, where, until the recent state of the economy, architects might look askance at that kind of employment.

RG: It's true now. In my time it wasn't like that.

BLDD: So, freed from those old strictures, in this new place, what did you do?

RG: I worked for a publishing company and became art director first of a magazine called *Interiors,* then of *Industrial Design.* I worked for a few years doing that and enjoyed it.

BLDD: What did you learn from it? Did it in any way influence your later practice of architecture?

RG: I don't think it did. I always kept in the back of my mind the fact that I was thinking as an architect and contributing to architecture in some form. Work is always good, any kind of work. In architecture you learn from all sorts of experiences. Architecture is hard work in the context of art, if you wish. But it's essentially the hard work of putting people together, of developing something conceptually, of designing or drafting, of making drawings and sketches; then going to the field, learning about the materials and the methods of construction, and following up by talking with the people in the field. The last time I was in Australia, most of my time was spent with a construction manager, a field manager, and our team leaders. You have to become responsible in architecture for all sorts of things. You have to feel responsible. Otherwise you are not an architect. You mentioned architects who eventually follow some other path—that is fine, but they are then no longer architects, they are something else. An architect who has a good conceptual thought and promotes the idea but never really touches the mud in the field does not experience the full spectrum of the art of architecture. To a great extent it is an art. Architecture is like a river that starts from a very small spring and doesn't become substantial until it joins other streams. Without the participation of many elements and many people, architecture remains the demonstration of theory, and this is not good. You make a theory, you make a box, and that's the end of it. But people have to live in these boxes, they have to submit to a certain way of life only because there's nothing better. This makes life in the long run quite miserable. It's not for architecture to illustrate the contradictions of life, but rather to come spontaneously from the resolution of opposing

Wright Brothers Memorial Visitor Center, Kill Devil Hills, N.C., rendered perspective

forces. There have been buildings of pure architecture that were not designed by architects. You find a shelter in the country and you marvel at how wonderful it is. That's because there has been a real confluence at that point. No genius has designed that particular shelter, but it gives a tremendous aesthetic experience and has value. I wish I could do something like that—become like the anonymous group of people who conceived that shelter.

BLDD: In 1958 you started an architectural firm, Mitchell/Giurgola, with Ehrman Mitchell. Its first building received nationwide recognition. Before we talk about the Wright Brothers Memorial Visitor Center, though, could you tell us about your firm? To begin with, how did you and Ehrman Mitchell come together?

RG: We'd met in Philadelphia in an office where he was working.

BLDD: Were you working in the same office?

RG: No. I never really worked for anyone in any office. I was working with Kahn at school. For some strange reason I had never worked in an office with another architect. Only in the very beginning, in Brooklyn, when I was at Columbia as a training peer of the school. But Mitchell and I met in Philadelphia. It was during a period of economic depression, and at that time the government was very generous in providing jobs. Our designing the Wright Brothers museum wouldn't have been possible if it weren't for the good intentions of the government.

BLDD: Tell us about this first project. What were your major concerns?

RG: The place where the Wright Brothers took off, Kitty Hawk, North Carolina, is in the middle of sand dunes in an open field. It was a difficult site since there was nothing that made it recognizable from a distance. The problem was to erect a shelter for the first motorized kite. From the beginning we wanted to make a gesture from a great distance, so we made the roof of the room a peculiar shape. From a distance you can see that something different is going on there; it serves as a signal, like a white handkerchief. Then we divided the space into the exhibit proper, the terrace where people would look at the field, and the small museum. It was a very small building, but very firm, contrasting with the shifting environment of the sand dunes.

BLDD: Who did what in that project? How did you and Ehrman Mitchell divide or share your duties? How do you do that now?

RG: We still work in the same way. We are sort of complementary to each other. He has more administrative and technical talent, so I have found a great deal of help in the collaboration. Every architect wants criticism all the time, and the best help is criticism from someone with a different point of view.

BLDD: From the beginning your perspective has been a very open one. More than twenty years ago you wrote in the Yale architectural journal, *Perspecta,* an essay entitled "The Realism of the Partial Vision." What were some of the ideas in that influential essay? Are they still central to your work?

RG: Yes, they're still important. The title of the piece refers to the fact that I don't think of architecture as a whole. I don't think we can conceive some absolute form that we then force people to fit into. We should think in terms of separate elements, parts that we can bring a human scale to, parts that are friendly, parts that you can touch and relate to—starting with the door, the entry, and moving on from there. You have to study the parts well. The architecture of the Renaissance was born that way. Before Brunelleschi arrived at the design of the Church of San Lorenzo, he was very much concerned with a single element, the arcade of the Ospedale degli Innocenti, a unit he found perfectly proportioned in terms of the size of the column, the capital, the dimensions of the arch. Once that element was clearly established, it became part of the whole. I always feel that the whole is something to work towards.

BLDD: You still feel that the building is a fragment of the larger whole and not an object that is complete unto itself.

RG: Absolutely right. In the city, in particular, our buildings really are fragments, a variety of instants that exist in the city as well as in nature. I think one of the future tasks of architects will be rediscovering that wonderful symmetry between natural and man-made elements that the Greeks, for instance, achieved in the positioning of architecture in space, the scale of elements, the choice of land, the character of growth, and so forth.

BLDD: Then what is the function of a place in the city, particularly in a city of monumental scale?

RG: The way the program develops within a city today, most places are not self-sufficient. An auditorium, for instance, could be made to serve different functions—one day for a school, another day for another kind of organization—and there could be a continuous exchange of similar situations throughout the city. In terms of offering something to the city, you see more of this today in office buildings, many of which have tremendous atriums. But at the moment they all seem to be parts that are dissociated from one another. The task is to find those connections.

BLDD: What ideas do you have for making the human element more predominant in a dense urban center?

RG: In architecture it's the quality of the space rather than the taste that matters. We have interior design, but how much do we work on making rooms where you can isolate yourself and develop some kind of interior life? The room becomes not something casual, simply a place to spend your time in a particular way, but a very intimate event of your making. The room is probably the form that best conveys the potential to improve all possible human characterization in architecture. Space has always talked to people with the same quality of language that is used to express the most vital concerns. When a farmer goes into a cathedral, he doesn't care if it is neoclassic, Renaissance, or Gothic. What remains in his mind is the emotional experience produced by the quality of the space. Either it is evocative or it is simply a void. In this sense space is the fundamental constituent of architecture. Taste is not. Taste could be the circumstantial description of a specific moment. It is too little to rely upon. I'm not denying that function of taste, but in architecture it doesn't have the role we sometimes pretend it has.

BLDD: One prevailing taste in architecture today is the notion that buildings should fit into the surrounding context. How important to your own work is contextualism?

RG: Very much so. A building should have resonance, the ability to develop links with the past as it is represented by other forms and other buildings. It's not a question of being a good neighbor but of establishing a continuity so that the city presents itself as history, as a living place, and not as an assortment of competing elements. You see, I never consider New York as an assembly of buildings. It's just one building.

BLDD: And Philadelphia?

RG: Well, Philadelphia is a little different. Philadelphia has a history that still maintains a characterization in parts that are clearly discernible. In the few projects we did there we tried to be sensitive to that.

BLDD: I mention Philadelphia not only because you have taught and worked there, but also because you were a con-

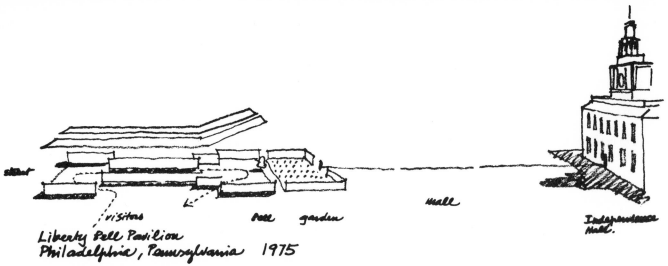

Liberty Bell Pavilion, Philadelphia, Pa., rendered sketch/diagrammatic section

sultant to the City Planning Commission. Would you describe your buildings in Philadelphia that are mindful of their context?

RG: There are a few. One was the pavilion for the Liberty Bell in Independence Mall. It was originally located under the tower of Independence Hall. For the bicentennial year it was decided to move the bell outside. Because of the tremendous number of people who come to see the bell, the first question was the location. Another consideration was what the bell represented. The bell is really a folk tale, not a monumental object. We received recommendations that the bell should be displayed in an amphitheater with guards in front and all sorts of rhetoric surrounding it. We elected to make something more like a gazebo in a park, but to design it so that the bell would be inside the building. We protected the bell with a roof, and there is a little garden in front so it also can be seen from the outside. The most important element was the placing of the bell to be visually related to the tower so that there would be a discourse. We developed a room around the bell so that people could get close and have a good time and good reminiscences looking at it. I was quite happy with the experience, and I've been told that people enjoy it. That's most satisfying for an architect to hear.

BLDD: The significance of order in architecture is critical to an understanding of your work. Could you elaborate on the architectural function of order, especially within an urban environment?

RG: I think of order not as a preconceived geometrical assessment, but as a sublimation of many aspects—of certain dynamics of life, certain views and conceptions. The city develops an order of its own; it is a body that survives by being organized in a particular way. It's difficult to disrupt that order; it can only evolve and change. When you build, you have to be very concerned with this urban order and at the same time concerned with the natural, geological order, the configuration of the land. It's funny to see houses and buildings designed for flat land but sited on a hill, suspended in air. What makes it seem funny is the lack of a sense of order, of relationship with the natural land configuration. You see, there *is* an order to things. Even an old part of town has a kind of order. If you look at New York's Chinatown, for example, it has an order all its own, a fabric that you have to be concerned with if you build there. You cannot design totally contrary to that order.

BLDD: You once said that you object to the use of an architectural vocabulary that is patined by time. What did you mean by that?

RG: I was talking about trying to camouflage yourself with the environment.

BLDD: Let's use Chinatown as an example. What would be a desirable sense of order? To what would you object in that environment?

RG: The sense of order there is in the particular configuration of Chinatowns all over the world. There is a proximity and rhythm of shops open to the street all the time. It's not a curlicue or any other kind of decoration that creates its special impact.

BLDD: It's not the pagoda?

RG: Not the pagoda. That's right. It's a particular order to which the rhythm of the inhabitants' lives is adjusted—or perhaps it is created by the rhythm of their lives. When you create a building in a natural environment, you don't do better by using natural wood or by trying to minimize the building's impact by disguising it in nature. You can be absolutely independent, but you can't ignore the environment. An element built in a particular place has to respect the order of nature: the difference between the levels, the sloping of a surface, the character of surfaces, but especially the overall configuration of the natural site.

BLDD: Is architecture essentially a personal vision or is it a joint vision shared by the client, the banker, the developer, and even the community?

RG: I would say that it consists of *many* personal visions, many different perceptions of architecture.

BLDD: But who has the last word?

RG: The person who uses the place, really. It's strange, but when I finish a building I always feel that something is gone. People ask if I ever go back to see a building.

BLDD: Do you?

RG: Very rarely. I should go more, but I feel a detachment—something is finished, and I am already developing certain moments for somebody else.

BLDD: Are you also saying that the process is more important for you than the result of that process?

RG: Both are important, but the result is not the final, frozen result. If you go to Rome and you live in a Renaissance building, you will find it perfectly comfortable if you have present-day amenities. It is perfectly agreeable to live in a room of the Renaissance with a painted ceiling. That is essentially because although it wasn't intended to be a bedroom, it was meant to be a space that would last forever. To develop a dimension that has value in time forever—that is the permanence of architecture. That is why when we talk of architecture that could be obsolete in twenty-five years, we are not really talking of architecture. We are perhaps talking of an efficient capsule for the moment, but it doesn't have anything to do with architecture.

BLDD: Are you interested in the use of historical elements in architecture, or are you opposed to it?

RG: I'm not interested in the use of historical elements per se. I'm interested in the dimension of architecture that has permanence. People in the past have also thought in that way. In a medieval village some things had temporary value, others permanent value. People were very concerned with that difference. I think we lost something when architecture started responding to one function and developed an aesthetic that relied on that alone. When this function is over, everything is finished. Architecture is too important to be confined to the pettiness of our circumstances of life. From the worker to the architect, there's too much of an investment of effort and initiative. You wouldn't apply that to a painting: you know that once you have painted it, it will remain forever.

BLDD: Can we talk specifically about some of your projects? Some of your better-known academic buildings include a high school in Columbus, Indiana, and buildings at Swarthmore College and Columbia University. How is this kind of institutional work different from commercial work? How do your priorities change with that kind of assignment?

RG: I really don't think that there is much difference—they are both instances of life that you have to respond to—but it is true that all our commercial work has been more time-consuming and difficult. We have to go through more exploring to try to convey the different possibilities. For instance, we have been considering several projects for urban shopping centers. We don't know definitely yet if we are going to build one, but one seems to be almost in construction. This is a project we are doing in Boston that includes a shopping center and a hotel. It's near Jordan Marsh and Filene's, at the end of Washington Street. The value of being in the middle of the city had to be assessed, as well as the value of this kind of activity as a substitute for or an extension to the street. We started with the usual mall, two or three stories high, with different levels of shops, but when we scratched the surface and looked at the context of the particular place, we found that this was not the most appropriate way of looking at the project. We elaborated on the integration of open and closed space. We reduced the conventional mall to a shopping alternative that is more typical of an urban environment—the arcade. What is

Sherman Fairchild Center for the Life Sciences, Columbia University, New York, N.Y., rendered perspective elevation

good for Texas is certainly not good for Boston. I hope not, anyway! That would be the end!

BLDD: The architectural critic Ada Louise Huxtable has said in her assessment of the skyscraper that it is "this century's most stunning architectural phenomenon." Is this a view you share?

RG: It's stunning, all right. I don't know if it's important, but it certainly covers most of the world. We've just returned from Singapore, where towers are mushrooming. Yes, skyscrapers are a stunning fact.

BLDD: It's not one that pleases you, though?

RG: No. I don't think any architect really likes to do tall buildings. I would ask Philip Johnson if even he really likes to. There is nothing to them.

BLDD: There is a top and a bottom.

RG: Yes. It is all dictated by the speculative idea of taking the lot and multiplying the floors. You have to get out of it as many square feet as possible.

BLDD: How does that differ from an apartment building?

RG: At least in the apartment building there is the condition of a kind of space, a different orientation. In an office building there is not. All you have is the exploitation of a form. You can jazz it up, but it's basically a box. This is not wise architecture. It passes as architecture, but it's an exploit. It's a mechanical construction, let's say, that consists of face-lifting in some form or another. You can probably name five or six tall buildings in the history of architecture that are really important.

BLDD: What would they be?

RG: Probably one of the Chicago School buildings would be first. I would say the Reliance Building by Burnham & Root, or one of Sullivan's buildings. Perhaps Rockefeller Center, which is not just a single building but a complex. And there are pleasant ones, like the Seagram Building, which is important because it belonged to a way of seeing architecture in general, not because it's a tower. But that's about it. The rest are a merging of different kinds of ideas. But there is another issue: space being what it is, you have to build high. That is a very important factor, but how should architecture respond to those restrictions? The best answer would be to deeply and seriously reinvestigate the conditions in which man has to work, to find the values of orientation and interaction between people. Do you have to be isolated all the time in that office, or could you, for instance, have relatives come for lunch? Does the place have to have the same height of nine feet from floor to ceiling repeated forever? Could it be integrated with spaces of different dimensions? Something is changing now in that regard, especially concerning the needs of individuals within that kind of structure. Much of architecture stems from the individual's attempt to fit in, to make a place part of himself, to be at home. That's the real issue. You can say that man adapts to anything, but that is precisely the responsibility of the architect. You *can* adapt to anything, but you can also end up being crippled by adapting. You have to take things slowly in order to develop the kind of environment that makes life enjoyable. The fundamental task of architecture has always been to create an aspiration to a better life. When the Greeks built their temples—the Parthenon, for instance—at the end of the Persian Wars, there was great hope for the future of Athens. Building represented these aspirations. The building of the Vatican Palace represents a way of life, not just public relations for a cardinal or pope. Within that building there is an ordered structure of life, from the shops on the ground floor to

Competition entry for the American Institute of Architects National Headquarters Building, Washington, D.C., rendered interior perspective

the reception areas above to the place where you have an audience with the pope. It symbolizes an aspiration to a better life that everybody could take as an example. It's like that in New York, too, where people look up at penthouses because everybody wants to live in a penthouse. That is perhaps why the best parts of New York buildings are the penthouses. This kind of fundamental issue always comes up when you build, and you must take it into account—you must sit down and face the problem.

BLDD: Let's face that problem for a moment. Has architecture in modern times made for a better life?

RG: That's a very good question. In many ways it has. The modern movement has been chastised so much recently . . .

BLDD: By you too?

RG: Yes, but in a different way.

BLDD: You seem as determined as Philip Johnson to get away from the Miesian box, even though you made reference to the Seagram Building.

RG: Sure, but I've wanted that since the very beginning. It was our generation that invented that kind of building—and now our students are making the big fuss, but in a different way.

BLDD: Why is it a fuss when they discuss it and a debate when you did?

RG: Because they got off the track of sticking to fundamental issues.

BLDD: What *is* the fundamental issue?

RG: First of all it is the perception that the purpose of architecture is to continuously enhance life, not just to create a physical statement of a more comfortable life. This means we can develop unimagined attitudes toward life that are much more intimate and more relevant to our own experience. Until this attitude is everpresent, all the rest is circumstantial, as Kahn would say. All the rest is simply manipulating what the public would like to have because of their habits and their desire to be entertained. Some may object to this treatment, but they keep quiet because they don't have the strength to say anything.

BLDD: Or the forum in which to be heard. Would you answer the original question—has architecture made for a better life?

RG: Yes, and to a great extent the modern movement did do that. The activity of searching for a good home is very important for everyone, and the notion of the importance of a place to live has spread all over the world. The problem is that it was presented to people as a preconceived notion. Now that this is understood, the idea of a place to live could be more related to local conditions and local character. If you go to the middle of the Pacific—the Fiji Islands—you find the government building houses like those in Frankfurt, Germany! That's ridiculous. On the other hand, they have created an environment superior to the existing conditions, when people lived half in the sewers and half under a leaking piece of metal. In many ways architecture has done very good things for cities. We have been fortunate enough to work in Canberra, which is a stupendous new town.

BLDD: You have won numerous architectural competitions: for the American Institute of Architects National Headquarters in Washington, D.C.; the Wainwright State Office Complex in St. Louis; and, most recently, the Australian Parliament House in Canberra, on which you are now working. What is the value of the architectural competition?

RG: I think architectural competitions are always valuable. They have always existed. It's natural to compete. They held a competition for the dome of the cathedral of Florence. We submitted a design for a competition sponsored by the Fine

Arts Commission in Washington for the headquarters of the American Institute of Architects.

BLDD: That's the commission you eventually turned down?

RG: That's right. We won the competition, but then the Fine Arts Commission started to discuss things that were not, in our opinion, pertinent.

BLDD: For example?

RG: Oh, details about the configuration of the building being in an interior part of the court and so forth. This dialogue went on for quite a while. There was no dignity whatsoever in continuing this, so we decided to quit. That was it.

BLDD: You had a happier experience with the Wainwright Building in St. Louis. What was that assignment? How did you redeem the landmark Louis Sullivan building, which was close to demolition?

RG: The merit should go to the public that reacted against its demolition and to the governor, who took it on himself to buy the building, make it a state office building, and add the extension. I enjoyed doing the addition because it's serving the city very well. It's a fragment of urban environment around this queen, Sullivan's building.

BLDD: Would you describe the important project for the Australian Parliament House in Canberra? What were your design considerations? How long will construction be going on?

RG: Until 1988. We started several years ago. We have planned charts for completion of the building by the spring of 1987. All indications are that it can be built in that time, so we are quite optimistic.

BLDD: What's the scale of the project, in size and in cost?

RG: In cost it's about $300 million, and in size it's 1.5 million square feet. It's not too big. There are complexes in this country that are much bigger, but the significance of these these million-and-a-half square feet is something else. This building is a parliament house, and every inch of it belongs to the public. It's a place of work and debate for the whole nation. In that, it's a pure architectural problem. What happens there is very significant. First of all, you have to believe in what happens there, and in the particular location, too, which was defined by the basic plan that Walter Burley Griffin did for Canberra, an exceptional plan for a new city. Griffin won a competition in 1912 to design the capital for Australia. I got very excited looking at those plans. It was a plan for a garden city with a tremendous sensitivity to the articulation of the land, the configuration of the hillside and the valley.

BLDD: That is an ongoing concern of yours—the relationship of the built environment to the natural landscape.

RG: And I must say, it came very much from Griffin.

BLDD: So the 1912 plan influenced your design?

RG: Very much so. In fact our premise, in part, was to continue that plan in spirit because Griffin hadn't conceived of Parliament in that particular location. In principle we followed that plan very closely and the form itself resolved a certain condition of the geometry of the city. It's a project that completes, three-dimensionally, certain ideas that were set in the original plan for Canberra—the axis of the land and the lake and, finally, the culmination of a triangle at that particular point. But we were not imposing a structure on top of a hill. That was possible only during the Enlightenment, or with the United States Capitol and other capitol buildings throughout the country—imposing a building, making an assertion with a physical statement.

BLDD: Using buildings that way you end up with New Delhi.

RG: In a way. It happened in New Delhi with a certain sophistication. But in Canberra we felt that we had to work with the land and the site, with the confluence of different avenues and the movement of traffic. We chose to maintain the continuity between the axis of the city plan and the background so that nothing arrests a visual perception of this axis. This, I think, is the aspect of our plan that was especially appreciated. The sensitivity that the public is developing toward their land is a unique factor nowadays, and a wonderful one, especially when the land is not yet massacred by construction. Architects get very bad press now because they have been building terrible things all over the place.

BLDD: Your plans for Canberra are obviously important, but are there other places where you would like to make your statement or leave your mark?

RG: Oh yes! I'm not the kind of architect who has a vision only for a tower here or there—no. Recently we were asked, for instance, to design a subway. I thought this was a wonderful problem. I prefer to do things that come from a desire to make something better, not to create something new just for the sake of novelty.

BLDD: Is there any dream project that you haven't done yet that you'd care to?

RG: I'd like to work on a place where young people convene, a student place, a place of learning. These are the ones that I feel more inclined to work with, where young people are searching for themselves, for their own lives.

BLDD: You've written extensively on the work of architect Louis Kahn and a book on the work of Eliel and Eero Saarinen. What do you see as the Saarinens' most significant contribution?

RG: I became interested in them a long time ago. They are very much akin in temperament to some of my work, and one thing strikes me. The older Saarinen, Eliel, brought modern architecture to Scandinavia in some ways. By reassessing and working with certain traditional elements in architecture, he also introduced new characteristics into contemporary architecture. In his work there was a quality of resonance, of making a link. This was often despised during the modern movement because there was an idea that everything had to be different, new, and absolute. Saarinen realized, for instance, that craftsmanship was a very important factor. I think it's something we have to reexamine. Craftsmanship essentially means an approach to the world, making forms that are basically honest. It has to be absolutely honest, because it has to

Wainwright State Office Complex, St. Louis, Mo., rendered site plan

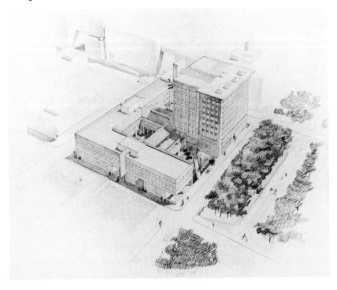

Parliament House, Canberra, Australia, rendered site plan

deal with the material and follow the nature of it very carefully. When you start to betray the material, it falls to pieces, and you cannot afford that in craftsmanship. Craftsmanship symbolizes the honest approach to work and to labor in general. I think that is very significant. Unfortunately, the modern movement took industry as its model. We submitted to the values that industry brought us. Now there is a reassessment. In many areas industry is looking again to craftsmanship. I was very interested in that in the early work of Eliel Saarinen. Eero brought that tradition into this country. He understood the industrial character of production here but also introduced the sense of craftsmanship into industry. There is a continuity in the Saarinens' work that makes a direct link with the period before the modern movement and that seems of tremendous value to the modern movement.

BLDD: Now that we've talked about model architects, what do you think makes for the model client?

RG: The ideal client—whether a person or a community—is one that is willing to sit down and think with you about the resolution of problems or about the manifestation of aspirations. The ideal client is one who presents you with an incomplete program. You have to make an assessment and a judgment yourself. If your judgment tells you that the client's is a good aspiration, then you work with him. That's a good client, not the one that presents you with a preconceived, finished program. Since it's been preconceived without a forum, without elaboration and the test of the program itself throughout a forum, it remains an abstract program and is of no value whatsoever. A vague gesture does not make architecture.

BLDD: Did you ever expect your life to unfold the way it has?

RG: In many ways, yes. I always wanted to be an architect; it was in the blood of my family, I suppose. I never thought of being anything else. Now I wish sometimes that I had done less, and better. I wish that I had taken even more time on certain things than I did. It seems that time is always lacking to arrive at a conclusion. Sometimes I feel that if I had had more doubts it probably would have been better, because both doubt and certainty make your life work.

JOAN GOODY

Joan Goody, a principal of the Boston firm Goody, Clancy & Associates, Inc., is best known for designs that are sensitive not only to the needs of their users, but to the history and fabric of the environment as well.

BLDD: You've said that you approach architecture as part of a continuum in time and space. What do you mean by that?

JG: Every building has to be regarded not only as an expression of its own era, but also as a chapter in the history of the city or locale in which it is sited. It is not an isolated object in time or space. The building should relate to the past and to the future, whose inevitable changes the building should be prepared to accommodate.

BLDD: You've also said that how we relate to what has been done before us and how we prepare for what may come is of particular interest to you. Do you think that the traditional concerns of architects are of much use in preparing for the future?

JG: By looking at how we can relate our work to that of previous eras, we get the best clues as to how we can prepare for the future. When you are asked to add a building to an existing group of buildings, looking at how previous generations of architects have added their wing or layer to the total composition provides clues as to what makes a building receptive to future changes. In that regard, I believe, we can learn from past architects.

BLDD: I know that you consider planning and building a potential problem in urban areas of the late twentieth century. Why is that?

JG: Simply because we're so much more powerful now. We have the tools to build bigger, to span further, to dig deeper, and to use a greater variety of materials than ever before. So if we make mistakes or go by rules that don't work now, it's going to be more visible. The potential for chaos is greater if each person tries to be different or creates whatever he or she thinks would be fun to do, rather than what's appropriate for the location. A greater degree of anarchy is possible now than in previous centuries.

BLDD: How are you using the word "anarchy"?

JG: I was in Japan a few years ago, and that word certainly came to mind when I was in Tokyo. In some ways that city is an example of what happens when there are no restraints, no rules, and no good manners. Japan is a country with a marvelous architectural heritage and with a current sensitivity to design on the small scale. But there seems to be a lack of regard for the urban landscape as a whole—an anomaly in a country where good manners are so strong everywhere else in society.

BLDD: Your ideal image of a community is the small European city with a sense of history, a diversity of scale, and a day-to-day social life that is accommodated in comfortable streets and squares. Is such an ideal applicable to the American community?

JG: It really is. In the American community, we call it the neighborhood. In Boston we're particularly familiar with it; Boston is a city with distinct and old neighborhoods.

BLDD: More so than other cities?

JG: The neighborhoods are geographically, ethnically, and architecturally more distinct than in many other cities. We're all aware of some of the social features—knowing your local grocer, having your kids on a Little League team, passing familiar faces en route to work every day. Those characteristics are common across the country. It's knowing the people around you, feeling as if you belong to that specific place and it belongs to you, and having some pride in it and some desire to protect it that makes a sense of community. That's typical small-town America. My ideal is what has been called the "village in the city," meaning the cohesive spirit of that small town in a large city.

BLDD: Is that an overly romantic idea? What changes would be necessary to make this ideal a reality today?

JG: It sounds more romantic than it is. Neighborhood feeling exists to an extent even in Manhattan. Many people here know the people at their local grocery and newsstand and have an allegiance to a particular block or building. It's very difficult to isolate what makes it work, but architectural form is one

Gymnasium renovation, Radcliffe College, Cambridge, Mass.

element that can either obstruct it or help it. In a place where neighbors see each other regularly, people are more likely to recognize each other and thus notice strangers. If there's a place where people stop to sit in the sun, read a newspaper, and watch others go by, this also encourages the casual social interaction that leads to a sense of community. By providing spaces for it, as opposed to streets, corridors, and lobbies that are hostile to anyone stopping and pausing, architects can foster this interaction.

BLDD: What combination of architectural features does it take to make a street or a neighborhood appealing?

JG: Going back close to home, Beacon Hill—where I live—is very successful, partly because of the scale of the streets. They're comfortable for pedestrians, narrow enough for you to greet your neighbor on the other side. There are alleys that dead-end in mews, creating shared courts and gardens. The doorways, steps, and tiny gardens right outside the houses encourage some lingering or minor maintenance work that provides an occasion for conversation and acquaintance among neighbors. It's a pleasant place to be. There's a richness in the texture of the area. It's a predominantly red brick area, and yet there's an enormous variety in the types of brick, in the details of the houses within that limited range. It's not anarchy; it's variations on a theme. And within limits, the scale invites the people who live there to make minor modifications in their environment, whether it's painting their front door, planting

some flowers around the base of a nearby tree, or putting in a window box. That personalizes the place and gives it character.

BLDD: How important is that variety of materials and forms?

JG: It's enormously important. If you ask anyone what they find wrong with the typical housing project—why the word "project" makes people shudder—words you'll usually hear are "sterile," "monotonous," "all the buildings are the same." It's anonymous and impersonal. In these projects it is very difficult to orient oneself, to distinguish one area from another, to feel that "I live *here* rather than *there*." The problem is twofold. First, the past was totally erased and the project was built all at one time; it is difficult to create variety in one grand sweep. Second, of course, is that the minor changes people tend to make to their dwellings are often discouraged by the management of housing projects, so that the important things people do to distinguish their places of residence are eliminated.

BLDD: A good deal of your firm's work has been commissioned by New England colleges. What are the particular challenges and responsibilities connected to this kind of work? How did you get so involved with educational institutions?

JG: Both my late husband, Marvin Goody, and I taught—Marvin at MIT and I at Harvard. We did many little renovations at those institutions, particularly MIT, when the office began. Later we expanded and did work at Radcliffe, Harvard, Simmons, and many other schools in New England. These are schools with a large stock of turn-of-the-century buildings.

Some of them are quite handsome, some of them quite ordinary, but all of them now need something—whether it's tightening up to conserve energy, creating access for the handicapped, or just adapting to current programs. The challenge has been to find more usable space in these buildings, some of which were built to generous proportions but not as efficiently as possible. It has often meant peeking into attics and basements to claim space that wasn't being used, to add to the building the layer of our era without eradicating the architectural characteristics of the period in which it was built.

BLDD: Let's go back to a specific project—your renovation of a gymnasium at Radcliffe College designed by McKim, Mead & White. It illustrates some of the limits and opportunities presented by older buildings. Can you tell us about the genesis and evolution of that design?

JG: It is a lovely 1902 building. The original Radcliffe gym was on the second floor. The locker room was on the first, and a pool was in the basement. The pool had been superseded, and a new gymnasium had also been created. There was a need for different kinds of spaces in that area of the campus: storage space for manuscripts and books to serve an adjacent library; a research center; and facilities for a dance program, to name just a few. The gym was part of a three-building complex linked by a colonnade on one side of Radcliffe Yard, and the programming and architectural development were done for all three buildings simultaneously. The McKim building presented a particularly interesting example because the gym itself was a beautiful high space, with wood trusses and wood paneling. Some people on campus were eyeing that area, thinking that they could build several new floors in there. I felt one of my duties as architect was to say, Oh no, you can't. That space is a treasure, and it would be criminal to subdivide it. The president of Radcliffe, Matina Horner, heard me. Instead of subdividing we found we could use the abandoned swimming pool in the basement for the heavy, high-density stacks, which weigh less than the water the pool once held but more than the design load of any other part of the building. Then we converted the old locker rooms and bathrooms into office space. They presented a very different challenge from the gym. The gym was so complete and so beautifully detailed that our work there was simply to install new lighting, upgrade other systems, and make acoustic changes, without letting it be seen we'd done anything. My pride is that you could go there and think that nothing had been done, that it had just been restored. But the locker rooms, which had no details worth preserving, were completely gutted and were redesigned to echo some of the characteristics of the older portions of the building. A symmetrical plan reflects and respects the facade's symmetry. Heavy new moldings, although not an imitation of those of a historic period, have a weight equal to the older ones. The new acknowledges the old while clearly adding its own chapter to the building's history.

BLDD: Does working with educational institutions require a specific set of skills?

JG: I don't think so. This kind of work has some particular characteristics in that the educational institution is building for itself and for the long term, as opposed to, for instance, a speculative builder who may be trying to put up something fairly flashy that will rent quickly. The educational institution is more concerned with a building that wears well, that fits into the campus well. I have found in recent years, with the diminution of the student-age population, that educational institutions are competing with each other by providing more attractive physical facilities, such as bigger gyms or better dormitories. Apartment-style housing, which was unusual a few years ago,

is being built now as an attraction. Also, some schools are trying to give character to some of the nondescript buildings that were built in the fifties. Some of the institutions are looking at themselves and realizing that the architectural character of the campus is important.

BLDD: Were they practical considerations that forced them to address that concern, or an emerging design aesthetic?

JG: Perhaps it's a greater appreciation for the value of what they have. The elaborate older building, which might have been seen as "that old white elephant" a few years ago, is now seen as a symbol of the school or just a very lovely piece of their history that they'd like to preserve.

BLDD: How do we ensure that there will be no conflict between development, be it urban or campus-related, and historic preservation?

JG: Believing as I do that part of the quality of any place is its visible history, I don't want to eradicate the past while building for the present and preparing for the future. We should plan in such a way that we enhance those parts of an environment that have a distinctive quality, make an effort to reuse them, and build the new in a scale and with materials and forms that are sensitive to the past. That doesn't mean no building at all, but it means perhaps building less than some developers and some schools would like. I think it requires self-restraint—or governmental regulation.

BLDD: You've characterized your firm as conservative. That's hard to believe, listening to you. Yet you've said that you don't want to be the first on the block to experiment with something new. What do you mean by that?

JG: I don't mean the way the firm thinks is conservative; we're willing to consider all options. But we feel a great responsibility for what we build—that it last and that it work. The firm has been around for almost thirty years, and we have done repeat work for many clients. We try to think about what the project will be like after we've left it, given the quality of maintenance one can expect. We want places that look good after the photographs are taken. If we'd like to use a new material and we feel there's some risk because it's not been tested over a period of ten or twenty years, we share that information with the client and make the decision together. We say that this seems like a good idea, but we can't be absolutely sure its going to work. And we are probably slower to try unproven systems and building materials, although we are always open and looking for new and better products.

One of the ways, in fact, that the office distinguished itself in its early years was by research in new building materials and methods of construction. Two of the partners, Bob Pelletier and Marvin Goody, worked on a variety of building materials and construction research. Projects, both at MIT and in our office, included solar heating and plastic and concrete prefabricated modules for housing and schools. Because of that, we really understand how difficult it is to introduce new systems and to make a building that wears well. It is because of our respect for the complexity of the construction process that I characterize the firm as conservative in that area.

BLDD: How did the firm originate? What was it called, and what were your first projects?

JG: The firm was founded in 1956 by my husband, Marvin Goody, and Richard Hamilton, who had died before I joined the firm in 1960. Their first project was to build a plastic house that had been developed from their joint research at MIT. The research was sponsored by Monsanto, but as the research became a specific building project, MIT suggested that these two young professors start a firm to carry it out. It turned out to be something called the House of the Future, which was installed in Disneyland and visited by over seven million people. It was an interesting beginning, one reason I find it so amusing to call the firm conservative. Very innovative things were done in that house, one of them being the first molded-plastic bathroom. That was part of our tradition of research, which was maintained in the office for quite a number of years. We're doing less of that now.

BLDD: For any particular reason?

JG: My husband died in 1980. He had stopped teaching at MIT in the late sixties. My academic connection at Harvard in the seventies was strictly in teaching design studios. So there was less connection to academic research, for one thing. And our time became increasingly taken up with building. Our interest didn't slacken, but the time to go out and get the research grants just wasn't there.

BLDD: What were your architectural concerns when you first started out, and how have they changed?

JG: I don't think they've changed radically. The approach was always the same, which was to look at the totality and see how the piece we were doing would fit in and be used. In the early years we did smaller pieces, very often the renovation of a room or an older building. Now it's often a new building or a group of buildings, as in some of our housing projects. There I've discovered that the space between the buildings is one of the most interesting things to be dealt with, particularly where there is not a great deal of money or need for large interior spaces. The way the site plan is developed and the way the buildings are organized in relation to each other can make

positive, useful exterior spaces and create a community, instead of just creating objects in space. I've expanded my horizons, but I don't think I've lost my earlier concerns.

BLDD: Has most of your work centered in Boston?

JG: A lot of it has. That's not a limit that I'd like to continue, but it has just happened that way.

BLDD: How diverse is the practice of the firm?

JG: Very. That's one of the things I enjoy most—learning about new building types. We do office buildings, teaching and research facilities, housing. There was a recent groundbreaking for the rehabilitation of a thousand-unit public-housing project in South Boston, which will become seven hundred bigger apartments through creative demolition.

BLDD: "Creative demolition"? Is that your phrase? Now *that's* creative!

JG: This is one of those typical housing projects of thirty years ago: identical three-story-high red brick buildings on a superblock. Sometimes by removing a floor or a wing instead of a building, we are able to reshape the project. By adding pitched roofs here and gables there and projecting bay windows in other places, we are able to introduce some of the variety I've been talking about. By discovering the ghost of an old street pattern in that superblock, we've been able to demolish the superblock and create a pattern of small neighborhood blocks and streets. It's a fascinating project. It has also involved a lot of work with the tenants, who were marvelous: active, constructive, and vocal.

Also under construction right now is the Whitehead Insti-

Harbor Point, Boston, Mass., rendered site plan

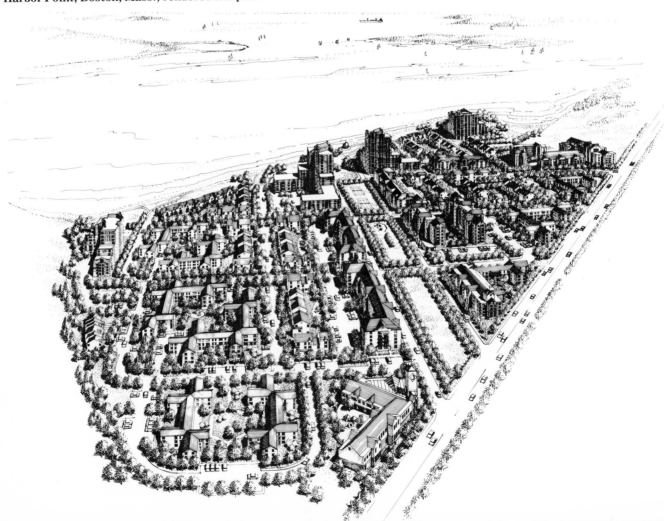

tute, a biomedical research facility associated with MIT but independent from it. We are building a simple shell with some extraordinarily complex laboratories inside. My partner, Bob Pelletier, is one of the nation's experts in translating complex technical programs into architecture. The architecture also expresses the importance of the people who are working and creating in those laboratories. Curved forms enclose their meeting and eating places, libraries, and lounges and weave around the rectilinear laboratory and office forms. In downtown Boston we also have two office buildings under construction.

BLDD: How many projects do you have going on right now?

JG: Probably eight or ten in the office right now.

BLDD: And can you give us some idea of the dollar amount those projects represent?

JG: Given a $70 million state office building and a $30 million subway station—easily over $200 million.

BLDD: How does that compare to the work of other firms in the United States?

JG: To my surprise, I've discovered we're among the larger firms. We have about fifty people now. There were about six when I started, and we've grown slowly but continually. We didn't have the great expansion-contraction cycle typical in many architectural firms.

BLDD: Do you know of any other firms on that scale that have women as principal partners?

JG: Sarah Harkness is one of the principals in The Architects Collaborative, which is a much bigger firm, with many more partners and employees. Also Chlothiel Smith in Washington and, more recently, Laurinda Spear of Arquitectonica in Miami. There are many more younger women coming along.

BLDD: I keep hearing that younger women are not going into architecture as much as development and other fields ancillary to architecture, fields that provide them with a greater opportunity for earlier recognition, satisfaction, and participation. How does that square with your experience?

JG: Both young women and young men trained as architects are going into these ancillary fields more often than my generation did, and it's wonderful that people feel they can use their architectural skills in a broader way. But many women are continuing in architecture. About a third of our office is women architects right now.

BLDD: Is that your own "affirmative action" program?

JG: I wasn't aware of it as a conscious program. I think the fact that the firm has a female principal has attracted more women applicants. And the male partners have never in any way shown prejudice against women, which has meant that we've hired women when good women have shown up.

BLDD: Did the male partners start out that way, or did they evolve to that point of view? Were you, as the wife of another principal, in a somewhat protected role?

JG: I was in a protected role, although I don't think I needed protection from my partners. I was helped by them very much in terms of dealing with clients in the outside world. The character of the office and the partners is very supportive for males and females. I never sensed, in regard to myself or anyone else, any lack of confidence because the person was female. But I don't diminish the support I got from my husband and my partners in the early years, when it was less common for women to be architects.

BLDD: From whom did you feel you needed protection?

JG: There were clients who were surprised to see a woman running a project, but by the way I was presented I felt that protection was given. It was clear my firm stood behind me and had every confidence in me.

BLDD: Has being a woman been a help to your career, a hindrance, or both?

Whitehead Institute, Cambridge, Mass.

JG: I would say both. There were prejudices—and still are—that women couldn't handle certain things. And now, as I get to do larger projects, I find that most people don't question that I might handle a $5 million or $10 million or $20 million project, but when people are talking $70 million or $80 million, they may want to know where my male partners are. I'm enough of a businesswoman to say, "If you want me to bring my male partners, fine."

BLDD: Does that still happen?

JG: Yes, on some very large jobs, but not always, not with every client. I have some clients, usually ones I've known for a while, who have absolutely no qualms. But with some new people, it can be a problem.

BLDD: What other problems did you encounter along the way with regard to your gender?

JG: In the earlier years there were questions about whether I ought to go on the construction site.

BLDD: Who asked these questions?

JG: The construction supervisor. Blue-collar workers often have a more limited and possibly protective view of women than some of our middle-class colleagues, and there was genuine concern, I believe, that I would overhear offensive language on the site. I assured them I wouldn't understand it, so it was O.K. I think a sense of humor helped an enormous amount in my early years in the field.

BLDD: How did you manage to escape the woman architect's ghetto of renovating kitchens?

JG: Mostly because I don't cook and don't know much about kitchens. What you choose not to learn can be significant. I never learned to cook or to type, but I'm pretty good with a hammer.

BLDD: Are there advantages for the woman architect today?

JG: I think so. There certainly have been for me, after having gotten over the hurdles. There are now some advantages in terms of visibility. I find that being slightly different can be used to my advantage, and I'm not afraid to use that advantage. Some of the things that are considered characteristic of women—although there are many men who have these characteristics—help in architecture.

BLDD: For example?

JG: Listening, learning how to hear other people's needs. Most women of my generation were brought up to listen, perhaps more than most men were. So it's easier to pick up clues—whether from users or clients—about their real, if not necessarily stated, desires.

BLDD: Were there ever any self-imposed limitations that related to the fact that you are a woman?

JG: I was as much a victim of society's views as anyone else, and in the early years I tended to do more things in the background—to write letters and suggest that one of the men in the firm sign them because their signature would have more weight. The women's movement and an organization called WALAP—Women Architects, Landscape Architects and Planners—which came about in the early seventies in Boston, were very helpful in building self-confidence. I realized that although I wasn't perfect, neither was anybody else, and I might dare to do more. As I grew more confident, I discovered people listened to me.

BLDD: Is WALAP a national organization, or is it located only in Boston?

JG: It was just Boston-based, and it seems to have faded. The dozen of us who were the founding members—there were two dozen active members at most—enjoyed talking to each other and learning that, indeed, we had similar problems. And I suspect that our problems were those common to architects in general. It was just good talking to other women. When we tried to recruit in the schools a few years back, we found there was not that much interest. The women didn't seem to feel themselves a beleagured minority now that there are so many of them.

BLDD: Is that really true, that there is no longer a need for aid to women in architecture, a profession that historically has militated against women?

JG: No. I think there's still a need. But for some reason the perception of the need was not there among the students at the time. Women do need encouragement, and I sometimes have to give a little extra encouragement to some of the women in my office to take on a certain task. But when they know that I'm behind them, they do it.

BLDD: You've been very generous in your description of the help your late husband gave you. I wonder if you would talk about that for a moment—what was it like to be partners in both work and marriage?

JG: It was very successful because of both of our characteristics. My husband had launched his career earlier than I, so he was established by the time I joined the firm. John Clancy had just been made a partner. I came in as an employee, though obviously one with a special position. But in a six-person office everybody is special. I developed strengths of my own, and Marvin and John were respectful of those things that I did well. I found that Marvin and I complemented each other more than we competed with each other. Quite early on he felt he could turn to me for advice on certain issues, and I knew that there were things about which I would go to him for his opinion. Right through our joint careers, that seemed to me to be of particular value. That mutual system was beneficial to both of us, an extra boost that most architects don't have. Fortunately much of that exchange has developed between John Clancy and Bob Pelletier and myself. We are each in charge of separate projects, but we turn to each other for design crits or technical consultations, and I find that very important.

BLDD: Your father encouraged your design interests when you were young. Could you talk about your earliest involvement with architecture?

JG: My father helped me set up a drafting board when I was about ten years old and growing up in New York City. I attended the Ethical Culture School, where we had wood shop, and I decided to make a drafting table. As I recall, we handwrote and handbound books, and I first used a T-square in drawing the lines for my book. The use of the T-square was something my father had suggested to me as a less laborious method of doing whatever the other students were doing. My father is an industrial engineer. He had more to do with designing policy than with designing objects, but he has also always had a turn of mind that is interested in how things are made and put together. I was encouraged to feel that I could do whatever I wanted to do, and when I showed an interest in something such as building a drafting table or doing some sort of design, it was encouraged by both of my parents. There was no suggestion that I should be playing with dollhouses instead of designing houses.

BLDD: Did you intend, at that young age, to choose architectural design as a career?

JG: I don't think I clearly focused on it until I went to college. I was a history major but always interested in design and drawing. I was at Cornell, where the drawing classes were held right next to the architects' studio. I saw what the architects were doing and thought, this is for me. So it was while I was an undergraduate that I realized that was the natural focus. I decided to finish my liberal arts education first, and I'm very glad I did.

BLDD: Was there a particular person or event that was the catalyst for your decision to switch from history to architecture?

JG: I think, in fact, there is a particular place. When I was a college junior spending a year abroad, I visited the Alhambra. I found a sequence of spaces there that was so beautiful and satisfying that I later bought a little plan of the Alhambra. I realized that plan recalled for me the character of the space, which confirmed the feeling that I wanted to work with three-dimensional design. When I went back to Cornell for my senior year, I took the architect's first-year design studio just to test myself. And I found that it was one of the most satisfying courses in my academic career to that date.

BLDD: And you've never regretted the switch?

JG: Not for a minute.

BLDD: You've said that you especially love designing structures where there's a mix of the old and the new. How did you first become interested in historic preservation?

JG: My early work was often the renovation or rehabilitation of older buildings; for instance, some townhouses on Beacon Hill that I designed early in my career were behind a beautiful old fire station facade. I realized that what I was doing was adding to buildings that had a past life and adjusting them for current needs. I came to appreciate how many lives a building can have, each the richer for the past ones. I am currently on the Boston Landmarks Commission and play a more formal role in the attempt to preserve Boston's architectural heritage.

BLDD: You're a long-term member of the commission—you've been on it for many years. What do you see as the importance of your role there? Why do you spend so much time and energy and effort in this public service, which is sometimes a thankless task?

JG: I guess it's because I love Boston and I think there's much worth preserving. It's a beautiful city. It had the good fortune to be poor in the sixties, when some of the worst demolition was done elsewhere.

BLDD: Are you saying it's been the happy recipient of benign neglect?

JG: In a way, yes, and now it's appreciated for having those old buildings. On the other hand, it's increasingly prosperous, and the threats to its scale and to the character of the downtown are growing. As an architect and someone who's involved in some new development, I think I have a balanced attitude, one that sees the need for development as well as the need to preserve the essential characteristics of the old.

BLDD: How does Boston compare—as both a preservation community and a development community—with other significant urban areas in the United States?

JG: Boston stands up quite well. We have a lot more to preserve than some other cities, through the luck of being an older city and having a real history.

BLDD: How has the Landmarks Commission evolved in the years you've been there?

JG: We've stopped fighting fires. At first all of our time was taken up reacting to emergencies—good buildings threatened by imminent demolition. Now we've had time to do a little more than that. We have done a survey of the entire downtown of Boston, in a sense grading every building. That is one of the things I am most pleased with. It's so difficult when a building is considered as a possible landmark, unless it's one of the absolutely obvious ones, to decide how it stands in the big picture. It's difficult to determine how you would really classify it if it were not an emergency, or if you were not influenced by some other outside factor, such as a developer who's going to put an ugly building instead of a nice one on that site. And the survey at least enabled us to specify the buildings we've always thought of as potential landmarks. It also ensures that those who believe that any building more than fifty years old should be saved will not throw an obstacle in the way of any possible construction.

BLDD: The way you talk, I'm led to believe that you think of landmarks as a useful, or potentially useful, planning tool.

JG: I don't think a landmarks commission should do "back-door" planning, but by default it has become that way. The statutory limits of the commission are really just to select landmarks. I don't think we should be planning for the city or deciding on urban development policy. That wasn't why we were selected.

BLDD: What is the size of the commission?

JG: It's a big commission. There are nine members and nine alternates, with people from both groups equally active. We probably get eight to ten people at most meetings. We meet every two weeks, with many subcommittees and other things in between. I find I can't keep up with every item, so I pick specific issues and try to follow through on them.

BLDD: How has your involvement in historic preservation affected your design aesthetic?

JG: It has sharpened my eye for buildings from some periods that I previously didn't know much about. It's clear that Faneuil Hall and the Old State House are landmark quality, but I've looked more closely at the less spectacular real estate in Boston and have come to understand its importance in the city.

BLDD: What effect has the preservation movement had on the fabric of American urban areas—Boston, New York, and the like?

JG: First of all, it's made the public aware of its architectural heritage and its history, and that's marvelous. It's affected almost every project now going up in Boston in terms of increased sensitivity in relating to an adjacent building or neighborhood or in terms of reshaping a project site in order to preserve buildings of quality. For example, the largest project our office is doing is the Massachusetts Transportation Building. John Clancy is the partner in charge. It's an office building housing the state's transportation agencies, with a retail arcade on the ground floor. It is almost a million square feet set in

an older section of downtown. Its site was a much blighted block, where the removal of many structures was a blessing but where there were a few really fine old buildings. The shape of our new building is very odd; it bends, twists, and turns on an irregular site that was shaped to conform to the old street pattern and to save those buildings of quality in the area. The Transportation Building also steps down from a height of eight stories (equal to the tallest building on its block) to six stories to meet the height of its immediate neighbors. It's clad in a red brick that relates to those existing buildings' facades and enhances them. In a way, it sets an example of how a very large new building can acknowledge and enhance the value of nearby older buildings, both visually and economically. It has been very well received by the public in Boston. I've heard comments like "I can see it's really big and new, but it seems to belong here." That way of thinking about new construction is spreading, and for that we can thank the preservation movement.

BLDD: To the work of what other architects, historic or contemporary, do you respond?

JG: I certainly find myself delighted to be able to walk by the work of H. H. Richardson frequently—Trinity Church, for one—and the only Aalto building on this continent—Baker House, at MIT.

BLDD: Does the work of Aalto particularly interest you?

JG: Very, very much. His forms, his use of materials and light are very hard to talk about but very easy to respond to. And architecture is a sensual art more than an intellectual art. It can be intellectual in the way it's conceived, but it's got to appeal to the senses once it's built. Aalto's work does that very much.

BLDD: You seem to describe a number of buildings as either sensual or sexy. I like the idea, but what does it mean?

JG: I mean that that these buildings evoke a response from one's senses. It feels good when light enters in such a way that it opens up space rather than making it oppressive or cramped; when the proportions of a facade feel comfortable, in harmony; when materials, colors, textures are appealing to the eye. This is a sensuous reaction, as opposed to an intellectual one, where you need a scorecard to understand that one piece of a structure alludes to something that's three blocks away and another is an ironic comment on something else three centuries away. I think one should be able to respond to a building directly with one's eyes and one's body, although certainly it is an extra benefit if the content provides food for further thought.

BLDD: What is your favorite of the projects you've done?

JG: Always the next one! I always aspire to do something better than I've done before. I think that 265 Franklin Street, a twenty-story office building we're doing, is going to be really exciting as a link between old and new Boston. Located between a preservation district with low brick buildings and Boston's financial district with thirty- and forty-story concrete towers, the building mediates between the two. Its base, in a six-story rough red granite, follows the old street line, which is not quite rectangular, and relates to the older red brick structures. The tower that rises from this base is a polished pink granite rectangle that relates to the lighter-colored, higher towers in the financial district.

BLDD: This building has been described as "sort of Art Deco." Is that accurate?

JG: Yes, it's been called Art Deco, but I've objected to that description. It's also been called "art décolletage," which I find more amusing and in some ways more accurate. It can be viewed as an outer red layer pulled back to reveal a polished pink core.

BLDD: Is this the largest building you've ever designed?

Massachusetts Transportation Building, Boston, Mass.

JG: No, the tallest. The Transportation Building is larger in area (almost two acres per floor). But 265 Franklin is exciting to me because of the materials used. I've always wanted to work with granite, and I'm thrilled to have had the opportunity to do so here.

BLDD: How involved are you with each aspect of the design process?

JG: I'm involved with *every* aspect of the design process, from the earliest meetings with the client to checking that the bathroom fixtures look right. On the other hand, there are a host of other people who are involved with me in most stages. It's a myth that any single person builds any complex building today. But I am interested in all phases. I don't tune out after the design. I love to see the project under construction.

BLDD: What are your future plans? What project that you have not already done would you care to do?

JG: I'd love to do a whole community.

BLDD: Not a new town?

JG: I have problems with new towns. Perhaps I'd rather do a whole neighborhood in an existing town. And, in fact, there is a possibility, should one of our proposals come through, that I will be working on a whole new neighborhood in Boston.

BLDD: If you had all the resources, staff, and funds that you needed, what would be your ideal project?

JG: A project that allows adequate design time. Time means even more than budget. As long as we're working with a reasonable budget, I don't find costs as constricting as the deadlines that we face, particularly with developers, when something has to be submitted to a planning board in a hurry. You think to yourself, Don't worry, we won't build that, but all of a sudden you've frozen the footprint and have to design something that fits within the constraints that were agreed to at that zoning meeting. Then you have to get together quickly a set of plans to establish a budget, perhaps with the construction manager, which becomes your lid and against which everything is measured for the rest of the design. I would love to do a project that had a reasonable schedule, allowing you to work on each piece lovingly and refine each detail and put the whole together in proper order. To be able to make changes during construction, to make the most of possibilities I hadn't envisioned when the building was on paper—those are luxuries that architects don't have any more.

BLDD: What do you see as the major problems facing architects in the eighties?

JG: Making the public, the clients, and government agencies understand how important high-quality design is to the long-lasting success of a project. I often feel that what we do best is what the people who pay us appreciate least. We have to sneak in the aesthetic qualities on the sideline while we're satisfying the functional needs, the budget, and so forth. I feel that we have to satisfy those things, but it would certainly be more gratifying for us, and it would be easier for us to work, if we could educate the public to the difference between a good design and something that merely solves a problem.

BLDD: Do you see an increased public awareness and appreciation of architecture and design?

JG: There's certainly been more media attention to architecture lately.

BLDD: How do you explain that?

JG: I think it's a release from the strictures of the International Style. A lot of people, myself included, are using color and form more freely, and that makes better copy. And things that make good copy get published. The trouble is that the more extreme it is, the more exciting the copy. I'm not sure that makes for better architecture. I think it's training a public

Paine Webber Building (265 Franklin Street), Boston, Mass.

to look for pop symbols, rather than lasting design quality.

BLDD: What do you see as the role of architecture? Is it public sculpture? Is it haven? Is it shelter?

JG: I see architecture as a setting for life, for the lives of the people who use it. It's a good setting if it makes that life more satisfying and more exciting than it would have been otherwise. It's a bad setting if it obstructs that life and it makes itself the star. I don't like abstract projects. It is *not* ideal not to have a client. There are some wonderfully talented people designing today who are creating things that are beautiful but are more like sculpture because they don't seem to have any client or user in mind.

BLDD: Who are these innovators?

JG: I suppose Peter Eisenman is a good example of someone concerned less with the ultimate user of the building than with putting forth some very interesting ideas about space. I think people like him have made a very important contribution to the art of architecture, but I'm not sure I would call them architects. I see an architect as someone who creates a place that is meant to enhance the lives of its users.

BLDD: Did you expect your life to unfold the way it has?

JG: No. I don't think I had a strong or a clear plan. I've been delighted at many turns—not at every turn, but at a large number of professional turns.

BLDD: What would you do differently if you were given the chance to start over?

JG: I'd get a little bolder a little younger! I was slow in expressing and developing my own thoughts on architecture.

BLDD: Do you think you're bold enough now?

JG: No. I hope I continue to grow in that direction. Architecture is a wonderful profession from that point of view.

BLDD: You mean in which to grow old?

JG: Yes. I certainly feel as if there's lots of room to improve and lots of time in which to do it.

BRUCE GRAHAM

In the years following World War II, Skidmore, Owings & Merrill became America's premier architectural firm in terms of size, the dollar value of its commissions, and, most important, the aesthetic and functional excellence of its designs. Bruce Graham, SOM's chief design partner, is internationally renowned for such structures as Chicago's John Hancock Building and Sears Tower.

BLDD: You were born in Calí, Colombia. What was your family doing in South America at that time, sixty years ago?

BG: My mother was Peruvian; my father was in the banking business in South America. He started with an American bank, then had his own bank in Peru, near Lima, and later in Puerto Rico. We spent very little time in Calí. We just happened to be there when I was born. My family is really Peruvian. Most of my childhood was spent in Peru. We moved to Puerto Rico when I was a teenager, and I went to school there until I came to Dayton, Ohio, to go to college.

BLDD: When you came to the United States from Puerto Rico, why did you choose Dayton?

BG: I had a scholarship to go to college at Dayton University. After my father died a scholarship became very important. Those were the years just after the Depression and at the beginning of the war. I got a scholarship to Dayton, so I went there. I knew nothing about the town.

BLDD: Why did you choose to study engineering?

BG: I really didn't know the difference between architecture and engineering. I was pretty young—only fifteen—when I made up my mind. I was just interested in cities and building. A year after entering Dayton I volunteered for the navy. After two and a half years, the navy sent me to the Case School of Applied Science, in Cleveland, to study flight science. So I was still studying engineering. When I was out of the navy, I decided to study architecture. I'd matured enough to know that there were schools of architecture and that it was a different course of study from engineering. So I went to the University of Pennsylvania, where I got my bachelor's degree in architecture.

BLDD: Was there anyone teaching there who especially influenced you?

BG: Probably the professor who taught architectural history was the most influential. The architecture school was not in terribly good shape at that time. It had gone downhill, although it used to be a great school. We had to learn pretty much on our own. That's why the history class was one of the most interesting. We traveled a lot to see the work of other architects.

BLDD: Did you see anything during that period that particularly engaged you? Whose work did you find interesting?

BG: The work of Frank Lloyd Wright, Mies van der Rohe, and Gropius.

BLDD: Did you know any of those architects?

BG: Later I got to know Wright and Mies. I met Wright when I went back to Chicago after I graduated.

BLDD: Did you have an ongoing relationship with him?

BG: Nobody had an ongoing relationship with Wright. I happened to meet him a couple of times in Chicago. I was asked twice to be on a platform with him, in which he would talk and a panel of young architects would respond. We spoke about the philosophy of architecture. Wright was a very introverted and selfish person. He was intolerant of anybody who thought differently than he did, which was not unusual. Particularly as he got older, he became just plain unkind. He was unkind to Mies van der Rohe, even more so to younger architects, to everybody, in fact.

BLDD: And your relationship with Mies—how did that come about?

BG: It was simply a friendship. In Chicago, architects get to know one another. There was, and still is, a community of architecture in Chicago. I got to know a lot of the young men who worked for Mies, which is how I got to know him.

BLDD: Did he say anything that you've found particularly enduring over the course of your life?

BG: Almost everything Mies said was enduring. Mies was very generous, and also very conscious of his responsibility as a great artist. It's that sort of consciousness that I was most impressed with. It was the art that was important to him, not the individual. Art has a life of its own, which you have to be willing to commit yourself to.

BLDD: Do you think of architects as artists, or would you describe them another way?

BG: There are people who build but are not necessarily architects. If you're truly an architect, then you're an artist. Architecture is the combination of three-dimensional art and technology. Architecture is the art of space, as sculpture is the art of solids and painting the art of surfaces. When you just build shelter, it isn't architecture. It becomes architecture when you are somehow concerned with the cultural aspects of man. If I could verbalize what architecture is about any better than that, I would be a poet. Architecture speaks for itself. You can't explain a painting; you can't explain a sculpture; you can't explain architecture, either. You have to feel these things, just as with music. You can talk to me forever about a Beethoven sonata and it won't mean a thing until I actually hear it.

BLDD: Were there other ways that Mies influenced you?

BG: It was Mies who recommended that I apply for my first job in Chicago, at Holabird, Root & Burgee. He advised me that they were the firm to work for, because they had built permanent buildings. Most other firms at the time, just coming out of the Depression and the war, had not done permanent buildings. They also knew how to detail buildings.

BLDD: During the period that you were at Holabird, Root & Burgee, what was the emphasis? Could you describe the work of that firm during your years there?

BG: I'd be kinder if I didn't. The work was really being done by a cadre of people who had been assistants to John Holabird and all of a sudden owned the firm. But they were *not* architects. Now it's become a much more viable firm, a very good firm.

BLDD: You spent two years there and then chose to leave. What precipitated that decision?

BG: I felt that I had learned everything I was going to learn at Holabird, Root & Burgee, and there was a young firm, Skidmore, Owings & Merrill, that was demonstrating some interesting and innovative ideas. Also, their notion about practicing architecture—as a group practice—was quite different. Owings and Skidmore went into practice in 1936 and Merrill, an engineer, came on about two or three years later. Skidmore, Owings and Merrill believed in architects working together as teams rather than a few principals organizing everything. They quickly expanded into a rather large partnership, which is not passed on from father to son but is owned by the principals alone. Firms like Holabird & Root have survived by passing the practice on from one Holabird to the next. But Skidmore, Owings & Merrill is similar to a law firm or medical group practice. It's less disciplined than a pyramidal structure, which has a boss, then his assistants, and so forth down the line. At Skidmore, Owings & Merrill we have no boss. Each office has its own chief of design, but there's no overall chief.

BLDD: Is it fair to say that you are the principal among principals?

BG: No, that's not true anymore. We don't work that way. Each firm, each office, has a number of partners. And certain partners are design partners and certain are manager partners. We have three design partners in Chicago, for instance, and each is responsible for his own projects. In New York we have two, in San Francisco we have three, and so forth.

BLDD: How does it all work then? Who makes decisions for the overall SOM?

BG: Nobody decides overall. Each office is autonomous. In fact, each partner is autonomous. We're exactly like a law firm. A law firm doesn't have a chief partner. We have committees that make certain management decisions. It works very well.

BLDD: When a project is offered, who decides whether you take it or not?

BG: Each individual partner.

BLDD: How do you select the people to carry that project forward?

BG: We use a pool of people. We share the talent and knowledge of our people, and we share space. That's why it's so efficient. That's why the Mayo Clinic is such a good clinic—it's a group practice.

BLDD: Do you still see the teamwork approach as appropriate to the kinds of projects and problems we're faced with today?

BG: Teamwork is even more appropriate now. But don't be confused about the team approach. Every project is still overseen by an architect and a manager partner, who have the artistic and the business responsibility for each individual project. We don't use sixteen hundred people to work on every project; each project has a small team. In Chicago, for instance, we've divided the office into twelve studios, which are rather small. The office is like twelve small offices put together. A specific group works on each project from beginning to end. It's not as if you're sharing the project with a lot of other people, but you do have a tremendous amount of resources to call on—technical, financial, international, and so on.

BLDD: SOM is known for the efficiency of its organization. How has this teamwork, this group effort, continued successfully as the firm has expanded? To begin with, what was the size of the firm when you joined it over thirty years ago?

BG: There were about thirty people in Chicago, thirty in New York, and twenty in San Francisco.

BLDD: About eighty architects in three cities. What is the scale now?

BG: We're about sixteen hundred now, with nine offices—Chicago, New York, San Francisco, Portland, Los Angeles, Houston, Denver, Boston, and Washington. We have no overseas offices because it's very difficult to practice outside the U.S. Most countries try to keep us out. There are Canadian architects working all over the United States, yet we can't even take a drawing across the border to Canada. We get taxed the cost of the building for taking one drawing across the border. As a result, when we have done buildings in Canada, we've always collaborated with Canadian architects, who do the working drawings. Architects are much more organized elsewhere than they are in America. The Royal Institute of British Architects, for instance, is extremely powerful. You can't practice architecture in England without their permission. The American Institute of Architects, on the other hand, may have been efficient at some point, but that was a long time ago, when top architects were running it. Now it's run by small-time architects who are more union-oriented than architecture-oriented. I wouldn't even call them architects, frankly. Young architects and smaller firms are being ripped off by the AIA. The AIA budget is huge, but they give nothing back. It's become a bureaucracy with a life of its own, but I'm not going to worry about it.

BLDD: What *do* you worry about?

BG: Just architecture and cities. You know, I make beautiful cities. That's my charter.

BLDD: In what direction is urban architecture going?

BG: I think there's far more consciousness of the need to create cities and places rather than buildings, a concern of mine since I started in architecture. I have not been so concerned with the building of objects, which I think is more like sculpture. Freestanding buildings in a meadow are not the real opportunity for architects today. This epoch will be known as an urbanized epoch. The Industrial Age is dead, but a new society is emerging, particularly in the United States, that is concerned with building cities. What architects are really talking about today is creating a total society, a total city in which there are meaningful relationships between buildings and interesting spaces for human habitation. They are thinking more along the lines of medieval or Renaissance cities than industrial cities, which were disastrous.

BLDD: What issues do you think architects, particularly architects who work in urban areas, will have to address in the next twenty years?

BG: Creating a common cultural language that belongs not to any one architect or to architects alone. There is a very clearly defined cultural language in all beautiful cities. You don't have to be an architect to see that Paris is beautiful.

BLDD: Today people are moving to urban centers, not outlying areas in smaller towns, as was the pattern in the past. I think that reveals that the world many people prepared for hasn't turned out the way they expected. What are the implications of this shift, in terms of demographics, cultural patterns, and economics?

BG: People are changing. Young people are looking for a different kind of life than that which seemed inevitable after the war. They have fewer children. They want to enjoy life while they're young. They're more interested in filling their lives with meaningful experiences. Those desires cannot be satisfied in suburban bedroom communities. So young people are moving to urban centers, where they have access to simple pleasures like restaurants and movies, but also to theaters, operas, symphonies, libraries, adult education, and the presence of other people who have the same interests. Large urban centers offer diverse opportunities for everyone, not just the wealthy or the elite. There is a broader cultural base in cities, and the more available the cultural opportunities are to the general public, the more they will thrive. The Philadelphia Museum of Art was placed in a park, which is terrible, because the museum is inaccessible to the people. Since it's not accessible, it's not supported. The Art Institute of Chicago, on the other hand, is placed so that it is convenient to the subways, to the streets, to all the people who want to use it. Therefore, it's successful and has a very strong financial base.

BLDD: Chicago enjoys the distinction of being responsive not only to its cultural institutions, but also to its architects and its architecture. In spite of that fact, it has managed, like other cities, to destroy a part of its distinguished built past.

BG: You are assuming in what you just said that everything in the past was distinguished.

BLDD: No, I did not make that assumption. I said "*part* of its distinguished built past." I assume you will concur that all new things are not necessarily better, nor are all old buildings necessarily excellent. But to get back to my question, would you comment on the significance of the preservation movement as it has evolved over the last twenty years or so?

BG: There are certain buildings and parts of cities that are part of a cultural heritage and should be protected, maintained, or reused. On the other hand, there is also a great deal of ugliness in American cities. American cities are ninety-five percent ugly. The great cultural magnates who built these industrial cities had a vision of great empires, but they built essentially ugly cities. Their model was Newcastle, and they built quickly and efficiently for the mass society. Now the mass society, both the communist and the capitalist ideals of it, has been discredited; it doesn't exist. There is now a realization that technology in the hands of the people can serve very small units of society, down to the individual. But to do that, you have to be able to do away with our ugly cities. The models that we so revere as residences do not serve the individual. They're not safe, not private, and they're segregated by race and economic level. We've further splintered the society by separating the workplace from the home, the school, and cultural facilities. We have to work toward a much more integrated city. To do that, we're going to have to tear out a lot of the city. You just can't save it. It's obsolete. It's not a viable place for the next century.

BLDD: So what do we do?

BG: We build.

BLDD: Should we save any aspects of the past?

BG: Some areas you can save, some you can't. Certainly most slums in America are not salvageable. Many types of construction used in old buildings are simply not safe. They would be outlawed today. Most fires don't take place in high-rise buildings. Check the paper every day and see how many people die in fires in these marvelous row houses we want to save.

BLDD: So you don't think we should be conserving row houses?

BG: Of course not. They're dangerous.

BLDD: Not even fit to be brought up to standards?

BG: How do you do that? You'd have to take out all the wood. If you take out all the wood, you've torn down the house.

BLDD: You play an important role in the Chicago community. One of the many civic positions you hold is president of the Chicago Central Area Committee. Can you elaborate a little on the tradition of Chicago's architecture and on the purpose of the Chicago Central Area Committee?

BG: Chicago architects have been part of the building of Chicago from its inception. Probably the best known was Daniel Burnham, who did the general plan for the 1893 Columbian Exposition and then the master plan for Chicago in 1909, around which the city was actually built. Architectural planning has been a continuing tradition in Chicago. The Chicago Central Area Committee is the present-day equivalent of the old Commercial Club, which at that time consisted of the leaders of industry who sponsored the plan for Chicago. The Commercial Club has broadened considerably to include a lot of other people in the private sector, people from the academic world and from government. The Central Area Committee, though, is strictly private sector—the chief executive officers of corporations. The committee is sponsoring the new plan for Chicago. I was a member of that group, and I was made president because we got involved in a plan they were all very enthusiastic about. The leaders of industry in Chicago are quite different nowadays from how they were before, and I think that's true all over the United States. It's not the old families who are running corporations now, it's professionals.

BLDD: You've been with SOM since 1951. That's quite extraordinary, being with a firm for that long a period.

BG: Not if you're happy, it isn't. We actually have a lot of people who have been in the firm that long.

BLDD: You began at SOM with a bachelor's degree in architecture, in contrast to the master's degrees that many other architects have. Did you ever consider that any limitation?

BG: Mies didn't have a degree, Frank Lloyd Wright didn't, Sullivan didn't, Adler didn't, Holabird didn't, and I don't!

BLDD: Would young architects without degrees do as well today?

BG: They would, except for our preoccupation with being systematic in America. We're keeping architects in the schools too long; they're even giving doctorate degrees now, which is ridiculous. It's like keeping a painter in school until he's thirty-

Inland Steel Building, Chicago, Ill.

one before he can start painting. Or keeping a doctor in school until he's thirty-one before he can practice medicine. Anyway, I think the degrees we received then were the equivalent of today's master's degrees. You were in school longer—for five years in some schools—to get a bachelor's. Now they give you the same education and call it a master's program.

BLDD: What do you think of architectural education today? What kind of architects are we turning out?

BG: The architectural education system is a disaster right now. Some schools are temporarily successful, but for very short periods. The main problem is that the architect is not accepted on the campus as part of the academic community. Neither is the painter or sculptor. If you don't write or publish, you're not accepted. So to get ahead in the academic community, architects try publishing. Some publish things they've never built. But I do think we are seeing better students going into architecture. In that sense we're graduating better architects, because the quality of the students is higher in the first place. They're interested in making the city beautiful and the planet beautiful, and architecture is the ideal field in which to do this.

BLDD: What do you think would make a difference in architectural education, other than sending people out to work at an earlier stage? Are you suggesting that students' time be divided between academic courses and work programs?

BG: No. I am suggesting that the teachers be practicing architects.

BLDD: Do you have time to teach?

BG: Sure. I've taught from time to time, but I'm really not welcome on the campus. The idea of an architect having a practice and making money while also being a professor is unacceptable to the rest of the professors on campus. Architects make a lot more money than professors.

BLDD: Where have you taught?

BG: I taught for a while in my last year at Penn and I've taught all over the country since then. Recently, I taught at the Chicago Circle campus of the University of Illinois. And I'm constantly teaching in the office. We still get students who know nothing when they come out of school. We teach them architecture. They have no idea of scale or structure or space. They've never really traveled. They don't know what a beautiful square is like. They can't tell a good proportion from a bad proportion. It doesn't matter how long they've been in school; we still have to teach them when they arrive.

BLDD: How do you select the people who work with you?

BG: Mainly by interviewing. The most attractive are those who produce drawings that convey good ideas; not necessarily those who are facile at drawing, but those who can communicate. Interestingly enough, someone who conveys ideas will also know how to draw well, though there are a lot of people who know how to draw well but can't convey ideas.

BLDD: The inclusion on your staff of lawyers, economists, social scientists, and management specialists indicates an awareness of the complexity of contemporary society and of the many factors that go into creating an environment for that society. What do those who are not architects or engineers contribute to any given project?

BG: A lot of people contribute to architecture. When the great cathedrals were built, the master builder would have a meeting with the townspeople—craftsmen, religious people—to talk about the building. The architect would draw from their ideas a general notion of what the building should be. We don't do it quite that way, but we do have things like programming sessions with the owner. The participants in building are more than just those who pay the bills. They're also the members of the society within which you are building. You have to do a lot of listening. I enjoy open community hearings. It's better to talk to people before you design; they may very well verbalize ideas that would enrich the project.

BLDD: There's a special relationship between the architect and the client on every project. How involved do you want clients to be in a project? Some architects would like to be told the programmatic requirements and then not see the client again; some involve clients in every aspect of the project. How does it work best for you?

BG: I think the client should be an integral part of the project. Of course, we have very good clients at SOM. When they come to us, they've already made a serious decision that they're committed to good design. In many cases the client expects you to educate him as to what kind of architecture would be appropriate. You may open up a world they've never been exposed to. To most clients who are not developers, a headquarters building, for example, is a once-in-a-lifetime experience.

BLDD: And by the time you've educated them, the project is over! You've had an important relationship with Hyatt International Hotels. Were they your clients before they were based in Chicago? What kind of contribution—in design or otherwise—was SOM able to make to the Hyatt corporation?

BG: Hyatt became our client when they moved to Chicago. My main work with them has been international, with a branch of the Hyatt group. We worked with Pete Detulio, who has since died. He was quite knowledgeable, probably the best hotel man I've ever met. He knew what he was looking for. He was not somebody that you had to train. He'd been building hotels for a long time. One of the projects we worked on with him was the Cairo Hyatt.

BLDD: How long ago was that project?

BG: It was begun in 1973, but it's still not open. Building in Egypt is very slow. This project includes a national bank, an apartment building, and a hotel. They have a huge bureaucracy in Egypt and it takes a long time to get anything done, anything of significance. If it's an unimportant project it can progress just as quickly as it would here. But the slowness doesn't bother me. I don't think everything has to be done tomorrow. I'm quite happy taking the time to think out a building; in fact I prefer it. In the United States you have to do everything so fast you don't have time to really think out a problem.

BLDD: How do you temper the demands of the banker/developer?

BG: For one thing I don't feel compelled to come up with a new idea for every building. I think of buildings as a body of work, so at any given time I'm following through with ideas from earlier buildings. In most cases, and certainly in Chicago, the relationships between various buildings are easy to establish. That's more difficult if you are doing a unique building in a unique city in a unique country. Then you should have a lot of time to think things out. Similarly, if you are doing a project of social and cultural importance beyond the norm, you should have more time. Saarinen used to complain about the lack of design time, and he used a lot of tricks to stretch the design period. He would ask a corporation what their organization was like; he used to say that was good for at least six months!

BLDD: What are your tricks?

BG: Well, I've used that one, too! I try to buy as much time as possible by showing alternatives that force the owners to ask a lot of questions.

BLDD: You said that it's not necessary for you to come up with a new idea each time you build something. In the *Encyclopedia of American Architecture*, it is noted that each of the firm's designs is an attempt to perfect the preceding ones. Do you see your designs as a refinement or an evolution of previous ones?

BG: Obviously every building you do is a learning experience in that different problems are posed each time, and from solving those problems you learn something for the next building. Also, the location of every building is different. The corpus of a building may always be basically the same, like the human body, but you're trying to find what's unique about that particular site, how the building will relate to other buildings around it, what kind of space you're going to create. That search is not very apparent in most American cities because most of the work has been too egotistical. Certainly in New York that's the case, and it's destroyed some of the better streets. They're now in the process of destroying Madison Avenue. The character of Madison Avenue was its sidewalk. That was always one of the nice things in New York—that sidewalk experience—and I think it's tragic that it's being destroyed rather than enhanced. In Chicago it's a little easier, because there are all kinds of clear clues to tell you what a building should be, how it should meet the sidewalk, whether it should have shops on the ground floor, whether it should be set back, whether it should have a plaza. And in most European cities it's very clear what a building solution should be.

BLDD: You liken the building to the human body. Speaking in those terms, your work has sometimes been called the "skin and bones" approach to design, a reference to the use of structural cages to encase buildings. What models of architecture have inspired that notion?

BG: Man's built environment is made up first of structure. Whether it's a tent, a grass hut, the Eiffel Tower, or a Gothic cathedral, structure is the primary articulator of space. That's true of all great architecture of the past and of contemporary architecture. And if that's so, it's also the element that gives the participants—the people who inhabit it, without whom there is no architecture—a sense of scale, of space, and of time. The structure gives them an understanding of what's going on. Buildings without structure tend to have no scale. There's a lot of that in New York. For example, you have all these glass walls that have no sense of scale. The building could be a hundred stories high or twenty stories high, but there's no way to tell, particularly with reflected glass. The scale of these buildings is overwhelming; it has no relationship to man.

BLDD: During the time you've been with SOM, there has been an evolutionary refinement and unfolding of your work. Looking at it in a more critical light, some people have made reference to the "sameness" of many of SOM's projects. Do you think that evaluation is fair or accurate?

BG: I don't listen too much to critics. In the first place, most of them are not educated enough to be critics of architecture. They come from other fields and are still learning. And most critics in America today are more interested in their own careers than they are in architecture. So they invent clever words. They use architects, and when they're through with them they spit them out. The only one who has survived it all is Philip Johnson, simply by the pure power of his personality. In most cases the critics are not interested in architecture, they're interested in sensationalism. They promote one architect, and in the process they feel they have to destroy another. So the architect tries to play to the critic, tries to be different for the sake of being different. That's what the critics love, but it's uncivilized. A building can't be good in 1948 and bad in 1983. I think architecture, as Mies said, is epochal, that it's not of the time of one life.

BMA Building, Kansas City, Mo.

BLDD: But what's your view of the assessment that there is a certain sameness to SOM buildings?

BG: There isn't. Critics say that, but there isn't. There's nothing similar in the work of Walter Netsch and that of Gordon Bunshaft. Nothing. There is nothing in Walter Netsch's buildings that resembles in any way what I'm doing.

BLDD: If you were to describe your work to the public, what would you want them to know?

BG: Buildings should have a language of architecture that's epochal. That means they have to fit into the culture of a city. So a building I did in Chicago would be different from one I did in Boston or Guatemala.

BLDD: So the context is very important to you?

BG: Extremely important. In all cases a building's structure should fit its context. You don't use a suspension bridge to span a creek, but the San Francisco Bay requires a structure as big as the Golden Gate Bridge. The same is true of buildings. The rocks of Chartres Cathedral seem right at the limit of collapsing because they are enclosing a big space. And the Hancock Building has diagonals on it because it is a hundred-story building. If it was twenty stories, you wouldn't need them.

BLDD: The diagonal slash of One Magnificent Mile, which cuts very dramatically across the Chicago skyline, is an unconventional . . .

BG: It's not. I had done it many years before in Boston at 60 State Street, and there's a simple idea behind both buildings—they're tubes of structure. If you look from the ground you don't see that it's a tube. But if you see where the sides were cut, you can then see that it's a tube. That's why I did it that way. From the beginning, it was a tube.

BLDD: Is this a notion that you'd like to pursue even further?

BG: Certain ideas lead into other ideas. Sometimes you may have a slightly different solution to the same problem in two buildings, because you've learned something in building the first one.

BLDD: What would you say are the most distinguishable features in any Graham design?

BG: Thickness and structure.

John Hancock Center, Chicago, Ill.

BLDD: Are there specific design details, such as some kind of fenestration, that you particularly like?

BG: Thickness and structure distinguish my work. Fenestration is a result, but for me it's not an a priori idea. It might be for Michael Graves, but it isn't for me. Each problem elaborates the whole. If you saw a photograph of just a little corner of one of Mies's buildings, you would be able to visualize the whole building. You couldn't do the same with one of Graves's buildings. You couldn't tell whether it was a big or small building, a horizontal or vertical building. A photograph of a corner of the Hancock Building will tell you it's a hundred stories high.

BLDD: You talked about how contemporary architecture doesn't relate to human scale.

BG: I was referring to building an object without any defining elements to tell you how big it is. All great architecture has defining elements. You can always tell how big a Gothic cathedral is by observing certain clues. Now, with the developments of new technology, we build buildings for which there is no definition of scale. They are not necessarily dehumanizing, but they are certainly not satisfying to look at. They're devoid of some of the romance of architecture, which is space. If a building has no definition of space other than its relationship to another building, it's devoid of the real pleasures of architecture.

BLDD: Your firm has been involved with sculpture, paintings, and other artworks in many of its buildings. Is this an area in which you are particularly interested?

BG: Yes, but it's not unique to me. It's quite common among leading architects to involve other artists, and it always has been historically. Before I came to Skidmore, Owings & Merrill they had hired Miró to do a mural in Cincinnati. That was his first mural in the United States. Before that, when I was a student in architecture, Eero Saarinen and his father, Eliel, had involved artists in a major way at Cranbrook, the school they started. They had painters, sculptors, weavers, and pottery makers in the same school. Even at Penn we were very much involved with the arts. I worked with artists in the fifties through the seventies, and so did Gordon Bunshaft.

BLDD: There is a well-established relationship between Bunshaft and Noguchi. Is there any artist with whose work you have been particularly involved?

BG: I didn't specialize as they did, but I've worked with Calder and with Henry Moore, and with many other artists and painters as well.

BLDD: How involved is the artist in the design aspect of the project? How does the association work? Why commission the artist, as opposed to collaborating?

BG: The architect has a sense of space. Most painters and sculptors don't have a sense of space. They can't tell how big a painting or sculpture should be in a room. The architect has to be the coordinator, not only describing the place but also helping the artist with scale and even color in some cases.

BLDD: Are the works of art you use in your buildings specifically commissioned, or do you sometimes acquire existing works because you think they're appropriate and would enhance a project?

BG: There are certain parts of a building that are inherent to its personality, whether they include sculptures in the courtyard or murals on the wall. Those are the areas we should be concerned with. Nobody can stop you from hanging a painting in a room, but that's a different experience completely. The first case has to do with integrating the art and the architecture. In the second case, the building should have room for more independent art—sculpture, painting, music.

BLDD: You've said that you really don't pay attention to the media. But SOM has received a great deal of attention, not only in professional publications but also in other forums, print and electronic, that have more broadly based audiences. It is probably, in fact, one of the best-known architectural firms in the world. How important has media coverage been to the recognition of the firm's work, or of your own work?

BG: The most important medium for us—and it's brought us every client who has walked in the door—is the buildings themselves. Media coverage comes and goes, but when people see a building that's thirty years old and still looks like it's an important building, *that's* significant. People come to SOM because our buildings have lasting value. That's what we're most interested in—not fashion but very, very good buildings. If some of them happen to be great, so be it. I can't talk about my own as being great, but I can say that Lever House and the Pepsi-Cola Building in New York are still a lot better than any buildings being built today. Bunshaft was a great architect. A lousy PR guy, but a very good architect.

BLDD: Some have called the Sears Tower SOM's best building effort. Do you agree with that assessment?

BG: No, and I don't know why anybody thinks it is. I don't think there's any such thing as the "best" SOM building.

BLDD: For what would you most like to be remembered?

BG: For a continuous body of work.

BLDD: Are there any specific buildings of yours that continue to give you pleasure?

BG: Yes, practically all of them. The Hancock Building I enjoy a lot, the BMA in Kansas City, Banco del Occidente in Guatemala.

BLDD: Is there any specific project or building that you haven't done yet that you'd care to do?

BG: The National Gallery in London. I won the competition for that building, and then Michael Heseltine, a secretary of state, decided to give it to one of his friends.

BLDD: What was the point of the competition then?

BG: I think he was just anti-American.

BLDD: What are your favorite unbuilt projects, other than the National Gallery in London?

BG: A university for the Arabs I designed for Mecca. We had some marvelous Islamic consultants working with it who loved it, but it will never be built because it's too appropriate. I designed it as an Arab village, but the Arabs visualize a Stanford University in the desert, which of course is inappropriate.

BLDD: An article in *Vanity Fair* discussed what they called "The Fountainhead Syndrome"—the emergence once again of the strong, individualistic, public persona of the architect. Do you see that kind of trend emerging? If so, what does that portend for architecture?

BG: I think the critics are creating that trend of individualism, and it portends nothing but evil. Architecture is a participatory art, not the art of an individual. It's the art of a society, and it's epochal. It takes a long time to build cities. One man can't build cities. If it were true that architecture was a product of one man, then Houston would be heaven—and we all know it isn't. It's a disaster because every architect has done his own thing on each block, and there's no relationship between them.

BLDD: It's not only architects but also the developers who have done their own thing in Houston.

BG: Developers today are making high-profile buildings not because of their own egos but to serve the egos of the client. The oil magnate doesn't want his building to look like another oil magnate's. He wants *his* picture on the wall.

BLDD: You're obviously an activist architect, and you serve on

One Shell Plaza, Houston, Tex.

many civic boards. How do you find the time, and what compels you to do so?

BG: Architecture is a product of society, and without being involved in that society you wouldn't know much about it. You have to assume the responsibilities that go with being an architect—to serve the society and to make people aware of what you have learned. It's like a doctor who gets involved in society to teach people about health.

BLDD: What do you consider to be your most important civic endeavor?

BG: Right now it would certainly have to be the Central Area Committee, because it deals with a whole new plan for the city of Chicago.

BLDD: If you had your life to live over, what would you do differently?

BG: Not much.

BLDD: Really? You have no regrets at all?

BG: Not really.

BLDD: Could things have been easier for you?

BG: I am not interested in doing easy things. If everything is easy, you're not living a full life. You're not being challenged.

BLDD: Did you expect your life to unfold the way it has?

BG: No, but do you know anyone who did?

JOHN HEJDUK

In his roles as architect, author, educator, and dean of the Irwin F. Chanin School of Architecture of the Cooper Union, John Hejduk is known for his creative blend of professional rigor and intellectual vision.

BLDD: You grew up in the South Bronx, where poverty was no stranger to your family. Was there anything in this environment that gave you the inspiration to choose architecture as a career?

JH: The interesting thing about being in tight straits and living in that special neighborhood is that one is not conscious of the horror of the situation. What strikes me, in retrospect, about that area during the mid-forties is that there was always a sense of place and a sense of neighborhood. There was a strong community spirit. Other neighborhoods at the time didn't have that characteristic closeness; they were simply poverty-stricken and terrorizing.

BLDD: Was there a particular event that inspired you to study architecture?

JH: I went to the High School of Music and Art in New York City.

BLDD: How did that come about?

JH: A public school teacher of mine saw that I had an ability to draw and suggested that I apply to the High School of Music and Art. So I did.

BLDD: Was there a specific person that influenced you?

JH: My uncle was an architect. He was trained at Cooper Union in the early part of this century. When I was about seventeen, I worked with him. We did a lot of different kinds of housing right after the war. His name was John Adamic. A wonderful man, one of the old school. I learned from him a characteristic way of drawing—drawing with a sense of the material you were working on. I'm the last of a small group of people who still draw the way they did at that time. The 1980s architects don't draw that way anymore.

BLDD: How would you describe the quality of the drawings that you make?

JH: I might almost call it classic, but it also had a sense of probing architecture. I think it was a way that architects did

things at the end of the thirties.

BLDD: Did your uncle inspire you to become an architect?

JH: Yes and no. I had a deep admiration for him and he did inspire me, but I started at Cooper Union in graphic design. Then just being at the school, and taking an introductory architecture course led me to transfer into the architecture program, which was then just beginning full force at Cooper Union.

BLDD: While you were attending Cooper Union in the late 1940s, you also worked for several New York architecture firms. Which offices were they?

JH: One of them was Fellheimer & Wagner, who did the Cincinnati Railroad Station, a great piece of architecture. After I worked for them I went to the University of Cincinnati and was able to see the station in operation. I was amazed by the incredible way the circulation worked. The train came in, you went up the stairs, down a concourse, and then there was a whole series of levels for buses, taxis, and other transportation. The circulation was so smooth; it always impressed me. I also worked on the New Jersey Turnpike, where we did many access and egress roads into the Howard Johnson's sites. It was all curvatures. Because each site had a different access/egress road and a different topographical condition, I learned how to handle curves. I attribute a lot of my sensibility for curves to that experience. I also worked for Bancel La Farge, one of the last of the old-type architects. I often remember him saying, "I am perhaps the last of the old gentlemen architects." The beauty of his office as a place to work was that the people there were not only gentlemen but also gentle men. The architects shared a blend of passion and deep cultural concerns.

BLDD: What characterized that gentleman architect? To what do you attribute his disappearance?

JH: They understood the word *humanitas*. They were humanists, vast in the knowledge of their own field of discipline as well as other aspects of the arts such as literature and painting. They were well-read. The disappearance is probably due to a number of factors, but I suspect it's mostly due to the waning of the idea of the single individual controlling his own area.

Old-style architects did as much as they thought they could control. Their own hand was always involved in their work; responsibility wasn't delegated to anyone else. Once work is delegated and not followed through by the original hand, it's not architecture anymore. It's something else.

BLDD: How significant is the loss of the gentleman architect? Has he been replaced?

JH: Something will replace him. We're in a period of architectural search and re-search that is most interesting because of the present distinction between building and the forces that really make architecture. Architecture will perhaps be clarified. We are on the edge of the invention of a new architecture, but in a form that will encompass other fields as well. New spatial probes are not by and large being done by architects. They are being done by people in other disciplines, particularly literature. Literature is now the most beautiful of the arts, especially as practiced by someone like Jay Fellows, a creative and original spatial investigator.

BLDD: How did you incorporate the practical experience of working in architectural firms into your formal education and, later, into your own practice?

JH: Between the ages of seventeen and twenty-two, I worked for many New York architects who were very pragmatic in the sense of putting buildings together. Schools and universities are the outposts of freedom; your mind is free to expand. Those two things, the hard-nosed practical aspect and the expansion of the mind, made me look at architecture in a special way. I was not anxious to build until I was *ready* to build. In these times everybody is very anxious to get right out of school and start to build. I'm in my mid-fifties now, and I feel I am just ready to build.

BLDD: Isn't that part of architecture—that everyone has to accumulate time, experience, and wisdom in order to practice the art?

JH: Yes. It's an art that needs time, that needs mellowing. I am always shocked that graduate schools take people for three years and then say, "You've got your education." That's nonsense. Even in school you need time.

BLDD: Would you make professional students out of people interested in the design arts? How do they live while they're distilling and mellowing?

JH: If they have a love for what they're doing, they will exist, and will exist well. I don't believe people should be in architecture unless they have the will to endure.

BLDD: Are you saying it's more than an occupation, almost a divine calling?

JH: It's a calling of life. I would hope it to be.

BLDD: In your last year of college, you were commuting between New York and the University of Cincinnati. How did you manage this? Did it give you any advantages as a fledgling architect?

JH: There were a couple of very good teachers in Cincinnati, particularly in the art school. At that time, Cooper Union gave only a certificate after three years. So I finished my degree requirements elsewhere. The only way I could afford it was to go to a co-op program out in Cincinnati, where you studied for seven weeks and then worked for seven weeks. I don't think that's a good program, again because of the time element. By the time you started work you were already on your way back to school, mentally at least. I don't know if that system has changed, but then it was a way of finishing certain requirements, not an education. I loved going to Cincinnati, though. It was a beautiful town, and still is.

BLDD: In the mid-1950s, after graduating from the Harvard Graduate School of Design, you taught at the University of Texas, where you were involved with a group known as the Texas Rangers. Where did the name originate and who made up the group? What were some of its central ideals and goals and what part did you play in it?

JH: The name is a Harvard expression. I have always been intrigued by names other people put on groups. You generally dismiss things by naming them.

BLDD: Who named it the Texas Rangers?

JH: I have no idea. A group of people went to Texas, invited by Harwell Hamilton Harris, an architect and then dean of the architecture school at the University of Texas. They were to bring new blood into the school. Among the original people there was Bernhard Hoesli, a Swiss architect who worked for Le Corbusier on the house in La Plata. I met him in New York while working for Fellheimer & Wagner. He took a tour to look at all the Frank Lloyd Wright houses in America and ended up teaching in Texas. He asked me to come to teach. That's how I got there. In the meantime, somebody else was looking at Frank Lloyd Wright, American religious architecture, and American architecture in general. This was a man from England via California, Colin Rowe. Harwell Hamilton Harris asked King Lui Wu at Yale to recommend people to teach freehand drawing. The two people he recommended were Lee Hershey and Bob Slutzky. They arrived from Yale, Colin from California, I from New York, and Bernard Hoesli was there already. These five people were asked to establish a new architecture program.

BLDD: What did you do once you were there?

JH: We began to establish an architecture program with a European orientation. I had just come back from a year in Italy on a Fulbright. We were all new to teaching and we had intense discussions. At the end of the first year Colin Rowe, Bob Slutzky, and I were fired. We had introduced a program that had horrified the people there because we brought in drawing and collage and talked about Braque and Mondrian.

BLDD: If you were to begin work on the project today, what would you change?

JH: Nothing. I wouldn't have changed anything at that time. It had an organic life. Unfortunately what has happened is that the program has become academicized at Cornell. Colin pushed it to the limit. Colin is wonderful, but he sets up things and then goes about destroying them.

BLDD: You went on to work in the office of I. M. Pei & Partners in New York City. How did you come to work there? With which projects were you involved?

JH: I. M. Pei was my teacher when I was at the Harvard Graduate School of Design. He was inspiring; he created a kind of electricity. Also important was the fact that he was helpful. The first project I worked on at Pei's office was Roosevelt Field. I wasn't too involved, but I worked on row housing.

BLDD: What caused you to leave that firm?

JH: I wanted to be independent, to do what I had to do.

BLDD: More than ten years later you became part of the now legendary group—if it ever was a group—known as the New York Five. I assume it was your early concern with purely formal abstraction that led to your association with them. What was the genesis and evolution of that relationship?

JH: That group started in a strange way, by the making of a book. We all knew each other: Richard Meier was teaching at Cooper Union when I came; Charlie Gwathmey I knew through his father; Peter Eisenman I met through Colin Rowe, who I had taught with in Texas in 1953; Michael Graves I met later. It was a group loosely connected through education—for instance, Peter had worked with Michael at Princeton. One day Peter called and said, "Let's make a book." The first thing you do when Peter calls is to ask how much it will cost. "How much?" I asked. He said, "Two hundred dollars apiece." The absurdity of thinking you could make a book for a thousand dollars! But we said, "O.K., let's make a book for two hundred dollars." That's how it really came about.

BLDD: How much did it end up costing?

JH: It cost each of us three thousand dollars—about fifteen thousand for the book—because of lawyers who got involved at the end.

BLDD: Was it a worthwhile investment?

JH: Yes. We're still getting royalties from it today. We've certainly gotten back the original three thousand. Why did that book take off? It grabbed hold at that particular time, 1970, because we were five independent architects quite willing to put our own work together in the same book. That was what made the impact. If any one of us had done it singly it would not have worked out.

BLDD: Was it perceived as a school of architecture or point of view, rather than a literary effort?

JH: It was not a school of architecture but a point of view. It showed our commitment to modern architecture, whatever "modern" might mean. It was not a very popular position to take at that time.

BLDD: How would you characterize the position that the book presented?

JH: Europe-oriented, but transformed in America with an overlay of anti-intellectualism. I'm still trying to put that together.

BLDD: Do you think the group still has any similarities?

JH: We still talk to each other. I think each of us has gone his own inevitable way.

BLDD: Could you imagine the five of you being in the same book together by your own choice now?

JH: No. I think I could still be in a book with Peter Eisenman, because of his independent search. He really probes. It's fresh stuff. But the rest have gone their own special ways. People think that Michael Graves's work has changed. To me, it's exactly the same work that was produced in *Five Architects*.

BLDD: Can you elaborate what you mean? It is often said that there has been such a distinct shift in his work.

JH: There was no shift. Michael is an extremely talented man. The problem with his work, then and now, is that he cuts the paper covering the tub of butter, without ever going into the butter. Peter Eisenman goes into the depths of the butter. I go into the depths of the butter, too. Richard Meier I admire for his doggedness, his perseverance. He's onto something that he is very good at, and it's amazing in these times to have that consistency of commitment. Richard is in a realm he controls entirely. He's incredible. I just wish he would allow the innate expression and sensibility of his colleagues to be introduced to his architecture. Charlie Gwathmey is always strong and tough,

Diamond House

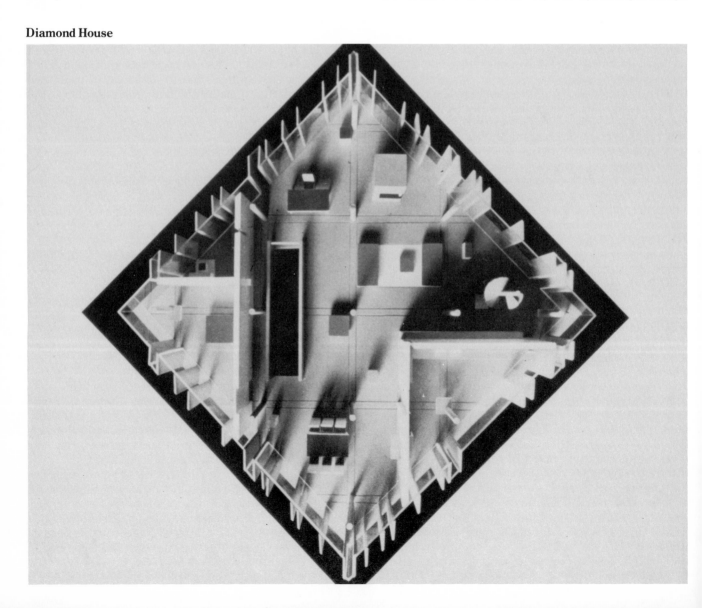

his architecture solid. His interest is in building and he knows how to; he does it simply. Charlie and Richard predictably are continuing on those paths, with slight modifications. Michael will have to make another surface shift. The architecture will have to appear to be something new, although the underlying forces will be the same.

BLDD: Someone once pointed out the similarities between your career experience and that of another influential teacher, architect, and philosopher—Louis Kahn. How accurate or appropriate is that comparison?

JH: I met Kahn around 1953. I always admired him. When I look at his work, I am struck by how solid and strong it is. It's entered the realm of forever and will always stay there. It's so simple, yet also intellectual. I liked Kahn on another level, too. He was always accessible; anybody could visit him, and he would always have time for them. You never felt you had to have an appointment. He was also a passionate teacher and had an aura about him that touched those around him.

BLDD: That commentator also compared your work to Kahn's in its concern with both the abstract and the particular. How important are these two things in your current work?

JH: They are inseparable. I'm ready to build at this time in my life. The life of a drawing is the life of a building now. The drawing, the idea of construction-fabrication, now has every nut and bolt organically tied to the concept. For instance, you can build from my drawings for the Berlin project; the sense of material is in the drawings. The drawing is not just representational or illustrational—it *is*. I am also for the abstract. Starting with a commitment to the abstract can lead you to an architecture filled with psychological, political, social, and aesthetic ramifications.

BLDD: What other architects or artists have most inspired or influenced you?

JH: Certainly Braque, Mondrian, and Léger. In the last ten years I've been fascinated by Hopper, the only truly American painter.

BLDD: Is it because of his use of light and shadow, or the fact that architecture is such an integral part of his painting?

JH: It's both, but it's also because of the after-sense, the feeling you come away with.

BLDD: It's obvious that the concept, the aura, the mystique, the metaphysical is as palpable to you as the physical.

JH: Oh, absolutely.

BLDD: When did you become so philosophical, so metaphysical? Have you always been that way?

JH: I've often thought of myself as philosophical and metaphysical. But I'm not a theoretician.

BLDD: How *would* you describe yourself?

JH: I want to say I'm an architect, in the full meaning of that word. Architecture is the art of approximation. You could have pure painting, perhaps pure sculpture, but never pure architecture. The beauty of architecture is that it's an impure art, that it allows the option of adjusting things. If I put in a window somewhere and have to move it by an inch or two, I can do that in architecture. I'm not so sure painters could do the same with their work.

BLDD: Throughout your career you've been intimately involved in architectural education. You've taught at the University of Texas, Cornell, Yale, and Cooper Union, where you've served as dean since 1975. What does teaching architecture teach you?

JH: Plenty. People ask, "How can you keep teaching the same thing all the time?" Well, you never teach the same thing all the time. It's a process; teaching is constantly revelatory. I've always taught at places where I have been excited by the contact with talented faculty and really bright, talented students. Teaching also allows me to question on a personal level; I'm able to throw out thoughts, and the students don't even realize it. I never tell a student how to design. I hate that; it never works. I always teach by implication, by inference.

BLDD: What are your major concerns in teaching?

JH: To keep society free in the deepest sense.

BLDD: Is this what you think is most important to pass on to a younger generation of students?

JH: Yes. I believe in the idea of the transferability of thought—Le Corbusier said that the only thing transferable is thought.

BLDD: What advantages have you found in returning to, and teaching at, Cooper Union?

JH: That's a good question. There's a mystique there, and that mystique is Peter Cooper. His conception was a powerful one in the nineteenth century. Frank Lloyd Wright admired Cooper very much, which is interesting because Wright wasn't generally keen on education in schools. Peter Cooper obviously impregnated the place with an educational concept that still prevails as a tradition.

BLDD: Was that always the case? Has that tradition always been there?

JH: It's been there as long as I can remember. I went to four other schools, but I went there first, and there was something special there. I don't want to sound mystical, but being there is carrying on a tradition, a commitment to a place where those who could not afford it at that time, or any time, had the opportunity to get a so-called college education. For me this was important. At the time of my graduation from high school I could not have conceived of going to college if there hadn't been such a place. And I had some of the greatest teachers in the world.

BLDD: Who were they?

JH: For example, Charlie Gwathmey's father, Robert Gwathmey, taught drawing. His eyes were like those of the Furies. Another teacher, Henrietta Schutz, trained my architectural sensibilities on how to work with a brush and how to build.

BLDD: Your renovation of the Cooper Union Foundation Building, completed the year you became dean, features a new building deftly inserted into an existing shell. How did you come up with that solution? How do you think it works, now that you've lived with it?

JH: That's some question. The basic form and structure of this building is isolated. It's one of the few isolated, completely freestanding buildings in New York. The site is an unusual shape. I have difficulty drawing it sometimes, because I always get thrown off between Third Avenue, which is right-angled to Eighth Street, and the acute angle at Fourth, where the structure shifts. Peter Cooper and Frederick Peterson's original building is a double structure. The shell of the building is strong and dominant, and so is the structural modulation of the internal gap. The renovation was predicated on keeping both the strong structural grid and the existing peripheral conditions. The renovated building's spaces recall the volumes that were there originally. It's an anonymous architecture setting up anonymous space. Ten years later it still has that anonymity, which allows you to work in it. It's without style.

BLDD: Color has always been a crucial element in your work. How has your sense of color changed over the years? Which problems about color currently engage you most?

JH: What I think is antithetical to what might be the general impression. Architecture is fundamentally a monochromatic art. It's black, white, and gray—like movies. I'm very uncomfortable with color movies. I prefer black-and-white ones, although some color films are beautiful because their structure

Cooper Union Foundation Building renovation, New York, N.Y., entrance lobby

Cooper Union Foundation Building renovation, New York, N.Y., elevator shaft

dictates color. As a kid it never occurred to me that films should be in color. You never questioned it. Are our actual thoughts monochromatic or chromatic?

BLDD: Do you think in color?

JH: I'm going to say no, but I know it's not true.

BLDD: In addition to your building, you're also known for writing poetry. Have you always worked with words as well as with the built environment?

JH: Yes. In Berlin I'm doing a project for the victims of the Gestapo. It's filled with words and language that are not only architectural but also literary. It's a new project, new in its idea. While I'm doing the project I also write in a diary, which consists of fiction, nonfiction, and semifiction, a self-analysis as the work progresses.

BLDD: How does the writing inform the architecture, and the architecture the writing?

JH: They are inseparable. This is very important. I'm probing a new architecture—the inseparability of thought and written language. This is the social/aesthetic/psychological condition that architecture really is. I can no longer look at any architecture without seeing it from this perspective. We have to change our programs today to accommodate a new architecture. The old programs are not valid or authentic for our time and have to be questioned. Architects are facing a crisis now. The question is, What are they to build? Architects must spend time searching out new institutions appropriate to our time.

BLDD: You've said that you don't agree with the emphasis of

some architects today on building. Why is this? What is your alternative?

JH: What I don't agree with is the emphasis on *building* rather than *architecture*. The very thing an architect can do is to affect your psyche and spirit—that's his job. It's simply not enough for him to answer only to the physical. Unfortunately, that's what is being done today. We have builders, not architects.

BLDD: How have your concerns changed over the course of your career?

JH: I'm constantly amazed that there is always something to do. The well is full. I cannot predict what I will do in architecture a year down the line. I'm an incrementalist; I build from what I have, so I imagine what might be.

BLDD: If you were to live your life over again, what would you do differently?

JH: Nothing. I just want time. Methodologically, I'd continue in the exact same ways to produce work. An old-fashioned view, but I believe in it. I'm fortunate that I've been able to work in a free atmosphere that permits me to continue. I feel privileged. Architecture is a mellowing art, and one should get better with time. I used to believe in Gide's thesis that you could never separate body and soul, neither in life nor death. But now, even though I look in the mirror every day and see myself aging, my soul and my mind feel as fresh as when I was seventeen. When I came to that realization, I no longer believed in Gide's theory. I now believe in the possibility of transcendence.

HUGH JACOBSEN

Hugh Jacobsen, who has been accurately described as a gentleman architect, is a four-time winner of the National Honor Award of the American Institute of Architects. He is deeply concerned with the thoughtful arrangement of space and sees the order and progression of the entire street as more important than any individual building.

BLDD: You espouse, at least architecturally speaking, a very well-mannered approach to one's neighbors. Can you tell us why that view also brings about good architecture?

HJ: From the beginning, I've looked at all architecture as a matter of good manners, being part of the whole street, being part of the fabric of the city. Good architecture, rather than beating its chest or shouting at neighbors, behaves like a well-mannered lady. There is politeness in every great city—Florence, Rome, and especially Paris. The streets have continuity, but each building also has its own individuality. The buildings are at once proud and humane, standing strong in their mutual respect.

BLDD: Can you give us some examples of bad manners?

HJ: Surely. The Pan Am Building in New York City, for one. The Whitney Museum is basically outrageous—as a building, as architecture whose purpose is to encourage one to observe art, to observe people. It's a marvelous event to go to the Whitney, but the architect was arrogant in assuming that history was bad, history was out, and modern architecture was absolutely correct. If this was the case, then for miles to the south and miles to the north on Madison Avenue, every other building was out of touch. But time has proven that those dear little row houses on either side of the museum have a much greater sense of humanity, scale, and purpose than that provided by the Whitney's vulgar "look-at-me" arrogance.

BLDD: The Whitney has its eye on one of those rows of houses for an extension to the museum, a multipurpose building to be designed by Michael Graves. What would you advocate that the design look like?

HJ: Michael Graves is without a doubt one of the most important architects in the world today. I can't wait to see the

extension. I think it will provide humanity at last. I'm positive his building will identify with the scale of the avenue and the progression of the street and will also, of course, respect the purpose of the building. In Michael's work there is really an understanding of what postmodernism is. His buildings are not just appliqué, but are intrinsic wholes. Postmodernism can't be described simply by witticisms like "tacked on the outside." When architects talk with architects, we never discuss style. We never refer to our work that way. It's only referred to that way when those outside our profession try to describe what we're trying to do as architects. They can only explain it in terms of style.

BLDD: If architects don't talk about style, what is it that you do talk about to one another?

HJ: In presenting a building, a concept, or a scheme, architects use a vocabulary that describes the tools we have used since we first started putting rocks on top of each other. We talk about the basic components of architecture as they've been defined so many times: scale, order, light, proportion, wholeness, mass, strength, unity, honesty, integrity. These are words that architects use. When an architect is actually working on a design, whether it's an 1890s romantic style, classic modernist, postmodernist, or representative of some other trend, he's not saying, "I think I will do this style or that . . . maybe a little Ionic."

BLDD: Not even ironic Ionic?

HJ: No, not even in a whimsical sense.

BLDD: You've said there are no bad architectural periods, only bad buildings, but you must have some favorites. What periods, buildings, and architects do you consider the most distinguished?

HJ: In answer to which era, my choice would be pre–World War I, anywhere. Just look at what was going on in Edwardian America, for instance, or with Stanford White and the impact of the Beaux-Arts on the United States. This self-conscious nation, desperately waiting for a style to arrive, embraced the Beaux-Arts whole and built it all the way across the United

States. There was a marvelous gusto and romance about buildings as the expression of our spirit, our pride, our hope, our aspirations. The era was a very rich, educated, and fruitful time for many architects.

BLDD: What architect had the most influence on your career?

HJ: Louis Kahn, although, unfortunately, you can't see his work in mine. But I still hear the teaching and the words that Lou gave me at Yale.

BLDD: In fact, you've said that you hear the voice of Lou Kahn talking to you all the time. What does he say?

HJ: To try harder. But he was also very funny and would say things like "If it isn't worth doing, it isn't worth doing well." He also said that the difference between a good architect and a bad architect is that both architects solve the problems they set out to solve, but the good architect solves the right problem. The whole essence of design is isolating the correct problem and solving it. The approach to a solution is infinitely easier than trying to identify the problem.

BLDD: How did you decide that you wanted to practice architecture?

HJ: I really loved being a student and I was terrified of going to work. As an undergraduate, I majored in fine arts and I studied painting. When I was about to graduate, my father found out that I was painting instead of studying business administration. He pragmatically put business and art together and said, "Would you like to be an architect?" I hardly knew what the word meant. However, I did know it meant four more years of staying out of the job market, four more years of beer and misbehaving. I applied to Yale and, miraculously, they accepted me. Within the first two weeks there, I found that everything I had ever studied as a kid began to make some sense. Architecture touches every walk of life. It is the whole reason for man's efforts. It reflects everything man has done. As Mies said, it is the translation of an epoch into space, and that is the joy of it. Architecture turned me around, so that everything finally had some reason.

BLDD: Do you still rely on such a range of information when you start a project?

HJ: Oliver Wendell Holmes said that everything you do before the age of forty is preparation for what you do after forty. When I was a younger architect it seemed I spent all my time looking things up in books. It seems like yesterday that I discovered that a two-by-four is not just two inches by four inches. Now I don't have to do all that research because those words, those relationships are in me. It comes easier now, and I've gotten a lot more daring because I feel more competent.

BLDD: One of the things you did as a young architect was to work as an architect/draftsman in the New Canaan, Connecticut, office of the very daring Philip Johnson. How did you get there? What were the most important things you learned?

HJ: Philip was on my thesis jury, and when I left Yale I went to work for him. I was very honored to be included because he was really a heavyweight then, as he is now. The thing I learned there is how to keep a job, because he fired me!

BLDD: Why did he fire you?

HJ: I was the most recent person taken on, so when the Hirshhorn project in Canada dried up, I was fired. It is a tradition in most architects' offices that in times of crisis, the last hired is the first fired. No matter what rationale you take home with you, though, getting fired is a terrible experience. But I learned other things, as well. It was my first experience in an office. Many young architects forget when they go to work that it's continuing their education. If you work for an architect without principles, for instance, you learn to sell out. It was by listening to Philip fight with his clients and defend his buildings that I

realized how vital the principles he was trying to put forward were to the integrity and scale of the work. It was a very good lesson. If a client is upset with a design, some architects might change it without a fight, but that would be a mistake since clients know nothing about design.

BLDD: That's an interesting statement coming from you, because you've often been described as a client's architect, sympathetic to the needs of the client, rather than an architect's architect. How do you reconcile what you've just said with your reputation?

HJ: You *do* listen to the client. It is his building. He is going to live in it. You listen to his program and try to isolate the problem, identify the important needs. Every time I meet a client, I am interviewing him as much as he is interviewing me.

BLDD: What do you look for when you meet this new client?

HJ: How far down the garden path I can lead him.

BLDD: And how quickly?

HJ: That's right. Setting a budget is important; good architecture does cost more. And talking with the client helps you find out how much freedom you really have, how much risk he is ready to take with you.

BLDD: Are there often surprises?

HJ: With clients? It's *always* a surprise. When you present the scheme and he says, "Let's build it," it's always a marvelous new experience. It's never repetitive.

BLDD: What's the ideal client?

HJ: All my clients have been nearly ideal. They participate and they make me listen. Lou Kahn said that if you present two schemes you don't have one. You don't go in and say to the client, "Which one do you like?" or "What style would you like it in?" You isolate and solve the problem as they perceive it and as you perceive it. Architects know much more about architecture than any client. We should only lose an argument about architecture to another architect. I wouldn't take on a lawyer and argue the law. All architects have an arsenal of weapons. One of the most common is to say that what the client wants is terribly expensive, and that what we want is absolutely free. But they catch on to that rather soon. So then there's the weapon of shaming them unmercifully for how little they know about architecture, the mother of the arts.

BLDD: How do you do that?

HJ: They come to me and to my colleagues because we are professional architects. People don't tell the doctor how to set an arm, but they have a misconception about architects: because we're all born in buildings and we all live, work, and die in buildings, everyone feels an innate right to behave like an architect. "Give me that pencil and let me try that for you," they say.

BLDD: But don't clients have some right, and responsibility, to alter and mold the places where we live and work?

HJ: Yes, and the first discipline of the architect is to listen to the client. But we, after all, are the professionals, the tour guides. It's very hard to listen because we are always building up walls between our preconceptions and the clients'. When I got out of Yale, everybody was doing flat-roof houses, but one of my first clients said, "I must have a pitched roof." No one had done a pitched roof in ages, but there it was: I had to do it. It's important not to shut yourself off as an architect but to listen to the client, because he is rarely stupid about his needs.

BLDD: What about the role of the client who knows not only about the way he or she would like to lead a life but also about architecture and architectural history?

HJ: I'm doing a house now in Michigan for a couple who can really outdo me in the knowledge of architectural history. I'm finding that what gives me the strength to stand against this historical background is what architects do have—a perception of space. If somebody says that a room is twenty-eight by thirty-six feet, the ceiling is twenty-two feet high, and there are three windows on an axis facing southwest, I know reasonably well what the light in that room will be like at 4:23 on October 4. And I can tell them about that.

BLDD: Light is something you know a lot about. If there is a recurring theme in your career, in fact an obsession, this is it.

HJ: It's an unending, beautiful thing to play with, one of the many tools architects use. There's little that is new in architecture; men have been playing with light for centuries.

BLDD: Why do so few architects use light properly?

HJ: Light has order. Architecture has order. Glass has integrity unto itself. Light has integrity unto itself. The architect has to recognize all of these factors within the palette in order to use light as a tool. Most people don't understand this. They seem to think that glass in an opening is a void. This does not take into account the aesthetic of glass—that it is a sheer, taut tension of reflection, not a void. It's holding a space on the inside. Mies's glass buildings weren't empty spaces. You could feel the volume within his buildings, which brought them to life. By reflecting light you can actually hold it, contain it, manipulate it as you will. It is incredible to me how Louis Kahn could fill a room with light and then sparkle the spaces within with little slits in the skin. I have also learned a great deal about light from the Egyptians.

BLDD: At what point in the design process do you start considering the role of light in animating space?

HJ: Oh, I can't say. In the design process you're working inside, outside, in plan, elevation, section; you're creating the spaces and the order of the architecture. Light must not be thought of as just another element. It is primary, like gravity. The quality of light in a house should be important all the time, even after the sun goes down. The same integrity of space must be allowed to exist day and night. There may be an awful lot of theater in achieving this, but there's an awful lot of theater in very good architecture.

BLDD: During this conversation you've managed to humanize architecture, relating it to the way it is used. How much of architecture is designed not by architects, but by planning commissions, bankers, zoning laws, concerned citizens, and all sorts of external factors? In the end, how much of a building belongs to the architect?

HJ: American cities are not any worse or any better than cities in Europe or elsewhere, in spite of the good intentions of zoning, height restrictions, and so forth—design curbs to which I do not object at all. The more restrictions, the more an architect has to try to get within the framework of what surrounds his site. Good buildings don't come about by zoning committees. You can't zone design. It isn't something just anybody can do.

BLDD: Is design also conditioned by economic . . .

HJ: Not necessarily. Vincent Scully used to talk about how the greatest buildings in history were built in times of economic depression. Federal Triangle in Washington, perhaps one of the best complexes in a city, was built in 1931–34, very grim economic years indeed. When times get tight monetarily and nobody is building, they think very carefully about how to spend money when they finally do decide to build. Therefore, there is a tendency to select better architects. It's during boom periods that money manipulators put up junk all over our country, giving very little care to the selection of architects.

BLDD: And, from time to time, they turn to historic preservation. Economic realities, as well as more high-minded motives, have recently turned the interest of a number of architects to

historic preservation. You long ago emerged as an architect doing very sensitive and successful restoration, and you served on the Landmarks Commission in Washington, D.C., for five years. What first sparked your interest in adapting historical forms to new uses?

HJ: Again, contextualism, that sense of belonging. Historic preservation has become a bizarre scene now. It's become a weapon used by landmarks commissions, preservation groups, and citizens' groups as a reaction to the tremendous egg my profession has laid on this beautiful green earth. It used to be that when you saw a sign announcing that an old building was coming down and a new one was going up you would say, "Hot dog! Grand Rapids is coming into the twentieth century!" In those days it was usually a very good building, better than what they pulled down, anyway. But now when you see that sign, you know what's going to follow: the odds are that the new building is going to be infinitely worse than the one they're taking down. So we've started saving buildings that ought to be torn down—shouting "Save that cinder block garage!"—because we have seen a ghastly preview of what is likely to replace them.

BLDD: Obviously, everything cannot and should not be saved. What kinds of buildings should be designated as landmarks?

HJ: The really truly classical, beautiful pieces of architecture. You do not have to explain good architecture. It simply is. Everybody agrees that you don't tear down the old Custom House in New York, for instance. It would be insane. There are other buildings that have maintained the humane scale of an entire area, although nobody knows who did them. A building may not have a particularly distinguished sense of proportion or scale, but it has made one corner what it is, and you love that building because of it. If a McDonald's had been built there, the whole corner would have gone, then the block, the neighborhood, the town. There are also background buildings that just quietly form the avenue. Warehouses, mills, and bridges across the country have addressed that problem in a very quiet, elegant way.

BLDD: Your best-known building in Washington, D.C., is a restoration. I'm referring to the conversion of the old Corcoran Gallery, designed by James Renwick, into the Renwick Gallery of the Smithsonian Institution. It's strategically located diagonally across from the White House and directly opposite the old Executive Office Building. Will you tell us about this project?

HJ: Old buildings are saved because you find new uses for them. The Smithsonian, thank God, found a new use for this building. It became the architectural success that it is because it was designed by James Renwick. Jack Warnecke and I helped along the way. Renwick's client was William Wilson Corcoran, a banker who bet on the right side in the Mexican War and made a fortune, then eventually bet on the wrong side in the Civil War and had to leave the country. In the mid-1850s he hired the fabulously successful and talented architect James Renwick, who had already completed St. Patrick's Cathedral in New York City, as well as Trinity Church and the Smithsonian castle on the Mall in Washington. Corcoran took Renwick to Paris, where they stood outside the great pavilions of the Louvre. I can just hear that American banker saying, "Bet you can't get it on the corner of Pennsylvania Avenue and Seventeenth Street." Renwick did exactly that. It's a little building of heroic spaces. How Renwick plays with the scale! It's always throwing you off balance, leading you into the building, up the incredible staircase as if with a roll of drums and a salute to the grand salon above.

BLDD: Did that question of scale affect buildings that you've worked on since?

Renwick Gallery renovation, Smithsonian Institution, Washington, D.C.

Georgetown University Housing, Washington, D.C., elevation drawing

HJ: If there is any constant in my work it's the quality of not knowing what size it is until you get near it. It is the human figure that gives my buildings their scale. Traditional elements that architects have used to indicate scale include stringcourses, moldings, steps, and the height of doorknobs. Since working on Renwick's building I have learned it's O.K. to change the size of the clapboard or the height of a doorknob. Or I will include no horizontals whatsoever, so that you don't know how tall a building is until your eye can measure against something in front of it. It has helped me a great deal. If a building looks like it grew out of a hill, you're kinder to the hill if you can manipulate the building's scale and break up its massing so that it looks smaller. It's much more polite. As old man Wright said, "Never build on the hill, but be of the hill." The object is to make the hill look better rather than worse.

BLDD: Until 1976, you served on Washington's Landmarks Committee for the Fine Arts Commission and the National Capital Planning Commission. You were also the editor of *A Guide to the Architecture of Washington, D.C.* What are the architectural treasures of Washington, D.C.?

HJ: The book was both a great deal of fun and an awesome responsibility. You have to look at your city and objectively determine what belongs in the book. The book truly is an architectural guide, not a guide to the politically or historically important things that happened in particular buildings. We did not feature Watergate, for instance, because we didn't think of it as significant architecture. We did not include the Jefferson Memorial. The importance of the guide was in the buildings that we left out.

BLDD: By the way, why did you resign from the Landmarks Commission after serving for five years?

HJ: I got awfully busy. Because I'd been jumping to France and Greece about once a month for the past five years, I couldn't attend all the meetings. Later on I'd see this turkey come up on the corner and know that if I'd been there, I could have helped cut two floors off of it. The members of the board are all overworked. You've got to be there all the time.

BLDD: What about the level of architectural dialogue in Washington? Has the commission helped raise the standards or open the debate?

HJ: Oh, most certainly. If it wasn't for the Federal Fine Arts Commission, the grandfather of architectural review boards in the United States, our city would be something else entirely. It would have gone right down the tubes. Right now the commission is really very good. Its character changes with each administration and depends a great deal on the strength of the chairman. J. Carter Brown, the current chairman and the director of the National Gallery, is terrific. I urge everybody to go to those hearings. They're high theater. They're intelligent but not arrogant; philistines get their legs broken quickly. But the plight of Pennsylvania Avenue is sad. The best architects' work has been crippled and hobbled. The developer has won, really, all down our avenue.

BLDD: Is there a specific project on Pennsylvania Avenue that you have in mind?

HJ: No. The new architecture on the north side of the avenue is not in the same league with the buildings that were built in 1931 to form the Federal Triangle. Certainly not distinguished work.

BLDD: Before the early 1960s, Washington was very much a southern city. In the last twenty years it has changed both in terms of its tempo and its design. How do you think the city has evolved? How would you evaluate it today, architecturally and functionally?

HJ: The great nineteenth-century monuments are based on an eighteenth-century plan. The plan, which Charles Pierre L'Enfant modeled after Versailles, is the best thing about the city. The order of French landscaping, with strong diagonals placed over a grid, gave us a grandeur to grow into. It is the only way to lay out a city. The problem now is that every hack in the country wants to build in Washington as a step toward immortality. When we had a stronger Fine Arts Commission (the commission was formed in the beginning of this century) and a stronger Parks Commission, we selected the best architects in the country to work in Washington, D.C. Now it's something else. There's a great deal of developers' money moving in and a far lower quality of architect. The best architects in this country are very little in evidence in our capital, which is outrageous. Lou Kahn never built there. Frank Lloyd Wright never built a monumental building there, nor Louis Sullivan, H. H. Richardson, or the Saarinens. You can go down the list. It's absolutely shocking who is omitted. Those American architects of world renown who have made such a contribution to our art and our profession have regularly been denied a place in our sun.

BLDD: As you are based in Washington, have you had the desire to do much work there, either privately or for the federal government?

HJ: Oh sure—anyone would love to. There are plenty of sites and commissions in Washington; it's challenging to work there; it even promises some immortality. However, I have a hang-up about working for developers. I've never met developers who take pride in their buildings. I'm suspicious of any developer who won't put his name on the sign. Is he ashamed? I don't know how to do a beautiful building for a rat.

BLDD: Why did you choose to establish your practice in a city that has not been known recently as a citadel of architectural excellence?

HJ: For all the wrong reasons. I got out of the service, I had finished Yale and, like every young architect, I dreamed of having my own office. I had not lived in Washington for a long time, but I had finished high school there, my family lived there, and I knew more people there than in New Haven or New York. But, as it turned out, every client I have met in the past twenty-two years I've met since I came back, so I really could have gone to any city.

BLDD: Since you do so little work there now and most of your work is elsewhere, why do you choose to remain there?

HJ: Oh, it's a terrific and stimulating town. My office is a block away from my house. Georgetown is an extremely humane neighborhood: the domestic scale, the mixture of styles. Everybody thinks it's like Williamsburg. It is not. There are only eight federal houses and four colonial; the rest are nineteenth-century. It's a series of little houses. You live in a city, yet you feel like you're living in a neighborhood, almost a village—you walk to dinner, you walk to work, you're seven minutes from the airport. Besides that, it is the nation's capital, and it's become a real cultural center as well. With all of my jumping around, I'm now doing my first project in Washington since 1976, housing for 360 students at Georgetown University. It's a handy four blocks away from my house—no jets, just a civilized walk to the site. Unbelievable.

BLDD: Most of your current projects aren't quite so handy. In fact, you soon leave for Moscow, Paris, and Greece. What will you be doing there?

HJ: In Moscow the American ambassador lives in a pre–World War I house. A textile merchant built it in what is called the Moscow Regency style, but he had the misfortune of finishing it in 1913, not a very good year for a capitalist, and never lived in it. When Roosevelt recognized the Soviet Union in 1933, the house was given as a personal gift to our president, but he couldn't accept it. So our ambassador has leased it from the Soviets ever since. Right now I am generally rehabilitating the building, relighting it and redoing interiors using rich empire blues and gold leaf. It's a remarkably good building, neoclassical, more federal than anything else. In Paris we are completing a $9 million renovation of l'Hotel Talleyrand, which is on the Place de la Concorde and designed by Ange-Jacques Gabriel, and for the embassy we are working on the residence and two buildings designed by Delano & Aldrich. In Greece we just completed an 850-seat theater. We are also building three houses and a mausoleum in Athens. Not since the Beaux-Arts heyday has an architect been given a commission to design a mausoleum. It's a fascinating experience. My client, who is in his seventies, owns a site on a small quiet cove south of Athens, where I am to build the mausoleum. He said, "Why should it be a sad event for people to come out to visit and remember me? Considering the beautiful site—the mountains and the sea—why don't we build a little cabana, a bedroom, a living room, and make it something wonderful?" I thought about this and began to loosen up a little from the heavy image of mourning usually associated with a mausoleum. He wanted to put only a few objects of any real value into the mausoleum: a fourth-century bronze urn and four portraits of himself by Andy Warhol. The concept, the site, and these objects are so expressive of this remarkable man.

Greek Villa, Athens, Greece, rendering

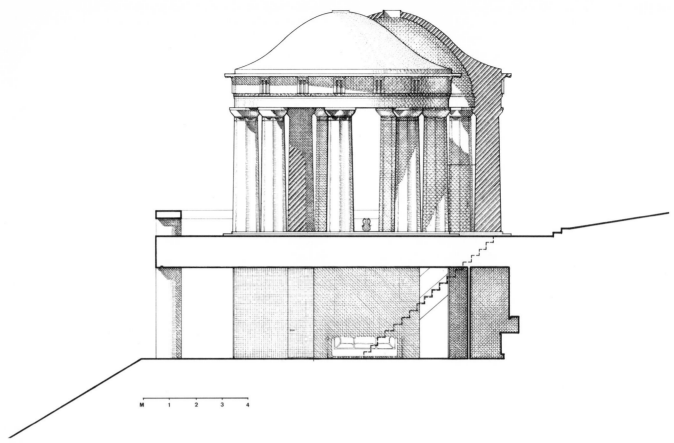

Mausoleum, Athens, Greece, section

BLDD: How did you get a commission like that?

HJ: I don't know. I never know what makes the phone ring—and, right now, what makes it stop.

BLDD: How do architects get clients?

HJ: I have no idea. I am always trying to figure it out. Sometimes people have called me right out of the Yellow Pages. Potential clients that hear of me from magazine articles usually want to buy plans and are not very serious about architecture. Who actually reads the glossy magazines? You usually only look at the pictures.

BLDD: But isn't it important for architects to have their work published?

HJ: That depends on where it is published. Most of my clients come through referrals. If they're serious about building, they will ask an architect. An architect may tell them that they don't do that kind of work but to look in the professional journals, some of which publish special annual issues on specific building types. Most of my clients have come to me through that kind of research. A few have seen or been in my buildings and will come because of that.

BLDD: In addition to receiving the National Honor Award of the American Institute of Architects four times, you've won over seventy-six AIA design awards. You've also been juror for nearly fifty AIA award programs. How important are architectural awards, honors, and competitions in ratifying the work of architects?

HJ: After you leave school you don't get crits as a practicing architect. Your client isn't going to criticize you—he's bought you. The kids that work with you are not going to criticize you. Also, there is precious little criticism in the press. Therefore, the only way to get a crit is to trot out your work before your peers. It's the only valid judgment available. I'm very proud

that we've won seventy-six awards, but it should also be stated that I have entered hundreds of competitions. When I lose it's very hard on me; I feel that I'm not keeping up anymore, not contributing, not thinking, not challenging myself. When I get shown down, it calls for a great deal of introspection about just what I am doing. There are good juries and bad juries, and there are good and bad awards programs. The serious ones are entered by all good architects. All good architects enter competitions.

BLDD: Are competitions important for generating new ideas?

HJ: Sure. America has a notoriously bad reputation for holding design competitions and then never building the projects, whereas in Europe they generally do build them. Anyway, competitions give younger architects a chance to challenge the current way of thinking.

BLDD: Are you ever typecast as a certain kind of architect?

HJ: Yes, as one who can only do houses.

BLDD: Is that fair or accurate?

HJ: What is fair? It's not accurate. Less than forty percent of my buildings for the past ten years have been residential, but my larger-scale buildings have all been abroad, in Egypt, Greece, and France. They're coming out in the journals soon, which might help change people's perceptions. We've also done hotels. But people don't understand that building houses is something very intricate. I did a project for thirty-five row houses in Baltimore that was very successful. It cost, in those days, about $7.5 million. If you stood it on end, it would be an infinitely complex thirty-five-story building. But I didn't get a large commission until seven years afterward because I had done only houses. It's very difficult. Some people think all I do is houses, others think all I do is historic preservation. That's O.K., I love working.

BLDD: A few years ago you built a remarkable house—or would you say it was seven houses?—in Pennsylvania. It has been described as a synthesis of tradition, modernism, and postmodernism. What were your intentions there?

HJ: I'm really pleased with that house because it expresses so much of what I've been trying to do. In the interior it addresses itself responsibly to the quality of the light and to the scale. The exterior is a response to the particular site, in a well-established neighborhood, surrounded by twelve houses overlooking a parklike area. The houses, large homes for executive types, were built between 1905 and 1970, in Tudor or Georgian styles. When the neighbors found out that a lot across the street had been sold and that a modern architect had been hired, it nearly caused a series of cardiac arrests. In order to be kind to the neighbors, like a well-mannered lady, I abstracted the beautiful regional vernacular houses. Eighteenth-century Amish families would start off with one little house; when children came along, they would add a small house next to the first, and sometimes a third one. These were called telescope houses. We did a telescope house made up of seven units, each one four feet smaller than the one before.

BLDD: And ended it with a surprise.

HJ: The end of each house was in reflective glass, so that the big gabled end was a forty-two-foot-tall mirrored surface. On the outside, the house is very historicist and almost disappears in an inverted perspective. The facade is truly a facade, built to be kind to the street and the neighborhood. Yet when you open the front door, you realize it's an extremely modern house: the second-story windows are part of the entrance hall, the basement is also part of the living room. Of course,

you knew all along that it was a modern house because of its essential irrationality. The use of mirrors on the outside certainly tells you it wasn't built in 1753. We deliberately made the facade look like it was a decal stuck on this mirrored series of boxes, a house form like the houses in Monopoly. Whenever a kid is asked to draw a house, it always takes that form. I've used that form a great deal in my work because it says "house," not "factory," "insurance headquarters," or "school." This is very important.

BLDD: How did the neighbors react?

HJ: I feel happy if a third of the people like my work. In this case most of them liked it on the outside, but some didn't like it on the inside. Some liked it all the way around. Nobody hated it, however.

BLDD: Is the inside very modern?

HJ: Yes, no moldings, no trim—like being inside origami with skylights.

BLDD: How does what architects design for themselves differ from what they design for others?

HJ: Very few of us live in houses we have designed for ourselves.

BLDD: Can't afford them?

HJ: That's certainly one reason. When an architect designs his own house, not only the profession but the community is saying, "Now we'll see what he really wanted to do. He's really free." But we're not free at all. One, your budget is never as high; two, it's difficult to isolate a problem and solve it within yourself. You can freeze someone else's problem at a given time, but you're too intimate with how you are changing to do this with yourself. Unfortunately, most architects' houses

Private Residence, Eastern Pennsylvania

Jacobsen Residence, Washington, D.C.

have also had a tremendous influence on how buildings are designed. Something I'm working seriously on now is based on the fact that when I was born my life expectancy would have been about fifty years. Now that I'm in my fifties my life expectancy is seventy-eight. By the time I'm seventy-eight, I hope it will be a hundred. This means that all our buildings must be designed to take care of very old and, I hope, very independent people. We have to come to terms with this, or our buildings are going to be destroyed by the introduction of ramps, chair-lifts, and the like. It's valid as a design problem to make these things part of the architecture.

BLDD: How important is it for architects to meet their budgetary allowances?

HJ: If architects don't meet their budgets, they don't build. Setting a budget is one of the primary problems to solve. Buildings look the way they do because of the site, the program, the way people live, and the budget. It's the architect's responsibility to consider those four things, as well as things like gravity, wind, and light, to make architecture. If you violate any one of them, you're not going to build.

BLDD: What's it like to have famous and distinguished clients? You've had a number of them.

HJ: I've been asked that a lot. They're people, too.

BLDD: But are their needs and schedules different from those of other people?

HJ: No, not when it comes to addressing themselves to the problem of a house. Lou Kahn used to tell us never to build a house that's too special for a person, since you don't want the house remodeled once that person is gone. It's really quite true. And the rich, the famous, and the powerful have budgets like everybody else. An architect has never been given carte blanche, never.

BLDD: If you had sufficient funds and assistance, what dream project would you like to build?

HJ: I'd love to do an art gallery.

BLDD: What would the design look like?

HJ: I don't know. It would depend on the site and the budget. The problem involves the grace of looking at fine art and how one perceives it. The architect must establish a space for looking at little pieces as well as big pieces and must bridge the gap between the intimate way an artist sees his work and the way he would like other people to perceive it. We just got a commission to do a very large Roman Catholic church. I'm very excited about it because, as in designing an art gallery, you're dealing with symbols. All architects do is make space. When you're dealing with symbols, it helps those spaces contain a spirit. Good architecture holds the spirit of the architect and of his time, the era when the building was designed and built. All the great art galleries hold the spirit of their time. Civilizations are measured not by wars or technology but by the achievement of our art and how we perceive it. It's that understanding of symbols that is so vital to what man is, to where we are going and where we have been.

BLDD: Is there a commission or an assignment that you would decline, a project that you'd flatly refuse to design?

HJ: No, except if someone wants an exact replica of something else—"I want you to do exactly the same building you did last week" or "Would you do a Tudor house?" Otherwise, I don't think there's anything I would refuse. We even tried to do a shopping center. We designed what I thought was a beautiful little shopping center, but I lost the client. He just walked away because it didn't look like other shopping centers and he couldn't understand it.

BLDD: I suspect that very often architects get work because the potential client has seen their last project and wants a

really do shout, because they express everything the designer knows at that moment. The house may be absolutely terrific when it's built, but it will date quickly, and the architect will then have to live with that awful echo.

BLDD: You're one of the few architects fortunate enough to live in a house of your own design. If the architect's house does serve as a showcase for his or her work, how has yours survived?

HJ: Mine had a rationale: it was designed for a speculative client. A friend of mine who lives on the next block bought the house because he was tired of backing down the narrow little alley and wanted a place to turn his car around before he destroyed too many cars. Then he asked me to fix the house up for sale, since the Republicans were coming to town in 1968 and we knew, of course, that they wanted to move into Georgetown. So we sat down one evening and wrote a Republican program: Republicans have 4.3 kids, Ethan Allen furniture, and so on. I was living a block away with my wife and children, and we were outgrowing our house. So we decided to buy this thing. Not only did I buy my own work, but then I had to pay back my own fee, on which I had already paid taxes! If anything works in that house, I say thank you very much. If anything doesn't, I blame it on the Republicans. So it's O.K.

BLDD: In the twenty-five years that you've been designing houses, how have the needs or demands of your clients evolved?

HJ: It was much easier to design buildings before they invented energy. Problems of security and the rising crime rate repetition of it, while the architect is ready to move on to the next one. How do you satisfy that desire on the part of the client and still move forward?

HJ: Most clients, especially commercial ones, approach architecture as a money-making venture. That doesn't necessarily mean it's evil. Our whole system is based on the profit motive, and a commercial project must make money for the client. That's why he's doing it. Unfortunately, he often approaches a building with the attitude that the last one was a howling success and should be re-created. If you can't describe to the client how much better this building could be than the one down the road, you don't deserve the commission. You've got to communicate with the client. People think that the design process consists of the architect sitting up in the middle of the night, slapping his forehead and saying "Eureka, I've got it," and rushing to the drawing board.

BLDD: How *does* it happen?

HJ: It is a long, difficult process of questions and answers with clients. The architect can describe the spaces that only he can see, the spaces that constitute the potential of what can be done. But the client must explain why he wants things a certain way. That's how he's going to make his money. If you don't understand this and you build something that he loses money on, you've made a terrible mistake. The building could even be torn down, which would be an awful thing to happen.

BLDD: Has it ever happened to you?

HJ: No.

BLDD: It's quite clear that you love your profession but that you also see putting up a building as an awesome responsibility.

HJ: Oh, it's fun. It really is. I feel sorry for anybody who's not an architect. Once you get a building up and walk into it, you can't believe that it all began on the back of an envelope at 31,000 feet. It goes from a silly little sketch, then moves onto paper, and then years later the bloody building is finished.

BLDD: What is the biggest surprise you've ever had in designing and watching a building of yours unfold?

HJ: That they're going to build it at all is always a tremendous surprise. Aside from that, I usually have a sense of how the light is going to work, but it's always better than I expected. That has happened in practically every building I have done. After having worked it all out—the back lighting, the fore lighting, lighting the trees, and so on—it still seems like magic when you turn the switch on. It's always an extraordinary experience. Clients will call you ten years after you've done a building for them and say, "We just had four people for dinner. God, it was marvelous." That's worth more than any fee.

BLDD: Did you expect your life to turn out this way?

HJ: My life is so much better than I ever dreamt it would be as a kid, all because of this incredible profession I stumbled into. The very idea that I'm working in fifteen states, in Russia, Greece, and France, jumping all over the world, and building what I think are serious buildings that are making a contribution . . .

BLDD: What would you do differently if you were to start over again?

HJ: Listen to Lou Kahn more. Try harder. The awful thing—and I hear this a great deal from my colleagues—is that you get going and you don't have time to make decisions. You have to shoot from the hip, and you wish you could be a lot more contemplative about isolating a problem before you jump into solving it. If you overthink the solution to a problem, you can strangle it and take the spirit from it. To isolate the correct problem is always hard—where the building sits, how it faces the light, how you get in, what you do and why you do it there. You never have enough time for that. You *never* have enough time. You want to be on that yellow paper all the time, moving it and moving it. But pretty soon you've got to stop and make decisions to actually build.

HELMUT JAHN

The designs of Helmut Jahn have become increasingly varied, complex, and expressive. His firm, Murphy/Jahn, known for works that combine a sleek modernism with a respect for historical form, is the major new presence in Chicago skyscraper design.

BLDD: You were born and educated in Germany. It's a long way from Munich to Chicago. How did you wend your way?

HJ: I was born in Nuremberg, Bavaria. I went through high school there and studied at the Technische Hochschule in Munich from 1961 through 1965. In Munich I worked for the architect Peter von Seidlein, who had worked for a couple of years at the Illinois Institute of Technology and then in Mies's office in Chicago. That fact, together with my education at the Technische Hochschule, generated my desire to see some of the buildings here firsthand and to meet some of the people involved. I applied for a scholarship from the Rotary Club—and was fortunate to get it. In 1966, I ended up in Chicago. I came for one year, but I'm still here.

BLDD: How has your background affected your style?

HJ: There was a definitive value to my pragmatic, functionalist-oriented education in Munich, one way of approaching architecture. My subsequent education was essentially at IIT, where I was for one year, though I was working part-time. IIT was oriented towards principles based on the Miesian curriculum: the study of materials, forms, and value judgments on architecture—something lacking in German education. I find that having both backgrounds—the pragmatic, problem-solving aspect and the more visual, aesthetic, and value-oriented aspect—has helped me make judgments that have directed our architecture from being strictly functionalist to being more image-conscious.

BLDD: How did you first get interested in architecture?

HJ: You probably enter a profession for the wrong reasons. As a child I could draw rather well; what I saw I could draw. I also watched buildings going up for hours. Sometimes during vacations I worked on construction sites.

BLDD: Was there any particular building or individual that had a strong influence on you?

HJ: None that I can remember. I didn't even know of Mies van der Rohe until I started at the university. Maybe I had an aversion to doing the obvious. My father was a teacher in a school for handicapped children. He always wanted me to become a teacher. He was a teacher in the traditional sense of a pedagogue, very much geared toward the process of teaching people something and getting them to do something. I wanted to do something freer, to express myself more.

BLDD: Your designs are strict and formalist. Do you feel that they have also given you the opportunity to express yourself?

HJ: There are really two continuing styles in our work: low-rise "mat"-type buildings and high-rise buildings. As with the work of every architect exposed to large audiences, our tall buildings have generated a great deal of interest lately. They're in the centers of cities and very visible. The functional and technological rationale of our low buildings was important for the tall structures because they generated the knowledge to deal with a building's various systems and components. Free of specific programmatic constraints, tall buildings can be manipulated to make a more expressive statement. The tall building is shaped to a greater degree by external forces, in contrast to the internal forces that affected the low buildings. The facade and the boundaries the building establishes in the larger urban context are generators of its form and expression. Within that expression, though, there's a strict adherence to functional and technical principles—the pragmatics of building.

BLDD: How did you first become involved with the Murphy firm, best known for their connection to Mies?

HJ: When I was at the Illinois Institute of Technology, I didn't spend all my time in the most fruitful way. There was a requirement that you had to go through an introductory year if you hadn't studied at IIT. I asked for permission to work part-time, to get exposure, which they granted me. I started to work for Gene Summers, one of Mies's closest assistants who worked on some of the major buildings such as the Bacardi

Building, the Federal Center in Chicago, the New National Gallery in Berlin, the Seagram Building in New York City, and the Toronto-Dominion Centre. Gene had just established his own firm. For a couple of months we had a great time designing some of the biggest buildings in the world for people Gene knew in Canada, but the projects never got off the ground. In January of 1967 McCormick Place burned down, which turned out to be a fortunate accident for me; I was in the right place at the right time. The Murphy firm got the job to design McCormick Place and they brought Gene in as a partner to direct the project. I came with him as part of the package. The two of us worked closely. I was Gene's right-hand man. I was only twenty-seven and just out of school, but I worked so hard that he had me direct the team. We worked on that building from 1967 to 1970 and went through several designs. The building turned out to be a $100 million job. It was very exciting to work on, and I decided to take a leave of absence from school. I never graduated from IIT. When the building was finished in 1970, I was involved in so many other things I felt I should continue and never thought of going back to Germany. Gene left the firm in 1973 to form a partnership with Phyllis Lambert in a company called Ridgway in Los Angeles. I took over from Gene to head up the design in the office. A few years ago we changed the name of the firm to Murphy/Jahn.

BLDD: Do you consider it unusual to have had the opportunity to practice architecture at such a young age?

HJ: Many people think I had a grand master plan to come here and accomplish what I did. I never set out to achieve this particular goal. I thoroughly enjoyed the challenge of what I was doing all the time. I thrived on solving certain problems, and I still do.

BLDD: *Is* there a grand design to your life and your work?

HJ: Looking back, it might seem more like a grand design than it actually was. We're always smarter when we make judgments from a historical perspective. But I couldn't tell you what I'm going to do next year, or even in the next two months. It's a varied profession and the challenges and opportunities are numerous. You can't control them, especially if you're following a single direction like speculative tall buildings, a type that arose quickly and could disappear just as fast. It's not a very broad field. These buildings respond to economic and social conditions. Everybody builds at the same time, everybody stops at the same time. Right now there's a proliferation of ideas and quite a variety of pursuits. But there's also a reaction setting in against these tall buildings and their effect on the city and the environment. It's not architects alone who determine the way those buildings turn out. Architects are sought out today both to create a diversity of visual expression and to satisfy the economic goals behind buildings. Design statements are very much related to marketplace consumption.

BLDD: You've become strongly identified with Chicago, but in many ways your work is curiously outside of the Chicago tradition. You don't have the strong adherence to structural expression that buildings in that city have had from the Chicago School and Louis Sullivan through Mies van der Rohe and Skidmore, Owings & Merrill. In the last few years it seems you've moved away from structural expression altogether. Do you see yourself as an architect in the Chicago tradition, or as someone in Chicago changing that tradition?

HJ: I don't agree that I am not of the Chicago tradition. This tradition has been constructed by historians who have a tendency to promote points of view that fit their theory. The tradition started with Sullivan, the first Chicago School, which is directly connected to Mies van der Rohe, the second Chi-

cago School. There's a great deal associated with technological breakthroughs and structural expression in both those schools. But there is also a lot of ornamental expression, especially in Sullivan's buildings. Mies's buildings—especially his low buildings—are not just structural statements; they are also aesthetic statements. There is a strong preoccupation with visual elements, which goes beyond structural and technological interests. The German word *struktur* best describes those intentions. In Mies's Lake Shore Drive Apartments, the structure is clearly subordinate to the ornamental expression of the skin, which is in a visible dialogue with the structure. In the Federal Center and the IBM Building the structural expression is totally subordinate, except for the columns at the ground floor. Mies fit technical capabilities of a particular time to his aesthetic intentions like no other architect in history.

What's peculiar about the way historians have established the Chicago tradition, with the connection between the first and second Chicago Schools, is their omission of the Art Deco buildings from the twenties and thirties—the Chicago Board of Trade, the Palmolive Building, 333 North Michigan Avenue, the Tribune Tower—and even the Beaux-Arts buildings like the Wrigley Building. The twenties and thirties showed an indulgence in more experimental, formal, and ornamental elements; architects often willfully created picturesque buildings that made reference to earlier periods of history. These buildings are symbolic and expressive structures that create urban excitement and drama. We appreciate these buildings more today than we did ten years ago during the high modernist period. They are landmarks on the urban scene in a way that many modern or even early Chicago School buildings are not. Chicago architecture has been innovative aesthetically as well as technically, but that part of Chicago's architectural history has been suppressed or omitted from history books because it doesn't further the idea of Chicago's steadfast structural expression and pragmatic attitude. We often make the mistake of relating what we do to something we know from the past. That's a very regressive attitude. Our buildings do connect with the Miesian tradition. They are made out of walls, steel, and glass, which, in its relentless gridding, often represents the essential elements of a Mies building. But sometimes this "Mies box" is classicized or alludes to something else—an object or ornament. Sometimes it is new, different, and inventive, contrary to conventional representation. For the State of Illinois Center we looked for a new typology but also tried to express ornamentality, which a government building ought to represent, without resorting to classicism. We are "typically" Chicago in the way we try to orient ourselves to the past by making historical connections; to the present by using tools and techniques peculiar to our time; and to the future by applying materials and techniques, forms and colors that are unconventional, explore new limits, and could serve as models for things to come.

BLDD: Your work does have a devotion to Miesian ideals. How do you think that Miesian influence has worked over the course of your career? How has it been tempered?

HJ: The first buildings we did, our low buildings, were Miesian in the way they expressed the modularity of the plan and elevation and in their subdued use of color; they also explored technology—for instance, using exposed steel. The primary effort was to solve the planning, functional, and technical problems through a rational, objective analysis that resulted in an appropriate aesthetic expression. Function and technology were the generators of form in these buildings. Many of them were skin buildings, exploring variations in the facade based on different exposures, different uses behind it, and different

North Western Terminal, Chicago, Ill., rendering

materials or methods of construction. Other buildings used circulation as a form-giving element. Some buildings dealt with large plans and column-free spaces; these used the structure as the primary basis for the architecture. Today I consider many of these buildings "one-liners": they pursued single ideas exclusively. Our later buildings are more inclusive: they bring together various aspects having to do with function, structure, skin, and technology and synthesize them with other interests. All these buildings deal with image as well as function—plan, structure, and services. We consciously draw on pursuits we characterize as "formal" (geometry, surface treatment, and ornament), "intellectual" (meaning, metaphor, and symbol), and "social" (resources, context in time and place, and people's use and perception of buildings).

BLDD: How important is the integration of the building's exterior and interior? Is that a top priority for you?

HJ: The integration of the form of a building and its interior spaces, not generally important in high-rise buildings, is very much part of our latest work, such as One South Wacker, the Board of Trade addition, and the State of Illinois Center.

BLDD: Many of your exteriors speak explicitly of the building's content and purpose. A good example might be the 1980 Area 2 Police Headquarters, "uniformed" in regulation dark blue. What was the inspiration for the design?

HJ: Our buildings are sometimes very literal about what they pursue. In a number of projects, for instance, we used color to represent the uses and functions of the building. The Area 2 Police Headquarters Building is "clothed" in a blue uniform. The Oak Brook Post Office is like a piece of post-office equipment—a mailbox or a mail truck—colored red, white, and blue. The tectonics of these buildings are enhanced by the representational values that create the image of the building, which, in turn, is enhanced by the social goals of creating a more humane and resource-conscious interior.

BLDD: What do the bright yellows, oranges, and greens of your 1981 De La Garza Career Center communicate about the function of that building?

HJ: Color is a very important ingredient in that particular building. The building is located in East Chicago, next to oil refineries that provide very little context for the building. The idea of using color to make a statement about the functions and the processes in the buildings was very much on our mind. The yellow was used to evoke the color with which much large-scale machinery and equipment in refineries is painted.

BLDD: You are known, among other things, for playful experiments with natural light. How important is natural light to an urban structure? Is there a feasible and attractive alternative to natural light?

HJ: In tall buildings, where you're stacking more or less identical floors, there are limited possibilities for bringing in daylight. Atriums or other spaces bring in light, but only to a certain extent. Exploration with light can be done more in one-, two-, or three-story structures, which allow architects to determine the size, height, and interior arrangement of a building for maximum natural light. This is done as an environmental concern, as well as a concern for resource-consciousness.

BLDD: Would you describe the space in which you work?

HJ: In the office I have two spaces: one for business functions, the other for privacy, for my thinking and architectural work. It is an open and accessible area, where much of the drafting work evolves. It's like a big laboratory, filled with artifacts, samples of glass and stone, old and new models. It gets me in the right frame of mind to reflect on what I've done before and what I want to do now.

BLDD: You've said that it's possible for you to work anywhere—at home, in the office, in a car or plane—because your work relies more on ideas than on drafting. Where do you work most often and most productively? How do your designs evolve?

HJ: Over the years my way of working has changed. Like any architect who gets involved in a lot of projects, I spend less time in the office, less time at a drafting board. Today I find myself thinking more than before. Earlier I explored a lot of different ways. Now I am more sure of what I aspire to, what I

Oak Brook Post Office, Oak Brook, Ill.

accept, and what is right for a particular problem. I am also surrounded by people who are loyal to the approach I pursue. Working on a multiplicity of jobs allows you to see a continuum of ideas evolving. The exploration of these ideas has a lot to do with the way individual jobs work out. When you work on a few jobs, especially in a large office, there's an element of competition. When I was just beginning to work and there were more design heads in the office, I found that because one group did something one way, another group would try to do things differently. Today we are a different firm with one design approach. Everybody is oriented to those goals, everybody adheres to that overriding philosophy. I conceptualize a lot through small and large sketches. When I work on ideas, I tend to visualize them in terms of those drawings, which can easily be done outside the office. The drawings often serve to generate architectural ideas. The latest works we are involved in are tall buildings, which are unique in that they are without a program; they have as their only programmatic determinant to provide as much square footage as possible on a given site. You don't know the tenant; you only provide a vertical infrastructure of elevators, stairways, and services for a nondescript space. Following the notion of the tall building as a modernist idea, expressive of functional and structural requirements, really leads to a dead end. There is only a limited number of ways to express particular systems and components.

BLDD: Do you design different kinds of skyscrapers for different cities? Do you tend to design for specific sites or programs, even though you say that most skyscrapers don't have a program?

HJ: The underlying notion of your question is the element of context. "Context" is probably one of the most misused words in architecture today; everybody uses context as a justification for what they are doing. To try to do the right thing in a particular place and time is probably the wrong idea, but it is very much an underlying goal of modernism. Modernism tried to come up with an architecture that would end the agonizing search for the right building in the right place. Of course we design a building in a particular place and at a particular time to relate to what we consider important, but it doesn't have to be commonly received as such. When we did the State of Illinois Center in Chicago, we were aware of the building's location in relation to the urban corridor formed by Clark and Dearborn Streets, in relation to La Salle Street as a "walled" street, and in relation to the Civic Center and the City/County Building. We wanted the building to be a statement of governmental presence and symbolism in downtown Chicago but also something unconventional and new. We're doing a midblock building in New York, between Fifty-fifth and Fifty-sixth Streets, about a hundred feet off Park Avenue. There are many difficulties with a midblock building, especially with street-wall continuity

State of Illinois Center, Chicago, Ill., model

and fitting a larger structure into a smaller-scale urban fabric. We are also very much aware of the location of our building in relation to the AT&T Building, which is just to the west.

BLDD: This is your first building in New York City, and it is on a very important site. What specific concerns did you have in taking on this commission? How did the commission come about?

HJ: The developer talked to various architects. We were very interested in doing a building in New York, as any New York architect would be in doing a building in Chicago. We got the job a few years ago. It was delayed because of the economic slowdown and also because of the zoning change in midtown that has taken place in the last few years. The client is Park Tower Realty, headed by George Klein, who is known for doing quality buildings responsive to the urban context. He hires architects who have a certain design reputation.

BLDD: Is that the new "Good Housekeeping Seal of Approval" in architecture, to design a George Klein building in New York?

HJ: No. Architects are probably not as choosy as you may think. People often ask us how and why we accept a certain commission. We always have a belief that we can solve the problems, so it's nice to work for a client who is known for aspiring to something more than absolute minimum requirements, which unfortunately is what many developers do—or must do—because of economic necessities.

BLDD: That's not a very exalted standard—anything beyond the minimum . . .

HJ: Developing a building for commercial purposes is a phenomenon of the last fifty to sixty years, even more so of the last five to ten years.

BLDD: Do you see that phenomenon, the need for that kind of building, increasing?

HJ: At a time when building is so expensive and will probably become even more so, there is a need for people whose profession it is to build for profit. They have replaced sponsors like the Medici or the popes. Developers are the Medici of today. They pick and choose architects, and there is a lot of competition to get selected. Developers will undoubtedly increase their influence on the built environment.

BLDD: How much of a building's design is created by zoning laws?

HJ: There have always been zoning laws and limitations. I don't necessarily consider these limitations harmful. In fact, I think they are good, helping to narrow down the possibilities on a particular problem.

BLDD: So you don't feel particularly hampered in your midblock site with the limitations imposed on you?

HJ: I often talk about the building as one that shouldn't be built anywhere but New York City. I'm not saying this in a derogatory way but in a responsive and understanding way. New York is known for overcrowding. I think overcrowding is what makes New York work. Ten years ago everybody said that too many buildings were being built, and in the last three to four years many new buildings have been put up. But they seem to help the city. Still the city seems to thrive.

BLDD: Do you think the city can support new neighborhoods that bring on problems of critical mass, transportation, garbage, and so on? Have we finally reached the point of overdoing it?

HJ: I'm not advocating higher density, but it's not architects who make those laws—it's politicians or planners. Planning has become a lost art. Today planning is nonexistent in cities; there's only land management. There's definitely a need to bring architecture and planning together again. It can be done.

Park Avenue Tower, New York, N.Y., model

Xerox Centre, Chicago, Ill.

We may have overdone it, but in the past we often thought we had overdone it and we somehow still found a way out. Also overcrowding does have a balancing effect in that it eases the load on an infrastructure because it fosters development in other directions. When the Hancock Building was built in Chicago, everybody thought it would mean the end of Michigan Avenue. Now, even with four or five more large buildings on that avenue, sometimes you can drive up Michigan Avenue faster than up Lake Shore Drive. I've always been amazed by that. I think it has to do with the ongoing life of the city. Architects don't create the infrastructure. All we can do with our buildings is to create monuments in a particular time and place; we can't change the infrastructure. Within the fixed grid of streets the building process continues, based on socio-economic forces, technical possibilities, catastrophic events.

BLDD: What do you think about postmodernism, and where do you place yourself in the modern-postmodern debate?

HJ: A lot of people call me a postmodernist and, like many architects, I refuse the label. Postmodernism, if it can be quickly characterized, is a catch phrase for a concern with history, context, ornament, and decoration. Often it implies a tendency to use elements from the past and assemble them in a contemporary context. Postmodernism started as a reaction to modernism but fails in the end because of its own orthodoxy. Just as modernism refused to acknowledge anything that had to do with history, postmodernism refuses to acknowledge anything that has to do with modernism and looks back strictly to historic elements. There's no effort to explore contemporary possibilities.

BLDD: How would *you* describe yourself?

HJ: I see myself as a synthesizer, as somebody trying to bring together divergent issues and complexities. Architecture deals with very contradictory elements: the pragmatic and the ideal, form and technique, intellectual rigor and commercial acumen. Architecture also deals with art and social purpose. Many efforts we see today, especially those associated with postmodernism, deal only with one element. The synthesizing activity—which both respects modernism and sees room for exploring it further by merging it with a historic responsibility—has a certain future in architecture.

BLDD: Recently you've been called "the Flash Gordon of American architecture." I assume that's a reference to more than the fact that you're an avid runner. What do you suppose it means?

HJ: When *Newsweek* coined that phrase I called my wife and asked her, "Who is this Flash Gordon? Is this good or bad?" She said, "It's not really so bad. He's almost like Superman." I really don't get excited about those phrases. They call me other things, like "Baron von High Tech," but I don't like to dwell on those things. There's no doubt that some of us today are made into stars, just to be knocked off our pedestals later. Architecture is a profession subject to a great deal of criticism, especially because of architects' presence and involvement in highly visible urban developments. Architects promote a certain idea about design quality, partly because of the fact that we work on many buildings: we are forced to come up with something new, something marketable, and something different from other buildings. This search for new forms and new techniques is a very dangerous assignment; it's left up to the architects to develop a continuity within those parameters and to strive for a direction that promotes new issues.

BLDD: What about that ultimate urban pedestal, the American skyscraper? Do you think the skyscraper aesthetic still has room for growth and development?

HJ: The skyscraper is responsible for a new vitality in architecture because it offers never-ending possibilities for exploration in terms of its urban symbolism, its form, and its image. It's not a question of whether or not the skyscraper is here to stay. The skyscraper is the urban phenomenon of the twentieth century. With land values and zoning the way they are, the skyscraper is definitely going to stay, and the technological possibilities exist to extend its limits even further. It's up to architects to take those possibilities and form the skyscraper into something that is specifically about our time. There are various kinds of skyscrapers built today: the abstract, late-modern geometric skyscraper, a derivation of the modernist movement; the historicist skyscraper, which uses past images and forms to evoke a kind of symbolism; and the buildings in between, which are trying to reach back to the historical prototype of the American skyscraper and at the same time explore modern materials and techniques. Our latest work is in the last category; it makes an attempt to link those goals.

BLDD: Which of your buildings do you think will be remembered best?

HJ: The next one.

BLDD: Are there any that you would like to forget?

HJ: Not every building is a masterpiece, but there is no building in which I would deny my involvement. You have to stand by your record. You have to take the buildings for what they are. There are a lot of buildings that didn't turn out quite the way we wanted. And there are others that, for all kinds of reasons—client's wishes or costs, or a combination of the two—couldn't be built how we wanted to build them. But an architect should never use the excuse of a client or an influence beyond control. If you have to use that excuse, you should quit.

BLDD: What's the best or most satisfying job you've ever done?

HJ: Probably the small buildings. One of our nicest buildings is a gymnasium we did at St. Mary's College in South Bend, Indiana. It was done in the 1973–74 recession when we didn't have much to do; we took any job we could get our hands on. It turned out to be something very straightforward, but it also went beyond the pragmatic, making both a rational and a poetic statement. The Xerox Centre, which was our first tall building, turned out to be a very satisfying experience because all the way along there was very little dispute. The building went up quickly, and it was architecturally successful, as well as economically successful for the developer. That building helped get our foot in the door of the high-rise market. We secured other commissions from that success.

BLDD: What are your best unbuilt projects? Why weren't they built?

HJ: I always liked a competition we did in Abu Dhabi. It was an underground building about three miles out on a peninsula in the Arabian Gulf. It had a huge movable painted screen above the desert. I always related the strength and simplicity of this form to that of the pyramids. That may sound pretentious, but it had a disarming simplicity, especially in relation to its site, that you seldom find in a building.

BLDD: Architecture is no longer an image of the world as the architect wishes it to be, but as the world is. What happened to the idea of the architect as reformer or revolutionary?

HJ: The role of the architect today is not nearly as powerful as it used to be. I think that is primarily because we do not work for nobility, popes, the rich and famous. Their architects were able to transform whole cities. What Baron Haussmann did in Paris whole planning departments would not be able to do today. The architect has little opportunity to be the leader in creating a responsive environment. He has to rely on the cooperation of the social and political environment to bring many often contradictory goals together.

BLDD: Did you expect your life to unfold the way it has?

HJ: I haven't had a lot of time to have any qualms or frustrations about my life. I'm very happy with the way things have gone this last decade, and I look forward to a similar time in the future.

BLDD: Given the chance to live your life over, what would you do differently?

HJ: That's a difficult question to answer. If I say I wouldn't do anything differently, it would mean that I did everything right. If I wanted to do it over again in a different way, that would assume that now I know how to do it better. I have an underlying belief that a lot of things an architect does, a lot of your actions and reactions, especially at the time of creation, are intuitive. In addition to the conscious act of controlling what you know when you build, there is an intuitive act that you may perceive only with the benefit of distance and time.

PHILIP JOHNSON

Philip Johnson is recognized by virtually everyone as the dean of American architecture. His influence began in the 1930s, when he founded and was director of the Museum of Modern Art's Department of Architecture. Since then, his role has been central—as master builder, critic, historian, patron, and gadfly of contemporary architecture.

BLDD: How does it feel to have evolved from what you yourself have described as the bad boy of American architecture to its current most eminent figure?

PJ: I'd just like you to repeat that introduction again and again. I didn't know I was such a famous and delightful person! But I suppose being dean just means I'm old.

BLDD: Venerated . . .

PJ: Venerated because of old age!

BLDD: Hardly. Venerated because of your continuing accomplishments.

PJ: Anyhow, it feels fine. I advise everybody that life doesn't really begin until you're seventy.

BLDD: Let's discuss the level of the dialogue about design that exists today. Do you find it more impressive now than it was at the time you brought your now-legendary International Style exhibition to the Museum of Modern Art in 1932?

PJ: I don't think there's any question about that. In our day nobody talked about architecture. Our first show wasn't reviewed in any magazine, no newspapers would touch us, there were no discussions. There were no interviews like this one.

BLDD: How do you think the public feels about the built environment today?

PJ: I think they hate it, cordially.

BLDD: Do you think they notice it?

PJ: Yes, some subconsciously, but most of them consciously. At least the people who write to me or call me find enough to scream about, especially when I build something they resent. They seem to notice buildings they don't like much more than those they do like.

BLDD: Are you saying that the public really cares?

PJ: They're starting to. One example is the landmark preservation movement. There was no concern for preservation in my day. I marched with six people to try to save the old Pennsylvania Station—that was only twenty years ago. Even the *New York Times* took the side of tearing down Pennsylvania Station. I think of what would happen now if anybody dared touch a building like Pennsylvania Station—it would be worse than the cries raised over the issue of saving Grand Central. That shows how much the consciousness of the general public has changed.

BLDD: How do you explain the increasing interest in preservation, not only here but throughout the world? Is it nostalgia—a love of history—or is it caring more for what we have than what we might be getting?

PJ: I doubt whether anybody can answer that question. I don't think it's just a fashion because the preservation movement has been going on now for fifteen or twenty years, at least since we started it that cold day in front of Pennsylvania Station. Today people notice buildings more than they ever did. Look what happened when we first published the plans for the AT&T Building. All those outcries of shame and horror—that's a good sign. It shows that the public is interested in what kind of buildings are being put up.

BLDD: Your early influence was as a teacher and a curator. In 1932, you and Henry-Russell Hitchcock were the curators of an exhibition at the Museum of Modern Art entitled "Modern Architecture: International Exhibition." The exhibition defined a new movement in architecture. How did you come up with the idea for the show?

PJ: It was a perfectly natural one. The International Style was a very severe, highly defined movement such as we haven't seen since the Gothic. It was a discipline of architecture that avoided ornament, used flat roofs, lots of ribbons of glass, and stucco or other plain materials. The International Style castigated the architecture of the Beaux-Arts school. It was almost a moral movement. We thought we had saved the world.

BLDD: So in addition to being a style of architecture, it was a philosophy. You really believed that architecture would make a difference.

PJ: We did. Le Corbusier once said that people will be better people if they live behind glass. Today, of course, that sounds absurd, but in the twenties, when the best International Style work was done in Europe, the rules were very strict and the hopes for the future were endless. It was the old socialist dream, that everybody could be happy. We don't have these illusions anymore.

BLDD: What has replaced them?

PJ: A perfectly delightful sense of living in the real world.

BLDD: Have you enjoyed your roles as teacher and curator? Have you ever really abandoned them?

PJ: No, I'm still doing that. I still tell everybody what to do. Just ask me. I'm still pretty cantankerous. I have my likes and my dislikes—pretty strong ones—and I guess I'm the most hated architect in America, which is a perfectly normal reaction against anyone too outspoken.

BLDD: In 1979 you were the first recipient of the Pritzker Prize, the most distinguished prize given in architecture. How did you feel about receiving that prize?

PJ: I'm very proud of it. The Pritzker Prize is the Nobel Prize of architecture. It is indeed a great honor, and I'm appreciative of that.

BLDD: When did you first become a practicing architect, and under what circumstances?

PJ: I was practicing long before I was actually allowed to. I couldn't wait for a little thing like a license; that would have meant going to school, writing a thesis, and drawing—I still can't draw today—so I started building buildings.

BLDD: Did you practice without a license?

PJ: Yes, and they threw me out of New York. A man came around and tapped me on the shoulder and said, "You're going to have to close this office and leave New York State."

BLDD: Where did you go?

PJ: I went to New Canaan, Connecticut, where they didn't have any silly laws, and went right on building until they passed a law there, and then I had to do something else, so I went to Harvard. It hurts very much to go to school after the age of thirty. I was thirty-four and my classmates looked all of fifteen, although I suppose they were a little older.

BLDD: Who were your teachers?

PJ: Lots of kids younger than I was, and some people my own age. Marcel Breuer was my favorite. He was the best teacher I ever had. And he was just a couple of years older than I was.

BLDD: Who was the dean of the school then?

PJ: Joseph Hudnut was dean, but the leading man was Walter Gropius, the spirit of the Bauhaus and one of the creators of the International Style.

BLDD: To whose work did you respond then? By whom were you most influenced?

PJ: I disliked Walter Gropius so much that I had no trouble getting inspiration from other places. The man who influenced me the most was Mies van der Rohe, my guru, who was the head of the Illinois Institute of Technology in Chicago. I saw him all the time. But at Harvard there was only Breuer.

BLDD: Most architects today reject Mies van der Rohe's austerity but seem to rejoice in the underlying classicism of his work. What do you see as his most lasting contribution to architecture?

PJ: To me the most significant quality of his work was its classicism. Naturally, we see that aspect a lot more now that we're all classicists—we slice the bread differently at various times, and right now it's sliced that way. We don't consider him an austere, monotonous man. We consider him a productionist-classicist—a "contaminated classicist."

BLDD: A contaminated classicist?

PJ: A marvelous new phrase.

BLDD: But what does it mean?

PJ: It's my present philosophy. I accept it because it was invented by somebody else—Peter Eisenman, actually. It describes what Mies did. His very careful balancing of parts in the Seagram Building, for example, was almost thrown out of the canon of the International Style because it was too symmetrical. Our sense of balance in the International Style came from Mondrian and Cubist spatial lapping, whereas Mies's came from Schinkel, the great Prussian classicist, and from his own historic sense. Mies was an historian. He and I always spent our vacations looking at classical architecture, never bothering with the modern. Now we see him as the leader of the antimodern protoclassical revolution.

BLDD: What is most important to you about his work?

PJ: His sense of organization and order, of clarity, and his sense of detail. As he said, "God lies in the details." I still believe that. A lot of architects say the idea is the thing. But it isn't. The detail is what carries the building. It shows in the Seagram Building, which I watched him design. I was listed as a codesigner, but that isn't fair; he designed it, and all the little parts. Next time you go by, look at the little mullion—the thing that holds the windows apart—see how it is sculptured. That was hand-sculptured by Mies van der Rohe himself. The shape of that thing is not simple. It only looks simple.

BLDD: You do not take credit as codesigner of the building, but you do list yourself as the designer of the Four Seasons Restaurant, which is in that building.

PJ: I did that, yes. Mies had left—he was tired. He said, "Why should I design restaurants?" I couldn't have agreed with him more. But he was older than me and I didn't know enough to leave restaurants strictly alone. Restaurants are too hard! I spent a long time doing the Four Seasons.

BLDD: It's obviously a place and a space that you enjoy enormously—it's also your lunchtime club.

PJ: Yes, I have a permanent table there; I always eat there. The food's good, too!

BLDD: How does the room hold up for you after all these years?

PJ: I still like it, although I wouldn't do it that way again. It's too barren and too square—too cubic. But we did use a lot of rich materials.

BLDD: What was your first architectural endeavor, and who was your patron?

PJ: Myself, of course. You always have to build for Aunt Matilda if you're lucky enough to have a rich Aunt Matilda. The first rule of architecture is to be born rich; the second rule, failing that, is to marry wealthy. There isn't any third rule—you've got to do one of those two things. Architecture is one of those very difficult professions. When I started building for my family, I built a barn out in New London, Ohio, where we had a farm. If nothing else you could always build farm buildings just to store machinery.

BLDD: One of your first buildings was a house you designed for yourself in Cambridge in 1942.

PJ: I finished it and went off to the war. I didn't live in the house very long.

BLDD: What if an architect doesn't have the luxury of commissioning himself?

PJ: Then he has to be very patient. Or a genius. We don't have that type of genius anymore; we're not in that kind of a period. We're not in what the English call a "heroic" period. There's no Le Corbusier, Mies, or Frank Lloyd Wright. Nobody would dispute that. We granted these people a genius status as you would Michelangelo and Veronese. Today I don't think any of us measure up to that standard. Architects today don't think of themselves that way. Mies was convinced that he was the greatest architect in the world, and when Frank Lloyd Wright was young, he believed that there were only two architects that ever lived—Michelangelo and himself—which he wasn't at all hesitant to tell you.

BLDD: And you did not hesitate to argue that point with him at least once in his career. . . .

PJ: That was embarrassing. I told him he was the greatest architect of the nineteenth century, and it was way into the twentieth when I said it. That was very unfair, because he did a lot of his best work after that, but, as I told you before, the International Style was a moral movement as well as an intellectual one, and Wright didn't fit. We were very mean to him. I apologize, Frankie.

BLDD: During 1948 and 1949 you designed the now-famous Glass House for yourself in Connecticut. How does that look to you today?

PJ: It's marvelous. I wouldn't want to live anywhere else. But I also wouldn't build another like it. It isn't interesting enough. Our sense of what's interesting has been greatly influenced by Venturi. The Glass House is too simpleminded. I spent all my time thinking, "How do you hold up glass? With a piece that size by that size." It took months, years, to do every one of those little details. It wasn't one of your broad-brush, interesting shapes. It was all so strict.

BLDD: What was the most important aspect of that design for you at the time that you were creating it? Were there any elements that were more significant than others?

PJ: Yes, the siting. If you have a glass box without any character and without any interesting details, then it had damned well better look well placed. So I found a glorious site in Connecticut, which I've never tired of.

BLDD: After building the glass box, you continued to expand that environment. How many houses are there now?

PJ: Five or six. Every time I get an idea I build it there for myself. There's only one good client and that's oneself! You don't have anybody bothering you about budget or telling you that their closet isn't big enough. That's the worst thing you can hear from a client.

BLDD: Many people are under the impression that an architect comes up with an idea, works long hours to execute the design, and then, presto, it gets built. I'm afraid that's often not the way it works. How do you take an idea and translate it into a reality?

PJ: Like porcupines making love: with difficulty. There's no way to become a good architect. You certainly don't do it by going to school. In this country we cannot afford to waste five years of kids' lives, at public expense, training them to be architects. Of course, it's all a waste of time.

BLDD: What is the alternative?

PJ: What did the good architects do? They just hung out their shingles or went to work for another architect. Frank Lloyd Wright never went to school. Mies never went to school. Le Corbusier never went to school.

BLDD: But when you didn't go to school in this country . . .

PJ: I was disbarred and thrown out of the state. Things change. You have to have a license now to be a barber. You have to be licensed to be an elevator operator.

BLDD: In the end does that help establish standards, or dilute them?

PJ: I certainly don't think it makes any difference at all if you have those pieces of paper. I think you learn after you get out of school, in the school of hard knocks. You learn by conceptualizing a building and then trying to get it built. Then you

work on the engineering side and you work on the history side. In another area, I'm a great lover of art history, but I didn't learn it in school. I just picked it up. You learn through the pores of your skin. What great artist ever went to school? If they did they probably were ruined. Jasper Johns never went to school. Matisse—how ridiculous! Picasso—heavens, he started painting great pictures when he was eight or ten years old.

BLDD: You are noted as a kind of patron of younger architects. You send work their way and you follow their careers closely. By your own admission you have favorites among them.

PJ: Oh yes. And you seem to be interviewing most of them, so I can't talk to you about them. It's too bad, because it would be fun to say mean things. But it's impossible because I picked them all.

BLDD: Who *are* some of those favorites?

PJ: Robert Venturi seems to me the most important architect in the world today. You'll notice I use the word "important." I don't care so much for his work as I do for his thinking. He revolutionized architecture in 1966 with his book *Complexity and Contradiction in Architecture*. It was a seminal book. It freed architects, loosing all the chains with one brief stroke. He is a great architect, too, but he just hasn't yet had a chance to get into the big time. Another favorite is, of course, Michael Graves, who's also a "classicist."

BLDD: You were helpful in getting Michael Graves the commission for the Portland Municipal Building in Oregon—a building that is almost as controversial as your own AT&T Building. What do you think of Graves's building now that it is finished?

PJ: Don't forget another building that I was the cause of—the Beaubourg in Paris. I was the man who picked that one, so I've had my troubles! I'm not going to be judge and jury anymore. I think Graves was up against an impossible situation. The Portland Municipal Building was a hopeless endeavor from the beginning, but a very important one, because it signals the first public building in the after-modern, after–International Style period. It's a very important building, but Graves didn't have a chance.

BLDD: Why? Were the architectural community and the general public opposed to that notion?

PJ: Everybody was opposed to it, except me! But the point is that he was given a squat, cubic building with much too much to go in it, and a budget with which no one could build a building. With so little money there was no chance of using any decent materials or of designing a decently shaped building. Everything that possibly could fit was jammed in.

BLDD: In light of those limitations, how do you think the building turned out?

PJ: Pretty well. I want people to realize when they see it, though, that it would be more fair to Graves to judge the building by looking at his sketches. But he'll have plenty more chances; he's building lots of buildings. In the next five years he will be the leading architect.

BLDD: What other architects do you consider major today? What makes each of them important?

PJ: Richard Meier's work is entirely different, but I like it just as much. I also like the work of Frank Gehry and Peter Eisenman. There's a whole slew of them.

BLDD: What about each of them engages you—the ideas, the detail, the aspiration?

PJ: No, it's certainly not the aspiration; it's the accomplishment, the shapes that they are able to make. You can only judge them as you judge any work of art. Mondrian was better than anybody who copies him because he had a way with the thickness of a line versus the square of white or the square of red—there was a balance that looked correct. He's recognized as better and his works are priced accordingly. The marketplace is not so bad after all. These people that I mentioned are not all appreciated now, but I think someday they will be. We're setting up better standards. This conversation could not have been held ten years ago. There weren't five or six architects to choose from in that generation.

BLDD: How do you explain this difference over a period of ten years?

PJ: There's the freedom that Venturi gave us. Now it's no crime to copy Le Corbusier. It's no crime to enjoy looking at Schinkel. Even in Pittsburgh it's no particular crime to build the classic skyscraper.

BLDD: A concern of every architect is the initial perception of a space, be it a room or a building. What do you think about when you plan for that first impression? How are your concerns different in the design of a building and that of a room?

PJ: A room is the opposite of a building. We always talk in our office of our "inside buildings" and our "outside buildings." Some of our buildings are very successful outside, but the interiors are not exciting; others have great rooms, but the outsides are just tacked onto the great rooms. The trick in architecture—and I don't think I've ever totally succeeded at it—is to combine the two. The Parthenon, for example, is an outside building; it hasn't any inside. On the other hand, many of the cathedrals of the Middle Ages have no exteriors at all, only that incredible Gothic space. The outsides of those cathedrals were not important. This wasn't the point—the point was the great room.

BLDD: Which of your buildings do you think comes closest to combining the outside and the inside?

PJ: It's hard to say, because most of my work in the last ten years has been skyscrapers, which don't have interiors. You can't make architecture out of an elevator.

BLDD: But you have managed to do that in one of your most celebrated and controversial current buildings—the new AT&T Building. As I recall, the lower stage doesn't even have a lobby. Why did you choose to do that?

PJ: That building *may* have an interior. Have you looked in the door? There's a gold-leaf cross-vaulted ceiling. The statue from atop the old AT&T Building is right underneath the gold vault. It stands there to symbolize what was the biggest company in the world for quite a while.

BLDD: I heard recently that the headquarters building of AT&T is about to take in boarders. They're going to rent almost half of the 700,000 square feet to an outside tenant. If you had known that in advance, would you have designed the building differently?

PJ: I think it's a strange decision. It's not a question of economics—AT&T simply doesn't want the building. I think they regret having built it. But there it is, and I think they're going to have a hard time renting it. Now it's quite a different company than when we started.

BLDD: Did you ever expect the public furor that erupted when the design for the AT&T Building was originally announced?

PJ: I thought it was perfectly natural. I was given the job because I had worked on the Seagram Building twenty years before. We promised AT&T that we were going to give them the most important building in the city of New York, which was only their due as the biggest company in the world. We designed it and they loved it. We started the building and, all of a sudden, all hell broke loose. Ada Louise Huxtable hated it. If

AT&T Corporate Headquarters, New York, N.Y.

Ada Louise hates a building you're in deep trouble. It's that simple. Fortunately, Paul Goldberger likes it.

BLDD: Let's talk about a controversial part of the building—what you have referred to as the "highboy pediment."

PJ: No, I have not. I resent that phrase very much. It had nothing to do with a highboy and I resent the fact that they thought we were building a small building and blowing it up to scale. It is a hoary old tradition in classical architecture to break a pediment, and there are many ways of breaking it. Throughout the Hellenistic period and the Baroque age pediments were broken, twisted, bent, curved, kicked—this happens to be our way of dealing with a pediment. We placed it up there to call attention to the building and make it identifiable. If you look down from the Empire State Building, all the buildings form an unintelligible mass. You're going to recognize our building the way you do the great buildings in New York like the Chrysler Building and the General Electric Building, and all the downtown buildings with beautiful tops on them, like the Woolworth Building. All buildings that are of a great period—like the 1890s or the 1920s—have tops on them. So we said, "We're going to give you a top." That was where we had problems, even with our clients. So we showed them other tops.

BLDD: It certainly became the most notorious unbuilt building in America. What were you trying to do there, and do you think you succeeded?

PJ: I was trying to recall some of the great periods of New York architecture without worrying that the design was eclectic. For instance, the colonnade is the same as that of the New York Municipal Building built by McKim, Mead & White

Transco Tower, Houston, Tex.

in 1911. There was nothing unusual or new about a colonnade of that kind. There's nothing unusual about windows cut in a hole. The top is unusual, but it used a classical theme.

BLDD: Opening a client's eyes to new ideas must be difficult under any circumstances.

PJ: Once I walked in and the chairman said, "What's it made of?" I said, "It's made of granite." That's the length of time it took to get that building accepted.

BLDD: You have also done something in that building that is either revisionist or a very fresh idea: instead of overhead fluorescent lighting you have used incandescent desk lamps. Why did you decide to do that?

PJ: To reduce the glare of fluorescent light ceilings, the bad color of fluorescent tubes, the boredom of the office world. Now you go in and pull a little chain; if there's too much light you push the lamp away; if there's not enough you bring it a little closer. That's what you do the minute you get home. It's the original way of doing it.

BLDD: What innovations have you developed in response to financial or technological constraints?

PJ: The best thing we did was that we got rid of the elevators. There are thirty-five elevators in the building, but only four main elevators. At the end of the great room on the ground level are the four doors into the four "shuttle cars," as we call them. They go up to the real lobby, on top of the big arch. That's why the great big arch is such a great big arch: when you get up to the real lobby you're still under the arch itself. The lobby of the building is ten stories high.

BLDD: What informed your sensibility in the construction of that monumental arch and unusual lobby?

PJ: The public. We had a big building to construct on too tight a site. There's no question about that. I still resent the fact that they didn't buy the land that IBM is built on. They couldn't; IBM wouldn't sell. We had to take second place and jam our building up with everybody else. We wanted to give as much of this ground back to the public as we could, so we took the elevators—which would normally have taken up practically the whole ground floor on a small site like that—and just lifted them up.

BLDD: How much will a building with 700,000 square feet add to the traffic flow in that already dense part of town?

PJ: Absolutely nothing. You'll never know it is there.

BLDD: Have you planned something to alleviate that kind of congestion?

PJ: Yes, we left the whole ground floor open. It's like a garden except it's not as light. What people object to today, and they're right, is the shadowing of the street, the feeling that you are moving around in canyons. They're trying to make laws to alleviate that, but I don't know how it can be done.

BLDD: What is it that you think makes the city unlivable?

PJ: I don't find cities unlivable. Any of them. Tokyo, yes. Tokyo has ugliness. But New York has beauty. We don't have such a shift in scale. You learn to use your feet. If you come from outside of New York you can't believe the fact that people don't use cars. Of course, that's the best thing about New York—if you want to go somewhere you walk. If you lived in Kansas City you'd take your car. In Houston once, I told a friend I was going to take him to visit a future client—and so we got into his car and drove across the street! It doesn't cross a Texan's mind not to get in the car first. I find New York, therefore, a great experience.

BLDD: You've built a number of buildings in Texas, one of which has transformed the Houston skyline; I'm thinking of Pennzoil. Currently you have a commission that will be the tallest building in Houston's Galleria, the Transco Building, which will dominate the city like the Eiffel Tower does Paris. Will you tell us how the design evolved?

PJ: It's a delightful story. Gerry Hines, the developer, wanted to make his mark in the development park he did near Houston. If you put a skyscraper in New York, you hardly see it. But if you take a sixty-five-story building and put it out in the country, that's the Eiffel Tower effect. That's what we've done. All the rest of the buildings are ten stories tall, and you don't see them. So this great big building sticks up there—it's a lot of fun.

BLDD: Was Hines the patron of the Pennzoil Building as well?

PJ: Yes, he was the instigator of that building, and it gave him such a kick he thought he'd do it again.

BLDD: How important is a patron to an architect? Who is the best patron you ever had?

PJ: Gerry Hines. Should I say that with all my new clients around?

BLDD: They have something to aspire to now.

PJ: Everybody wonders how Gerry does it.

BLDD: How *does* he do it?

PJ: Smart. Smart. Patrons are more than half of architecture. Architecture is much too important to leave to the architect, because we get fantastic and silly ideas. We aren't as willing as artists are to tear up our work. So we build it. If there's a mistake, you have to cover it with ivy—or move to another city. But if you have a patron, he'll stop you short and say you can't afford that, and you'll go home and cry.

BLDD: But is architecture too important to be left to the bankers, the developers, the planning officials, and the government agencies?

PJ: Of course.

BLDD: In the end, how much of a building is designed by each of the above?

PJ: That's an interesting question. We'd have to work at that one. I think the architect is gradually gaining importance. Twenty years ago we didn't have a chance—then the only great patron was Sam Bronfman of the Seagram Company. Now, there is J. Irwin Miller in Indiana, a number of other single patrons across the country, as well as developers like Gerry Hines and George Klein.

BLDD: I've heard you describe even the most powerful architects as the employees of the developers. That isn't a very flattering description of the architect's role.

PJ: A more flattering word than "employee" might be "whore." I don't think that's a very nice word either, but it's apt. I wish we *were* employees, because architects don't get paid as well as most employees. Developers know they can get architectural work done quite cheaply because we're dying to build and would do it for nothing, as long as we could still eat. Developers don't like us to starve to death, but as employees we're on a pretty low echelon.

BLDD: You've said, however, that there *are* commissions an architect can and should refuse. What would be an example of this?

PJ: My own experience is the commission for Lever House, which is going to be redone. I mean it's up for grabs. They haven't used their air rights, so they can build on top of the existing structure. In another two months, the Landmarks Preservation Commission will make it a landmark, and the air rights will be gone. I also refused the St. Bartholomew's commission. But anyone would. I didn't want to hurt Bertram Goodhue's great building. Great architecture has to be preserved at all costs. The addition to St. Bart's didn't seem to be worth it. The people that own that church are very rich. They owe it to New York to preserve that building because it

Fort Hill Building, Boston, Mass., model

provides open space on Park Avenue and because Goodhue is a great architect. This may not be recognized now, but just wait five years. I wouldn't overshadow the church or tear any part of it down. I refused other, more important jobs, including the tower over Grand Central Station. That was my first statement of principle, because I felt it would have defaced Grand Central.

BLDD: You've said before that you do not know of any great period in architecture that paid no attention to detail. Earlier in this conversation you said you still believe God is in the details. To which details should the architect be most attentive today?

PJ: The details change with the period. The details that Mies van der Rohe paid most attention to were the frames of the windows, the spandrels, and the doors. Mies was a bear on corners, which, of course, he learned from Schinkel. Le Corbusier had a different set of details. Today I don't worry about window details so much. In my latest building I'm worrying about the relationship of a circle to a cylinder to a rectangle. I'm talking about the Fort Hill Building in Boston. It is going to be one of the largest buildings in the country, a new attempt at

PPG Industries Headquarters, Pittsburgh, Pa.

skyscraper design. I'm very proud of it. It's based on a village concept. There are six buildings of different types, round ones and rectangular ones. They bump into each other, making only two buildings with a garden in between. It's the tallest building in Boston, as tall as that famous glass one, the Hancock Building!

BLDD: Who was the client for that village?

PJ: Donald Chiòfaro.

BLDD: In Pittsburgh you have designed a structure that is in some ways very different from the AT&T in New York, in its proportions, its scale, and its use of materials.

PJ: Yes, the Pittsburgh Plate Glass Building is almost the opposite of AT&T. AT&T is a classical building, built of granite, with little windows in it. PPG is built of glass, and you can imagine why: it's the headquarters of the Pittsburgh Plate Glass Company. So the entire building is glass, but the details are Gothic. It has delicious little four-corner spires. The building has peaks like Pugin's Houses of Parliament or any English church.

BLDD: You've designed buildings in glass before. In fact, one of them is the world's first drive-in church, the Crystal Cathedral in Garden Grove, California. It's longer, wider, and higher than Notre Dame. How did you manage to fulfill the Reverend Dr. Robert Schuller's request that you "tie the religious experience to nature"?

PJ: Over protests. We designed a perfectly sensible church with a nice roof and solid walls. It creates that nice mysterious feeling of being in a church. When he said, "I want it all glass," I said, "Dr. Schuller, you certainly don't want to sit here and look at all the parked cars." He said, "What is wrong with cars? You live in your car all day long. Are you ashamed of it? Is God

not in the car?" It's an entirely different way of looking at religion from the way I look at it in a Gothic cathedral.

BLDD: How do you think that type of building works as a place of worship, in contrast with the more traditional form?

PJ: I was surprised: it works marvelously. There is a very religious light because we used almost opaque glass. It's like being under water. The interior sparkles with little white lines—actually they aren't little, they're great big things, but there are so many of them so far away that they look very small. You look into one of those corners and it's a long way away. It does work religiously.

BLDD: Do you ever set out to design a building in a particular style?

PJ: Yes, with the Dade County Cultural Center in Miami, which is right in the middle of the city, we decided to build a little acropolis at the square, heavily influenced by the Tuscan style, I guess. But if you get pictures of enough Tuscan farmhouses and put in enough arches, it looks like a de Chirico. Maybe I hope it does. De Chirico is a much maligned and much undervalued influence on architects. He had more influence on architects than Picasso did. It isn't counted but it should be.

BLDD: Much of your life has been involved with the visual arts and the design of museums. As a member of the Board of Trustees of the Museum of Modern Art, you served on the architecture committee that commissioned another architect to design the new museum tower. In addition to approving the work of another architect, you sacrificed a building that you had codesigned in an earlier period.

PJ: That sounds like such a good story.

BLDD: How do you feel about the museum tower?

PJ: It's very nice. I'm going to live there because I can see several other buildings I like to look at. I can see the garden I designed. I can see the Seagram Building I had something to do with. The AT&T stands right in front of me. I wanted to build the new museum tower, but I got fired. That's why I didn't do that building.

BLDD: How did you get fired?

PJ: It was very difficult, but I managed.

BLDD: Weren't you a likely choice?

PJ: I thought so. They wanted to go outside the Board of Trustees to get an objective view. I don't blame them. It was a lot of fun working at the museum all those years. I miss Alfred Barr so much. He started me off in life. It's all different now.

BLDD: How important has your involvement with artists been during the course of your own career—not only in terms of aesthetic pleasure, but also in terms of your work as an architect?

PJ: I don't learn anything from the young artists. We're just friends because I collect their work and I like to look at it on the wall. But I don't learn from them. I mostly learned from Mondrian and de Chirico.

BLDD: Can you learn anything from younger architects?

PJ: Oh yes, I learn from Venturi, Meier, Stern, Graves, Eisenman.

BLDD: You often use the adjective "inevitable" to describe great architecture. What does that mean?

PJ: Great architecture has to be so fitting for its site—like the Parthenon—for its purpose, and its age that it *seems* inevitable. But objectively there's no such thing as inevitable.

BLDD: People call your style of architecture classical, traditional, historical, eclectic. What would you call it?

PJ: All of them. It's not postmodernist. Did you notice that neither of us has used that word throughout the entire interview? That must be some kind of record!

BLDD: You have alluded to the idea that architecture is a

Garden Grove Community Church ("Crystal Cathedral"), Garden Grove, Calif.

profession of money and patrons. What are some of your feelings on developing and upgrading housing for the poor?

PJ: I am a plaything of the rich and therefore don't know enough about that field. I regret that deeply. To my own moral sense, especially before I threw it all over and became a success boy, it did seem that the only important project for an architect was to house the people of the United States. Why is it that a country with more money than the rest of the world put together has people living the way they do? It doesn't make any sense. This is why I supported Huey Long when I was young. Huey didn't help much, but I thought he might. I was grasping at straws. I didn't become a communist the way all my classmates did, but I still believed in the social values that they were concerned with. The scandal of the age is that neither the Democrats nor the Republicans have built housing. What's keeping this country in the present depression just as in the last one is the failure to spend money—I don't mean spending cash money, but putting people to work. What are the millions of people who used to be employed building automobiles going to do now? We don't need any more automobiles. What we need is housing. Why don't we build according to need instead of according to the laws of the marketplace—building offices that we cannot use? It sounds like a topsy-turvy civilization. If I came down from Mars I'd think these people were absolutely insane. I don't often talk about that because I'm not on a soapbox anymore, and there's very little I can do about it.

BLDD: Now, at the age of seventy-eight, you are still as active as most people half your age.

PJ: That's right. More so. But I think we've got to mention here that it isn't all me. I was very clever in 1967 and began working with John Burgee, who's a good deal brighter than I am in many ways, as my partner.

BLDD: Recently you've changed your relationship with your firm of Johnson/Burgee and have become a consultant. After hearing and reading about all the assignments and commissions you're involved in, I wonder if there's really a difference in role, or if it's merely in title.

PJ: It's just a change in title. My partner says that eventually—and it's true, *eventually*—it will be a change in fact. But nothing has changed yet. I did it to help him. There's no point at all in a middle-aged man who does half the work always having his work described as "Johnson's AT&T Building" or "Johnson's Transco Building." That isn't fair. I couldn't get the jobs, I couldn't carry them out, I couldn't design them without sitting down with John on every single detail. There was no other way to give him credit. No journalist will ever use the plural credit line. Scott Brown and Venturi have the same trouble. She's an architect, too, and yet they all say "Venturi's house," "Venturi's plan," "Venturi's Westway." It isn't. It's Venturi *and* Scott Brown, but who is going to say all those words? I'm well known and John Burgee isn't. So now John Burgee is beginning to get some valentines without my name on them, which is good, because then in a few years—let's not specify when—he'll have his start in life. I think every older architect should do that.

BLDD: What do you think of as your greatest contribution—is it a building, a theory, an idea, or even an attitude?

PJ: It infuriates me to believe it, but probably my main influence is that I talk so much. And I also favor the young, so naturally they reciprocate by thinking I must be good, or I wouldn't favor them. There's a lot of mutual admiration between me and five or six young architects whom I like. If they're going to be good architects, then my reputation is perfectly safe, because that will mean good architects will say I'm good. What I most desire in this world is to be known as a great architect. Instead I'm going to be known as the great influence of the 1970s or the 1980s because I helped a whole slew of architects.

BLDD: For what would you most like to be known?

PJ: For my buildings, naturally.

BLDD: Are there any you would cite especially?

PJ: I guess I can't help being known for the Glass House. And there's always the next one—in Boston, for example, or even the project that's coming up in Times Square.

BLDD: What *is* coming up in Times Square?

PJ: The city and the state, mainly through the brilliance of Richard Kahan, a former head of the Urban Development Corporation, have laid out the boundaries of Times Square and let it out for developers to re-create the section from Forty-second Street up to the Portman Hotel. We're building four buildings that are more or less the same, a Rockefeller Center for that part of town, only somewhat larger. We're putting up some four million square feet. It should be a new center for New York.

BLDD: Is there a particular type of building you haven't yet designed and would like to?

PJ: Yes, I had hoped to get a commission for an architectural school. I did the design, but I guess we aren't going to get the job. I'd also like to design a museum. I haven't been asked to do a museum for twenty years. It seems that every day somebody else is building a museum. I'd also like to do a house. I wouldn't have time, but I would like to.

BLDD: If you were to do it all over again, is there anything you would do differently?

PJ: I wouldn't be such an ass as I was in my youth and run off to Huey Long, nor would I become a farmer. I did that for a while, and I was a lousy farmer. And a lousy politician. Unbelievably bad. I couldn't make a public speech, and Huey Long was crazy. I wasted a lot of years in which I could have been designing. I was already old when I got to Harvard. I said to Breuer, "I'm not so sure I can go to Harvard." He said, "What's the matter? Let me look at your hands. Well, they aren't very pretty, but you seem to have the right number of fingers. You can be an architect." So I can advise everybody that's thinking of becoming an architect to start before they're forty.

BLDD: You say that both historians and architects make very bad prophets. If there was a prophecy you'd dare to make, what would it be?

PJ: That we are entering an unbelievably glorious age of mélange, eclecticism, random choices, and leadership. It's impossible to pin down, but it should be the greatest period architecture has ever seen.

BLDD: And you have helped to make it so.

PJ: I blasted a few things a little . . .

RICHARD MEIER

Since the publication of *Five Architects* in 1972, Richard Meier has been identified with the New York Five, also called the Whites, contemporary architecture's most adamant—and prominent—purists. In the intervening years, each of the five architects has developed a style distinct from that of his fellow neo-modernist practitioners. Sculptural and pristine, Meier's work is the epitome of architecture as high art. It represents the harmonious coupling of form and function, of the literal and the figurative.

BLDD: It's been said that you're a rather curious figure in the architecture world, an anomaly: at a time when almost everyone is questioning the modernist aesthetic, you are celebrating it. Just who is out of step with the times?

RM: Perhaps none of us. What some people have reacted against in recent architecture is not the essence of the modern movement, but its overgeneralized manifestations. Mainly as a result of architectural practices common in the fifties and sixties, people have come to associate modernism with the commercialization of architecture and with unspecific, nondescript built forms that lack human scale. This has been true not only in this country but throughout the Western world. Architects began to use the available forms simply because they were expedient and economical, and the result has been disastrous. They failed to take into account the bases of modernism: creating a relationship between open and closed space; expressing structure as differentiated from a planar sense of enclosure; incorporating aspects such as natural light in addition to more formal organizing elements. These things make up the essence of modernism, as well as the essence of architecture, and are relevant not only to the modern movement but to the entire history of architecture. Architecture today is not isolated in its own time; it's part of history. And that means more than just an assemblage of past forms to give a building symbolic or allusive value.

BLDD: Your work is strongly identified with that of Le Corbusier. Did you ever meet him?

RM: I did meet him, twice. The first time was when I was traveling in Europe after having graduated from architecture school. I had the idea that I might stay in Europe and work for a while. I went to see a few architects, the first one being Le Corbusier. I knocked on the door of 35 rue de Sèvres in Paris, and was told, of course, that it was not possible for me to come in. I said, "I have my portfolio with me. I'd like to have an interview for a job." But that didn't work either. After staying in Paris for a while, I went one day to the Cité Université, where the dedication was going on for the Maison du Brasil by Le Corbusier and Lucia Costa, the Brazilian architect. Le Corbusier was there an hour or two before the ceremonies were to take place. I went up to him and said that I'd tried to see him and was interested in working for him as an apprentice. Since he didn't have much else to do at that moment, he explained to me why he wouldn't want an American in his office at this time.

BLDD: Why was he so disenchanted with Americans?

RM: It went back to the League of Nations competition, when he was almost disqualified for using the wrong ink, which he attributed to the Americans on the jury. The ink he used on the drawings was different from the black India ink prescribed. He wasn't exactly disqualified, but he didn't get the commission, and he was told that he didn't follow the rules of the competition. Later he was asked to be on the committee for the planning of the United Nations in New York. When it was time to make a presentation of his scheme, his notebooks were suddenly lost. Harrison and Abramovitz ultimately were the architects for the building, which was based essentially on Le Corbusier's scheme. This is well documented—it's in all of Le Corbusier books. He was a member of a larger group involved in the planning of the United Nations. There were many discussions, and the eventual building was a scheme that he had more or less proposed. It was generally acknowledged that it was Le Corbusier's scheme, although Harrison and Abramovitz became the architects of record. Later, when UNESCO was being planned for Paris, Le Corbusier thought that at least he would get to do that project since Paris was his home. It went, again, to an architect practicing in America, Marcel Breuer, and not Le Corbusier. Le Corbusier attributed these three events to the influence of American business interests as well as to the fact that his work was not exhibited at the Museum of Modern Art until very late in his life. It was a great disappointment to him.

BLDD: How did you respond to all of this?

RM: I just listened! There wasn't much I could say. I did protest that all of that had nothing to do with me and that I just wanted to work for him, but he said it was impossible. I left, with great disappointment, and went to Finland to see Alvar Aalto. I waited two weeks but never got to see him. When I returned to New York I went to work for Skidmore, Owings & Merrill for a short time and then for Marcel Breuer.

BLDD: You've been called a "second-generation Corbusier" and a "neo-Corbusian." What was it in his work that interested you?

RM: When I was in school, every student of architecture was influenced by four architects in a major way: Le Corbusier, Frank Lloyd Wright, Mies van der Rohe, and Alvar Aalto. Le Corbusier had a very strong effect on the students at Cornell when I was there. His pilgrimage church at Ronchamp and his monastery at La Tourette—two great works—had recently been completed and his influence was in the air. There's not an architect practicing today that has not been influenced by Le Corbusier in some way.

BLDD: Descriptions like "neo-Corbusian" and "second-generation Corbusier" suggest that your work is derivative. Do *you* think of yourself as a second-generation Corbusier?

RM: No.

BLDD: Is his work still compelling to you?

RM: Oh, of course. There are certain aspects of my work that are similar to his, probably the most obvious being that many of my buildings have been white, although Le Corbusier used color to a far greater degree than I have in my work. In terms of the use of materials, Le Corbusier, like Prouvé, experimented a great deal with prefabricated materials, as I have with metal-panel wall systems. The separation of skin and structure is one of Le Corbusier's five points of architecture; in much of my work there is a separation of structure and enclosure. But I also see my work as being very different from Le Corbusier's. For some reason people want to make that association. That's all right. I don't deny having learned from Le Corbusier, but the conceptual and spatial organization in my work is very different. I think of my design for the High Museum in Atlanta, for instance, as being much more related to the ideas of Frank Lloyd Wright. In terms of the use of the ramp as a major circulation element and the organization of spaces around the perimeter of the atrium, the High Museum is much closer to the Guggenheim Museum than to anything by Le Corbusier. Yet the building is partially white; has porcelain-enameled steel panels and granite at the base; establishes a column/wall plane relationship; and uses handrails—all of which are in some way related to the work of Le Corbusier. So there are many aspects to my work, and when people say it's "neo-Corbusian" or whatever, that's simply what they want to read into it.

BLDD: What other architects, besides Le Corbusier and Wright, were an influence on your work? Whose work do you admire?

RM: I've also been inspired by Borromini and Bramante and by German Baroque architects like Balthasar Neumann. Architects today are not wary of learning certain essentials from past architecture. There's much we can learn, for instance, from the way natural light enters the spaces of those great

Baroque churches in southern Germany. That does not mean that we have to use Baroque forms and applied decorations; we can simply try to re-create the essence of that quality of light—the way it filters through the clerestories and comes in from the side—and the relationship between that light and the structure of the building.

BLDD: You have criticized much of the recent trend toward historicism as "a stylizing of architecture as mere decoration" and suggested that it is a manipulation of elements without a guiding principle. What is your criticism based on?

RM: I was saying that for me that is not an appropriate way of making architecture. If someone else wants to do it that way, that's up to them, but I think architecture is more profound. I need a sense of order, a sense of intention that has to do with more than simply stylizing. The use of decoration is fine, but decoration in and of itself should not be the end product.

BLDD: To go back to Wright, in a conversation you and I had in 1980, you described the Guggenheim Museum as the most important work of contemporary architecture in New York City. Do you still think that is the case?

RM: I'd be hard pressed to come up with a better single building in New York. I remember saying that, now that you mention it, and that was long before I designed the High Museum.

BLDD: That's why I'm reminding you of it now. If that is the case, would it be a more accurate assessment to say that you were more heavily influenced by Wright than by Le Corbusier?

RM: Certainly Falling Water at Bear Run was a very, very strong influence in the design of one of my first commissions, a house for my parents in Essex Fells, New Jersey. I learned that enclosed interior space is very different from space that is out in the open, and that the idea of extending space from interior to exterior is a myth, as is the notion that materials are organic. Materials are not organic, they are inert; they don't change, they don't grow. The minute you cut down a tree it's no longer a living substance, and the wood has to be treated and protected. When Wright talks about material being organic he's talking about it in a philosophical sense, not in the sense of actually making architecture.

BLDD: One of the complaints leveled against the Guggenheim is that it stands so independent from the art, that it is too much of an object in and of itself.

RM: The problem with the Guggenheim is not its object-like quality or its sculptural quality or its independence as a work of architecture; the problem with the Guggenheim Museum is that the contemplation of a work of art is almost impossible there. Because of the propelling force of the winding ramp and the sloping walls, ceilings, and floors, it is very difficult to look at a work of art up close or from a distance, in relationship to the other works. The fact that a museum is a wonderful work of architecture, a great space, does not have to preclude its ability to function well as a contemplative place for viewing art. The two can be compatible.

BLDD: Like Le Corbusier, you are an artist as well as an architect. Before you started your architectural practice in 1963, you were deeply involved in painting and collage. How did the transition from artist to architect come about?

RM: It wasn't so much a transition as two things happening simultaneously. While I was working as a young architect I was also painting, for the most part in the evenings or on weekends. I realized that I could not comfortably do both with the same seriousness of intention, that I could not be both a practicing architect and a devoted painter. I studied painting with Stephen Greene, who had been a teacher of Frank Stella's. Frank and Stephen and I used to spend a lot of time together.

High Museum of Art, Atlanta, Ga.

Frank let me work in his studio in those early days, when he had a part-time job painting houses.

BLDD: Have you ever exhibited your work?

RM: I did in the early sixties, and I guess it was exhibiting that made me realize I was not able to pursue two careers at one time.

BLDD: But you still do artwork, now in the form of small collages.

RM: That's right. I began making collages when I was taking a trip around the world. I had a sketchbook in which I made notes and put things down. Now I make books rather than individual collages. I have a box about sixteen by eighteen inches that holds a book, collage materials, glue, and whatever else I need to work with. It's much easier to carry around. And when the books are finished, I can keep them on the shelf.

BLDD: How does your so-called artist's sensibility affect your architectural work?

RM: For the most part, my work is very rational, disciplined, and ordered. But I am not so rigid that I can't modify the inherent conceptual framework of a building if something outside of that order needs to make its presence known. I have the ability to create an order but also to pull out of it. It's like doing a collage, when you have an idea about what you're doing, but each step leads you further, leads you to something else. In architecture there is a process of action and reaction between the architect and the client. Other elements come into play that either make your design better or make you rethink it. You are forced to work over and rethink the interrelationships until they're right.

BLDD: Is architecture an art or a business?

RM: It's certainly not a business! There's no way, unfortu-

nately, that the time that goes into making a work of architecture is in proportion to the compensation received.

BLDD: But think of the psychic rewards.

RM: That is what keeps all architects going. The recent public response to the High Museum, for instance, really made it all worthwhile for me.

BLDD: The High Museum has been described as a stark white Corbusian structure. Would you describe it that way?

RM: No.

BLDD: How *would* you describe it?

RM: Basically the High Museum is a building in which there are four squares, four corners of a building, one of which has been removed. The auditorium is placed in the quadrant where that square has been removed, and the volume of the auditorium comes out of that cubic form. Is it the relationship between the cubic volume of the building and the more playful, sculptural elements such as the auditorium and entrance that people identify with Le Corbusier? Is it the density of the planar walls against the more open, translucent walls that people identify with him? Perhaps it is the whiteness and the ever-changing quality of the natural light within the building.

BLDD: Would you tell us about your design for the newly opened addition to the Museum für Kunsthandwerk in Frankfurt? What was the program?

RM: The Museum für Kunsthandwerk, which is a decorative arts museum, is approximately the same size as the High Museum in Atlanta, but the two museums differ a great deal. The High Museum is an introverted building in which all the spaces are organized around a central top-lit atrium space; this was done as a response to the site, the nature of the collection, and the program for that particular building. The Museum für

Kunsthandwerk, in contrast, is very outward-oriented. It is located in a parklike setting on a river—the Main—with hundred-year-old trees all around it, and all of the gallery spaces have windows that provide views of the park and the city across the river. This museum is an addition to a neoclassical villa, which has been incorporated into the design of the new building. Although the new building is nine times the size of the villa, it doesn't overwhelm it; it relates to it. Some of the materials, for example, are similar: stucco from the neoclassical villa is repeated in the museum. The villa happens to have been white, which is also the color of the new building. The scale of the new building is related to the scale and proportions of the old building, and the cornice lines of the new and old buildings are identical.

BLDD: How do you design a museum that works as a piece of architecture as well as a showcase for art?

RM: It's the relationship between the person and the art that's important, and that can be dealt with in a variety of ways. One thing I've tried to do in a number of museums is to make it possible to see a work of art in more than one way. Viewers should not be restricted to the one-to-one relationship you have when you're in front of an artwork; they should have an opportunity to see it again from different perspectives, to revisit the work in a sense. This was my intention in the exhibition I did in Albany with Tom Hess on the New York School of painters and sculptors, in which the design of the interior space was a metaphor for New York City. There were streets, alleys, windows, doors, always providing vistas. When you were in a space looking at a de Kooning, a Pollock, and a Kline, you could look across and see a Rauschenberg and a Johns. You could see the relationship between various people working at various times, which was appropriate because people working in New York City did influence one another.

BLDD: How did you first get involved in working with artists? Was it through your activities as a painter?

RM: I have had a long-term involvement with artists that goes back to when I was first living in New York. When Frank Stella let me work in his studio, he also allowed Carl Andre and Hollis Frampton, the photographer, to work there. It was the kind of place where a lot of people were always walking in and out. When I stopped painting there and was working on my own, I was very close with Alan Solomon, who was then director of the Jewish Museum. I worked with him during the installation of the Jasper Johns and Robert Rauschenberg shows.

BLDD: Did you do those installations?

RM: Alan did the installations, but I was involved in an exhibition on recent synagogue architecture during the same period. It was then that I met Barnett Newman. Someone told me he had designed a synagogue, and I went to see him about it. Barney eventually showed me sketches he had done for a synagogue; what he really wanted was to do a model for this exhibition. So Bob Murray, the sculptor, who was an assistant to Barney at the time, worked on the model, and I would go down and give him crits on what he was doing. This led to an involvement with a number of artists in the early sixties.

BLDD: What is the prevailing philosophy that informs your design of public institutions for the exhibition of art and artifacts?

RM: There is no single point of view, but many points of view. The design grows out of the nature of each particular place, and no two places are the same. There are very important distinctions to be made, for building in Atlanta is very different from building in Frankfurt, just as building on the East Coast is very different from building on the West Coast.

BLDD: What are some of the differences? Is it a question of regional taste?

RM: No. It has to do with light, location, climate. In the case of the museums it has to do with certain attitudes about the nature of spaces for exhibiting art and the relationship of natural light to the art object, attitudes that differ greatly in Europe and America. One has to consider the nature of the rooms, whether they should create a flowing organization or

Museum für Kunsthandwerk, Frankfurt, West Germany

separate discrete spaces; the scale of the objects to be exhibited; the purpose of the galleries, whether for permanent or changing exhibitions.

BLDD: You were recently awarded the commission for the arts complex of the J. Paul Getty Trust. The location selected for the Getty complex is 742 acres of what has been described as "gold dirt" on a promontory above Los Angeles, an arrestingly beautiful site, but one that presents a formidable challenge to the architect who will use it as the foundation for one of his designs. Have you ever designed a building for a site with similar difficulties?

RM: No. To the best of my knowledge, no one in recent times has designed anything for a site like that!

BLDD: Why is the site so extraordinary?

RM: First of all, the terrain is spectacular. Secondly, the site, on the corner of the San Diego Freeway and Sunset Boulevard, is highly visible: it's seen from great distances as well as from passing traffic in four directions. The hillside has magnificent views to the center of Los Angeles, to the Palisades, and to the Pacific Ocean. It is a very exposed site, with access from the freeway, and a great deal of thought has to be given to how to approach the site and get up into the museum spaces. The relationship of the built form to the landscape is also a major consideration. In terms of the program, one has to think about how to best utilize the site for all the diverse activities that are now planned, as well as for activities that may not even be thought of at the present time.

BLDD: What are some of the facilities planned?

RM: There will be a museum to house the existing collections of decorative arts and of sixteenth- through nineteenth-century painting.

BLDD: No contemporary art?

RM: No. There will also be a study center for scholars, with one of the most incredible libraries on art, architecture, photography, and graphic arts ever assembled, and an institute for conservation of works of art. Those are the three main elements of the program.

BLDD: The selection committee for the Getty commission included Bill Lacy, who was the chairman, Ada Louise Huxtable, Anne d'Harnoncourt, Craig Smyth, Reyner Banham, Richard Bender, and Kenneth Dayton, a businessman. Was this unusually well-informed panel more difficult than one you customarily face in courting a commission?

RM: Each situation has its own characteristics. It wasn't a question of being more difficult. This group was certainly well informed and very thorough, a group with whom one could talk about architecture. It was not a matter of simply showing one's work and having it either accepted or rejected. The unusual thing was the thoroughness of the process, a thoroughness I've never experienced before. First of all, the length of time involved was unbelievable. It was more than a year between when we first talked to the committee and when the selection was made. Normally the process takes maybe a month, six to eight weeks at the most.

BLDD: Were you asked to present specific design ideas to the selection committee?

RM: No.

BLDD: What were you asked to do?

RM: A lot of questions were directed at our previous work—both philosophical and practical considerations—and at what our concerns were for the Getty complex in terms of the site, the nature of the place, and the relationship between the built form and the site. This is something you can talk about in general terms, since the climate in southern California allows for the ability to move between indoors and outdoors more freely than in New York. What is the style of Los Angeles? It's very difficult to try to identify what is appropriate.

BLDD: Do you like California?

RM: Yes, I think it's terrific. The quality of light there is very special.

BLDD: What is the projected size of this complex?

RM: The program for the complex is still being developed.

BLDD: How do most architects get their assignments?

RM: By being lucky. But it is through a different process every time. One Saturday when I was working in my office, the telephone rang and it was Ed Logue, who was then head of the New York Urban Development Corporation. He asked if I would be interested in doing some housing. I said yes. He said, "We have a project we'd like to talk to you about on Monday morning." This resulted in three buildings housing over five hundred families in the Bronx. I didn't even know that I was being considered for that project. In another case, the High Museum, we went through committee after committee in the selection process and were very fortunate to be selected. Each situation is different.

BLDD: I assume the Getty complex is an assignment you wanted very badly.

RM: Very much.

BLDD: Is it the dream assignment?

RM: It is the most desirable commission for me to be working on for the next ten years.

BLDD: Why?

RM: For a number of reasons. First, as far as I can tell, this is perhaps the last major public institution of its kind. In the last ten years a lot of museum buildings and cultural institutions have been built. I don't see that continuing, and I can't imagine a museum or cultural institution that can in any way compare with the Getty. The purpose here is to make the best museum possible from everything we know at the present moment but also to go beyond what's been done anyplace else. Here there's a budget that won't force you to cut corners if it's important to do something right, with a certain level of quality. It's a project with both private and public aspects. I've never had a site that offers this kind of opportunity to explore the relationship between built form and natural form, between architecture and garden. The design will deal with movement and circulation, with ideas about how one moves through the landscape and how architecture relates to movement in the landscape. It's not just a question of how the building will be used; it's also one of how it will be perceived from a distance.

BLDD: How do you envision the process of developing the design?

RM: The process will be a long and complex one that will involve not only the staff and directors of the various components, but also the board of trustees. Many, many people are going to have input in this project in a major way. The architect's role is to try to balance all of this input, to make some sense of it all and bring it together in some relationship. It's not simply a conglomeration of various components, but elements brought together with a sense of order.

BLDD: How do you think your design will reinforce the unique quality of the Getty collection?

RM: I can't really say because I think there is an aspect of the Getty collection that may still be to come.

BLDD: Do you mean works that are not yet acquired, or works that have not yet been exposed to public view?

RM: Both. But I think there's a scale that works, especially in the case of the decorative arts. Those rooms will probably be dictated by the size of the objects and will have wainscoting and moldings that are already set. But that won't dictate the

Bronx Developmental Center, Bronx, N.Y.

Smith House, Darien, Conn.

relationship of room to room or the experience of moving from room to room.

BLDD: How will you infuse a sense of purpose into the Getty project?

RM: I think that will begin from the moment you enter the site—by car or bus or however. Moving up the hill through this site will be a part of the educational experience of going to that institution. Visitors will be able to walk, climb, or perhaps ride in some kind of vehicle to get to the top. The views will change as you move through the site; one's perception of the site and the city will be altered. Moving through the site, then through the museum buildings, looking at the art—will all be part of a total experience that will deal with one's perceptions and attitudes about the place.

BLDD: Currently your firm employs twenty or thirty people. For the Getty project, you will obviously require a great many more people than you currently have on staff. It may also take two decades to realize a project of that scope. Where will you find the extra personnel needed to address such a challenging assignment?

RM: You don't expand overnight; you grow gradually, as needed. There are a lot of people sympathetic to our aims and intentions that would be able to contribute in a meaningful way to a project such as the Getty. It's simply a matter of taking the time to find them.

BLDD: How will this assignment affect your firm?

RM: We will probably do relatively little else. The involvement, at least for me, will be fairly complete. I'm not interested in doing lots of building projects. I've found that by doing one or just a few at a time, I'm able to devote my energies and concentration. I would rather practice architecture that way than try to do a lot with less control. There are a lot of things that are just not worth doing, and it takes experience and time to learn what those things are.

BLDD: You've said that each structure receives instructions from all that have come before. What new possibilities do you envision the Getty will provide for you as an architect in general, and as a designer of museums specifically?

RM: There's no question that you learn from what you do, both good and bad things. The Getty affords me the chance to bring to its right place a certain knowledge I believe I have about the design of museums. Having done a European museum and an American museum in which there were very different points of view about ways of looking at art, I have come to feel that there's no one way that is appropriate. The Getty museum offers an opportunity to deal with many ways, and the opportunity to do this at a high level of quality. I've always operated with very limited budgets, trying to maximize the building within a narrow scope.

BLDD: You were recently given the Pritzker Prize, an award described as the Nobel Prize of architecture. What does this honor mean to you?

RM: It means that the work I've done is important not only to the people who use my buildings, but also to a larger public and to other architects. It's very gratifying to me to think that people go to Hartford to see the seminary or to Atlanta to see the High Museum.

BLDD: What will you do with the $100,000 prize money?

RM: I haven't earmarked it at this point for any particular purpose other than to try to make architecture.

BLDD: Has recognition of your work by fellow architects encouraged a similar recognition by the public?

RM: I don't think so. In fact, it seems to discourage clients. I don't get inquiries for lots of commissions because people assume I'm too well known, or too busy.

BLDD: You've said that a building can relate to its context in two ways: through textural similarity, and through recognition of and response to its surroundings. What determines how a structure should relate to its environment?

RM: Every situation, every environment, is different. For instance, if you are designing a building in an urban situation in which there are adjacent buildings and streets, you must obey what is dictated by the existing context. In environments in which there is no physical context to relate to, however, you have to *create* the appropriate context for the building. One of the possibilities in an urban environment is to go beyond simply creating an interior space and to make a building that reaches out, extends beyond itself, encouraging and motivating other things to happen so that it is not simply an object.

BLDD: How does designing a small structure inform your designs for larger structures, and vice versa?

RM: The houses I've designed have certain overriding principles—in the relationship of closed and open space, or public and private space, for instance—that relate to those in my larger structures. But other than that, I believe that the houses and the larger structures have different scales and conceptual frameworks. The considerations for an office building are very different from those for a private residence.

BLDD: You recently described a commission you are working on as having the ideal client. What is an ideal client?

RM: In this case I was describing a couple. They are very enthusiastic and very clear about what they want, but also very inquisitive. They ask why things are a certain way and what would happen if something were changed. This can be a little exasperating at times, but it forces you to not take anything for granted.

BLDD: Are you saying that the best clients are the most demanding ones?

RM: Yes—the most demanding, the most involved, the most curious.

BLDD: What elements in your work have garnered the kind of respect and popularity you now enjoy?

RM: There is a certain uplifting quality that people feel visiting, working in, or living in many of our buildings. I was recently at the Hartford Seminary, for instance, and it was wonderful to find that the new director is so enthusiastic, so jubilant about being in the building. He said that everyone who works in the building feels great about it. It was as though he had taken part in the whole building process, which he hadn't. That is what makes the effort gratifying.

BLDD: John Hejduk wrote, "Architecture can lift up the spirit and make life a little easier." Has contemporary architecture lived up to this idea?

RM: I think so.

Hartford Seminary, Hartford, Conn.

Westbeth Artists' Housing, New York, N.Y.

BLDD: Do you think architecture shapes or reorders society?

RM: I'm not sure it shapes or reorders society, but I think it gives some focus, some sense of purpose or meaning that otherwise might not be there in the chaos of our time.

BLDD: You once described architects as an "optimistic, idealistic lot." Would you still stand by that characterization?

RM: I think so. There are a lot of barriers to making architecture—practical, economic, structural—inherent in a process where you design something but don't actually build it. What you strive for is to bring together the myriad people involved in a project in an attempt to achieve a certain goal. I think that process requires a lot of optimism.

BLDD: The architect's work, like that of other artists, profits by experience. What has maturity brought to your architectural insight?

RM: There's a difference in the way in which I respond today than, say, the way in which I might have responded to certain situations ten or fifteen years ago. I used to think that if you conceived of something in a certain way, that's the way it had to be. What I've learned is that there may be a point where you have to reexamine your initial premise and find other ways to do things. It's a matter of responding to changes. Another thing you learn is that not everything you do becomes realized—and that hurts. You may spend two or three years working on the design of a project and be left with only the models and the drawings—no work of architecture.

BLDD: Some people suggest that the architect of the future must take a more active role in the design of our cities, in urban planning. Do you agree?

RM: No, I don't. If you want to be an architect, you do architecture.

BLDD: There is no crossover?

RM: Oh, of course there's crossover. When I do a building in an urban situation, I have to consider the planning of the city, the fabric of the city. But I don't think it's possible for an architect—or for anyone—to be involved in the design of cities. You're imposing a building or a group of buildings on a city, and that has an impact on the larger urban fabric. I, for one, wouldn't want to be involved in the planning, for instance, of the South Bronx or lower Manhattan.

BLDD: Which of your designs pleases you most?

RM: The one that pleases me most is the most recently completed, the Museum für Kunsthandwerk. You always feel closest to the thing you're working on.

BLDD: Which of your projects was the most challenging and the most innovative?

RM: When we did the Westbeth Artists' Housing in New York, a conversion of the old Bell Telephone Laboratories, I thought that it was the most difficult and innovative because we were doing things that had never been done within certain restrictions before. We changed the zoning, we changed the building code of the City of New York, we changed the requirements of the Federal Housing Authority; we designed the whole complex in nine months and built it in another nine. Everything was a first in what used to be called "renovation" and is now called "adaptive reuse." In spite of all of this, for me it wasn't architecture because it was working with such confined limits within an existing building. Some of the early houses were freer and more rewarding, and the most recent museums were more challenging in many ways.

BLDD: Did you expect your life to unfold the way it has?

RM: No, certainly not. I thought I would just go along and do my work. At this point I'm going through a period of reexamination, not only in looking at what I've done, but also in planning what I'll do in the future. It won't be like what I've done in the past.

BLDD: In what regard?

RM: I think the nature of the buildings will change.

BLDD: Will they still be white?

RM: Probably not.

BLDD: And how do you expect to expand your palette?

RM: I don't have the answer to that question.

BLDD: How will you diversify? Will we recognize the work as that of Richard Meier?

RM: You'll have to decide that. I don't think all my buildings are as recognizable as everyone tells me they are, but I do feel the need for a change. I think the change will come in the relationship of materials. I feel that my work with shiny white panelled building systems in relation to granite or stucco has gone as far as it can go, and that a new material relationship will necessitate a new area of investigation.

BLDD: If you had to do it all over again, what would you do differently?

RM: I don't know that I'd do anything differently. I've always tried to do as much as possible within any given framework, and at times I've felt I was trying to do too much. Now I feel I don't have to do so much. I simply have to concentrate on what I'm doing.

GYO OBATA

In 1955 Gyo Obata founded Hellmuth, Obata & Kassabaum, a small St. Louis architectural firm, with two other architects. Today HOK is ranked fifth in size among American architectural-engineering firms and has offices on three continents. It is recognized internationally for the diversity of its practice and the scope of its projects. Obata, the sole remaining HOK founding principal, is the firm's president and chairman.

BLDD: Did you grow up in an environment that influenced your decision to pursue architecture?

GO: My grandfather was a famous painter in Japan; he did silk painting and sumi. Both my father and mother were artists. They were born in Japan, but my father came to San Francisco in 1903 to study, which was very unusual because Japanese painters of the time generally looked toward Paris as the art mecca. My father was trained in the traditional sumi and silk-painting technique; he studied under one of the famous masters in Japan, Murata Tanryo. He felt that the growing new country of America was where he wanted to go, rather than Europe. So he came to San Francisco, dressed in his kimono, speaking no English. He suffered the racial abuse and ridicule often experienced by first-generation immigrants. But he was a very strong man. He came to love San Francisco and the whole West Coast and finally decided to settle there. He loved the nature of the West—the Sierra Nevada and the ocean.

BLDD: Was it reminiscent of any landscape with which he was familiar?

GO: He was from a town north of Tokyo called Sendai, where the Matsushima Islands are, beautiful little islands with lots of pine trees. I think places like Point Lobos and Carmel in California reminded my father of that area. But he really liked the grandeur, the tremendous scale of Yosemite and the Sierra Nevada range as well as the ocean scenes along the West Coast. He did a lot of landscape paintings.

BLDD: Where did he meet your mother?

GO: My mother was on a visit with her father, who was a businessman, and they met in San Francisco. She taught flower arrangement; in fact, she introduced ikebana to the West Coast. She's in her nineties, and she still teaches four days a week. Through my parents I learned about the culture of Japan and about artists. There were always other painters around as well as students—my father taught at the University of California at Berkeley. Until after the Depression, he somehow made a living painting sets for the San Francisco Opera, murals for the Gump Company in San Francisco, and so forth. Then he got an appointment at the University of California, and we moved to Berkeley when I was in the fourth grade.

BLDD: Didn't you spend a year in Japan when you were five or six years old?

GO: I went to Japan for a year with my parents. I lived in Sendai and went to a Japanese school. I forgot my English and spoke only Sendai-ben, a provincial-sounding dialect of Japanese. When we came back to the United States my English came back immediately because I started going to public schools in San Francisco. I grew up in the Japanese ghettos of San Francisco, where we had an apartment. The conditions weren't bad, but because my mother thought I should have a broader experience, she sent me to a predominantly white school called Redding. I had to take a streetcar every day and go downtown to get to school. I was about the only Japanese-American in the Redding School at that time.

BLDD: Was there anyone or anything that encouraged you to study architecture?

GO: We had flowers and painting in our house all through my childhood, and I became interested in painting. But very early on, from the sixth grade, I knew somehow I wanted to be an architect. I don't really know why that happened. I was interested in mathematics, physics, and chemistry, but also in the arts. I thought architecture was a little more technically oriented than just plain art. My older brother and younger sister were painters, but I went into architecture.

BLDD: You studied at the University of California at Berkeley but completed your B.A. at Washington University in St. Louis. Why did you choose to change schools?

GO: Pearl Harbor happened the day before the first final exam of my freshman year. I remember that dreary day. Over time the Hearst papers and many Californians began to express prejudice against the Japanese. I would be called a "Jap" in school and sometimes get into fights. There was always some kind of undercurrent of prejudice against Orientals on the West Coast. But the buildup was gradual until the war. When the war came, you could just feel the Hearst papers stirring things up, reporting another Japanese-American family caught in some espionage and so forth.

BLDD: How did you react to all of that?

GO: My parents were so broad-minded that we never got really anxious about it. But after Pearl Harbor and all this stirring up of public opinion, notices were posted on telephone poles saying that all Japanese-Americans had to get rid of all their belongings and report in a week's time to a certain bus terminal to be taken to camp. The ridiculous order by the army stipulated that if you were a Japanese-American living in Oregon, Washington, or California, you had to be moved. If you lived in Nevada or Utah, they didn't touch you. Then I heard that one of my friends in Berkeley was going to go to the University of Illinois, which had a fairly well-known architectural school, so I thought I would apply. But the Big Ten suddenly ruled that they would not accept any Japanese-Americans from the West Coast. So I tried to find an architectural school as close to the West Coast as possible, and Washington University in St. Louis was one of the closest. Washington University sent me a telegram saying they'd accept me, but I had to get permission to leave from the provost marshal in San Francisco, as well as from the university. I was denied permission. My father went to the president of the university and said, "I want to get my son out." The president spoke to the officer above the provost marshal; he gave me permission to transfer. The night before my family was moved to a camp, I got on the train. They were moved first to a racetrack called Tanforan, where they were put up in little paper shacks. They had public toilets outside. They stayed there for about three or four months. The Japanese-Americans were very law-abiding, and there were few dissenters. Now I think there would be more. But everybody went along, thinking this was a temporary thing. Then after the racetrack, they were sent to permanent camps.

BLDD: Even those who were economically and socially privileged?

GO: Everybody! Everybody was put together. We had to give up everything, including our car. We had one week to do this. You could only bring the smallest amount of belongings. It was incredible. It was based on nothing except for the army law. Roosevelt finally approved it, but Mrs. Roosevelt was totally against it. She was the only one who was a public conscience. She came to the camps.

BLDD: Did you ever visit the camp?

GO: Yes. I went to St. Louis in April and received special permission to go to visit my family at the camp at Christmas. They were behind barbed wire, with soldiers with machine guns walking around; it was just like a concentration camp. The real irony was that there was a small group of what they called Kibei—unlike Nisei, they were born in the United States, but they were sent to Japan to get their education—that was very vocal in the camps saying, "Look what the United States has done to you."

BLDD: What perspective do you have on this experience now?

GO: My father was a first-generation Japanese-American. At that time, you couldn't become an American citizen because of the Asian Exclusion Act that Theodore Roosevelt had passed for fear of the big "yellow peril" of China. There were only about a hundred thousand Japanese-Americans in California—a small minority, which is why the government could figure on moving them. Most of them were farmers and becoming prosperous. Their incomes were rising. Some recent books have pointed out that there was an economic justification for getting rid of the Japanese competition to American farmers. I think the internment program during the war was economically motivated, like a lot of prejudice.

BLDD: After you graduated from Washington University, why did you then choose to go to Cranbrook Academy in Michigan?

GO: In 1945, the two major graduate schools were Harvard with Gropius, the best known, and Cranbrook with Eliel Saarinen, a smaller school that wasn't as well known. There's only a handful of well-known people that have come out of Cranbrook—Eero Saarinen, Charles Eames, Harry Weese, Ed Bacon of Philadelphia, and Ralph Rapson, head of the University of Minnesota architectural school.

BLDD: Was Cranbrook less intimidating to you than Harvard?

GO: Maybe not going further east was less intimidating. Being from the West Coast, you think you're a little bit closer to home if you don't go all the way east! Being at Cranbrook was a marvelous experience because Eliel Saarinen was a really interesting teacher. There were only about eight or nine graduate students studying with him, and we all studied city planning. He felt that after you studied architecture you should take a broader, macro view. I undertook a master plan of the St. Louis metropolitan area since I was familiar with that city. Saarinen would come in every morning, dressed immaculately, and would walk around the studio, talking not specifically about your project but about broader issues. We would all sit around and talk. In the afternoon he would change his suit, come in again, and the same thing would happen. We worked night and day. Our dormitories were right above our studios. We would get up at eight and work until midnight every night.

I felt I got a tremendous education from Eliel because he made us take a micro-to-macro view of things. I remember him saying that you design a chair, then you design a room, then you design a house, then you design a street, and then you design a city. He would always ask, "What's the next relationship? What's the connection?" I've never been afraid of large projects, such as the Dallas–Fort Worth Airport, because of my experience with planning. A lot of people wrote Saarinen off as being too eclectic, not a minimalist, like most of the movement at that time. During that period, contemporary architecture was made up of simplistic diagrammatic solutions; there was no sense of enrichment. Some of the Cranbrook Academy of Art, like the museum and the library, *is* a little monumental. But the Cranbrook School for Boys is so beautiful, embodying just what everybody is talking about now: the ornamentation, the scale, the forms, the use of brick, the wonderful windows. He did the whole interior, too. I think I understood Eliel better than most of the students, although I probably didn't appreciate the details in his buildings then as I do now, having matured myself. There is a tremendous amount of detailing and humanizing of architecture in some of the Cranbrook design. So I learned a great deal from Saarinen, about overall planning, large-scale planning, all the way down to the detailing. What I appreciate most now is his detailing.

BLDD: Were your student projects on a large scale?

GO: I did a plan for all of metropolitan St. Louis that was related to the whole region of Missouri. Then I broke the master plan down into parts and did community planning in neighborhoods. So you went from macro down to micro studies. I felt I got a tremendous overview of architecture studying with Eliel.

BLDD: Were there other architects you were influenced by at the time?

GO: During that period, the late forties and early fifties, we were all influenced by the great masters. For example, when I was in school, Frank Lloyd Wright visited Cranbrook, and we were certainly influenced by him. We were influenced by Mies and by the whole Gropius school at Harvard.

BLDD: By the time you were twenty-five, you had lived in a number of visually distinctive places—San Francisco, Berkeley, Sendai, St. Louis, Bloomfield Hills. What elements in these environments do you find linger most in your thoughts?

GO: I was quite young when I lived in Japan, but I do remember things about my grandmother's house—the beautiful garden in the back, the sense of privacy, the paper shoji screens, the very clean straw tatami mat floors. I remember the simplicity, the beautiful detailing of the house, and the relationship of the living areas to the areas outside—the tight, walled-off streets, the good use of property. Cranbrook was an idyllic setting that Saarinen created with lakes, ponds, waterfalls, beautiful sculpture, and museums, both artistic and scientific. We were enclosed in our own little world there. I imagine that in some subconscious way all of these places have had some influence on me.

BLDD: Soon after graduate school, Japanese-American or not, you were required to join the United States Army. Did you feel particularly resistant or resentful?

GO: No. Having grown up with two artists, I never had any kind of grudge or any kind of resentment toward the United States. I knew that I was an American and that this was a passing thing. My family never really resented it, although I guess we could have. We saw it as a kind of bad dream that would pass. My family was always optimistic, never looking back. I knew I had to serve in the army. Since I had a master's degree in architecture, after basic training I tried to talk the assignment people into putting my education to some use in the army. They sent me to the Aleutian Islands to work on Arctic warfare equipment—can you imagine! We used to say there was a girl behind every tree, but there were no trees there, only tundra grass. We went camping in the cold, testing equipment and clothing and so forth. I had a miserable time. I didn't like the army at all.

BLDD: Were you making designs for your future there? What did you do after the army?

GO: I had an option to work for the Saarinens in Michigan, but I chose to go to Chicago because I had been in Michigan for almost two years. I got a job at Skidmore, Owings & Merrill. SOM at that time, 1950 or so, was like a postgraduate school with many veterans who had come back from the war. There were twenty-five young designers, and we all had a tremendous amount of freedom on projects. I had a very interesting project, working on standardized buildings for the army—PXs, housing, chapels, offices. I also worked on some buildings for Knox College in Galesburg, Illinois, and on a department store in Seattle. The Chicago office of SOM didn't have any strong direction like the office in New York, which was run by Gordon Bunshaft. I did a variety of work for SOM and got a very good look at how a large office operated. The difference between working in a small office and a large office is the pace and energy. At SOM you had to make decisions very fast. It was a good experience; I learned to work quickly and on a variety of projects.

BLDD: You were at SOM from 1948 until 1951, when you joined Hellmuth, Yamasaki & Leinweber as an assistant to Yamasaki. How did you meet Yamasaki, and what types of projects did you work on with him?

GO: Eero Saarinen had brought John Dinkeloo, head of production at SOM, to work for him in Bloomfield Hills. Eero's office and Yamasaki's office were very close, and when Yamasaki set up his own office with Leinweber and Hellmuth, he asked John about a designer in the Chicago office. Yama called me out of the blue and asked me to join him. They had offices in Detroit and St. Louis. My assignment was to work in Detroit for a while, but I was spending most of my time in St. Louis, which I knew very well, and headed up design there. I worked with Yama on the airport in St. Louis, one of my first assignments. When Yama became ill with ulcers, which he still has, he decided to close the St. Louis office. That's when Hellmuth, Kassabaum, and I decided we wanted to stay in St. Louis. That's how our office got started.

BLDD: How did your early experiences affect the kind of work you decided to do at HOK?

GO: One summer during Cranbrook I went back to San Francisco to work for a small office, which did houses and small commercial buildings. Working at Skidmore and then with Yamasaki led to my interest in working on large-scale projects. When we started our practice we resolved that we would never be known as specialists in any one field. We began as school architects, but that's what most architects did at that time—a lot of primary schools, then high schools, then college buildings. We were getting a lot of schools, but since we wanted to have as diversified a practice as possible, we still tried to get other kinds of buildings. We got a certain amount of press from some of our schools that won awards, particularly one in Webster Groves, Missouri, called Bristol School. Then we did the Priory Chapel, a very important commission for a new Benedictine boys school in a religious community. They were interesting clients to work with—Benedictine monks from a traditional abbey in England. They were very well educated, and what they wanted was a contemporary school. That's how the round chapel evolved. Because of that project, we began to get work outside of the Missouri-Illinois area—like the National Air and Space Museum in Washington, D.C. Then Stanford University asked us to do their library, on the condition that we open an office in San Francisco, which we did.

BLDD: You ended up as chief of design at HOK at the age of thirty-four—quite an assignment for a young man. Was that an undertaking you felt ready to manage so early?

GO: I didn't really think about it. Kassabaum headed up production, I headed up design, and Hellmuth headed up marketing. We took each step at a time. If we got an assignment, we tried to do the best we could. If we did a really good job, we got more assignments. There was no thinking about how enormous a task it was. It helped that, unlike many firms where each partner is in charge of a particular job or project, we had already established the idea of having one person in charge of marketing, one in charge of production, and one in charge of design. We worked together as a team. Once the job was in, it was totally my responsibility to do the best possible design. Once the design was approved, it would go into production. We really worked very well as a team. Now other architectural firms are beginning to use this idea of clearly distinguishing the various jobs; architecture is definitely a team effort.

BLDD: You have grown to a firm of 850 employees in ten offices.

GO: The major offices are in San Francisco, Dallas, St. Louis, and New York; we have smaller offices in Washington, Los Angeles, Houston, and Denver. We have an overseas office in

Priory Chapel, St. Louis, Mo.

Riyadh, Saudi Arabia, and we are now going to open an office in Hong Kong, in a region where we think there is tremendous potential for work. We think Southeast Asia is the next real growth area. I see it in Thailand, in Singapore, in Jakarta, in mainland China, in Taiwan. One of the things we have to offer is our tremendous technology, our knowledge in architecture, planning, interiors, engineering, and graphics programming.

BLDD: Are you implying that American architecture is now superior to that of any place on earth?

GO: Absolutely.

BLDD: Is there any competition, technologically or aesthetically?

GO: There are good architects throughout the world, but I think my firm, for example, knows how to put together large-scale projects and how to get them done on time and on budget. I don't think many other firms in the world can do that.

BLDD: How have you mastered those skills?

GO: Easily. We have come from an industrial age to one of communication, and our office is based on total open communication.

BLDD: You've said that HOK operates on the principle of an open society, which would imply that everyone knows what is going on in all areas of the office. How can this open society continue to exist with the rapid expansion of HOK? How do you maintain and promote that open society?

GO: HOK is essentially made up of a series of many smaller offices. San Francisco, for instance, has about 150 people. Within each office the structure is based on our firm's design, production, and marketing operations. At HOK, Inc., which is the top decision area, I have a small group called the Office of the Chairman. It consists of King Graf, who is in charge of marketing, Jerry Sincoff, in charge of operations, and me. We

can make decisions very, very quickly at the top. The key people from each of our offices, like San Francisco, Dallas, and New York, make up our board of directors. So we have this kind of matrix.

BLDD: One of the ways you promote communication, from what I understand, is through a house newspaper—a publication called *Network*—and through photocopying plans. Do you still do that now that you're such a large firm?

GO: Every month we photocopy all the designs of every office and send them to every other office. The heads of design get together at two-month intervals to discuss where we're going, what we're doing, what our strategy is. Marketing does the same thing, as does operations. We also have specialists in the fields of medicine, corrections, interiors, planning. We have, for example, the largest planning group in the country; there are 120 people in planning. We have the fourth or fifth largest interior design firm in the country. HOK sounds tremendous, but it's made up of a lot of smaller units or villages of people, and the villages are united.

BLDD: Given how extensive and wide-ranging the work of your firm is, how much of a hand do you have in each project?

GO: I work on the major projects in the firm. Having worked as a designer for thirty years, I have a huge amount of experience in arriving at directions fairly quickly. I concentrate on what the needs are and come up with concepts. This is where I am most valuable to the firm—not in managing a lot of people but in working on the design. So that's what I try to do, and I will continue to work on the major projects.

BLDD: HOK is an international firm with offices on three continents. Why have you chosen to keep your headquarters in St. Louis?

GO: For a practice in the United States, having a headquarters in the middle of the country is a real asset. In one day's time you can cover any part of the East Coast, the South, the North. The West Coast is maybe a little less accessible, a three-and-a-half-hour flight away. But I can have a meeting in New York and still get back to St. Louis that day. Having an office centrally located seems ideal.

BLDD: Considering the enormity of HOK's projects, and the impact they have had on the skyline of so many cities, have you ever felt that your firm doesn't get the kind of media attention that it deserves?

GO: I do feel that. We're known as a midwestern firm. I imagine much more media attention goes to eastern firms. But we'll get there eventually!

BLDD: Do you think your location has contributed to that lack of attention?

GO: Having St. Louis as our headquarters has probably hurt us. But we now have a hundred people in New York and have done a lot of work in the suburbs of New York. For some reason we haven't gotten a commission in Manhattan. I'd love to do an office building there.

BLDD: Do you feel a part of the architectural establishment?

GO: Yes, we feel that we are a part of the establishment. There are certain people, like Philip Johnson, who get a tremendous amount of attention, and the postmodernist group has been hyped tremendously. But that's not the real world. The real world of architecture is the many major corporations and developers who are very, very serious not about a passing style but about something appropriate and meaningful to them. These are our clients—major corporations, major developers, and major institutions.

BLDD: How many corporate headquarters have you done?

GO: We've done twenty-four headquarters, for companies like Squibb, Lenox China, Sony, Sohio, Levi Strauss, Phillips, McAuto, and Kellogg's.

BLDD: How would you describe the way HOK works with clients?

GO: We believe in communication, interaction, and understanding, unlike some architectural firms. We respond to the feelings and psychology of each client. We go in with no preconceived concept. We have programming people who look at the whole management structure of a corporation to make sure that their expressed needs are really what is required. We also do a tremendous amount of research. For the Riyadh Airport and the university there, I researched Islamic architecture in general and the architecture of that particular region of Riyadh.

BLDD: What does that do for an identifiable style?

GO: HOK's style grows out of the particular set of circumstances and the moment in time in which a project is designed.

BLDD: How do you contrast that to the work of other American architects?

GO: I think some American architects have a conception of a model in their head and impose that on the owner without a lot of interaction or communication. That may be an oversimplification, but that's how it seems.

BLDD: Architects are often thought of as having very strong egos that don't take pleasure in the anonymous.

GO: I'm not saying that we're anonymous. I'm saying that in the end you get everything you want as an architect if you really listen and understand, because then the client will go along with you. Empathy is the key word. If you have empathy, the client will go along with you.

BLDD: What do you see as the most important issues facing today's architects?

GO: Communications and the computer.

BLDD: HOK has received much attention in the industry for its commitment to using computers as aids for designing. How did HOK come to incorporate computers into its operation?

McAuto Headquarters, St. Louis, Mo.

GO: About three years ago we decided that it was about time for a firm like ours to go into computer-aided drawings. We asked headhunters to find the most knowledgeable software scientist in our field, and they came up with a fellow named Chuck Atwood. We told him to take his time and observe how we go about doing design and production drawings, and then develop a computer-aided drawing system. In two years he came up with what we think is the best software in our industry. It's custom-tailored to our needs, not designed by somebody who's simply marketing a software system. About a year ago we started using computers as aids in our production drawings. We're now on our fourth and fifth projects using this system. We're using computers as design tools, and they have humanized our process even more. This tool does so many more drawings than a person could do that we can study our projects more carefully.

BLDD: What do you think of the current debate about postmodernism? Where do you see your work in relation to postmodernism?

GO: There's been such a lot of dialogue about postmodernism that when you use the word it conjures up only a certain style or a certain group of architects. I think that's too limiting. I have always hated to be categorized, just as I disliked being categorized as Japanese simply by prejudice. I don't want to be categorized, I want to be free.

BLDD: How would you like to be described?

GO: As a very thoughtful architect whose solution fits the needs and aspirations of the client. The architect's ego gets in the way many times because he may be pushing for something

Galleria, Dallas, Tex.

that he wants, not something that solves a particular problem. I have just as much of an ego as anybody else, but I feel I really understand what I'm doing and get a lot from listening. In the end I can get everything I want as far as personal gratification goes because I'll get to do the kind of design I really think ought to be done.

BLDD: One of your design principles is the view that a building should fit in with the surrounding environment in terms of its height, scale, and materials. Have you ever found this goal aesthetically restricting?

GO: Never. I've never felt restricted on any of my designs. Naturally, in some cases I may have wanted a better budget, better materials, or something like that. But the kind of architecture we practice is one of process; it grows from understanding and gradually builds up. The postmodernist reaction has brought some good things. It's made modern architects look at buildings more carefully, to make them more humanized to the layperson. Recently I spent many days walking around London looking at existing older apartment buildings with their beautiful bay windows, their little towers, the brick buildings with great limestone trim. I learned a great deal from that kind of detailing. Balconies, bay windows, the use of certain materials like brick, limestone, copper, wood—I'm incorporating many of the things I saw in London. Architecture is now at a point where it has so much to choose from, a much wider palette than the boxes, rectangles, and flat roofs that came out of the modern movement.

BLDD: Do you think that's a temporary phenomenon?

GO: No. I think that architecture will continue to be enriched and that the public will really enjoy this.

BLDD: Is that how you explain the widening constituency for the preservation movement?

GO: Yes, absolutely. We're not going to continue to have these huge projects to do. We need to save and refurbish good old buildings.

BLDD: Do you do any of that kind of work?

GO: We just got an assignment in St. Louis—a huge old warehouse that we're going to turn into a very beautiful contemporary office building, using all the beautiful old detailing. We're retaining the whole exterior and much of the interior wood.

BLDD: Do you find working in preservation limiting as an architect?

GO: Absolutely not. Combining the old with the new gives tremendous enhancement.

BLDD: You've spoken of the need to bring variety and serendipity to contemporary architecture. How have you introduced those elements into your design?

GO: In terms of the locale, we really study. When we design in the Islamic world, we study the architecture in that area. We're also paying a lot more attention to interior design and we have built up a strong interior planning staff. In the past, modern architects used to just do a building and forget about the interiors. They weren't that interested in them. Now interiors are becoming richer, more beautiful

BLDD: In an effort to avoid the fluctuations of the market your firm has attempted to diversify rather than specialize. Has this diversification helped with the expansion and creativity of the firm?

GO: Architecture is probably one of the most cyclical businesses around. Right now, for example, there's a glut of office buildings, and firms that have specialized in office buildings will be feeling the pinch. Our diversification has really helped to fight that cyclical effect. It has also helped us in designing mixed-use centers like the Gallerias in Houston or Dallas, or

National Air and Space Museum, Smithsonian Institution, Washington, D.C.

even the Air and Space Museum, which was thought of almost as a shopping center to allow people to move easily through the building and see all the exhibits.

BLDD: What were you trying to achieve in your design for the Galleria in Houston, done twenty years ago when that part of the city was still considered a suburban area?

GO: Up to that time, shopping centers consisted of two department stores connected by a one-story mall. Working with developer Gerry Hines, we came to the conclusion that there was a better solution to the shopping center environment. We were thinking of the compactness, the density of many European cities, where places like the Galleria in Milan are crowded with office buildings as well as shops. We decided to make a city center, not just a shopping center, and to have office buildings, hotels, theaters, two levels of mall, and so forth. We also drew on the model of Rockefeller Center, with its ice-skating rink in the middle, to try to create some dynamic qualities in the shopping center. The rink turned out to be an incredible asset, and Houston has really taken to ice-skating because of it. The idea of making it more compact, more dense, more active came from the fact that people are always looking for interesting places to go. That's why we Americans are always running over to London, Paris, Rome, Venice, and Florence: we're looking for urban centers. In this country we're too spread out; people are not concentrated in smaller urban centers. Manhattan works so well because it's crowded. We need that in other cities.

BLDD: In the National Air and Space Museum you've managed to concentrate more tourists in one place than any other designer of public space. Is that a design, a project, that you still find compelling?

GO: Yes. I really enjoyed working on that project with Dillon Ripley, then secretary of the Smithsonian Institution, and Mike Collins, one of the astronauts, who was the executive director of the museum. I knew it was going to be crowded; I didn't know that it would become the most popular museum in the world, but I knew that the circulation system had to be excellent. We faced north on that area in the mall, so I knew I could have a lot of glass facing north to create open galleries. There are three of those, as well as closed galleries. The museum wanted to achieve a theater-like feeling, to create sets for the airplanes. It was always a wonderful project to work on.

BLDD: Until HOK got the commission for Moscone Convention Center in San Francisco, you were considered outsiders in that city. How did you get the project?

GO: Getting a project from the City of San Francisco was really the turning point that made us a San Francisco firm. Now, having done Levi Plaza and Saks and the Moscone Center, we have a tremendous office in San Francisco; we're probably the second-largest firm there, next to Skidmore. We're very much keyed in to that city and its unique urbanism, which creates places for people. In the Levi Strauss project, where we had four blocks to work with, we created not only a corporate headquarters but also a place where people could

Levi Plaza, San Francisco, Calif.

meet and enjoy the environment of a low-rise office building in the heart of the city.

BLDD: One of HOK's most celebrated and now widely admired foreign projects is the King Khalid International Airport, which stands in the desert twenty-two miles outside of Riyadh. Was this project your first attempt to utilize Arab architectural features? Did you work in collaboration with Arab architects on the project?

GO: We studied the history of Islamic architecture and brought in experts like Oleg Grabar from Harvard, a specialist in the history of Islamic architecture. We wanted to create the most contemporary, up-to-date terminal in the world but still retain the feeling that it's in the Moslem world. By using the slight curved forms, the arch, and elements from Islamic architecture, which is full of geometric patterns, we hit upon the triangle as the right form. That triangular form was broken down into smaller modules of triangles, reflected in the ceiling and all the internal decorative patterns. We're also doing a university in Riyadh for thirty thousand students.

BLDD: Which of your designs do you consider the most innovative?

GO: The one I'm doing now; it's always the latest one. I'm doing an office building in Dallas that has many interesting ramifications. Earlier projects were all creative efforts, but I don't look backward. I always try to look forward, and I do what's best for each moment in time. It's very Zen: I do the best I can for that moment in time, and then I go on.

BLDD: Do you think of yourself as being "very Zen?"

GO: Yes, I do.

BLDD: Is there a great Eastern influence in your life and your work?

GO: An influence through my parents. The way my father painted influenced me a great deal. He would totally free himself of all thoughts, and once he applied the brushstroke, that was it.

BLDD: Is that what happens to you at the drawing board?

GO: No, not quite. But I do a lot of designing on airplanes, because there are no disturbances and you can become totally immersed in a project and work on an idea.

BLDD: Your father preserved the disappearing landscape through his painting of California pastoral scenes. Do you ever think that instead of preserving a pastoral landscape, you are creating a twentieth-century urban landscape?

GO: That's a very interesting remark. My father always talked about nature in his paintings. As an architect I'm trying in a sense to create a man-made environment that's meaningful. Projects like Levi Plaza are important because we attempt to make humanized places.

BLDD: If you were to live your life over again, what would you do differently?

GO: You do the best you can at any given moment in time. Your viewpoint changes continually, so you can't look backward.

BLDD: Did you expect your life to follow the path it has?

GO: No, but I've always been an optimist!

WILLIAM PEDERSEN

In a profession in which competition is fierce and success hard won, Kohn Pedersen Fox Associates has evolved in less than ten years into a nationally celebrated architectural firm. Much can be attributed to William Pedersen, principal and senior partner in charge of design, whose designs have contributed significantly to a reconsideration of the aims of contemporary architecture and to a redefinition of the urban landscape.

BLDD: Your work has been called assemblage, collage, or organic architecture, for it recognizes the relationship between seemingly independent environmental elements and evokes a sense of each structure as part of a larger entity. Is that a reasonable assessment?

WP: Our work is based on the contributions of many talented people focused on a rather specific philosophical objective: to create buildings that generate contextual linkage within the urban fabric. While I have played a major role in clarifying our point of view, I am by no means a singular artist working in isolation. The formal vocabulary that we employ in our work to generate linkage has evolved over the years from many individual contributions. It is true that our work is essentially focused on perceiving and restructuring the urban environment and that we are heavily influenced by the model of the "traditional city." Our energies are aimed at creating a temporal and physical continuity within cities. The stylistic devices we employ to encourage this continuity vary from an extreme of assemblage in some buildings to a relative homogeneity in others. At this point our vocabulary is evolving. Our future work will be focused on the same general philosophical objectives of our past work, but a much greater emphasis will be placed on developing a stylistic language with which we can be identified.

BLDD: What originally gave you the idea to become an architect?

WP: My grandfather, Jens Pedersen. He came to the United States from Norway and practiced land surveying in St. Paul for a number of years. He was very much interested in the work of Frank Lloyd Wright. As a matter of fact his home, which he built on Summit Avenue in St. Paul, was influenced by Wright's Winslow House. Summit Avenue in St. Paul was, at the turn of the century, the dominant residential street. It ran from the capitol, in downtown St. Paul, to the Mississippi River. Along this street many of the aspiring families of St. Paul built their residences. To build on Summit Avenue was the hope of many, the achievement of few. My grandfather's house was a great influence on me; there were many family gatherings within it. It was a house that gave me, and still gives me, a great deal of pleasure. My cousin owns it now, so it's still within the family. My father was also involved in architecture. He studied architecture at the University of Minnesota and took a degree in architecture and civil engineering. He and my grandfather started a plan service called *Practical Homes*. They produced a series of editions of this publication beginning in about 1937, just about the time I was born. The last edition was produced in 1962. This book offered the houses that constitute most building in suburban America. At the end of World War II there was a tremendous demand for this service. The large tract builders had not yet come on the scene. I think my father's and grandfather's book was one of the first plan services offered in the United States.

BLDD: You were exposed to architecture from your early days but were not determined to become an architect. What did you want to be?

WP: I was a hockey player when I was a young man, dedicated to it with an enthusiasm I now have for architecture. At the time, I was very much interested in pursuing that sport; I played on the hockey team at the University of Minnesota. I was a rather good hockey player, but hockey and architecture couldn't exist together in my life. I had to make a decision; so here I am.

BLDD: Are there any analogies between the sport and architecture?

WP: I am sure that there are many, but the one that has meaning for me—it will probably sound trite—involves form. When I was young there was a hockey skate called the CCM Tackaberry. The blade of this skate had a magnificent profile, a profile far superior visually to any of the other skate blades that were on the market. If Brancusi had designed a skate blade, that was the one he would have created. I couldn't afford to buy the skate with the shoe and the blade, so I bought a pair of the blades separately—I think they cost fifteen or twenty dollars—and had the shoemaker attach them to my old skate shoes. My desire to possess these blades, just for their physical appearance, seemed a bit abnormal to me at the time. In retrospect the emotional response that elegant form generated in me was prophetic. Now maybe one can see similarities between the form of those skate blades and certain buildings I have designed, like 333 Wacker Drive. I still have the skates down in my basement.

BLDD: Are you a collector?

WP: I'm a collector, but not of sports memorabilia. I am a collector now, in a rather timid way, of English Regency and French Empire furniture. I enjoy the formal characteristics of the furniture. I enjoy things that are beautifully made. It gives me great satisfaction to live with these objects. The design of furniture is becoming an increasing preoccupation for me.

BLDD: Why Regency furniture? It seems in many ways to contrast with your design sensibility.

WP: For me it represents a high level of formal evolution in furniture, a great elegance of line. There are a number of architectural lessons to be learned from the design of furniture, lessons that can be experienced so much more quickly than with a building design. Buildings take years to initiate and finish. That is the great frustration of any architect, particularly an architect of large buildings. The final model of the building represents a certain state of completion and gives me personal satisfaction. Then there's a long process of waiting for the building to get built.

BLDD: You've had the opportunity to work with a number of different architects, particularly in the earliest part of your career. While you were a student you had your first professional experience as a designer for Leonard Parker. How did you manage to juggle school and professional work?

WP: That was a requirement of the school of architecture at the University of Minnesota. You had to work professionally, while you were in school, before you could receive a degree. I joined the office of Leonard Parker, a young architect in Minneapolis who was on the faculty. For a while I was his only employee, so I had an opportunity to see all facets of architecture very early in the game. I think that's important in the beginning. One needs to get a sense of the entire scope of practice as opposed to simply one small portion of it. I worked with Leonard for two years and was involved with a number of his designs in a rather significant way.

BLDD: Did you go on to graduate school after that?

WP: Yes. I was influenced by a friend who had studied at MIT with Eduardo Catalano and was enthusiastic about the experience. As a result, I selected MIT. While I was there I worked briefly for Dean Pietro Belluschi. He has been very helpful and encouraging to me. He has also been extraordinarily generous to other young architects, assisting them in starting their careers.

BLDD: It is also said that Belluschi developed a regional architecture in his use of stone and wood in many of the structures he has designed for the Pacific Northwest. Have his concerns influenced you? Like him, you seek to integrate your designs into the environment in which they are built.

WP: I may have been influenced by him. We, of course, are doing work on a larger urban scale. But one of the tenets of my philosophy is that a building must be able to gather its meaning specifically from its context. To make a building participate as part of its context and place is consistent with what Belluschi attempted to do—and succeeded in doing—with his residential and religious buildings around Portland.

BLDD: How would you describe the work of I. M. Pei & Partners during the five years you were there?

WP: I. M. Pei & Partners was loaded with talented people while I was there. Many of these people are still in the office; many have gone on to make major contributions to the architectural scene on their own. For all of us the training we received in that office was invaluable. To describe the office I must begin with I. M. as a person and as a leader. I have yet to meet anyone in architecture with his combination of abilities. His charm, his optimism, and his talent draw a remarkable devotion and dedication from his staff (and clients, for that matter). I. M. never told us specifically what to do, so when a solution was arrived at, we all had a great sense of personal contribution. Yet I. M. was able to get from us exactly what he wanted. His qualities of leadership have had a tremendous influence on me. I am, of course, a very different person, but I try to follow his example. The work of I. M. Pei & Partners was, and is, known for its elegance in detail and construction. Both my partner Arthur May and I worked at I. M.'s in the late sixties and early seventies. The concern we show for detail in our own work was developed there at that time.

BLDD: While at the Pei office you were a designer on the National Gallery of Art project. How did that assignment come about, and what special challenges did it provide?

WP: I was *a* designer on the project; Yann Weymouth and Tom Schmitt were other designers and, of course, Jim Freed. All of us worked together very much as a team. To explain how I was chosen for that project, maybe I should explain how I found myself at I. M. Pei & Partners in the first place. I. M. had been a chairman of the jury for the Rome Prize in Architecture the year I won it, 1965. The Rome Prize is given annually to a young architect, based on a review of one's portfolio and recommendations. The winner then spends two years at the American Academy in Rome, investigating anything of personal interest related to architecture. I spent a year studying D'Arcy Thompson's theories of the evolution of biological form, hoping to link them to architecture. After I finished at the American Academy, I. M. asked if I would be interested in coming to work for him. From the time I joined the office I always worked directly with him. I'd been there for about two years when the National Gallery project came in. It was a wonderful opportunity for me, both to continue to work with I. M. and to be working on a magnificent commission.

BLDD: What were your specific responsibilities?

WP: I. M. very quickly understood the basic geometry of the site and he soon came to us with an initial diagrammatic parti of his intent. The responsibility that Yann, Tom, and I shared was in the development of that parti. It was a long, exhausting, but ultimately rewarding process. I. M.'s initial diagram was severely tested, but it always held. In the end it produced a building that was responsive to both the site and the program. My personal frustration was that it all took *so* long.

BLDD: Did it turn out the way you'd anticipated? What were the most significant things you learned in a project of that magnitude and scale?

WP: The gallery is a beautiful building and it achieved its fundamental objective: to act as a significant piece of civic architecture first and foremost. Great numbers of people come to the gallery, and the internal space deals with that particular problem remarkably well. However, the gallery was designed within the confines of a strict geometry. In retrospect, the tyranny and inflexibility of that geometry were things I learned

Hercules Incorporated Headquarters, Wilmington, Del.

to resent. One did not have the latitude to manipulate as freely as one could. While I learned a great deal from the whole design process, I must say frankly that the purity and rigidity of geometry employed in that building was not what I wished to pursue in the further evolution of my work. I felt that I needed to find an approach that was more flexible, one that could deal with both the internal demands of a building's program and the external demands of a site and respond intimately to both. One pursues a design direction that is comfortable for one's own personality, one's own attitude, one's own objectives. I recognized then that I wanted to take a different tack.

BLDD: Is that why you chose to leave the firm?

WP: No, but I have always been impatient. I wanted to be able to do something on my own. The opportunity I was looking for was to do a building without any guidance. That chance was provided by my present partner, Gene Kohn, who was at the time president of John Carl Warnecke & Associates.

BLDD: How did you know one another?

WP: Through Jim Nash, who had been at Pei's office and then worked in the Warnecke organization. Gene had heard about me through Jim and asked if I would be interested in designing a major project. It took me a year to finally make up my mind because the experience at Pei's office was unique and I wanted to get everything possible from it. I also felt that I had an obligation to I. M. At the time I left, however, the gallery was well along in design.

BLDD: What was the initial assignment at the Warnecke firm that lured you there?

WP: It was a major project for the City University of New York, an 800,000-square-foot facility at C.C.N.Y. It involved an extremely complex client—City University, City College, and the State Dormitory Authority were all participating together. Jim Nash was the project architect, the administrator of the project. But the responsibility for designing and selling the design to this multipart client was mine. It was a very important experience for me. It is one thing to design a building and another to convince one's clients of that design, particularly when the client is as complex as this one was. My first presentation to them was a disaster. I presented what I thought was an excellent solution, but because it was the only solution I presented, I gave them no means of comparison. For that reason alone they were offended, and rightly so. An architect has the obligation, I learned, to uncover many possibilities. Then the logic of the right choice will be more evident. I went back and worked out six or seven alternate schemes and presented them in clay massing models. The next presentation went much better. I had given them the tools by which they could get involved in the problem. They could see the pros and cons of each solution as well as I could. I have used this method of design and presentation ever since that experience. Now the first design meeting is always a review of a series of alternative designs presented in clay massing models. These models are inserted into a large base model of the building's surrounding context so that one can get a sense of the building's ability to participate within that context.

BLDD: Did you expect to stay in New York when you first started working here?

WP: I came to New York after the Rome Prize and did not intend to stay long. But, as with most people, one good opportunity led to another. After all this time I'm still here.

BLDD: What regional differences in taste have you found between St. Paul and New York?

WP: There are certain regional differences in architectural taste, but I was not in Minnesota enough of my professional life to be completely aware of them. The greatest difference for me lies in the architectural climate. New York is an intense environment for an architect. That intensity has been essential to my growth. There are simply more architects here doing important work than there are elsewhere. One senses the competition. It may be subliminal, but it tends to increase your level of involvement. Without it I could never be as productive. I am in awe of an architect like Frank Lloyd Wright, who was able to return to Spring Green and essentially operate as an independent artist. But when one talks of Frank Lloyd Wright one is talking of a great genius. Those of us with lesser talents need the stimulation of a competitive climate.

BLDD: Have you been influenced by Wright's work?

WP: Yes, certainly, I am influenced by his work. It has such tremendous virtuosity. When you review his life's work and see the number of buildings he did and the incredible amount of inventive detail that each building contains, you can't help but be intimidated. The older I get the more impressed I am; to be able to contribute at such an elevated level throughout a lifetime is, to me, remarkable.

BLDD: Can you tell us about the genesis and evolution of your current firm, Kohn Pedersen Fox Associates?

WP: Our firm was brought together in 1976. Gene Kohn started an office after he left Warnecke's. When I left one month later, I did not have the intention of joining Gene. As a matter of fact, I was considering the possibility of going back to Minnesota; there wasn't a great deal to do in New York. But Gene had one or two opportunities and he asked if I would come and help out with them. That started the ball rolling, and it's been rolling ever since. Shelly Fox joined us about a month later. Patricia Conway joined us about that time, as well. Patricia is not an architect; she is a planner and a writer. Originally she was an investigative reporter for the *Washington Post*. She also wrote the book *Ornamentalism* with Robert Jensen. Now she's the head of KPFC, our interiors group. Patricia can do a great number of things well, and she is exceedingly helpful in balancing our organization. The four of us started together with a small office doing a series of studies for projects.

BLDD: The growth of KPF Associates has been impressive. To what do you attribute the firm's success?

WP: When we started the firm in the depths of the recession in 1976, we did not know that the country was coming out of it and that many opportunities would be available to us in subsequent years. The combination of personalities that our firm possesses has enabled us to take advantage of those opportunities. Gene Kohn, especially, worked very hard to bring us the opportunities. Our first big job came along when ABC asked us to remodel the St. Nicholas Armory, on Sixty-sixth Street. Shelly knew Robert Goldman, a vice president of ABC, and Bob gave us the opportunity to explore the feasibility of this project.

BLDD: Could you describe why this was such an unusal assignment, in terms of both location and program?

WP: At the time, ABC was bound by the inflexibility of their technical plant. They simply needed more studio space. They needed to be able to expand their entire facility, but at the same time they had to stay on the air. This was an exceedingly difficult and complex planning problem, building new facilities for them but at the same time allowing them to continue functioning in what had become an outdated facility. Initially we did studies for the armory, to transform that space into a studio. Subsequently we did a planning study related to all of their facilities within the area between Sixty-sixth and Sixty-seventh Streets and Columbus Avenue and Central Park West. The first phase of construction involved an administrative building and a studio space for WABC-TV, which is now on the corner of Columbus Avenue and West Sixty-seventh Street. Today we're in the second stage of construction, which involves another building on Sixty-sixth Street. So they amplified what they had on Sixty-seventh Street and enlarged what they owned on Sixty-sixth Street. It's very fortunate that they have been able to stay in New York and develop that entire area in such a way that it did not conflict with the essentially residential character of the neighborhood.

BLDD: How many projects do you have now? Are you personally involved in every design for which your firm is commissioned?

WP: I suppose we're doing ten or fifteen projects within the office right at the moment, but, no, I am not involved with every design. I think that was one of the most important early decisions I made, that we made jointly as partners. We were not going to dilute our individual capabilities as we grew. Our intent was to bring into the partnership group other individuals who had the ability to deal with projects and clients autonomously. Arthur May came to our office about a year after we had started. By then we had a significant body of work and we needed another design partner. Arthur and I had worked together at Pei's office and at Warnecke's office, and we have similar architectural objectives, although we've explored these objectives through somewhat different stylistic manifestations. We do not review or criticize each other's work; we work autonomously. Yet I think one sees through the body of work, as it's evolving, a certain continuity because we have similar philosophical objectives. Bob Cioppa, our administrative partner, joined us at about the same time as Arthur. He has taken on the heroic task of managing all of our staff and, in addition, manages several major projects. Recently William Louie joined us as our third design partner. Bill and I have worked together for over twelve years.

BLDD: Can you describe what your design objectives are?

WP: We do urban work primarily, although not exclusively. We love doing institutional and residential work, but we haven't had much of a chance to. We have done some suburban corporate office buildings, but the great bulk of our work so far has been doing high-rise urban office buildings. To do one building type so many times has allowed evolutionary growth within the firm's stylistic and architectural attitude. This attitude is founded first of all on the premise that for a city to be successful, it must have a well-defined public realm, meaning the streets and squares. That realm has to be dominant within a city; the private realm, as represented generally by the buildings themselves, should not dominate the public realm. Every individual building must contribute in shaping the public realm. The tall building must begin at its lower levels by acting as a facade that can join with other facades to create the urban walls that define a street. Once it meets that need, the tall building can rise as a freestanding object to fulfill the demands of its own program. The architects who first designed tall buildings, such as Cass Gilbert and Louis Sullivan, instinctively drew their buildings to the property lines so their buildings could join with others to frame the street. Above that, their buildings rose freely. Later, Rockefeller Center was, in a sense, the culmination of the evolutionary growth of the high-rise office building. There, for the first time, a group of tall buildings shaped a significant public realm. After Rockefeller Center, the proponents of modern architecture took the stage; the city of modern architecture was their intent. Streets for those modern architects were anathema. The street represented the evils of the industrial city. For them, a building was to be positioned freely in space with all sides completely exposed to view. This attitude, that a building stands as an object in space, has been prevalent for the last fifty years. While this attitude was originally well intentioned, it has decimated almost all of our American cities. Presently, urban buildings, as representatives of the private realm, are visually dominant over the spaces that represent the public realm. I consider that condition to be anti-urban. Consequently, our primary objective is to design urban high-rise buildings in such a way that they help shape the public realm. We do this by treating the tall building initially as facade and then as object.

Next, one must consider the nature of the facade. How do you create a facade that has the potential for establishing visual linkage? The street walls of the traditional city are largely based on the language of classical architecture, which, I feel, arose largely from a concern for boundary. A building resting on earth gave rise to a series of elements devised to express that condition; the boundary between building and sky generated other elements. My point is that *each* facade was composed of elements designed to resolve a common concern for edge or boundary, hence each shares ingredients with the others and allows for combination. Modern architecture, largely inspired by Cubism, dealt with its facades abstractly. Because they were abstractly conceived, these facades were never able to establish connections to each other.

Beyond the issue of developing visual linkage, an urban building must generate meaning, which should be drawn from the specific context within which it's built. That's somewhat difficult in American cities because most of them are very heterogeneous. Yet all cities present visual clues. That's how our firm's attitude of assemblage developed. We feel it is possible to draw together into the individual building various references from the context, some of which may have a retrospective leaning to conditions of the past, while others may have a prophetic leaning to conditions of the future. Assemblage allows for combining within an individual building a series of pieces, yet still creating an artistic unity.

These three principles—that the urban building must act as facade as well as object, that the facades must be developed with a concern for visual linkage to other surfaces, and that a building must be able to gather its meaning specifically from its context—are the lynchpins of our architectural philosophy. All our urban buildings emerge from that philosophical position. The evolution of my point of view toward the tall building began with 333 Wacker Drive in Chicago, a building that has been well received and of which I'm very proud. It is a building that generates a great physical presence and feels right for its unique urban position. However, now I don't feel that it represents a fully developed theoretical point of view. In subsequent works I have tried many things to accentuate linking the tall building to its place. Presently we're designing another building in Chicago, at 900 North Michigan Avenue, a building that I think represents the intent of this more developed philosophy.

BLDD: The building on Wacker Drive was one that gave you a high profile in Chicago. One review said that you had achieved what no outsider had ever before accomplished in Chicago. Did being an outsider afford you a certain freedom?

WP: Our relative anonymity at that time allowed us a certain freedom, because there was no pressure of expectation placed upon us. Urban Investment in Chicago hired us at a time when we had done very few tall buildings. They took a chance on us, and we are forever grateful for that.

BLDD: What inspired the design for the building?

WP: The site—and my skates, of course. This particular site was so special, both in its geometry and its position in the city grid, that there was no other possibility than to respond to it in a very powerful and dramatic way. It's the curving face at the bend of the river that is the building's salient characteristic, the element that gives the building its personality and establishes its presence. That gesture came instantaneously when I saw the site. The rest of it was a long, slow process of evolution and debate with all the participants.

BLDD: You've called architecture a service profession. How does that shape your work and philosophy?

WP: It's a service profession in that one is providing service to a client for which one is remunerated. Certainly one has a responsibility to that client to provide this service in their best interest. My definition of service is, first of all, to allow the client to see all the possibilities, all the alternatives. This is one of the most meaningful roles we play—assisting our clients in participating equally with us.

BLDD: Do most clients come to you because they want some variation on your last building? Does that present a problem?

WP: That has not been a problem for us. We have always prided ourselves on producing buildings that are unique to both their client and their site, and this will continue to be very important. Clients recognize that they're going to get from us not something that we have done before but something that is special to them.

BLDD: The unique work of your firm has received a great deal of attention, not only in professional publications but also in magazines like *Newsweek* and *GQ* that have broadly based audiences. How important is media coverage to the recognition of your work?

WP: Media coverage is extremely important. It brings our message, if one wants to call it that, to a wider audience.

BLDD: Just what is your message?

WP: I like to think we are known for buildings that are urbanistically responsive and responsible. It is also very important to me that we be known as architects of buildings that have a serious theoretical and philosophical basis.

BLDD: You've criticized some cities for not being urbanistically responsible. How did a city like Houston, which you have

333 Wacker Drive, Chicago, Ill.

described as having buildings that are "autonomously conceived, insular, and discrete," evolve?

WP: In American cities up to 1930 there was a strong understanding of what was necessary in the public realm. Individual buildings acknowledged the public realm and contributed to it. The destruction of American cities is largely the result of a philosophical point of view generated by the proponents of modern architecture, who believed that buildings ought to stand autonomously. That point of view has ruined our cities.

BLDD: Are you saying that American architecture is fundamentally un-American, in fact anti-American, in spirit?

WP: One can trace the formal genesis of the present condition to an attitude brought to us most passionately and inventively by Le Corbusier. The industrial city was choking itself; the streets that had been the lifeblood of the traditional city had become largely uninhabitable. A natural solution to these congested cities seemed to be to bring more sunlight into the streets. Hence the attitude that a building ought to stand freely within space, an attitude that formed the basis of modern urban architecture. Urban buildings as objects in space, rather than as facades defining space, create an inversion of the traditional city, whether European or American. It is this inversion that has been the most destructive to our cities because it leads to the dominance of the private realm over the public realm. In addition, when one explores the symbols of modern architecture, those that convey meaning, one is again faced with the dominance of the private consciousness over the public. The facades of early modern buildings are largely inspired by Cubism and the abstractions generated by that system of expression. The abstractions of Cubism, as I see them, tend to focus more upon one's private world, one's internal thought process. Renaissance and classical thought employed abstract symbols also, but they dealt more with universal experience than with private experience.

BLDD: Would you classify yourself as a classicist?

WP: Our work has turned for its inspiration to the traditions of the art of architecture, as opposed to the arts of painting or sculpture. Whether or not one calls our work "classical" is another question. I don't think one can be considered a classical architect unless one deals with the orders of architecture, because they were the essence of classical architecture. However, our work is increasingly involved with the assemblage of discrete pieces to create unity, also a characteristic of classical architecture.

BLDD: You've written that modern cities lack those physical qualities necessary to enrich the spiritual lives of their inhabitants. To what qualities are you referring?

WP: Our cities do not have enough opportunities for shared experience, a situation that won't change without a revised approach to the design of buildings, particularly the tall building.

BLDD: How do you redefine the architectural form of the skyscraper?

WP: One has to begin with the point of view that the skyscraper has the potential of making a contribution to urbanism. Before 1930 it certainly did. The tall building is a salient component of the urban landscape as we know it today. Anyone interested in urban architecture has to focus primarily on the development of the tall building. I'm dismayed by the lack of concern within the schools of architecture for developing a theoretical point of view toward this building type.

BLDD: What contributions do you make toward that end? Does your recent return to teaching represent part of that commitment?

WP: I've demanded from my own work a theoretical basis; it is natural to want to teach it to others. I taught at the Rhode

900 North Michigan Avenue, Chicago, Ill., model

Island School of Design a few years ago at Rodolfo Machado's invitation, and recently in the graduate division at Columbia University, with Robert Stern and Barbara Littenberg. Teaching a course on the tall building was not possible, but teaching certain lessons related to the tall building was. At Columbia we worked on one very interesting problem that related exclusively to issues of the facade. All of the students' projects were focused on the objective of creating facades that can establish linkage. The results took on a great number of stylistic variations but were generally remarkable.

BLDD: Obviously you pay a great deal of attention to facades and the achievement of external unity. How closely do you work with interior designers to ensure that a building's interior relates to its exterior? Do you think architects in general are becoming more conscious of that relationship?

WP: Architects today are more concerned with everything that falls within the province of architecture, including furniture design and interior design. I like to think of architecture as being a dialogue between internal forces and external forces. By that definition, the internal aspect of a building is half the problem; one simply *has* to be concerned with it.

BLDD: What do you consider the state of American architecture now?

WP: It's certainly in a provocative phase. The aesthetic atmosphere has been enriched by the contributions of a great number of people passionately interested in the creation of architecture. Architecture now is greatly concerned with its traditions and with the understanding of these traditions. Architects today wish to establish a relationship between what we build and what those who preceded us built.

BLDD: What features of contemporary architecture speak of their time?

WP: I think all architecture speaks of its time. Even if it is confused or misdirected, it still speaks of its time. It's a question of what speaks most eloquently.

BLDD: One of the voices that speaks most eloquently today is the voice of times past, that is, the increasing influence of the preservation movement in architecture. What do you think of the current emphasis on and growth of the preservation movement? How can you reconcile the old and the new?

WP: To reconcile the old and the new, one must begin with a respect for and understanding of both and then search for an architectural strategy that fuses these two poles. For me, architecture that excludes one or the other is profoundly pessimistic. Perhaps one sees in the work of certain architects today too great a preoccupation with traditional form, but this seems to be a necessary swing of the pendulum. As for the preservation movement, it's tragic that it didn't exist earlier. If it is an intrusion, it's an absolutely necessary one. If an architect takes down a building that has contributed to its environment for many years, he has to have an ironclad justification for doing so. One must be able to justify this in front of the largest possible audience; if one cannot, one should not be able to proceed further.

BLDD: What have been the most important developments in architecture during the last twenty-five years?

WP: A great deal of what is now developing in built form was called for in prophetic works of the sixties—*The Death and Life of Great American Cities* by Jane Jacobs, *Complexity and Contradiction in Architecture* by Robert Venturi, and *The Mathematics of the Ideal Villa* by Colin Rowe. These were enormously influential works. Each of them focused on the inclusion of both the past and the present and on what now has come to be known as contextualism.

BLDD: What do you see as the most important issue confronting today's architects?

WP: The restructuring of a public realm within our cities and the synthesis of past and present conditions. None of this will be possible if the primary component of our urban landscape, the tall building, is not given a tremendous infusion of creative energy. This has been, and will continue to be, my central focus.

BLDD: How do you see your work evolving?

WP: I would ultimately like to develop an architecture based on elements that are personally evolved from contemporary experience fused and combined with those that relate to a past condition.

BLDD: Have the early successes of KPF inspired greater experimentation or independence among the members of your firm?

WP: I see our work evolving, and I hope it will continue to evolve. We have contributed a great deal to the tall building at a point in time when the tall building has been largely neglected. We have been adventurous, but the adventure has followed a very rigorous path. Our future work will focus more upon the stylistic evolution of the elements that compose our buildings. Hopefully that will give to our work a greater personality, individuality, and identity.

BLDD: Do you have a secret or dream project that you'd like to work on?

WP: I'd simply like to do something very small very well. I'd love to do a chair, for instance.

BLDD: Which aspect of William Pedersen dominates your architectural efforts? Is it the artist, the engineer, the pragmatist, the philosopher?

WP: I cannot conceive of doing architecture without having a theoretical point of view. However, the theory must come from the buildings. Only then can it develop and change. If one is a prisoner of one's own theories, no growth is possible. Without artistic growth the agonies that one experiences in the practice of architecture would be intolerable. Doing meaningful architecture takes every ounce of one's artistic, philosophical, and pragmatic concern.

BLDD: Would you do anything differently if you were to start over?

WP: That question makes it sound as if I'm ready for pasture. I've just begun. I hope the best lies in front of me. From time to time I do look with envy at architects I admire who are doing smaller, more personal work. But I've worked for a long time to get into a position where I could do buildings that might meaningfully affect the urban condition. That is a most exciting prospect. I don't want to change course now.

NORMAN PFEIFFER

Norman Pfeiffer is a principal of Hardy Holzman Pfeiffer Associates, a firm whose designs are characterized by eclecticism more than any one architectural style or ideology. Through the substantial body of work it has created since it was founded in 1967—buildings distinguished by a bold use of color, an inventive structuring of space, and an innovative use of inexpensive materials—the firm has gained recognition for its unconventional solutions to functional challenges.

BLDD: Your office is often described as a place of controlled, almost choreographed chaos. Is that an assessment with which you would agree?

NP: It is probably a fair assessment, particularly to people who come in from the outside and have an opportunity to watch how the office works. As for the partners, having worked together for twenty years, we have developed a shorthand by which we communicate in a way that very few can understand. It's almost like a foreign language. Even people who work with us are not sure when the partners have made a decision and moved on to another topic or another design consideration.

BLDD: Are the partners sure?

NP: Oh yes!

BLDD: Can you describe this language?

NP: Our thoughts are not always articulated in a sentence like "I agree with that and let's move in that direction" or "I disagree." Sometimes the discussion isn't carried on that way. Sometimes we communicate by bantering or responding to each other almost as adversaries. Our language isn't necessarily even verbal. Most of the work that's done in this firm is through the construction of models and three-dimensional devices. Compared to other firms, we do a lot less drawing in the design process—less drawing and much more construction in three dimensions. Often we work things out in three-dimensional developments of the room, the theater, the building—whatever space we're working on. Usually we build maybe six or eight models of the same thing so we can take a look at it from slightly different points of view. In the course of reviewing those models, part of the more formal process that

the three partners use, some are rejected and some are accepted to be developed further. The process of developing any idea can be initiated verbally—by any one of the partners saying "I think this is the one we ought to develop" and the other two agreeing—or nonverbally, by the partners tearing the models apart, rearranging them, throwing them to the side, and leaving one finished model on the table. There is no standard design process; it just comes out in this shorthand we have developed among ourselves.

BLDD: You first began working with Hugh Hardy in 1964. How did you meet?

NP: I met him right after getting my master's degree at Columbia. Malcolm Holzman had joined Hugh shortly before I arrived. Hugh was practicing pretty much by himself; Malcolm had just come to work for him a few months when I arrived. After Columbia I had planned to go back to the West Coast, where I grew up, but had decided to stay the summer. I needed a job to support myself in New York.

BLDD: What was it that encouraged you to become an architect in the first place? Were there elements in your early environment—you were born in Seattle, Washington—that affected your decision?

NP: There were a couple of things. My family was involved in the building and construction business, so at a very early age I had a fascination with architects and drawings and those things I was surrounded by as a kid. Later on, there was the influence of the educational system at the University of Washington, where I got my bachelor's degree. They worked on a kind of open system. Rather than offering a group of strong, internationally known architects who imposed their design direction on students, the university encouraged students to explore in any direction. There was, of course, some emphasis on the indigenous qualities of the Northwest; one was always reminded to take that into consideration. But there was a great freedom in the educational system and a willingness to allow students to pursue courses in their own interests, rather than in some predetermined architectural style. That was further reinforced when I went to Columbia. In fact, I went there because the man I was going to be working with was very sympathetic with that school of thought. Victor Christ-Janer, who was in charge of the master's program at Columbia, had established a very close relationship with the University of Washington over a number of years. Historically, there was a migration of Washington graduates to Columbia's program. Christ-Janer always came to Seattle and worked with us. His free spirit about architectural education encouraged students to explore, not to perfect some sophisticated architectural approach. He was more interested in your mind and your ability to think through the same problem from five or six points of view than he was in achieving a finished product worked to perfection. I was very enamored of him and wanted to study with him, which is why I came to New York.

BLDD: You saw the job with Hugh Hardy as summer employment?

NP: Yes. I wasn't concerned about my professional future at the time. I knew that I was going to go back to the West Coast to start a practice and was going to get on with life there. To get a summer job in New York I went to the Yellow Pages and made lists of architects. I then organized my interviews so I didn't have to walk all over town. I met Hugh and Malcolm because I happened to be in the H's that day. When I got home from my interview, the phone rang—they were calling to tell me to come back and work. It was as simple as that.

BLDD: At that time how many employees were there?

NP: Malcolm, the secretary, and perhaps one other person.

BLDD: How did the firm evolve in the next several years?

NP: We all discovered early on that we worked very well in a collaborative way. Even at that time, the few commissions we had required some traveling, so all three of us were never in the office for an extended period of time. We worked well enough as a unit that it didn't matter who was gone; the others were always capable of advancing the work in their absence. When the one who had been away from the office returned, there was an exchange of information about what we had been working on, very much as in today's collaborative process. From the very outset there was a cooperative spirit. There were no extremely big egos involved; nobody adamantly demanded the credit for something, nor did any of us need to run things completely by ourselves. The discovery of this sharing in the development of ideas made us realize that we had an architectural partnership. Usually it happens differently—people say, "Gee, wouldn't it be nice if we went into practice together." We were already in it when we discovered that we had something quite special among us, which still exists today. It's still the basis for how all the major work is produced.

BLDD: For a long while your firm was known for its use of colorfully painted pipes and air ducts, multilayered floor plans, remnants of Roxy Theater carpeting—a style described by one writer as an "American melting pot" approach to design. Is that how you would describe either your present or your past work?

NP: That's still very much a part of the work we're doing today, although it may now be expressed differently. We've always felt that architecture, as it has been traditionally practiced, is very exclusive, eliminating and homogenizing to the point of becoming tyrannical. Everything had to have its own place or it was no longer in the proper order. Our underlying motivation has been to make architecture more inclusive. The use of color on a pipe or a curved surface, a remnant of something from the past—we continue to feel these things are important. Architecture, after all, is for people, and it should include things that people can relate to. An exclusive

architecture that reduces everything to the simplest forms is sometimes very tyrannical, denying the human being access.

BLDD: Your work has also been marked by refined, non-orthogonal plans. How important is that quality?

NP: When we first started out we were very much involved with trying to break out of the orthogonal box. It was very characteristic of our early work. When some of that work was built, we realized how powerful the juxtaposition of angles against rectangles could be. Because it is a very powerful geometric device, it is not always appropriate. When it is appropriate we still use it, but there are times when you don't want to set up such a violent tension between a rectangular, orthogonal organization of space and angular forms inserted within it.

BLDD: One critic has called your firm "the designated off-the-wall architect for the respectable middle." Is that an accurate or fair statement?

NP: It's relative to the architect's position in his professional society at any given time. If you take into consideration the kinds of clients we had—for the most part very well-established, well-known institutions—then our work of ten years ago was taking pretty extraordinary risks and making some unprecedented architectural statements. The Cummins Engine medical center in Columbus, Indiana, is a good example. While Cummins Engine is a sophisticated company, and very interested in architecture, it is also a part of a conservative corporate entity. We were hired to do a project with a new architectural vocabulary for Cummins Engine, but we were also doing it in a medical arena with the most conservative group of people you could find. In our concept, which was based on our belief that people get anxious when they go to doctors because everything has been cloaked in mystery and secrecy, we proposed to make the clinics a more open kind of environment. We were challenging the historical notion that medicine is best performed behind locked doors, but we chose to formulate this challenge from a practical point of view. The architectural statement was made up of a vocabulary of exposed structural and mechanical elements and two very distinct geometries in opposition to each other—two rectilinear grids turned at forty-five degrees to create a circulation pattern through the facility. Viewed in the context of the time it was built, the Cummins project may well have been seen as startling, although today it would surely seem less so.

BLDD: How much of that early image was the result of modest budgets that caused you to use inexpensive materials?

NP: It all goes back to a fundamental part of our thinking, still important today, that architecture can be made out of anything, not just a narrow palette of building materials. You can make buildings out of all kinds of things, and we have never been afraid of experimenting. Budget has been an issue on just about every one of our projects. But if you can take the elements necessary to hold a building up or make it functional and use them as decorative aspects as well, not only can you save money, but you can also introduce a richness into the architecture that would be eliminated if you covered up those elements.

BLDD: Who does what at HHPA? How are the various design, administrative, publicity, and financial responsibilities divided?

NP: Although the office now has eighty people, it's still a Mom and Pop operation. The three of us, the original founders of the company, realized early on that to practice architecture successfully there must be a very strong relationship between the architects and the clients that extends beyond the design process and into the management of the business. We have

Columbus Occupational Health Center, Columbus, Ind.

divided the administrative tasks of running the office among the three of us. Malcolm is primarily in charge of personnel and hiring and making sure that projects are appropriately manned. Hugh is assigned the area of the front office, the administrative staff. He handles all the publicity and public relations for prospective clients. I have been assigned the financial management. Those three areas cover the administrative chores of keeping the company solvent, organized, and moving through its work load in a consistent fashion. In terms of the running of the jobs themselves, every client needs someone they can count on. They may be interested in and encouraged by the collaborative process that goes on here and the fact that three partners are going to be fairly active in the creation of the architecture, but they still need one person they can always turn to. So every project has an administrative partner, a partner chosen usually because he has been instrumental in getting the job. Sometimes the choice has to do with geography. I, for example, have been responsible for a lot of the work on the West Coast. Since it is a long airplane ride to the West, it makes sense for one person to handle most of the projects there. Basically the work load has been equally divided among the three of us. The design process for all major commissions is begun by the three of us and a small staff. Once we know what the program is, we all go off in our own directions for a while and work up our own ideas about it. Generally we work on things for a few days and then bring all of the materials together to discuss them. Sometimes we'll talk about the interiors, sometimes the plans, sometimes how it will all fit into an urban site. At some point we talk about the outside of the structure, what we refer to as the "image." Once we reach a consensus as to what image this project is trying to convey, it's very easy for any one of the partners and the staff to go in that direction.

BLDD: Is this a good way to work? Do you think your working process is conducive to a fruitful method of design and problem solving?

NP: I think it is extremely good. It's very helpful to have people to talk to along the way, rather than having the design process go on completely in your own mind. You can bounce ideas off someone and get feedback. This method also allows us to consider an extraordinary number of possibilities for every job; three people with small staffs generate almost every conceivable approach to the problem early in the process. If there is a troublesome time in an architect's mind, it comes later on, when you wonder if perhaps you should have done things differently. Because of the process we go through, we always feel quite secure that we have explored most of the solutions to a problem. This gives us—and the client—the feeling that the problem has been well analyzed and that the direction we ultimately take is probably the best one.

BLDD: In the early days of your practice, the prevalent view was to tear buildings down and start anew, in contrast to the current view that a certain care should be taken to preserve our architectural heritage. How was your attitude toward preservation reflected in the firm's early projects and philosophy?

NP: The partners have always had a fondness for history and for old buildings, which has, of course, affected our attitude toward the preservation of buildings. From the outset we were involved with art institutions that had been in business long enough to have buildings that were part of their establishment. When we worked with these institutions, we had to work with their existing buildings. If you are an architect with a clearly defined architectural style and you have to work within an existing building, you are faced with a conflict that is almost insoluble: if you are here to create a new piece of architecture that is

uniquely yours, then how on earth are you going to do it within the confines of an existing building? But none of us ever felt the need to establish an architectural style, to pursue a "signature" architecture. We were totally free of that and felt uninhibited about going into an existing structure and adapting it to make a new piece of architecture. There are a variety of ways to do this. Some buildings are such architectural treasures that one has to restore them and be perfectly respectful of them. Others are worth preserving because the shell itself is of value, but the building may not be great architecture. Other historical examples need new buildings attached to them. We've found it quite a challenge to bring together a new architectural vocabulary with an historical building in order to solve a problem that wasn't anticipated when that building was built.

BLDD: Your firm was responsible early on for the adaptive reuse of many buildings, including a number of railroad stations. How did you become involved with railroads, and what was your intent in adapting these structures?

NP: The railroad idea came about simply because one of the partners wondered what would happen to all those wonderful stations because of the decline in passenger rail service in this country. Somehow that discussion escalated and found its way to some people from the National Endowment for the Arts. Eventually a study was funded to address the problem and to determine the inventory of significant railroad stations in the country: what was happening to them, what could be done with them if they were no longer going to be used for their original purpose of transportation. In our minds, because of the large volumes contained in railroad stations, there was a potential relationship between artistic uses and those buildings. There is a considerable number of artistic groups looking for places in which to make their homes, and these buildings are a natural consideration. Our involvement with railroads came out of that particular concern. We didn't just run around saving railroad stations for the sake of saving them.

BLDD: Recently your firm submitted designs for a proposed addition to the New-York Historical Society, a building with landmark status. Some people were surprised that your firm, which has been so identified with the preservationist movement, chose to take on that project. What was your firm's approach and philosophy in that assignment?

NP: We have been put in a difficult professional position because although we have been given a lot of credit for our care and concern for historic buildings, this does not necessarily mean that we should steer clear of a sensitive issue like the Historical Society. The challenge, and presumably our ability to solve that problem, pushes us in a completely different direction. You can take the position that Hardy Holzman Pfeiffer, because of the respect for history and old buildings that we exhibit in our work, should not now attempt to create a building on top of a landmark. Or you can take the position that if a building—any landmark building—will ultimately have to be built upon, who is better suited to tackle such a difficult problem than people who have spent most of their professional years worrying about such problems?

BLDD: Why would you say that *any* building would "ultimately have to be built upon"?

NP: The New-York Historical Society issue and the landmark building issue in general involve the difficulties the owners of some landmark institutions experience in trying to maintain or operate them. Some of the economic hardships that may be involved may be ameliorated if the institution is allowed to use its real estate to offset them. But if the landmarks preservation community takes the position, in every instance, that nothing can be built on or beside such a building, then ultimately one of those landmarks will have to be destroyed. I'm not sure that the Historical Society is the prime example of an extreme hardship case. But the point is that one of the ways to preserve what little history America has left is to figure out creative new ways to expand upon existing property, if owners are in fact entitled to do so.

BLDD: In presenting your proposal for the New-York Historical Society, your firm prepared a position about the balance between development and a covenant with the past. Could you recapitulate that position?

NP: Landmark laws must remain flexible to adjust to changing circumstances and new issues. Those who use the laws to block all change rather than to protect the best of our architectural heritage will ultimately cause great harm. The hands-off approach applied to a steadily increasing number of structures may result in the loss of many important buildings. Landmark buildings cannot all be viewed as isolated objects to be kept the same regardless of what happens around them. Each area of New York results from specific growth patterns and calls for different solutions in response to its particular character. Preservation and development cannot be at war.

BLDD: How important is it in your design aesthetic to integrate diverse elements and reconcile opposites?

NP: You have to see architecture as a composition. A very simple painting with a very simple form can be calm and restful. We feel that you can do the same thing in three dimensions, that you can create an equally simple, composed piece of architecture with many elements. It's a matter of where you put the final emphasis. It's a push-and-pull process; you set something in motion in one direction and then you counterbalance it in another. This can be difficult to achieve in three dimensions, where there are forms and surfaces above, below, and around you. You have to bring that chaos into some kind of equilibrium.

BLDD: How do you balance invention and convention?

NP: I'm not sure that we do. Any one project ultimately has to reconcile those factors, but in our practice as a whole we are not trying to come out even with so many projects in one idiom and so many in another. We take one project at a time.

BLDD: Can one ever be overly inventive?

NP: Oh yes. Invention just for the sake of invention is disastrous. If there is a simple way to solve a problem, there is no point in making it complicated by doing it differently. Being overly inventive can cause more problems than it solves. One always has to be very cautious about moving in new directions. The ability to do this comes with experience; it's part of a learning process that one can get only by working. We are just beginning to understand that in our own practice, now that we've had a chance to see a lot of the paper and cardboard models actually realized in building.

BLDD: Your work has often been described as theatrical—it has a high dramatic quality. Who influenced that style?

NP: The use of the word "theatrical" has me somewhat troubled. A lot of the work has a sense of humor, a sense of surprise, a sense of the unexpected. Those qualities, however subtly expressed, are very much a part of our work. We've resisted very strongly the one-sidedness of traditional architecture, the one "acceptable" vocabulary, by introducing exceptions, features that look like they don't quite belong to an order that has been established. That takes the seriousness out of the architecture. By that I don't mean that we're not serious or that the architecture isn't serious. Certainly a room designed for symphonic music has to be given serious consideration, but that doesn't mean that it has to be humorless, or

St. Louis Art Museum, St. Louis, Mo.

without surprise, or lacking in innuendo. In that sense the work is dramatic or theatrical. Perhaps the word "theatrical" bothers me because the very early work has sometimes been characterized as brash, and our intent was never to beat people over the head with a dramatic quality.

BLDD: How does a building have a sense of humor?

NP: Architecture generally has something very serious to accomplish, but if it does so in a regular, expected way, it misses part of its very reason for being. Architecture is for people, and it shouldn't be so homogenized that it provides no pleasure or interest. An unpredictable aspect in the design, an idiosyncrasy one discovers as one moves through a building, can provide a sense of humor. A consistent row of columns, for example, that suddenly changes in your visual perception is a very simple way of breaking a regular and monotonous pattern and turning it into something that is not so straightforward and predictable.

BLDD: Which projects do you consider HHPA's five or six most significant achievements? Would you describe their genesis, evolution, and execution?

NP: Our 1977 renovation of the St. Louis Art Museum is certainly one of them. It began with an ambitious master plan for the museum that addressed issues of concern to most museums in America over the past twenty years. In this case we were dealing with a very significant building, designed by Cass Gilbert and the only structure left from the St. Louis World's Fair. Having been designed for a fair in pre-automobile times, the museum was ill equipped to accommodate the automobile, which is how most people now come to museums. What was designed as the front door was no longer a viable entryway. So there was the initial problem of altering the museum exterior to accept twentieth-century forms of transportation. In terms of the interior, the original organization and character had been so obliterated by layers and layers of museum installation and new construction that it was almost unrecognizable as what it was—a very simple Beaux-Arts orthogonal plan based on a grand central hall with major horizontal axes leading to smaller galleries, all organized in a very simple, rectangular shape. In addition, because the museum activities would not fit inside the original building, a new addition was contemplated. So I would say that our solution brought about a successful renovation involving the rediscovery of the impeccable interior logic of the plan, the true restoration of the galleries to their original character, and the juxtaposition of a new exterior vocabulary that offered unity with the existing Cass Gilbert structure.

Another significant project was the Boettcher Concert Hall. There was no precedent in America for a symphony hall in the round, in which the musicians sat on a platform around which the audience was shaped. Several such halls had been built in Europe—one in Amsterdam, one in Rotterdam, and the well-known hall in Berlin. When we arrived in Denver we were asked by the people there and by the symphony to make a concert hall in the round. It wasn't something that Hardy Holzman Pfeiffer independently decided would be nice to do in Denver; it was a given when we arrived. The concept was not an easy one to carry out, and it was a very risky professional assignment. We had just finished a concert hall in Minneapolis,

so we had been through the problems of making a room for natural acoustics. But there we did it with a tried and proven form—the rectangle, the traditional shape of a concert hall. Everyone knew it could be made to work if it was done right. In the Denver project, though, there was an initial feeling that making a room for music in the round was not possible. But the result is quite dynamic. We created a very intimate room for the enjoyment of music.

It might be worth mentioning the Willard Hotel since you brought up the issue of historic landmarks. The Willard, designed by Henry Hardenbergh, also the architect of the Plaza Hotel and the Willkie Building, had a completely different problem from the arts institutions we had been working with. A major structure had to be added on the site adjoining the Willard in a way that would respect the older building. The first proposal was to add a hotel, which was much more compatible with the existing building in terms of architectural character than what the later proposal called for—the addition of an office building. The architectural problem of finding a new vocabulary that would be appropriate to the Willard was tough enough; the problem of integrating an office building made it even more complicated. Office buildings by their very nature require a lot of glass and a lot of window openings. The Willard, on the other hand, was full of small windows. The basic consideration, then, was one of relating a twentieth-century office building to the historic Willard Hotel, a problem of relating old and new at a

Boettcher Concert Hall, Denver, Colo.

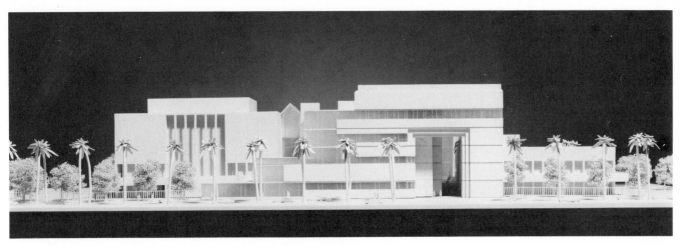

Los Angeles County Museum of Art, Los Angeles, Calif., model

very large scale. Although we subsequently redesigned it, we still believe the scheme had great merit.

An important project still in the works is the Los Angeles County Museum of Art. The initial assignment was to add a new wing for contemporary and modern paintings to the three-building complex designed by William Pereira. It was clear from the beginning that simply adding a wing into the context of the existing museum would create some severe problems with respect to the museum's support facilities. So what had to be done initially was to rework the existing three buildings, including behind-the-scenes support space for the museum—for cataloguing, photographing, and storage—to create a compatible relationship with the new facility. It was the firm's largest and most comprehensive planning assignment up to that point. One of the major weaknesses of the museum was that because it had been designed initially as three separate pavilions, the public never had a sense of where the real front door was. So aside from providing new gallery space, one of our tasks was to create both symbolically and in practice a new front entrance for the museum. We also had the opportunity with the new addition to create a central court, a place to concentrate all public functions—buying tickets, getting information, applying for membership, eating—all of the non-gallery-going activities. In the proposed design, when you come in the front door the three existing Pereira buildings are united with the new wing. The most difficult part of the project was dealing with an existing architectural vocabulary that we were clearly not going to repeat. The original museum buildings were done in a style of architecture very characteristic of that period, a style seen in, say, the Kennedy Center or the Seattle World's Fair buildings. The Pereira buildings were the last vestiges of a style that borrowed from the classical world to present a layer of elegance over complexes of enormous scale. We knew that we were not going to add a fourth element to the architectural composition in that particular vocabulary. On the other hand, we did want to make an architectural statement that showed respect for the placement and organization of the Pereira buildings around the common plaza. We expended a considerable amount of effort in shaping a building that did not obscure or compete with the architecture of the existing buildings. Only the built result will verify these design goals.

The performing arts center that we designed in Eugene, Oregon, is considered by that community to be an absolutely smashing success. A lot of that has to do with the fact that the architecture included as part of its vocabulary a number of works of art produced by the local community. They had asked

us from the outset to include works by local artists as an integral part of the building's architecture. They were interested not in turning the lobby into a pseudo-gallery for exhibiting works of art, but in a process that goes back to the Arts and Crafts movement, where artisans actually designed and participated in the making of the building. Now the people really feel that the building belongs to them. The wonderful sinuous wooden handrail on the stair has been sculpted and installed by one of their local artists; the ceramic tiles that line the wall surfaces of the restrooms were conceived and hand-painted by members of the community. They are small touches, but from the point of view of creating community spirit, they are very significant. And they provide something that is rare in the mainstream of architectural practice in this country—the acceptance of someone else's ideas about how things should be

Hult Center for the Performing Arts, Eugene, Ore.

WCCO Television Headquarters, Minneapolis, Minn.

made and how they should look. We plan to go through a similar process for our new project in Anchorage, Alaska, where we are designing a $50 million performing arts center.

BLDD: You, Hardy, and Holzman have been working together for twenty years. What do you consider to be the most significant changes in your practice and your design aesthetic?

NP: There have been no abrupt changes in the practice. The ability to move through the design process very quickly has probably been the most important aspect of the evolution of the company. This is due in part to the fact that our staff is now experienced, having been through it all a number of times. But it's also because a lot of the work is about similar issues. We do a lot of museum and performing arts work in the office, and many of the problems are quite similar from one project to the next. Now we can recognize and address the problems readily, whereas before it may have taken weeks of pondering the problems.

From an aesthetic point of view, there hasn't been a drastic change either. Probably what one notices is that we're doing bigger buildings. Also, for the most part, the detailing and the finishing of our buildings are becoming much more sophisticated, a development that also comes out of experience. We've made remarkable progress in learning how to bring dissimilar materials together, and our work certainly shows that. We have always, for instance, been involved in using a

wide array of materials in construction, but most recently we've become very interested in stone. Up until the last century stone was used heavily in architecture; recently it has been treated more as a skin, a material that could be applied as if it were a metal panel. Our investigations in stone in some of our recent buildings involve the traditional use of stone as major blocks of material piled on top of one another. The Virginia Museum is being constructed in this fashion; the WCCO Television station, which was just finished in Minneapolis, is a stone building; and the Los Angeles County Museum of Art will be constructed of a very thick coursing of what is known as sandstone.

BLDD: What do you see as the most dramatic changes in the profession in recent years? You've said that you learn from each of your buildings and that you can't wait to get onto the next one to incorporate what you've learned from the past ones.

NP: We are a bit naive. The longer we are in this business the more we discover that things we think are new to the world are really only new to us. Running an architectural practice that is given the opportunity to work on the kinds of commissions that we have done and are doing is a major business. Design is what the end result is judged by, and what the public that is not involved in the daily process of making buildings ultimately sees. But for the partners, it is the running of the architectural practice that is really the most demanding and time consuming. While we have staff and we have help, every job has to be run as if it were almost a business in itself; but in the public's mind what architects do is to make drawings. I think one change is that more of an architect's time now is spent in anticipating and organizing the course of a project, keeping in mind that construction dollars are a very real part of the success or failure of it. And the clients we work with seem increasingly involved in the process. They are not, by and large, people who hire you one day and then don't show up again until the groundbreaking. They like to meet on a regular basis and share in the development of the project. They like to know six or seven possible ways to do something and why you rejected some and chose others. They demand a lot of time in the creative process. So it seems that the profession these days is becoming much more demanding on the business side.

BLDD: What is an ideal client? Architects talk about clients who are really interested and informed, but how interested and how informed do you want them to be? When does their involvement intrude on your creativity?

NP: Obviously, we have encouraged involvement and participation on the part of our clients. It's more enjoyable when there are two parties in the conversation as the process is developing. But it is the architect's responsibility to make clear to the client that there are certain points where decisions must be made and that turning back is not possible after that point. I cannot recall a case, though, where a client has come to us late in the process wishing to change his mind in any drastic way, nor can I recall a case where a client has insisted on being intimately involved in the design to the point where you can't do your work. As for the ideal client, he has to be one who can see. It is amazing how difficult it is for people to read drawings and understand models, and it is rare to find a client who is capable of either projecting the reality of the finished product into those drawings or of anticipating what it is that the architects have in mind. A client who cannot see is a very disruptive client because he reacts to things he thinks he sees on paper that are not necessarily there. The ideal client is also one who comes prepared, one who can match the architect's own organization. It does no good to be extremely organized yourself if you have a client who's disorganized. It is not helpful to have a client who is inconsistent in the manner in which he responds to you—one day with a formal set of meeting notes and the next night at 8:30 with a phone call. The process takes discipline and organization on both sides.

BLDD: How do you discipline the client?

NP: It's a matter of discipline not in the sense of reprimanding them, but in the sense of giving them an idea of what the process will entail, what you expect from them at each meeting, how you would like to have the information conveyed to you. Since most clients don't build buildings every day, they're not in the business of thinking through the administrative duties that they should undertake to match what the architect is doing. It's an educational process that most clients are more than willing to go through. Some of them love it; some think it's a great thing. When I hear other architects talk about bad clients, my usual reaction is to think that it is the architect's responsibility, that he didn't get the client in the proper mood. It rarely is the case that a client is truly bad.

BLDD: Do you have a dream project that you haven't done yet?

NP: Yes, but it's more of an obsession than a dream project. We are desperate to do an office tower, a very tall urban office tower. In twenty years of practice, the tallest building we've done is something like three stories!

BLDD: Is there any advice you'd give to young architects?

NP: I would say that if I were going to do anything differently—a backhand way of giving advice—I would have gone to work in an architectural practice much sooner than I did. I would try to be involved very seriously in the profession while going through it academically. There are always pros and cons to any method, but I sometimes regret that the learning process the three of us went through was devoid of practical experience because by and large we had never worked for any other architect before we came together.

BLDD: What kinds of limitations does that bring about?

NP: It makes it very difficult to understand the practice side, the common-sense business side of running an architectural office. I'm not sure how much of a liability it's been in our case. A lot of good has come out of the fact that we've had to invent just about everything as we've gone along. But it would have been helpful to have followed a building from a design concept through a construction process before we were actually off and doing it ourselves. There are schools that have programs like that, where you have to work in an office while doing classwork.

BLDD: Did you expect your life to follow the path it has?

NP: No, I really didn't. I always knew I was going to be an architect and that I would work very hard at it and do my best. But the opportunities that have come out of starting a practice in this city at the time we did have been fortuitous and unpredictable. It was a stroke of luck that all of this came together at that particular point in time. New York has been a marketplace that has provided us with contact with so many different people. I wouldn't know how to do it differently, and I wouldn't want to! We've been extremely fortunate in working with people in the artistic world—our "specialty"—whose motivations are not unlike our own. They may be involved in different art forms, but their lives revolve around the creative process. It has been a rewarding and enjoyable experience working with them. It would be difficult to have a relationship with people who aren't interested in the process or aren't sympathetic to the value of architecture and what it can do for them.

MICHAEL PITTAS

In his role as architect, city planner, teacher, and director of the National Endowment for the Arts Design Arts Program from 1978 through 1984, Michael Pittas has shown a consistent dedication to improving the quality of our built environment.

BLDD: In talking about your childhood years you've described yourself as a "candy store kid." What does that mean?

MP: Having been brought up in a working-class ethnic neighborhood, the Lower East Side in New York City, I was one of those kids who had nothing better to do than hang out in a candy store and put nickels in jukeboxes.

BLDD: How did your early experience influence your choice of a career?

MP: Being brought up in New York City—an extraordinary environment, but one that can make you as provincial and myopic as an Iowan farmer—made me want to make changes, to exert some influence on the world around me.

BLDD: How did you make the transition from jukeboxes to the design arts?

MP: An elementary school art teacher recognized some talent that neither I nor my parents knew was there and suggested I apply to the High School of Music and Art. I was an art major there and felt I was going to be the next Picasso. But when I realized that I would have to make a living at one point or another, it was a natural transition to turn to architecture to fullfill the need to express myself.

BLDD: Your educational background includes training in architecture at Cooper Union and a graduate degree from Princeton University. Was there anything especially inspiring or influential in either of those environments?

MP: The technical education at Cooper Union was extraordinary. There was no finer school in the country for giving a student the ability to perform a task. There are very few schools like it now. It's the only private institution left in the country that does not charge tuition. Its student body is there by merit alone. It was quite a struggle for me. I entered with a class of fifty-four and graduated with a class of eight. The decline wasn't caused simply by attrition; students were asked to leave if they did not live up to the goals of the school. Princeton represented an entirely different kind of education. During that period the Anglo influence on architecture was just developing, as was the ascent of postmodernism as a major influence in this country. Peter Eisenman, Tony Vidler, Ken Frampton, and others were at Princeton at the time. Michael Graves was just beginning to work.

BLDD: Certainly an unusual group—controversial and sometimes contentious. What ideas were emerging there that influenced you?

MP: It was clear that the postmodernist movement was starting to have a great influence on the form of building, but by predisposition and background I was interested in the behavioral and social content of buildings as well. My feelings about postmodernism caused me to go in a somewhat different direction from that of many of my colleagues.

BLDD: Was your goal to practice architecture, to become an urban planner, or to follow a different field entirely?

MP: Most assuredly, I wanted to practice architecture. I wanted the feeling of immortality that goes with putting up great buildings. I wanted my name to go down in history.

BLDD: How did you make the transition from art to architecture?

MP: Through a recognition of economic necessity. There are an awful lot of talented artists out there who don't get recognized. If a person chooses the luxury and privilege of becoming a visual artist, he also takes on a great deal of pain and suffering. I made the choice of a limited degree of pain and suffering in an architectural career.

BLDD: Some people think there is luxury and privilege in pursuing a career in architecture. But it isn't the easiest field to succeed in, and it certainly isn't the most rewarding economically—at least not for the first forty years of practice.

MP: No doubt about it. Architects are among the most influential professional groups in this country and at the same time among the most powerless.

BLDD: Powerless?

MP: Certainly. Every few years *Fortune* magazine publishes a list of the top hundred or so professions in the country. They classify them in two ways: first by income, then by status. In terms of status, architects invariably are about third from the top, right after astrophysicists; in terms of income, they are about third from the bottom.

BLDD: How do you explain the great disparity?

MP: To some extent it has to do with the nature of the architectural profession. Roughly four percent of the large architectural firms in this country dominate between thirty and forty percent of the major commissions. So there are a limited number of people making money and exerting power and influence.

BLDD: Is that because only a handful of firms are equipped to carry out large-scale jobs and therefore continue to get more of them—a cycle that perpetuates itself?

MP: Undoubtedly. Although this country encourages competitiveness, it has not encouraged it in the commissioning of architecture. It's a *Catch-22* situation: if you have not done it before, you are not likely to be given the opportunity to do it. The issue here is opportunity in the design professions. It is an issue that has led me, with support from the National Council on the Arts, to put forward a program of active advocacy for design competitions.

BLDD: Do competitions make a difference? Do they change the quality of design?

MP: No, that's not what they do.

BLDD: Then what value do they have?

MP: Opportunity. Equity. Fairness. These are the issues that make competitions valuable.

BLDD: Are competitions in favor these days?

MP: Competitions are coming into favor partly because of a very pragmatic assessment by the architectural profession that they will not be able to do business as usual—with the large firms dominating the field—much longer. Two antitrust decisions by the Department of Justice—one regarding the setting of fees, the other concerning disciplining members of the American Institute of Architects through their own code of ethics—have led to a situation in which architects find themselves being exploited in private competition. They are producing design work—schematic, almost full-job development drawings—in order to procure a commission. Increasingly it is in the interest of the large firms that dominate the membership organizations to promote a situation in which there is competitiveness.

BLDD: How has equal opportunity legislation influenced the profession?

MP: Hardly at all. Roughly three percent of licensed architects in this country are women, and less than one percent are from minority groups. You have to conclude that it is not a broadly representative profession.

BLDD: Is the limitation due to the economic, cultural, and social hierarchies that are part of architecture?

MP: They certainly have some effect. Architecture is an applied art that has always been very closely associated with the establishment groups in almost every society, with the exception of the brief period during which the Bauhaus philosophy held sway. The International Style's early manifestation was as much a social doctrine as it was a new physical form.

BLDD: A social doctrine that led us to what beliefs?

MP: That doctrine had its roots in the European socialism of the early 1900s. Its adherents saw the working class, rather than the merchants or royalty, as its principal client. Aside from that exception, architecture has always been a profession that responds mostly to powerful and monied interests. This is certainly the case today.

BLDD: Is that because only certain people can afford to commission architects to work?

MP: That's an interesting question, since architecture is so pervasive.

BLDD: Inescapable.

MP: Yes, both the good and the bad. But to think of architecture as only the products of Philip Johnson and a handful of other well-known names is to avoid admitting that pervasive influence.

BLDD: How many architects are there in this country today?

MP: Somewhere between seventy and eighty thousand. We're not certain exactly how many are out there.

BLDD: How many of these actually practice architecture?

MP: All of them *claim* to practice architecture. The Bureau of Labor Statistics shows only a two percent unemployment rate among architects, which may mean that a large number work at other jobs—like driving cabs and other such occupations.

BLDD: You mentioned the sense of competition we venerate in this country. How does an architect compete for jobs? Is the architectural profession a meritocracy?

MP: Not really, though among architects who are already established the choice depends to a large degree on merit. You hire Philip Johnson and not some other known architect because you believe that Johnson is going to do a better job.

BLDD: Is it easier to get financing for a project that a well-known architect is going to be responsible for?

MP: Sometimes it can be a liability, since cautious investors may see brand-name architects as the cause of cost overruns. We architects don't have a particularly good reputation for handling our building budgets very well.

BLDD: Is that because of the artist in every architect?

MP: No doubt about it!

BLDD: For ordinary people who simply want to build a house, is it more expensive for them to do so with an architect or without one?

MP: In fact, almost all houses are designed by an architect. The idea that architects don't participate in subdivision tract-built housing in this country is a myth. We're just talking about a different type of architect.

BLDD: What distinction are you making?

MP: The architects that do standard types of designs that are replicated many, many times make a very good living, but they are different from those whose practice is widely celebrated and published.

BLDD: Is there now a greater awareness of architecture by the general public?

MP: Certainly. There are some broad reasons for it that have little to do with what architects are producing. The awareness has a great deal to do with a change in attitude toward our cultural traditions—a change that has come about in the last few decades in this country. I would link postmodernism, conservative politics, Broadway revivals, historic preservation, and natural conservation as part and parcel of a singular phenomenon.

BLDD: Are you talking about nostalgia?

MP: In part. That's one of its manifestations. We are a culture looking for roots, seeking our traditions and finding ways to preserve them. When you detect an interest in the artifacts of society, you may be seeing a shift in the whole cultural ethos of that society.

BLDD: Is it also because we prefer what we once had to what we have now? The tedious sameness of the glass-and-steel box is such that most folks see any alternative—even their

Old Post Office Building renovation, Washington, D.C.

grandmother's house, which they never particularly admired—as better than what surrounds them now.

MP: Indeed. It has always struck me as strange that the last fifty years—a period in which the palette of architecture has been so rich in terms of technology, materials, and a whole host of other elements—has seen so little richness produced in the form of enduring architecture that gains respect over time. Actually, I'm not sure that's altogether correct. I'm thinking of a line from the movie *Chinatown:* "Crooked politicians, prostitutes, and ugly buildings get more respectable with time."

BLDD: How much of an influence has the Design Arts Program of the National Endowment for the Arts had on the improvement of buildings? Do you think the program has had a real impact in the twenty years of its existence?

MP: In a therapeutic sense, yes. In a realistic sense, an agency with so few resources for advocating better public architecture can't really have an extraordinary effect. We're talking about principles, policies, and practices that take fifty to one hundred years to make a significant change in the environment. So it is hard for me to assess the changes that have already occurred as a result of the Design Arts Program. One significant change has been developing legislation.

BLDD: Would you talk about the National Endowment for the Arts in general, and specifically about the Design Arts Program?

MP: The initial legislation that created the National Endowment for the Arts in 1965 said that architecture was among the art forms the federal government ought to support and nurture.

BLDD: Whose idea was that?

MP: My suspicion is that it came about because of August Heckscher and Daniel Patrick Moynihan, who was then Deputy Under-Secretary of Commerce and the author of *Federal Principles of Architecture*. In fact, Moynihan is an unsung hero of architecture. He has done more in public life to support good architecture than most people know. He brought the issue of federal architecture to President Kennedy and later to presidents Nixon and Ford. As a senator he helped write and pass the Cooperative Use Act, which requires the federal government to look at a community's historically and architecturally significant buildings before putting up a new office building. The act also states that, if possible, the government should introduce new uses into old buildings. For example, the Old Post Office on Pennsylvania Avenue in Washington opened in June 1983 with some fifty retail establishments on the first two floors and three federal agencies on the upper floors, including, fortunately, the National Endowment for the Arts and the National Endowment for the Humanities.

BLDD: What does "design arts" encompass?

MP: There are eight distinct disciplines—urban design, architecture, landscape architecture, industrial design, product design, interior design, graphic design, and fashion design.

BLDD: How are they interrelated?

MP: The overlaps are humorous in many respects. For example, most architects today would submit that they do better landscape architecture than landscape architects. What they mean is that they do better garden design than landscape architects. Landscape architects do better city planning than city planners do today.

BLDD: The fracturing of disciplines into urban planning, architecture, landscape architecture, and so on in any one project or in any one city seems to create problems in making decisions. Are the divisions constructive or destructive?

MP: Historically those divisions didn't exist. The architect was the master planner, the landscape architect, the communicator, the graphic designer, the product designer; he was in charge of all aspects.

BLDD: Isn't it sometimes desirable to have unity—one sensibility, one hand, one eye—instead of so many competing disciplines?

MP: Even in periods when the architect dominated, building was a complex undertaking. The result was always a collaboration. It was a question of who was king of the hill.

BLDD: Who *is* king of the hill today? The architect?

MP: Unquestionably not.

BLDD: The developer?

MP: The developer may not even be. In this country today the banker or the insurance underwriter is probably more influential than the entrepreneur or the real-estate developer.

BLDD: What about the government agency?

MP: The federal government is certainly an important and pervasive influence, but one that is largely ignored by the architectural profession.

BLDD: How can it be ignored? In the end, a building is often designed more by external factors than by architects.

MP: You are probably correct. Zoning, minimum property standards, and codes of all sorts directly and indirectly influence the form of buildings everywhere. Beyond that, the direct cost of all public construction in this country is between $30 billion and $40 billion annually. That means that between $300 million and $600 million are awarded each year in architectural and engineering commissions. Why, then, are architects not wealthy? Because architecture is basically a service industry. You don't accumulate wealth in that kind of profession. The architect doesn't have a piece of the real-estate pie—with the exception of certain hybrids like John Portman.

BLDD: When the architect is also the developer?

MP: That's right. They changed the American Institute of Architects' code of ethics to allow that. In fact many of my students over the last ten years have gone on to business school or have taken real-estate development courses.

BLDD: Is that partially a measure of self-protection?

MP: I suspect that it's largely in self-defense. I worry a great deal about the degree to which the real-estate imperative takes over the design imperative.

BLDD: What is the Design Arts Program's most important function?

MP: To act as a national clearing house for design ideas. When something good and original occurs in the marketplace of ideas, there should be some source through which those ideas can filter down to those who can use that knowledge. Unfortunately the principal way in which we communicate ideas about design is visually. I say unfortunately because often we should be paying attention not to the artifactual result but to the *process* by which knowledge is transferred.

BLDD: What contribution does the Design Arts Program make to this process?

MP: The posture it takes with respect to ideas. It provides small amounts of money at the beginning stages of an idea for doing something in the design arena. There has been a consistent philosophy that if we just put a little bit of money here or there, something might bloom.

BLDD: What has bloomed? Any innovative ideas?

MP: Yes, some of the most influential ideas of this period. Most of the research for Bob Venturi and Denise Scott Brown's *Learning From Las Vegas* was supported by grants from the program. There you have an example of support for a theoreti-

cal work. At the other end of the spectrum, a small grant to the city of Lowell, Massachusetts, in 1974 produced very tangible, practical results. The grant enabled the school board to hire some designers to help change the citizens' opinion about something they considered a liability—the old mill buildings. What started as a small grant eventually generated $40 million in federal money, about $100 million in private investment, the designation of the first Urban National Park, and one of the lowest unemployment rates in the country.

BLDD: Isn't Lowell's industrial park now the model for other communities with similar resources and problems?

MP: Yes, in terms of historic preservation—that is, understanding how to use and reactivate historically significant buildings.

Another small grant was given to an industrial designer who wanted to redesign the wheelchair. It seemed like a worthy project and he seemed capable of doing it. Indeed, he did redesign the wheelchair. Wolf von Eckardt later pointed out that at least some of the billions of dollars we are now forced to spend in retrofitting architecture to make it accessible to the handicapped could have been saved if we had simply redesigned the wheelchair.

BLDD: What project that you've funded has had the most surprising result?

MP: The Vietnam Veterans Memorial competition. We did not expect the kind of national catharsis that project brought about. A group of Vietnam veterans went to Washington and asked for a joint resolution of Congress to allow the installation of a memorial on the Mall. No public funds were to be used in its construction. The memorial was to be dedicated to the memory of the 57,939 war dead in Vietnam, not a memorial to the war. This was a very important distinction. Representatives of the veterans' group came to the NEA and asked about hiring or commissioning a designer for this memorial. We suggested a design competition. The competition was open; the contestants didn't even have to be architects to enter. We received 1,450 submissions—the largest response to any competition conducted in the United States in the past hundred years. Andrews Air Force Base provided a hangar to display all of the entries. The judging took place over a five-day period. Most important was that this was a blind competition. This means that the judges do not know who has submitted any of the drawings. The winner was Maya Ling Yin, a young woman of Oriental descent and a second-year architecture student at Yale. Secretary of the Interior James Watt and several other individuals, both public and private, objected strenuously to the fact that the memorial did not have representational sculpture in it. A compromise was finally made in which a statue of three soldiers in heroic poses will be placed at some point near the monument.

BLDD: Maybe this tells us that people really need and want more graphic images, more representational forms.

MP: That's like saying that the Washington Monument ought to have a representational figure of George Washington on top of it.

BLDD: Did you tell this to any of the critics of the memorial?

MP: I'm sure that someone must have said something like that at some point or another. But the memorial as it exists today is highly personal. You can see that people have attached flowers near soldiers' names. People reach out and touch the names inscribed on the shiny black marble, the names of people who meant something to them. It's a moving experience and quite beautiful.

BLDD: What was the most controversial project you ever funded?

Above: Vietnam Veterans Memorial, Washington, D.C. Below: Submissions for the Vietnam Veterans Memorial Competition

MP: The NEA has certainly won its share of Golden Fleece awards from Senator Proxmire. I think some of the programs wear them as badges of honor. The Vietnam Memorial was one controversial project. Another was a design competition using environmental artists and landscape architects in New Orleans in a significant but little-known square. Bob Irwin and a local landscape architect won the competition. It was beautifully done. But the mayor refused to build the result, imposing his aesthetic on that of experts and community people who had been involved.

BLDD: Does this happen often?

MP: Unfortunately, yes. The reason is very simple: there are no rules of the game. In law, medicine, or most other professions, the opinion of the experts cannot be overturned by laymen. Would the owner of a football team step in and overrule the referee?

BLDD: So how do architects defend themselves?

MP: In forums, in exhibitions, in the popular press to some extent—and by good behavior.

BLDD: It has often been said that architects compound their difficulties by not making their work accessible to more people. Do you think that's a fair accusation?

MP: Yes, but it's also fair to say that that is the nature of any professional group in this country. The creation of jargon is an inevitable result of specialization, but it's a natural self-protective professional device as well. I believe architecture can be demystified and still maintain its magic.

BLDD: Some people say that's exactly what you've been doing for the last five years. In your travels throughout the United States, what have you found the state of American architecture to be?

MP: It's very vital, it's exuberant. You can see this not only in New York City, Los Angeles, and San Francisco, but in Phoenix, Tucson, and small towns all over the country.

BLDD: Do you really see activity all over?

MP: What most people see is what the popular press and the professional journals make public. What we don't see is the vitality that exists out there and the variety of formal manifestations of that vitality created by the thousands of practitioners working with contextual local problems.

BLDD: Are there any recurring architectural themes throughout the country these days?

MP: The restoration of historically and architecturally significant buildings and their reuse for new purposes. Another theme is a sense of humor. People like Stanley Tigerman, who produces wonderful buildings in Chicago, are showing a sense of humor that has been singularly lacking in the design professions.

BLDD: Are you suggesting that architecture can be based on sight gags or visual puns?

MP: To a certain extent it can be, and there is no reason why it shouldn't be. Whether or not this kind of architecture will endure is another issue. Certainly the economic life of a building is much shorter than its actual life. That's particularly true of private commercial ventures, which are often the buildings that contain humor.

BLDD: You've said that most architects today build for yesterday's problems and that what is lacking in the ideas of even the best architects is an underlying vision.

MP: Yes. Architecture has narrowed its vision to the morphology of the artifact. The social consequences be damned, say the architects, and with good reason: because the social sciences haven't been able to predict or foresee those consequences, they cannot be much help in informing what we do. It's natural to say that if we can't get answers we'll go off and do our own thing. We've become very good at working in increments, losing sight of the totality. I'm not talking about building utopias, although those kinds of models are significant and should be considered. Le Corbusier's Ville Radieuse was about the future, and so was Frank Lloyd Wright's Broadacre City. The fact that these models were not successful does not mean that architects should cease trying to envision beyond what they've done. Architects are the only professional group that can give formal manifestation to the new demographics of the country and reflect such factors as changing lifestyles, household formulations, age distribution. These are critically important issues that are not being discussed at all in the vocabulary of architecture. What does it mean when the predominant household type in the country is *not* Mom, Dad, two kids, and a dog? What does it mean when there are more elderly single-person households, more extended-family households? It means that certain functional relationships ought to be adjusted. The issue of the necessity of open space and recreational areas, for instance, has not had much attention over the last few years. These things have been considered a luxury when, in fact, they are a necessity.

BLDD: Given the present state of urban economics, what can we hope for in terms of urban design and policy?

MP: More patience, more vision, and a sense of the relativity of things. One of the great difficulties for architects is that they are trained to believe that every problem has a solution. When you design and build something, there's a brick-and-mortar result. But in order to create a future for this society, you have to take a more relativistic point of view. There are contingent futures, and that means differences.

BLDD: What does a relativistic point of view entail?

MP: It involves believing in more than one solution, being more catholic in approach. The postmodernists have something to offer; so do the contextualists, the regionalists, the behaviorists, the social scientists, and the economists.

BLDD: Do you advocate relativism only in your official role, or do you believe in it privately as well?

MP: Privately I believe in it too. But I characterize myself more as a catalyst than an author. I am less concerned about having a building named after me when I am dead than having some modest influence on the institutions and processes of society.

BLDD: How has your own training as an architect been useful in your role with the Design Arts Program?

MP: Because I was trained to believe that there are solutions to problems, I have not been hampered in the search for them. City planners, social scientists, and lawyers will seldom take anything more than an equivocal position. Because I believe there are solutions, I'm willing to test them or at least to put them forward.

BLDD: What major changes have you made since you've been director of the program?

MP: Survival has been a priority, despite the fact that architecture has been called the mother of the arts or the second-oldest profession. We're a tiny program in a vast array of much more powerful artistic influences at the NEA. Thus, it's important for us to maintain our position; this is often my major activity.

BLDD: You have established all sorts of innovative ideas, one being the recent Presidential Design Arts Program. What is your goal there?

MP: To raise the awareness of the effect of public design on the citizenry of this country by having awards presented by the president. There's nothing new about design awards, but this is a way of bringing them more public attention. Many coun-

Florida Art Deco: The Cardozo Hotel, Miami Beach, Fla.

tries use design awards from their prime ministers and premiers to raise public awareness.

BLDD: You mentioned that time can make beautiful buildings or spaces even richer. What is your view of the role of historic preservation?

MP: We have come a long way from seeing architecturally and historically significant buildings as needing fossilization. The heightened awareness has made a real difference. Concern with preservation is no longer restricted to the enlightened, well-educated people who you would expect to see standing before city councils and boards of estimate and fighting the good fight. It's spread to unexpected people as well. For example, Miami Beach, Florida, has one of the richest resources of Art Deco buildings in the country and one of the most galvanized preservation movements. But that did not come from people educated in the history of architecture; it arose from retailers, landowners, and long-time residents in the area. What emerged was the first twentieth-century historic-district designation in this country. The Design Arts Program, by the way, gave the early money to support that effort.

BLDD: What's the most important function of preservation today?

MP: Retaining our cultural heritage without fossilizing it.

BLDD: Do you see preservation ultimately as a tool for city planning?

MP: Yes. We have seen a significant turnabout from the clear-it-all-out-and-start-all-over attitude of the 1950s to a much more refined, gradualist point of view today, even to the extent that we are now re-creating, or trying to re-create, what was there before. Certainly the success of Harborplace in Baltimore, for example, has as much to do with retailing and marketing potential as it does with the sense of nostalgia the new construction creates. It's all brand-new—there's no restoration—but it gives the impression of being old.

BLDD: How has the field of architecture and design changed in the years that you've been involved with it?

MP: One significant change is that the architectural drawing is viewed now as an art form in its own right. In the past only those who collected the drawings of particular architects held that view. The present popularity of architects' drawings has had a major influence on the public's perception of what architects do. This has some liabilities associated with it, since what looks good on paper doesn't always look good when it's built. You can't proclaim anything the greatest building of the century just by virtue of its drawings, as some of our critics are fond of doing.

BLDD: Early in your career you worked as chief designer for a New Jersey firm known more for the quantity of its work than the quality. It had half the volume of all the work in the state. What did that experience teach you about the workings and possibilities of public housing and of architecture in general?

MP: It taught me about the degree to which the public sector influences design. My first experience in that area was developing an eight-story public housing superblock. I was constrained to such an extent—in terms of the square footage of rooms, minimum dimensions, size of windows and doors, distance to a fire escape—that I felt I was arranging plumbing. So I decided to play with the facade and worked out a system that mirrored the plans and created some diversity. I was promptly told by the public housing board that it looked too good. In a middle-class neighborhood it was inappropriate to make public housing look good, for reasons that were obvious at the time. Because of this I came to the conclusion that to make a difference you had to change some of the rules of the game. The public sector seemed to be the major arena in which this could happen. Those were heady days. John Lindsay was mayor of New York and the Urban Design Group had started up. I became intrigued by the whole process and joined the group shortly thereafter.

BLDD: Have you changed your mind about the influence of the public sector?

MP: No, not in the least. I have changed my mind only about the naiveté of some of the things we did. For example, the enfranchisement of the SoHo district was probably a bad mistake.

BLDD: Why? It's sometimes cited as a model of how to bring artists to the center of town and integrate them into the community.

MP: But the artists were there already and were . . .

BLDD: . . . quickly driven out by the dentists?

MP: Exactly. The Upper East Side alternative types were allowed to come in. By legalizing the process we created real estate in the area.

BLDD: But keeping it illegal prevented artists from living there.

MP: At that time there was a de facto hands-off policy by both the fire department and the HDA. A compromise had been reached. SoHo could have gone on for many years providing a place for artists to live. The mistake was to legalize the area in the first place.

BLDD: So you're saying that ambiguity in certain sectors of the city can be useful, even desirable?

MP: Yes.

BLDD: Are we about to make any similar mistakes?

MP: We do it all the time. New York's Local Law 10 said that you have to fix up all the loose cornices and ornamental details on a building. And what's the result?

BLDD: Buildings stripped bare.

MP: Exactly.

BLDD: Is communication part of the difficulty?

MP: Yes, and predicting the consequences. For example, when the theater district idea was put forward in New York, it was the crudest and most rudimentary form of incentive zoning. The idea was to trade off excess air rights to commercial developers in exchange for that uneconomic use called legitimate theater. Unfortunately, at that time there was little happening on Broadway and everyone was going broke. A couple of years later there was a magical season with enormous successes on Broadway. Theater is a business that goes up and down all the time, but we didn't acknowledge that.

Acting on the fallacious notion that theaters needed a continuous subsidy in order to survive, we gave an additional twenty percent of floor space to developers as long as they included a theater on the ground floor.

BLDD: What would be a better way to deal with a complicated situation in the theater district, an area that contains not only precious real estate but also a specific industry?

MP: The first thing I'd do in the theater district is to assert the public's right to downzone. It's nonsense to say that an individual landowner has an inalienable right to some fictitious air space above him, and that his right to it is immutable or untouchable by virtue of some law. Laws can be changed. New York should have asserted that right to downzone a long time ago. That means relieving property owners of that speculative real estate. This may sound fantastic in New York, but it has been done in other cities. The reason the North End of Boston—the old Italian community—exists at all today is because of three successive downzonings.

BLDD: Are there ever excess air rights in the center of a densely populated urban environment?

MP: Only to the extent that the public allows it. I'm saying this as a matter of law and right.

BLDD: How important is the role of the citizen or community activist in shaping the design of the places where people live, work, shop, and play?

MP: New York is probably the object lesson in this respect. Since the late sixties we have been into participatory democracy. Representative democracy was lost to the extent that courts were beginning to act like legislators, so it seemed necessary to involve as many people as possible. In fact, this became part of the federal and public legislation all over the country. But the process in which communities and lay citizens involve themselves is basically reactive: we have discovered how to stop things, but not how to start them or make them happen. New York is learning how to achieve that to some extent with the creation of community boards, which have some ability to move affirmatively rather than only reactively. I'm not sure whether it is for the best. It leads to one generation making decisions for another generation in a more widespread area, and I can't point to anything that has been better designed because of this process.

BLDD: After all your years of training and experience as an architect, is there a part of you that longs to design again?

MP: No, not at all. I've carved out my territory, and, despite the fact that what I do does not receive the rewards or professional acknowledgment that some people think it ought to, it's wonderful work and I wouldn't give it up for anything. I have the same feeling about teaching. It's thoroughly consistent with the way I want to be. I'm not going to make the mistake of going back to designing, as many of my colleagues in the public sector have done.

BLDD: You're obviously an open and innovative thinker. This is in direct contrast to the stereotype of someone who works in traditional establishment institutions—particularly those with which you've been associated. It always astonishes me that you manage not only to survive but to flourish. How do you explain it?

MP: I guess I'm basically a good bureaucrat. Despite the characterization of institutions as stuffy places in which creativity is stifled, like all human organizations, institutions go through cycles. Very often they call on people like me to do things, people who believe in institutions, or at least the power of institutions to accomplish certain goals.

KEVIN ROCHE

Kevin Roche is one of the country's most prominent designers of corporate and institutional buildings. His distinguished body of work is celebrated as much for its discipline and restraint as for its continuing inventiveness.

BLDD: After studying architecture in Dublin, where you were born, you left your home in County Cork to come to the United States. What prompted you to do that?

KR: I graduated from the National University of Ireland at the age of twenty-two and worked in Dublin and London until the age of twenty-five, when I had a mid-twenties crisis. I didn't know what to do with the rest of my life, so I decided that since I would probably live for another forty-five years, I would divide my time into three parts: fifteen years of study, fifteen years of practice, and fifteen years of teaching. For the first phase I decided to study with all the leading architects in the world. As you can see, I was very naive. It was a completely mad idea. I just woke up one morning and made up my mind; it came like a flash of lightning. But I set about it, and decided to start with Mies van der Rohe.

BLDD: Did you *know* Mies van der Rohe?

KR: Just by his published works. At that time he had just started the first buildings at Illinois Institute of Technology. He seemed to be the most promising of the practicing architects. I applied for entry into IIT, where he was teaching, and was accepted. That was the beginning of my forty-five-year plan, but as for the fifteen-year tour of study with great architects, I never got farther than Mies.

BLDD: Who else was on your original list?

KR: Oh, I had everybody: Wright, Aalto, Markelius, Neutra . . .

BLDD: As time went by, did you have the opportunity to tell any of them about your earlier intention?

KR: I met most of them subsequently but never had the nerve to say what I had been planning.

BLDD: What impressed you most about American industrial architecture, which you first saw in Chicago?

KR: Coming from an agricultural country, the whole panorama of American industrial society was overwhelming and extraordinary. Many of the trends of modern architecture originated in Chicago, were transferred to Europe, and then returned to Chicago. I really felt in the center of things on arriving there.

BLDD: What struck you about Mies van der Rohe?

KR: That he was truly a very great architect and had such an intensity about architecture. Working as an architect in England at that time was quite frivolous; people spoke of it as being fun. But for Mies it was no fun; it was a very serious art. It was interesting to begin my life in architecture with the sense that this was *the* most serious of all the arts, the one to which we must devote the most effort and time.

BLDD: Did you spend a great deal of time with Mies?

KR: As much as I could, but it was just a student-teacher relationship.

BLDD: Was there anything particularly important in your exchange with him?

KR: He imbued everybody with a sense of responsibility—almost a sense of guilt—about their performance. It took me years to live it down.

BLDD: Have you gotten over it yet?

KR: Not quite!

BLDD: From IIT you went to work for Eero Saarinen, who was perhaps America's most successful architect during the 1950s. How did you come to work for him?

KR: I first came to New York when the United Nations headquarters was being built, and I worked as an office boy on that project for about a year. I had some friends who knew Eero and were aware that I was anxious to get on with my world tour. They suggested that I talk to him. I did and, for some reason, he hired me. In 1950 I went to Detroit, where he was just beginning his independent career.

BLDD: It's been said that your buildings combine the romanticism of Saarinen's work with a greater discipline, that they are less theatrical and more restrained. Would you agree?

KR: I wouldn't aspire to have any building I worked on compared to Eero's work, but it's a nice compliment.

BLDD: Is there a particular design that publicly marked the distinction between your work and Saarinen's?

KR: The Oakland Museum, the first building we designed after Eero died, was in a sense a rejection of the monumentality of Eero's later buildings. I was in an antibuilding, antimonumental mood at that time.

BLDD: How pervasive was the influence of Saarinen's father, Eliel, the celebrated architect and founding president of the Cranbrook Academy?

KR: Eliel had a formidable effect on all Cranbrook graduates, among whom were Charles Eames, Florence Knoll, Harry Weese, and Harry Bertoia—very distinguished alumni. As for his influence on Eero, it's hard to say since Eero was very much his own person and had his own set of interests. I'm sure his father was an early influence, but he wasn't necessarily the *only* influence.

BLDD: Aline, Eero's wife at the time of his death, was a remarkable woman. She was one of the earliest cultural commentators, and one of the most incisive. Did she exert an aesthetic influence on him?

KR: I think so. She was a very good and forthright critic. He depended very much on her review and her opinion of a project. But he was nevertheless an artist. When he was in his creative mood he was completely independent of any influences whatsoever. When he needed something reviewed he would ask her. If she didn't agree with something she would certainly let him know, and he had high regard for her advice.

BLDD: Did they ever collaborate on anything?

KR: No, she didn't have any pretentions to being a designer. But they worked together every evening. They had a common workbench or desk; she worked on one side, he on the other. She wrote and he designed furniture.

BLDD: What was inspiring about working with him?

KR: It was his approach to the nature of an architectural problem. He always began at the foundations of the problem by considering the forces behind it, the elements bringing it about, and how to use these forces to generate a building. The best of Eero's buildings, and the most characteristic of the way he worked, was Dulles Airport, where he virtually invented a new airport type. He developed a completely original idea— that of the mobile lounge, around which a whole airport was planned. The exhaustive process he went through in that design is typical of how he designed everything. Eero and Charles Eames had very much the same approach to problems, something they discussed frequently. It was a thorough, investigative, and serious study of all the forces involved.

BLDD: A method very similar to the one you use currently. It seems you have a holistic approach to architecture, in which social, economic, and other factors are as important as aesthetics.

KR: Very much so. After all, in everything we do we are part of our society and our culture. We have a tremendous responsibility in what we pass along to our children and our grandchildren, the future of our society. If what we leave to posterity isn't done well or isn't done right, we are leaving the future with a problem. We should try to improve the environment, do better work, and make a contribution to culture.

BLDD: I've heard that Saarinen was a slave driver and that no one was more driven than he was. What was it like to work for him?

KR: In Detroit there wasn't much else to do aside from work. We worked long hours and we worked every day. We usually started around 8:30 A.M. and worked until one or two o'clock in the morning.

BLDD: Every day?

KR: Yes. Eero was very much a night person, but he expected all of us to be day people. He worked every day, including Christmas and New Year's. There was no such thing as a holiday. On Christmas morning you would receive a telephone call from him wondering why you weren't there.

BLDD: How did you reply?

KR: Oh, you got there!

BLDD: Who else worked there then?

KR: There was quite a succession of people going through the office: Bob Venturi, Cesar Pelli, Gunnar Birkerts; quite a number of architects who have become established in their own right.

BLDD: And designers, too. Niels Diffrient, the product designer, was recently telling me about his days there.

KR: Yes, Niels worked on the very first of Eero's furniture for Knoll. The reason so many interesting people worked for Saarinen was that in the early 1950s there really wasn't any place else to work in the United States. There was very little going on in New York, for instance, in 1950. Skidmore, Owings & Merrill did have an office there, but they weren't doing much. In Chicago there were a few offices. Mies was a very strong influence there, and so was Frank Lloyd Wright. If you wanted to work in an architectural office, Chicago was the logical place to go. But Eero had the largest private project since the war—the General Motors Technical Center, which was well over a million square feet. It was an enormous building for that time.

BLDD: What was so compelling about the environment of the office that it kept you all involved fifteen hours a day, 365 days a year? What were you doing that was so important?

KR: Actually we were having a very good time. We were doing what we wanted to do. Eero provided tremendous leadership, and we had a sense of total involvement. It was almost a religious experience, being so possessed by this activity.

BLDD: Was Eero a cult figure for you?

KR: In certain ways, perhaps, but he had no aspirations in that direction. He simply worked very hard and was relentless in his dedication to solving problems and finding answers. You can easily get wrapped up in that, particularly when you're young.

BLDD: When Saarinen died, at the age of fifty-one, you were his chief design associate and inherited a number of his unfinished projects: the TWA Terminal at Kennedy Airport in New York; Dulles Airport, outside Washington, D.C.; and the CBS Building in New York City. Did you change any of the original Saarinen plans when you took over the projects?

KR: There were twelve projects that were either not yet in construction or had just been begun. One of the terrible tragedies of Eero's early death was that, except for the General Motors Technical Center, he saw none of his important buildings completed. When he died on September 1, 1961, the TWA shell was just in place; the very first catenary arch of the roof of Dulles Airport was in place, one single cable and one of the posts; the St. Louis Arch had not been started; the Deere and Company headquarters had not been started; the design for CBS wasn't really even finished; construction on Bell Laboratories was just starting. So not only did he not see his buildings completed; most of them he didn't even see in the early stages of construction.

BLDD: Did you complete the design of the CBS Building?

KR: The concept and the details had been established. It hadn't gone into working drawings and final selection of materials had not been made.

BLDD: Frank Stanton, then the president of CBS, who was

deeply involved in the construction of the CBS Building, tells the story that one day Saarinen came to New York with one sample square of the dark gray granite to be used on the building and then returned to Detroit. Several days later he died.

KR: In fact, I was at a meeting at CBS discussing how many elevators were going to be in the building when I got the telephone call that Eero had died. It was a great tragedy that such an intense and creative architect never had the pleasure of seeing any of his major works completed.

BLDD: Were you involved with Charles Eames in any way?

KR: Yes. He did a number of films for us, which I worked on with him. The first was the one for Dulles Airport. Then when we were designing the National Aquarium—which never was built—we did an extensive film. There was also a film about a museum project for IBM that was never built.

BLDD: To the work of what architects, aside from Saarinen, do you respond?

KR: Among modern architects, I think Alvar Aalto was remarkable. Wright obviously was *the* great American architect, particularly in his early works. I like some of the Swedes: Asplund, for instance, was a very interesting man. And, of course, Le Corbusier. There are also many excellent younger architects today, such as Richard Meier and Michael Graves— very fine, even formidable, architects.

BLDD: Who do you consider to be among the most undervalued or overlooked architects?

KR: Those who produce indigenous architecture, people who don't qualify as architects at all but who really did build—the journeymen carpenters of the nineteenth century, for example, or the masons who built the small Greek villages and medieval towns. Those were the best architects of all.

BLDD: Your training as a Beaux-Arts student at University College, Dublin, left a slight Beaux-Arts inflection in some of your buildings. Does the work of the Beaux-Arts continue to inspire you?

KR: Fortunately, I've lived long enough to see it become respectable again; now I can bring my feeling for it out of the closet.

BLDD: Did you keep it there for long?

KR: Oh yes, it was well hidden. But almost everybody educated during that period in Europe or in America had a Beaux-Arts training. It wasn't until the 1950s that the schools discarded that kind of education. Princeton, I believe, had a Beaux-Arts program well into the fifties.

BLDD: Vincent Scully, our premier architectural historian, has described your designs as "Irish-American in the most syncretic sense, the scale pure grain elevator and the detail Dublin elegant." Is this a fair description?

KR: Vincent is a very romantic writer. I wouldn't dream of qualifying his descriptions at all!

BLDD: Do you think there's any evidence of an Irish style in your work?

KR: No, I feel that I'm very much an American responding to American problems. I fondly imagine that I have an American accent, and I hope that I fully improve myself in American culture. I don't think of myself as being Irish at all.

BLDD: Did the small town you grew up in have an influence on you? What was the architecture of that town like?

KR: It was interesting. The town had a very well worked-out plan, a legacy, I suppose, from English visionary planning of the early eighteenth century. But I don't think these things influenced me very much. I respond more to the immediate problems of the world I live in. I would say more important influences were Eero and Mies van der Rohe. I can't go back any farther than that.

BLDD: You've received numerous awards, honors, and prizes throughout your career, including the $100,000 Pritzker Prize. How did it feel to receive such an honor? How do you intend to use the prize money?

KR: As for receiving it, I didn't value it that much because— and this may seem very strange—I really don't believe in that kind of recognition. An underlying problem in architecture, as in many of the arts, is a star system, which this kind of prize tends to foster. It obscures the real issues we have to deal with. I very much wanted the prize money to be useful in education, so I proposed to Yale University to start a fund for a chair and a lecture series named after Eero Saarinen, the purpose of which will be to broaden the contact students have with the world at large. The visiting professors wouldn't necessarily be architects but would be from a variety of professions. They would work with the students and show them other parts of the world they're living in. When only architects are brought in to talk to architecture students, the whole thing gets too inbred. I'd like to open it up and get aspiring architects involved with the full spectrum of culture, with the rest of the world. Many people—painters, writers, people in the theater, economists, intellectuals of all sorts, shapes, and sizes—can pass some of their wisdom along to the students.

BLDD: What do you see as the value of architectural education?

KR: I would have to say it has very little value, although one would have to qualify what architectural education is. It varies a great deal. In this country it means to a large extent an education in art history. In Denmark it means an education in the trades as well as in art history. In other countries it means an education in architecture as a performance profession. Regardless of what it means, though, it's hard to pinpoint the benefits of architectural education. You can't make an architect any more than you can make a painter, a composer, or a writer. All you can do is teach some of the elements of composition. Being an architect is a creative act, after all. It is an art.

BLDD: Then what is the best way to prepare a young architect for work?

KR: Of course you have to teach the basic elements of architecture—the effect of gravity and how one counters it, the nature of materials, the concepts of planning, all of those things. And then you must teach the students the most important thing of all, that they are building for *people*. They have to understand their relationship to people, how they can provide what the people need. We are working in a democracy, in which the ultimate client is the people. We may imagine the client to be a municipality, a developer, or a corporation, but ultimately it is the people. Architects don't always understand this, nor do they understand their responsibility to perform for the people.

BLDD: You have said that this is a time of unique opportunity because we do not have a formal architecture or a formal civilization. Would you clarify what that really means?

KR: In civilizations or cultures prior to the emergence of the great social reforms and the idea of democracy and its application on a large scale, we were dealing with a patronage system. The patron was a king, a pope, a prince, a baron—a single person who was building for himself, for his own aggrandizement. Doing public good was incidental. Now we are building for communities. So we must have uppermost in our minds the responsibility of doing public good. That is the beginning point of architectural education, to hammer the idea into students that what they are doing is going out to serve the people. Their purpose is not to work out their frustrations, to make a lot of money, or to be artists; their goal is to serve the people.

BLDD: Do you think that's a widely held idea?

KR: I don't believe so. Our models are generally architects like the one described by Ayn Rand in *The Fountainhead*—the architect who has the right to do anything, even blow up a building if he doesn't like it. Or we use the model of Frank Lloyd Wright, the eccentric genius. We need to broaden the education of people to convey what architecture is. We need to train people to see their environment, to understand that they can use their influence to improve that environment, and to realize that architects can be the instruments in making that improvement.

BLDD: I know that an architect must have a good eye. But you've also said that an architect must have a good ear. What does that mean?

KR: An architect must listen. When you're planning something it is very easy to imagine that you know all the answers. People actually aspire to plan enormous buildings or even towns without ever having had as much as one conversation with the people who are going to use them. It's a terribly misguided notion. In the practice of architecture the starting point should be based not on your own grand concept but on the aspirations, expectations, and needs of the people for whom you are providing an environment. I believe very deeply in the idea of community service. Without that it is impossible to be an architect. Of course, all buildings result from an act of will, but you must also have a conviction that what you're doing is right.

BLDD: Of all the adjectives used to describe your work, the ones you least approve of include individualistic, original, and creative. What adjectives would *you* use to describe your work?

KR: I would prefer that people not describe it at all. I would rather that the work just be there as background, that people use it without it ever occurring to them that someone had designed it. That would be the ideal condition not only for myself but for all those architects we hear too much about.

BLDD: John Dinkeloo, your late partner, once said that it was more important to understand how your office does things than to understand the finished products. He said that design is the way something is carried out. Is that an approach you agree with?

KR: Yes. Design is not drawing and not conceptual moments, but guiding a slow, evolutionary process to the best of your ability and with considerable interest in the result. It is the opposite of making a few sketches and handing it over and saying, "Here, build this." The process also attempts to involve all of the elements and forces that make a building.

BLDD: Would you describe the way your office works?

KR: When John was alive we split the responsibility into the two aspects of building: I was responsible for the program design, the evolution of the concept of the building; John was responsible for the actual process of building, including the preparation of the final bid, documents, dealing with contractors, dealing with codes, getting the structure up. I usually start with a lot of research on the project, a lot of conversation and a lot of interviews, which I throw away when I finish. I never refer to them afterwards, because I am not really listening to the specifics of what people are saying, but to the overall impression of what they're saying. Then I look at the particulars of the project: the urban or rural nature of the site, the zoning considerations, the technology available, the economics of the project, the aspirations of the people paying for it, the imagery involved. The insights are very important; we tend to start every design with the interior and gradually work our way to the outside.

BLDD: How do you organize your work life?

KR: I'm an early riser and tend to start early. I often work until after 6 P.M., and always on Saturdays, but not on Sundays. That's a little less than what I used to do.

BLDD: Is it true, as it has been said about you, that you would not take a client that was a plane ride away because you didn't want to waste time traveling?

KR: No, it's not. I fly all over the country. I've read all of Dickens on planes in the last year alone, which is something like fourteen thousand pages. I'm working my way through all of nineteenth-century English literature this way.

BLDD: How does the reading influence your design aesthetic?

KR: Dickens is interesting because he was a great humanitarian, and because his descriptions of nineteenth-century London match any study you might make of estate planning and the growth of London.

BLDD: How large is your office staff?

KR: We have about eighty people, of which perhaps sixty-five are architects.

BLDD: How many projects are you working on now?

KR: About fourteen, in varying stages of construction.

BLDD: How do you manage to coordinate all that work and also have time for your family?

KR: Our five teenagers do keep us busy! I love the challenge of change. I get bored very quickly if I work on something for more than half an hour. I just keep going back and forth from one project to another.

BLDD: Don't some projects require sustained concentration?

KR: Yes. But if you sit down and start to think only about the problem, it becomes more difficult and goes away from you completely. My advice is not to sit down and look at the thing, but to work on it briefly and keep thinking about it as you do other things.

BLDD: Your office makes extensive use of models; thirty to fifty are often used for a single project. Why are models so important to the process?

KR: For several reasons. Since all buildings are three-dimensional, you should use models, also a three-dimensional medium, in designing. Also, from the point of view of organizing an office, it engages a large number of people—only one person works on a drawing, but ten people can work on a model. Another advantage to models is that you can create an image of the building in varying scales, move things back and forth quickly, changing the color or the size, which you can't do with a drawing. Drawings are too static. Architecture students are now studying things more and more in model form. The idea of just studying the drawing is almost obsolete. The practice has in fact gone a little too far—many students can't draw at all now.

BLDD: If you use models rather than theory, what is the impetus for that first model?

KR: It almost doesn't matter how you get it started as long as you get it started. Once you've done it two or three times, it is very easy to give a few directions to get something started. Once you have something, you can make changes. The panic about creating something comes from the sense that you have to finish it right away. If you manage to forget that you have to actually achieve this thing, it will come together some time in the future. It's similar to writing. When you're writing and you say, "This is going to be it," it never works. You have to write something, then cut it up and paste it together again—over and over. You design buildings the same way.

BLDD: How does your last model on a project relate to your first one?

KR: There's usually no connection at all.

Ford Foundation Headquarters, New York, N.Y.

BLDD: Are you saying that architecture isn't necessarily intellectual?

KR: I've always said that. It's intuitive as much as intellectual.

BLDD: You seem to approach each project without preconceived notions. If you don't begin with a set notion, with what *do* you begin?

KR: You can begin with a set notion, but you won't end up with that same notion. If you do, something is wrong, because the process of doing it involves other people. To a certain extent you are the captain of a ship that is heading in a certain direction, but you need other people to sail it and get it where it's going. There has to be a substantial contribution from people in the office and from the people for whom the building is being built. It really takes two groups of people to build: the clients and the architects. Both need to be enlightened in order to produce good architecture. A great deal of dialogue is necessary between client and architect.

BLDD: Let's talk about your long-term associate John Dinkeloo. How did the two of you come together?

KR: John was born in Holland, Michigan, and graduated from the University of Michigan. He was the first head of production at Skidmore, Owings & Merrill in Chicago, their very first office. He joined Eero just about the time I did in 1950. When we joined Eero's office it had twelve people; by the time Eero

died it had about sixty-five or seventy. John's role was to organize the production of the drawings and to supervise the building. Since I had been involved in design and John in construction, when Eero died we were able to continue just as before and complete the projects Eero had designed.

BLDD: Your office is housed in a turn-of-the-century mansion in Hamden, Connecticut. When did you acquire those headquarters, and why did you choose that location?

KR: It started when we were in Detroit, in Bloomfield Hills, a suburban area. Most of our work at that time was on the East Coast—in New York, Washington, and New Jersey. This was before jet planes, and with propeller planes it took four hours and a lot of martinis to fly to the East Coast. We all began to suffer, so Eero decided to move the office east. We made a survey of a number of sites: Washington, Princeton, Stamford, New Haven, New York, and Boston. We wanted to find a place that wasn't in a downtown area but also wouldn't require being located in a shopping center. We found a house in New Haven owned by a member of the local zoning board, who conveniently changed the zoning from residential to commercial to sell his property. So we were able to use the house as an office. We were planning to move the last week in August, 1961. Everything was packed in trucks and we had sold our property in Bloomfield Hills. So when Eero died we had to move anyway, which turned out to be very good because it meant a break with the past. The move also turned out to be a good thing because Connecticut was fast becoming a center for corporate headquarters, and there we were, already on the spot.

BLDD: The Ford Foundation Building, which was essentially a headquarters building, provides a monumental enclosed garden. It preceded the current spate of office and hotel atriums. What gave you the idea for that innovation?

KR: During the nineteenth century it was a common thing, and there are many hotels in the United States that use the device of enclosing a courtyard. But the Ford Foundation Building is probably one of the first in the postwar period to do so. The building presented an interesting problem to grapple with in New York. The site could have held a much larger building, but the foundation would not construct a building larger than they could occupy. So we had a unique opportunity in New York—building a small structure on a large site. The project allowed us to do a low-rise building, something I was very anxious to build. It had to fit in with Tudor City, a marvelous residential neighborhood. I like the scale, the character, the parks, and the very pleasant details it has. It was a very enlightened development for its time. We designed a C-shaped building with two scales, one for the Forty-second Street side and one for the Forty-third Street side. In looking for a solution to how to create public space, I knew I did not want a plaza because I loathe plazas. The word "plaza" is really a misnomer for that kind of space.

BLDD: What should it be called?

KR: Unused windy space. It seemed to me that since we were fortunate enough to be adjacent to the park in Tudor City, we should try to bring the park into the building. Suddenly, as I was driving one day—this is how things happen—it occurred to me that we should create an enclosed garden. This way the garden could be used year round and the building's offices could open onto it. At that time it seemed a very radical idea. Now it's commonplace.

BLDD: Is the idea still fresh and workable?

KR: It's still possible to use the garden in a pleasant way. I might say that as a public space the Ford Foundation garden is used less than I had hoped. We designed all of the planter walls so that people would sit on them, but shortly after the building was finished I discovered that the guards had been instructed to keep the planter walls wet so people couldn't sit on them. So our best intentions were deflected. The idea of providing retreats and communion with nature is so important and so difficult to achieve in the city. You can do it in parks, and there are many wonderful parks and small gardens in Manhattan. But it's also nice to have year-round places, which is not to say that I really advocate atriums. Just as plazas are generally unsuccessful spaces, not all atriums work, not all of them are desirable or pleasant.

BLDD: Which are most successful?

KR: Ones that have commercial life. I don't mean shopping centers.

BLDD: Like the IDS Center in Minneapolis?

KR: IDS is very successful. And I like to think the space in the Ford building is very successful, too.

BLDD: As part of New Haven's $96 million redevelopment program, you created the Veterans Memorial Coliseum. Was the intent of that project to modernize New Haven's decaying center?

KR: It was only part of a redevelopment project that also included a highway leading into the city center. We did not have a hand in establishing the site for the Coliseum; it was

already determined for us. We had to provide a location that would allow the people to come to the Coliseum without congesting the streets of the city with traffic.

BLDD: The car is an important part of most people's lives. Do you think it has a strong influence on architectural design?

KR: Not as much as it should. I believe very strongly that we have to recognize the presence of the car. We tend to design buildings as they were designed in the Renaissance—with a large carriageway entrance, a large front door—as if we were still stepping out of carriages that were then taken away by somebody else. The reality is that we drive up to a building and then are confronted with the problem of what to do with the wretched car. If it's an enlightened development the car is hidden somehow, perhaps put into a basement garage, where you see the pipes, the air-conditioning ducts, and all the mess.

BLDD: How have you dealt with this overriding problem?

KR: At the General Foods headquarters we made the visitor drive into the lobby. The parking space is a space that people are going to use. Employees drive in and park in the building. The ideal situation for American suburban office workers would be to drive directly into their offices. It is technically possible to drive onto the floor where your office is, and walk perhaps a hundred feet to your office. It can be dealt with in a very comfortable way. The cars can be put out of sight, and the process can be more elegant and pleasant. It is a very serious issue, and we have not faced it in a proper way.

Knights of Columbus Headquarters, New Haven, Conn.

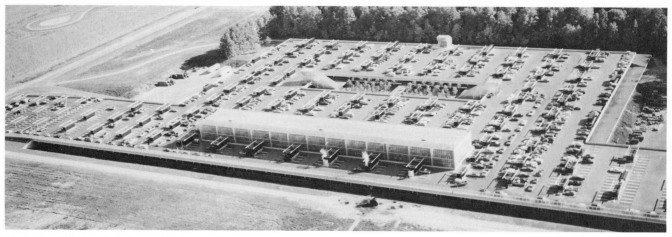

Cummins Engine Sub-Assembly Plant, Columbus, Ind.

BLDD: Haven't you also placed automobiles at the top of buildings?

KR: Yes, we have done that at the Coliseum. I am very concerned about land use—the loss of arable land, suburban sprawl, and so forth. When we build in the countryside I deplore the use of the parking lot, which is both ugly and destructive to nature. In an office building the car usually takes up about the same amount of space as the person, about 350 square feet. So we use the roof as the parking area, which gets a lot of cars out of sight and minimizes land use. We did a factory in Columbus, Indiana, for instance, where the workers drive onto the roof, take escalators down into a little garden courtyard, and then go to work. The employees have the luxury of convenient and pleasant arrival—and it didn't cost anything extra.

BLDD: The Knights of Columbus building and the Coliseum in New Haven, the Ford Foundation in New York, and the Power Center for the Performing Arts in Ann Arbor all seem to incorporate massive masonry piers and steel girders reminiscent of highway construction. What do you admire about those structural elements?

KR: This may sound peculiar, but one of the great art forms in America is highway construction, a most extraordinary achievement. If a sculptor were to make a highway from the East to the West Coast that included all those wonderful curves and bridges, books would be written about it, just as with Christo's *Running Fence.* I don't particularly like highway construction, but highways are remarkable manifestations of the twentieth century just as the aqueducts were of the Roman Empire. I'm sure that from a historical perspective highway construction will be considered one of the representative achievements of our civilization.

BLDD: Among your innovations is the use of a great deal of Corten steel. What do you like about that material?

KR: It is the nature of steel to rust, and the beautiful quality of Corten is that it rusts to a certain point, then stops, achieving a beautiful, deep color. If you put a weathering-steel building in a wooded area, for instance, its color fits in well with that of the tree trunks. It's a handsome material that requires no maintenance and is relatively inexpensive. Interestingly enough, it became a very popular material for sculptors after we had used it in building. So it also has some aesthetic merits.

BLDD: The new headquarters of the Worcester County National Bank in Massachusetts is a twenty-four-story twin tower covered in mirrored glass that literally reflects the city. What was your intention in that project?

KR: Worcester is an interesting town in that it is surrounded by hills, and on those hills there's a big ring of highways. I thought it would be appropriate to have a single needle that would establish the center of Worcester, just as the spire located the medieval city in the plain. We designed our building behind the handsome main street, with the entrance being a small gap in the street. It was designed to be a receding building, but before construction was finished they had torn down all of Main Street!

BLDD: Did you transform your design?

KR: We couldn't do anything with it. It was already built at that point. So we ended up with a plaza, which is what was left of Main Street. So much for contextualism!

BLDD: You've always tried to integrate the built form with nature. The project that comes to mind first is the Oakland Museum, but this also holds true for the Ford Foundation, the John Deere headquarters, and the Metropolitan Museum of Art. Has this been as conscious an effort on your part as it appears to be?

KR: Just as we need to commune with each other and with animals, we need to commune with the trees, flowers, plants, and grass. If you isolate people from that they suffer deeply. It is so easy to put growing things in our cities, in our towns, and in our houses—why not do it? It costs very little and it is a calming influence. It prevents us all from going mad.

BLDD: Can you describe the Oakland Museum for us?

KR: The original project was to build three museums: one for art, one for natural history, and one for cultural history. They passed a bond issue to build a museum, but they had no clear idea of what they meant by a museum. There were three small museums with virtually no collection. There was a good collection of art of the American West, but the natural history collection consisted of a number of large trunks filled with elephant skins in the basement of a house. In any case, when I went out there several things became apparent: one, they were very proud of their parks; two, they had a marvelous climate for growing things. Since the collection would take some time to get together, we thought it would be nice to have something else for people to visit in the meantime. The theory behind this museum was that it would be a regional museum, focusing on the culture of the United States from the Rockies to the Pacific Ocean. The collections would incorporate the art of the American West; the history and culture of American Indians and the eighteenth- and nineteenth-century migrations from the East; and the rich natural features of the region. This gave the whole museum a description and an organization.

From then on it was easy. We decided to build a park that would serve as a museum and a museum that would serve as a park. They now have an excellent curatorial program and a lively, active museum. It is a very successful regional museum.

BLDD: Among your other museum designs is the master plan and additions to the Metropolitan Museum of Art, constructed between 1975 and 1983.

KR: We are still working on it. We have one more wing for twentieth-century art to go, which is hopefully going to happen soon.

BLDD: Tell us about that commission. What were the conditions and limitations you had to concern yourself with in creating those spaces? And what about the ongoing concern of incursion into the park?

KR: We never incurred on the park. Let's go back in history for a moment. Before the first museum building was constructed, a section of land had been set aside in Central Park as the site for the museum, and Calvert Vaux and Frederick Olmsted had made a master plan. From 1880 to 1882 Vaux built the first section of the museum, which is now the Medieval Court. The western facade of that building now appears in the Lehman Wing. When that first building was finished the master plan was discarded. Weston & Tuckman then built another structure to the south, and Tuckman built one to the north. They also had a master plan, which was thrown away. The next person on the scene was Richard Morris Hunt, who decided this was not a building in the park, but a building on Fifth Avenue. He built the Great Stairs and the Great Entrance Hall. The next group of architects was McKim, Mead & White, who built the wings to the north and to the south over a period of ten or fifteen years. The final building program was the American Wing, built rather eccentrically on the northwest corner with no resemblance to anything else around it—it was out of alignment, had different

floor levels, and so on. A few other small buildings were built in the intervening years. A large master plan was developed in the early forties, but it collapsed. When Thomas Hoving became director and Douglas Dillon was chairman, they set their first priority as developing a master plan for the growth of the museum. It was very badly needed—there were some absolutely frightful conditions. Curatorial spaces were abominable; art was stored with no protection in hallways and basements. The American Wing alone had only eleven percent of its collection on view at any time. It was clear that a larger vision of the museum was necessary, especially in view of growing attendance. We were asked to reorganize all of the departments in the museum—establishing exhibition, storage, study, and curatorial spaces—as well as all of the service elements. Suddenly it all began to come together, almost before we had the plan completed. Robert Lehman came through with his collection. The Temple of Dendur was secured. We started to *build* the master plan almost before the plan was finished. It happened very quickly.

BLDD: Was this a good way to go about it?

KR: Yes, because it enabled us to plan and build at the same time. I felt very strongly that the move out on Fifth Avenue had been a mistake, and that the original Olmsted plan for a building in the park was the right approach. So the first decision was to give the Fifth Avenue side an urban setting with plazas, places to sit, fountains, and steps. These, of course, have proven to be very popular as spaces for people. As for the neoclassical facades on Fifth Avenue, which are quite successful—not extraordinary, but successful—I felt that there would be no justification for turning those facades around into the park. The kind of architecture needed there is what one would expect to see in a park—a botanical garden. And when it is all finished, when all the landscaping is in and all the ivy has grown, that is what you will see—beautiful botanical-garden

Metropolitan Museum of Art, New York, N.Y., plan

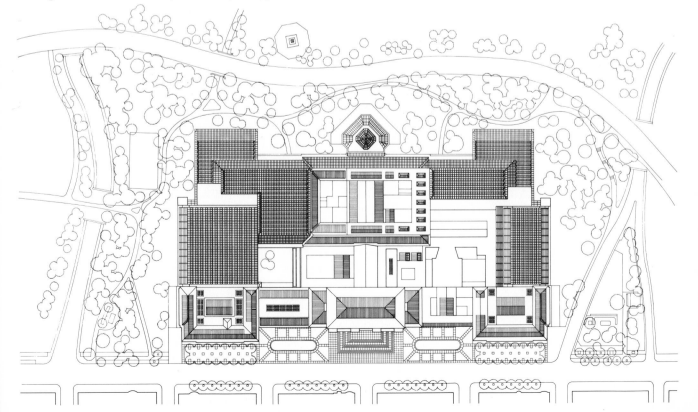

buildings. The Fifth Avenue side will remain as a very urban facade.

BLDD: One of your most controversial suggestions was the idea of removing the Grand Stairs.

KR: That's right. And I would still support that suggestion. There's a problem in people's minds as to what the Metropolitan Museum is, and the staircase has a lot to do with the confusion. Many people think of the Metropolitan as a collection of European paintings. But the art of many other cultures is included, although it's always been dealt with as secondary. Unless you happen to be particularly interested in ancient Egypt or Islam, for instance, you would never get back to those collections. As we built the museum we filled out the remainder of the space with the American Wing, Western European arts, and the Rockefeller Wing. In order to get another line of circulation—north/south circulation—the access to them would have to be right through the middle of the staircase.

BLDD: Do you think you'll ever accomplish that kind of circulation?

KR: No, I don't think so. But it does make sense, and that is why I proposed it. *I* like the staircase, too. But it is a case of the tail wagging the dog. What the staircase does is to lead you up to the European paintings, making them the major element in the museum.

BLDD: For a long time they were.

KR: They were. But now the setup tends to detract from the extraordinary range of the rest of the collection.

BLDD: One of your recent commissions is for the design of a new Central Park Zoo, in which you are replacing some of the rather harsh buildings that date from the 1930s. How are you planning to transform this area?

KR: Let me make one general comment about the difference between designing buildings for animals and designing buildings for people. People seem much more concerned about the living environment of animals than about the living environment of people.

BLDD: How do you satisfy the desires of animal lovers as well as those of people interested in architecture?

KR: One way is to work with a lot of advisers. We're working with the New York Zoological Society. Dr. William Conway, the general director and one of the leading figures in animal sciences, is an incredible man.

BLDD: So research in this particular project is fundamental?

KR: That's right. Dr. Conway and his staff are providing all the guidance with respect to the treatment of animals and the environments appropriate for them. The existing buildings were built as part of the WPA program in the early thirties. Some of them aren't bad—those we are leaving. The Arsenal, which is the headquarters of the Department of Parks, is within the park and not a part of the zoo. It was built prior to the park. The buildings flanking the Arsenal are the bird house and the monkey house, two quite handsome buildings, which we are saving. We're going to rehouse the seals and sea lions in a new pool where you will be able to see them better and they will have more water and better accommodations. There will be a much greater variety of animals in the new zoo. But they won't be the same animals that were there originally.

BLDD: In your scheme none of the animals will be behind bars. Whose idea was that?

KR: It is an idea now common in the most enlightened zoological gardens throughout the world. The animals' own limitations are used as criteria for designing the barriers. For instance, if an animal can jump fifteen feet, then you make a moat that's

Central Park Zoo renovation, New York, N.Y., model

sixteen feet long. The barrier is a moat or some other simple device. The big problem is keeping the people away from the animals; they can usually do more damage to the animals than the animals can do to the people.

BLDD: As I recall, the Bronx Zoo is 252 acres. Here you are working with a zoo of five acres. How do you deal with those space limitations?

KR: What we really have is a downtown zoo. When people think of the Central Park Zoo, they think of the central formal garden, which we are preserving. We're refurbishing it, re-planting it, and restoring it, but it will still be the main feature of the new zoo. We are removing the cafeteria, one of the uglier buildings, which will have a dual effect: it will take the service yard out of Central Park, eliminating a big mess, and it will open up the zoo to the rest of the park, making the western portion of the site more accessible visually as well as practically.

BLDD: Another new feature is an "intelligence garden." Is there an historical precedent for that?

KR: This was the invention of a Chinese emperor who created what is considered the first zoological garden; his concept was for a garden of intelligence, a garden for understanding our animal friends. Dr. Conway brought this idea to the project. We are calling it the temperate zone. We have three zones in the new zoo: temperate, polar, and tropic. The tropic zone is an enclosed glass house. The temperate zone holds those animals that live in our climate. The polar bears, penguins, and puffins will be in a separate polar-zone building. Forty penguins will be seen above and below water. It will be very exciting. A wonderful exhibit.

BLDD: One question raised by the New York City Landmarks Preservation Commission, even as they approved the plan, was whether the glass roofs you mentioned were appropriate to such a rustic or garden context. How did you respond to those questions?

KR: We have by and large concealed the glass. You will see mostly slate roofs. We do, however, have a wonderful arcade that is a combination of brick, wood, and glass and is trellised with wisteria. It will allow a visitor to go to all of the exhibits without getting wet, should it be raining.

BLDD: You have also been working on an addition to the CBS Building, located on Fifty-third Street between Fifth and Sixth Avenues in New York City. What was involved in the design of that project?

KR: It was a very difficult problem because, of course, it is adjacent to the existing CBS Building—a very strong, very formal building. We want to avoid the new building being called "little rock" or "white rock." [The CBS Building is referred to as "black rock."] The new building will go from Fifty-second to Fifty-third Street and will incorporate the Museum of American Folk Art, which used to be on the site. The interesting feature will be the space created between the existing building and the new building. We are hoping to do a public plaza that once and for all really works as a people place.

BLDD: Another Paley Park?

KR: Yes, something along those lines that will really be a pleasant place.

BLDD: With *public* access?

KR: Yes, one hundred percent public access.

BLDD: Where do you see architecture heading in the next decade?

KR: I'm very optimistic. People are becoming more aware that there is such a thing as architecture, an environment and a city that you can save and live in. While I sounded pessimistic about architectural education, it has improved considerably in recent years, and its focus is approaching what it should be. Interviews like this are very important in the sense of public education. We have made so many mistakes in American cities since the war. I hope that we won't have to relive the past and that we will benefit from those mistakes. The future holds the possibility of a resolution of urban problems, the fulfillment of what our living environment can be—ultimately, what the ideal conditions for life on earth can be.

BLDD: Is there an ideal project that you haven't done that you'd care to?

KR: Not really. I'm willing to undertake almost anything. There are some things I'm not interested in—hospitals, for instance. They're technically complicated and one should spend a whole lifetime learning the technical design aspects.

BLDD: As a man so committed to the notion of the public good, why have you never designed public housing?

KR: Because I don't believe in the way in which it is provided. First of all, since public housing is really dictated by legislation, the act of designing the housing itself is so constricted as to prevent you from providing decent habitation. Secondly, if what we call public housing is intended for people who other-wise wouldn't have a decent place to live, a better approach would be to provide the people with money and allow them to live where they want to live. We shouldn't pack people into some filing cabinet full of rooms and thereby absolve ourselves of our social responsibilities. Social problems are deeper. They don't begin or end with the act of building a housing project.

BLDD: If you were to start over again, what would you do differently?

KR: That's an unanswerable question. I started my career by making those naive plans to organize my whole life, but it doesn't work that way. People and circumstances form every-thing you do. So even if I had responded to all of the op-portunities and constrictions I faced in my life, I don't know that I could have done anything differently.

BLDD: Would you have completed that world tour?

KR: I'm glad I didn't!

BENJAMIN THOMPSON

For close to forty years, Benjamin Thompson's work has been synonymous with distinguished design. As a modernist and a preservationist, he has been responsible for giving new life and new usefulness to the built environment.

BLDD: More than forty years ago, with Walter Gropius and others, you founded Architects Collaborative. What was the origin of this unique group, and who else was involved?

BT: When World War II ended, a group of us were ready to start an architectural office. The group included Norman Fletcher and his wife, Jean, John and Sally Harkness, Robert and Louis MacMillan, and myself—all friends from graduate school days. I had sought out and met Gropius informally in Cambridge in 1944, on a navy shore leave. In 1946, when Harkness was offered a teaching job at Harvard, we all came to Cambridge to talk about starting an office. We met with Gropius and talked about joining forces. He was head of the Harvard Graduate School of Design, but since his wartime association with Breuer had terminated, he had not settled into a practice. He was extremely sympathetic to our idea of an office based on "creative teamwork." The outcome of our meeting was that we rented a small space and got started. That was the nucleus of TAC.

BLDD: What were your goals then?

BT: Not too different from what they are today. We were oriented toward a social architecture. We had finally gotten style, in the Beaux-Arts sense, off our backs and out of our schools. We didn't have to worship it any more. We discussed theories and programs for building a better city, a better nation, a better world. That's where we were headed after six years of war.

BLDD: What was it like to work with Walter Gropius, a figure who was already legendary?

BT: It was great. At that time we weren't very knowledgeable, so we were not terribly awed by his reputation as a world figure. The most fascinating thing about Gropius was his total intensity, the sense of purpose and seriousness he exhibited. But he was also a very natural fellow. He wasn't what the

legend says—a character who went around making great "form-follows-function" pronouncements. He was a person you could talk to about almost anything, and we did. He would talk about a leaking roof, a business problem, or a political situation, about books, or women, or love.

BLDD: How did he influence your career?

BT: Most importantly as a role model, a mentor, an example of an architect who was acting individually and independently within the profession. In architecture at the time there was a lot of discussion about esoteric aspects of aesthetics. But Gropius was anything but a formalist obsessed with "modern style." Everything he did he took seriously. He loved younger people and worked closely with them. A great deal of his influence was in his manner, the way he respected every individual. He was a true democrat.

BLDD: How long did you work with him?

BT: Twenty years. That's a long time. I may have worked more closely with him than any of the principals associated with him during his active career. He worked with Maxwell Fry in England for two years, then with Breuer when he came to the U.S.; then he joined The Architects Collaborative. That was a kind of two-dollar name. Nobody knew what "collaborative" meant then. They probably still don't.

BLDD: What did it mean to the collaborators?

BT: We had an idea, which was ahead of its time, that architecture today requires teamwork; no single mind or set of skills is equal to the comprehensive task that architecture is. I still operate on that principle.

BLDD: Was Gropius involved in Design Research, that remarkable idea you developed about thirty years ago?

BT: That came about in 1953. Gropius was involved only in the sense that he very much supported the idea. I proposed D/R and carried it out independent of the architectural firm.

BLDD: What was the idea behind Design Research?

BT: When writers interviewing me would ask that question, I used to insist that to understand it they had to see it, feel it, experience it. Words are no substitute for experience! The goal of

Design Research had to do with environment, with the idea of art being part of daily life. I've never thought of art as something museum-bound, something untouchable contained within sacred walls. I wanted to encourage a view that art is part of the house, the kitchen, or the whole environment of living, eventually spreading out to the cityscape and the landscape. We were trying to demonstrate that concept in Design Research, in its products, its arrangement, its spirit. So we began calling the shops "environments," even though that sounded a little too serious. After all, it was commercial—we did sell things. Because it was attractive people sometimes felt skeptical about it also being a business.

BLDD: Did it turn out to be commercially viable?

BT: Yes, it did. The company was always undercapitalized and had its economic struggles, but it did well and grew while I ran it. There was a take-over in 1969, at which point I resigned.

BLDD: Do you think it's possible for products to be both well made and mass-produced?

BT: Yes, and Marimekko is a good example of that. In 1957 I discovered a small company in Finland making printed fabrics with wonderful rich, vibrant colors. I introduced them in the U.S. in 1959. The fabrics were handcrafted by silkscreen, which gave them extraordinary color, and they had bold, imaginative designs. As the company grew into a worldwide concern, it moved to a machine-printing process. That limited some of the things that could be done, although the color and quality retained a level that no other firm has yet matched. Something was lost, but mass production also allowed Marimekko to become a large, successful enterprise reaching a world market with products that were nevertheless sophisticated in concept. With effort, quality can be combined with mass production, but it is usually a mixed blessing.

BLDD: Let's consider a Breuer tubular-steel chair, for example. Does our perception of it change when we begin to see it everywhere, both the originals and the copies? Does it become a cliché, or is it still a well-designed chair?

BT: That's a much argued point. Twenty years ago many of us were upset that manufacturers began to copy the Breuer chair and other designer chairs. The original manufacturers, of course, were the pioneers, making an advanced design for a selective audience, which always means a higher cost for development and promotion, and propery royalties for the designer. The result is usually a higher price, although I often argued that some manufacturers were too little concerned with reasonable pricing. When a good product that is exclusive and fashionable becomes widely known, somebody always tries to copy it, to knock it off at a lower price for a broader market. They do it by cheapening the product—it happens on Seventh Avenue every day—and the copy has more to do with a "look" than the quality of the real thing.

BLDD: Most modern architects claim that their goal is to bring quality design to a wider audience, and in so doing to revolutionize modern life. It seems to me that in your practice you've done more of what modernism is supposed to be about than almost anyone else. Was that your intention?

BT: I'd have to say yes, but I don't believe I thought of it as revolutionizing anything. My goal was to make the creation of a personal and individual environment easier for people, with freer choices than the marketing system was offering. I started Design Research out of a concern that the average citizen with a house or apartment to furnish in the 1950s could not buy a good modern chair, table, or bed without going to the exclusive trade showrooms of Knoll or Herman Miller. A person had to buy through an architect or decorator in the trade. That implied that the customer had no taste, couldn't make choices

without professional help. It was terribly limiting and inconvenient, as well as elitist. I set out to make a broad selection of good things, including many excellent products found only abroad, available to Cambridge customers—some of them friends and clients. They certainly had the judgment and imagination to assemble their own environments and to enjoy selecting everything they needed for daily life—down to ashtrays and casserole dishes. You might say I'm an aesthetic pluralist. I don't believe it is the prerogative of any person or profession to dictate what taste is and what "good" means. I have my own standards, but society is better if people find their own beliefs by having choices and making decisions.

BLDD: From a historical perspective your design for Boston's Faneuil Hall may be seen as one of the more significant projects of its time. Even now it serves as a model for every city's vision of adaptive reuse. To begin with, just what does the term "adaptive reuse" mean, and how does it apply to what you did at Faneuil Hall?

BT: Sometimes the word "revitalization" is used. I have had difficulty with the kind of strict restoration that we called "Williamsburging the place," meaning doing a totally strict historical restoration reproducing every detail, every paint color, every pane of glass, every floorboard exactly as it was, say, in the eighteenth century or, in the case of Faneuil Hall, in the nineteenth century. Even if we knew exactly how it was—and often we don't—strict museum-like restoration is not affordable and, in my view, not desirable in an urban situation. "Museumitis" stifles the spirit and kills the evolutionary growth that gives cities their sense of continuity. In older cultures abroad they take a much more organic view of history. Most great buildings of the past are like layer cakes, showing modifications and changes over time, accretions, accidents, repairs, all of which keep pace with technical and social change. If you applied the strict purist historical standards that have become the weapon of some preservationist groups in this country, the unmatched towers of Notre Dame would not be permitted! I suppose one would have to be torn down and rebuilt to conform. But who is going to decide which piece of history is real and which deserves to be wiped out for the sake of idealized revisionist symmetry?

Most old buildings are eminently worth saving because they speak to us about time and tradition and where we came from, and because they display materials and workmanship that we cannot afford to duplicate today. In the late 1950s I was able to convince Harvard to restore and reuse Boylston Hall and Emerson Hall, at great savings in cost and in the environmental character of Harvard Yard. Respectable modern architects then did not deal with old buildings except with a bulldozer. I became concerned with finding ways of adapting buildings to new uses, to functions that fit our time, because without an attempt to use some imagination in both preserving and updating them, most of our heritage buildings were clearly going to be disposed of. We came to Faneuil Hall in this spirit.

BLDD: How was it being used and what was its state when you first came upon it?

BT: Quincy Market and the two side blocks were built in 1825 as a wholesale city market, which was the commercial heart of the city in the nineteenth century. It was made obsolete by time, expansion, and modern trucking, just as Les Halles was in Paris. By the early 1960s the market was more or less empty and falling into ruin and was part of an urban renewal plan. There had been fires, and the roof leaked. A handful of merchants stayed on—the rest relocated to a new truck depot—without heat and with very little business. But they had a lot of life and character, some being from families that had

Faneuil Hall Marketplace, Boston, Mass.

been merchants in the market for fifty or a hundred years. They were worth saving as much as the buildings themselves.

The idea of making the Faneuil Hall area into a market was not very original, since that's what it had always been. The location within the city was still right, and it was a matter of adapting the market concept for our time. We had faith in the concept of markets in cities. We had seen working examples all over the world. In this country we were living in the postwar world of the A&P and the mall, where you went *out* of town to shop for food in plastic wraps and freezer containers. The forces of distribution, not sound planning for cities, had brought this about. Would anybody consider coming *downtown* again to a market? Most people said no, it would never work in an automotive and suburban age. What we proposed and pushed for at the outset was as much an economic and social belief as an architectural one.

BLDD: How many merchants are there in Faneuil Hall now?
BT: About two hundred, and they are mostly independent merchants in small private businesses. That was our concept. The largest shop is 8,000 or 10,000 square feet.
BLDD: Can you give us an idea of the size and scale of the project?
BT: The size of the project is 400,000 square feet of floor area on six acres of land. It's low, made up of five stories and a lower level, the basement, and it's 500 feet long. That means very low density for prime city land. We closed three streets, which had a substantial effect on what we call pedestrianization, but also on the environment and the feeling of safety in the internal character of the place.
BLDD: How does the Faneuil Hall project contribute to the life and well-being of Boston and its residents?

BT: It provides a real urban center for all kinds of people. Before the redevelopment—and this would also prove true in Baltimore, in our Harborplace project—there was no downtown center and no place alive enough to be safe at night. My wife, Jane, and I had written extensively about the need for a sense of place in the American city. We played songs, told stories, made films, and showed photographs of cities, both American and European, going back as far as the fifteenth century. We were trying to prove something that shouldn't have been hard to prove—that the American city was in decline, that there was a lack of faith in urban culture. We could point to Brussels, to Paris, to Helsinki, to Venice, to Copenhagen as vital, healthy cities that had not decayed at the center. But everybody always said, "Well, that's different. Nobody goes out to eat in Boston. . . . Puritans don't like to eat or enjoy themselves."
BLDD: Was the implication that Bostonians aren't interested in food?
BT: That's what people said—that Bostonians don't like food, that there is no restaurant tradition there, that only people in New York or Paris like to eat out. We said we wanted twenty restaurants within three blocks and they said that one was enough. Jane and I started four restaurants ourselves because we were trying to get something going, to show what kind of mix and diversity was possible.
BLDD: How did it all work out?
BT: It's been a huge success.
BLDD: Did you expect Faneuil Hall to receive such an overwhelming public response? There isn't a city in America that doesn't want its own Faneuil Hall.
BT: There is tremendous power in a working prototype. Once

people experience some new level of possibility, they make it part of their standard of expectation. Pioneering, doing anything for the first time, is the hardest work because you don't have the support, even the moral support, of other believers. It is true that every city now wants its Faneuil Hall. In 1967 and in 1975, even people with the most power and ability to change things in Boston did not believe it could happen. Today there is living proof, and that makes people everywhere more courageous and visionary. Still, I must say that these things do not happen by formulas, by copies, or by transplants. Each successful solution has some universal elements but must also have countless very special local elements. Each one has to do the right thing in the right way for its own place.

Of course we believed it would succeed—that's why we devoted ten hard and often lonely years to making it happen. The idea was right, humanly and economically sound. We knew intuitively that people would respond—they were hungry for new excitement, for all the best that a city can offer. We had no way to measure how rapidly they would respond, or even how they would *find* the place. Yet on opening day, in the heat of August 1976, there were two hundred thousand people there! That was a surprise, but it was really just a measure of the need, the hunger for a more dynamic approach to the central city. At Baltimore's opening there may have been a million people, but that was less of a surprise, although it's always a little like opening night in the theater, when you aren't quite sure that the audience will applaud, or even show up. You have to remain calm, obey your educated intuition, and not lose confidence.

BLDD: But isn't architecture a little more predictable than live performance? Would you liken architecture to the theater, other than the high sense of drama that many architects have?

BT: That leads into basic questions of what architecture is—a stage, a performance, a facade. How deep does it go? Those questions are timely today because there is a lot of "facadism" going on. I keep busy with serious stuff and have avoided involvement in that war. Architecture is *not* facades or stage sets in the illusionistic sense of a backdrop that isn't even a real building. That "decorator" approach makes a joke out of the complex thing that architecture really is. But drama is another matter when it is intrinsic to the use of buildings and streets and plazas, and when people create that drama.

BLDD: How do your results at Faneuil Hall differ from what you might have done in the late 1950s or in the early sixties? Would you have been more likely then to tear the whole thing down?

BT: Certainly not, though it was the trend in American urban renewal, and I was a distinct minority. I have always worked with what was there because invariably it was already a graceful part of a local context. That continuity is much more important urbanistically than the assertive and disruptive ego statements that are, unfortunately, thought to be the measure of architecture.

I remember the first Design Research in a small restored rowhouse on Brattle Street. With fairly simple means we turned it into a new place without doing violence to the street. A decade later we restored the more elegant Gallery Norval on Manhattan's Fifty-seventh Street, opening with fashion shows, flowers, and dancing girls—it was very colorful and warm, and people flocked there. Remember that in the mid-1960s we were in the middle of the Vietnam War. The whole world seemed gray, desperate, demoralized. The need for a place to go in the city with color and an uplifting spirit was suddenly greater than it had been since the years of World War II. Social upheaval and negativism brought certain things into focus. I

concluded that an architect's greatest service would be the expression of possibility, of potential. It was easy to mouth all the negatives, the "God's own junkyard" kind of criticism. But I am naturally positive, and I wanted to make real three-dimensional examples, which people could see and feel, showing how the world really could be put together if we worked at it. The Design Research shops stood for that optimism, right down to the flowers. Faneuil Hall, which I first put on paper in 1967, stood for that as well. So does everything we have done since, in cities and elsewhere.

BLDD: During that period in the mid-sixties, you were chairman of the architecture department at the Harvard Graduate School of Design, replacing Walter Gropius. What were your goals at that time, both for the school and for the community?

BT: If I had been the dean, I might have been able to control the financial resources of the school. Chairmen are financially powerless at Harvard. But, at any rate, I did have a fair go at it for four or five years, and I had a definite interest in changing certain traditions in the teaching of architecture. We had a couple of good years. I was very critical—I still am—of the jury system and the kind of Socratic tyrannizing of students that goes on. Juries put the student into a defensive state, which hampers his ability to think freely and respond creatively. We made some changes. We brought outside teachers into the school. Often the traditional architecture teacher is too stiff and one-dimensional. We needed women teachers and teachers from other disciplines—sociology, government, education—to convey broader attitudes and ideas about the real tasks of architecture.

What's happening in the schools today is a lot of talk and not much action—the architecture of theory, false history, cults, and papier-mâché. I would have to call it a mean, petty, and self-centered period in education and in the field, lacking the largeness of spirit or grandeur of vision that a professional brotherhood should provide. There's too much concern about the self and not enough about our responsibilities to mankind. Among the other things that have been lost, or hopefully just set aside, in professional schooling is the idea of building as craft, of craft and materials as the genesis of any architectural aesthetic. It is vital to learn how to build beautifully, to know the quality of materials through which buildings live, speak, and endure. Without caring about craft, we are building a world of insubstantial junk. And we will see such buildings fall apart within the designer's lifetime. Speculative builders create junk because they don't care. It is alarming to see architects throwing away the sense of enduring quality in pursuit of cheap, fashionable gimmicks of self-expression.

When I was at Harvard we were on a completely different track. I felt that students should know everything possible about the craft of architecture, about skills, structure, materials, purpose, expression, about with whom and for whom you are building. Did I succeed? There are a lot of people who now feel that it was the right direction, but they're not teaching because they were driven out of the universities, mostly by the academics who resent practitioners in education.

BLDD: What did you bring to your role as chairman from your twenty years of architectural practice and experience?

BT: It's very important that the schools have a percentage of people teaching who work at the actual profession. That is something I did. Of course, we brought our own concerns into the studios. We tried to infuse the school with the knowledge and values of the real world. We would take students into our offices. We wanted to mix it up—make the school part of the office, make the office part of the school—but that's much too impure for most universities. I'm optimistic that it could be done, but I haven't seen it done very well in the American university.

BLDD: You once said that most schools of design seem to be stuck in the fifteenth century. Do you see that changing in the near future?

BT: I'm hopeful that since there is so much controversy now, some breakthroughs may be coming. The students coming out of the schools will surely discover that they have not been especially well served by their expensive training. Back in the 1960s, our new educational approaches were all mixed up with old academic hang-ups. They were still running "studies" on how to train architects. They talked endlessly about it. The students were unhappy and the teachers were unhappy, but at least they were looking at the questions of what an architect should be and how best to achieve that. My impression is that now those things are not open to question in certain institutions. The lines are drawn between what's in and what's out. Positions are narrow, monolithic, and dominated by personality cults; they lack tolerance, inquiry, and a certain humility before the vast questions that architecture raises. That's a very unhealthy atmosphere for students. You can't provide a professional education without teaching people to build and without instilling a sense of social responsibility and ethical behavior, as in the study of law and medicine.

BLDD: What would your old partner and mentor, Walter Gropius, make of the current scene? Do you think he'd be surprised at the vehemence with which many architects now reject his ideas, or would he take pleasure in the intense level of dialogue and interest on the part of the broader public now?

BT: I'm not convinced that people *are* rejecting his ideas. They're rejecting myths created by other people in his name, and most people—especially the most outspoken—haven't taken the trouble to learn what his ideas really were. They were a great deal broader, wiser, and more tolerant than what is going on now. For instance, Gropius did *not* invent or promote the International Style. The Museum of Modern Art did, in order to foster a movement in the U.S. that worked on "acceptable" rules of modernism—acceptable to the museum, that is. There was a great deal that was practical, sensible, and constructive in early modernism. It responded to the critical needs of the times and established an ethical framework for the first time. But it seems that it will take an historical revival of modernism fifty years from now before its meaning is again taken seriously. Gropius himself was always open-minded, intellectually inquiring, and *against* rules, which are really crutches. He was always enthusiastic about what he would call energy—he would say, "Look at all that energy!" I suspect that because he took things seriously he'd be depressed about the stuff we see today. He was not superficial, irresponsible, or egotistical. He did not dictate answers; he always encouraged the search for better answers. He certainly would be interested in all the conversation and debate and would be part

Design Research Headquarters, Cambridge, Mass.

of it. Harvard's Graduate School of Design under Gropius was very much a school of participation and people. If he felt you were a good teacher he would give you freedom to work in your own way—he was famous for that from his Bauhaus days—and he respected a student who would think for himself, even if it was to disagree. He was more interested in the quality of exchange than in abstract philosophical theories. If you came around with a manifesto, he would say, "Let's get five good teachers and forget the manifesto. Even with one hundred manifestos you still won't have a good school." So Gropius brought in Breuer and Giedion, Perkins, Martin Wagner, Serge Chermayeff, and lots of younger architects as teachers. What they were interested in was serious stuff, not mannerisms and styling. If a group sat around to talk about a chair, we'd talk about the structure of the chair, the form, the cost, the angle of sitting. We'd seldom talk about how the chair looked, but rather what it was all about. Anyone could understand the conversation and learn from it. It was not esoteric. I have difficulty understanding the private languages being used today, and I suspect students do too.

BLDD: Your firm has always been a hothouse for ideas about how to design. You're known for encouraging your staff at the start of a project, be it a hotel or a marketplace, to think like a guest or a consumer—anything but an architect. What do you want to foster with that kind of thinking?

BT: I've been very concerned since my Harvard days about a lack of awareness on the part of the designer, an inability to put himself in the position of the person for whom he is designing. Architects must get outside themselves and become sensitive to the problem itself. If I were going to design, say, a house in a beautiful field, I'd want to stay in that field for a year or two to understand the wind, the rain, the seasons, the sun, the animals—the whole environment—before I picked up a pencil. And I would have to know and understand the people who were going to live there. After that, maybe we could talk about design. I have found that most designers want to rush right into the solution without understanding the problem. They say, "Just give me the pencil and I'll tell you what you want." It's not easy to stop that process and teach people to ask, to listen, to think. In considering the needs of a guest in a hotel, we do some role playing. I put the designer in the role of the guest or in the role of the cook or the waiter or the maid or the desk clerk. As the user of the place, he has to go through a kind of mental transference, living out in his mind the actual experience of being in this building. If he does this, he's not going to be a Howard Roark character who says, "Aha, I'm going to create this great dream about your house. I'm going to tell you how to live. As an artist, I'm superior."

BLDD: So many architects I've spoken to have made reference to the fictional architect Howard Roark. Do you think the general public was as affected by that characterization as the profession itself was? Was it an accurate description? Maybe it's time to update the image of the architect.

BT: I think it is. Very few novels or movies have been created about architects. *The Fountainhead* happens to be one of the few. For better or worse, it was the first popular book that told the public that architecture is something of consequence. It also gave a generation of aspiring architects an unfortunate role model—the aloof, unbending creative genius who answered to no one but himself and his sacred talent. The issues of self and society were, of course, ludicrously distorted. But that fawning portrait of Architect as Self-Serving Artist was just what a lot of young architects—and now not-so-young ones too—wanted to believe in. That kind of image has a lot to do with the mess the profession is in today.

BLDD: You've made several references to your wife, Jane Thompson, who is also distinguished in the field of architecture as an editor, curator, writer, and lecturer, and as vice president of Benjamin Thompson and Associates. Most recently she has become known in the restaurant business. How did you and she first become involved in that endeavor?

BT: I have to tell you that in assessing Gropius I was thinking of Jane, because she shares some of his characteristics: a great sense of seriousness and an intellectual ability to deal with many problems on various levels. As for the restaurant business, in dreaming up Faneuil Hall, we began to realize that we wanted not only shops but restaurants as well. But what kinds of restaurants? We said, "Let's reinvent the best seafood restaurant we've ever been to." And we would try to replicate one—in Paris or Marseilles or New York. What about a French café? We'd describe a wonderful café in Helsinki or Montmartre. Pretty soon we found we were designing and planning all of the restaurants because we couldn't imagine that anyone else would do it. That's how we dove into this enterprise. The restaurants at Faneuil Hall in the early phase were pretty much patterned on the American formula of the time, combining singles bars and a kind of standard steak-lobster menu. We wanted quality restaurants with serious kitchens. We also wanted individual proprietors throughout the marketplace, not restaurants owned by chains. From our point of view, the new retailing really had to be personalized, so we got into it very deeply.

BLDD: I'm sure your wife has had considerable influence on the development of your work. What is the most important thing you've learned from your collaboration with her?

BT: The seriousness of her approach to life, on almost every level, is something you don't find in many people. The English, who are a wonderful group of people, tend to make a joke over anything that's serious, a quality that has been picked up in this country through our English heritage. Gropius, a Berliner, was absolutely not like that. He may have been one of the first older people that I'd run into who was objective and straight, with a balanced view. And Jane is like that. She claims some English background, but I think her influence probably comes from Austria or Italy. She has a tremendous willingness to be serious and a great ability and discipline, but she also has passionate beliefs and a sense of humor. On the level of aesthetics, she is a good critic and commentator. We're in an age when the definition of architecture is discussed a lot. It's time to define what architects really are. I call Jane one of the better architects I've known. In aesthetics, in practical planning, and in social values, she's had a tremendous background. All those skills have been of great help. Her contributions are an integral part of our firm's work and can't be separated out. We have an open process of creative exchange.

BLDD: As you mentioned before, for all its diversity, Baltimore lacked much in the way of any place to go. So it was not suprising that the mix of bars, restaurants, and shops was welcomed by more than one million visitors on the opening day of Harborplace in the early 1980s. Harborplace seems to be a sort of combination Design Research and Faneuil Hall. How did that project come about? What were your intentions?

BT: When Jim Rouse came to me to talk about doing Harborplace, he said, "Can you do a kind of Design Research in Baltimore?" I asked him what he meant because I didn't see the connection. He said that he liked the effervescent, glittering, flowing feeling of the all-glass D/R building. I kept asking questions and found that what he really liked was the four-sided openness of the place. There is no dead back side—it is front all the way around. For Baltimore we wanted a place that

Harborplace, Baltimore, Md.

looked not only into the harbor, but also back into the city. Harborplace was built in a park, separated from the rest of the city by a frightening twelve-lane road, one of the most dangerous roads in America, particularly at five or six o'clock in the evening. To get across is an act of heroism. You might not have believed we could build anything in that park that would attract crowds of people. Yet we managed to make Harborplace a *destination*. In other words, it's not tied integrally to the city in the way that Faneuil Hall is. Harborplace is a place you go *to*. It's not exactly in the mountains or up on a hill, but it's an island in the sense that it's almost self-contained between highway and harbor.

BLDD: What existed at Harborplace before you came?

BT: For ten years, the City of Baltimore had been working on Charles Center, which contained banks, office buildings, and one hotel. A little life was put into that part of the city. Along the harbor edge there was a field that they called a park. It was about 200 feet wide and planted with rye grass although it had few trees. The city had built a walkway along the harbor edge, and there was one tall building by I. M. Pei. The harbor itself was a serene lagoon, but the area around it was still empty and isolated, and people used it only for annual neighborhood festivals.

BLDD: How did you transform it? What was your key idea there?

BT: The key idea was not dissimilar to the idea for Faneuil Hall: it was based on food in its many forms. People eat and market every day. Food is one of the constants and essentials of life, as well as one of the greatest sources of pleasure and satisfaction. Yet with urban development, food-centered activity had been pushed out, off the streets, in favor of banks and airline offices on every corner. In Baltimore there was clearly a need and a desire for this kind of activity, so in Harborplace we set the proportion of food stalls and restaurants at thirty-five to forty percent of the retail area.

BLDD: Was this emphasis on food based on your previous experience?

BT: Food is the critical ingredient in any real marketplace, from Mexico to Manchuria. At Faneuil Hall food was the central idea. In addition to about fifteen restaurants, we programmed many shops selling food-related products, from tea and spices to pots and pans, china and glass. We wanted no conventional department store in Faneuil Hall. It wasn't easy. A major commercial project costing $25 million without a large anchor for leasing is something no insurance company will finance. To prove that we had critical mass, we demonstrated that the anchor was made up of this collection of food merchants occupying about 100,000 square feet, the equivalent of a medium-size department store. This was similar in Baltimore. It also proves to be a popular approach, providing variety and a pleasurable experience for people.

BLDD: How is your project at New York's South Street Seaport different from your projects in Boston or Baltimore?

BT: The plan is a lot more comprehensive in New York, although it's a little smaller in terms of square footage. The variety is wonderful. Not only is there a new Fulton Market—a fresh-food market—with restaurants above it, but the old buildings along Fulton and Front Streets have shops of different kinds, and the wholesale fish market remains. Streets are closed off for walking. On Pier 17, which extends out into the East River about 450 feet, there is a pavilion for shops and cafés right on the water. It's more diversified than Boston and richer than Baltimore in the mix of activities, because New York has such fantastic resources.

BLDD: With New York as a forum for experimentation, what innovations have you tried at the Seaport? How is South Street different?

BT: It is more natural, more an organic piece of a city, but a piece that happens to be historically intact. In Faneuil Hall parts were restored to their pure 1825 condition before we took over, which is a falsification of the natural evolution of buildings. I argued that most of the buildings should have been repaired but left with their sequence of styles. The New York Seaport district should be an integral part of the city and should not start or stop at South Street or Fulton Street. The Seaport represents various periods of the past, not one artificially selected time frame, and contains the entirely new buildings that we have designed to fit into the historic continuum. It is very rich architecturally.

The marvelous Brooklyn Bridge is overhead and Brooklyn is across the river; Wall Street and the Battery are to the south; the new development is to the west; and Chinatown and Little Italy are to the north. Once it is revitalized, the Seaport, which used to be situated in lower Manhattan like a hole in a doughnut, will bring the area together with an exciting sense of unity and orientation. Once this catches on—provided New York corrects past mistakes in zoning that allow the wrong buildings to overwhelm sensitive districts—I envision great new things happening to make the whole waterfront of Manhattan something unique and, at long last, accessible to the public.

BLDD: If food shops and restaurants bring people to the Seaport or to Harborplace, what keeps them there?

BT: At Faneuil Hall we circulated a questionnaire asking why people were there. Most replied that they were there for the place and the quality of the experience. Why do they go back frequently? Because it is a wonderful place to be. It is a place in the city where they feel safe, even at night. It is a place to sit, watch other people, feel in contact. There are varied age groups, and everyone is welcome. There is a choice of places and activities, ranging from free to expensive. For many people, it works like a clean city park with conveniences.

BLDD: What is the estimated number of visitors annually to Faneuil Hall, and how many do you anticipate at the South Street Seaport?

BT: They say about twelve million come to Faneuil Hall every year. The South Street number may be close to that, or it may be less because there is less commercial space. But then, New York is a big place. You can't plan the number of visitors to Times Square or Greenwich Village. You can't draw a line and say that people are going only to the Seaport. There are thousands of people already there just a few blocks away. The real change will be in people staying downtown after work hours.

BLDD: Since there are so many people in the area, how have you planned for quality control and some standard of order and tidiness?

BT: Cleaning and security are very much part of the design. The two projects we've been talking about are being run by the Rouse Company as developer. And their management and maintenance has been fastidious. Their security is provided by a private internal police staff. Municipal police also patrol the

Fulton Market, South Street Seaport, New York, N.Y.

project, but definitive security is controlled by the developer. The developer has made a real effort to design effective security. We architects may have a fair amount of control in these projects, but the number of people making decisions is literally in the hundreds. At times you feel like a little cog in a big wheel. There's a maintenance department. There's an operational department. There's a leasing department. There's an advertising department. There's a tenant inspection department. And then there are the architects, trying to solve all their problems and act as a catalyst to relate departments to each other.

BLDD: After all of these influences come into play, how much of the design is in the hands of the architect and how much is governed by zoning or, in this instance, preservation law?

BT: That's very hard to say. It takes a tremendous team to put these things together—neighborhood groups and tenants; preservationists; city, state, and federal agencies; developer departments. If you see a successful project, chances are that everybody worked unusually well together. There are *no* one-man projects these days, and no such thing as "personal control."

BLDD: In revamping and revitalizing the old marketplace or harbor or seaport, there is, of course, the need for modern amenities ranging from lighting to garbage disposal. How do you update features of the old seaport, for example, to accommodate today's visitors and still satisfy the needs of city agencies, preservationists, concerned citizens, and the original inhabitants of a neighborhood?

BT: Over a period of years we developed a vocabulary of materials to suit this place. Materials of enduring quality, like stone and brick, iron and wood, lend themselves to designs of timeless quality. We use them because they fit in with what has already shown lasting value. We presented our vocabulary of street materials to the Landmarks Preservation Commission, to the city, and of course to the developer.

BLDD: Which was the most rigorous test?

BT: Probably the developer, because you're dealing with cost and budget, which impose real discipline on the imagination. It's easy to pick materials without regard to cost, but it takes exhaustive work and research to find design materials that meet both aesthetic goals and budgetary limits. Often simplicity is the solution. Modern urban landscapes and cityscapes, plazas and pocket parks tend to be much too complex in detail. Landscape architects seem incapable of designing a street without overdoing the details, including too many parts and an unnecessary array of materials. For the Faneuil Hall streetscape we used only two materials—brick and granite—then added some benches, lights, and trees. Simple, but not simplistic: quality materials and subtle organization. We put the benches where people would want to be and designed walks so people could conveniently look in shop windows. We wanted a naturally integrated place, not overdesigned in a directive way. I didn't want it to feel like Disneyland, like an artificial place. We haven't designed and dictated every move. There is room for experiment and individual choice.

BLDD: Are you saying the projects, like cities, must evolve, must allow for spontaneity in how they are used?

BT: That's what I'm saying. What you have to do to encourage spontaneity is leave some places empty, like a stage, for people to perform on. If you set every scene, it begins to feel artificial and doesn't work like a real city.

BLDD: You once said that people no longer see the ugliness that surrounds them. What did you mean by that?

BT: I said that in 1968 in a talk in New York on the first Earth Day. I had become acutely concerned about the physical and psychological impact of the monotonous, hard, overbuilt city environments and the chaotic, ugly roadscapes of America to which people seemed to have become blind. One day a cab driver started talking to me about the asphalt jungle and the Wall Street canyon. I was impressed by the man's sensitivity to things that were harmful to him, and I realized I wasn't alone. If you live in an environment of fluorescent light, asphalt streets, raw concrete—where all contact with nature has been removed and you are deprived of a sense of living under the stars and breathing clean air—it has a strong effect on your ability to feel. You have to feel in order to live, to survive. It has now been well demonstrated that not only noise, smog, and pollution, but the alienation from nature caused by the hard, overscaled man-made environment have direct effects on the human nervous system.

BLDD: You've also spoken of America's mediocrity in its physical creations. What do you think has caused that?

BT: I am concerned about American mediocrity in the planning and development of our cities. There is a lack of vision and leadership that starts at the top. So few of our presidents have shown any real understanding of urban culture or dynamics. Take Calvin Coolidge—not a very inspiring guy to have as a client. Or Hoover, Truman, Johnson, Nixon, or Carter. They've all thought like small-town people, unaware of the problems in our cities. An architect might like to have P. T. Barnum as a municipal client, or Thomas Jefferson. A sense of priority in environmental issues comes from the top and affects the whole spirit in which we build.

BLDD: What is the ideal client for an architect?

BT: We architects go through life dreaming of finding the ideal client, sort of like the ideal woman. I find that the best client is very intelligent and brings a considered viewpoint to a problem, can question, can give you a lot of response and feeling born of experience. He will give freedom and responsibility, yet will take responsibility as a client for what he gets.

BLDD: Doesn't it complicate the process to have a client with a strong point of view?

BT: My best experiences have been with strong, decisive people open to new ideas. Jim Rouse, for instance. Committees are always hard to work with, although sometimes you're lucky and get to work with unusual committees led by one or two strong people. But every client is different. That's something never spoken about in design schools. They don't seem to recognize that a client is central to the process.

BLDD: The diverse practice of your firm ranges from building individual structures, complex renovations, and rehabilitations of old buildings to large-scale hotels, commercial-area developments, and comprehensive urban plans. What ties all these interests and projects together? Is there a common thread in your work?

BT: I suppose the common thread is a way of *seeing* a problem. We always formulate an answer within a basic value system. Architectural consistency comes from a core of beliefs, ideas, and goals. You don't start from scratch every time; you work with a vocabulary of materials and ways of putting them together that have taken years to discover, consider, and improve upon. That vocabulary conveys meaning, a sense of craft, an attitude toward sensual values and human use. We always start by considering connections—the connection of a building to its site and its community. No matter what the job, we view it in terms of the life and activity that will animate the building, and in terms of how people inside will experience views and light and nature. We are extremely concerned with scale, size, comfortable distances—the dynamics of human experience in using a building. I don't undertake each new design as a monument or as a supreme struggle for absolutely original form or exterior image. Space, material, and experience are of much more lasting importance.

BLDD: What inspired you to become an architect?

BT: I kind of backed into it as an undergraduate. I knew what I didn't want to do, and I knew a few things that I liked. The things I liked seemed to fit the description of architecture, so I just signed up for the B. Arch. program one day.

BLDD: You make it sound like the army.

BT: It wasn't very stimulating, and it wasn't very serious. They operated on the Beaux-Arts system, which was superficial at best. After a time I felt I should go to a more professional school, so I went to Yale. But I found that rather out of touch, too. For the first two years Beaux-Arts classicism prevailed. Then in my last year the school began to come out of its fantasy world and discover the twentieth century. The students used to gang up to move all the school's Beaux-Arts statuary to the basement. The next day the faculty would move it all back again. That was one of the first revolutions I was involved in, and though it was not an important one, it was symbolic.

BLDD: Do you have any dream projects that you'd like to do?

BT: I'd love to do a major park, as Olmsted did, something like Central Park, although I'm afraid that opportunity won't come. It's much more important to revitalize built areas, to turn old buildings and city districts into new and humane places. Not that the whole world should consist of restorations, but we must avoid another round of urban destruction like that caused by the disastrous urban renewal laws of the fifties and sixties. The optimum result is a happy blend of old and new, evolving over time. I don't favor new towns; cities are not born in a day or a decade. They must evolve organically in response to complex factors, and a multitude of people must participate. I enjoy working within the existing cityscape, where human experience takes place. I love challenges that involve many elements and many things happening.

BLDD: Did you expect your life to turn out this way?

BT: No. As Casey Stengel used to say, "I play them one at a time." If you're in business, which architecture really is, or even in teaching, which is considered more elevated, you get up every day saying, "I'm going to get through this one." It is a high-pressure business, in which you are held accountable in many directions. Some days are better than others, but it is not all pleasure or doing what you're best at. Jane has a saying: "The secret of happiness is a poor memory and no foresight." The creative process is full of improvisation. It consists of dealing with a multitude of elements, mostly unknowns, as they happen, bringing meaning out of chaos. There are limits to what can be accomplished by planning, and the tighter the planning, the more it hampers creative responses. That is the reason I live one day at a time. It works.

BLDD: Is architecture a business or an art?

BT: Architecture is a profession, which means it provides a service to others and has a base of ethics and responsibility. A business structure is required these days to practice this profession. Architecture's relation to art has been grossly misunderstood, with some help from Howard Roark. An artist is categorically different from an architect, at least since the fifteenth century in the Western world. An artist has no external responsibility, no licensing requirements, no accountability for public health and safety. He works alone and answers only to his own vision. Whereas an architect is part of society and its values, an artist may stand apart from those values as a detached commentator. If an architect were to work as a pure artist, the end result would be abstract form, nonutilitarian sculpture, and not purposeful building. That does not mean that architecture cannot occasionally become art, but it is in a special category of utilitarian art, which has its own distinguished tradition. The trouble today is that too many people, including theorists, critics, and practitioners, are going about architecture with the wrong idea: they see it as art, as form and facade or as commentary and literal quotation. The idea of architecture as pure art seduces with promises of prestige and personal freedom and ego gratification. It's a myth that can easily corrupt the architectural profession.

BLDD: You've mentioned the word "lucky" several times during our conversation. Do you think luck was an important element in your career?

BT: Of course. From a career standpoint, I was lucky to be born when I was. I managed to finish architecture school by 1940, before going into the service. As soon as I left the navy, I was ready to go forward with starting my practice. Starting work in that postwar period was very productive. Everyone felt mature and ready to move after the wasted war years. It was a dynamic time to have new ideas and get things done. Today's students complain that it's hard to get a job and that the world is too competitive. I get impatient with that attitude and tell them, "It was tough and competitive when I started, too. You have to be awake and energetic and seize your opportunities." I believe in luck, but I also believe that luck favors the well prepared. You have to actually *do* it yourself.

BLDD: If you had your life to live over again, what would you do differently?

BT: I'd like to be Darwin. I was enchanted by the story of Darwin's trip in the *Beagle* to South America and the Galapagos Islands, observing and documenting animals and growing things. I was impressed that Darwin started without much formal scientific education and didn't really know what he wanted to do in life. But he had the ability to look and listen. He had acute powers of observation that allowed him to see nature in its reality and its beauty. When he came back to England with his collection of shells, fossils, skeletons, and skins, he studied it for years, making connections, leaping to imaginative conclusions. Of course he had an intense inner struggle about the meaning of his new "truth," because he apparently knew that what he had discovered contradicted centuries of religious orthodoxy. But finally truth won out over myth and tradition. Darwin's life encapsulates my philosophy that the world is full of marvelous, magical, and often mystical things, which are ours to experience if we can free our senses and feelings to understand. For future generations of architects, I would wish such a continuing, tireless quest for truth about life. They will find it bit by bit—if they can bury myths, open their eyes, ask questions, and listen to the answers.

STANLEY TIGERMAN

Stanley Tigerman is known for both his unusual ideas and his irreverent approach to building. In the architectural establishment of his native Chicago, he is an eclectic in a city dominated by the work of Mies van der Rohe. Although he is looked on as something of a maverick, Tigerman's work has earned him many awards and honors from the American Institute of Architects.

BLDD: What first gave you the idea to become an architect?

ST: I read *The Fountainhead* when it was first published, in 1943. I was in the eighth grade, and I fell for the message of the book.

BLDD: What were you doing reading a book like that in eighth grade? Were there architects in your family?

ST: No, but it was a dirty book. Eighth graders always read dirty books, generally in the bathroom. So I read it because I'd heard it was dirty, but it also turned out to be very interesting.

BLDD: Did you ever meet Ayn Rand?

ST: Yes, much to my regret, I met her many years later when I was a graduate student at Yale. I attended a symposium she was doing at the Yale Law School because I had always wanted to meet this woman who had changed my entire life. After the symposium I told her that it was because of her book that I had become an architect. She put her hands on her hips, cocked her head, looked at me, and said, "So what?"

BLDD: And what was your reply?

ST: I was crushed, I really was.

BLDD: What was so influential about her book that it determined your career?

ST: My interpretation of the book was a very idealistic one, which I think was her intention: to produce an idealistic alternative to the way she saw culture developing in America and in the world. You also see that attitude in her later books such as *Atlas Shrugged*. It wasn't just architecture that she was using as a conduit for her somewhat elitist ideas. But *The Fountainhead* presented an interesting thesis, particularly for someone as highly impressionable as I was at the time.

BLDD: How did your family react to your choice of career?

ST: There have never been architects in my family nor, for that matter, any artists. They understood neither what architecture was nor why I wished to become an architect. It was alien to my family.

BLDD: Were there circumstances in your early environment that influenced your choice to become an architect?

ST: My parents were very poor, and I grew up with my paternal grandparents, who had a boarding house. It was fabulous being surrounded by all the different kinds of people living in that place. I was immensely spoiled; not only was I my parents' only child, but I was also the only child in that boarding house. I grew up with a lot of attention.

BLDD: You seem to be a nice, amiable fellow, yet you have been called "the seasoned guerrilla leader" and the "enfant terrible" of midwestern architecture. What has prompted the use of such labels?

ST: Do I look like one of those?

BLDD: Not to me.

ST: I'm just a very quiet person, a short, fat Jewish architect practicing in Chicago. I have no idea what all that means.

BLDD: You've said that it clarifies your existence to inhabit a city filled with enemies. Do you mean that?

ST: When I came back from Yale, Chicago was a product of what can only be called the German invasion: Mies van der Rohe and his elite troops from the Black Forest. I really wanted to make a home for myself, my own home, in the city where I was born. It was important for me to do that. So I saw that group as the enemy, in a sense. On the other hand, of course, much of my work has been couched in their language. But Chicago has changed dramatically, not because of my actions, but because of the work of a number of architects and the changing concerns of our times.

BLDD: For quite a while you involved yourself in an open battle with the Chicago architectural establishment, the most extended battle being with the firm of Skidmore, Owings & Merrill. Are you opposed to the idea of large firms in general, or just to the kinds of projects they do?

ST: I've always felt that architecture was a human activity, an activity concerned with people, and I see Skidmore as operating only on a corporate level. That generalization is obviously simplistic, but there's some truth in it. SOM is concerned with pragmatism and the bottom line, things that I feel have precious little to do with architecture. For many years, one saw nothing idiosyncratic in their work. A normative system of architecture in the hands of someone who creates that system, such as Mies van der Rohe, is one thing. But Skidmore's architecture is the product of eclecticism and refining other people's work, in this case predominantly Mies van der Rohe's, and I object to that.

BLDD: While we're on the subject, would you say a word about Mies? He is the *real* establishment in Chicago, isn't he?

ST: He is. But he was a wonderful man and, frankly, I miss him. When he was alive, those who were influenced by him—which was damned near everyone in Chicago—were closer to the source of the flame. When he died, he became canonized in simplistic ways, both in the *details* and in the *parts* of architectural form. Without his presence, the laws became even more rigid than when he was alive. He would be the first to structure change in his own work. After he died, his descendants didn't allow for that change because he wasn't there to lead them.

BLDD: We seem to be going beyond postmodernism to the point where we can now reevaluate the earlier reevaluation of Mies. In that light, is his influence on the decline or on the rise?

ST: It's on the rise. All of the early books on Mies van der Rohe were written by sycophants: at the time Philip Johnson wrote his book, he was a sycophant; Arthur Drexler was a sycophant. Ludwig Hilberseimer, Peter Carter, Werner Blaser—all of their books are sycophantic, written by descendants attempting to prove a point through simplistic thinking. Now, after some time has elapsed, Mies is being looked at critically for the first time, in much the same way that Charles Jencks in his first, and I think only truly brilliant, book looked at the tragic figure of Le Corbusier. Mies is being looked at by scholars now as a flawed figure, and he becomes even more significant, more consequential. Mies is being seen in an entirely new light.

BLDD: What influence did Mies have on your own career?

ST: Enormous influence, first of all because I knew him.

BLDD: What was he like?

ST: He was like the cut blocks of stone that his stonemason father in Aachen worked on. He was a big bear of a man, with a great, huge square-jawed head, but he wore very elegant silk suits. At the end of his life he was in a wheelchair. He was very gentle and kind at the stage of his life when I knew him.

BLDD: Did you ever visit him at home? In what kind of environment did he live?

ST: He didn't live in a Mies building. It was a building like one you could find in Berlin or in Munich or Frankfurt today, an old mannerist building with rusticated stone. He loved to watch TV westerns. He drove a two-tone Oldsmobile, or had it driven by Gene Summers, who was his chauffeur as well as his employee.

BLDD: Did Mies live with Mies furniture?

ST: He had Mies furniture, but he also had very comfortable and large overstuffed furniture, furniture that was scaled appropriately for him. Mies alone fit perfectly in the Barcelona chair, which is really big enough for two people to sit on comfortably. He was a big man, and the chair was designed for him. We all design for ourselves. It's impossible not to.

BLDD: Was there anything particularly striking about how he lived?

ST: Before he left Germany he had an enormous library.

According to his own perhaps apocryphal story, the Nazi government forced him to leave with only twenty-odd books. He didn't buy many more books in America and still read St. Thomas Aquinas, St. Augustine, Ortega y Gasset. He had a very small, select, and precious library that he reread constantly. Architects work in different ways. Some architects frantically draw and draw and draw, producing billions of sketches and drawings, until it finally all comes together. Mies didn't do much drawing. He thought a lot. He actually thought about buildings. There's a wonderful photograph of him puffing on a cigar, looking out one of his glass walls. It's accurate. I once went to his office and saw him sitting in his wheelchair at one of his employees' boards. The man had a problem with some coping detail, and Mies looked at it and said, "Yah, I will think about it." I came back maybe a month or six weeks later, and there he was at the man's board showing him how to do the detail. He had spent all that time on a detail, had thought it out. It was not a snap decision.

BLDD: What's your style of working? Do you draw frantically? Do you read?

ST: I draw a lot, because that's what I do for a living. I started out as a draftsman; I'll die as one. I draw on airplanes. I do sketches and cartoons. And I read.

BLDD: What do you read?

ST: When I wrote my book, *Versus,* I started reading some interesting literature. I had a lousy education—I didn't get a proper undergraduate liberal arts education—so I'm doing it now. I'm reading Plato, Aristotle, St. Thomas Aquinas, St. Augustine, everything that people should read in their pursuit of education. I read Talmudic exegeses and cabalistic theory. What I really like is our friend Roland Barthes. He is fabulous, he knocks me out, as he does many other architects.

BLDD: Why is his work so compelling for architects?

ST: Because of his concentration on syntax, as opposed to a concentration on a symbolic message through some sort of semantic reading. I'm very interested in the syntax of architecture, the structure of the language of architecture. Other architects are, as well. Reading Barthes and then thinking about symbolism creates an interesting juxtaposition.

BLDD: What continues to make Chicago compelling for you?

ST: Being an architect in Chicago is like being born wealthy. Chicago is architecture's mecca. Chicago is a builder's town. Many years ago Paul Goldberger wrote a very interesting article, maybe his best piece ever, on the difference between Chicago and New York architecture. It is not that Chicago architects are better than New York architects but that Chicago developers are much better than New York developers. They are less venal. Some years ago, I saw a poster at LaGuardia Airport that had a frontal photograph of the Seagram Building. The only type on it was: "This is the only building in New York City by Mies van der Rohe. Isn't it a shame?" In Chicago there are forty-five buildings by him completed while he was alive. There are over fifty by Frank Lloyd Wright. There are over seventy-five by the first Chicago School—John Wellborn Root, Louis Sullivan. And then there are buildings by the descendants. One is confronted by this enormous tradition everywhere in Chicago. Even our hack architects, of which there are plenty, are inevitably influenced by such brilliant work so that their work isn't so bad. It's a fabulous city. It's an architectural city.

BLDD: Whose work has most influenced you?

ST: Probably John Hejduk's. He is a brilliant architect, and not simply on a conceptual level. He deeply influenced me. So did Bob Venturi. Architects today affect me in a real way.

BLDD: What ideas of Hejduk's have had a strong effect?

ST: I'm interested in the dialectic, the dialogue in architecture and antagonistic toward the totemic tradition of architecture that speaks of traditional values and deals with monumental sorts of systems and beliefs. Hejduk was probably the first architect to influence that kind of thinking. His Wall Houses spoke of a future and a past and a thin present, which was the wall. They were very surrealistic. I was stunned by them because of the implications of the dialogue about the thin present.

BLDD: Tell us about the Chicago Seven, with whom you are identified and whose members hold ideas similar to yours. Who are they, and what goals and ideals do you share?

ST: There *was* a group called the Chicago Seven, but they really had few ideas in common. It began in 1976 with the show "Chicago Architects," which we brought back to Chicago from Cooper Union. It was a show that contrasted with "One Hundred Years of Architecture in Chicago: Continuity of Structure and Form," the canonical Mies show that was going on at the Museum of Contemporary Art at the time.

BLDD: Was this your Armory Show?

ST: Right. Larry Booth, Ben Weese, Stuart Cohen, and I put that show together and based a book on it, and the show traveled extensively. We expanded the group to include Jim Nagle, Tom Beeby, and then Jim Freed, who was at that time the dean of the Illinois Institute of Technology and has since gone back to New York. We later expanded to eight architects, with the addition of Helmut Jahn, then added three others—Cindy Weese, Ken Schroeder, and Gerry Horn—to make it eleven. Since Jim is in New York, now we're ten. We don't have a great deal in common, but the fact that there isn't an awful lot of backbiting makes the situation a bit different than New York.

BLDD: Is there a lot of backbiting among New York architects?

ST: Yes. Look at the backs of the people you interview—you can see all the scars and blood through their jackets. It's quite incredible. You shouldn't look at them from the front, those people in New York.

BLDD: To me they look cheerful and in good spirits and health.

ST: I know, but they're in great pain.

BLDD: How do they manage to survive?

ST: Gingerly. It's been very hard for them. Paranoia is their middle name.

BLDD: Is that how New York architects are perceived?

ST: I would say that to some degree it's an exaggeration. That quality was perhaps stronger years ago. But the point is that in Chicago there is a genuine confluence of interests. It's like a navy wives' club. We hang out together.

BLDD: But navy wives, if one is to carry the analogy further, hang out together because they have no place else to go.

ST: Well, that's probably true. At least that's what New York architects think about us.

BLDD: Where is the center of architectural thought these days, and where is the center of architectural practice?

ST: New York architects think that the center of architectural thought is in New York and that the center of architectural production is in Chicago—that it's the East Coast versus Middle America. This is simply not true. Bob Venturi's office, for example, produces extraordinary working drawings, and Bob Stern's buildings are very beautifully made, belying the idea that New Yorkers cannot build well. And in Chicago there are people like Tom Beeby, who is utterly brilliant at an intellectual, conceptual level, writes wonderfully, draws very romantically and evocatively. I think the distinction made between the East Coast and the Midwest was a simplistic way of putting people in boxes. Notice that we entirely avoid mentioning the West Coast, which is like another country. It's really a never-never land. They're very funny people out there. They make me look like Grandma Moses. West Coast architects seem to be in a perpetual state of angst. I think a lot of California architects never really grow up. Nothing ever gets finished; buildings never quite get completed. Speculation is definitely a part of what architects do, but there is also a time to build—if not permanently, at least for a bit more than the fifteen minutes of fame Andy Warhol said we should all have. The West Coast is a complex society, very different from the rest of the country.

BLDD: How has your notion of architectural quality evolved over the years?

ST: I no longer believe in the totemic value systems that make buildings monuments. Architecture seems to me to be a series of oppositions; it's dualistic. Everyone wants to leave behind children, books, buildings—things that will give us a sense of continuity, that will leave a trace of our existence. On the other hand, life is finite and imperfect. The juxtaposition of those opposites is very interesting to me. The best way I can express that sense of dualism in my own life is that although I was trained in architecture, which I believe to be based on a Hellenistic set of disciplines, I also happen to be Jewish. I started *Versus* by asking the question, How come no Jewish mother ever says "my son, the architect"? How come she always says "my son, the lawyer" or "my son, the doctor"? Because architecture is not a Jewish discipline. It's a gentile discipline.

BLDD: How do you explain that? Do you think professions come in denominations?

ST: Christians believe in life after death, and their buildings are based on monumentality and other perpetual value systems. That's where the interest in zeitgeist, a spirit of the ages, comes from. Jews, on the other hand, are interested in the sanctification of life itself. Those are contradictory propositions. That schizophrenia makes me the perfect architect for post-Vietnam America, since America is also in a fragmented condition.

BLDD: What was the original title of *Versus*?

ST: *Post-Modernism is a Jewish Movement,* which is now the title of its last chapter.

BLDD: How important a role does your religion play in your work?

ST: In terms of the scholastic side of my work, it plays a large role. I think the Jewish tradition teaches you the ability to come to terms with disparate conditions without letting one side overwhelm the other. Also very much a part of the Jewish religion is studying things without an end point in mind. But I am not simply a Jew; I am also an architect. Architecture has an entirely different set of values than Judaism. The juxtaposition of these different systems is fraught with difficulty.

BLDD: How have you worked it all out?

ST: I haven't worked it out. That's the point. What I have done is to attempt to do a series of buildings that are ruptured, sheared, pulled apart, left apart—to find different representations of struggle that invite participatory involvement from people, from strangers as well as users, so that the building is not a finite end in and of itself. At its worst, architecture presents itself as the unchanging answer, to be worshiped because it promises life after death. Often the reason clients build buildings is that they wish to leave something monumental behind to show that they were here.

BLDD: Why did you change the title of the book?

ST: Because *Versus* is a more descriptive title. It describes a confrontational set of propositions. The book is a study of opposites, something that has been done in all of the disciplines but the visual arts. Philosophy, literature, physics, medicine, law—studies of those disciplines have been undertaken without an overriding zeitgeist position. Architecture, painting, and sculpture tend to advance an attitude that says that there is one correct, overriding answer, often couched in the language of the era in which the works are created. I no longer believe in that single answer. The struggle of combining all the things that produce a work of architecture, especially the accommodation of a client, has become much more important to me than that early vision presented by Ayn Rand.

BLDD: You've said that concern for the client is an aspect of architectural morality that is seldom considered. Is that something that interests you a great deal?

ST: Yes. The philosophy that included service as a part of architecture was thrown away at the end of the sixties. But even Bob Venturi has often said that in many ways he considers himself a hired gun.

BLDD: What do you see as the ideal client?

ST: The toughest son-of-a-bitch out there, the one that really works you out, not the one that lets you get away with murder.

BLDD: Do you try to get away with it?

ST: Of course. We all do. We hope to find the path of least resistance. What you see in front of you is a sloth! If I can find an easy way, I'll take it. But a tough client, a mean bastard—that's fabulous. That kind of client forces me to think it out again and again until I get to a deeper level of understanding of the problem and of the project.

BLDD: Charles Moore has said that his clients are the starting point for all of his designs. Kevin Roche, on the other hand, has said that his best clients tell him nothing at all.

ST: I think it shows in both of their work. Charles's work shows that his clients are the starting point, and Kevin's shows that he didn't need them at all. I think they both told the truth.

BLDD: Now that we know your conception of the ideal client, what's your conception of the ideal house?

ST: I don't think there is an ideal house. That would imply a right, legitimate way to produce something. But people are different and, to the extent that architects accommodate their clients, their houses are different. Michael Graves's houses look different from Bob Stern's, which in turn look different from Richard Meier's.

BLDD: What role does irony play in your houses?

ST: Architecture is by nature optimistic. You can't believe in the bomb and produce a building, because architecture's an optimistic, constructive act. On the other hand, blind optimism alone no longer is sufficient for me. I'm also skeptical. The skepticism combined with the optimism—Talmudic theory and Hellenistic ideality—produces irony in my work.

BLDD: Is there a philosophy behind such houses as the Hot Dog House and the Daisy House?

ST: Both of them are wall houses. Like Hejduk's Wall Houses, both of them have a future and a past. One way to read the Daisy House, of course, is to see it as a phallic symbol. If Claes Oldenburg had designed the Daisy House, it would have been made out of a monolithic, uniform material. But architecture is not that way. The house's copings and downspouts and gutters and siding give it an ambiguity, an ambivalence, because of the

Daisy House, Porter Beach, Ind.

Weekend House, Lakeside, Mich.

scale contradiction. So there are simplistic readings of the Daisy House that see obvious sexual overtones in plan alone, but I often wonder if anyone would have read it that way if I hadn't said that it was shaped like an erect phallus with steps of semen. When seen under normal circumstances, it is simply a beach house. It's a wall house, with one facade made of a different material that's dematerialized. The house is a study in dematerialization versus measurability.

BLDD: How would you describe your style?

ST: I have no style. It's the one thing I've always argued about with Richard Meier. He is a brilliant, wonderful architect who creates elegant, lovely objects. But his theories override the idiosyncrasies of site and the other conditions that make a house individual. I am an American architect. This is an individualistic society. I am that individual. I could not be a European architect. The buildings I do would hardly be at home in Georgian London. Contextualism is not my middle name.

BLDD: What *is* your middle name, by the way?

ST: I don't have any. My parents were too poor.

BLDD: Your architectural middle name . . .

ST: Schizophrenic. I am a true, deep schizophrenic, if the truth be told. I have no style because all my clients are different. I don't feel compelled to design something that fits into a continuum. It's true that in addition to considering the special needs of the client I bring my own set of interests to a building, but the buildings still end up being very different from one to the next. Some are postmodern in the sense that they use premodernist symbolic imagery. Some are completely based on syntax and the structure of the work itself and have nothing to do with presenting any imagery.

BLDD: What sort of spaces have you designed for yourself over the years? Do they represent the central ideas of your work?

ST: The only thing I've ever really designed for myself I'm now in the process of doing, with my wife, Margaret McCurry, who is also an architect and my partner. We're building a weekend house in Michigan on the lake. She's an Episcopalian from Lake Forest and graduated from Vassar, so we're an odd combination. You can imagine that juxtaposition in architectural terms. The house is a bit more hers than mine. She has great taste—with one incredible exception, me—so the house is very beautifully detailed and proportioned. It's the only thing I've ever designed for myself. It's actually much better than most other things I've done because she's tough. She's a good architect.

BLDD: How does your professional collaboration work? Who does what?

ST: There are three of us. We have a third partner named Bob Fugman. We're all very different people and we all do different things. We all fight and argue, as any sort of collaborators do, and eventually one or another of us wins. It's an unusual experience for me to be in a partnership. I haven't done it since my first two years in practice two decades ago. But I really like it. They press me on to do better things. Working alone is simply not enough for me, no matter what other architects may feel. I need critical dialogue and argumentation, a constantly unsure condition. My graduate students provide that in one way; my partners and my office do it in quite another.

BLDD: Are you working on other projects with your wife?

ST: We're working on a Knoll showroom in Houston. She's doing a lot of the interiors, and Bob Fugman is very involved in that design as well as in producing the building. We're also working on a house in western Connecticut. Margaret and I are not doing an awful lot of collaboration, although we're designing a number of objects—vases and things like that—which we've always worked on together.

BLDD: You're designing a line of everyday objects for Swid/Powell Designs, who have commissioned work from a number of architects and designers. What objects are you working on, and what is your design intent?

ST: At the moment the series includes Richard Meier, Charlie Gwathmey, Bob Stern, Jim Polshek, and Margaret and me. We are designing flatware, candlesticks, salt and pepper shakers, and oil and vinegar cruets. It's a great deal of fun. What's really interesting, in terms of a critical discourse, is that we're our own design review board. We present work to each other at design gatherings and then critique each other's work.

BLDD: What interests you in making these small objects? They're certainly on a different scale than the work to which you're accustomed.

ST: In fact, at the same time, I'm working with Helmut Jahn, Bruce Graham, and Tom Beeby on planning the World's Fair for 1992 in Chicago, which is on a gigantic scale, and on a central area plan for the City of Chicago. I have a short attention span, and I like doing different things. I like working on little objects, on buildings, and on enormous planning projects. I like detailing, I like drawing, I like writing. I no longer want to be simply an architect in the tradition of making finite objects as so many icons to be placed in the landscape. Planning for urban spaces and designing small objects—both provide interesting lessons.

BLDD: I suspect that there were some interesting lessons learned by cities that have been host to the World's Fairs of the last several decades.

ST: Chicago did the first cohesive national World's Fair in America, and it was brilliant. One hundred years later, on the 500th anniversary of the discovery of America by Christopher Columbus, Chicago's going to do it again. Bruce Graham at Skidmore is the planner and has asked Tom Beeby, Helmut Jahn, and me, as well as a few others, to be involved in making it a national event and bringing in the best architects. Bruce wants to produce a cohesive fair, one that addresses the subject of what the American city will become. Of course, it will have to take the form of a mammoth conceit, since by law nothing can remain at the end of the fair but the residual park system. But what better place to confront this issue than in an architectural mecca like Chicago, where the Columbian Exposition, the balloon frame, the Chicago style, the exposed structure, and the skeleton frame all evolved? I don't know the answer yet, but the question is, What is the ultimate American city and how can it best be represented symbolically?

BLDD: Do you have *any* notions about how it will evolve?

ST: Zero, absolutely zero. If you want the truth, that is the way I go about architecture most of the time, which is a little scary. I envy someone like Richard Meier because he has the answer, his own answer. I don't. Ever. I don't know what the hell's going to happen. But certainly, as far as the fair is concerned, we all are interested in the American city and its many typologies. We're trying to leave it as open as we can and also to include as many people as possible outside architecture—philosophers, academicians, and so forth.

BLDD: During the past five years there has been a noticeable shift in your work, from straight to curved lines and from black and white to color. What caused the change?

ST: It has simply developed. What's happened can best be seen in the difference between my work in two Venice Biennales, in 1976 and 1980. The confrontation is between American and European values—or individual and collective values. I am becoming more and more the sort of individual American architect represented by people like Frank Gehry, Charles Moore, or Bob Venturi. I genuinely respect them because they are truly American architects, not European at all. They embody individual values much in the spirit that Jefferson did in his design of the University of Virginia. That is becoming more clear in my work as time goes by; my work is becoming more American. When I was a young boy, I loved America in a very simplistic way. In World War II I followed the advances and retreats of the war with maps and flags and pins. Then, during the Korean and Vietnam wars, I hated America because it no longer had values that I respected. When America failed in the Vietnam War, I came to love America again, as I would any fallen giant, but in a much more comprehensive way. America's schizophrenia, its struggle to encompass pluralistic conditions—high and low art, the legitimate and the illegitimate—now seems noble. In the bumbling way that any one person can, I would like to replicate that struggle in architectural form, to express the complex set of conditions that provide nobility, as opposed to the simplistic belief in perpetual value systems.

BLDD: In the late 1960s, you widened the perspective of many of your fellow architects and other observers with a concept you called "instant city." Could you describe these experimental megastructures?

ST: They were megastructures in the form of tetrahedrons. Most young architects have grand dreams but build very little. The actual projects I had were very small, but I had these enormous idealistic concepts based on geometric megastructures, which would span expressways and rivers and God knows what. They were a well-intentioned but slightly misdirected use of structure to absorb eccentric human conditions into an overriding, correct system. It was a part of the time. I was very much a part of that time.

BLDD: Have your views on the possibilities of instant cities changed?

ST: Dramatically. Occasionally I still hear from people who want to use the concept of these megastructures for housing in Calcutta or hotels in Miami. Luckily for all of us—certainly for me—they never got built. It's easy to refute one's dreams as a young man, which I don't want to do. I loved doing those

Instant City

Illinois Regional Library for the Blind and Physically Handicapped, Chicago, Ill.

things. It was a fabulous concept as far as visionary architecture goes. But I had no awareness of the deeper values of
the American structure. At least now I am aware of those
issues, although I still barely comprehend them.

BLDD: One of the buildings you did realize, and one of the
major contributions you've made to Chicago architecture, was
a library for the blind. That structure is notable for its use of
very bright colors. Isn't that an odd thing, given the building's
users?

ST: No, on the contrary. It may look like an ironic building by
good old ironic Stanley Tigerman, but it's really a very straight

building. The color is there because less than five percent of
people who are pronounced legally blind are totally blind.
Ninety-five percent of them have some kind of vision. The last
thing people who are partially blind see before they go totally
blind is bright colors bathed in light, so I used color to code the
building: yellow indicates structure, blue software, and red the
perimeter of the building. When people see red they will know
that it's the edge of the building, outside or inside. Color can be
coded and used as a device for communication, as opposed to
simply using it to make a building pretty.

BLDD: What else makes that building special?

ST: Everything is fixed; there are no movable pieces of furniture. Everything is also linear so that people can find their way, so that they can memorize the plan and know quickly where things are.

BLDD: Among your most recent projects is a house in western Connecticut that features two perpendicular rectangles. On what is this plan based?

ST: Edwin S. Prior, an English architect who was a contemporary of Sir Edwin Lutyens, did a project in 1899 called The Barn, which is based on something called a "butterfly plan." Two rectangular objects are juxtaposed with each other perpendicularly. In the Roman and Christian tradition of the basilica plan, a simple rectangular form has a predominant axis which leads to something beyond—the landscape in the case of Roman architecture, the altar in the case of Christian architecture. If you juxtapose two rectangles perpendicularly, the axes lead to points beyond each building, so that a series of spaces is created outside. It's interesting to me that one can be led to things beyond architecture, that the perception of space can lead one beyond the containing walls to assimilate something else.

BLDD: You've described another recent project of yours, a house on the North Shore of Long Island, as being influenced by Lutyens in its design.

ST: That design also had the sense of axes terminated by walls that aren't based on a basilica plan; your orientation is forced in another direction, which is again terminated. This is basically a big U-shaped house. It looks as if the entrance to the house is through the U, but in fact this is deceptive. The house is sheared—it's a two-story building with two one-story wings that telescope out of the two stories. The two-story gables become one story, which in turn becomes bay windows. The point of the rupture is the place between the sacred and the profane, the lawn versus the parking space. On the inside of the house all the rooms are entered on the diagonal, in a Hellenistic way. But in the interiors of the rooms are a series of symmetries reminiscent of Roman architecture. Inside the building there is a juxtaposition of Hellenistic and Roman elements.

BLDD: Has Lutyens been an important influence on your design?

ST: Yes, but so has Frank Lloyd Wright, in more formal ways. In simplistic terms, Western architectural thought has been based on two trends, the Hellenistic and the Roman/Christian. The Roman/Christian tradition incorporates a predominant axis and is characterized by formal qualities. The Hellenistic system is more perceptual, having to do with looking at an object from different perspectives and points of view. One is formal, the other perceptual. The combination of the two provides spatial involvement with the place, as well as a perceptual involvement. Wright was involved with both; so was Lutyens.

BLDD: Earlier you mentioned a design you are doing for a new Knoll showroom in downtown Houston. Are you enjoying that project?

ST: I love it. It's one of the best things we've ever done

Knoll Showroom, Houston, Tex., conceptual sketch

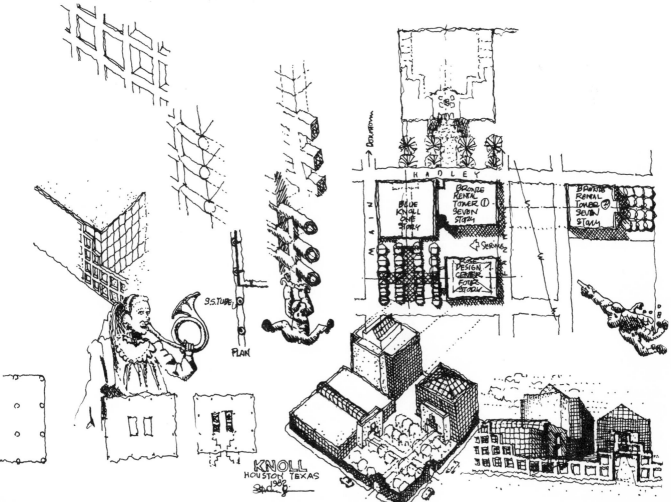

because the clients are fabulous. It's been an incredible, wonderful experience, and the building shows it. The building is really good—my typical immodesty!

BLDD: You've compared the building to an archaeological dig that shows the traces of what it used to be. What was it originally, and what is it now?

ST: It's a remodeling of a 1917 building as part of a project on a block that Knoll has purchased in downtown Houston. The first phase is the Knoll showroom, which is being done, as it turns out, in a building that was originally a furniture showroom. It fell into disrepair and was used as a storage building and a warehouse. In the process of pulling the building apart and seeing what the structure was, we discovered that it had been a showroom in the first place, which is something I tried to replicate architecturally. The building has been ruptured, in a sense, by a jagged line; it has been pulled apart, leaving the traces of the showroom's columns in the raw concrete floor. Another reading entirely is that when one enters the showroom one is thrust on stage. Furniture is arranged in tiers on either side, so the spectator becomes a kind of performer in front of this mute audience of modernist furniture.

BLDD: Among other things, your book *Versus* describes the twenty-year period between 1960 and 1980. What characterizes this period? What will its architectural legacy be?

ST: As I recall, I say in the book that Bob Venturi was to architecture what Vietnam was to America, in the sense that they both made the subject fall from grace.

BLDD: Is that meant as a compliment?

ST: Yes. America and architecture were thought about simplistically before Vietnam and Venturi. They both made the subject fall from grace but gave it a great poignancy. The Vietnam War was one of the most stunning examples of a country coming to grips with its own imperfection. Similarly, architecture was thought to be high art, the aristocratic descendant of a highly refined English sport, until Venturi came along and pointed out that Las Vegas was part of our heritage and that this was O.K.

BLDD: In what direction is architecture going now?

ST: What's beginning to take place is a struggle to present the many contradictory conditions in operation today—America versus Europe, syntax versus semantic symbolism, any number of dualistic oppositions. Bob Stern works in his way, Graves works in his. Little will change them, I would hypothesize, and almost nothing will change Richard Meier. Because these very forceful and important people represent differing attitudes, and because none of them represents the single right way to do things, one begins to reflect on the condition of the dialectic, the dialogue, the interaction not just between those people but within the work itself. The struggle is between the process and the product. Before the late sixties, American architecture was very sure of itself. Mies and Le Corbusier had won, and their descendants were everywhere. But at the end of the sixties, the cultural revolution, inner-city problems, black revolutionaries, advocacy planning, and numerous social concerns caused a rejection of prior products. It was at that time that the Vietnam War was taking place and that Venturi's book—*Complexity and Contradiction in Architecture*—came out. We tend to forget about all that struggle, but I would contend that the situation today is a product of the struggle among all of those trends. It is as yet unresolved, which is the part that interests me.

BLDD: What is the architectural spirit of our time?

ST: That struggle. For the first time, it's acceptable to admit that one is not sure of one's values, that change is part of the process of life. For example, fashion has always been a dirty word in architecture. To be interested in such things is to trivialize architecture, to destroy the notion of architecture as permanent. I am very interested in fashion simply because it represents what people are interested in, and I'm interested in people. But one is also interested in value systems based on a sense of permanence. It is the conjunction of those two things, I think, that makes American architecture. For the first time, it is showing its frailty, and it is that unsureness that is the most interesting part of it. Architects are no longer that sure of themselves.

BLDD: If you had access to unlimited funds and assistance, what would your ideal project be?

ST: I don't think that way. Many years ago I taught with a very talented man who was trained at the École des Beaux-Arts, and he had that very opportunity. A rich man in Bucks County, Pennsylvania, had a fabulous two-thousand-acre piece of terrain in rolling mountains and commissioned this architect to do a mountain retreat. No budget, no program, no size, no nothing. The architect couldn't do it. Most architects do best with a very well-defined set of conditions. Some architects, like Kevin Roche or John Hejduk, are self-starters and don't need those things. But a lot of us need other people to be tough on us. I'm one of those guys; so is Charles Moore. We're both overweight. We're both lazy. We need clients to work us out.

BLDD: If you had your life to live over again, what would you do differently?

ST: I may yet do what I would have done. I grew up in the house of my grandparents. My grandmother was a chef at a hotel in Chicago, but my grandfather never worked for a living. He spent his days in his bed in the attic, wearing his long johns, reading Kant, Descartes, Hegel, and Talmudic exegeses. If I ever grow up, I'd like to do that. I still may—I'm finding that I'm reading less architecture and more philosophy, literature, and history as time goes by.

BLDD: Does that make you a better architect?

ST: I don't know. It makes architecture harder, it adds more dimensions, but I don't know whether that leads to better work. Nothing is ever satisfactory, nothing is ever enough. Ultimately, no client and no set of constraints is ever sufficient. So you always seek things to enrich, to ennoble, to elaborate, to embellish work. And that's what I find in those readings.

BLDD: Did you expect your life to unfold the way it has?

ST: No way. I've been very lucky. But it's also been hard. Attempting to struggle with things beyond the nature of the work has been very difficult.

BLDD: Are these the best years of your life?

ST: They're the best in the sense that there is a genuine exchange between architects that I find very rewarding. Architects are willing to give and take criticism, and I like that very much. I also think that for the first time an authentic American architecture is developing. American architecture is coming to recognize the place of the individual and the collective. Martin Buber talked about the fine line between collectivism and rampant individualism, which is a line American architecture is beginning to walk, without falling for an overriding system of beliefs that allows only one "right" way of making things. That's the best thing about this period—being around at a time when what's evolving in our country is a unique and marvelous experience.

ROBERT VENTURI
AND
DENISE SCOTT BROWN

Robert Venturi and John Rauch have been business partners since 1964. Denise Scott Brown joined the Philadelphia-based architecture firm three years later. At about the same time Venturi and Scott Brown became partners in marriage as well. In the late sixties their theories were instrumental in launching the postmodernist movement. Today their work and their many fresh ideas—involving a nondoctrinaire and accommodating approach that uses architectural forms from many different periods and gives them new meaning—have made them major leaders in contemporary architecture.

BLDD: Bob, you recently commented that your rather complex message has to be viewed more simply. What is your message, and how has it been misinterpreted?

RV: One of its important characteristics is that it is hard to simplify. That means it's hard to explain, hard to teach, and hard to write about. But one way to understand it is by referring to the titles of the two books I have written: *Complexity and Contradiction in Architecture* and *Learning from Las Vegas* (the latter I wrote with Denise and with Steven Izenour). *Complexity and Contradiction* was concerned essentially with architectural form, and *Learning from Las Vegas* was more about architectectural symbolism than about Las Vegas. What I was trying to say in those books is that in our time architects should acknowledge complexity, contradiction, and ambiguity more than simplicity, unity, and clarity. The word "accommodation" describes this approach in a nutshell. Another way to put it is that I was advocating mannerism in architecture. The book on Las Vegas emphasizes our belief that one should go to many sources of symbolism for architecture, and that the symbolism of Las Vegas and the commercial strip are as important a source of reference today as industrial symbolism was for the heroic period of modern architecture or historical symbolism was for nineteenth-century architecture. This makes for a nondoctrinaire approach to architecture.

BLDD: Denise, how would you describe *your* philosophy of postmodernism?

DSB: It's related to what Bob said, but I approached the problem from several other angles as well. I came to America with an interest in architecture that transgressed the rules. In 1958 I took a course in urban sociology with Herbert Gans in which he suggested good reasons why architectural dogma should be questioned. During the civil rights and social movements of the sixties, Gans and other social scientists criticized the architecture of urban renewal in America. They pointed out that the new towers in the centers of our cities, although reminiscent of social housing in Europe, did not house the poor, and that the beautiful utopian vision of the planners have become a nightmare in which the poor were removed to make way for urban renewal. The architects' vision of the good city seemed to conspire in this situation. Without intending to, architects were aggravating the social ills of cities. Their views of what architecture should be were part of the problem. I began to feel that if we architects could tolerate complexity and variety, we might be more sympathetic and receptive to the needs of people in the cities.

BLDD: It's been twenty years, Bob, since you and John Rauch formed a partnership to practice architecture. How did that partnership come about?

RV: I didn't start out with a grand idea or a very particular plan. I had worked by then, like most young architects, for several firms. Then at a certain point, not realizing all of the difficulties involved, I decided to try working on my own in order to get the satisfactions inherent in being your own boss. It was important for me to team up with a congenial fellow architect whose talents complemented mine. I wanted to establish a firm that worked on a practical as well as an aesthetic level. John Rauch has always been the practical, technical business partner; his abilities are complementary to my more theoretical and artistic abilities—although it's not quite that simple, since John is the intellectual on our team and a brilliant critic.

BLDD: Now that the firm has fifty people and offices in New York and Philadelphia, how are responsibilities divided?

RV: Generally the division remains pretty much as it was in the beginning.

BLDD: And what do you concern yourself with, Denise?

DSB: Too many things to describe. Technically I am the principal in charge of planning and urban design. But I also work with Bob on everything from the design of a teaspoon to that of a region. My social planner friends say that architects who believe they can design everything from a teaspoon to a region have delusions of grandeur. Since I agree with that, I'm surprised to find us doing it all! I'm involved at many different levels in the office. The three partners share office management, but we're trying to get other people to take over some of that. I have also been trying to plan for our increasing staff, trying to keep VRSB the kind of organization we want it to be.

BLDD: You were born and raised in Zambia, South Africa. How has your background influenced your architectural style and your ideas about planning?

DSB: Living in Africa I think I acquired a xenophobia about Africa that was translated into a xenophobia about America when I came here. I've always felt that we must look to the artifacts and environment of our own culture for inspiration.

BLDD: Both of you bring pluralistic cultures, rich lives, and very eclectic sensibilities to your work. How does that affect your practice of architecture?

RV: It makes it exciting. It allows us to understand what being different is all about. It's forced us to be open-minded, with no specific ideology that we try to impose on everybody. Our approach involves adaptation. In a sense, most architects have to work for varieties of clients with varieties of taste cultures, to use Herbert Gans's term, and we acknowledge this plurality. It makes our architecture varied and, we hope, rich. It also makes it difficult to accomplish.

BLDD: Philip Johnson has cited *Complexity and Contradiction* as a seminal force in creating the movement away from the simple austerity of the architecture of the modern movement. That book, published in 1966, is often described as the most important contribution to architecture theory since Le Corbusier's *Towards a New Architecture.* What did you write that so influenced your fellow architects?

RV: I'm not sure. In struggling through the writing of a book or an article I get it out of my system and almost forget later on what I said. But I always write in relation to practice, and I know I wrote what I thought at the time. I love the phrase of Jean Labatut, my teacher at Princeton, who referred to the "creative forgetfulness" you must use to forget your previous theories and your preconceptions. In our case, we must forget what we've written.

BLDD: Did you ever imagine that the book would have such a great impact?

RV: No, I never thought about it. I just thought of writing a book because I had something to say and I wanted to get it out. The book also came out of frustration. I was a young architect without enough work, so I got my ideas out in words rather than in buildings. I don't think anyone who does something that turns out to be valid or influential starts out by saying, I'm going to create an influential book or a great masterpiece. He or she starts out by saying, Here is a problem or a challenge. What is the best way to deal with it?

BLDD: Younger architects often write articles or books while waiting for work to come along, hoping that the writing will encourage it. I've often wondered in the case of this book, which was on the one hand so praised and on the other so maligned, if it lost you as much work as it brought.

RV: I'm sure it did. *Learning from Las Vegas,* even more than *Complexity and Contradiction,* lost us lots of work because it was so easy to misinterpret, to see it as *advocating* Las Vegas rather than *learning from* Las Vegas. Some critics and journal-ists liked to make us out as controversial because that made their story easier to write. We weren't controversial, we were just commonsensical. But simply writing books or teaching or being perceived as an intellectual does diminish an architect's chances of getting jobs and big commissions.

BLDD: That book served to enrich the language of architecture. What were some of the phrases from the book that have now become a part of the language?

RV: "Both-and," "allusion," "accommodation," "messy vitality." The aesthetic ideal of orthodox modernism was a combination of unity and clarity. This was a perfectly valid ideal. Renaissance architecture was based on the same ideal—the Pazzi Chapel is remarkable for the unity and clarity of its forms and symbols. But there is another, equally valid ideal apparent in Byzantine architecture. In terms of unity or clarity, a Byzantine chapel is a disaster in its combination of materials, media, symbols, and forms. But it is appealing because of its richness and ambiguity. This "messy vitality" is an ideal we think is valid for today. This is what people want—an architecture that has many levels of meaning and that achieves its effect through richness rather than unity, ambiguity rather than clarity.

BLDD: You said that *Learning from Las Vegas* had a different kind of impact from that of *Complexity and Contradiction.* How did your intent differ in writing that book, published ten years later? Do you think the title is a bit misleading?

RV: Yes, it is. It was the wrong title, in the end, because it made people think the book was about Las Vegas. When you write you learn that most people don't really read—at least architects don't. They often get a superficial, if not mistaken, idea of what a book is about. In general, the book was about the forgotten element of symbolism in architecture; in particular, about the validity of ordinary and commercial symbolism for architecture. Because we were also architects with a sense of the history of Western architecture—including high art and monumental architecture—we found we could look at the current American scene with a clear and vivid perspective. Denise used the wonderful phrase "from Rome to Las Vegas" to describe our range of interests.

BLDD: Who introduced whom to popular culture in the everyday environment?

DSB: We probably both knew about it from our different backgrounds and experience. But I invited Bob to visit Las Vegas with me. At the University of Pennsylvania, I had learned that California—Los Angeles especially—was an area serious urbanists should study. So I moved to California to teach at Berkeley and UCLA because it was an extremely interesting area. On my way I stopped in Las Vegas and found that the environment there was fascinating and relevant to my interests in architecture. Bob and I had taught together at Penn and shared our ideas about architecture and popular culture, and I knew that Bob would like Las Vegas. I invited him to come and lecture to my students. Then I gave them a design assignment that lasted four or five days, while we went to Las Vegas.

RV: I think our appetites had been whetted by Tom Wolfe's brilliant essay on Las Vegas, as well as by the brilliant work of the New York Pop artists of the time, which had expanded our sensibilities in an important way. Very often in the last decades painters and sculptors have been far ahead of architects in terms of sensibility.

BLDD: What do you think of the state of architectural criticism nowadays?

DSB: It could be a lot better. Sometimes the critics' lack of understanding amazes me. If one more person asks why I didn't mention the evils of gambling on the Strip, I don't know what I'll do! My answer to them is: Why didn't they mention the evils of medieval Christianity when they wrote about the cathedral at Chartres? Our work and theories are much more socially concerned than those of most of the architects who ask that question.

BLDD: As you mentioned, you are interested in designing everything from a teaspoon to a region. You have worked in recent years on the design of a line of furniture. How did this assignment come about?

RV: Very simply, we love furniture. We own something like eighty-seven chairs.

BLDD: Are you collectors of chairs?

RV: I guess you could say so. We just bought another chair. I don't know why. I guess that's one definition of a collector.

BLDD: Any specific kind of chairs?

RV: No, all kinds. Only they can't be too expensive. They are mostly straight chairs. The evolution of chairs is fascinating because the program is limited and almost constant. Since a chair must accommodate the adult human body in a sitting position, even the smallest variations in the form, scale, and symbolism of the design become important. For several years we have been designing a line of furniture with Knoll and for Knoll, and it has been both thrilling and frustrating. As an architect, it's hard to work in a scale involving fractions of an inch. We're used to fractions of feet or acres.

BLDD: You were recently commissioned by an Italian manufacturer to design a tea service. It has been compared to a very generous English teapot with a round belly.

RV: We were rather angry when that design was published because it represented a very early study and was not very refined.

BLDD: How do the published designs resemble what was finally created?

RV: They're more or less the same except that the final pieces are now more refined in their design. It is important to em-

phasize the simple idea of quality in design because most of the critical writing about architecture today dwells on philosophy and theory and polemics over simple matters of quality. What really distinguishes good architects is not so much the originality of their ideas or the frequency with which they coin quotable phrases or identify new schools but how well their work succeeds in its aesthetic and its purpose. Critics shy away from critical assessments of proportion, tension, and usability because this is dangerous ground, but that's where an architect's sweat and struggle should go. Unfortunately at this level of creation you have to work one hundred percent harder to do ten percent better.

BLDD: It has been said that the buildings of Venturi, Rauch and Scott Brown are not easily labeled, that there is no one set style to which you adhere. Do you see it that way? What would you identify as the trademarks of your work?

DSB: I feel there are definite themes and categories visible in our architecture. At one point there were two different lines of development: complex and contradictory buildings, and ugly and ordinary buildings. The character of the client strongly affects the building, as does the environmental context. Yet common themes emerge from the variety. There's always a strong influence of Palladio in what we do. You could say that many of the houses Bob has designed are Palladio in the front, Le Corbusier inside, and Aalto behind. Common themes and consistent relationships recur in the houses, although superficially they may not look alike.

BLDD: You've spoken of the role of the "ugly and ordinary building" in the landscape. Obviously you don't intend to *make* ugly and ordinary buildings. That idea is, of course, full of paradoxes. What do you really mean when you use the phrase "ugly and ordinary"?

DSB: It sounds simple and it's complex. It *is* paradoxical. Basically, the idea is that with everyone striving to be revolutionary, you will be most revolutionary if you try to be ordinary.

Silver tea service with gold plating and ebony handles

BLDD: What sets Venturi, Rauch and Scott Brown buildings or projects apart from those of other firms?

RV: Well, I think a VRSB building is very *good*. That sounds banal, but . . .

BLDD: You're known for having very high standards. How did you achieve that reputation?

RV: Thinking is important. We do a lot of thinking. But in the end, the proof is in the work, in succeeding very well in doing what you set out to do. I am happiest looking at a work of art that succeeds in doing what it set out to do, even if I don't agree with the aesthetic of the artist. This is true in assessing almost all historical art: you don't have to be a proponent of Christianity to appreciate a medieval triptych. That's because content is only one ingredient in art; in the end, quality is important too. As an artist you are a craftsman and you have to do well what you want to do. It's a very simple idea but something that's lost today in all the polemics, the verbosity, the self-conscious naming of schools and styles. Inventing styles or provoking polemics or doodling on napkins just isn't our way. Inventing styles and adjusting your work to fit them isn't a good thing. Bernini didn't know he was Baroque. Architects should leave the naming of what they do to future historians.

BLDD: You said that in the end the proof is in the work. With your very high standards and distinguished reputation, do you ever turn down jobs?

RV: Very rarely. On the other hand, we seldom accept invitations to lecture, teach, be on panels, or engage in theoretical projects because we want to devote our energy and time to concentrating on the real work in our office. Work requires focus.

BLDD: What type of project interests you the most?

DSB: That's very difficult to say. We don't define our interest according to building type but according to the challenge involved. I've often wondered what links our interests in the teaspoon and the region. It's a demand inherent in the problem itself, a challenge in the approach.

RV: You don't think in terms of preferring houses to corporate office buildings. You want a commission that allows you as many opportunities and dimensions as possible. And you want a client who is a collaborator. Most good buildings derive from an understanding collaboration between architect and client.

BLDD: Is there any type of project that you would particularly enjoy working on, given that it provided ample challenges? What circumstances do you think would provide the most fruitful collaboration and exchange?

RV: Probably what would interest us most now is the kind of project that has a high degree of symbolism, such as a religious building—a church, a mosque, a cathedral, a synagogue—or a civic building. Buildings like that are particularly attractive to us because we are now more interested in symbolism than in purely formal and structural aspects of architecture.

BLDD: Denise, is there anything you haven't designed yet that you would like to?

DSB: I would like to design a synagogue. I would also like to design an office building—a tall one.

BLDD: How would you infuse the architecture of an office building or a synagogue with a new spirit?

RV: You don't really know until you try.

DSB: A synagogue would be interesting to work on because it's not a church. It has an open question mark regarding religious expression. It hasn't developed a form. Forms have developed in different times and in different countries, but there really isn't one here now. It would be interesting to try to work out what an archetypal synagogue should be; given that it's a meeting house, what would the religious meaning of

meeting entail in terms of form? In the design of an office building, the mass repetition of small units would be interesting to investigate. The art involved in such a design is impressionistic: you are putting together ordinary industrial components in repetitive combinations to give an impression greater than the individual elements themselves.

BLDD: You've mentioned the importance of the client. Who is the ideal client?

DSB: I have a theory that clients choose architects just like themselves. Perhaps for us the ideal client is also someone very much like us. But that could be many different kinds of people.

BLDD: How would you describe that client?

DSB: Usually it's a person with considerable entrepreneurial flair. That doesn't necessarily mean a corporate executive; it may mean the president of a college or the head of an urban renewal agency. The client could be in the private or the public sector. He could be a poet, which one of our best clients was, or a would-be professor running his family's factory, like another. But they all have an entrepreneurial sense, a view that they're going to do it themselves, and the architect is very special to them. They also like to match ideas, to match wits. They ask telling questions: You said such-and-such, but look what you did. Why this contrast?

RV: They should be demanding and understanding at the same time. The most difficult client is the characteristic client of today, the committee. A committee works by consensus and therefore seldom achieves anything new or first rate; its role is one of compromise. This goes for choosing an architect: committees choose everyone's second choice. It's hard to be an outstanding architect and present yourself to a selection committee. Kafka would understand. I think architects had an easier time in the days when they had a single client—a prince or a cardinal or an entrepreneur—and a one-to-one relationship. There is today, though, a creative dynamic that can evolve when working with citizen groups as clients.

DSB: I like very much working with community groups, especially in small towns.

BLDD: Isn't one of your specialties "small-town therapy" and community participation? How does that kind of client go about selecting you?

DSB: We seem to be selected (or not selected) for many different reasons, but I think there's always a chemistry involved. We try to help our client to achieve the democratic participation of the town or the neighborhood in the project, to involve people who ought to be involved. If they're not involved they can't know the issues and can't make good decisions. They may also veto what you propose. So we help set up a representative democracy through some kind of steering committee and a direct democracy through public meetings. We hope that the two together will keep the community informed. Communities have their own particular personalities, which are fascinating—in some communities people will debate until midnight; in others only two people will come to public meetings.

BLDD: You mentioned that you're now interested in designing a building with strong symbolic content. If that is your concern for the eighties, what most absorbed you in the seventies?

RV: We're so involved in what we're doing now it's kind of hard to remember! We have become more and more interested in symbolism, representation, and decoration and have increasingly turned toward historic sources to learn lessons about application.

DSB: In the seventies we designed most of our constructed architectural and urban projects. We further developed our thinking about symbolism by examining symbolism in housing. We worked on several houses and on several Main Street revitalization projects. We also designed four exhibitions, which was fascinating.

BLDD: One of those exhibitions, at the Renwick Gallery of the Smithsonian Institution in Washington, D.C., was particularly influential. Can you tell us something about your intent and design for that exhibition?

DSB: The exhibition, called "Signs of Life: Symbols of the American City," was based on the ideas we'd developed between 1968 and 1975 through our analysis of symbolism in city streets, suburban areas, and on the strip.

BLDD: What were the most prevalent symbols?

DSB: In housing, the most salient symbol was probably the American eagle, although the meaning-laden pitched roof and green lawn occurred even more frequently. The American flag was not far behind.

BLDD: And the most surprising symbol?

DSB: I'm not surprised by *anything* anymore, but when I saw that first mailbox on a stiff metal chain, I was pretty surprised. Also the plastic wagon wheel, or half a wagon wheel that looks as if the other half is in the lawn. Perhaps my favorites, though, were the mixtures of symbols—patriotic, religious, and sentimental—to be found in old ethnic neighborhoods.

RV: I think those were also my favorites. We had a good time doing that project. We did not feel condescending toward the material, though we were accused of being so. We learned lots of lessons from the work we did, the main one being that by acknowledging the plurality of American life and culture and accommodating to it, we can get richer effects than we can by imposing some ideals based on personal predilections.

BLDD: What are some of the historical precedents that most engage you?

RV: I love, above all, Italian architecture. I particularly love Italian Mannerist architecture. Michelangelo is my favorite architect; Palladio and Bernini are also important. I also love English architecture, which embodies the pragmatic English quality of adapting a set order or system, a kind of English muddling-through. These generalizations are dangerous, but they indicate my preferences. There is also Sir Edwin Lutyens, whom I feel I rediscovered in a sense and learned very much from. These are some of my historical mentors.

BLDD: In addition to learning from Lutyens, who are some of your most significant teachers or mentors, Denise?

DSB: I start with my mother, who studied architecture. There are so many others they're hard to name. There was Arthur Korn, my teacher in London at the Architectural Association. He had a vast influence on a great many architects and prepared me for the kinds of lessons I learned at the University of Pennsylvania. I came to Penn because of Louis Kahn, but in the end the social planners there—and Bob Venturi—were more important to me. For both of us, J. B. Jackson, the philosopher of landscapes, was very important, and for me, Charles Seeger, the ethnomusicologist.

BLDD: Like many young architects, Bob, you once had a member of your family as a client. I'm referring to the now legendary house that you designed for your mother in Chestnut Hill, Pennsylvania, about twenty years ago. That design has become a sort of icon among architects. Some people describe it as one of the earliest postmodern buildings. Did you expect the house to become such an important part of architectural history?

RV: No. I don't think most people work that way. I just worked very long and very hard on the project. I had the time then, and I was able to concentrate and work on that house for about five years. It was a significant learning process. In a sense, almost everything that I've done and everything our firm has done since has come out of that house—at least our highly spatial and formal buildings. Now we are interested in the idea of the decorated shed and applied decoration. That is a whole new thing and I'm now engaged in another major learning process involving symbolism and ornament, but the other is still important. That house was important to me because through it I could really work things out. It was a seminal experience. While designing and redesigning that house (which I did a great many times) I confronted most of the issues with which I've been involved since as an architect.

BLDD: How did your mother feel about the house? What influence did she have on the design?

RV: I'm afraid not much direct influence—I was rather arrogant at that age. But she had a big influence on me in the sense that she had been interested in architecture all her life—also in clothes and furniture. So the design of the house connected with her taste in general and, in particular, I designed it with her furniture in mind.

BLDD: Do you still find the house a satisfying design?

RV: Yes, I love it.

BLDD: You referred to the decorated shed, which calls to mind the office building you completed in 1978 for the Institute for Scientific Information in your native Philadelphia. That design features a plain brick box decorated with patterned color tiles on the surface—on the shed, so to speak. How did the design for that building evolve?

RV: The design of that building involved a process that is not atypical in office building design. Essentially the dimensions of the building were dictated by the site and the client, and they produced an awkward shape: a rather low, squarish box. There were other determinants to the design. We had to use a certain kind of brick required by an aesthetic deed restriction. We also had a very low budget. That building came in at thirty-seven dollars a square foot when it was built, which would have been low for even a speculative office building at that time. We decided that since we could not achieve an effect through expensive and dramatic structural or spatial means, what we could do was to adapt the architectural conventions of the loft building, with strip windows and highly flexible interior space. These conventions are traditional and appropriate expressions for an office building, of course, but in this building, a more explicit architectural effect was derived from applied ornament. The combination of these elements evoked an effect of contradiction: the body of the building was conventional, indeed ordinary, although we very carefully designed the proportions of these elements, and the independent ornamental pattern was unique.

BLDD: You managed to build it in something like eleven months. How did you do that?

RV: We pride ourselves on being a practical as well as arty firm of architects. It involved careful planning, including a fast-track method of organization where certain elements of design and construction overlap.

BLDD: That design is very different from other buildings you have worked on, such as a bank in Stratford, Connecticut, which is a kind of enlarged Palladian pavilion with all the elements just slightly out of proportion. What was your intent when designing that bank? How does it reflect some of your firm's theoretical notions?

DSB: It was a small building in an automobile environment. There was a great deal of "messy vitality" around it. To make the bank visible in that environment, Bob added a large cupola

Installation view of "Signs of Life," Renwick Gallery, Smithsonian Institution, Washington, D.C.

to give a symbolism and a scale that would suit both its function and its environment. I think the planners in the town felt that we were too historical, but our idea was to refer to local history and at the same time to make a small building noticeable. But to go back to the Institute for Scientific Information in Philadelphia, there is also a Palladian influence there. The ornament is placed symmetrically about the center line of the building, and there's a contradiction between the centralized ornament and the placement of the entrance on the side. Richness comes from the interplay between the symbolic-ornamental elements and the functional dimensions of the building. It isn't a one-idea

building. It has many different themes, which sometimes overlap and sometimes clash.

BLDD: But the building seems less tied to architectural history than many others you have done.

DSB: Less visibly tied. On close analysis you'll see that it has historic referents, even in its checkerboard pattern.

RV: The composition of the building's facade juxtaposes two kinds of rhythms. Because it is an office building with repetitive spaces inside, it presents an even rhythm of bays outside—the facade has six identical bays defined by the location of columns. Juxtaposed to this system is another kind of rhythm that involves a crescendo focusing at the center. The rhythm of windows and bays has a consistent A-A-A beat. That of the pattern involves a hierarchy, where the center is more important than the edges, and has an A-B-C-B-A configuration. This juxtaposition reflects both the nonhierarchical spatial organization of the modern office building and an image of a definitive whole, appropriate to the single institution that the building houses and represents.

BLDD: Does the decoration wrap around the sides as well?

RV: We couldn't *afford* to wrap it around the sides.

DSB: But the pattern shouldn't go around the side anyway because it is a decoration on a facade with a shed behind it.

BLDD: The choice of VRSB for New York's Westway project was something of a surprise, particularly considering the firm's vehement objections to large-scale urban renewal projects in cities like Miami. How did this assignment come about?

DSB: We were invited to join the project through a member of the prime consultant team who felt that a new scale and a new type of civic urbanism were needed for that area. He was interested in harking back beyond the asymmetrical railroad-tie-and-concrete playgrounds of the fifties and sixties to the great parks and parkways of the thirties. He felt that we had the ability to produce a civic landscape at that scale and a knowledge of the environment to help weave this park into its surroundings, to understand the relation between river, park, and city. We had successfully fought an expressway on South Street in Philadelphia, but the differences between South Street and Westway were considerable. On South Street about six thousand people were slated for removal, and there was no place for them to go because no public housing was being offered. For Westway there would be no human removal, and the context seemed to us to be quite different—for one thing, the highway would be mainly underground.

BLDD: Is Westway ever going to happen? What's the current status?

DSB: We think it will go ahead.

BLDD: What do you have in mind for us, if and when Westway *is* built?

DSB: A quiet, urbane park, with an esplanade along the water where people could stroll. Beyond that, toward the city, a lawn and trees, simple and abundant. Within that plan there is the intention to locate specific community-related facilities, but programs for these will be developed nearer to the time Westway is built.

BLDD: Most of your work in the past reflects your view of the city as a slowly developing mixture of old and new, with a scale that is suitable to people. Is Westway a departure from that?

DSB: Towns have always had juxtapositions of scale. And great works of engineering are a part of all towns. Expressways or fortifications or river embankments must be built on a certain scale, which forms part of the contrast that makes up the city. The river edge requires a sturdy scale to meet problems of flooding, to contain waves and tides, and to avoid the pollutants in the river. Strong engineering is needed whether or not there is an expressway underneath, but especially for a park on Manhattan at that point. We're not designing an estate upriver on the Hudson that is occupied by ten people. Urban-scale use calls for something sturdy and tough. Another real urban issue is that certain decisions must be made now and other decisions will be made ten years from now. Decisions about the overall configuration governed by the location of the expressway under the park must be made now. Therefore an overall decision must be made now about the river edge. Specific community uses of and relations to the park will be decided in detail much nearer to the time of construction. Who knows now what the communities will want then? Ten years beyond that time community requirements may change yet again.

BLDD: So it is an incremental and ever-changing process.

DSB: On one level. And on another level a decision must be

Institute for Scientific Information, Philadelphia, Pa.

Esplanade for Westway, New York, N.Y.

made and maintained, particularly when the plan includes a waterfront, when you have to make strong edges to deal with the water. Westway needs an urban scale, even a national scale, as well as a local scale that relates to small-scale environmental change. The two go together. That's typical of all cities.

RV: In European cities there is a grand tradition of urban amenities along the river. That's seldom the case in the United States, where the riverfront is used almost exclusively for commerce, for docks that run parallel to railroads and highways. Since the docks and the railroads are no longer there, why not have a beautiful amenity that could have an effect on the edge of Manhattan comparable to the effect that Central Park has on the heart of Manhattan?

BLDD: Given the state of urban economics, where will urban design go over the next ten years?

DSB: I think we will learn to value what we already have, which will be a great achievement. Devising methods of maintenance that cities can afford will be a great challenge to creativity.

BLDD: Are you neo-preservationists?

DSB: I'm certainly a preservationist.

RV: We are balanced, not fanatical, preservationists. Ten years ago there was too much demolition for the sake of progress and urban renewal, but today we are sometimes prone to the other extreme—a fanatical stress on historic preservation that does not connect with the inevitable urban evolution. To achieve the Piazza San Marco, after all, they had to demolish then-existing historic buildings. There has to be a balance between tradition and progress in the growth of cities, the kind of balance you find in most good old cities. Unfortunately, the American way seems to be to fluctuate between extreme enthusiasms rather than to keep a pragmatic sense of balance in matters of taste.

BLDD: How do you account for the enormous increase in public interest in historic preservation? Is it due, in part, to a denial of contemporary architecture?

RV: Probably, yes.

DSB: People feel that life isn't as great now as it used to be. Hard times make us nostalgic for easier times. There is also nostalgia for the natural. The guiding notion of the ecological movement was that natural was better.

BLDD: You've mentioned that, particularly during the fifties and sixties, in the name of progress and urban renewal much of the past was swept away. As a result, there are those who feel that planners and architects have sometimes done more harm than good. During that period socially concerned architects tended to leave architecture and enter the fields of planning and public housing. Thirty years later, is architecture still lacking in social relevance?

DSB: I find social issues are now dismissed, viewed as an outdated concern of the sixties. There has to be a way for us to be socially concerned in the eighties; the pendulum has swung so far away from social concern that it must swing back again.

BLDD: How does the architect reconcile formal concerns with social ones?

DSB: One way is by supporting an aesthetic of "messy vitality" for social reasons, among others. The social planner who asked for our help on South Street in Philadelphia said to me, "If you can like Las Vegas, we trust you not to try to neaten up South Street at the expense of its residents." She thought architects in general were elitists—and various other ugly things—but she felt that because of our aesthetic predilections we could help South Street without hurting it.

BLDD: A few years ago an exhibition was held of twenty-five years of your architectural drawings. What did you learn from that exhibition? Were you pleased with it?

RV: As we went through our files we found that the drawings that had the most quality and that were most interesting to us were sketches that were made very unselfconsciously—studies of designs as they evolved. Their purpose was purely to inform the designer while working, and the most successful ones were those in which the hand was informing the mind. They're quite different from the usual architectural drawings, which are made essentially to communicate between architect and client and to explain or even sell the design. I enjoyed reviewing the drawings; I thought a lot of them were very good.

BLDD: What is it in the act of drawing, or even doodling, that helps further the architect's plan?

RV: Architects work in different ways, so you can't generalize. I never draw for the sake of drawing or to make a beautiful picture. I learn a lot from the drawings. There are moments well into the process of design when your hand guides your mind and does things that your mind wouldn't do. The best moments are when you let your hand go off on its own. I learn a lot as I draw, but other architects learn more from models or photography or other means of developing their designs.

BLDD: What buildings of the last twenty years reflect the best in architecture?

RV: That is hard for an architect to answer because he will always like his own buildings the best. But architects whose work I love and whom I've learned the most from include Alvar Aalto, Louis Kahn, and Le Corbusier, as well as Sir Edwin Lutyens, Philip Webb, and other architects of the Arts and Crafts movement in England. Armando Brasini, although he was a Fascist, did very significant work. Also extremely interesting are the highly eclectic architects who practiced in Milan at the turn of the century. And, of course, there are the other decorative schools of early modern architecture, like the Viennese. We also learn a lot from American architects of that period, like William Price. And we learn an awful lot from looking at ordinary architecture. I don't look at many architectural magazines today. We don't learn too much from them. We have learned much more from architecture of more than twenty years ago.

BLDD: Which of your own buildings do you think will be best remembered?

RV: I don't know. I like them all almost equally.

DSB: I have a theory that the addition to the Allen Memorial Art Museum, which is difficult for people to understand now, will have considerable staying power.

BLDD: Can you tell us a bit about that project, which was an addition to Cass Gilbert's splendid museum? Some people see the design as a gesture of respect; others see it as a gesture of defiance, an "ironic Ionic" design. What did you have in mind?

RV: Denise has pointed out elsewhere that this building, more than others, resulted very little from preconception and quite directly from difficult site constrictions, program restrictions, and the immediate architectural context. As the design developed we found we did not like what was evolving, yet we were convinced that the hard decisions we had made were correct on rational grounds. Buildings that evolve this way are often the best. Louis Kahn used to say, "I like to be surprised by what I design." Eventually we liked it, but it was an acquired taste. Our building involves nothing but respect for the building next door, the great Cass Gilbert building of 1915. The new wing achieves harmony through both contrast and analogy with the old building, both in its form and its symbols. The stylized Ionic column is an incident as you circulate within and around the building. That was certainly one of the first representations of a classical order in late modern architecture, but it appropriately does not take itself too seriously.

BLDD: Are there any of your buildings that you think will be forgotten, or any *you* would like to forget?

RV: I imagine all architects have some they want to forget about. It's usually the fault of the client or of too small a budget, of course.

BLDD: Ada Louise Huxtable has described your firm's contribution as "beyond debate" and has said that it passes the one conclusive test of art and history: as a result of your work we are never going to look at the world the same again. That is very high praise, particularly from such a respected source. How *should* we be looking at the world today?

RV: We should look at it with very open eyes, and we should be both tolerant *and* critical. As an architect you have to have some kind of love and enthusiasm for your time; you have to be part of it and work from within it. At the same time you have to be critical of your time in order to enhance or focus it. So you have to be respectful *and* disrespectful of your era. That's the way we were with Las Vegas. We loved it and we hated it. This kind of love-hate relationship can be healthy for an artist. Observing one's environment and involving one's environment, working within it and working against it are all important.

DSB: A sense of irony helps, although that's something you really develop only as you reach middle age.

BLDD: What do you mean by a sense of irony?

DSB: One way to meld respect for, love for, and criticism of your age is through irony. With a sense of irony you can laugh rather than cry about the phenomena you both hate and love.

RV: I think one of the problems of the early modernists was that they would have none of that. They were evangelists who spoke the gospel. They detested a lot and admired little. They were reformers, but they were not receptive, which is one of the most important things for an artist to be. Artists must learn from many sources, including the ordinary—the ordinary can lead you beautifully to the extraordinary.

BLDD: In a lecture at Harvard you said that architects are still too tied to dogma despite their breaking away from the restraints of the International Style. Has postmodernism now become too much of a dogma?

RV: Yes, I think it has. *Plus ça change, plus c'est la même chose.* The postmodernists may use pink, green, and other pastels instead of white, but they are still dogmatic and ideological. They see only one way—their kind of neoclassicism, which comes out of their limited perspective more than the multifarious circumstances of their time. They are still modern architects big on unity, with a yen for the universal; they're bent on an International Style, this time in pastels. We're living in a time of intense communication that promotes unity in one sense, but there is a concurrent trend of people trying to acknowledge and understand their own heritage, their own unique qualities. This is a time when heterogeneity reigns over homogeneity, eclecticism over neoclassicism, when many kinds of symbolism and formal systems can be employed in architecture. But the postmodernists don't get it.

BLDD: Sir Hugh Casson, the director of the Royal Institute of British Architects, once referred to the nineteenth-century architect Colen Campbell, who designed Burlington House, as "the Venturi of his time." Did you ever imagine your name would be so invoked?

RV: I think you just do your job. That's really what a good artist must do. You must want to work, to sit down and do the best you can when you get the opportunity. That's really the best approach.

BLDD: If you were to start over again, what would you do differently?

RV: Be rich!

DSB: That's too abstract a question for me. If I had tried to do something differently, something worse would probably have happened!

JAMES WINES

As the president and cofounder of SITE, the architectural and environmental arts organization known for its exploration of innovative, often shocking ideas for buildings and public spaces, James Wines combines the vision of an artist with the pragmatism of an architect.

BLDD: You were born in Chicago, one of the country's architectural vital organs. How did your early observations or experiences in Chicago influence your later involvement in architecture?

JW: Almost anyone brought up in Chicago has a heavy dose of exposure to its architectural legacy. I was brought up in Oak Park, where Frank Lloyd Wright buildings sprout like trees. So much of even the best Chicago architecture prior to Wright's time was still European derived, but Wright used the American landscape as his source and really made architecture into an American statement. His liberation of architecture was an early influence on me. Also, I suppose the idea that buildings like Wright's could generate dialogue and controversy was an inspirational incentive. For example, to this day my mother still sees Wright's domestic architecture as "those buildings that ruined the neighborhood." Wright's challenge came in plunking down these structures right in the midst of fairly conventional, turn-of-the-century houses. This notion of architecture as a focus of controversy, which SITE has also been connected with—intentionally or not—may have influenced my views on the role of architecture as a public art. Surely one of Wright's accomplishments was to change architecture from something people reacted to passively into something people could really get excited about or find reason to comment on.

BLDD: You graduated from Syracuse University in New York with a degree in sculpture and art history. Then for more than ten years you lived in Rome and worked with a sculptor, exhibiting your work in London and New York. A number of your works of that period were commissioned for large-scale architectural settings. If the large-scale architecture projects that you do now should be considered art, what did you see as the role of the buildings that housed your sculpture?

JW: That's a really good question, because I think the issue of sculpture versus architecture was the turning point in my conceptual development. It always seemed to me that contemporary architects dealt with artists only in a token way, asking them to provide merely an object in a setting, bringing them in after the fact to embellish, to add a decorative element, to "humanize" a space, or to perform whatever specific service the artist was expected to deliver. But the existing historical context in Italy was conceptually and aesthetically exactly the opposite—art and architecture were synonymous. So there I was, working in a situation where my everyday experience was this unified aesthetic but being asked to produce an assortment of token amenities for architecture. I came to feel that somehow there had to be more to the relationship between art and architecture. When I returned to the United States, I was still doing architectural sculpture, but that lingering memory of Italy remained, that incredible legacy of architecture as an integral part of its context and art as an integral part of architecture. It left an indelible imprint on my aesthetic subconscious.

The U.S. was also experiencing the beginning of the environmental art movement. I became friends with people I admired, like Gordon Matta-Clark and Alice Aycock. During the late 1960s and early 1970s a number of artists around New York were engaged in an intense dialogue about the future of sculpture in an outdoor context, sculpture *as*, rather than simply *in*, a context. Many artists were also becoming interested in architecture. Architecture itself was in the process of becoming an extension of art and the second interest of artists, because it gave one the public scale that traditional sculpture had never provided. The next step for me was to simply realize that buildings are the only intrinsic public art. When you build a work of architecture, the need for it is implicit. You don't have to self-consciously plunk it down like a piece of sculpture. The public, too, acknowledges the organic and natural existence of a building. It looks inevitable in its place. When you place a work of art in a public space you always feel it has come from someone's studio. The sensibility for working in interiors is totally different from the public sensibility needed to work outside. Even when you put a bad building down, it still performs as a needed artifact.

BLDD: That's very generous of you.

JW: Yes, I know—too generous, considering the proliferation of bad buildings.

BLDD: How have these experiences affected the nature of your present work?

JW: The basic innovation of SITE's work is our fundamentally different perspective on architecture, the notion of architecture as the subject matter of art, rather than the traditional notion of architecture as the objective of a design process. Whereas most architects think of a building as a product to be totally designed, SITE approaches architecture as something that, in effect, has already been designed. It is just information to be recycled through an art-making process and sensibility. Even if we do design a building in terms of its practical functions, we still treat this information as if it were elements of a found object, as a collagist painter might take a series of prefabricated ingredients or common objects and assemble them into a new reality. SITE uses the rhetorical notion of a building as the raw material for art. If you took away, for instance, all of the innovative aspects of our buildings you would find that they are nothing but mundane prototypes of certain kinds of structures. A house we are doing now is almost a ranch house, but it's not quite like any ranch house you have ever seen. Another example would be some of our buildings for Best Products, which stand as nothing more than the most ordinary shopping center warehouses. There is nothing exotic about them in terms of architectural design. They exist as common objects, identifiable almost by reflex on the highways of America. They are typologically familiar, commonplace, acceptable. In each of our Best projects we always depended upon the fact that people would just walk up to them and say, "I know what kind of building this is."

BLDD: In what ways does your work differ from that of an architecture firm?

JW: It's a question of attitude and viewpoint. Considering architecture as subject matter is a lot different from considering it as a design problem. Design and art imply very different states of intention. Generally architects begin with the problem of orchestrating the services of a building in terms of space planning. Whatever the aesthetic contributions might be, the manipulations of form thereafter are usually at the service of some sacred notion of function. Architects are generally delighted by working out a stairway that both services a room effectively and looks like a piece of abstract sculpture. SITE's alternative would be to put in the most mundane stairway possible and then take a unique look at the entire idea of a stairway, to make it serve the subconscious, while still giving people access between two floors.

BLDD: SITE became a corporation in 1970. What inspired you to incorporate at that time?

JW: SITE started as a theoretical group growing out of environmental art. We had a lot of ideas we wanted to publish and we set up originally as a nonprofit corporation so we could get grants to produce pamphlets and books.

BLDD: Did you get any?

JW: Yes, we did. Strangely enough it was less difficult then than it is now, when grants to support new ventures have pretty much dried up. Then it was fairly easy—or at least easier—because there were a number of emerging nonprofit corporations of interest with experimental missions, and the National Endowment for the Arts and the New York State Council on the Arts had just gone into action. These endeavors

had a special kind of charisma surrounding them. You could even go to a private foundation with some real hope of securing funding. For example, we got support from the Rockefeller Foundation, the Graham Foundation, the Noble Foundation, the Kress Foundation, and others.

BLDD: Was that important to your beginnings?

JW: Of course. It was the basis of our survival because it started us out and gave us the opportunity to look into theoretical matters. SITE came out of that combative discourse of the 1960s that dealt with the mutual roles of art and architecture. Finally SITE got its first job. This was a renovation for Best Products—we actually had something to build. Our first patrons were Sydney and Frances Lewis, the chairman and vice president of Best. They simply said, "Why don't you operate on one of our buildings?" The first project was for an existing structure. We experimented with a number of ideas and finally built the Peeling Building. We asked ourselves, Why try to design these buildings, since they are already designed, in effect? Why not try to bring in another psychological ingredient that might be more interesting than merely designing a building or adding public art? This was the beginning, and it led to a series of Best Products buildings, a theme with variations. The prototype was a fixed entity that could be dealt with environmentally or sociologically. We chose various themes—building and unbuilding, fragmentation, kineticism, commentary on consumer culture—developing architecture as extensions of various ideas or as reactions to the immediate world. We explored buildings as a kind of theater. But we were getting increasingly involved with architecture, and less so with environmental art. When we decided to expand our enterprises we were joined by architects. Soon we were clearly an architectural firm. Somehow it all came together.

BLDD: You've referred several times to "we." You founded SITE with artist Alison Sky. How did the two of you come together? In the creation of SITE, were you responding to a perceived need?

JW: We started with a dialogue and, of course, a personal interest in each other. We became a couple, started talking a lot about ideas. She had been doing concrete poetry and conceptual art and I had been doing large-scale constructivist sculpture, but we both felt these areas had dried up for us. We were dissatisfied with the scale and the lack of communication to a wide audience. We started to get interested in architecture, which had been pretty inactive conceptually since the formative years of modernism. In 1910 lots of ideas in architecture exploded with a new energy, but since the 1930s everything seemed to be basically a rehash of earlier ideas. Unlike art, which went through a series of important revolutions and continued to be vital, architecture had stood still. At the time that we became interested in architecture, it seemed to offer a good potential for new directions. In 1970 Michelle Stone joined us. She was interested in helping us publish some of these ideas. We started a series of magazines and books called "On Site," which dealt with subjects like conceptual architecture, energy, environmental art, philosophical issues, and ended with a book called *Unbuilt America,* which recorded two hundred years of architectural ideas that never got off the ground. Then Emilio Sousa, an architect, joined SITE and suggested we put together an architectural production division to produce working drawings for buildings. The organization grew from there.

BLDD: What surprises have there been for you in the evolution of your unique organization?

JW: It's all been surprises. I think if we had known how difficult it would be to survive, none of us would have em-

Paz Building, Brooklyn, N.Y., rendering

barked on this enterprise. It is insane to persist in the face of so many reasons not to. We wanted to experiment in a field that does not welcome much experimentation, especially when it comes to questioning the basic purposes or aesthetic principles. The surprises have come, first of all, in the fact that SITE ever managed to get anything built to begin with. Sometimes when a project is under construction, I'm amazed that we are actually being permitted to proceed. The other surprise has been how limited the market is for creative services, even once you are famous and successful. I was a participant in a conference about five years ago where a number of the now most famous architects were in assembly. We estimated that the total amount of enclosed space we had all built up to that moment proved to be less than that in one SOM skyscraper. That really gives you pause. It makes you wonder what the hell you are doing.

BLDD: What *are* you doing? How would you describe it?

JW: I don't exactly know. Fortunately SITE has acquired some very interesting and patient clients, but I often feel that, collectively, none of us know what we are doing. The joy of it has been that our clients have been so broad-minded and supportive that the issue doesn't seem important.

BLDD: Who have been some of your clients?

JW: Now, for example, we are doing an office building for the Hasidic community in Williamsburg, New York. It is a study in contrasts. On one hand the Hasidic religious life is pious and ritualized; on the other hand, the people have an ability to deal practically with the secular world. This duality, the fact that

they have so successfully reconciled these two worlds, makes them exciting clients from the outset. In a way, SITE engages only with their economic life, since their whole creative life is their religion and its rituals and scholarship.

BLDD: How do you envision this Hasidic office building?

JW: This project includes the conversion of a 1904 YMCA building in Williamsburg into commercial space for offices, a health club, a bank, and a *glatt* kosher restaurant. The new building will, in effect, emerge from the old structure, but we also have to respect the many rituals and traditions of the people of the community. The health club, for example, will be difficult because men and women cannot be in the building together. The entire space has to be oriented for occupancy at different times. As far as the aesthetic concept is concerned, SITE's idea will deal with the spirit of the enterprise and its level of public communication. Our project will be about Williamsburg in a state of renewal, the cultural contrasts of the immediate neighborhood (the combination of Hasidic and Hispanic lifestyles, for example), and the dualities of Hasidic existence. This theme of dualism seems to be the dominant and unifying concept so far. Since everything is a duality in Hasidic life—religious/secular, meat/dairy, black/white, open/closed, practical/pious, and so on—we decided to celebrate these contrasts through architecture. Even though Hasidim are turned inward in terms of religious contemplation, they are also extremely visible because of their way of dressing. You can spot a Hasidic five blocks away. They have also reconciled a life dedicated to the Torah with the survival necessities of political and economic life. SITE's work often deals with conflicts and paradoxes, so this project seemed like a natural. I think we could make a genuine contribution to the community with this project. I can't think of a group of people I have ever liked more in terms of their spirit and what they are trying to accomplish. I am amazed by the fact that while they are a very protective and private people, we have learned so much from each other.

BLDD: How important is it for you to steep yourself in their religion? Do you know anything about it?

JW: I was very curious, obviously. SITE always does a very thorough site and community analysis before starting to develop ideas for a building, an analysis that is probably more psychological than physical, since all of our ideas come out of a dialogue with the people of a particular location. Even the Forest Building for Best Products in Richmond, Virginia, evolved out of a general sentiment of the community, which felt that if we destroyed the existing trees on the property, the showroom would be very unpopular. So SITE made the trees integral to the idea, an intrinsic part of the architecture. We hope that through this kind of sensitivity to community interests, we will erect structures that will provoke thought—even controversy—but will still be in harmony with the instinctual wishes of the neighborhood. In the case of the Hasidim of Williamsburg, it was very important to incorporate ideas, directly and indirectly, from their religious life. We did a good deal of homework on rituals and customs. This attention to details and sources other than architectural form and tradition is characteristic of how SITE works.

BLDD: How does the community react to your process?

JW: So far communities have never been a problem in terms of negative reactions. Nobody ever asks us how we got *that* built, implying that we shouldn't have been allowed to, although they sometimes question how we got it through the building department. If there has been a difficulty, it has invariably been voiced by a conservative architect who happened to be sitting on a selection panel, a review board, or a building department advisory group—a professional who felt threatened or competitive, who was being protective of his own interests and didn't want a SITE structure going up in his town. He would always find petty reasons to delay our acceptance or proper permits and, in one outrageous case, prevented us from continuing on a park project and then ripped off our idea and built his own modified version. Fortunately, because of the influence of very supportive clients, we have managed to get some things constructed. Once our clients get started, they don't want to stop.

BLDD: Has your most significant client been Best Products, your best known one?

JW: The Lewises of Best Products were the pioneers who took the first long-shot chance on SITE. But they are unique among clients; they are more patrons than clients. In fact, they generally hire us and then simply show up on the opening day of the building to see what we have accomplished. They just toss us the ball and tell us to call them when the concept is complete. Most architectural clients don't have that kind of confidence and constantly question what we are doing all along the way. The Lewises are a rare case—patrons with enough confidence in their judgment in hiring an architect to also trust his talents to produce something exceptional. They like to be challenged, as opposed to merely confirming what they already know. We have had the other kind of client as well, the kind whose endless questions and intrusions can destroy the very creative process they are paying for in the first place. Usually these projects remain on the drawing board.

BLDD: How many buildings did you do for Sydney and Frances Lewis?

JW: Eight—two renovations and six new buildings.

BLDD: How did you first come to work with them?

JW: The Lewises have always been active in the arts. Alison and I were circulating in the art world in the early 1970s and we became friendly with them—I had already known them as personal friends some years before. At that time their catalogue/showroom business was beginning to expand and they had to build new showrooms. We really hit the beginning of the building boom of that company. The Lewises were both art collectors and extremely astute businesspeople. They seemed to see the potential of using their corporation as a living extension of their art interests. There have been some poorly researched critiques of the Lewises and Best Products suggesting they used art strictly to promote business. It sure didn't hurt business, but their early patronage of SITE, for instance, was an act of such courage and caused such critical controversy in the beginning—even within their own company—that it had to be a much more idealistic mission than mere commercialism. The Lewises intuitively understood that Best Products, as an entity, could become the subject matter for art. They were great collectors of Pop art, so they had a familiarity with the concept of common objects and commercial products becoming the raw material of art.

We stopped building for Best a few years ago during the period of high interest rates, but now they seem to be starting again and have called us in. What I would really like to do now,

Forest Building for Best Products, Henrico, Va.

in addition to their showrooms, is to pursue some other ideas for totally different types of buildings.

BLDD: They've done enough of the showrooms, you think?

JW: The first group of showrooms stands as a total work in itself, a collective work, or a theme and variations. If you consider the innovations within that context, I think we accomplished something pretty impressive. These projects set us off in many different directions—dealing with nature as an invading force, fragmentation, process as finished building, sculpture as a commentary on architecture, architecture as theater—a lot of issues we might not have had a chance to experiment with otherwise. This, in turn, expanded our vision of what was possible in architecture. We got into the habit of thinking of buildings in a nonformalist, narrative, metaphorical way. It's rare to be given that kind of mandate from a client.

BLDD: Now that you may be starting a new chapter with them, what do you think their next direction should be?

JW: I really wish the Lewises would do a museum or some kind of personal monument that SITE could be involved in. I think they are presently working with Hardy Holzman Pfeiffer on an extension of the Virginia Museum to house their furniture collection. But they also have a collection of several thousand works of art that needs a home, and I am hoping that they will want to build an even bigger museum somewhere else.

BLDD: How would you characterize the fusion of art and architecture that you're trying to achieve? Which elements from each field are retained? Which are dropped?

JW: That varies with each project. Clearly, sometimes we are dealing with art as a kind of commentary on architecture. Other times it's more like art invading architecture, or architecture invading art. What makes our view quite different from that of, say, Richard Serra, Mark di Suvero, or other artists who create public works is that we really are not interested in making identifiable objects that can be defined as "the art" and other, larger objects that can be defined as "the architecture." We are not interested in such formalist issues as directionals in space or scaling geometric shapes in response to certain similar forms on a building. We are interested in the more abstract and subconscious psychology with which people arrive in a public situation or confront a building. We use that information as the raw material for both art and architecture, or a fusion of the two. It is the *attitude toward* a building that integrates our art with our architecture. It is integrated by a narrative or allusive process, more than a specifically physical one. But SITE has not been alone in this direction. Gordon Matta-Clark, who "operated" on buildings, and Bob Smithson, with works like *Buried Shed,* dealt with the issue of architecture as a raw material. Scott Burton, in his furniture, also works in this never-never land suspended between art and design, a situation where design is the subject matter.

BLDD: Are there collaborations between architects and artists that you think have been particularly successful?

JW: Truly successful collaborations respond to the larger needs of a community and reflect a universal agreement in what constitutes a communicative imagery. In this epoch I think it is very hard to bond people together with any single philosophy or mission. Nothing seems universal anymore. Everything is fragmented, disparate, and pluralistic. Great collaborations have always come out of situations where there was a church or state with a universal mandate. There was a central idea or philosophy to be celebrated that took precedence over all of the potential petty interests of self-expression and ego (which, of course, plague most contemporary attempts at cooperation between artists and architects). Artists and architects in the twelfth century were unified by a sense of communal purpose, so the final work implied a natural collaboration from the outset.

BLDD: Are there any specific examples that inspire you?

JW: Gothic cathedrals, naturally. These were inspired collaborative projects that required the dedication of communities for hundreds of years. They were successful because people were collectively inspired by the celebration of their religion. Collaboration was implicit. No one felt sociologically or psychologically separated from the total effort. Our society is too fragmented now to inspire that kind of cooperation between artists and architects.

BLDD: SITE's work has been described by some critics as an endeavor to get rid of architecture altogether. What is your response to that assessment?

JW: Certainly a number of our works have been humorous commentaries on architecture. Many architects feel that buildings are too serious to be treated in a cavalier manner or as a "throw-away" ingredient. But all advanced art is a critique of conservative art, so SITE's efforts are merely part of a long legacy of change. Since we are not applauding architecture for its own sake, in a sense we must be breaking it down. Metaphorically, at least, I guess one could say we are trying to get rid of architecture. SITE's work has generated a certain amount of hostility over the years, but I think a lot of that has subsided now. I have always thought of Arthur Drexler at the Museum of Modern Art as a supreme arbiter of status in architecture; it seems that without his endorsement, one could be assigned to oblivion forever. He took a long time to notice SITE, but I think I can safely say that he now views us with cautious acceptance. We found out we really could get along when he realized that we admire so many of the same architectural heroes, Mies van der Rohe in particular.

BLDD: What caused SITE's shift to a more architectural focus?

JW: The belief that buildings are the most natural part of the real world and the best vehicle for creating public art. I would find it very difficult now to be assigned a plaza without also being given the building to work on. I can't separate these things because I want to be involved with every aspect of a context. I am not sure SITE's work is understood generally by colleagues and critics. The view still persists that SITE does facades or environmental art when, in fact, we have been working recently on some of the most complex of architectural solutions. During the environmental art movement many artists produced large-scale architectural works. But their creations exist primarily as objects imposed on a space, without the larger sociological implications associated with actual buildings.

BLDD: For the past decade SITE has been celebrated as being on the cutting edge of conceptual and experimental architecture. Was that your intention when you first started out?

JW: More so than it is now. To a certain extent we came out of the ideas and attitudes of the conceptual art movement in the late 1960s. At that time one wasn't supposed to "produce" art—it was considered almost obscene to do something that showed the artist's hand. So we tended toward "idea" architecture, as opposed to "made" architecture. For a few years Alison and I spent most of our time writing and publishing pamphlets and treatises. There was a lot of support then for an idea-oriented architecture as an alternative to the commodity architecture being turned out by developers. We were a little self-conscious about it all because we wanted to assert the difference between sculptural/formal design and what we were trying to accomplish. Now we are much more relaxed with the whole polemic and not as dogmatic as in the early seventies.

BLDD: You've said in the past that when you first began, there seemed no reason beyond academic convenience for the use of such geometric elements as cubes, cones, spheres, and cylinders or such historic elements as columns, pediments, and arches. What did you propose as a substitute?

JW: What I was saying, in effect, was that there is a kind of architecture-school version of design that has traditionally judged the success of all buildings by how cleverly these ingredients have been used. I was making a case for a reexamination of the virtues of the simple rectangular enclosure, the unarticulated box that is both practical and allows a lot of wall space to carry the ideas, references, and associations that give a building meaning. These views relate back to an artist like Duchamp, who liberated art from the prejudices of limited definitions. He expanded ideas through a series of reductions. By removing the craft and formal composition skills from painting and sculpture, he opened them up to other meanings and potentials. Similarly, if you think of architecture only as a composite of formal means, only as a building, then you are leaving out a whole range of ideas and sources. Duchamp's most progressive concept was to assume that you can create art without making a crafted artifact, that you can just assign art value to something and, in time, the audience will accept this redefinition. Duchamp placed certain objects in rooms almost as semaphores of information. In the beginning, they were denounced by the public as "not art." But if something is placed in a legitimate art context, it takes on the characteristics of art and eventually becomes as much a part of the definition of art as even the most conventional productions.

BLDD: How have your ideas about the use of formal elements evolved since that early period?

JW: We view them quite differently, in a more relaxed way. When we started out the mere mention of formalism gave Alison and me a spasm of apoplexy. Now we use whatever we deem necessary to communicate an idea. We recently completed a concept for the Frankfurt Museum of Modern Art competition in which we clearly use historical references. But in no sense did we approach these references in a decorative, postmodernist way. Someone like Charles Moore, because his work is about sculptural form, would have tried to create new shapes and contours based on history and interpretive of history. The winning entry for this competition by Hans Hollein is a supreme example of this interpretive approach and, of course, the opposite of everything SITE's work is about. SITE's treatment of this project allowed the ambience to invade the exterior and the interior of the building in the most psychological and informational way, but the actual forms used to convey ideas were selected because of their commonplace characteristics. Decorative surfaces and pretty forms had nothing to do with our approach.

BLDD: You've used several convenient labels to identify various movements—postmodernism, formalism. What label would you apply to your firm?

JW: There really isn't a label as such. We have used the term "de-architecture," but this is just a phrase of our own and related more to a philosophical position.

BLDD: What does it mean?

JW: It implies a different perspective toward architecture. If you take away or subtract from something, you are both disintegrating and redefining it. We hope that our "de-architecture" will establish new definitions. We deconstruct traditional axioms, methods, and attitudes to arrive at altered meanings. "De-architecture" is a conceptual tool. Since SITE is a firm that deals with socio-psychological content, we felt the need of a method of evaluation. One critic, early on, called our work "arch-art," and there have been a lot of such labels applied to the work of SITE. Although labels are convenient, we rather hope we can escape this limitation. With the general discontent expressed now about postmodernism and the deluge of facile spin-offs, it goes without saying that in the next few years there will be a combination of backlash and future-oriented changes in architecture that will make the whole label and movement passé. All the ins will be outs. This is tragic; I would rather circumvent such trauma.

BLDD: Can you describe the process of designing a typical SITE project? How are responsibilities divided?

JW: Alison Sky and I are the conceptual side of the group. We usually put our heads together, working very closely in digesting information and bringing the many ideas and attitudes we might have about a situation into focus. We make notes, jot down impressions in the form of sketches, discuss endlessly. When the germ of the idea for a project seems ready, we share it with everyone else on the architectural team to get their reaction and input on its feasibility, what method of design development should be used, and so on. We have an incredible group of people in our office now and they bring valuable insights.

BLDD: How large is your group?

JW: It fluctuates around ten or twelve. We have a core of main contributors who have been with us for a while. Even our bookkeeper is a contributing member in terms of insights. Michelle Stone is the partner primarily in charge of developing new business and taking care of ongoing survival. However, she will often walk into a creative session where we have been laboring with an unresolved idea for days and offer some astute observation that encapsulates what we should have been thinking about. Alison and I usually do the early conceptual sketches and models that define the general direction of a project. But, as I said, we have a very interactive group. John DeVitry works on interior planning and design development. Josh Weinstein is primarily in charge of working drawings, but he also uses this technical process as part of design development and has come up with innumerable innovations that have strengthened concepts. We all bounce ideas off one another. When it comes to presenting an idea to a client, John DeVitry is a master at reassuring clients that everything will be O.K., that they won't be shunned by neighbors or run off the block if they build an unusual structure. The basis of the working process is that all of the main people at SITE are tuned into a central sustained sensibility.

BLDD: There must be advantages as well as limitations to the kind of close collaboration, professional and personal, that you have had with Alison Sky during the life of your organization.

JW: The biggest advantage is that we have become totally integrated in terms of the flow of ideas and the completion of projects. The problem is that Alison and I are never free of work.

BLDD: Do you take your work home with you?

JW: Always, and that's definitely a disadvantage. Work is everpresent in our lives. We never seem to be able to take off without some overriding guilt or compulsion to do "just a little more work" on this or that. Neither of us can go home and complain about a hard day's work, since we have usually had the same day. Two people in different professions can come home, complain, maybe even have a little healthy argument about who had the worse day; at least they have had different days and, in the end, can wind up sympathetic to each other. In our case, we take every problem right into the home. We have to conscientiously try to cut it off—usually without much

Inside/Outside Building for Best Products, Milwaukee, Wis.

success. Often one of us will have a sudden revelation in the middle of the night and want to share the idea, while the other wants to sleep. On the other hand, the spirit of collaboration can be very exhilarating, especially when we are both on a roll, when things are unfolding in rapid succession. There is no excitement like this process. These are truly high moments— that period of inspiration and idea development. It's the first of several highs in the process. There is also the period when a building is about three-quarters constructed, when you are impressed with your ability to move things along this far. It's usually not until the project is finished that you become depressed—that's when you see everything you did wrong. The self-critique is very painful, but it makes you want to start on something else that will be better.

BLDD: You both have such singular ideas. Is it ever difficult for you to accept some of hers?

JW: We're so homogenized at this point that it's very hard to say. It's like a bottle in which the cream has blended with the milk.

BLDD: When you have a really strong difference of opinion, whose viewpoint prevails?

JW: On questions of sensibility and aesthetics, we really don't ever have arguments. We both instinctively know when a concept is right or wrong. When a project is going badly we may discuss its failures, but it isn't like an argument or a critique. A few years ago we had some employees whose contribution to projects was always the staged critique. These critiques became arguments in the stupidest and most unproductive way because they were not based on an understanding of the objectives or the sensibility. These employees are long gone, but the situation did impress me with the fact that Alison and I never really argue—and certainly not on this pedestrian critique level. We are always bound up in the optimism of the final objective and, however painful and difficult the process, all of our dialogue is constructed toward this objective. The only things we get distressed about are projects that are clearly not resolved, and even then we always agree on this fact. We know when ideas are not connected to larger meanings. I am sure this is a situation common to collaborative people of all kinds—rock and roll bands and filmmakers all have the same procedural problems.

BLDD: Is there such a thing as a typical SITE project?

JW: Since an inordinate amount of publicity has attended a very small portion of our work, to the general public there is probably a certain image attached to our work. I notice that critics have used the term "SITE-like" when referring to certain ideas in other people's work. This usually boils down to some category of fragmentation, since this is a persistent theme in our work. But considering our range of built and unbuilt projects, that is just one of a number of recurrent themes. The press coverage has been both an advantage and a disadvantage. On one hand it made us famous, but on the other, it pigeonholed us as architects who do shopping centers, funny buildings, conceptual art, or whatever. Taking into account everything we have designed and are in the process of designing, I don't think these limited SITE profiles hold up very well. We have dealt with a wide range of projects.

BLDD: How wide?

JW: Now we seem to be doing one of everything—a private house, an apartment, an office building, a fast-food restaurant, clothing showrooms for Williwear, a new Best Products showroom in Milwaukee.

BLDD: Is there a typical SITE client?

JW: Usually our clients have a certain sympathy with the arts, but even that isn't necessarily true now. We used to attract collectors who happened to be in some form of real estate. Now we have clients who are only peripherally interested in art, although we hope to increase their awareness as the projects proceed. Our client is usually a person with inherent imagination and courage. After all, architecture is a big investment and stands in the public domain as a statement about the owner. Our work is not for the faint of heart to undertake. We work very closely with clients; it is often their intimate feelings and observations that form the substance of our ideas. We need a forthright and self-assured person to share the kind of information we need. In almost every case recently the final concept has been triggered by something the client said. In the final analysis we build as an extension of the client's notions about the world, but interpreted in a sometimes inverse way. We are presently dealing with a residential client who looked at the pictures of our former work on the walls of the office and remarked, "I don't want anything like that!"

BLDD: So why did they come to you?

JW: They came through the recommendation of someone who told them we were innovative.

BLDD: So they are pushing themselves as well?

JW: The clients are a couple with a sense of adventure and strong egos. They told us that they definitely did not want the loudest house in the neighborhood, that they did not want to attract an inordinate amount of attention. But they also didn't want to thwart our creativity. We encouraged them to keep talking at our initial meeting and prodded them for more information on what kind of house they were looking for. Finally they said, "You know what I think we really want? I think we want an invisible house." My answer was, "You've got it." We proceeded on that premise, and it's diametrically opposed to everything that the Best Products high-profile stores were about. And yet it is, in my view, equally unusual.

BLDD: One SITE project that has received widespread attention is the Highrise of Homes. Could you describe this unique concept?

JW: The Highrise of Homes is a concept that emerged out of a dialogue Alison and I initiated during a charrette we had conducted with some students. We eventually dismissed it as somewhat silly and put it away in a drawer. But somehow the memory and the implications persisted in our minds, so we decided to reinstate it for investigation. There had, after all, been a series of historical precedents, such as Le Corbusier's Algiers housing proposal and several Victorian individualized high-rise projects. But to our knowledge nobody had ever approached the multistory matrix in what Duchamp referred to as the "canned chance" frame of reference. Our concept became more serious and evolved into something like a game of chess. The final structure was supposed to be like a chessboard, where certain rules must be respected but the choices are infinite. The matrix provides the typology of the building—the typical urban condominium—while paradoxically offering another kind of living environment—the suburban tract house or other kinds of freestanding houses. Since traditional architects can't usually deal with paradox, hybridism, inversion, chance, and the potential for the inhabitants' self-expression, they hated this proposal with a vengeance. Everything they detested was the essence of the project's innovation. They felt it "had no design." Certainly the Highrise of Homes is not "designed" in the old modernist sense of the term. It is the idea of seeing what happens that makes it intriguing. The most interesting inquiry someone posed was, "What if every tenant decides to build in a colonial style? Wouldn't that ruin the project?" My answer was that it would on one level, but that if the architect maintained the true Duchampian attitude, this outcome would be a perfect fulfillment of the goals of the project. Duchamp commented that the breaking of his *Large Glass* made it better than ever. The notion of surprise, even to the artist who created the work, is the essence of the Highrise of Homes. It transfers the emphasis in architecture from controlled design to a condition of infinite choices.

BLDD: Do you see the project at this point as primarily a fantasy—a paper statement—or as a workable option?

JW: It's definitely not only paper architecture. It is a workable option, especially for the adaptive reuse of old factory struc-

Highrise of Homes, drawing

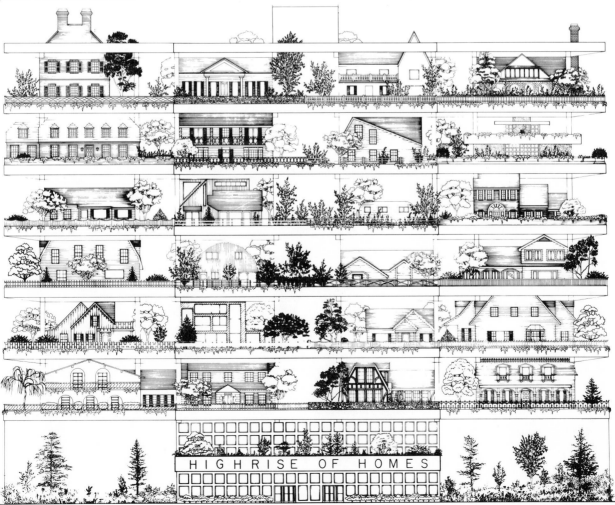

HIGHRISE OF HOMES

tures that occupy central space in practically every city in this country and are usually destroyed. SITE's work is different from that of past conceptual architects. We have always intended to build our ideas. We may not build something for reason of cancellation or lack of funding, but the intention to build is inherent in everything we produce. It is that intention that has kept our work alive. When students and scholars go back through our drawings they often remark, "I didn't know you designed that!" Their surprise is always based on the perception of SITE's work as ultimately buildable. That is the tension that generates the interest.

BLDD: You have said that your work differs from that of other architects because you treat architecture as a subject matter. But you also create structures. How do you make certain that the art you create is structurally sound?

JW: For one thing, we work with good structural engineers, like Matthys Levy at Weidlinger. But also our structures don't really deal with anything that requires an inordinate amount of experimental engineering, with the exception, perhaps, of the tilted wall in the Best showroom in Towson, Maryland. There we floated 450 tons of concrete block, so it required some innovative structural work. But the way I see it, more conventional architects and engineers have built life-endangering disasters in the past few years than any of the recognized "creative" architects have perpetrated. We have just designed a commemorative McDonald's restaurant for Berwyn, Illinois, the home town of the chain's founder, Ray Kroc. According to

Weidlinger, this is the most complex example of small-building engineering their firm has encountered. The structure is built in such a way that the parts of a standard McDonald's are dislodged and suspended in space a few feet above the ground, although all of the corporation's instant symbols of identification are kept intact. The actual engineering needed to accomplish this feat was quite extraordinary.

BLDD: You've said that it's the arbitrary or fragmentary aspects of urban life today that constitute its true vitality. What do you mean by that?

JW: This was a symbolic way of stating that SITE's work is the opposite of formalized architecture. Even the most die-hard glass-and-steel-tower advocates would have to admit that the tendency to overdesign has been a major cause of the decline of interest and, indeed, quality of life in this country's urban centers. All but the most fascist and intractable of designers have to finally concede that diversity is the only ingredient that makes a city livable. The modern movement's insistence on clarity, technology, functionalism—all of those organizational mandates—has led to dismal failure for most people. These ideas have benefitted the members of corporate board rooms whose interests are clearly served by organizing everything to their convenience, but the visual and psychological results have been a disaster unparalleled in architecture history.

BLDD: In your attempts to do away with design control, so to speak, and conventional good taste, how do you avoid bad taste and trivia, or a kind of Disneyland?

Floating McDonald's Restaurant, Berwyn, Ill.

Indeterminate Facade Showroom for Best Products, Houston, Tex.

JW: What we do is change or reinterpret the meaning of "design control" so that it doesn't end up looking like design control. I have a feeling that most people who are in a position to react to architecture know the difference. It is the difference, for example, between junk lying around in someone's basement and the same materials organized into a Rauschenberg assemblage. As for "good taste," however, it is nothing more than a residual of once relevant and dynamic art. Good taste is what lesser talent thinks of as good art. It is a compendium of accepted values and, in this sense, is the death of art. SITE seems to have done something that has already registered with an awful lot of people on many levels. We have used themes like fragmentation, banality, and the junk environment, but I would hope what we have accomplished is to give these sources a new order and a new perspective that is neither oppressive design control nor Disneyland.

I have a favorite story concerning this question of good or bad taste and the condition of acceptance. When the Houston Indeterminate Facade project was first completed, a German magazine interviewed a woman living in a tract house facing the structure and asked her what she thought of the new showroom. She questioned the "good taste" of the structure and also expressed confusion about its appropriateness in the neighborhood. Five years later the same magazine in Germany wanted to conduct another survey to see if the building had been accepted by the surrounding residents. The reporters asked this woman what she would think if Best Products Company decided to straighten out the indeterminate walls. "Oh, I wouldn't like that," she replied. "Then it wouldn't be normal." I feel that this assimilation process is the really important issue here. If the structure had been only an example of Disneyland or trivia, it would have always stood apart from its surroundings as an intrusion. It would never have

communicated the intellectual or aesthetic substance that would have made it acceptable, somehow right.

BLDD: You have been known for your work with students, whose participation on SITE projects you often encourage. What do they get out of working for SITE?

JW: I assume that the benefit is that they are exposed to an open-ended situation they don't get in school. We bring up issues in daily discourse at SITE that are not part of the usual academic environment. We don't use the words, references, and sources that are normally part of an architectural context. We don't refer to architecture-related issues of good taste, good design, formal relationships, harmonious relationships, decorative elements, historical references, modernist principles, articulation of space, and so on. SITE's vocabulary has to do with ambient and sociological elements. We also talk a lot about poetry, performances, current events—practically anything but "good taste" architecture. We are always relating architecture to other arts.

BLDD: What do you get out of working with students?

JW: It keeps us abreast of the times and changing sensibilities. What is nice about having young people around is that sensibilities are emerging all the time and kids are in touch with these changes. Obviously we're all getting along in years and the *enfant terrible* image is no longer applicable to SITE. I don't think we're really in that position any more.

BLDD: You're part of the establishment now?

JW: Probably so.

BLDD: How does that make you feel?

JW: You have more time to deal with the poetry of the profession and don't feel compelled to break ground every ten minutes. I find myself very interested in issues of communication, that is, making architecture more imagistically intense. As I have mentioned, I feel architecture is the ultimate public art, even more so than television if you consider how unavoidable architecture is in our daily lives. People can choose not to buy a television set, yet buildings cannot be removed from our existence for a minute. Even a camping trip includes a form of architecture.

BLDD: You were named chairman of the Department of Environmental Design at Parsons School of Design in 1983. Why did you take the job, and what is this interdisciplinary department about?

JW: The involvement SITE has had with students and education over the years logically led to this decision. I look at all my colleagues who have performed in academia and they seem to have survived it, so I hope I will too. The environmental design branch of the school has had a lot of problems in the past and has been the weakest of all of the departments. It shouldn't be, because architecture and design are among the hottest subjects of the day in terms of general interest. The design fields are making a big impact these days, and I don't think there has been as natural and widespread an interest in any subject as there has been in architecture in the last five or six years. People are still drawn to the visual arts in a big way, but there seems to be a lot of hype needed to sustain it. I think people are genuinely interested in buildings now.

BLDD: Then do you see this as a good period for architecture?

JW: In terms of the energies being focused on creative architecture, yes. The times never feel quite that way while you're living them, though. When you look back at Paris in the 1920s and muse on how wonderful it must have been, you have to also speculate on the possibility that perhaps you would not have been able to discern the magnitude of the creativity. I can't believe how excited people get over the topic of architecture nowadays. It is the expression of this collective energy that is the most important thing of all. The fact that Leon Krier practically punched me out one time at a symposium is an indication that these times are intriguing. The various positions being defended are the basis of all the vitality. I wouldn't have it any other way. This does not mean I agree with even half of what is going on, but I would defend the general excitement with all of my energy. There are sour notes in all of this, though. I went to some occasion—I believe it was at the Institute for Architecture and Urban Studies—where it was "attack Michael Graves night." The body of people organizing the attack were defending over-the-hill issues and were clearly grasping at straws to maintain certain conventions. God knows, I take issue with all of Michael's historic and decorative references, but here he was simply doing the most interesting work because of his unique talent and being blasted by unquestionably inferior talents. I thought to myself, Why not let it be? What is anyone going to do to prevent genuine ability from succeeding? You can't make it go away by sour grapes.

BLDD: Twentieth-century architecture, you've said, has mainly been about formalism, functionalism, rationalism, standardization, and economy, "all of the things," you went on to say, "that make life oppressive and tedious." How can we move beyond the "repetitive reshuffling of volumes and spaces"?

JW: I hope that SITE is making some meaningful moves in that direction. We don't get enough commissions or opportunities to try all of the ideas we have in mental storage. To think that the biggest commission given in the architecture-as-art category has been Michael Graves's Portland building! For SOM that would be a minor civic job. All the fuss made about Graves's structure is because truly interesting buildings are so rare. Think of all of the attention our little shopping center boxes received. Imagine what would happen if SITE got a major urban-scale project to do. It all boils down to the fact that

the architect/artists most capable of investing buildings with a high level of interest and revolutionary aesthetic ideas are the least likely people to get big jobs. There is a vast amount of construction in this country that SITE has no access to because of politics, money, and prejudices about things that are too "artistic" or too controversial.

BLDD: Choice, chance, and change are elements that appear again and again in your statements about your work. How important are these concepts for other contemporary architects?

JW: Not very. Possibly Frank Gehry shares this interest with us. In general, though, I don't think the notion of letting things happen by chance has been implicit in much, if any, architecture under the influence of the modern movement. People like Tigerman and Graves and Stern, as brilliantly talented as they are, perform clearly as formalist designers. They talk of fragmentation, for instance, but as an architectural device, not as a psychological force. Everything in their work boils down to the creation of very determinate shapes. The top priority is always the celebration of architecture itself as a successful orchestration of forms and spaces. Architects, in general, don't feel comfortable with the elements of chance. When Alison and I were driving around L.A. recently, we witnessed how Frank Gehry must have gotten a lot of his ideas for raw, open-frame structures. We saw hundreds of half-finished frame houses near the beach, and Frank must have at one time observed how much more interesting these dwellings are when they are half-finished than when they are complete. But this is clearly an artist's, not an architect's, response. The celebration of the unresolved is not the stuff they teach you in design schools.

BLDD: Do you see your work as representative of innovative architecture today, as something that already has its own conventions and traditions, or as something that's outside of architectural tradition? Where do you place your work in the spectrum of architectural history?

JW: I guess you could say we have our conventions, but I hope our period of innovation is not over yet. Duchamp once said that even a genius usually has not more than three breakthroughs in an entire lifetime and that all the rest is filler between these seminal ideas. I always maintain hope and keep trying. Certainly our major innovation has been the use of architecture as the subject matter of art and the new perspective on the profession that such a commitment implies. It is a concept that is being understood increasingly by younger-generation architects and can be very useful when evaluating how to approach a new project of any kind. But SITE has been working, from the beginning, outside of the mainstream of the architectural profession. Even a casual overview of international architecture magazines is enough to establish the differences. Cubism, rationalism, constructivism, historicism—the same clichés still dominate virtually everything illustrated. Our position outside these influences has created a certain amount of hostility toward our work, but it has also gained us a formidable following. For instance, during the past few years I have contributed information and interviews to about a dozen master's and dissertation papers being done on SITE in universities here and in Europe. I am feeling ever more confident that the misunderstanding of SITE's efforts will become less and less.

BLDD: What do you see as the most crucial issues or the most challenging problems that face architecture in the next decade?

JW: The continuation of an open-ended dialogue and the emphasis on visual diversity are incredibly important issues, lest we again succumb to the notion of architecture as pure functionalism. In terms of practical applications, the emphasis on energy conservation and on housing the people of emerging and Third World countries in economical and attractive shelter are both urgent issues. But diversity is the key word. The ever-increasing homogenization of architecture that has resulted from industrialization and modernist canons of taste has been the most destructive influence. Diversity implies options. Everything does not have to look the same. The pragmatists usually assume that diversity is somehow frivolous, never thinking that enjoyment and mental stimulation are two of the most essential elements of human existence. Functionalism has gotten a bad name because many interpreters have destroyed the most pleasurable aspects in pursuit of the goals of commerce and profits. Pragmatists have a tendency to say, "Let's attack *real* problems," and in the process completely destroy the psychological and aesthetic appeal of what they're building. This is the reason that housing projects begun with humanitarian platitudes end up looking like prison camps. Artists, for their part, remain aloof from these everyday problems because of the sympathy their work finds in an elitist world of patronage. But if we can bring the art attitude, the art mission, into the building industries we can hope for an architecture that is responsive to the most ordinary and nonelitist levels of life, thereby creating this much-needed diversity in our daily environment. This involvement of the arts in life processes is an important mission for the 1980s.

BLDD: In what direction would you like to see future SITE projects and efforts move?

JW: I would like to be a main participant in the open-ended situation I just described. Now, for example, we are very interested in the natural environment. We seem to be dealing increasingly with preservation as an ingredient of aesthetics. There is also the topic of energy to be dealt with. I don't know quite how to use art to communicate the urgency of this issue or, on a more basic level, how to demonstrate practical savings of energy in normal buildings in terms any more meaningful than token gestures. Society has to first face the crisis in realistic terms. Then the financing will become available for architects to make progressive moves in fuel conservation. But just as important is the basic problem of housing people. I am not talking about economical and energy-efficient enclosures that may be admirable from the standpoint of such functions but are visually oppressive in the extreme. I really wish SITE could have a crack at a low-cost housing concept. This is the kind of challenge that would really interest me at this point in SITE's development.

BLDD: Did you expect your life to unfold the way it has?

JW: I think SITE is still in the process of evolving. I would like to live long enough to see how it turns out myself. I would like for SITE to have more and more diversified work. The limitations on the amount and type of work we can do are very distressing. Having a narrow frame of reference to work within forces you to push yourself too hard to generate interesting works and sustain creativity. We don't want to do showrooms and interiors and things like that for the rest of our lives. We want to have something more sociologically challenging.

BLDD: Do you still enjoy it all?

JW: Some days. Some days it is truly exciting. But there are also moments that are unbelievably depressing. We had a wonderful interior project shot down recently because we got ourselves sucked into a situation where the client simply didn't share our interests or enthusiasm from the outset. The demise was really our own fault since we pursued the project in the first place. We tend to think the best of clients and overextend ourselves. Our commitment is a dangerous vulnerability that lets us in for crashing disappointments. You must remember we have had a lot more ideas unbuilt than built over the years. There's no question that architecture can exist on paper; but it has a whole other existence in the reality of construction. To get so near and then not to build is frustrating beyond belief. Every once in a while we get sucked into a project where the person isn't in earnest. It is painful indeed.

BLDD: And, happily, you never learn.

JW: You are right, never!

RICHARD SAUL WURMAN

As a teacher, an urbanist, an architect, a cartographer, and a publisher, Richard Saul Wurman has probably produced more information on the city in the last twenty years than has anyone else in this century.

BLDD: You've been described as an architect, a graphic designer, a writer, a collector and organizer of information—how do *you* describe what you do?

RSW: Once you're trained as an architect, that so infuses your consciousness that when people ask me what I do or what I am—the typical cocktail-party question—the first thing that comes into my mind is that I'm an architect. That's an honest response, since my definition of architecture is very broad.

BLDD: How would you characterize an architect?

RSW: An architect is a person who rigorously and creatively solves problems. In that sense, I'm an architect. What I do is to try to respond to my own ignorance. I find things that I don't know about but that interest me. Then I set out to do a book or an exhibition about those things.

BLDD: One of your favorite terms is the "architecture of information." What do you mean by this phrase?

RSW: In that phrase I'm using the word "architecture" in a creative way, implying an artful patina over life. The "architecture of information" simply means the artful, creative, and performance-oriented structuring of information.

BLDD: How did you learn to manage a body of information so as to simplify it and expand its content at one and the same time?

RSW: It's very easy. It derives from my ignorance. Everything I do comes from my inabilities rather than my abilities. From embracing my ignorance and inabilities, I've come to live with the fact that the only way I can move ahead is to put information in a form that I can handle. That's my life—trying to understand. I know that I will not grow at all except by understanding my failures. These are the only moments of learning—when things don't work. It's when the television set breaks that you find out how to fix it. Success tells you nothing; you learn nothing from success.

BLDD: If there's a subject that you want to find out about, do you then proceed to do your research and eventually share it with other people?

RSW: No. I share it with myself. I don't do things for some audience out there; my measure is always myself. I know that sounds arrogant—it's not what you're supposed to say—but what I try to do is simply to make something understandable for myself. I'm not very smart, but I'm fairly clever. I try to put things in terms that are comprehensible, so that I can walk away and feel a body of information literally coursing through me, so that I truly know something more. I also give in to my emotions. I give in to my fears—my fears of things like disorientation in a strange city, not knowing where I am and how to find something. When I gave speeches I used to suggest that I be introduced this way: "The speaker this evening is Richard Saul Wurman, and he's simple-minded." Then I would try to describe what I meant by simple-minded. I use "simple-minded" as Lou Kahn used the word "dumb," that is, not as a pejorative term but as a word that describes a certain essential way of looking at things. One can find the essence of things by being dumb.

BLDD: Does "dumb" mean innocent?

RSW: It means innocent or naive. But a naive solution to a problem can be right or wrong, whereas a dumb solution is always right. It's very important to me to discover over and over again that something is simpler than I had thought.

BLDD: How would you now like to be introduced?

RSW: Now I would tell somebody to introduce me as a publisher, knowing that the description lacks the artistic associations that "architect" has about it.

BLDD: And at a cocktail party how do you identify yourself?

RSW: I guess just as a publisher.

BLDD: You no longer identify yourself as an architect?

RSW: I'm still doing architecture. I'm doing a house now and a major exhibition. And I'm chairman of the Department of Interior Architecture and Design at the Otis Art Institute / Parsons School of Design in Los Angeles. So I'm involved in architecture in that sense.

BLDD: Which aspect of your career do you enjoy the most? Do you prefer designing? Teaching? Publishing?

RSW: I'm really insatiable. I love it all. I love making a deal and working out a contract—I get as much of a rush from that as I do from working out and designing a whole Access book.

BLDD: Why did you choose the word "access" for the series of guidebooks you have been working on for several years? What meanings does that word have for you?

RSW: The word was a fortuitous choice. It's a word that is technologically appropriate today, since people talk about accessing a computer, accessing information, access channels for cable T.V. People also use it in referring to access for the handicapped. It's a terribly current word, like "environment" was in the sixties. It's certainly a 1980s word. But I don't think it will sound old-fashioned for at least ten years. So it was a good choice in that way. It's also a simple word. We played around with a lot of words. "Access" was a short word that was current and also went well with the name of any city—or, as it's turned out, with other subjects.

BLDD: Could you describe the process of putting together one of your Access books?

RSW: I try to give myself only one day to design an Access book. That's the way I produce them. After everything is compiled—a process that goes on for seven or eight months—I sit down and design the book.

BLDD: Aren't you distilling the design of the book during the entire seven- or eight-month process?

RSW: No. The system I've worked out is to develop the parts, which are then put together at one time.

BLDD: What was the genesis of your Access books? What was the first step?

RSW: Lou Kahn used to say that he was infatuated with beginnings. He once gave a speech that started, "Beginnings, beginnings, beginnings—I love beginnings." What I've learned from that is that at the moment you think you have begun a project, you still have to move backwards to find a more basic beginning. You can't move forward yet. Even when it seems logical to go ahead, you have to have the discipline to move backwards. What I do essentially is to formulate in my mind the simplest image I have of the book, and then work very hard at trying to make it simpler. The guides themselves are fairly complex. The movement backwards in this case was to attempt to embrace certain feelings about the city and the desire for access—hence the title of the books. The most basic decision we made was to organize the book's entries by their location in a given city, rather than by their category—restaurant, shop, building, or whatever. The categories of all the entries have been mixed up.

BLDD: So that if you were to describe New York's Fifth Avenue, you would not have separate sections for department stores or churches, but would organize them according to their arrangement on the street?

RSW: Right. Now, that may not seem terribly brilliant, but apparently it had never occurred to anybody else before; I know of no other guidebooks that have done that. In visiting a city I've always wanted to use a guidebook to see the immediate surroundings of any given point of interest—a terrific building, a restaurant, a theater, a museum—whatever is in this neighborhood. That is why we don't have a chapter on museums, a chapter on architecture, a chapter on restaurants. We order subjects as if you were moving through the city. This is truly the way you enjoy a good city. You may want to go to a bookstore, but what is wonderful is what you pass on the way; what you see next door. It's those things that enrich the experience of visiting a city or living in a city.

BLDD: You've said that you build the guidebook the way a city is built. What do you mean by that?

RSW: A city is the most complex of grids. It's not a single-level grid, but a plaited grid with things on different levels, with things all mixed together. It's wonderful that in New York you have such varied places as Orchard Street, Fifth Avenue, and Madison Avenue, and that each place incorporates a mix of elements. I would hate to walk on Madison Avenue and see only art galleries, no restaurants where you can stop for a cup of coffee. Just as a city is this complex grouping of things, our books bring together myriad elements. Our books are simply a mirror of what's out there. But then we put the information into a format that allows you to form memories. Learning is remembering what interests you. A map is a pattern you've made understandable. Our books try to make the patterns of various areas in the city simpler and simpler, so that you can find what you want to find but also find things you never knew were there. If you use these books only to find a review of a restaurant you already know about and its phone number and address, then it really is a failure. If you can't find in the book something you weren't looking for, you should buy somebody else's book.

BLDD: Have you always been fascinated by cities?

RSW: Always.

BLDD: What sparked your interest?

RSW: I could never find anything more complex. My curiosity was never satiated; there was always more to find out.

BLDD: Was an Access book to Philadelphia high on your list, since that is the city in which you were born and raised?

RSW: No. I did two guidebooks on Philadephia—*Man-Made Philadelphia* and *Philly, Pa. Abbrev.*—but I haven't done an Access book for the city yet. These books are so complex and so expensive to produce that the initial ones are absolutely dependent on the largest market possible. The choice of which ones to do first is determined by business considerations—it is necessary to sell fifty thousand copies of each book per year for it to be worthwhile. I couldn't sell that many Philadelphia books a year.

BLDD: You and your staff have expanded our notion of creative marketing. You've placed your guidebooks in novel places, not the traditional locations such as tourist offices and bookstores. Is this a plan you'll expand on in the future?

RSW: I'll expand on the plan as long as it works; when it doesn't work anymore, I'll learn how to do it better. But I don't think we've done such a remarkable job. The most remarkable thing about our distribution system is that we survived at first by selling the books ourselves. Now we have national distributors. Once you have national books the cottage industry system breaks down, unfortunately. I say unfortunately because I like controlling what I'm doing. I think there is a big market for certain books, ours included, in places other than bookstores—car washes, the counters of good men's stores, any place where you have five or ten minutes waiting time or where you'll pick something up. We are going to continue to place books in those specialty markets.

BLDD: Your partner at Access Press is Dr. Frank Stanton, president emeritus of CBS. How did the two of you come together, and how do you divide responsibilities in your current partnership?

RSW: We met through Lou Dorfsman, through the Aspen Conference. But that is less important than the fact that when Frank Stanton saw our first book, the first edition of *L. A. Access,* he thought it was a good product and that it was worthy of expansion. In conversations with me, he said that he felt I could do permutations of it that would be worthwhile. Our connection came out of the fact that he realized my approach made sense and that he wanted to participate in the further development of that idea. His enjoyment and my enjoyment in developing that idea on some business-like basis is the foundation of our company. He contributes his expertise in marketing and his contacts with individuals, but he also serves as my conscience. In the New York book he's reviewed every drawing, looked at the entire text. He is not the editor—he gives me full control of that—but he is my conscience, and that is a hell of an important thing. It's very lonely without a conscience. And your own conscience is not enough. Other people have been my conscience as well—Lou Kahn, for instance, or my late friend Gene Feldman. Gene Feldman had a printing press and taught me the business. I learned the craft of printing from him, so that I am now heavily involved in the printing of my books. I am at every press run. I make color corrections. I know the printing presses. That's been useful for me because I know what's possible.

Cover of Hawaii Access, published by Access Press

BLDD: Why do you choose to be so involved in the technical aspects of your books?

RSW: Control. The media you use affect what you're able to do. We do everything ourselves, including the typesetting. If we do our own typesetting, I have much more flexibility in what I can do with type—make it big, small, cut it in shapes. It allows me to have ideas I wouldn't think of if I had to send type out.

BLDD: Where do you get the equipment and the manpower to do that?

RSW: I bought the equipment. Last summer there were six people working in my office, whereas previously there had only been my secretary. And they're trained to set type. One person runs my office, another is designing an exhibition for me. My current secretary spends half the day working on the Compugraph typesetter. Everybody in the office does a lot of things.

BLDD: How many people work for you now?

RSW: There are about a dozen in my office, and about ten or fifteen who work on the Access books in various cities.

BLDD: The dozen people who are part of your ongoing staff—what do they do?

RSW: They develop maps, do graphics and copyediting, set type, take care of the business, sell my books. There are secretaries who work on an exhibition I'm doing and on other projects as well.

BLDD: What are you working on now?

RSW: One of our current projects is a book called *Movie Access*.

BLDD: What is that about?

RSW: How to watch movies on television. I don't think people get as much out of a movie as they could.

BLDD: What is the ideal way to watch a movie?

RSW: For one thing, the average person doesn't even understand what the credits mean or how a scene is constructed.

BLDD: Is it necessary that they do? What relevance does it have for the average viewer?

RSW: No, it's not necessary. Edwin Land once said that what he did was to work on issues and problems that nobody really cared about. Nobody was asking him to do what he did, and he spent his whole life trying to find solutions for problems people didn't need solved. It wasn't until after the problems were solved that people realized the solutions were necessary. To invoke Lou Kahn's name again, he said, "Did anybody need Beethoven's Fifth Symphony before he composed it?" No, but you can't think of a world without it now. So I don't think you need *Movie Access* now, but because of the advent of cable, movies will become more and more important to us. I think the book will help you enjoy much more the form of a movie and how it's constructed. People don't need my *Football Access* book either, but I think they will enjoy the game much more by reading it. The subject will take on a new meaning if people know more about it. That's what fascinates me. I'm doing it for myself. I would like to know more about the construction of movie form.

BLDD: What else would you like to learn more about?

RSW: Weather fascinates me. My older son is getting his doctorate in meteorology at MIT, and in talking with him at great length, I have become fascinated with how little we know about the weather despite how much we talk about it and how much it affects our lives. We can be right in the middle of a bad rainstorm, which affects us tremendously, and we don't even have good protective devices. They're terrible. Weather is the most primitive of the sciences at the moment. I'm going to try to develop a way of understanding it better on television. I want to try to create a really good weather show, completely different than any that are on now—different not simply to be different, but to make the subject more understandable.

BLDD: Have you started to work on that yet?

RSW: I've been thinking about it, yes. I don't work very hard, but I think about what I think about all the time.

BLDD: What other projects are occupying your thoughts these days?

RSW: Aside from the Access books, I'm doing a book with Rizzoli called *What Will Be Has Always Been*—which is the complete speeches of Lou Kahn—and a major book called *A Paperclip and 299 Other Things*. The book covers three hundred products that have been designed and manufactured in the United States over the last two hundred years. A lot of them have been chosen by people in the design field in the United States today. We give biographies of a lot of these products, and each one is a surprise. The biography of a light bulb is much different than you might expect. The light bulb is thought of as synonymous with having an idea. But the light bulb was the result of five separate inventions that were pulled together by Edison. That was the new idea. My feeling about ideas is that it's O.K. to steal them because ideas are part of our civilization. Good ideas are public. One should be free to do whatever one can with an idea to make it better. I talk to my students about this a lot. If you have an idea and another student takes it, two things can happen. They will either do it better than you did, or they will do it worse. If they do it better, there is something to be learned: not only can you learn what they did to improve upon your idea, but you can also learn that ideas can always be improved upon. If they take your idea and somehow lessen it, you haven't lost anything.

BLDD: You have been called the "Barnum of the design and architectural world," a phrase coined by Massimo Vignelli. How accurate is that description? Does it displease you?

RSW: It doesn't displease me.

BLDD: What does he mean when he says that?

RSW: He means that one of the things I've done is to run a lot of conferences and bring a lot of people together, in a sense to put together one aspect of design communciations, which occurs in meetings. For example, my long-term involvement with the Aspen Design Conference—running the conference in 1972 and being involved with it for many years—running the American Institute of Architects national convention, running the Pacific Design Center conference for a couple of years, starting the Monterey Conference and running that for three years, and so on.

BLDD: Do you still have time to do that sort of thing?

RSW: I am now setting up a conference, instead of running one for somebody else. Working with Harry Marks and Frank Stanton, I am establishing a yearly conference called the T.E.D.—Technology Entertainment Design. Its subject is video and computer technologies in the entertainment and advertising industries—graphics in motion pictures and network television, for instance. We're trying to see the interrelationship and interdependence of technology and information. I believe that information in its highest form is both art and entertainment, and it's something I would like to know more about. I also have a lot of anxiety about computers and computer graphics because I don't understand them well enough. I hope that I will come to understand it all much better. We have already gotten a rather extraordinary slate of people interested in coming. I think it's going to be a very exciting conference, using technology in the most wonderfully elaborate way to communicate information. It's not going to be just a trade show.

BLDD: You've spoken and written at length about visual information systems. Certainly one system that is very important today is computers. To what extent do you use computers in your work?

RSW: I have the same basic computer anxiety that an awful lot of people in the United States have. I am overcoming that anxiety to the extent that I have a computer typesetter that will soon be enlarged to include programs for editing material, a dictionary for correcting type, and so on. And my involvement in establishing this conference will undoubtedly teach me quite a bit about computer technology.

BLDD: What do you see as the current role and importance of computers in architecture? How do they contribute to the design process?

RSW: The computer is really a magic pencil and eraser that will eventually provide opportunities to envision and design spaces that were previously inconceivable. The growing use of computers in design is not unlike the development of Renaissance perspective, which allowed people to explore relationships between interior and exterior spaces and groups of buildings in a manner that they were not able to conceive of before because they could not portray them.

BLDD: Why don't we go back to something that you touched on briefly before—your training as an architect. In the short while that we've been talking, you've mentioned the name Lou Kahn a number of times. Why don't you tell us a little bit about his influence on you, as both a student and a practitioner?

RSW: Lou's my mentor. He allowed me to be more of myself, and in so doing he gave me an extraordinary gift. He gave that not only to me; he gave it to hundreds of people that came in contact with him. I'm just one of those people. I'm not suggesting a more special relationship with Lou than many other people had. However, I did do the first book on Lou.

BLDD: How did you first become absorbed in his work?

RSW: I was at the University of Pennsylvania, and I was nineteen. That was the second half of my freshman year, 1954. There was this funny little professor—he was short; his face was scarred; he spoke in a high-pitched voice. He talked about architecture in a completely different manner, a different tone, than anybody else in the school. There were rather prominent people involved in the school at that time—Romaldo Giurgola was there, Bob Geddes, Bob Venturi, Tim Vreeland. It was a very special school then. Kahn spoke in terms so simple that half the people laughed at him, and the other half were in awe. I remember that after hearing him talk to some upper classmen one day, I was so struck by him that when I came home to my parents I felt compelled to tell them about him. I said, "I'm going to tell you something that will have no meaning to you, but I feel like I have to put it on record. I just heard somebody speak today, and although nobody knows who he is and a lot of students laugh at him and he has no money and he's not successful, he is going to be very, very famous someday, because he says something. When he speaks he is clear."

BLDD: What did he say that day that so engaged you?

RSW: The most marvelous thing he said at that time was that architecture was the thoughtful making of spaces, that there was a hierarchy of spaces, spaces that served other spaces—simple language. It seems almost ridiculous now. He said that although he didn't like mechanical equipment, he had to make a place for it in his buildings, but not by covering it up—it's too much a part of the building. He said that anything that is part of something has to be expressed. Nobody else bothered to make statements like that at that time. The typical problem given to architecture students was: "You have a thirty-by-forty-foot space with a hung ceiling. Subdivide it with partitions and make it into a house." Nothing was shown; spaces weren't made. Kahn, in contrast, was talking about the making of something. I had never known anybody who talked that way. I could understand very little of what most philosophical people were saying. But here was a man who was talking philosophically in a way that I could understand. It was accessible to me. It was simple. He had a way of saying things that were so dumb, so simple, that you could understand them. He had a marked effect. I had never met anybody like that.

BLDD: Have you since?

RSW: No.

BLDD: Anyone who comes close to it?

RSW: No. I have met other people whom I respect a great deal and have gotten many things out of knowing. Schuyler Van Ranseleer Cammann, another faculty member at Penn, a professor of Oriental studies, had a thoroughly encyclopedic knowledge. He opened up another part of the world for me and showed me a level of learning and scholarship that I knew I couldn't attain, but I was much the better for knowing it existed. He was very special. Today, Frank Stanton, a person I deal with often, has a simplicity and clarity when he talks that I respect a great deal. He's very direct, very honest. I guess it's his honesty that I like so much. I think people lie continuously, so much so that we almost don't know when we're lying. When you find people who speak with simplicity and clarity, not for the purpose of shocking you, but because this is their only method of expressing themselves, it really comes as a surprise. They are not like the rest of us. It warms me to encounter someone like that. I would like to be that way, and yet I know it's not something you can try to be. Maybe someday I will become that way, but it's nothing I can work towards.

BLDD: As a young architect, what gave you the idea to publish the work of Louis Kahn?

RSW: In 1962, when I was twenty-six or so, I had been working for Lou and I felt it was just something I had to do. I was just a young squirt in his office and I'd never done a book before, but I said to Lou that I wanted to do a book on the drawings he had done that I liked and the words he had spoken that I understood.

BLDD: What were you doing in Kahn's office?

RSW: I'd had Kahn as an undergraduate, I'd had him for my thesis, and I'd had him for my master's degree. I wanted to work for him very badly after I got my master's degree, but he didn't have any work and I started to work at another office. When he called later and asked me if I'd work for him nights and weekends on a couple of strange projects, I said sure. One project we worked on was a proposal for the GM pavilion at the World's Fair in New York, for which he didn't get the commission. Later he asked me to work on the design of a barge that was to go up the Thames in England and hold orchestral concerts. I had been working on that nights and weekends for about a month when Lou asked if I would work for him fulltime. I said yes. When I came to work for him—it was a Friday—he said that I had to go to London on Monday. We worked all weekend on yellow tracing paper sketching with charcoal. On Monday I went off to London to find out about this project, to see what was going on, who could build it, and so on. When I started meeting with the people there I found that Lou was not really up on what the situation was or that he simply wanted me to take care of it and felt I could. But the barge was scheduled to be completed in ten weeks, and the concerts were already scheduled. So I had to decide whether to come home or stay and work on the project in London. It was a trial by fire, but it turned out to be another gift he gave

me. By being put in an impossible situation, I learned a great deal.

BLDD: How many other people were working in his office at the time that you, the newly arrived employee, were dispatched to London?

RSW: I guess there were about fifteen or eighteen people.

BLDD: Why did he select you?

RSW: I guess that was his gift to me.

BLDD: Are you engaged primarily by his works, his philosophy, or his life as a teacher?

RSW: What is most meaningful to me is the process he went through, how he thought and expressed himself. I do love his buildings, though. I've been all over the place, including India, to see his buildings, and they're truly wonderful. They're considered wonderful buildings in the trade; he's the architect's architect in that way. Even a work like the Kimbell Art Museum in Fort Worth, which is certainly not perfect, is special. There is nothing in it that says, "I am facile" or "I can do pretty things" or even "I'm a designer." It's a building that came out of trying to solve a problem in the most artistic and the most basic way. His handling of light was like no other architect's. He said that even a closet should have a little natural light and that the change of light during the day should be perceived even when you're inside a building.

BLDD: What is Kahn's legacy for present-day architects? What can they learn from his work or his approach?

RSW: He's touched a lot of people who are practitioners now. But I suspect that right now everybody is so caught up in the styling of things that his influence will pass this generation and hit a later one.

BLDD: Are you saying that current students or practitioners of architecture are not as interested in his ideas as they ought to be?

RSW: No, I don't think anybody *ought* to do anything. I just think that they're not as interested as another generation will be. And that's O.K.

BLDD: You once said that Kahn's approach resembled poetry more than philosophy. What does that mean?

RSW: A philosophy teacher I had at Penn spent the first month of class trying to define what philosophy is. He said that what most people call philosophy is more poetry—it's made up more of feelings and thoughts about things. A philosophy, he said, had to have a certain rigor. By that strict definition of philosophy, Lou was no philosopher. What he voiced was his thoughts, his opinions, his stories—it was his own poetry. He did give serious thought to things, which in a vernacular sense could be defined as having a philosophy, but he had no rigorous, worked-out philosophy.

BLDD: It was about twenty years ago that you founded GEE!, the Group for Environmental Education, a nonprofit corporation that reflected many of your own philosophical ideas and approaches. The goals for the group's secondary-school program, called "Our Man-Made Environment," included making the child aware of his environment, strengthening his confidence in his own judgments, and broadening his perspective to provide greater aspirations. How did you hope to achieve these goals? What were your methods?

RSW: At that time I had a great belief in building a better mousetrap. I had faith that if you created something better—something clearer and cheaper than what existed before—people would say, "Hey! Let's get one!"

BLDD: Have you abandoned that notion?

RSW: Oh yes. But I kept that notion going for fifteen years, failure after failure.

BLDD: How would you characterize the approach you used?

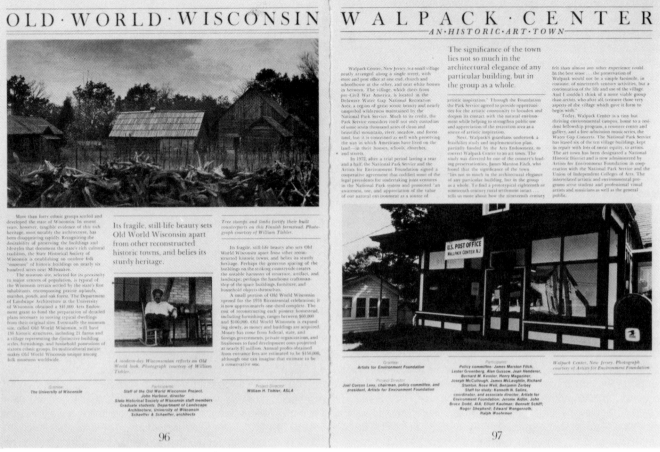

Pages of Design Arts, issue designed by Richard Saul Wurman

RSW: It was at the time that the word "environment" became popular. The Group for Environmental Education was trying to show the "gee whizness," the joyousness, of discovering everything around you. Bucky Fuller described the environment as "everything but me." GEE! was an attempt to respond to the attitudes of the sixties, a period when the word "environment" for most people meant clean air and clean water. For us it meant everything around you, including the city. Cities were becoming squalid, and there was no understanding of them. We were making an effort to say that before you can effect change, you have to understand the city, how the man-made environment was built. That's why we did this series of books, including *Our Man-Made Environment, Process of Choice, Learning to Get Around: Guidebook to Guidebooks,* and *The Nature of Recreation.*

BLDD: Who were your students? How did they respond to your philosophy and approach?

RSW: We didn't convert anybody. There were teachers around the United States who already had similar thoughts.

BLDD: So you preached to the converted?

RSW: We preached to the converted teachers, who then got our books and gave them to their students, who loved them. But there was no true movement because there was, and is, no place in the educational system for a new subject.

BLDD: How successful were you in that attempt? How do you gauge the success of a project?

RSW: The most success came in clearing my head. Otherwise I don't think we were successful. The converted know of our work, and the nonconverted have never heard of it and never will. The average person thinks of our educational system as God given—that there has always been a public school sys-

tem; that it has always taught certain subjects; that students should go to school nine months of the year, from nine o'clock to four o'clock; and so on. They think you can't change the system because it has always been this way. What they don't know is that it was not always like this. The present system is a creation of the last hundred years. The only method to change it is to do so violently and completely. The way school is structured today is not conducive to learning. There should be a Department of Learning, not a Department of Education. There is no consideration now of how and when people learn. People do not learn continuously; they learn in isolated moments. There's nothing in the system now that gears you up for those moments of learning. There's also no way to customize the system, to minimize the guilt people feel about situations in which they don't learn and to maximize the situations in which they do learn. I try to maximize in every way the situations in which I can learn something, but there is not even a hint of that in our present system. The situation is so bad that it can't even be modified—you can't get there from here. You have to begin with a whole new thought.

BLDD: As head of the Department in Interior Architecture and Design at Otis Art Institute / Parsons School of Design in Los Angeles, how have you tried to make use of your ideas about education?

RSW: The reason I still teach is that I believe so strongly in what I was just saying. Also, because I'm chairman of the department, I have some control over the system in which I teach. What I talk most about in my teaching is the problem of designing your life, especially designing your life for those moments of learning. The dialogue I have with students is very much along those lines.

BLDD: Do you learn a great deal from your students?

RSW: No, I don't learn from them. I learn from the situation. I learn by being in front of the students and talking all the time. I am constantly learning something. The moment I am learning less than they are I'll stop teaching.

BLDD: Is that moment approaching?

RSW: No!

BLDD: In the early seventies you published an influential issue of *Design Quarterly* called "Making the City Observable." What were some of the problems involved in the "invisible" city? How did you propose to resolve them?

RSW: That publication—along with the urban atlas I did with Joe Passonneau—probably had as much of an effect as anything I've done up until these guidebooks. The idea occurred to me by accident. I was doing an exhibition with Evan Turner, who was then director of the Philadelphia Museum of Art and is now director of the Cleveland Museum. I developed an exhibition called "City/2: Half the City Belongs to You." It was my premise that half of the total land area of every American city—streets, sidewalks, public buildings, parks—was owned by the citizenry. If we understood that, we would have a feeling of ownership of the city. We would have a higher stake in it and would want to find constructive ways to change it. While I was doing the exhibition, *Design Quarterly* asked me to do an issue. I said that I wanted to do an issue that would serve as a kind of catalogue for the show, but they didn't want that because the show was affiliated with a museum. So I had to come up with another idea, which was their gift to me in a sense. Because I had to develop an idea fairly rapidly so as not to miss out on this opportunity to publish, I decided I would use the things that had been accumulating on my shelf—maps, guides, and things like that—to create a catalogue analyzing their strong and weak points. As I worked on it, I realized there was a bigger subject involved, a special idea that I had always missed. "Making the City Observable" ended up being not just about guidebooks and maps. I found that a map was more than just a map, that it was like looking out the window of a tall building, having access to the tops of buildings. Seeing the city, in other words, was as much a guidebook as a guidebook is. What I did in *Design Quarterly* was to develop a method for making the city observable, making information about the urban environment understandable. It was a broader subject than it had previously been seen as. People appreciated that. We did a traveling exhibition that went to twenty cities, and there have been a lot of spin-offs from it. Marc Treib did another *Design Quarterly* that was a spin-off; Susan and Michael Southworth recently put out an excellent book called *Map*, although unfortunately they're making the definition slightly narrower again. I think there could be a course of study called "Making the City Observable" that would explore the graphics, the technology, the pedagogical devices, the way of seeing and walking and hearing—all the devices that allow us to perceive information about the physical environment of a city.

BLDD: What changes have you observed in the accessibility of cities in the years since that book was published?

RSW: I've been told that that book has influenced a number of graphic designers and urbanists, and I believe it's so. Recently a number of wonderful guidebooks have been published that seem to be influenced by that book. People who have worked for me, like Joel Katz and Stefen Geisbuhler, and people I've worked with, like Peter Bradford, have gone on to be more concerned with information in that form. Although I don't know how you would trace it, I think the book has had an effect.

BLDD: With such extensive knowledge of and experience in cities throughout this country—from New York to Aspen,

Philadelphia to Los Angeles—what have you concluded about what makes these places special?

RSW: The special thing about each city is the relationship between the curiosity it evokes and the availabilities it presents. When I lived in Raleigh, North Carolina, where I taught for two years, I was obsessed with the fact that they didn't have a symphony orchestra and that I couldn't get good pastrami. When I moved back to Philadelphia I would occasionally eat pastrami, but I never went to the symphony. But availabilities are very important. They are a mark of our civilization and the mark of a good city. Availabilities occur on several levels. That they're there is one thing. That you have access to them by foot or in some convenient way is another. Where L. A. breaks down is in its lack of a pedestrian environment.

BLDD: If you were to plan a city from the beginning, how would you begin?

RSW: I think you can plan the nucleus of a city, but not a whole city. The best a planned city has offered so far is some reasoned geometry imposed on the landscape, with some major buildings. This is not a city, it is a diagram. Reston, Virginia, is not a city. Even Washington, D.C., was more a geometry of interstices with some major points than it was a whole city. The city is more than just an opportunity to form a mental map and an organizing principle. The city is dependent on cultural and social things to make it great, to make it special. All you can do in planning a city is to develop an appropriate geometry, appropriate to the place and to the people, with moments of emphasis. You have to feel that it is a creative grid that allows the freedom for something to develop that you can't predict. A city is an infinitely long design problem.

BLDD: What do you see as the biggest urban problems we face currently?

RSW: There are only a few big urban problems, and none of them has to do primarily with physical design: crime, fear, hostility, and ignorance. They are all at some level the same problem. The present system is not one that allows people, from an early age onwards, to feel the joy and the gift of learning. Imbuing the spirit with curiosity would do a lot to reduce hostility, disorientation, crime, and disorder. Until we design a system in which people can see that gift of learning, those problems will persist. The physical problems are very interesting, but they are of lesser importance than the architecture of learning.

BLDD: How do you see the needs of urban areas evolving in the coming decade?

RSW: I think the architecture of public places, which contribute so much to the feeling of a city, will become more important as people have less need to leave their homes. Whether it will be in a kind of shopping center that we cannot even imagine yet, or in new types of lobbies, we will have to work on establishing unique solutions to the problem of designing architecture where people can gather together. Lobbies, for instance, can become bigger and bigger—they don't always have to be within a hotel. People must be given spaces in which they can have conversations. People don't talk to each other anymore. Conversation will one day come back as a radical alternative to watching television. But the situation will have to get really bad before that happens. Change comes only out of a desperate need for radical alternatives. When the simple desire for talking to people occurs, that will affect the physical design of cities: we will develop places for meeting.

BLDD: You've said that we can no longer address urban ideas as we have in the past—with speeches, visual presentations, or literary forms. How should we be addressing those problems?

RSW: How we address those problems is, of course, dependent on what effect the public can have on the decision-making process. I think that up until five years ago, citizens could have an effect on policy and decision making in the cities. They can have less effect now. It depends on government policies—on what monies come to the city through community development, urban renewal, or other things like that—and on where people can enter the process. My concern is that during the time when huge amounts of money were being spent on urban renewal and so on, the public had tremendous power to effect change, but their power was caught up in emotional reactions to superficial headlines rather than a true understanding of what the overall issues were. In order to make constructive changes you have to have understanding. I was deputy director of Housing and Community Development for the City of Philadelphia, so I'm talking from the experience of a public role.

BLDD: How long did you fill that position?

RSW: One year. I was head of Planning and Communications, and we had $100 million to spend—$2 million a week. That was a lot of money! I saw things that went ahead for the wrong reasons and others that were stopped for the wrong reasons. There was no understanding of what could have a positive effect for citizens in need. And neither the federal government nor the local governments did much to make information understandable. We did try: one of the things I did was to produce a newspaper called *Comm=unity* that I think was significant. It was also published in Spanish as *Comunidad*. These newspapers were quite different from any other public communication in any city at that time.

BLDD: During that period you spoke about the difficulty of trying to resolve urban problems with products rather than performance. What do you mean by that distinction?

RSW: It's so easy to buy a product—you can go into a store and buy a lamp. But you can't buy lighting. Lighting is a performance. It's so easy to look at something and not consider its performance. Automobiles are probably bought more on the basis of their look as a product than because of any genuine testing of their performance. Yet performance is what we want out of people; it's what we want out of products.

BLDD: What do you think, then, of the current emphasis on designing things to "look good"?

RSW: Right now we're in a stage in which people want buildings to look good and don't care about how they perform. It is a travesty of the definition of architecture and the architect as a servant of the client, of the user, of the people. Critics sharing a bed with architects reflects a level of irresponsibility that shocks me.

BLDD: Why don't you describe that clandestine relationship?

RSW: It all has to do with what's easy. It's easy to talk about the look of something and the styling of something; you don't have to back up that judgment because you can say to yourself, "I don't know what's good, but I know what I like. I like this." The Museum of Modern Art has products in its design collection that look pretty but don't work! That's antithetical to what design should be about. Design has to do with responsibility, and it can be done with great art. That doesn't mean function, but performance. Performance includes art and function. The art of function is performance. I believe that a building should perform like a great musical, which causes you to leave the theater humming the songs. With a building, too, remember the performance—the whole thing—and not just the look of something.

BLDD: What do you see as your greatest "performance," the most significant accomplishment of your career?

RSW: The first accomplishment that comes to mind is simply that I've survived doing things that I like to do. But it's nothing you can point to. I really can't say that I am motivated to do what I do for anybody else. I can only say that I hope that some of my curiosity has rubbed off on somebody, and I suspect that inevitably it has. That's about the only contribution I've made. I also have four nice kids.

BLDD: If you were given the necessary assistance and funds, is there any one project, any secret dream, that you'd like to realize in the future?

RSW: If I had funds I'd do so many more things. I would try to set up a dynamic urban observatory, an active museum for understanding what's happening and learning how to manipulate what's happening. I would certainly establish a museum of failure. It would probably be the most popular museum in the United States. A museum of failure would be a tremendous psychological breakthrough. It would be a spectacular achievement—a museum to promote consciousness of why things don't work and what occurs as a result of failure.

BLDD: What was your most important failure?

RSW: I have failure every day. Life is like learning how to walk. When you walk, you take a step, lose your balance, and fall on the other leg. Walking is really a constant process of losing your equilibrium—and that's like life. So, I don't have an important failure; I have continuous failure. I don't think you have important successes either. You have little successes between little failures.

BLDD: If you had your life to live over again, what would you do differently?

RSW: If I had it to do over again, one of the things I would do is go into advertising. I would be able to have more influence, to do things more responsibly and touch more people with ideas. But I know none of the experiences I've had—running an office in Philadelphia, designing a lot of beach houses, doing some books, and teaching; my relationship with Lou, with my partners, and with all the people I've come in contact with; the disappointments I've had, like making no money and not being given things to do—can ever be taken away from my life. They all affect my decisions now, and they affect my view of myself.

BLDD: Did you expect your life to unfold the way it has?

RSW: When I was eighteen I wrote a plan that took me to the age of fifty-four, outlining what I was going to do in six-year blocks of time.

BLDD: How are you doing?

RSW: I screwed up. I kept on the plan pretty well for a long time. I was going to graduate first in my class. I was going to take more courses than anybody had ever taken at Penn. I was going to teach at Cambridge. I was going to have two boys. I was going to do a book when I was thirty. Those worked pretty well. But then I didn't make a million dollars by the age of forty-two. . . . There are some things I feel remorseful about now, like my lack of fulfillment as an architect. I designed a house for myself which, for a number of reasons, I didn't build, although I was about to. The day I was going to get the loan to build it, I decided not to do it. Had it been built at that time, it would have satiated my architectural desires—for fame, fortune, a clarification of my ideas. But I never did it, and I never had the opportunity to do anything that good again.

BLDD: Do you envision designing major buldings again?

RSW: My career has gone off in such a different direction, but it is probably inevitable that at some point I will develop a house for myself in which I will try to incorporate my feelings about architecture. I still love architecture. I just spent three-and-a-half hours at the Maison de Verre in Paris, and I can't tell you how it moved me.

PHOTOGRAPH CREDITS

Peter Aaron/Esto Photographics, Inc.: p. 176
J. Alexander/Courtesy Conklin Rossant Architects: p. 45
Aldo Ballo: p. 233
Adam Bartos/Courtesy Museum of Modern Art: p. 69
Tom Bernard: p. 237
Brian Burr: p. 80
Piero Casadei: p. 19, 26
Louis Checkman: pp. 22, 23, 24, 25
Courtesy Conklin Rossant Architects: pp. 47, 48
George Cserna/Courtesy Museum of Modern Art: pp. 63, 68
Courtesy Cummins Engine Co: p. 27
Robert Doubek: p. 198 (top)
Bill Engdahl/Hedrich-Blessing: p. 126
Esto Photographics, Inc./Courtesy Ulrich Franzen & Associates, Architects: p. 86
Dick Frank: pp. 72 (top), 78 (top), 79, 81
Y. Futagawa: p. 175
Guy Gillette: p. 72 (bottom)
Courtesy Goody, Clancy & Associates: p. 114
Gorchev & Gorchev Photography: pp. 38, 94
Daniel Haar/Courtesy Museum of Modern Art: p. 70
Bob Harr/Hedrich-Blessing: p. 34
Jack Horner: p. 57 (top)
Courtesy House & Garden/Condé Nast: p. 91
Wolfgang Hoyt/Esto Photographics, Inc.: p. 155
——Courtesy Conklin Rossant Architects: p. 50
——Courtesy Ulrich Franzen & Associates, Architects: p. 90
R. Greg Hursley, Inc.: p. 55
David J. Kaminsky: p. 200
Howard N. Kaplan (© HNK Architectural Photography): pp. 226, 228
Barbara Karant: p. 179
Paul Y. Keating: p. 185
Kate Keller/Courtesy Museum of Modern Art: p. 66
Lilian Kemp Photography: p. 36
Balthazar Korab: p. 227
Andrew Lautman: pp. 196, 198

Robert Lautman: pp. 141, 142
Nathaniel Lieberman, New York City: p. 157
William Mathis: pp. 168, 174
Norman McGrath: pp. 182, 187, 190, 191 (bottom), 192
——Courtesy Ulrich Franzen & Associates, Architects: p. 87
Jay Meisel (© 1983): p. 133
Merrick/Hedrich-Blessing: p. 123
Joseph W. Molitor, Architectural and Industrial Photography/Courtesy I. M. Pei & Partners: p. 37
Courtesy Museum of Modern Art: p. 64
Keith Palmer and James Steinkamp: pp. 147, 148, 149, 150
Bo Parker: p. 52, 57 (bottom), 58
Richard Payne AIA: pp. 31, 33, 100, 156, 158
Irving Penn: p. 161
Russell B. Phillips: pp. 246, 248
Wendy Reid: p. 102
Cervin Robinson (© 1980): p. 189
Courtesy Kevin Roche, John Dinkeloo and Associates: pp. 202, 207, 208
Steve Rosenthal: pp. 41, 112, 115, 118, 214, 218, 219
Rothschild: p. 85
Julius Shulman: p. 159
George Silk: p. 173
Theodore Spagna: p. 130
SITE: pp. 243, 249
Ed Stoecklein: p. 78 (bottom)
Ezra Stoller/Esto Photographics, Inc.: pp. 125, 127, 163, 164, 166, 167, 168, 216
——Courtesy Conklin Rossant Architects: p. 46
Stuart-Rogers Photographers: p. 120
Judith Turner: p. 132
Courtesy Venturi, Rauch and Scott Brown: p. 236
Jonathon Wenk: p. 61
Wheeler Photographics, Inc: p. 119
Wilfried Wietstock: p. 96
Marek Zandmer: p. 40